$83.00

REFERENCE -- NOT TO BE
TAKEN FROM THIS ROOM

D1788385

# Poetry for Students

# National Advisory Board

**Jennifer Hood:** Young Adult/Reference Librarian, Cumberland Public Library, Cumberland, Rhode Island. Certified teacher, Rhode Island. Member of the New England Library Association, Rhode Island Library Association, and the Rhode Island Educational Media Association.

**Christopher Maloney:** Head Reference Librarian, Ocean City Free Public Library, Ocean City, New Jersey. Member of the American Library Association and the New Jersey Library Association. Board member of the South Jersey Library Cooperative.

**Kathleen Preston:** Head of Reference, New City Library, New City, New York. Member of the American Library Association. Received B.A. and M.L.S. from University of Albany.

**Patricia Sarles:** Library Media Specialist, Canarsie High School, Brooklyn, New York. Expert Guide in Biography/Memoir for the website *About.com* (http://biography.about.com). Author of short stories and book reviews. Received B.A., M.A. (anthropology), and M.L.S. from Rutgers University.

**Heidi Stohs:** Instructor in Language Arts, grades 10-12, Solomon High School, Solomon, Kansas. Received B.S. from Kansas State University; M.A. from Fort Hays State University.

**Barbara Wencl:** Library Media Specialist, Como Park Senior High School, St. Paul, Minnesota. Teacher of secondary social studies and history, St. Paul, Minnesota. Received B.S. and M.Ed. from University of Minnesota; received media certification from University of Wisconsin. Educator and media specialist with over 30 years experience.

# Poetry for Students

Presenting Analysis, Context, and Criticism on Commonly Studied Poetry

*Volume 17*

*David Galens, Project Editor*

*Foreword by David Kelly*

LONGWOOD PUBLIC LIBRARY

Detroit • New York • San Diego • San Francisco • Cleveland • New Haven, Conn. • Waterville, Maine • London • Munich

Poetry for Students, Volume 17

**Project Editor**
David Galens

**Editorial**
Anne Marie Hacht, Julie Keppen, Ira Mark Milne, Pam Revitzer, Kathy Sauer, Timothy J. Sisler, Jennifer Smith, Daniel Toronto, Carol Ullmann

**Research**
Sarah Genik

**Permissions**
Margaret Chamberlain

**Manufacturing**
Stacy Melson

**Imaging and Multimedia**
Lezlie Light, Dave Oblender, Kelly A. Quin, Luke Rademacher

**Product Design**
Pamela A. E. Galbreath, Michael Logusz

© 2003 by Gale. Gale is an imprint of The Gale Group, Inc., a division of Thomson Learning Inc.

Gale and Design® and Thomson Learning™ are trademarks used herein under license.

*For more information, contact*
The Gale Group, Inc.
27500 Drake Rd.
Farmington Hills, MI 48331-3535
Or you can visit our Internet site at
http://www.gale.com

**ALL RIGHTS RESERVED**
No part of this work covered by the copyright hereon may be reproduced or used in any form or by any means—graphic, electronic, or mechanical, including photocopying, recording, taping, Web distribution, or information storage retrieval systems—without the written permission of the publisher.

For permission to use material from this product, submit your request via Web at http://www.gale-edit.com/permissions, or you may download our Permissions Request form and submit your request by fax or mail to:

*Permissions Department*
The Gale Group, Inc.
27500 Drake Rd.
Farmington Hills, MI 48331-3535
Permissions Hotline:
248-699-8006 or 800-877-4253, ext. 8006
Fax: 248-699-8074 or 800-762-4058

Since this page cannot legibly accommodate all copyright notices, the acknowledgments constitute an extension of the copyright notice.

While every effort has been made to ensure the reliability of the information presented in this publication, The Gale Group, Inc. does not guarantee the accuracy of the data contained herein. The Gale Group, Inc. accepts no payment for listing; and inclusion in the publication of any organization, agency, institution, publication, service, or individual does not imply endorsement of the editors or publisher. Errors brought to the attention of the publisher and verified to the satisfaction of the publisher will be corrected in future editions.

ISBN 0-7876-6036-1
ISSN 1094-7019

Printed in the United States of America
10 9 8 7 6 5 4 3 2 1

# Table of Contents

*Guest Foreword*
"Just a Few Lines on a Page"
by David J. Kelly . . . . . . . . . . . . . . . . . . .ix

*Introduction* . . . . . . . . . . . . . . . . . . . . . . . . . .xi

*Literary Chronology* . . . . . . . . . . . . . . . . . . .xv

*Acknowledgments* . . . . . . . . . . . . . . . . . . .xvii

*Contributors* . . . . . . . . . . . . . . . . . . . . . . . .xix

*The Arsenal at Springfield*
(by Henry Wadsworth Longfellow) . . . .1
    Author Biography . . . . . . . . . . . . . . . . . . . . .2
    Poem Text . . . . . . . . . . . . . . . . . . . . . . . . .2
    Poem Summary . . . . . . . . . . . . . . . . . . . . .3
    Themes . . . . . . . . . . . . . . . . . . . . . . . . . . .5
    Style . . . . . . . . . . . . . . . . . . . . . . . . . . . . .7
    Historical Context . . . . . . . . . . . . . . . . . . . .8
    Critical Overview . . . . . . . . . . . . . . . . . .10
    Criticism . . . . . . . . . . . . . . . . . . . . . . . . .10

*La Belle Dame sans Merci*
(by John Keats) . . . . . . . . . . . . . . . . . .17
    Author Biography . . . . . . . . . . . . . . . . . . .17
    Poem Text . . . . . . . . . . . . . . . . . . . . . . . .18
    Poem Summary . . . . . . . . . . . . . . . . . . . .18
    Themes . . . . . . . . . . . . . . . . . . . . . . . . . .21
    Style . . . . . . . . . . . . . . . . . . . . . . . . . . . .22
    Historical Context . . . . . . . . . . . . . . . . . . .22
    Critical Overview . . . . . . . . . . . . . . . . . .24
    Criticism . . . . . . . . . . . . . . . . . . . . . . . . .24

# Table of Contents

*Guest Foreword*
   "Just a Few Lines on a Page"
   by David J. Kelly . . . . . . . . . . . . . . . . . .ix

*Introduction* . . . . . . . . . . . . . . . . . . . . . . . .xi

*Literary Chronology* . . . . . . . . . . . . . . . . .xv

*Acknowledgments* . . . . . . . . . . . . . . . . . .xvii

*Contributors* . . . . . . . . . . . . . . . . . . . . . . .xix

*The Arsenal at Springfield*
**(by Henry Wadsworth Longfellow)** . . . .1
   Author Biography . . . . . . . . . . . . . . . . . . .2
   Poem Text . . . . . . . . . . . . . . . . . . . . . . . . .2
   Poem Summary . . . . . . . . . . . . . . . . . . . .3
   Themes . . . . . . . . . . . . . . . . . . . . . . . . . . .5
   Style . . . . . . . . . . . . . . . . . . . . . . . . . . . . .7
   Historical Context . . . . . . . . . . . . . . . . . . .8
   Critical Overview . . . . . . . . . . . . . . . . . .10
   Criticism . . . . . . . . . . . . . . . . . . . . . . . . .10

*La Belle Dame sans Merci*
**(by John Keats)** . . . . . . . . . . . . . . . . . .17
   Author Biography . . . . . . . . . . . . . . . . . .17
   Poem Text . . . . . . . . . . . . . . . . . . . . . . .18
   Poem Summary . . . . . . . . . . . . . . . . . . .18
   Themes . . . . . . . . . . . . . . . . . . . . . . . . . .21
   Style . . . . . . . . . . . . . . . . . . . . . . . . . . . .22
   Historical Context . . . . . . . . . . . . . . . . .22
   Critical Overview . . . . . . . . . . . . . . . . . .24
   Criticism . . . . . . . . . . . . . . . . . . . . . . . . .24

## Table of Contents

*The Blue Rim of Memory*
**(by Denise Levertov)** . . . . . . . . . . . . .37
   Author Biography . . . . . . . . . . . . . . . .38
   Poem Text . . . . . . . . . . . . . . . . . . . . . .38
   Poem Summary . . . . . . . . . . . . . . . . . .39
   Themes . . . . . . . . . . . . . . . . . . . . . . . .40
   Style . . . . . . . . . . . . . . . . . . . . . . . . . . .41
   Historical Context . . . . . . . . . . . . . . . . .42
   Critical Overview . . . . . . . . . . . . . . . . .43
   Criticism . . . . . . . . . . . . . . . . . . . . . . . .44

*The Cobweb* **(by Raymond Carver)** . . . .49
   Author Biography . . . . . . . . . . . . . . . .50
   Poem Text . . . . . . . . . . . . . . . . . . . . . .50
   Poem Summary . . . . . . . . . . . . . . . . . .51
   Themes . . . . . . . . . . . . . . . . . . . . . . . .52
   Style . . . . . . . . . . . . . . . . . . . . . . . . . . .53
   Historical Context . . . . . . . . . . . . . . . . .53
   Critical Overview . . . . . . . . . . . . . . . . .54
   Criticism . . . . . . . . . . . . . . . . . . . . . . . .55

*Driving to Town Late to Mail a Letter*
**(by Robert Bly)** . . . . . . . . . . . . . . .62
   Author Biography . . . . . . . . . . . . . . . .62
   Poem Text . . . . . . . . . . . . . . . . . . . . . .63
   Poem Summary . . . . . . . . . . . . . . . . . .63
   Themes . . . . . . . . . . . . . . . . . . . . . . . .65
   Style . . . . . . . . . . . . . . . . . . . . . . . . . . .66
   Historical Context . . . . . . . . . . . . . . . . .67
   Critical Overview . . . . . . . . . . . . . . . . .68
   Criticism . . . . . . . . . . . . . . . . . . . . . . . .68

*Early in the Morning*
**(by Li-Young Lee)** . . . . . . . . . . . . . .74
   Author Biography . . . . . . . . . . . . . . . .74
   Poem Text . . . . . . . . . . . . . . . . . . . . . .75
   Poem Summary . . . . . . . . . . . . . . . . . .75
   Themes . . . . . . . . . . . . . . . . . . . . . . . .76
   Style . . . . . . . . . . . . . . . . . . . . . . . . . . .78
   Historical Context . . . . . . . . . . . . . . . . .78
   Critical Overview . . . . . . . . . . . . . . . . .79
   Criticism . . . . . . . . . . . . . . . . . . . . . . . .79

*For Jennifer, 6, on the Teton*
**(by Richard Hugo)** . . . . . . . . . . . . . .85
   Author Biography . . . . . . . . . . . . . . . .86
   Poem Text . . . . . . . . . . . . . . . . . . . . . .86
   Poem Summary . . . . . . . . . . . . . . . . . .86
   Themes . . . . . . . . . . . . . . . . . . . . . . . .87
   Style . . . . . . . . . . . . . . . . . . . . . . . . . . .88
   Historical Context . . . . . . . . . . . . . . . . .89
   Critical Overview . . . . . . . . . . . . . . . . .90
   Criticism . . . . . . . . . . . . . . . . . . . . . . . .91

*Having it Out with Melancholy*
**(by Jane Kenyon)** . . . . . . . . . . . . . .97
   Author Biography . . . . . . . . . . . . . . . .98
   Poem Text . . . . . . . . . . . . . . . . . . . . . .98
   Poem Summary . . . . . . . . . . . . . . . . . .99
   Themes . . . . . . . . . . . . . . . . . . . . . . .102
   Style . . . . . . . . . . . . . . . . . . . . . . . . . .104
   Historical Context . . . . . . . . . . . . . . .104
   Critical Overview . . . . . . . . . . . . . . . .105
   Criticism . . . . . . . . . . . . . . . . . . . . . .106

*I Go Back to May 1937*
**(by Sharon Olds)** . . . . . . . . . . . . . .111
   Author Biography . . . . . . . . . . . . . . .112
   Poem Text . . . . . . . . . . . . . . . . . . . . .112
   Poem Summary . . . . . . . . . . . . . . . . .113
   Themes . . . . . . . . . . . . . . . . . . . . . . .115
   Style . . . . . . . . . . . . . . . . . . . . . . . . . .116
   Historical Context . . . . . . . . . . . . . . .117
   Critical Overview . . . . . . . . . . . . . . . .118
   Criticism . . . . . . . . . . . . . . . . . . . . . .119

*Knoxville, Tennessee*
**(by Nikki Giovanni)** . . . . . . . . . . . .130
   Author Biography . . . . . . . . . . . . . . .130
   Poem Summary . . . . . . . . . . . . . . . . .131
   Themes . . . . . . . . . . . . . . . . . . . . . . .132
   Style . . . . . . . . . . . . . . . . . . . . . . . . . .133
   Historical Context . . . . . . . . . . . . . . .133
   Critical Overview . . . . . . . . . . . . . . . .135
   Criticism . . . . . . . . . . . . . . . . . . . . . .135

*Mind* **(by Jorie Graham)** . . . . . . . . .144
   Author Biography . . . . . . . . . . . . . . .145
   Poem Text . . . . . . . . . . . . . . . . . . . . .145
   Poem Summary . . . . . . . . . . . . . . . . .146
   Themes . . . . . . . . . . . . . . . . . . . . . . .147
   Style . . . . . . . . . . . . . . . . . . . . . . . . . .148
   Historical Context . . . . . . . . . . . . . . .148
   Critical Overview . . . . . . . . . . . . . . . .149
   Criticism . . . . . . . . . . . . . . . . . . . . . .150

*On His Having Arrived at the Age of Twenty-Three* **(by John Milton)** . . . . . . . . . .158
   Author Biography . . . . . . . . . . . . . . .158
   Poem Text . . . . . . . . . . . . . . . . . . . . .159
   Poem Summary . . . . . . . . . . . . . . . . .160
   Themes . . . . . . . . . . . . . . . . . . . . . . .160
   Style . . . . . . . . . . . . . . . . . . . . . . . . . .162
   Historical Context . . . . . . . . . . . . . . .162
   Critical Overview . . . . . . . . . . . . . . . .164
   Criticism . . . . . . . . . . . . . . . . . . . . . .164

*Poetry* (by Marianne Moore) . . . . . . .173
    Author Biography . . . . . . . . . . . . . . .174
    Poem Summary . . . . . . . . . . . . . . . .174
    Themes . . . . . . . . . . . . . . . . . . . . . .176
    Style . . . . . . . . . . . . . . . . . . . . . . . .178
    Historical Context . . . . . . . . . . . . . . .178
    Critical Overview . . . . . . . . . . . . . . . .179
    Criticism . . . . . . . . . . . . . . . . . . . . .180

*The Rhodora*
(by Ralph Waldo Emerson) . . . . . . .190
    Author Biography . . . . . . . . . . . . . . .190
    Poem Text . . . . . . . . . . . . . . . . . . . .191
    Poem Summary . . . . . . . . . . . . . . . .191
    Themes . . . . . . . . . . . . . . . . . . . . . .192
    Style . . . . . . . . . . . . . . . . . . . . . . . .193
    Historical Context . . . . . . . . . . . . . . .194
    Critical Overview . . . . . . . . . . . . . . . .195
    Criticism . . . . . . . . . . . . . . . . . . . . .196

*The Singer's House*
(by Seamus Heaney) . . . . . . . . . . .204
    Author Biography . . . . . . . . . . . . . . .205
    Poem Text . . . . . . . . . . . . . . . . . . . .205
    Poem Summary . . . . . . . . . . . . . . . .206
    Themes . . . . . . . . . . . . . . . . . . . . . .208
    Style . . . . . . . . . . . . . . . . . . . . . . . .209

    Historical Context . . . . . . . . . . . . . . .210
    Critical Overview . . . . . . . . . . . . . . . .212
    Criticism . . . . . . . . . . . . . . . . . . . . .213

*Wild Swans*
(by Edna St. Vincent Millay) . . . . . .220
    Author Biography . . . . . . . . . . . . . . .221
    Poem Text . . . . . . . . . . . . . . . . . . . .221
    Poem Summary . . . . . . . . . . . . . . . .221
    Themes . . . . . . . . . . . . . . . . . . . . . .222
    Style . . . . . . . . . . . . . . . . . . . . . . . .223
    Historical Context . . . . . . . . . . . . . . .224
    Critical Overview . . . . . . . . . . . . . . . .225
    Criticism . . . . . . . . . . . . . . . . . . . . .226

*Glossary* . . . . . . . . . . . . . . . . . . . . . . .235

*Cumulative Author/Title Index* . . . . . . . .255

*Cumulative Nationality/Ethnicity
Index* . . . . . . . . . . . . . . . . . . . . . . . . . .261

*Subject/Theme Index* . . . . . . . . . . . . . . .267

*Cumulative Index of First Lines* . . . . . . .273

*Cumulative Index of Last Lines* . . . . . . . .279

# *Just a Few Lines on a Page*

I have often thought that poets have the easiest job in the world. A poem, after all, is just a few lines on a page, usually not even extending margin to margin—how long would that take to write, about five minutes? Maybe ten at the most, if you wanted it to rhyme or have a repeating meter. Why, I could start in the morning and produce a book of poetry by dinnertime. But we all know that it isn't that easy. Anyone can come up with enough words, but the poet's job is about writing the *right* ones. The right words will change lives, making people see the world somewhat differently than they saw it just a few minutes earlier. The right words can make a reader who relies on the dictionary for meanings take a greater responsibility for his or her own personal understanding. A poem that is put on the page correctly can bear any amount of analysis, probing, defining, explaining, and interrogating, and something about it will still feel new the next time you read it.

It would be fine with me if I could talk about poetry without using the word "magical," because that word is overused these days to imply "a really good time," often with a certain sweetness about it, and a lot of poetry is neither of these. But if you stop and think about magic—whether it brings to mind sorcery, witchcraft, or bunnies pulled from top hats—it always seems to involve stretching reality to produce a result greater than the sum of its parts and pulling unexpected results out of thin air. This book provides ample cases where a few simple words conjure up whole worlds. We do not actually travel to different times and different cultures, but the poems get into our minds, they find what little we know about the places they are talking about, and then they make that little bit blossom into a bouquet of someone else's life. Poets make us think we are following simple, specific events, but then they leave ideas in our heads that cannot be found on the printed page. Abracadabra.

Sometimes when you finish a poem it doesn't feel as if it has left any supernatural effect on you, like it did not have any more to say beyond the actual words that it used. This happens to everybody, but most often to inexperienced readers: regardless of what is often said about young people's infinite capacity to be amazed, you have to understand what usually does happen, and what could have happened instead, if you are going to be moved by what someone has accomplished. In those cases in which you finish a poem with a "So what?" attitude, the information provided in *Poetry for Students* comes in handy. Readers can feel assured that the poems included here actually are potent magic, not just because a few (or a hundred or ten thousand) professors of literature say they are: they're significant because they can withstand close inspection and still amaze the very same people who have just finished taking them apart and seeing how they work. Turn them inside out, and they will still be able to come alive, again and again. *Poetry for Students* gives readers of any age good practice in feeling the ways poems relate to both the reality of the time and place the poet lived in and the reality of our emotions. Practice is just another word for being a student. The information given here helps you understand the way to read poetry; what to look for, what to expect.

With all of this in mind, I really don't think I would actually like to have a poet's job at all. There are too many skills involved, including precision, honesty, taste, courage, linguistics, passion, compassion, and the ability to keep all sorts of people entertained at once. And that is just what they do with one hand, while the other hand pulls some sort of trick that most of us will never fully understand. I can't even pack all that I need for a weekend into one suitcase, so what would be my chances of stuffing so much life into a few lines? With all that *Poetry for Students* tells us about each poem, I am impressed that any poet can finish three or four poems a year. Read the inside stories of these poems, and you won't be able to approach any poem in the same way you did before.

*David J. Kelly*
*College of Lake County*

# Introduction

## Purpose of the Book

The purpose of *Poetry for Students* (*PfS*) is to provide readers with a guide to understanding, enjoying, and studying poems by giving them easy access to information about the work. Part of Gale's "For Students" Literature line, *PfS* is specifically designed to meet the curricular needs of high school and undergraduate college students and their teachers, as well as the interests of general readers and researchers considering specific poems. While each volume contains entries on "classic" poems frequently studied in classrooms, there are also entries containing hard-to-find information on contemporary poems, including works by multicultural, international, and women poets.

The information covered in each entry includes an introduction to the poem and the poem's author; the actual poem text (if possible); a poem summary, to help readers unravel and understand the meaning of the poem; analysis of important themes in the poem; and an explanation of important literary techniques and movements as they are demonstrated in the poem.

In addition to this material, which helps the readers analyze the poem itself, students are also provided with important information on the literary and historical background informing each work. This includes a historical context essay, a box comparing the time or place the poem was written to modern Western culture, a critical overview essay, and excerpts from critical essays on the poem. A unique feature of *PfS* is a specially commissioned critical essay on each poem, targeted toward the student reader.

To further aid the student in studying and enjoying each poem, information on media adaptations is provided (if available), as well as reading suggestions for works of fiction and nonfiction on similar themes and topics. Classroom aids include ideas for research papers and lists of critical sources that provide additional material on the poem.

## Selection Criteria

The titles for each volume of *PfS* were selected by surveying numerous sources on teaching literature and analyzing course curricula for various school districts. Some of the sources surveyed included: literature anthologies; *Reading Lists for College-Bound Students: The Books Most Recommended by America's Top Colleges*; textbooks on teaching the poem; a College Board survey of poems commonly studied in high schools; and a National Council of Teachers of English (NCTE) survey of poems commonly studied in high schools.

Input was also solicited from our advisory board, as well as educators from various areas. From these discussions, it was determined that each volume should have a mix of "classic" poems (those works commonly taught in literature classes) and contemporary poems for which information is often hard to find. Because of the interest in expanding the canon of literature, an emphasis was also placed on including works by international, multicultural, and women poets. Our advisory board members—educational professionals—helped pare down the list for each volume. If a work was not selected for the present volume, it was often noted as a possibility for a future volume. As always, the editor welcomes suggestions for titles to be included in future volumes.

## *How Each Entry Is Organized*

Each entry, or chapter, in *PfS* focuses on one poem. Each entry heading lists the full name of the poem, the author's name, and the date of the poem's publication. The following elements are contained in each entry:

- **Introduction:** a brief overview of the poem which provides information about its first appearance, its literary standing, any controversies surrounding the work, and major conflicts or themes within the work.

- **Author Biography:** this section includes basic facts about the poet's life, and focuses on events and times in the author's life that inspired the poem in question.

- **Poem Text:** when permission has been granted, the poem is reprinted, allowing for quick reference when reading the explication of the following section.

- **Poem Summary:** a description of the major events in the poem. Summaries are broken down with subheads that indicate the lines being discussed.

- **Themes:** a thorough overview of how the major topics, themes, and issues are addressed within the poem. Each theme discussed appears in a separate subhead and is easily accessed through the boldface entries in the Subject/Theme Index.

- **Style:** this section addresses important style elements of the poem, such as form, meter, and rhyme scheme; important literary devices used, such as imagery, foreshadowing, and symbolism; and, if applicable, genres to which the work might have belonged, such as Gothicism or Romanticism. Literary terms are explained within the entry, but can also be found in the Glossary.

- **Historical Context:** this section outlines the social, political, and cultural climate *in which the author lived and the poem was created.* This section may include descriptions of related historical events, pertinent aspects of daily life in the culture, and the artistic and literary sensibilities of the time in which the work was written. If the poem is a historical work, information regarding the time in which the poem is set is also included. Each section is broken down with helpful subheads.

- **Critical Overview:** this section provides background on the critical reputation of the poem, including bannings or any other public controversies surrounding the work. For older works, this section includes a history of how the poem was first received and how perceptions of it may have changed over the years; for more recent poems, direct quotes from early reviews may also be included.

- **Criticism:** an essay commissioned by *PfS* which specifically deals with the poem and is written specifically for the student audience, as well as excerpts from previously published criticism on the work (if available).

- **Sources:** an alphabetical list of critical material used in compiling the entry, with full bibliographical information.

- **Further Reading:** an alphabetical list of other critical sources which may prove useful for the student. It includes full bibliographical information and a brief annotation.

In addition, each entry contains the following highlighted sections, set apart from the main text as sidebars:

- **Media Adaptations:** if available, a list of audio recordings as well as any film or television adaptations of the poem, including source information.

- **Topics for Further Study:** a list of potential study questions or research topics dealing with the poem. This section includes questions related to other disciplines the student may be studying, such as American history, world history, science, math, government, business, geography, economics, psychology, etc.

- **Compare and Contrast:** an "at-a-glance" comparison of the cultural and historical differences between the author's time and culture and late twentieth century or early twenty-first century Western culture. This box includes pertinent parallels between the major scientific, political, and cultural movements of the time or place the poem was written, the time or place the poem was set (if a historical work), and modern Western culture. Works written after 1990 may not have this box.

- **What Do I Read Next?:** a list of works that might complement the featured poem or serve as a contrast to it. This includes works by the same author and others, works of fiction and nonfiction, and works from various genres, cultures, and eras.

## Other Features

*PfS* includes "Just a Few Lines on a Page," a foreword by David J. Kelly, an adjunct professor of English, College of Lake County, Illinois. This essay provides a straightforward, unpretentious explanation of why poetry should be marveled at and how *Poetry for Students* can help teachers show students how to enrich their own reading experiences.

A Cumulative Author/Title Index lists the authors and titles covered in each volume of the *PfS* series.

A Cumulative Nationality/Ethnicity Index breaks down the authors and titles covered in each volume of the *PfS* series by nationality and ethnicity.

A Subject/Theme Index, specific to each volume, provides easy reference for users who may be studying a particular subject or theme rather than a single work. Significant subjects from events to broad themes are included, and the entries pointing to the specific theme discussions in each entry are indicated in **boldface**.

A Cumulative Index of First Lines (beginning in Vol. 10) provides easy reference for users who may be familiar with the first line of a poem but may not remember the actual title.

A Cumulative Index of Last Lines (beginning in Vol. 10) provides easy reference for users who may be familiar with the last line of a poem but may not remember the actual title.

Each entry may include illustrations, including a photo of the author and other graphics related to the poem.

## Citing Poetry for Students

When writing papers, students who quote directly from any volume of *Poetry for Students* may use the following general forms. These examples arc based on MLA style; teachers may request that students adhere to a different style, so the following examples may be adapted as needed.

When citing text from *PfS* that is not attributed to a particular author (i.e., the Themes, Style, Historical Context sections, etc.), the following format should be used in the bibliography section:

"Angle of Geese." *Poetry for Students.* Eds. Marie Napierkowski and Mary Ruby. Vol. 2. Detroit: Gale, 1998. 5–7.

When quoting the specially commissioned essay from *PfS* (usually the first piece under the "Criticism" subhead), the following format should be used:

Velie, Alan. Critical Essay on "Angle of Geese." *Poetry for Students.* Eds. Marie Napierkowski and Mary Ruby. Vol. 2. Detroit: Gale, 1998. 7–10.

When quoting a journal or newspaper essay that is reprinted in a volume of *PfS,* the following form may be used:

Luscher, Robert M. "An Emersonian Context of Dickinson's 'The Soul Selects Her Own Society.'" *ESQ: A Journal of American Renaissance* Vol. 30, No. 2 (Second Quarter, 1984), 111–16; excerpted and reprinted in *Poetry for Students*, Vol. 1, eds. Marie Napierkowski and Mary Ruby (Detroit: Gale, 1998), pp. 266–69.

When quoting material reprinted from a book that appears in a volume of *PfS,* the following form may be used:

Mootry, Maria K. "'Tell It Slant': Disguise and Discovery as Revisionist Poetic Discourse in 'The Bean Eaters,'" in *A Life Distilled: Gwendolyn Brooks, Her Poetry and Fiction*. Edited by Maria K. Mootry and Gary Smith. University of Illinois Press, 1987. 177–80, 191; excerpted and reprinted in *Poetry for Students*, Vol. 2, eds. Marie Napierkowski and Mary Ruby (Detroit: Gale, 1998), pp. 22–24.

## We Welcome Your Suggestions

The editor of *Poetry for Students* welcomes your comments and ideas. Readers who wish to suggest poems to appear in future volumes, or who have other suggestions, are cordially invited to contact the editor. You may contact the editor via E-mail at: *ForStudentsEditors@gale.com*. Or write to the editor at:

Editor, *Poetry for Students*
The Gale Group
27500 Drake Rd.
Farmington Hills, MI 48331-3535

# Literary Chronology

**1608:** John Milton is born in Cheapside, London.

**1632:** John Milton's "On His Having Arrived at the Age of Twenty-Three" is published.

**1674:** John Milton dies in November, apparently from complications arising from gout.

**1795:** John Keats is born.

**1803:** Ralph Waldo Emerson is born in Boston.

**1807:** Henry Wadsworth Longfellow is born on February 27 in Portland, Maine.

**1819:** John Keats's "La Belle Dame sans Merci" is published.

**1821:** John Keats dies.

**1839:** Ralph Waldo Emerson's "The Rhodora" is published.

**1845:** Henry Wadsworth Longfellow's "The Arsenal at Springfield" is published.

**1882:** Henry Wadsworth Longfellow dies on March 24 in Cambridge, Massachusetts.

**1882:** Ralph Waldo Emerson dies at home in Concord, Massachusetts.

**1887:** Marianne Moore is born on November 15 in Kirkwood, Missouri.

**1892:** Edna St. Vincent Millay is born on February 22 in Rockland, Maine.

**1919:** Marianne Moore's "Poetry" is published.

**1921:** Edna St. Vincent Millay's "Wild Swans" is published.

**1923:** Denise Levertov is born on October 24 in Ilford, England.

**1923:** Richard Hugo (born Richard Franklin Hogan) is born December 21 in White Center, a poor working-class neighborhood on the south side of Seattle, Washington.

**1923:** Edna St. Vincent Millay is awarded the Pulitzer Prize for poetry for *The Ballad of the Harp-Weaver*.

**1926:** Robert Bly is born on December 23 in Madison, Minnesota.

**1938:** Raymond Carver is born May 25 in the tiny logging town of Clatskanie, Oregon.

**1939:** Seamus Heaney is born on April 13 in Mossbawn, in County Derry, in Northern Ireland, in the same year that Irish poet William Butler Yeats dies.

**1942:** Sharon Olds is born on November 19 in San Francisco, California.

**1943:** Nikki Giovanni is born in Knoxville, Tennessee.

**1947:** Jane Kenyon is born on May 23 in Ann Arbor, Michigan.

**1950:** Edna St. Vincent Millay dies of cardiac arrest on October 19 in Austerlitz, New York.

**1951:** Jorie Graham is born on May 9 in New York City.

**1957:** Li-Young Lee is born on August 19 in Jakarta, Indonesia.

# Literary Chronology

**1962:** Robert Bly's "Driving to Town Late to Mail a Letter" is published.

**1969:** Nikki Giovanni's "Knoxville, Tennessee" is published.

**1972:** Marianne Moore dies.

**1975:** Richard Hugo's "For Jennifer, 6, on the Teton" is published.

**1978:** Denise Levertov's "The Blue Rim of Memory" is published.

**1979:** Seamus Heaney's "The Singer's House" is published.

**1980:** Jorie Graham's "Mind" is published.

**1982:** Richard Hugo dies of leukemia.

**1986:** Li-Young Lee's "Early in the Morning" is published.

**1986:** Raymond Carver's "The Cobweb" is published.

**1987:** Sharon Olds's "I Go Back to May 1937" is published.

**1988:** Raymond Carver dies from cancer on August 2 in the new house he and his second wife, Tess Gallagher, had bought.

**1993:** Jane Kenyon's "Having it Out with Melancholy" is published.

**1995:** Jane Kenyon dies from leukemia.

**1995:** Seamus Heaney is awarded the Nobel Prize for literature.

**1996:** Jorie Graham is awarded the Pulitzer Prize for poetry for *The Dream of the Unified Field*.

**1997:** Denise Levertov dies on December 20.

# Acknowledgments

The editors wish to thank the copyright holders of the excerpted criticism included in this volume and the permissions managers of many book and magazine publishing companies for assisting us in securing reproduction rights. We are also grateful to the staffs of the Detroit Public Library, the Library of Congress, the University of Detroit Mercy Library, Wayne State University Purdy/Kresge Library Complex, and the University of Michigan Libraries for making their resources available to us. Following is a list of the copyright holders who have granted us permission to reproduce material in this volume of *Poetry for Students (PfS)*. Every effort has been made to trace copyright, but if omissions have been made, please let us know.

**COPYRIGHTED MATERIALS IN *PfS*, VOLUME 17, WERE REPRODUCED FROM THE FOLLOWING PERIODICALS:**

*PMLA*, v. 87, 1989. Reproduced by permission.—*Poetry*, v. cxlix, January, 1987 for "Comment: The Tune of Crisis," by Alicia Ostriker. Reproduced by permission of the author.

**COPYRIGHTED MATERIALS IN *PfS*, VOLUME 17, WERE REPRODUCED FROM THE FOLLOWING BOOKS:**

Bikerts, Sven. From *The Electric Life*. William Morrow, 1989. Copyright (c) 1989 by William Morrow. All rights reserved. Reproduced by permission.—Carver, Raymond. From *Ultramarine*. Random House, 1986. Copyright (c) 1986 by Random House, Inc. All rights reserved. Reproduced by permission.—Cook, Martha. From *Southern Women Writers: The New Generation*. University of Alabama Press, 1990. Copyright (c) 1990 by University of Alabama Press. All rights reserved. Reproduced by permission.—Engle, Bernard F. "The Armored Self: Selected Poems," http://www.galenet.com (1999).—Garner, Dwight, "Sharon Olds," http://www.salon.com (July 1, 1996). Reproduced by permission of Salon, http://www.salonmagazine.com.—Graham, Jorie. From *Hybrids of Plants and of Ghosts*. Princeton University Press, 1980. Copyright (c) 1980 by Princeton University Press. All rights reserved. Reproduced by permission.—Heaney, Seamus. From *Opened Ground*. Farrar, Straus, and Giroux, 1998. Copyright (c) 1998 by Farrar, Straus, and Giroux. All rights reserved. Reproduced by permission.—Hirst, Wolf Z. From *John Keats*. Twayne Publishers, 1981. Copyright (c) 1981 by G. K. Hall & Co. All Rights Reserved.—Hugo, Richard F. From *What Thou Lovest Well, Remains American*. W. W. Norton, 1975. Copyright (c) 1975 by W. W. Norton. All rights reserved. Reproduced by permission.—Kenyon, Jane. From *Constance: Poems*. Graywolf Press, 1993. Copyright 1996 by the Estate of Jane Kenyon. Reproduced by permission of Graywolf Press, Saint Paul, Minnesota.—Lee, Li-Young. From *Rose*. BOA Editions, 1986. Copyright (c) 1986 by BOA Editions. All rights reserved. Reproduced by permission of BOA Editions, Ltd.—Levertov, Denise. From *Life in the Forest*.

New Directions, 1978. Copyright (c) 1978 by Denise Levertov. Reproduced by permission of New Directions Publishing Corp.—Millay, Edna St. Vincent. From *On Wings of Song: Poems about Birds*. Knopf, 2000. Copyright (c) 2000 by Knopf. All rights reserved. Reproduced by permission of Alfred A. Knopf, Inc.—Olds, Sharon. From *The Gold Cell*. Knopf, 1987. Copyright (c) 1987 by Knopf. All rights reserved. Reproduced by permission of Alfred A. Knopf, Inc.—Wasserman, Earl R. From *The Finer Tone: Keats' Major Poems*. Johns Hopkins Press, 1953. Copyright (c) 1953 by Johns Hopkins Press. Copyright renewed (c) 1981 by Eleanor B. Wasserman. All Rights Reserved. Reproduced by permission of the Johns Hopkins University Press.

**PHOTOGRAPHS AND ILLUSTRATIONS APPEARING IN PfS, VOLUME 17, WERE RECEIVED FROM THE FOLLOWING SOURCES:**

Bly, Robert, photograph by Chris Felver. Reproduced by permission.—Carver, Raymond, photograph (c) Jerry Bauer. Reproduced by permission.—Emerson, Ralph Waldo, photograph. UPI/Corbis-Bettmann. Reproduced by permission.—Giovanni, Nikki, photograph. Reproduced by permission.—Graham, Jorie, photograph. AP/Wide World Photos. Reproduced by permission.—Heaney, Seamus, photograph. AP/Wide World Photos. Reproduced by permission.—Keats, John, painting. The Library of Congress.—Levertov, Denise, photograph. AP/Wide World Photos. Reproduced by permission.—Longfellow, Henry Wadsworth, photograph. AP/Wide World Photos. Reproduced by permission.—Millay, Edna St. Vincent, photograph. The Library of Congress.—Milton, John, engraving. The Library of Congress.—Moore, Marianne, photograph by Jerry Bauer. Reproduced by permission.—Olds, Sharon, photograph. Reproduced by permission.—Teton River, in South Dakota, at Fort Pierre, Where the Lewis and Clark Expedition stopped, photograph. (c) Dave Muench/Corbis. Reproduced by Permission.—Whistling swans in flight, photograph. (c) Lowell Georgia/Corbis. Reproduced by Permission.

# Contributors

**Adrian Blevins:** Blevins has published essays and poems in many magazines, journals, and anthologies and teaches writing at Roanoke College. Original essays on *Driving to Town Late to Mail a Letter* and *For Jennifer, 6, on the Teton*.

**Jennifer Bussey:** Bussey holds a master's degree in interdisciplinary studies and a bachelor's degree in English literature. She is an independent writer specializing in literature. Entries on *The Rhodora* and *Wild Swans*. Original essays on *The Rhodora* and *Wild Swans*.

**Kate Covintree:** Covintree is a graduate of Randolph-Macon Women's College with a degree in English. Original essay on *Having it Out with Melancholy*.

**Carol Dell'Amico:** Dell'Amico is a college instructor of English literature and composition. Original essays on *Knoxville, Tennessee* and *On His Having Arrived at the Age of Twenty-Three*.

**Pamela Steed Hill:** Hill is the author of a poetry collection, has published widely in literary journals, and is an editor for a university publications department. Entries on *The Blue Rim of Memory* and *Having it Out with Melancholy*. Original essays on *The Blue Rim of Memory* and *Having it Out with Melancholy*.

**David Kelly:** Kelly is an instructor of creative writing and literature at Oakton Community College. Entries on *La Belle Dame sans Merci* and *Knoxville, Tennessee*. Original essays on *La Belle Dame sans Merci* and *Knoxville, Tennessee*.

**Sheri E. Metzger:** Metzger has a doctorate in English Renaissance literature. She teaches literature and drama at the University of New Mexico, where she is a lecturer in the English department and an adjunct professor in the university's honors program. Entries on *I Go Back to May 1937* and *On His Having Arrived at the Age of Twenty-Three*. Original essays on *I Go Back to May 1937* and *On His Having Arrived at the Age of Twenty-Three*.

**Marjorie Partch:** Partch is a Jungian astrologer, writer, and graphic designer. Original essays on *The Blue Rim of Memory* and *Mind*.

**Frank Pool:** Pool has published poems and reviews in several journals and teaches advanced placement and international baccalaureate English. Original essay on *The Singer's House*.

**Ryan D. Poquette:** Poquette has a bachelor's degree in English and specializes in writing about literature. Entries on *The Arsenal at Springfield* and *The Singer's House*. Original essays on *The Arsenal at Springfield* and *The Singer's House*.

**Michelle Prebilic:** Prebilic is an independent author who writes and analyzes children's literature. She holds degrees in psychology and business. Original essays on *Mind*, *The Rhodora*, and *Wild Swans*.

## Contributors

**Tamara Sakuda:** Sakuda holds a bachelor of arts degree in communications and is an independent writer. Original essay on *The Arsenal at Springfield* and *The Cobweb*.

**Chris Semansky:** Semansky is an instructor of literature and composition. Entries on *The Cobweb, Driving to Town Late to Mail a Letter, Early in the Morning, For Jennifer, 6, on the Teton, Mind,* and *Poetry*. Original essays on *The Cobweb, Driving to Town Late to Mail a Letter, Early in the Morning, For Jennifer, 6, on the Teton, Mind,* and *Poetry*.

**Erika Taibl:** Taibl is an English instructor and writer. Original essay on *Early in the Morning*.

**Carey Wallace:** Wallace is a freelance writer and poet. Original essay on *The Cobweb, On His Having Arrived at the Age of Twenty-Three,* and *Wild Swans*.

# The Arsenal at Springfield

## Henry Wadsworth Longfellow
## 1845

Henry Wadsworth Longfellow's "The Arsenal at Springfield," first published in 1845 in America, is considered by many critics to be Longfellow's most effective antiwar poem. The idea for the poem came on Longfellow's wedding trip to the famous arsenal in Springfield, Massachusetts, which supplied many of the guns used during the American Revolution. At the suggestion of his wife, Fanny, and inspired by the writings of his friend, the peace crusader Charles Sumner—who was also present at the tour of the arsenal—Longfellow wrote a poem that offered a desperate plea for peace. The many rows of guns in the arsenal, which in Longfellow's estimation resembled a pipe organ, provided a vivid image to launch his poem. In fact, many critics have commented on the effectiveness of the images in the poem, which offer a gritty tour through the ravaging effects of human war, as well as a preview of what a peaceful society could be like.

The poem was widely known in its time. Sumner was one of many engaged in a vigorous antiwar—and in some cases antislavery—debate, so Longfellow's poem was timely. The poet's reputation declined after his death, and the debate over the worth of his works still rages. Still, "The Arsenal at Springfield" forever commemorates the actual arsenal, which today is housed in the museum of the historic Springfield Armory. The arsenal is known as the Organ of Muskets—as a result of Longfellow's depiction in the poem. A current copy of the poem can be found in *Henry Wadsworth Longfellow: Selected Poems*, published by Penguin Classics in 1988.

*Henry Wadsworth Longfellow*

## Author Biography

Henry Wadsworth Longfellow was born on February 27, 1807, in Portland, Maine. His father, Stephen Longfellow, was a member of the Eighteenth Congress of the United States. In 1822, Longfellow enrolled in Bowdoin College, a new academic institution where his father was a trustee. However, Longfellow went against his father's wish, which was for his son to study law, and chose to pursue a literary career. A prolific writer, Longfellow published poems in several different publications while in school. In 1825, the poet was offered the position of chair of the new modern languages department at Bowdoin. In an effort to prepare for this post, Longfellow took a trip to Europe, which stretched into three years. From 1829 to 1835, the poet taught at Bowdoin, where he spent much of his writing time working on textbooks, essays, and other academic endeavors.

In 1835, Longfellow and his wife, Mary, pregnant with their first child, set off for Europe. However, later that year, Mary died of complications from a miscarriage, an event that greatly affected Longfellow. The poet soon gave up his academic publishing in favor of his poetry, and, in 1836, he accepted a teaching position at Harvard University. He renewed his former practice of publishing his poems in several different magazines. In *Voices of the Night* (1839) and *Ballads and Other Poems* (1841), Longfellow reprinted many of these poems. During this time, the poet was also trying, in vain, to win the hand of Frances Appleton in marriage. In 1843, however, Fanny relented, and the two were married. While they were on their honeymoon in Springfield, Massachusetts, the couple—along with their friend, public activist Charles Sumner—visited the city's famous arsenal, where Fanny suggested that Longfellow write a peace poem. Struck by the way the rows of guns resembled a pipe organ, Longfellow used this idea as the dominant image in the resulting poem "The Arsenal at Springfield," which was first published in *Graham's Magazine* in May 1845 and gained a wider audience when it was included in 1846's *The Belfry of Bruges and Other Poems*.

Following the publication of several more works, including poetry, a novel, and even a verse drama, Longfellow resigned from his position at Harvard in 1854. It was not long afterwards that his prolific output slowed down. In 1861, Fanny Longfellow's dress caught on fire while she was sealing some memory bags with wax, and the poet was unable to save her; she died from her burns the next day. At the same time, the poet's attempts to put out the flames had given him massive burns on his face that almost killed him. In time, the poet recovered physically, although with permanent scars on his face, he hid for the rest of his life behind the bushy white beard that many came to associate with the poet. Longfellow died in Cambridge, Massachusetts, on March 24, 1882.

## Poem Text

This is the Arsenal. From floor to ceiling,
   Like a huge organ, rise the burnished arms;
But from their silent pipes no anthem pealing
   Startles the villages with strange alarms.

Ah! what a sound will rise, how wild and dreary,    5
   When the death-angel touches those swift keys!
What loud lament and dismal Miserere
   Will mingle with their awful symphonies!

I hear even now the infinite fierce chorus,
   The cries of agony, the endless groan,    10
Which, through the ages that have gone before us,
   In long reverberations reach our own.

On helm and harness rings the Saxon hammer,
   Through Cimbric forest roars the Norseman's song,
                                      15

And loud, amid the universal clamor,
    O'er distant deserts sounds the Tartar gong.

I hear the Florentine, who from his palace
    Wheels out his battle-bell with dreadful din,
And Aztec priests upon their teocallis
    Beat the wild war-drums made of serpent's skin;   20

The tumult of each sacked and burning village;
    The shout that every prayer for mercy drowns;
The soldiers' revels in the midst of pillage;
    The wail of famine in beleaguered towns;

The bursting shell, the gateway wrenched asunder,   25
    The rattling musketry, the clashing blade;
And ever and anon, in tones of thunder
    The diapason of the cannonade.

Is it, O man, with such discordant noises,
    With such accursed instruments as these,   30
Thou drownest Nature's sweet and kindly voices,
    And jarrest the celestial harmonies?

Were half the power, that fills the world with terror,
    Were half the wealth bestowed on camps and courts,
Given to redeem the human mind from error,   35
    There were no need of arsenals or forts:

The warrior's name would be a name abhorred!
    And every nation, that should lift again
Its hand against a brother, on its forehead
    Would wear forevermore the curse of Cain!   40

Down the dark future, through long generations,
    The echoing sounds grow fainter and then cease;
And like a bell, with solemn, sweet vibrations,
    I hear once more the voice of Christ say, "Peace!"

Peace! and no longer from its brazen portals   45
    The blast of War's great organ shakes the skies!
But beautiful as songs of the immortals,
    The holy melodies of love arise.

## Poem Summary

### Stanza One

"The Arsenal at Springfield" begins with a clear statement: "This is the Arsenal." By using such a blatant form of speech, Longfellow immediately establishes his setting. This is important to him, because he wishes to build on the setting: "From floor to ceiling / Like a huge organ, rise the burnished arms." The guns that reside in the arsenal are so numerous that they take up the entire wall space in the building. Furthermore, the "burnished," or polished, guns resemble an organ, in this case a pipe organ. A pipe organ is a large instrument that uses pressurized air, forced through rows of pipes, to create musical sounds. By saying that the collection of guns is like an organ, Longfellow is being metaphorical. A metaphor is a technique by which the poet gives an object a secondary meaning that does not normally belong to it. Longfellow does not mean that one could play music on the guns as one could on an organ. However, his reference to the organ invokes a powerful image in the reader's mind. Although he has not stated so explicitly, the reader can infer from the organ reference that the arsenal's guns are all standing upright, arranged in rows with their barrels sticking up—like the pipes of an organ. This is the power of Longfellow's metaphor.

The image is even more powerful since the metaphor gives the reader a meaning that is contradictory to the objects' original meaning. Guns are, by their very nature, used to create violence, whereas organs are usually found in peaceful settings, such as churches, and used to create melodies. In the next two lines, Longfellow elaborates on the fact that he is using a contradictory meaning: "But from their silent pipes no anthem pealing / Startles the villages with strange alarms." Anthems are a positive form of song meant to praise something or somebody, and they often have holy meanings. These guns, however, have "silent pipes" and offer no consolation or assurance. Likewise, for now, they will not inspire any "strange alarms," which happen when a startled village is attacked.

### Stanza Two

However, the next line says that things are about to change. Says Longfellow, "Ah! what a sound will rise, how wild and dreary," indicating by the use of the word *will* that the peace is only momentary. Some "wild and dreary" tragedy is about to happen. At this point, it is possible to infer a time for the setting. Although some might guess from the start that the "Springfield" from the title is Springfield, Massachusetts, a famous town that helped supply guns to the American Revolution through its arsenal, this line confirms it. The guns from the first stanza are "burnished" and "silent," because they have never been used. The reader is getting a picture of the arsenal as it was in 1777 before the guns had been used. In this second stanza, Longfellow, writing from the 1840s but looking back to 1777 with the benefit of hindsight, can tell readers for a fact that once the "organ" starts to play, things are going to get bad.

He refers to a "death-angel," who will touch the "swift keys" of the organ. Normal organs are sounded through the use of a keyboard. However, for this organ of death, the keys are the triggers for the guns. Referring to these keys as "swift" underscores the fact that people are going to die quickly in the American Revolution. By using musical language such as "keys," Longfellow is sustaining the metaphor of guns as organs of death. In the next two lines, he magnifies this effect: "What loud lament and dismal Miserere / Will mingle with their awful symphonies! *Miserere* is French for "Have mercy," so these two lines are saying that cries for mercy of those who will be shot will be a form of music—which will blend in with the "awful symphonies" that the organ of death creates.

## Stanza Three

In the third stanza, Longfellow builds on this idea, saying that these "cries of agony" and "the endless groan" will form an "infinite fierce chorus." These guns are not just going to kill a lot of people; they are going to uphold a tradition that has been going on "through the ages that have gone before us." Furthermore, the horrible music that will come from them will be made even more horrible from the "long reverberations," or echoes, of violence from times past.

## Stanza Four

At this point, Longfellow goes back to the past to explore this violence in detail. He starts with the Saxons, members of a Germanic race of people who, along with the Anglos and the Jutes, staged a massive invasion of Britain in the fifth century. The Saxons fought with hammers, which Longfellow notes would ring on "helm and harness." The use of the ringing sound makes the depiction of the battle more intense and provides a fifth-century equivalent to the organ of death in Springfield. Longfellow continues his exploration of ancient battles by discussing the "Norseman's song," a roaring battle cry that tears through the "Cimbric" forest. The "Cimbric" people were a Germanic or Celtic people who were thought to have originated in Jutland, the continental portion of modern-day Denmark. The Norsemen, commonly known as Vikings, were another Scandinavian warrior culture, known for their boisterous battle songs. All of these sounds combine to help create the horrible music of battle, which is such a "universal clamor" that it extends over "deserts" to the land of the Tartars. Tartars, also known as Tatars, were a warrior race in the area of modern-day Turkey. Their "gong" is their particular contribution to the battle "music."

## Stanza Five

Like the previous stanza, this stanza highlights other warrior cultures that have helped to contribute to the war song. The "Florentine," located in modern-day Florence, Italy, uses a "battle-bell" during conflicts. Likewise, the "Aztec priests," a particularly notorious warrior culture that was active in Mexico in the sixteenth century, stand "upon their teocallis" and beat their "wild war-drums made of serpent's skin." A "teocallis" was a ceremonial space on the flattened and terraced top of a pyramid, which was used for rituals such as the beating of their war drums. In this case, their drums are made of "serpent's skin," an even more dangerous image, since snakes can be very deadly.

## Stanza Six

In the sixth stanza, Longfellow stops his listing of warrior cultures and focuses specifically on the war sounds that create the awful music of a death organ. These sounds include the "tumult" created from ravaged villages, the "shout" that covers up every cry for mercy, the "revels" of the victorious soldiers who are in the midst of pillaging, and the "wail" of people who are hungry—a common side effect of war.

## Stanza Seven

To these sounds of human suffering, Longfellow next adds sounds of various weapons from different eras in military technology. These sounds include "the bursting shell," explosive projectiles that can tear structures apart; the "rattling musketry," guns like those in the arsenal; "the clashing blade," or sword; and of course, as he emphasizes in the last two lines, the "tones of thunder" that accompany the firing of a cannon. This "cannonade" is a "diapason," a musical term that normally means a fixed level of sound. In other words, when people are at war with modern weapons like cannons, the assault is relentless; the "music" reaches a certain pitch and stays there.

## Stanza Eight

In this stanza, Longfellow poses a question:

Is it, O man, with such discordant noises,
With such accursed instruments as these,
Thou drownest Nature's sweet and kindly voices,
And jarrest the celestial harmonies?

Here, Longfellow once again identifies all of the previous descriptions as "discordant noises." *Discordant* means "inharmonious," so Longfellow is saying that, while these war sounds are creating a form of "music," it is not a good one—it is not harmonious with the rest of human life. Longfellow questions the reader, asking if it is possible that, with these "accursed instruments," the reader—and all of human society—is drowning out the natural harmonies found in the sounds of nature. Longfellow takes it one step further in the last line, where he suggests that this "discordant" noise might be so destructive that it is jarring the "celestial harmonies." This refers to an ancient philosophy in which people believed that the heavenly bodies, or spheres, were arranged in such a perfect way that they created divine music. By suggesting that human fighting could throw off the celestial song, Longfellow is underscoring the fact that war has colossal consequences.

### Stanza Nine

As if he is providing an answer to his own question from the previous stanza, Longfellow now makes a plea to stop the fighting. He poses a hypothetical situation: if "half the power that fills the world with terror" and "half the wealth bestowed on camps and courts" were reallocated, then humanity would not need "arsenals" or "forts." In other words, military campaigns and empires require enormous resources, which would be better spent in educating the human mind into a more peaceful condition.

### Stanza Ten

In this hypothetical new society, the tables would be turned. Whereas in the old society warriors like the Vikings and the Aztecs would be revered, in this new, peaceful society, they would be outcasts, and nobody would even want to speak their names, much less support their militant actions. In the last two lines of this stanza, Longfellow takes it even further, increasing from one warrior to an entire "nation." If a nation should dare exhibit violence toward another nation in this new society, it would "wear for evermore the curse of Cain!" Here, Longfellow calls on one of the classic stories of the Old Testament to support his case. The story of Cain and Abel is one of jealously and war-like rage. Cain becomes jealous when the Lord accepts an offering from Cain's brother, Abel, but does not accept an offering from Cain. As a result, Cain kills Abel. When the Lord finds out, he banishes Cain from civilization, giving him a mark that will discourage others from killing him. This eternal banishment will be the punishment of anybody who dares murder in this new, hypothetical, culture, Longfellow tells his readers.

### Stanza Eleven

Now that he has sketched out his plan for the perfect, peaceful society, Longfellow moves on into the future and tries to paint that future as a reality. He takes the reader down "the dark future, through long generations." Here, in this distant future, "The echoing sounds" of the war music that has been played for millennia now "grow fainter and then cease." Instead of these "discordant noises," this future once again holds "sweet vibrations," which sound "like a bell." Invoking the Bible once again—this time the New Testament—Longfellow says that he can "hear once more the voice of Christ say, 'Peace!'" By invoking both the Old and New Testaments, Longfellow is trying to underscore the fact that war is wrong and that both sections of the Bible will back him up on this idea.

### Stanza Twelve

Longfellow starts this stanza with the word "Peace!" after ending the previous stanza with the same word. This emphasizes Longfellow's message, forcing the reader to sit up and take notice. Now that Longfellow has sketched out his dream of a peaceful society, he takes one more look at the death organ, which is quiet once again: "no longer from its brazen portals / The blast of War's great organ shakes the skies!" At this point, although he has started out by discussing the organ of death at the Springfield arsenal, the "great organ" now refers to the collective instrument of death that has been forged throughout the countless battles like those described in the poem. Finally, at the end of the poem, Longfellow, having silenced the music of war, has freed up space for the "holy melodies of love," which are as "beautiful as songs of the immortals." Humanity may not be able to hear the music of the celestial spheres, but it has the ability to create melodies that are equally as beautiful, if it will just learn to focus on love, not war.

## Themes

### War

The theme that is most obvious in the poem from the beginning is war. Humans have been in countless wars in their history, and Longfellow samples some of these wars—from various points in humanity's past—to totally explore the brutality and horrors of war. When the poem starts, Longfellow introduces the arsenal at Springfield, which is quickly shown to resemble a ghastly type of musi-

## Topics For Further Study

- The American Revolution earned the United States independence from Britain. Research one other culture from any period in history that has successfully won its independence from another nation through military conflict. Compare this conflict with the American Revolution, paying special attention to the types of military strategies used to win each conflict.

- When Longfellow wrote his poem, America was experiencing a strong antiwar movement. Compare the attitudes toward war in the 1840s with the Vietnam antiwar movement in the late 1960s and early 1970s. What were the positive and negative effects of each movement?

- Choose a modern nation, other than the United States, that is currently embroiled in a military conflict. Research the background of the conflict, then use a map to plot out the major events that led to the strife. Finally, write a short prediction of how you feel the conflict may end, using your research to support your claims.

- Today, America is engaged in a debate about whether the portrayals of violence in television, movies, and other media should be censored. Those who want censorship believe that these portrayals of violence have a desensitizing effect on children, which may be leading to the increased violence in schools. Research both sides of this debate, including the legislation that may aid or hinder each side from reaching its goals. Using this information, give an argument for either side in the form of a newspaper-style editorial.

- Choose a war that has taken place sometime over the past five hundred years and research the economic and social effects that the war has had on the participating nations. Imagine that you are living in one of these nations at the time. Write a journal entry that describes how you feel about the conflict and how your life, and the life of your family, has been affected.

- Traditionally, wars have drastically affected the tone of the artistic works produced at the time, as writers, artists, filmmakers, and other artists try to document, support, or protest the conflict. Research other nonliterary works that have either a war or peace theme. Choose one of these artworks and compare it with "The Arsenal at Springfield."

---

cal organ. But this organ does not play an inspirational or spiritual "anthem." Instead, it offers a "wild and dreary" form of music, the music of brutality, suffering, and death. Longfellow describes the act of playing this organ—the guns—as if an evil force, a "death-angel" is playing "awful symphonies." When the poet starts to take the reader back "through the ages," he explains what forms some of these symphonies, invoking the Saxons, a Germanic race that—along with the Anglos and Jutes—invaded Britain. The Saxons used such basic weapons as a "hammer," which makes a ringing sound when it hits the metal "helm" or "harness" of a foe.

Besides actual violence, Longfellow also describes the auxiliary sounds of war, the songs, shouts, and drumbeats that announce a war is coming. These, says Longfellow, are still signs of war and so add to the "universal clamor" that has become the organ of war, as do the many advancements in military technology. From "the clashing blade," which has limited destructive power, humans have moved on to heavy artillery such as the "bursting shell" and the "cannonade," which can destroy ever-greater targets. However, these sounds are destructive to more than just humanity, Longfellow suggests. He poses a question to the reader, asking if it might even be possible for such "accursed instruments" of war to affect the divine music of the spheres.

### Peace

It does not have to be this way, Longfellow says in the last four stanzas. Instead, he suggests that if "half the power, that fills the world with terror" and "half the wealth bestowed on camps and courts" were put to good use, then humanity would not need war. In this peaceful world, precious resources would go to education, redeeming "the human mind from error." More importantly, in such a peaceful society, the idea of war would be a taboo, and those who engaged in such acts would be punished severely. Longfellow is so passionate about this idea of peace that he uses the word "Peace!" twice in a row—at the end of stanza seven and at the beginning of stanza eight. Instead of war, Longfellow says, humanity should focus on love. Unlike the "discordant noises" of war, which could potentially jar the celestial harmonies, love's "melodies" would "arise" to join the celestial music. This future is more appealing to Longfellow.

### Music

Whether he is talking about war or peace, Longfellow follows the theme of music. "War's great organ," "the celestial harmonies," and "Nature's sweet and kindly voices" are all described exclusively in musical terms. The war organ plays "awful symphonies," a "fierce chorus," which at times has "tones of thunder." This music travels "through the ages" in "long reverberations" to reach Longfellow's society. In addition to making the sounds of strife or peace sound like music, Longfellow also uses actual musical instruments within the poem, such as a "gong," "drums," and "a bell."

## Style

### Metaphor

The most obvious technique that Longfellow uses is metaphor. The organ of war comes to life from the moment he describes the guns as a musical instrument. This thought is compelling, especially since it is a contradictory metaphor. The idea of using a peaceful instrument to describe items that are used to create violence immediately engages the reader's attention. However, Longfellow takes it several steps further by sustaining the metaphor. The "huge organ" with its "burnished arms" takes on an even more sinister connotation when the "death-angel touches those swift keys!" Once this horrendous piece of death machinery is activated, the war organ seems to explode into the "awful symphonies," which drown out the "loud lament" of people who are suffering. As Longfellow takes his readers through the history of human warfare, he continues to speak in musical terms. There is a "fierce chorus" composed of "cries of agony" and an "endless groan." For the rest of the poem, Longfellow discusses the "endless" nature of this "fierce chorus" with several examples of the sounds of people suffering, weapons clashing, and barbaric victors celebrating their violent acts. All of these "musical" sounds serve to strengthen Longfellow's original metaphor of war as a giant organ that creates horrendous music.

### Imagery

While Longfellow is fleshing out this metaphor, he is also leaving the reader with some lasting mental images. The types of words that he chooses to use invoke images of extreme violence, brutality, and suffering. "On helm and harness rings the Saxon hammer," says Longfellow, and the reader can imagine a Saxon warrior bludgeoning somebody in the head or knocking the person off his horse. Longfellow also builds up images of powerful war chants. A "Norseman's song" is not just a song; instead, it "roars" through the forest, a weapon in itself. Likewise for the "Tartar gong," which is so powerful that the reader can imagine the noise traversing "deserts" like some huge sonic war boom. When Longfellow describes the human suffering that results from war, he gives the reader such images as a "sacked and burning village," a "prayer for mercy" drowning in an invader's shout, and "the wail of famine." These are all vivid and lasting images, as are the effects of a "bursting shell," a projectile explosive that can "wrench" a gateway from its original shape. Although the majority of the poem is composed of horrendous images such as these, Longfellow does offer some relief at the end, when he describes how things could be if people embrace peace, not war: "But beautiful as songs of the immortals, / The holy melodies of love arise." This image, of melodies taking on physical form and rising up—presumably to join the music of the celestial spheres—helps to take away the sting of the other negative images and to leave people with a hope for peace.

### Rhyme

When one looks at the structure of the poem, the rhyme scheme becomes immediately apparent. In each stanza, every other line rhymes. In other words, the end word in the first line rhymes with the end word in the third line. Likewise, the end word of the second line rhymes with the end word of the fourth line. So, in the first stanza, the word "ceiling" rhymes with the word "pealing," and the word "arms" rhymes with the word "alarms." Although Longfellow uses this type of rhyme scheme in much of his poetry, it works particularly well in this poem. When a poet uses such a predictable rhyme scheme, in which every stanza follows the same pattern, it affects the way a reader reads or speaks the poem. Since the reader's mind starts to pick up on the rhymes, the poem takes on a sing-song effect, much like that of a musical piece. Since Longfellow is using music as a metaphor for the horrors of war, this effect intensifies the reading experience.

## Historical Context

### United States War of Independence

Longfellow's poem is a plea for peace. However, instead of setting the poem in the modern day and talking about conflicts the world is currently facing, he chose to go back in time to 1777, when the fledgling American nation built its federal arsenal at Springfield. The new arsenal supplied many of the muskets that helped America win its freedom from England during the United States War of Independence (1775–1783). The war, which is also commonly known as the American Revolution, officially began in 1775. However, its roots can be traced back to 1763, after the conclusion of the French and Indian War (1754–1763)—the American phase of a much larger, worldwide conflict to establish territorial dominance in North America. Following Britain's victory, the British government, heavily in debt from its worldwide military campaign, decided that the American colonies should pay more taxes to help shoulder the load.

Subsequently, in 1764 the British Parliament passed a number of laws—collectively known as the Sugar Act—to raise taxes on sugar, molasses, and other commodities in the American colonies. However, the colonists, themselves struggling from an economic recession that resulted from the war, were opposed to the taxes. This was especially true since, unlike other British citizens, they had no representation in Parliament. Over the next decade, the British government continued to pass various taxation acts, and on April 19, 1775, the tension erupted into war when British forces killed several colonists. In 1776, the colonies declared their independence from Britain with the Declaration of Independence. On September 3, 1783, after several years of bloody battles, Britain signed the Treaty of Paris and acknowledged the independence of the United States.

### War of 1812

Though Longfellow was not alive during the American Revolution, his life did span the first three wars in the new American nation. And though the nation initially only stretched to the Mississippi River, the boundary lines soon changed. From 1793 to 1815, Britain was fighting on and off with French forces in the Napoleonic Wars. Although America was neutral, in 1807 British naval forces began to impede American trade by blocking French ports, as well as by forcing American seamen into service in the British navy. America warned England to remove its blockades and stop the impressment of American sailors, but Britain was slow to respond. At the same time, a group of United States congressman, known as the War Hawks, pushed for war with Britain, in an effort to win more territory for the United States—specifically Florida—from Britain's Spanish allies. These factors culminated in a declaration of war from United States President James Madison on June 18, 1812. American forces were ill equipped to fight a war against Britain and Spain, although they did win some key battles. In the end, the war was a stalemate, although it helped to inspire confidence in the citizens of the fledgling American nation.

### Mexican War

As the years passed and America began to build itself into an established nation, the quest for land continued. In 1845, the United States annexed Texas from Mexico. Texas had previously gained its independence from Mexico in 1836, and the citizens of Texas overwhelmingly voted to become part of the United States. However, Mexico and the United States disputed the actual borderline of Texas. In an effort to resolve this dispute—and buy more Mexican lands—President James Polk sent an emissary to Mexico. However, Mexico was not interested in losing more land and refused to see the emissary. Angry, Polk sent American troops to hold the disputed border area, which incited Mexican forces to attack. Although the area was disputed, Polk told the United States Congress that it was an attack on American soil, and on May 13, 1846, Congress authorized a war.

The Mexican War, also known as the Mexican-American War, was extremely one-sided, and America's more modern military easily won against Mexico's forces. The war, which ended on March

# Compare & Contrast

- **Late 1770s–Mid 1780s:** Outraged by massive taxation without representation and seeking to gain their independence from Britain, the colonies in America band together to fight against the British in the struggle known as the American Revolution.

  **1840s:** Anxious to gain more land for the young American nation, President James Polk helps to instigate a war with Mexico by sending troops into a disputed borderland. The American victory results in a substantial increase in lands for the United States, although not all Americans support the conflict.

  **Today:** Following unprovoked attacks on the World Trade Center in New York and the Pentagon in Washington, America leads an international war against terrorism. The military conflict, centered in Afghanistan, has wide support from the American public.

- **Late 1770s–Mid 1780s:** Neither of America's initial ruling documents—the Declaration of Independence and the Articles of Confederation—address the issue of slavery.

  **1840s:** The issue of slavery increases in importance, and the country becomes largely divided into northern abolitionists and southern slaveholders. In 1842, Longfellow publishes *Poems on Slavery*, a collection that proclaims slavery to be evil and warns of a future conflict over slavery.

  **Today:** Although discrimination is illegal, it still exists in certain areas, and many still fight to ensure equal rights for all, regardless of race, color, creed, or gender.

- **Late 1770s–Mid 1780s:** The federal arsenal at Springfield is built in 1777. In 1786, as a protest against high taxes from the state of Massachusetts, Daniel Shays, a local farmer, leads more than a thousand farmers in a months-long attack on the arsenal. Although the attack is ultimately repelled, the conflict, known as Shays's Rebellion, does inspire changes in Massachusetts tax law.

  **1840s:** Longfellow immortalizes the arsenal with his poem "The Arsenal at Springfield."

  **Today:** The arsenal, today known as the Organ of Muskets as a result of Longfellow's poem, is displayed in the museum of the historic Springfield Armory.

---

10, 1848, with the Treaty of Guadalup Hidalgo, resulted in a massive increase in land for the United States. In addition to conceding its claim on the disputed Texas borderland, Mexico also sold the United States much of the territory in the current states of New Mexico, Utah, Nevada, Arizona, California, Texas, and western Colorado, all for $15 million. However, even though the war was easily won, the American homefront was largely divided. Many slave-holding southern states appreciated the new land, which could create more slave-holding states in the South; however, some in the northern states, especially those against slavery, opposed the war.

## American Civil War

This division in thinking between northern and southern states increased over the next decade, especially surrounding the issue of slavery, an institution that Longfellow had spoken out against in some of his poems. In 1860, Abraham Lincoln—an antislavery candidate—was elected to the presidency. Southern states, which relied on slave labor to fuel their lucrative cotton industry, feared that Lincoln's intervention might hurt their business. As a result, from 1860 to 1861, eleven southern states, starting with South Carolina, seceded from the Union. The South tried to establish its independence, but when the Union failed to recognize the new Confederacy, war broke out. From 1861 to

1865, the American Civil War, also known as the War Between the States, consumed the lives of more than six hundred thousand Americans. It is, to date, the single most bloody fight that America has ever experienced.

## Critical Overview

The critical reception of Longfellow has changed over time. When his poems were published during his life, he was revered for them. His inspirational verses and folk themes struck a chord with audiences in both America and Europe, both of which were undergoing rapid change. However, after his death in 1882, his reputation was not as good, and it has been a constant debate since then as to whether or not Longfellow is a great poet.

"The Arsenal at Springfield" was originally published in *Graham's Magazine* in May 1845; it was reprinted at the end of 1845 in *The Belfry of Bruges and other Poems*, a volume that technically has a copyright date of 1846. As for the poem itself, it is widely known that the poem was not Longfellow's idea. As Cecil B. Williams notes in his 1964 book, *Henry Wadsworth Longfellow*, the poet's second wife, Fanny, was "at least partly responsible" for the writing of the poem. As Williams explains, on the Longfellows' "wedding journey in 1843, they visited, among other places, the arsenal at Springfield, Massachusetts, with the result, Fanny said, that 'I urged H. to write a peace poem.'" Likewise, as Thomas Wentworth Higginson notes in his 1902 book, *Henry Wadsworth Longfellow*, Fanny sometimes "suggested subjects for poems."

Fanny was not the only inspiration for the poem, however. As Higginson notes, on the trip to the arsenal, Longfellow and his wife were also joined by "Charles Sumner, just then the especial prophet of international peace." Sumner was a noted crusader for peace, and, as George Lowell Austin notes of the poem in his 1888 book, *Henry Wadsworth Longfellow: His Life, His Works, His Friendships*, a large influence on the poem. Austin, who had known Longfellow, recounts a conversation in which the poet told him that "The Arsenal at Springfield" "was suggested by reading Mr. Sumner's eloquent address on 'The True Grandeur of Nations.'"

As for the poem itself, critics have given it mixed reviews. Some, like Edward Wagenknecht, liked the poem. In his 1986 book, *Henry Wadsworth Longfellow: His Poetry and Prose*, Wagenknecht calls it an "admirably constructed poem" and says that it "is perhaps Longfellow's most effective plea for peace." However, others, like Newton Arvin, in his 1855 book, *Longfellow: His Life and Work*, have faulted the poem somewhat. Says Arvin, the poem "is only half successful if only because the anti-war theme is developed so fully in direct rhetorical terms." Still, in the end, Arvin approves of the poem, since it "takes off from a fine image—the burnished gun-barrels at the Arsenal rising to the ceiling like the pipes of a huge and ominous organ." Many other critics have been struck by the vivid imagery of the war organ.

In 1916, during World War I, George Hamlin Fitch notes in his essay, "Longfellow: The Poet of the Household," that the poem is "an eloquent plea for peace." In addition, citing the current state of affairs in the world, Fitch says that Longfellow's verses "have special force at this time when more than half the civilized world is engaged in the most destructive war ever known." However, not all critics praised the poem. The most scathing review comes from George Saintsbury, whose 1933 essay, "Longfellow's Poems," notes that while he likes many of Longfellow's verses, he did not like "The Arsenal at Springfield." Says Saintsbury, the poem "is a piece of mere claptrap, out of harmony with some of his own most spirited work, and merely an instance of a cant common at the time."

## Criticism

### Ryan D. Poquette

*Poquette has a bachelor's degree in English and specializes in writing about literature. In the following essay, Poquette discusses Longfellow's manipulation of structure, tenses, and sounds to emphasize his antiwar message in his poem.*

When one reads "The Arsenal at Springfield" for the first time, Longfellow's plea for peace is obvious. The gritty images from past wars send a very clear statement that Longfellow wants peace. Some critics, like Newton Arvin, have criticized the poem for this fact. In his 1855 book, *Longfellow: His Life and Work*, Arvin notes that the poem "is only half successful if only because the antiwar theme is developed so fully in direct rhetorical terms." However, once readers dig into the structure of the poem and start to see the ways in which

Longfellow has magnified the effect of his poem, they can see that it is this blatant quality that makes the poem so powerful. Instead of forcing the reader to dig deeply for the meaning, a requirement when reading some other poems, Longfellow's poem embraces its meaning. And in the end, even Arvin approves of the poem, since it "takes off from a fine image—the burnished gun-barrels at the Arsenal rising to the ceiling like the pipes of a huge and ominous organ."

At first sight, the entire poem appears to be uniform in structure. Each of the twelve stanzas contains four lines, and the poem uses a rhyme scheme in which the even and odd lines in each stanza rhyme with each other. However, even though the stanzas are standardized, the actual poem can be broken down into sections, based on what Longfellow is trying to achieve in each one. The first stanza is set off on its own, a description of the Springfield arsenal when it is completed and waiting for action. The collective guns sit "Like a huge organ," waiting to be played. In stanzas two and three, this "organ" bursts into activity, as it is played by the "death-angel," and the resulting "symphonies" are anything but pleasant. In fact, they are "awful." In stanzas four through seven, Longfellow increases the uncomfortable quality of his verses. Instead of reading about nameless "cries of agony" and other generic forms of suffering like he does in stanzas two and three, Longfellow now gets very specific, detailing the sights and sounds of violence in various warrior cultures, such as the "Norseman" and the "Aztec." The next stanza, stanza 8, also stands on its own, just as stanza 1 does. Longfellow does this intentionally because he wants to draw attention to it. In this stanza, Longfellow poses his question:

> Is it, O man, with such discordant noises,
> With such accursed instruments as these,
> Thou drownest Nature's sweet and kindly voices,
> And jarrest the celestial harmonies?

With this question, Longfellow suggests that war is so dangerous that it can destroy nature and even rock the heavens themselves. However, the structure over these four lines is somewhat odd for a question. In particular, the "Is it" seems to stick out, so it forces the reader to slow down and take notice of what comes after it. If the "Is it" were removed and the question mark were changed to a period, the statement would read more clearly. However, Longfellow does not want to make a statement. Instead, he would rather lead the reader—under the guise of a question—to adopt his view, that war is destroying both heaven and Earth.

> *Although Longfellow was criticized by some for his blatant antiwar message in 'The Arsenal at Springfield,' that was exactly his point. He did not want to bury his message within thick, literary language that needs to be deciphered.*"

The question mark is important for another reason, too. Since Longfellow is posing a question in this stanza, the reader will expect him to answer it. In fact, he does in the next two stanzas, in which he outlines how life could be in a peaceful society. The first of these stanzas in particular contains the overall message that Longfellow is trying to convey with his antiwar poem:

> Were half the power, that fills the world with terror,
> Were half the wealth bestowed on camps and courts,
> Given to redeem the human mind from error,
> There were no need of arsenals or forts:

If people will focus half of the power and wealth in the world on education, humanity will learn from its mistakes and will not need war anymore. Stanza 10 develops this idea even more. In this hypothetical society where peace rules, a "warrior's name would be a name abhorred," and any nation that dares attack another would "wear for evermore the curse of Cain!" In the final two stanzas of the poem, Longfellow imagines that he is traveling far into the future, "through long generations," to see this peaceful community come to life. When he hears the voice of Christ proclaiming the peace, he is joyous. In this future community, humanity will not need the "blast of War's great organ," which no longer "shakes the skies." Instead, "the holy melodies of love," which Longfellow notes are as "beautiful as songs of the immortals," prevail.

The effect of the poem's structure is one of a slow buildup, moving the organ from a standstill,

## What Do I Read Next?

- War poetry was common in many of the ancient societies of Europe, but no writer is more well-known or revered than Homer, a Greek poet who is believed to have lived during the eighth century B.C. Homer's epic poems, *The Iliad* and *The Odyssey*, have helped to form a basis for all of Western poetry and, many argue, Western literature in general. *The Iliad*, in particular, which details events of the Trojan War, is a good example of the type of heroic war poetry that antiwar poems like "The Arsenal at Springfield" rebelled against.

- Longfellow's *Evangeline*, originally published in 1847, is one of his best-known works. Like "The Arsenal at Springfield," the narrative poem details the effects of war, in this case on two lovers who are separated by the politics of the French and Indian War.

- While military technology has advanced rapidly over the last two millennia, military theory often has not. *The Art of War*, a military strategy book written by Sun Tzu in Japan roughly 2,500 years ago, is still used today to demonstrate everything from military tactics to how to get ahead in the business world.

- Henry David Thoreau, a contemporary of Longfellow's and also an antiwar activist, chose to go to jail instead of paying taxes that would support the Mexican War. Although Ralph Waldo Emerson paid the debt and Thoreau ended up spending only one night in jail, that night transformed Thoreau. He wrote about his experiences in jail and his antiwar beliefs in his essay "Civil Disobedience," which was first published in 1849 as "Resistance to Civil Government."

- Leo Tolstoy's massive novel, *War and Peace*, was originally published in Russia in six volumes from 1863 to 1869. Although the book requires a significant amount of time to read, the rich landscape and vivid characters that Tolstoy paints warrant the effort. Although the book tackles epic themes such as the grand scale of the Napoleonic wars, it also offers portraits of just about every aspect of human experience.

---

into action, then into more specific and increasingly horrible visions. By the time the reader reaches the question, in which Longfellow poses the possibility that war could have drastic consequences even beyond those already mentioned, the reader is primed to hear Longfellow's real message. This real message, located in stanzas 9 and 10, is the central focus of the poem and is the blatant message that Longfellow hopes to emphasize even more.

In addition to manipulating the structural breakdown in the poem to build up to the message, Longfellow also employs tense shifts to underscore the importance of stanzas 9 and 10. For most of the poem, Longfellow speaks in the present tense. "This is the Arsenal," he says when the poem starts off. With few exceptions, Longfellow maintains the present tense throughout the poem, drawing his readers directly into the conflicts that are described. Regardless of whether these conflicts are from the past, Longfellow wants his readers to feel them as if they are in the present so that they are harder to ignore. If something is in the past, nothing can be done about it, but when it is in the present, it must be dealt with. Since the present tense is the dominant mode in the poem, when Longfellow deviates from this pattern, it is noticeable. The only stanzas that do not use the present tense are stanzas 2, 9, and 10.

The second stanza is in the future tense, describing a sound that "will rise," once the organ is played. Why does Longfellow use the future tense here? It is important to establish the setting of the poem. Although readers may recognize that the arsenal is in Springfield, Massachusetts, they may not realize that Longfellow is taking them to the arsenal before it was used in the American Revolution. If the action took place in 1845, the poem would be less exciting because there were no wars going on, and so the arsenal would be relatively inactive at that time. Instead, with the benefit of hindsight, Longfellow is describing the calm moment before the storm of revolutionary war. While Longfellow needs to place this stanza in the future tense to properly establish the time of the poem, he does not want to stay there, and he jumps into the present tense starting with the next stanza: "I hear even now the infinite fierce chorus." From this point on, he does not return to the present tense until stanzas 9 and 10—the main message of the poem. Just as the structure of the poem builds up to these two stanzas, which provide Longfellow's hypothetical society, the tense shifts again from present to future tense. Once again, instead of burying his intentions, Longfellow is underscoring his message as much as possible.

He places this emphasis on stanzas 9 and 10 in one other way: through the manipulation of sounds. The poem is saturated with sound. Playing off the idea of an organ that creates death and suffering instead of music, Longfellow then finds corresponding sounds that reflect this grim organ and sprinkles these sounds throughout the poem. At various times, the war organ produces a "fierce chorus." Some of the many sounds in this chorus include "cries of agony," a song that "roars," a "battle-bell," the "wail of famine," and "tones of thunder" created by a cannon. These sounds are so pervasive that even when the pipes of the organ are technically "silent," Longfellow makes mention of an "anthem" and "strange alarms." In fact, there is only one spot in the poem that includes no sound references—stanzas 9 and 10. Instead, the poet focuses on his plea for peace. Though the sounds have served their purpose up until stanza 9, providing graphic images to make his readers uncomfortable, by the time readers reach stanza 9, Longfellow is ready to talk straight to them, without relying on sounds to get their attention. Because the rest of the poem is saturated with sounds, the lack of sounds here does get the reader's attention.

Although Longfellow was criticized by some for his blatant antiwar message in "The Arsenal at Springfield," that was exactly his point. He did not want to bury his message within thick, literary language that needs to be deciphered. Instead, he planted his message—his blueprint for a peaceful society—in stanzas 9 and 10 and then manipulated the structure, tenses, and sounds to draw the most attention to these two stanzas.

> *He wants readers to understand the devastation and wastefulness of war—and they do."*

**Source:** Ryan D. Poquette, Critical Essay on "The Arsenal at Springfield," in *Poetry for Students*, The Gale Group, 2003.

## Tamara Sakuda

*Sakuda holds a bachelor of arts degree in communications and is an independent writer. In this essay, Sakuda discusses how Longfellow makes expert use of rhyme, meter, and imagery to express his feeling on social issues.*

Henry Wadsworth Longfellow published "The Arsenal at Springfield" in *The Belfry of Bruges and Other Poems* in 1845. In his time, Longfellow was a much-loved and popular poet. For the most part, everyone easily understood and accepted his poems. Today, Longfellow is remembered for his most popular poems, which include "Evangeline," "The Midnight Ride of Paul Revere," and "Hiawatha." These entertaining and approachable poems are verse narratives depicting historical figures and events. "Evangeline" tells the sad story of an Acadian maiden, separated during the expulsion of French settlers by the English in Nova Scotia, who searches for her true love, only to find him years later dying on a hospital bed. However, Longfellow also used his popularity and literary genius to express his feelings and opinions about social issues of the day. "A Psalm of Life" contains images of Longfellow's grief over the death of his first wife. "The Arsenal at Springfield" is Longfellow's statement on the horrors of war. His poems are often full of dynamic historical imagery and a swinging meter, making them vivid and lively to read.

Longfellow was born in Portland, Maine in 1807 and was descended from well-established New England families. Cecil B. William's book, *Henry Wadsworth Longfellow*, credits the poet's father, Judge Stephen Longfellow, with strongly encouraging his son's academic lifestyle. Williams also notes that Longfellow's mother, Zilpah Wadsworth Longfellow, "was fond of poetry, and music." Longfellow was educated at Bowdoin College in Maine and then became a professor of modern languages there. He later held the same position at Harvard. In addition to family influences, Williams feels that growing up in the major seaport of Portland affected Longfellow's poetry. Williams writes in *Henry Wadsworth Longfellow* that "Probably much of his facility for verse rhythms came to him through his responsive listening to the lapping of the waves and the sighing of the wind in the lofty pines nearby."

Longfellow experienced death first-hand when his first wife, Mary Potter Longfellow, died due to complications from a miscarriage. He learned how to appreciate life because of his loss. Longfellow's religious faith sustained him during his period of grief. This faith along with his sense of loss over Mary's death shaped Longfellow's feelings about death of any kind—even the senseless deaths of wartime. During his career, Longfellow wrote numerous volumes of poetry and prose. As a professor of modern languages, Longfellow traveled to England and Europe and was fluent in several languages. Longfellow's historical imagery in "The Arsenal at Springfield" reflects his European influences.

Longfellow had strong beliefs about the sanctity of all human life. In his book, *Henry Wadsworth Longfellow: His Poetry and Prose*, Edward Wagenknecht notes that while Longfellow participated in many sports growing up, he had a strong distaste for blood sports of any kind. He opposed capital punishment and faithfully followed the Unitarian Church. These strong beliefs shaped Longfellow's poetry and inspired him to write such moving works as, "A Psalm of Life," which depicts his grief over the loss of his first wife and his "peace poem" "The Arsenal at Springfield." Again, Wagenknecht states in *Henry Wadsworth Longfellow: His Poetry and Prose*, "He felt the nearness of God in both nature and human life, and it was because God informed it and manifested Himself through it that life was sacred to him."

Shortly after his marriage to Fanny Appleton, Longfellow wrote "The Arsenal at Springfield." While on their honeymoon trip in 1843, Longfellow and his wife toured the Springfield Armory. Built in 1777, The Springfield Armory remained a munitions facility until 1968. At the time of Longfellow's visit, the armory contained racks for storing the M1861 musket. These racks in the Storehouse contained 2,000 guns each. The sheer magnitude of such a display reminded Longfellow and his bride of a huge pipe organ. According to Williams in his book, *Henry Wadsworth Longfellow*, Fanny urged her husband to write a peace poem and he created "The Arsenal at Springfield." Williams remarks that "Fanny seems to have been even more of a pacifist than he was, but his lifelong belief in biblical 'faith, hope, and charity' made him readily responsive."

Longfellow used the elegiac form in writing "The Arsenal at Springfield." The poetic form consists of a four-lined stanza in iambic pentameter rhyming on alternate lines. Longfellow's use of this form of poetry is appropriate since the word elegiac expresses mourning or sorrow. Elegiac comes from the word elegy, which means a poem or song composed especially as a lament for a deceased person. Longfellow is using "The Arsenal at Springfield" to express his sorrow and grief over civilization's penchant for war, especially in the poem's most famous stanza: "Were half the power, that fills the world with terror / Were half the wealth bestowed on camps and courts / Given to redeem the human mind from error / There were not need of arsenals or forts."

Longfellow also uses historical references and images to create vivid pictures for his readers. In discussing *The Belfry of Bruges and Other Poems*, Wagenknecht states in *Henry Wadsworth Longfellow: His Poetry and Prose* "The shifting between past and present is very characteristic of Longfellow in general but especially in this collection." "The Arsenal at Springfield" is full of such historical images. In the fourth stanza, Longfellow references the great Norsemen of Scandinavia, the Cimbri of Germany, and the Tartars of Asia. All these tribes were known for their war-like culture of invasions and domination. In the next stanza, Longfellow gives the reader the sounds of war. He speaks of the Florentines who wheel out a battle bell during combat. This bell, called a Martinella, rallied the knights during the Florentine and German battles in 1260. Longfellow mentions the Aztecs as they beat their war drums on their pyramidal temple mounds called teocalli.

Perhaps the most vivid pictures from "The Arsenal at Springfield" come from the poem's sixth stanza: "The tumult of each sacked and burning village / The shout that every prayer for mercy drowns / The soldiers' revels in the midst of pillage / The wail of famine in beleaguered towns." Longfellow's words allow the reader to picture the flames and smell the acrid smoke of a burning village. Readers can hear the shouts as soldiers carouse and plunder in the midst of the chaos. He also casts a pall of sorrow as the reader learns of the famine that inevitably follows war. Longfellow uses these powerful pictures to elicit strong emotions. He wants readers to understand the devastation and wastefulness of war—and they do.

In addition to the vivid pictures Longfellow creates, he fills the next stanzas with religious references. He mentions the biblical character Cain, who murdered his brother in jealousy and anger. Longfellow compares warring nations to the fighting brothers, Cain and Abel. Longfellow believes human life is sacred. Just as people abhor the murder of human beings in anger, Longfellow believes people should abhor the warrior who murders in the name of battle or conquest. As Augustus H. Strong states in Wagenknecht's book, *Henry Wadsworth Longfellow: His Poetry and Prose*, "I know of no poet who has written so little that is professedly Christian and whose poetry is notwithstanding so shot through with Christian spirit."

Longfellow opens "The Arsenal at Springfield" with grim images of weapons stacked high, "like a huge organ, rise the burnished arms;" and the angel of death playing, "those swift keys!" He then references the 51st Psalm with the word: Miserere. This is from the opening line of the Psalm, "Miserere mei, Deus" (Have mercy upon me, O God). From this bleak beginning, Longfellow leaves the reader with words of comfort and hope at the poem's conclusion. As in previous stanzas, Longfellow uses his skill to invoke images of sight and sound. He juxtaposes his previous images of death, war-drums, and anguished cries with images of light, "sweet vibrations," and music. Instead of the battle-bell mentioned in the fifth stanza, readers hear Christ's pure, bell-like voice say, "Peace!" Instead of the sounds of, "The bursting shell / The gateway wrenched asunder / The rattling musketry, the clashing blade" from the seventh stanza, Longfellow gives the reader images of sweet sounds, "But beautiful as songs of the immortals, the holy melodies of love arise." This consistent and fitting use of imagery characterized Longfellow's style and endeared him to his readers. As Cecil Williams writes in his book, *Henry Wadsworth Longfellow* "He is hardly the most figurative of poets, yet his similes, metaphors, personifications and symbolism are abundant enough to lend an extraordinary imaginative quality to many of his poems." "The Arsenal at Springfield" is no exception.

As in Longfellow's day, war still haunts modern civilizations. Its horrors continue to shock and sadden. Longfellow opposed war both because of his religious convictions and because of his deep love for his fellow man. This love was evident in the depth and breadth of his poetry. Longfellow used his skill as a writer to unite his fellow man and to show what wonderful accomplishments they can create. Williams comments on Longfellow's love for both his art and his fellow man in his book *Henry Wadsworth Longfellow*:

> A patriot, he wanted his country to recognize literature and to encourage it, but he did not believe that literary art is primarily national. Rather it is universal and each nation can contribute most by understanding first the general nature of humankind and then its own special nature.

Through his powerful poem, "The Arsenal at Springfield," Longfellow strives to show humankind the wastefulness and anguish of war. He uses vivid images to draw the reader into the poem and to speak to the reader on an emotional level. Longfellow ends the poem with a vision of peace, a vision of a world where the pipe-organ of muskets is forever silent. Just as in 1845, war still haunts the world today, and Longfellow's poem lives on with a voice for these times.

**Source:** Tamara Sakuda, Critical Essay on "The Arsenal at Springfield," in *Poetry for Students*, The Gale Group, 2003.

## Sources

Arvin, Newton, *Longfellow: His Life and Work*, Atlantic Monthly Press, 1963, p. 75.

Austin, George Lowell, *Henry Wadsworth Longfellow: His Life, His Works, His Friendships*, Lee and Shepard Publishers, 1888, pp. 294–95.

Fitch, George Hamlin, "Longfellow: The Poet of the Household," in *Great Spiritual Writers of America*, Paul Elder and Company, 1916, pp. 58–67.

Higginson, Thomas Wentworth, *Henry Wadsworth Longfellow*, Houghton, Mifflin and Company, 1902, p. 173.

Longfellow, Henry Wadsworth, "The Arsenal at Springfield," in *Henry Wadsworth Longfellow: Poems and Other Writings*, Penguin Putnam, 2000, pp. 33–34.

Saintsbury, George, "Longfellow's Poems," in *Prefaces and Essays*, Macmillan and Company, 1933, pp. 324–44.

Wagenknecht, Edward, *Henry Wadsworth Longfellow: His Poetry and Prose*, The Ungar Publishing Company, 1986, pp. 76–77, 198, 213, 215.

Williams, Cecil B., "Household Lyrics, Ballads, Odes, Elegies, Sonnets," in *Henry Wadsworth Longfellow*, Twayne Publishers, 1964, pp. 27, 29, 129–47, 192, 196.

## Further Reading

Apfel, Roberta J., and Bennett Simon, eds., *Minefields in Their Hearts: The Mental Health of Children in War and Communal Violence*, Yale University Press, 1996.

> This book collects firsthand accounts from mental health professionals who have worked with children exposed to war and violence. Contributors include psychiatrists, psychologists, and social workers, who address the issues faced by children in war zones and other violent environments and who discuss the types of interventions and treatments that are used in these situations.

Collopy, Michael, and Jason Gardner, eds., *Architects of Peace: Visions of Hope in Words and Images*, New World Library, 2000.

> Collopy and Gardner combine stunning photographs of seventy-five of today's most prominent peacemakers with quotes and stories from the public figures themselves. From Nelson Mandela and the Dalai Lama to Carlos Santana and Maya Angelou, this volume offers a sweeping view of the various efforts that are being made to achieve peace in the world.

Godwin, Joscelyn, *Harmonies of Heaven and Earth: Mysticism in Music from Antiquity to the Avante-Garde*, Inner Traditions International, 1995.

> This book examines the powerful effect that music has on people and explores the underlying metaphysical reasons for these effects.

Leckie, Robert, *From Sea to Shining Sea: From the War of 1812 to the Mexican War, the Saga of America's Expansion*, HarperPerennial, 1994.

> Leckie examines this rich period in America's early history as an independent nation. The shape of the modern continental United States was largely determined by the end of the Mexican War, and the book offers many anecdotes that illustrate the major events during America's territorial growth and highlights the major people involved in the expansion.

LeShan, Lawrence, *The Psychology of War: Comprehending Its Mystique and Madness*, Helios Press, 2002.

> Although it was first published in 1992, this book was brought back into print after the terrorist bombings in September 2001. LeShan is a former military psychologist, and his study demonstrates why people choose to fight wars and why military conflicts happen so frequently. The new edition includes a new introduction that comments on the war on terrorism.

Underwood, Francis H., *Henry Wadsworth Longfellow*, Haskell House, 1972.

> Underwood's biography of Longfellow gives a thorough overview of the poet's early life, his academic pursuits, and his studies abroad. The book also offers in-depth studies of several of the poet's better-known works and includes genealogies, correspondence, and a bibliography.

# La Belle Dame sans Merci

## John Keats
## 1819

"La Belle Dame sans Merci," written in 1819 and published the next year in a form slightly different from the one here, depicts a knight-at-arms who has been seduced and abandoned by a capricious fairy. Told in the form of a dialogue, the poem recounts the experience of loving dangerously and fully, of remaining loyal to that love despite warnings to the contrary, and of suffering the living death of one who has glimpsed immortality. At the beginning and end of the poem, the knight remains on "a cold hill's side," a world devoid of happiness or beauty, waiting for his love to return. Some readers maintain that the poem is really about Keats's confused feelings for Fanny Brawne, his fiancée, to whom Keats could not commit fully. Others claim the story is symbolic of the plight of the artist, who, having "fallen in love" with beauty, can never fully accept the mundane. Either way, the conclusion is the same: however self-destructive intense love may be, the lover has little choice in the matter. Further, the more one entertains feelings of beauty and love, the more desolate and more painful the world becomes.

## Author Biography

Born in 1795, Keats, the son of a stablekeeper, was raised in Moorfields, London, and attended the Clarke School in Enfield. After Keats's mother's death in 1810, Richard Abbey took care of Keats

*John Keats*

and his three younger siblings. Although Keats was apprenticed to an apothecary (pharmacist), he soon realized that writing was his true talent, and he decided to become a poet. Forced to hide his ambition from Abbey, who would not have sanctioned it, Keats instead entered Guy's and St. Thomas's Hospitals in London, becoming an apothecary in 1816 and continuing his studies to become a surgeon. When he reached the age of twenty-one, Keats was free of Abbey's jurisdiction. Supported by his small inheritance, he devoted himself to writing. Keats also began associating with artists and writers, among them Leigh Hunt, who published Keats's first poems in his journal, the *Examiner*. But, within a few years, the poet experienced the first symptoms of tuberculosis, the disease that had killed his mother and brother. He continued writing and reading the great works of literature. He also fell in love with Fanny Brawne, a neighbor's daughter, though his poor health and financial difficulties made marriage impossible. He published a final work, *Lamia, Isabella, The Eve of St. Agnes, and Other Poems*, which included his famous odes and the unfinished narrative, *Hyperion: A Fragment*. Keats traveled to Italy in 1820 in an effort to improve his health but died in Rome the following year at the age of 26.

## Poem Text

O what can ail thee, knight-at-arms,
   Alone and palely loitering?
The sedge has wither'd from the lake,
   And no birds sing.

O what can ail thee, knight-at-arms,    5
   So haggard and so woebegone?
The squirrel's granary is full,
   And the harvest's done.

I see a lily on thy brow
   With anguish moist and fever dew;    10
And on thy cheek a fading rose
   Fast withereth too.

I met a lady in the meads,
   Full beautiful—a faery's child,
Her hair was long, her foot was light,    15
   And her eyes were wild.

I made a garland for her head,
   And bracelets too, and fragrant zone;
She look'd at me as she did love,
   And made sweet moan.    20

I set her on my pacing steed
   And nothing else saw all day long,
For sidelong would she bend, and sing
   A faery's song.

She found me roots of relish sweet,    25
   And honey wild, and manna dew,
And sure in language strange she said—
   "I love thee true."

She took me to her elfin grot,
   And there she wept, and sigh'd full sore;    30
And there I shut her wild wild eyes
   With kisses four.

And there she lullèd me asleep,
   And there I dream'd—Ah! woe betide!
The latest dream I ever dream'd    35
   On the cold hill's side.

I saw pale kings and princes too,
   Pale warriors, death-pale were they all;
They cried—"La Belle Dame sans Merci
   Thee hath in thrall!"    40

I saw their starv'd lips in the gloam,
With horrid warning gapèd wide,
And I awoke and found me here,
On the cold hill's side.

And this is why I sojourn here,    45
Alone and palely loitering,
Though the sedge is wither'd from the lake,
And no birds sing.

## Poem Summary

### Lines 1–12

The ballad consists of two parts of dialogue, each uninterrupted by the other and each uncouched by the normal story-telling mechanisms

## Media Adaptations

- A reading of "La Belle Dame sans Merci" is available on a compact disc called *Conversation Pieces*, released in 2001 by Folkways Records. This recording was originally released in 1964 in LP format by Folkways.

- A compact disc named *Songs*, released in 2001 on the Hyperion label, has a version of "La Belle Dame sans Merci" set to music and sung by Sir Charles Villiers Stanford.

- Lexington Records released a recording of Theodore Marcuse reading "La Belle Dame sans Merci" along with others by the same author on an LP called *The Poetry of Keats and Shelley*, produced in 1950.

- The 1996 two-cassette set *The Caedmon Collection of English Poetry* features various poetic masterpieces, including "La Belle Dame sans Merci," read by famous actors such as Sir John Gielgud, Richard Burton, James Mason, and Boris Karloff.

- Sir Ralph Richardson reads "La Belle Dame sans Merci" on a 1996 Caedmon audiocassette release called *The Poetry of Keats*.

- HighBridge Co. of St. Paul, Minnesota, includes "La Belle Dame sans Merci" on *John Keats, Poet*, a reading of Keats's poems by Douglas Hodge. It was released on audiocassette in 1996 as part of the HighBridge Classics series.

- Listen Library Inc. included "La Belle Dame sans Merci" on its 1989 audiocassette *The Essential Keats*. Poems for this recording were selected and read by poet Philip Levine.

- A 1963 LP recording from Spoken Arts Records entitled *Robert Donat Reads Favorite Poems at Home* includes the famous actor's rendition of "La Belle Dame sans Merci."

---

for identifying speakers ("I said," "he said," etc.). Because of this, the identity of the first speaker, whose part is completed in the first twelve lines, remains cryptic. Though he (or, it could equally be argued, she) reveals the identity of the other (the "knight-at-arms"), the first speaker says nothing, at least directly, about himself. He does, however, give plenty of information about the situation of the poem. The time is late autumn, the annual grasses having already "wither'd" and the birds having departed on their winter migration. The place, one can infer, is not always as forbidding as it seems to be now—its desolation is simply due to the time of year. There has been a "harvest," but it has ended. There is latent life present around the two characters: "the squirrel's granary is full." Therefore, if the setting symbolizes the knight's emotional desolation, one must understand it as a function of an individualized circumstance: of a very specific but not necessarily permanent condition. Come spring, after all, the cycle of the harvest will begin again.

Yet, this seems little consolation to the knight the speaker describes. He is "alone and palely loitering," "so haggard and so woebegone." His pallor is described metaphorically in terms of a "lily" on his brow and a "fading rose" on his cheek. Further, he appears physically ill, "moist" from the "fever" of some "anguish." Though through these observations the speaker has already foreshadowed the reasons for the knight's grim condition, the form's rhetoric demands the question be asked: "O what can ail thee?" A knowledge of chivalric lore should prompt the correct guess. Of a knight's three profound allegiances—to his God, his lord, and his lady—only the last would be described in terms of lily-pallor and a faded rose.

### Lines 13–24

The story's twist occurs in the first stanza of the knight's speech. Though a "lady" was bound to figure into the poem, that she is a "faery's child" changes the expectations of the tale's outcome and causes readers to reinterpret the nature of the knight's desolation. Literature and myth are filled with examples of humans who fall in love with gods, and with little exception, such relationships bode disastrously for the mortal party. Particularly in that area of mythology dealing with fairies or fairy-like creatures, humans who become enamored of fairies, elves, pixies, and the like generally suffer extreme emotional consequences once their affairs with the capricious beings have ended. Having loved an immortal, these hapless humans discover that mere mortal beauty—which can include not only human lovers but also life itself—will no longer do. Based on thse conventions, readers understand immediately that this is the knight's fate, and through his descriptions of his fairy-love's beauty, readers see the caprice that brings on his doom. In keeping with fairies' quick and unpredictable behavior, "her foot was light." Her long hair suggests the sensual nature of such creatures, who in lore are given to continual pleasures, and "her eyes were wild." The knight confesses he was taken in by his lady's fairy-penchant for "seeming:" She looked at him "as she did love." In the terms of chivalric belief-systems, earthly love is a mortally serious concept: it is at once an all-consuming renunciation of and at the same time the earthly manifestation of heavenly love. As such, it is considered by the knight to be eternal. Yet for the lady, who as a fairy has no such ideas about heaven or about chivalry, love is a purely earthly proposition. To her, it is merely an expression of her fairy-embodiment of nature, which begins and ends with the erotic. Thus, she makes a "sweet moan," which readers have no reason to believe is falsely manufactured. Thus, as well, she responds favorably to his gifts, which all represent natural or sensual pleasure: a "garland," "bracelets," a "fragrant zone." Her hold over the knight becomes complete when she sings to him her "faery's song," the type known to hopelessly enchant mortals' souls.

### *Lines 25–36*

The lady's gifts to the knight represent her closeness to nature: she is able to find him "roots of relish sweet," "honey wild and manna dew." She professes to him, "I love thee true." But, she does so in a "language strange" whose words may (and, it turns out, do) not hold the same meanings as the knight's. Still, the knight believes because, in the truest fashion of the romantic sensibility, he wants and needs to believe. At this point, readers might examine the various allegorical meanings readers have attached to the knight's story. While some believe it is a representation of the perils of earthly love—whose desire and randomness can seem to have the qualities of fairy-love—others maintain Keats is really talking about the poet's infatuation with immortal concepts such as beauty. In either case, the lover—whether of another human or of some aesthetic concept—has little choice in the matter. To him, the experience of love is all-encompassing, transcendent and, at least briefly, immortal. How many lovers, after all, have behaved rashly, even self-destructively, in the belief that their love took precedence over the normal modes of conduct. In addition, how many disappointed lovers carry with them the belief that they can never love the same way again? Still, new lovers proceed despite the warnings of previously disillusioned lovers. So, the knight proceeds into the fairy-cave, where, he says, "I shut her wild wild eyes"—the repetition suggesting a euphemism for sex —"with kisses four." In a poem devoid of many particulars, the number of kisses seems overly specific. Though there are many numerological interpretations of this detail, one simple explanation for the knight's specificity may suffice: it is the last thing he remembers. Moreover, it is his last act before the disillusionment and perhaps his last pure act. After the kisses, he is "lulled" to sleep, has his final dream, and awakes "on the cold hill's side."

### *Lines 37–48*

In his dream, the knight is warned by previous lovers to beware "La Belle Dame sans Merci"— the lovely lady without pity. They come to him from the land of death, for once they have glimpsed immortality, all life seems a walking death to them. There are "pale kings and princes," "pale warriors"—all heroic characters whose romantic spirit led to their demise. Yet, the knight cannot head their warnings. He too is a hero, and in the romantic tradition, a hero is often someone who cannot learn from his mistakes. Regardless, he has already experienced a heightened state from which he cannot return to any previous existence. When he awakens on the hillside, he can only "loiter," waiting for the experience to return. After his fairy-romance, the world is pale and devoid of charm, yet to the poem's initial speaker the knight's vigil, however inevitable, seems to be pointless and grim. The poem concludes with a recollection of the first stanza: "though the sedge is wither'd from the lake / And no birds sing." This not only frames the poem; it also confirms that the knight agrees with the first speaker's assessment of the setting. At the same time, the knight cannot agree with the speaker's implication that no human ought to remain in such a godforsaken place. For the knight, who has glimpsed the immortal and will probably never do so again, any other place would seem equally desolate.

## Themes

### Unrequited Love

With its forlorn, heartbroken narrator suffering the pangs of embarrassment, "La Belle Dame sans Merci" appears to tell readers about the universal situation known as unrequited love. While love felt equally by two parties is a celebrated event in stories and song, unrequited love occurs when the love felt by one person is much stronger than that felt by the person who is loved. The root "requite" comes from "to repay," which indicates a balance that one expects in a love relationship and the sense of unfairness when one person "pays" love out but is not paid back.

In the poem the knight's disappointment would be less severe if he did not believe from the beginning of their affair that the fairy child loved him in equal measure. As it is, she appears to fall in love with the knight just as he is falling for her. The look she gives him in line 19 and her "sweet moan" in line 20 might be read as signs of her love, and the presents she gives him are further proof they are equally balanced in their feelings for one another. She even takes him back to her home, her "elfin grot," and makes him feel comfortable. It would be natural for him to assume she is as interested as he is in continuing their budding romance when he awakes.

It is unclear whether the knight's intense feeling when he finds his lady gone is caused primarily by the loss of the woman herself. It could be that he is suffering from the disappointing conclusion that she never really loved him as much as he thought she did. By the end of the poem he clearly feels alone, but he does not show any anger toward her. The only clues the poem gives about whether or not the lady may have felt love for the knight come from the spectral images who visit the knight in his dream and tell him the lady is pitiless, that she has no mercy. The presence of these dream images may be explained psychologically, as if the knight subconsciously knew the lady had left him, and his mind had already started shifting the blame toward her. The dream might just be his rationalization, a way of making her out to be evil in order to cope with the pain of learning his love is unrequited.

## Topics for Further Study

- Find a contemporary song you think has the same message as Keats's poem. Compare the song with the poem to comment on the ways people of the nineteenth century and the twenty-first century view love.

- Research why it is significant that Keats wrote the title of his poem in French. Based on your research, do you think the French title has the same significance now that it would have had when Keats were living? Why or why not?

- Write a sequel to this poem, explaining what will happen when the spring comes again. Will the lover return to the knight? If not, will he continue waiting, or will his attention fade as the seasons change?

- Keats used a supernatural setting to explain his idea of romance. Find a folk story from a non-European culture that involves lovers in a supernatural setting and explain what the supernatural elements tell you about each culture.

### Nature

The love story told in this poem is framed within images of nature. The lady with whom the knight falls in love is described as the child of a fairy. Fairy stories often stem from rural folklore traditions. The lady is described as having "wild" eyes and as living in a cave on a hill side. When they are together, the knight and the lady give each other presents made from flowers, roots, honey, and dew. After the knight awakens to find the lady gone, the world is described as one from which life has receded, using images associated with nature's death each winter: the squirrels have stored their provisions for the long dead months, the grass in the lake has withered, and the birds have quit singing. The only signs of living nature after the lady disappears are the fading ones on the knight's face. The "lily" that the poem's other speaker sees on the knight's brow is a sign he once was blessed with the delicate beauty of a flower, although lilies are associated with death. The rose color in his cheek is another sign he has been touched by beauty, but it, like the rest of nature, is "fading."

### Despair

Despair is the state of having lost all hope, of finding oneself unable to believe life will ever be good again. The knight in "La Belle Dame sans Merci" falls into despair when he learns a relationship that seemed to be just starting has abruptly ended. His situation is clear from the very first line, when a stranger finds him out in the forest and can tell just by looking at him that something is gravely wrong. The stranger sees how pale he is and, noticing he has chosen to live by a dead, frozen lake, wants to know what ails him, by which he means what has made the knight so sick in spirit.

In the middle stanzas of the poem, the knight describes the romance, which meant more to him than anything that happened before it or since. The brief romance ended with the lady lulling him to sleep. Readers can assume that, comfortable and happy beside her, he expected their love to continue and even to grow when he awoke.

In the real (as opposed to magical) world, the knight's despair would take time to develop, because he would not know for sure that the woman he loved was gone forever. In the magical world of this poem, though, he is visited in his sleep by pale figures of noble men who describe the woman as merciless. When he wakes to find her gone, he readily believes her absence confirms the damning things the figures said about her. The poem does not have the knight looking for his lady or trying to find out why she has left; he is as certain she had no intention of staying with him just as surely as he knows he loves her. There is no hope they will be reunited, and therefore there is no hope that he can ever be happy again. His life is doomed to despair.

## Style

"La Belle Dame sans Merci" is a ballad, an old form of verse adapted for singing or recitation. The ballad form originated in the days when most poetry was memorized rather than written, and the typical subject matter of the ballad reflects a folk sensibility. Ballads are usually narrative, or storytelling, poems, and early ballads often addressed themes important to common people: love, courage, the mysterious, and the supernatural. Though the ballad is generally rich in musical qualities such as rhythm and repetition, it often portrays both characters and events in highly dramatic but simplistic terms.

Additional characteristics of the typical ballad include a set rhyme scheme and alternating line lengths. Formally, the ballad stanza is a quatrain, or a group of four lines, in which the first and third lines contain four stressed syllables while the second and fourth lines contain three stressed syllables. "La Belle Dame sans Merci" consists of twelve such stanzas, with a slight variation: the last line of each stanza contains only two stressed syllables, creating a dramatic suspension between stanzas. Aside from this, the quatrains exhibit the typical ballad stanza pattern of rhyme: the second and fourth lines are set in perfect end rhyme with one another, giving the poem the musical sound most ballads feature.

## Historical Context

### Romanticism

John Keats is considered one of the central figures in the English romantic movement. Romanticism was a philosophical and artistic ideal that spread across Western civilization in the late eighteenth and early nineteenth century. It sprang from the ideas of French writer Jean Jacques Rousseau and German writer Johann Wolfgang von Goethe. Rousseau, a major figure in the Enlightenment, wrote eloquently and convincingly about theories of social equality. At the time, most governments were arranged in a system that divided the opportunities for social success available to commoners from those available to people considered to be of noble birth. Rousseau's writings presented society as a corruption of humanity's natural state. His theory that every citizen participates in society willingly, as part of an implied "social contract," created a cult of individual freedom that celebrated the human spirit and led to the French Revolution in 1789. The Revolution's ten-year struggle to overthrow the monarchy and the nobles was one of the most direct influences on the romantic movement.

Goethe was trained as a lawyer, but he became a celebrated poet, playwright, and novelist. In 1775 he, along with German philosopher Johann Gottfriend von Herder and historian Justus Möser, published a collection of essays called *Of German Art*

# Compare & Contrast

- **1819:** America is a small, new country with only twenty-two states. The nation battled Great Britain for its freedom in the American Revolution from 1776 to 1783, and fought them again for maritime rights in the War of 1812, which lasted until 1815.

  **Today:** America is an economic superpower, and Great Britain is one of its closest allies.

- **1819:** The entire population of England is around 21 million, leaving much open, unpopulated land.

  **Today:** The population of England is around 46 million. With about 917 people per square mile, it is one of the most densely populated countries in the world.

- **1819:** England has the world's greatest navy, making it one of the most powerful countries in the world.

  **Today:** The Royal Navy is thirteenth largest fleet in the world and second largest in Europe (after Greece).

- **1819:** Ordinary people rely on poetry to convey physical experiences.

  **Today:** Technological advances in photography, sound recording, and computer-generated virtual reality make it possible to give people experiences without using words.

- **1819:** Vast areas of the globe, such as the two poles, have not yet been explored.

  **Today:** Any areas not currently populated are monitored from the ground and from space.

---

*and Style.* Their theories about art's relation to traditional folktales and about the place of love and longing in art later evolved into romanticism.

Many literary critics consider the formal start of romanticism to be the 1800 publication of *Lyrical Ballads*, a collection of poems by William Wordsworth and Samuel Taylor Coleridge. In the preface to that book, the two poets spelled out the principles of romantic thought. They emphasized the importance of feelings and emotion over intellectualism in poetry, and urged writers to cast away traditional forms and follow their inspirations. Their call for writers to focus on the natural and spiritual aspects of the world were mirrored throughout all the arts at the turn of the century, including painting, music, and architecture. They were strongly influential with the next generation of British poets.

The names most commonly associated with romanticism in literature are Keats, Lord Byron, and Percy Bysshe Shelley. The three were friends and associates. Their poetry combined elements of the various romantic strains that had come before them: the thirst for social justice of Rousseau, the mysticism of Goethe, and the emphasis on nature of Wordsworth and Coleridge. In addition, Keats, Byron, and Shelley lived lives of freedom dedicated to the pursuit of love and adventure, a lifestyle often associated with romantic poets in general.

## Chivalry

The fact that the character in "La Belle Dame sans Merci" is a knight is no coincidence. One of the key elements of romantic poetry is an interest in the folk traditions of one's home country. The chivalric tradition, concerned with knights and their relationships to the women they loved, had been familiar in European poetry for centuries. Chivalry was a code of ethics for knights that developed in the south of France in the twelfth century. It required knights to commit themselves to living by the virtues of loyalty, chastity, honor, and valor. It bound the knight to be loyal to God and to follow Christian ideals; to be loyal to the feudal lord under whom he served; and to be loyal to one mistress to whom he promised his love.

For knights of this tradition, love was considered more of an abstract ideal than something that could be experienced in this world. Women were to be loved from afar and to be considered unattainable. Knights chose women who were married, or who were of a higher social rank, who could be worshipped for their beauty and integrity but could not become involved in any sort of physical relationship without diminishing their appeal. A knight sworn to a lady would be bound to suffer in her name, to work hard at making himself worthy of her affection. This aspect of the chivalric ideal served to make knights good servants and citizens, directing their energies away from desire and toward a higher good.

In practice, the idea of chivalry was short-lived, falling to abuse and corruption. It was an idea more often talked about than acted upon by knights. It carried on in literature, however, in the songs of troubadours, who traveled from town to town singing poems for a living. In England, chivalry became crystallized in the legends of King Arthur and his Knights of the Round Table during the fourteenth century. The suffering of the knight in this poem, his all-consuming desire for the nymph, and his relationship with her all refer back to the English chivalric tradition.

## Critical Overview

"La Belle Dame sans Merci" is one of Keats's most beloved poems and one of the few important works that seems to evade the kind of critical argumentation invoked by the odes and long poems. Typical of critics' magnanimity toward the ballad is T. Hall Caine's 1882 assessment of the poem as the "loveliest [Keats] gave us." He writes that the ballad is "wholly simple and direct, and informed throughout by a reposeful strength. In all the qualities that rule and shape poetry into unity of form, this little work strides, perhaps, leagues in advance of 'Endymion,'" one of Keats's most noted poems. Caine further argues that the ballad's strength comes from the poet's ability to "(move) through an atmosphere peculiar to poetry, lacing and interlacing . . . combinations of thought and measure, (and) incorporating . . . meaning with . . . music." In a 1913 essay, Mary de Reyes notes Keats's fascination with the doomed nature of love in "La Belle Dame sans Merci." She compares the poem with the work of another principle romantic poet in both tone and technique: "In the magical touch of this picture of desolation and gloom, there is much of the spirit of Coleridge. There is no full description. The poem is lyrical rather than narrative." De Reyes points out that the spare description of the landscape "gives the very spirit of the old romance world. And in the intense lyrical feeling we have the climax of passion."

## Criticism

### David Kelly

*Kelly is an instructor of creative writing and literature at Oakton Community College. In this essay, Kelly examines the many ways in which Keats explores subjective reality in the poem.*

One of the most notable things about John Keats's ballad "La Belle Dame sans Merci" is the sly way it presents one of the key issues of romantic philosophy, that of objective versus subjective reality. The quick, simple understanding—the encyclopedia version—is that romantic poets favor subjectivism, particularly those who, like Keats, wrote at the height of the romantic period and helped define the movement, but also those aligned with romanticism to this day. Their world view is generally characterized as a writer focusing on his or her own experience, with no regard for the variety of perspectives that can occur when other points of view are considered.

The central figure in "La Belle Dame sans Merci" is a medieval knight-at-arms who has suffered one of the worst relationship scenarios imaginable. As he explains it, he met a woman and they fell in love, leading to a brief, passionate romance. After he fell asleep, the unreality of the situation assaulted him in two ways. First, he was visited in his dream by figures who warned him the lady was insincere in her love, and then their warning proved true when he woke up and found her gone.

All of these events, the disappearing lover and the warning he received about her, could just be in the knight's mind. Keats, however, establishes a level of objective reality in the poem by opening it with a second character who meets the knight in the woods and talks with him. It is the interplay between reality and fantasy, and the poem's refusal to clearly define what is and is not real, that makes this one of Keats's most compelling works.

Another poet might have used the uncertain existence of the phantom maiden herself as a test case for reality. There is, after all, no proof she ever existed anywhere but in the knight's imagination, while at the same time there is much evidence that she did not. To begin, she appears to the knight in the wilderness, where no one else could experience her. He describes her as a "faery's child," giving her, at the very least, mythical antecedents. The romance that transpires between them is too perfect too quickly to be thought of as the type of relationship that might develop in the "real" world. But, this poem does not really make much of the unreal aspects surrounding the woman and her sudden appearance and disappearance; they are taken as a given, as the natural course of the mysterious ways of love. It is a fairly standard conceit in romanticism to identify love as a part of the internal self, as more a matter of one person's mind than as a meeting of two. In terms of human relationships, this poem makes no effort to focus on more than one person's perspective, and so the mysterious nature of the faery child is not very telling. She might be a figment of the main character's imagination, or she might just be the catalyst that inspires it, but the reader can presume from the tone and from Keats's other works that this is always the case when one is in love.

The basic story of the poem could easily have been conveyed by the knight narrating his experience directly to the reading audience, if all that Keats were trying to do was to capture the dizzy high and unexpected plummet that can happen when one is in love. Instead, he adds another character, one whose worldly existence is never questioned. This second character defines the reality that surrounds the knight, giving readers another philosophical level against which to compare the love relationship.

Readers are not given any details about who is speaking in the first three stanzas of "La Belle Dame sans Merci," and so this speaker can hardly be thought of as a character in the poem. While undeveloped, this stranger adds several vital elements to the poem. First, having another person in the real world offers the poet an opportunity to give readers a visual description of the knight. This is important because it gives details about the knight's state of mind that would not otherwise come out. The knight's attitude is more optimistic, or at least defiant, than his looks reveal: he himself is not aware of the toll that his ordeal has taken on him. In another type of poem, it might be possible for the knight to tell readers what he looks like without even being aware of how worn out he is. There are ways for a writer to have a character think about his own appearance, by seeing his reflection or by feeling his face with his hands. But in this case, having the knight take time from his broken-

> *"The poem's presumption of a jump from the emotional to the physical world shows that, for Keats, the boundaries between the two were not as fixed as readers think of them today."*

hearted misery to think about his own looks would have toned down the intensity of his love. His role in the story is to concentrate on his lover, not himself. While it is important for the poem to show what the knight looks like, that description has to come from someone who is not as deeply immersed in the situation as the knight is; therefore, the stranger is necessary.

The stranger's objectivity is also important for letting readers know just how odd the knight's behavior is. As is always the case in issues of subjectivity and objectivity, there is no way of knowing, from just one point of view, if the events are mundane, shocking, or just as they should be. If the knight's perspective were the only one given in the poem, readers could come away from it thinking that the quick romance was sad, unfortunate, but in some respect normal. Keats starts the poem with someone expressing shock at the knight's pale complexion and at the fact that he is loitering around the empty forest. The knight can express the agony of love, but he by himself could not put this agony into a social context without the presence of another person.

In addition to the knight's subjective view of his situation and the objective perspective the stranger gives to the same situation, the poem also provides several other elements to blur the line between internal and external reality. One seldom noted element is that the poem takes for granted a relationship between mental and physical well-being. The knight suffers in romance, and as a result, he is dying. His emotional turmoil leaves him pale and sweating, the color draining from his face. The images of dying nature that surround him can be accounted for easily enough if one believes that, in his misery, he would choose to pass his time in a miserable setting. Even though psychologists believe that mental states affect one's health, the relationship between the two is not generally considered as direct as Keats presents it. According to biographer Aileen Ward, Keats and his contemporaries believed "that emotional agitation, especially that of an unhappy love, could bring on consumption," or tuberculosis, which was the disease Keats had, and the one from which the knight seems to be suffering. The poem's presumption of a jump from the emotional to the physical world shows that, for Keats, the boundaries between the two were not as fixed as readers think of them today.

One final way that Keats blurs the line between subjectivity and objectivity is the appearance, in stanza 10, of the pale images who speak the poem's title to the knight. There can scarcely be any question about whether they exist in the outside world or only in the knight's mind: they appear in a dream, they appear in a crowd (the way kings, princes, and warriors never do), and they are even in the faded colors of a dream. There is no sign of them in the woods, only in the knight's mind. Keats complicates the question of existence by having them interact with the outside world in a way that goes past the range of the knight's subconsciousness.

To understand the significance of the ghostly figures, one must assume that the faery-child was in fact real and not just a figure of the knight's imagination. This is a more substantial interpretation than assuming that one fantasy is warning the knight against another fantasy. If the knight had in fact met a girl in the woods and shared a quick romance with her, then the figures in his dream could just be interpreted as his subconscious warning him, presumably because it had picked up some negative sign from her that his conscious mind had not noticed. That would only explain the fact that she would *eventually* be bad for him. In the poem, though, they are warning him she will abandon him *at the same time* she is abandoning him in real life. Dreams sometimes are thought to have the ability to predict reality, but granting them the ability to know what is going on in the outside world while the dreamer is dreaming raises a whole new question about where the mental world leaves off and the physical world begins.

Romantic poets are famous for describing the world as a subjective experience, one in which the important things happen in the human heart. There is certainly plenty of that in "La Belle Dame sans Merci," with the knight-in-arms either creating a fantasy love affair or not, creating his own tuberculosis within his mind, and then warning himself about the dangers of going beyond his own mind by entering into a relationship with another person. There is also a strong representation of the objective world, in the unnamed stranger who encounters the knight in the woods. The poem provides no clear-cut answers about how the world of emotion affects or is affected by the physical world, but it does raise substantive questions that cannot be easily ignored.

**Source:** David Kelly, Critical Essay on "La Belle Dame sans Merci," in *Poetry for Students*, The Gale Group, 2003.

## Wolf Z. Hirst

*In the following except, Hirst illustrates how Keats intertwines the diverse elements of "La Belle Dame sans Merci."*

With an inimitable magic Keats depicts another cheated soul in "La Belle Dame sans Merci." Flight into visionary experience and back again is expressed by means of the well-known motif (to be used once more in *Lamia*) of a mortal's ruinous love for a supernatural lady: a knight encounters and falls in love with a beautiful "fairy's child", dreams in her "elfin grot" of "pale kings, and princes" and "Pale warriors", and wastes away "On the cold hill's side." The poet may have dashed off this masterpiece of the literary-ballad genre straight into the journal-letter on 21 April 1819, which gives us the version usually preferred to the one printed in Hunt's *Indicator* in May 1820. (The latter, among other things, substituted "wretched wight" for the "knight at arms" of the first line, and in stanza eight omitted "kisses four," the expression Keats singled out for the banter quoted in chapter 2.) Whether Keats was most inspired by Spenser, the popular ballad "Thomas Rhymer," Dante, vampire literature, Celtic lore, Wordsworth and Coleridge, his own earlier poems, a painting by William Hilton, or his relationship with Fanny Brawne is less important than the skill with which he conjures the most diverse elements into a unified impression of spellbinding mystery.

The poem comprises three concentric dream circles. The outer frame (dream 1) consists of a weird encounter between the poem's first speaker and a haggard knight on whose cheek the rose is fading, while the knight's ride through the mead and the kisses in the grotto form an inner frame (dream 2) to the dream about the pale kings with the starved lips (dream 3). The aura of a transcendental experience which pervades the meeting with the fairy lady (dream 2) is undermined by the knight's dream of the death-pale kings and warriors (dream 3) with its suggestion of mortality and betrayal. This dream within the knight's dream in the dream poem—this third dream of the starved lips and horrid warning—comes true when the knight awakes on the cold hillside pale and enthralled as the dream prophesied. The realization of this dream of deathly pallor and starvation has moved in the opposite direction from Endymion's and Madeline's dreams, where fulfillment signified a shift from the actual to some ecstatic transcendental realm. Within the overall dream frame of the first speaker's words to the fantastic knight-at-arms and the latter's reply, the transition from the dream within a dream in the supermortal elfin world to the world of the withering sedge (from dream 3 to dream 1) has a touch of harsh reality. On the other hand the entry into, journey through, and sojourn in the elfin world itself remains pure dream throughout (dream 2). This dream comprises the poem's six central stanzas from the knight's encounter with the fairy's child till she lulls him to sleep; and the encroaching domination of the fairy world is reflected in the transfer of the initiative from the knight's "I" in stanzas four to six to the lady's "she" in stanzas seven to nine. The lady's ambiguity (does "as she did love" in stanza five mean that her love is true or sham? is she a flirtatious seductress or a caressing mother-figure?) and eccentricity (her sidelong bending, unusual food, strange language, and sore sighing), though explicable in a supernatural and perhaps even a natural context, yet create an atmosphere of dreamlike vagueness. The knight has evidently never entered a grotto and never left "the cold hill's side," for here, we are told, he dreams "The latest dream", so that instead of awaking in the grot he finds himself in the setting of the outer frame.

In the final stanza the knight tries to explain his sorry condition to the questioner. A folk ballad such as "Lord Randall," structured on question and reply, solves its mystery in the last stanza. In "La Belle Dame," however, the explanation ("And this is why …") raises more questions than it answers. The knight explains his haggard appearance and why he does not go home in the inclement season: he is "in thrall." But this explanation merely confuses the questioner, who sees that the knight is under a spell and wonders what the nature of this spell is. It is unclear whether the knight himself knows exactly how, why, and what things have happened to him. The dream in the grotto (dream 3), which is supposed to provide the key to the riddle, tells

> *It is unclear whether the knight himself knows exactly how, why, and what things have happened to him."*

the questioner at the most what the knight himself has learned but what the reader has known all along from the title: the knight is entranced by a cruel lady. By only pretending to provide a solution to the enigma, this ballad calls attention to the indeterminacy and frequent mystery of its genre just as "St. Agnes" showed how the author of romance manipulates his reader. But whereas in "St. Agnes" the last stanza cast us abruptly back from romance to reality, the last six lines of "La Belle Dame," though apparently returning us to a realistic level, leave us in fact still within the dream world of the outer frame, which makes rational explanation of what has happened impossible and superfluous. The solution that does not solve anything merely confirms our initial impression that we have here the presentation of something felt on the pulses, of a beauty seized as a truth by the imagination and expressed in a language of sensation inaccessible to consecutive reasoning.

The poem pushes negative capability to a new extreme. Since we have to guess even at what has happened, it is not surprising that readers fail to agree upon what the lady, the knight, his journey, and his dream might symbolize. In this "most mysterious and evasive of all Keats's poems," we cannot know whether the fairy's child is a Cynthia who has failed to "make / Men's being mortal, immortal" (*Endymion*, I.843–44), a vampire, a Circe, "a fairy mistress from hell," or "neutral as to good and evil." If we conjecture that she stands for the poetic imagination, we still do not know whether the knight's lapse from vision is due to her refusal to keep up the deception or to the knight's own failure to sustain the transcendental experience; and in the latter case, whether this failure is, as Wasserman suggests, the inevitable concomitant of his mortal condition or the result of some particular deficiency on his part—for instance, as Richard Benvenuto argues, his fear of facing death. The lady may stand for any of the four intensities that attract

## What Do I Read Next?

- All of Keats's poetry is available in one volume entitled *The Complete Poems*. This book is edited by John Barnard and was published in 1977 by Penguin. The Modern Library also has a volume entitled *The Complete Poems of John Keats*, published in 1994, but it uses a revised version of "La Belle Dame sans Merci" that almost no other publisher uses.

- Sir Walter Scott's novel *Ivanhoe* was published the same year as "La Belle Dame sans Merci." It is a tale of knights and sorcery set in the Middle Ages and began a trend in historical fiction that has come to characterize the romantic movement.

- Since Keats presents his knight as turning pale and drawn, literally dying of lovesickness, students might want to read Susan Sontag's groundbreaking 1978 essay "Illness as Metaphor." It was republished in 2001 by Picador USA in one volume with the sequel essay, "AIDS and Its Metaphors."

- Keats's own death at the young age of twenty-six is the subject of John Evangelist Walsh's 1999 book *Darkling I Listen: The Last Days and Death of John Keats*, published by St. Martin's Press.

- Andrew Motion's acclaimed biography *Keats* provides one of the most thorough portraits of the poet available. It is available in a 1999 paperback edition from the University of Chicago Press.

- Keats's name is almost always mentioned along with that of his friend and fellow romantic poet Percy Bysshe Shelley. The most dependable, authoritative text of Shelley's poetry available is the 1977 edition entitled *Shelley's Poetry and Prose*, selected and edited by Donald H. Reiman and Sharon B. Powers and published by W. W. Norton & Company.

Keats in "Why did I laugh tonight?": verse, fame, beauty, and death. She may represent the fatality of beauty or of what in "Ode on Indolence" the poet sees as "a fair maid, and Love her name", no less than the allurements of what in the ode he calls "my demon Poesy", especially since the perils of love have repeatedly appeared in Keats's poetry, notably in "Isabella" and in the Romeo and Juliet motif of "St. Agnes." But Murry's assertion that behind the poem lies "the anguish of an impossible love" (of Fanny Brawne) is only one more conjecture and his assumption that the joking comment on the four kisses in the letter "is the detachment of a man who has uttered his heart and must turn away from what he has said" can be proved no more than Jane Rabb Cohen's contrary (and more extravagant) suggestion that the comment indicates the humorous mood in which the ballad itself was written. The supposition that the knight's journey symbolizes the tragedy of Faustian rejection of human limitations is appealing, because the "starv'd lips" echo a passage in *Endymion*: "There never liv'd a mortal man, who bent / His appetite beyond his natural sphere, / But starv'd and died".

We only know for certain, however, that the knight is a victim of his supernatural adventure and no longer finds his bearings in the natural world of birdsong, harvest, and decay. While he was journeying through the fairy kingdom, birds sang and the squirrel filled the granary; now the harvest is over and the knight is left unprovided for. (In the first two quatrains the truncated stanzaic close echoes the finality of this loss.) Those who boldly confront this world of growth and decline (as Keats does in "To Autumn") not only see the withered sedge but also experience the joys and fulfillment of harvest-time. In his vain attempt to die into the life of fairyland the knight separates himself from the natural order and thus becomes a double loser: cheated of both the wonders of elfin land and of nature, he suffers a kind of death-in-life. The Romantic journey into vision vindicated in *Endymion* and still depicted as a worthwhile risk in "St. Agnes" here proves disastrous.

**Source:** Wolf Z. Hirst, "Dying into Life: The First *Hyperion* and 'The Eve of St. Agnes'," in *John Keats*, Twayne, 1981, pp. 92–118.

### Earl R. Wasserman

*In the following essay, Wasserman explores Keats's techniques, stylistic choices, and probable sources for "La Belle Dame sans Merci."*

It would be difficult in any reading of Keats' ballad not to be enthralled by the haunting power of its rhythm, by its delicate intermingling of the fragile and the grotesque, the tender and the weird, and by the perfect economy with which these effects are achieved. Snared by the sensuous workings of the poem, one is greatly tempted to evaluate it entirely as a poem whose function is not the expression of human values, but whose end is attained when it fulfills its own stylistic requirements. Nevertheless, out of the dim sense of mystery and incompleteness that its artistry arouses there rise not only richly suggestive overtones, but also dark hints of a meaning that might be available to us could we penetrate its mystery. The imagination, for example, seizes upon the sedge that has withered from the lake and upon the absence of the birds' song, and elaborates the pictorial connotations of these stark images into all barren and desolate autumnal scenes that ever were. And yet, one senses an insufficiency in these affective and image-making energies of the poem, for the overtones also drive the mind to ask questions of conceptual intent. What, one wonders, is the larger meaning couched within the absence of song? why a knight-at-arms and an elfin grot? and what are the significances of the cold hill side and the pale warriors?

Nor are these probings of the mind without justification, since the poem contains within itself the power of compelling us to such questions. For Keats' symbolism is almost always dynamic. His poetry does not lie inert, waiting, like the poetry of Blake and some of the early work of Yeats, to yield itself up to a symbolic reading. Such poetry as theirs assumes that the world is symbolic, and therefore that if the poet selects images of symbolic import and orders them into an artistic intertexture that corresponds to the meaningful relationships in the cosmos, he has created a symbolic poem, let the reader read it as he will. However, we have seen that Keats' world is not symbolic; it is his vision of the world that is symbolic, and a greeting of the spirit is required to transmute image into symbol. Since "every mental pursuit takes its reality and worth from the ardour of the pursuer—being in itself a nothing," Keats must entice a pursuit of his images by the reader, whose ardor will transform them into symbols, "ethereal things."

In the ballad, therefore, Keats not only dramatized a myth, but also dramatized the fact that the narrative and its component images are symbolic. The first three stanzas are introductory in that they are addressed by an anonymous someone to the knight-at-arms, whose answer will then constitute the narrative body of the poem. These three stanzas consequently serve to set the story of the knight's adventures in an additional narrative framework, a dialogue between the knight and the stranger, with whom the reader tends to identify

> "Keats conceived of a poem as a perfectly ordered cosmos, an experience not only completed but also self-contained by reason of its circularity."

himself; and thus the reader is drawn more intimately into the knight's experiences, for he feels himself to be present as the knight speaks in his own person. But even more important, in the introductory stanzas images and human values are gradually blended stereoscopically until at length the reader's mode of poetic vision has been adjusted to see the symbolized value as the third-dimensional projection of the image.

The first two stanzas have identical patterns: the first half of each addresses a question to the knight-at-arms about his spiritual condition; and the second half comments on the natural setting. The similarity of the gaunt, pale appearance of the solitary knight to the desolation and decay of nature is clearly implied, but the absence of any explicit relationship leaves the connection vague and therefore fluid enough so that nature and the knight may later be welded into an organic, instead of a synthetic, union—a method reminiscent of the first stanza of the "Ode on a Grecian Urn." The second half of each of these stanzas is built around a coordination of two natural images (sedge and birds, the squirrel's granary and the harvest); and it is noticeable that the first pair are the natural images themselves, while the second are the materials of nature as shaped and molded by creatures for themselves. The progress is toward a closer integration of nature and man: the granary and the harvest are what creatures make of nature for their own use. Corresponding to these pairs of images are two pairs of adjectives in the halves describing the knight, the first pair exactly paralleling the natural images: alone, no birds sing; palely loitering, the sedge has withered. All these balanced details, equally distributed to nature and the knight, now coalesce in the third stanza.

This stanza takes its structure from that of the second halves of the first two stanzas, for its pattern, too, depends upon the coordination of two natural images, lily and rose, and each image dominates half of the stanza, just as each image in the first two stanzas governs a single line. In other words, the structure of the third stanza is precisely that of the second halves of the first two, expanded to the length of a full stanza. The subject matter of the third stanza, however, is not the appearance of nature, but the spiritual condition of the knight-at-arms, which has been the theme of the first halves of the first two stanzas. By this absorption of the knight into the structural pattern of the natural imagery, the movement from a suggested but unstated relationship of man and nature in stanza one to an implied interrelationship in stanza two has now been completed. In the third stanza the two terms are organically integrated, and human values and natural images have been molded into interchangeable expressions: the lily and the rose are present in the knight's countenance, and his withering is theirs. This structural drama of their coalescence now compels a symbolic reading of the poem, and we cannot well avoid questioning the human relevance of the garlands, the elfin grot, and the cold hill side. If, to use Coleridge's definition, a symbol "partakes of the reality which it renders intelligible," the work of the first three stanzas is to make the symbols a living part of that reality.

## II

The first three stanzas, which make dramatic the subsequent narrating and excite a symbolic reading, introduce nine precisely balanced stanzas containing the main narrative (4–12). The progress of the knight in the first four (4–7) comes to a climax in the central one (8) when he is taken into the elfin grot, and in the last four (9–12) he withdraws from the grot. The withdrawal brings the poem back to the scene with which it began, the completion of the circular movement being marked by the fact that the last stanza echoes the first.

Whatever the specific source may have been, the narrative clearly belongs to a folk legend best known in the form of the mediaeval ballad "Thomas Rymer." In the version available to Keats in Robert Jamieson's *Popular Ballads*, 1806 (the variant in Scott's *Minstrelsy* differs in a few important details), Thomas encounters a beautiful lady whom he thinks to be the Queen of Heaven, but who identifies herself as "the queen of fair Elfland." She takes him upon her milk-white steed, for he must serve her for seven years; and for forty days and nights they ride through blood while Thomas sees neither sun nor moon. Forbidden to touch the fruit of this strange country lest he suffer the plagues of hell, Thomas eats the loaf and drinks the claret that the elf-queen has brought. At length they rest before a hill, and the elf-queen, placing his head on her knee, shows him three wonders—the roads to wickedness, to righteousness, and to fair Elfland. It is the last of these that they are to follow, and for seven years "True Thomas on earth was never seen." The relations of this narrative to a story of a knight-at-arms carried by a fairy's child to an elfin grot are too obvious to underscore. Apparently the myth of a journey to a mysterious otherworld that is neither heaven nor hell nor earth, and of capture there by the fairy magic of love for one who seems to be "Queen of Heaven," constituted a pattern that evoked from Keats a body of speculation ripe for expression and helped give these speculations an artistic shape.

Keats did not simply recast this folk legend into another artistic form but molded it into an expression of his deepest and most vivid conceptions. The legend was not merely an esthetic design that he felt he could bring closer to his idea of literary perfection; to him it was also a meaningful narrative in which he recognized his own journeys heavenward. Since, then, the substance of the folk ballad constitutes mainly the raw materials of Keats' creation, his modifications of the legend and his additions to it are the more obvious clues to his motives. It is noticeable that nearly all the larger narrative elements of the first four stanzas of Keats' central narrative (4–7) are present in the folk ballad also: the meeting with a fairy lady of great beauty, the implication of the lady's desire for Thomas, their sharing the pacing steed, and the knight's eating of the magic food. To these Keats has added three major details that do not appear in the folk ballad, even by implication: the knight weaves for the fairy's child a garland, bracelets, and a girdle of flowers; the lady sings "A faery's song"; and at length "in language strange she said—/ 'I love thee true.'"

What Keats has woven into the narrative, it appears, is another version of the pleasure thermometer, a series of increasing intensities that absorb the self into essence: nature, song, and love. We have already seen the important role of the pleasure thermometer in the "Ode on a Grecian Urn," and we shall have occasion to see how functional it is in other poems of Keats. It was "a regular stepping of the Imagination towards a Truth," towards that beauty-truth which was his heart's desire, and each aspiration towards it carried him along the route that his heart had marked out. When, for example, Endymion had traveled the "journey homeward to habitual self" and was buried in his own deadly selfhood, he was prepared for deliverance from "this rapacious deep" in three stages. First, the riches of nature appeared before him: "the floral pride / In a long whispering birth enchanted grew / Before his footsteps." Then music: "This still alarm, / This sleepy music, forc'd him walk tiptoe." At length, surrounded by cupids, he observed the love-visitation of Venus and Adonis. And now at last "some ethereal and high-favouring donor" has presented "immortal bowers to mortal sense." By ascending the ladder of intensities, Endymion, too, has been released from the prison house of his mortal self and has attained insight into the mortal-immortal nature of heaven's bourne.

In Keats' ballad these increasing enthrallments of selfhood appear in successive order, each occupying one of three successive stanzas (5, 6, 7); and they lead finally to the heaven's bourne of the elfin grot (8). In folk literature the interiors of hills are often the dwelling places of fairies and elves: Tam Lin dwelled in a green hill, and in the romance of "Thomas of Erceldoune," which deals with the same Thomas Rymer, the hero was led "in at Eldone hill." Apparently the tradition of elfin grots was especially appropriate to Keats' purpose. Earthly in its form and yet "elfin" in its nature—within the cold hill side of the physical world and yet being the otherworld mystery within the physical—it corresponds to the oxymoronic realm where life's self is nourished by its proper pith and to which man can ascend by a ladder of intensities. It is the earth spiritually transfigured; its fairyhood is the "leaven, / That spreading in this dull and clodded earth / Gives it a touch ethereal."

In calling upon another analogue to Keats' ballad I do not mean to propose that Keats was directly influenced by it, despite the possibility that he was. Even proof of Keats' indebtedness, could it be found, would be irrelevant to our purpose, for it could not charge his ballad with values not already inherent in it. Nevertheless, it is illuminating to observe what significances the legend of Thomas Rymer held forth to one of Keats' contemporaries, an intimate friend of John Hamilton Reynolds and therefore one who was undoubtedly known to Keats. In the summer of 1818, nearly a year before Keats composed "La Belle Dame Sans Merci," John F. M. Dovaston wrote his "Elfin Bride, a Fairy Ballad," although it seems not to have appeared in print until 1825. Its source is not the folk ballad but the mediaeval romance "Thomas of Erceldoune," which is a more extended version of the same legend.

The argument of the "Elfin Bride," Dovaston wrote, is that "Time has no existence but with motion and matter: with the Deity, 'whose centre is everywhere, and circumference nowhere,'—and with 'millions of spiritual creatures' ... Duration is without Time." Apparently the legend of Thomas has the power of provoking speculations about a condition in which love is forever warm and still to be enjoyed. In Dovaston's ballad Merlin is substituted for Thomas Rymer, his fellow in many mediaeval legends. Merlin meets a "White Lady" and begs of her that he may see "that airy country / That wots not of Time nor Place." They ride away on palfreys to fairyland, where Merlin is treated to a multitude of "pleasures refin'd." The passing time seems only a moment, but Merlin is informed that "to Man in the dull cold world thou hast left, / Seven times four Seasons are gone." When, however, Merlin attempts a physical consummation of his love, the ideal vision is shattered, and he finds himself once again in the world of time and place, which now seems to him insipid and decayed although the memory of the fairy music still rings in his ear:

*He gazed all around the dull heathy ground,*
*Neither tree nor bush was there,*
*But wide wide wide all on every side*
*Spread the heath dry brown and bare.*

Returning once again to fairyland, Merlin remains for seven more years until at last a longing grows in him for the mortal and mutable world: he thought

*on the vales and green mountains of Wales*
*And his friends so long forgot.*

*For blithe are the vales and green mountains of Wales*
*And its blithe sojourn there.*

The wish is sufficient to free him from the land without time and place.

*Then suddenly there small shrilly and clear*
*The Fairy-folk ceas'd their singing,*
*And the silvery swells of pipes and bells*
*No longer around him were ringing.*

*And the Fairyland gay all melted away*
*In a misty vapour curl'd;*
*And his opening eyes beheld with suprize*
*The light of this long-left world.*

Driven back to earth by his human desires, Merlin awakens to find that his life in fairyland has been a vision, that but a moment has passed, and that he is still in the summer bower where he was when his dream began. Although Dovaston, unlike Keats, drew from his narrative the conclusion that man should be content with his mortal lot, it is obvious that he also found in the legend of Thomas Rymer a myth of a spaceless, timeless realm of pleasure from which man withdraws when the mortal world beckons him and from which he is cast out when he attempts to realize physically the ideal pleasures. In all this one cannot avoid hearing echoes of the "Ode on a Grecian Urn."

With Dovaston's ballad in mind we can see even more clearly the meaningfulness of the narrative pattern into which Keats wove the increasing intensities that mark the journey to the elfin grot. Now, dreams often perform in Keats' system of thought the function of the imagination. It is, for example, in dream visions that Endymion is united with Cynthia and hence gains insight into the beauty-truth of heaven's bourne. "The Imagination," Keats wrote, "may be compared to Adam's dream—he awoke and found it truth." "Real are the dreams of Gods," for to them beauty is truth, not merely a foreshadowing of it, as the visions of the human imagination are; but for the man who lives a life of sensations, dreams may at least be prefigurative visions of the beauty-truth reality to come. Therefore, ideally, having ascended the pleasure thermometer, the knight should perceive an immortality of passion, especially since his vision-making imagination is aided by fairy magic.

But the tug of the mutable world is too strong for mere mortals because "in the world / We jostle" and, as Dovaston wrote, we are drawn away by thoughts of "the vales and green mountains of Wales / And … friends so long forgot." Even in the heart of his prefigurative visions of heaven's bourne earthly man recalls that human passions leave a heart high-sorrowful and cloyed; his spirit clings to the vision until "the stings / Of human neighbourhood envenom all." Merlin found that the desire to consummate physically his love for the "White Lady" cast him upon "the heath dry brown and bare," the cold hill side from which one sees only withered sedge and hears no song of birds. And yet, this is a fate that must befall all mortal aspirations, for so long as man is earth-bound his life is made up of

> *the war, the deeds,*
> *The disappointment, the anxiety,*
> *Imagination's struggles, far and nigh,*
> *All human.*

Mortal life must necessarily be an incessant struggle against these ills, which are ineradicable; living is the very act of being militant against the dimensional restrictions of the world. And thus all mortals who engage in "Imagination's struggles" are knights-at-arms. But man cannot gain his quest in this world. No knight-at-arms can remain in the elfin grot because, since he is mortal, he cannot wholly yield himself up to this extra-human realm and agian visionary insight into its nature. He will be impelled to make the visionary physical or will long for "his friends so long forgot." This is precisely the realization that came to Keats when he wrote of his visit to Burns' country:

> *Scanty the hour and few the steps beyond the bourn of care,*
> *Beyond the sweet and bitter world,—beyond it unaware!*
> *Scanty the hour and few the steps, because a longer stay*
> *Would bar return, and make a man forget his mortal way:*
> *O horrible! to lose the sight of well remember'd face,*
> *Of Brother's eyes, of Sister's brow…*
> *No, no, that horror cannot be, for at the cable's length*
> *Man feels the gentle anchor pull and gladdens in its strength.*

It is man's bond with mankind that prevents him from lingering beyond the bourne of care. There is nothing in Keats' ballad even suggesting the frequent interpretation that the fairy's child is responsible for the knight's expulsion from the elfin grot; only his own inherent attribute of being mortal causes his magic withdrawal, as only the call of Merlin's human and physical impulses caused "the Fairyland gay" to melt in a misty vapor. The vision of the mortal-immortal can only entice mortal man towards heaven's bourne; it cannot aid him in his aspirations or preserve his vision, which must inevitably be shattered. By this fair enchantment mortal man can only be "tortured with renewed life."

It is in this sense that la belle dame is sans merci, without tenderness; this is a description of what provokes man's aspirations, rather than an evaluation of it. Like the lady of the tradition of courtly love, she is the ideal whom the lover must pursue but whom he can never possess; and hence he is doomed to suffer her "unkindness," which is her nature although not her fault. Only the inherent meanness of man's dreams, then, draws him back from heaven's bourne, for, instead of being visionary penetrations into that final essence which is beauty-truth, they are only of mutable things. Aspire though he will, the stings of human neighborhood envenom all.

Instead of dreaming of the "ardent listlessness" which is heaven, the knight finds that death-pale kings, princes, and warriors intrude into his dream, mortal man being the necessary symbol of transitoriness and decay. What man calls living is truly the act of dying, since it is an incessant progress towards the grave; it is what Pope described as "that long disease, my life." Only after death, when man can exist in heaven's bourne, does he truly live; and therefore all earthly men are death-pale. Being mortal, and therefore death-pale, is also the condition of being cut off from that realm of pure being where life's self is nourished by its own pith. As death-pale man lives his existence of decay he can only yearn for that region from which his spirit comes, from which it has been divorced, but in which is the vital principle which will hereafter feed his spirit with "renewed life." Thus the lips of all mortal men are starved for lack of their spirit's own pith, for lack of the germ of spirit that is to be sucked from "mould ethereal."

Yet, instead of aspiring to this spiritual food of heaven, as the knight does, mortal man has circumscribed himself by the physical world, and though death-pale and spiritually starved, fears the attraction of heaven's bourne. The impulse in that direction, Keats wrote in *Endymion*, leaves one "too happy to be glad," "More happy than betides mortality." "It is a flaw / In happiness to see beyond our bourn." Therefore, fearful of the aspiration that agonizes and spoils the apparent splendor of the material world, mortality, despite its own sufferings, warns the knight that "La Belle Dame sans Merci / Hath thee in thrall!" How strange it is, Keats once mused,

> *that man on earth should roam,*
> *And lead a life of woe, but not forsake*
> *His rugged path; nor dare he view alone*
> *His future doom which is but to awake.*

It is significant that the warning comes from those who seek to battle the world's ills (warriors) and from men of power (kings and princes). "I would call the top and head of those who have a proper self," Keats wrote, "Men of Power"; that is, men who cannot ascend the pleasure thermometer and lose their selves in essence because they are self-contained.

The knight's inherent weakness in being unable to exclude from his visions the self-contained and world-bound mortality dissipates the ideal into which he has entered momentarily, just as the need for the world of men and the desire to materialize the ideal destroy the fairyland for Merlin. The elfin grot once again becomes the cold hill side which is the physical, mutable world, where the knight has been all the while, but which, by means of his visionary insight, took on the magic splendor of the elfin grot, the mystery within the mutable. The vision had momentarily transfigured a real thing into an "ethereal" thing. Exactly so, it was the poet's vision that transformed the marble embroidery on the Grecian urn into the unchanging vitality of a realm without space, time, and identity; and the shattering of that vision once again froze the immortality of passion into cold, motionless marble. With the dissipation of the vision in the ballad and with the consequent return to the cold physical world, the ladder of intensities which the knight had ascended to reach the ethereal world now crumbles beneath him: love has gone. "the sedge has wither'd from the lake," and "no birds sing." Love, song, and nature fade and disappear as the knight's capacity for the passionate intensity for fellowship with essence becomes enervate and he returns to normal human weakness.

Now that the knight has been awakened from his dream by the stings of human neighborhood, he is as pale, death-pale, as the kings, princes, and warriors, for he now shares their mortality. Being mortal, his very existence is a progress towards death, and death therefore is in his nature, although in the elfin grot existence, being without time, is without death. Indeed, Keats originally wrote, "I see *death's* lilly on thy brow ... And on thy cheeks *death's* fading rose." By withdrawing from the elfin grot, the knight has also become a Man of Power; the withdrawal is the act of reassuming his own self-containing identity, and thus he is "alone," being his own isolated self. His aloneness is the opposite of a fellowship with essence which absorbs the proper self, that self which is cut off from its selfless origin in heaven. At heaven's bourne there can be no aloneness because there are no individual selves, no proper identities; there it is irrelevant to ask, "Who are these coming to the sacrifice?" Earthly life, then, is a spiritual solitude overcast with the pallor of death, and a denial of the "honey wild, and manna dew," the heaven-sent food which is life's proper pith; all mortal living is a movement towards the sacrificial altar. "Living," therefore, must be a biding of one's time, a meaningless exhausting of one's mortal lease, since man is only a temporary resident in this world. The elfin grot being truly his home ethereal, mortal man, in the solitude of his self, can only "sojourn here, ... palely loitering" on the cold hill side of the world. And the unfinished, hovering quality of the metrics of each stanzaic close ("And no birds sing," "On the cold hill's side") perfectly reinforces the aimless solitude with which Keats is investing mortal life.

## III

We have already noticed the organization of the poem into two discourses—the questions of the stranger in the first three stanzas, and the knight's reply in the following nine. But within this pattern, another, more intricate and significant, is at work. In this inner configuration the poem falls into four equal groups of three stanzas each, the first of which is the symbol-making address of the stranger. The next six stanzas, the narrative core of the poem, tell of the direct relations of the knight and the fairy lady; of these the first three constitute one unit, and the last three another, the grouping and distinctness being marked by the two opening patterns: "I met," "I made," "I set"; and "She found," "She took," "And there she lulled me." The final unit of three stanzas in the poem is a kind of epilogue telling of the aftermath of the encounter with the fairy's child and thus answers the stranger's questions in the three introductory stanzas and brings the poem round full circle so that the final stanza may be an approximate repetition of the first. This last unit is also bound together, nearly as the second three stanzas are: "I saw," "I saw," "And this is why I sojourn here."

But with these balances and intricacies Keats is not merely carving his narrative into fascinating arabesques. His artistry is almost always functional to his meaning and is seldom an end in itself. In stanza four it is noticeable that the only actor is the knight. In the next stanza the knight controls the action of the first two lines, and the lady that of the second two. In stanza six he truly governs only the first line, and it seems significant that Keats altered the action of the folk ballad, where it is the lady who takes Thomas upon her horse. Apparently there is a special intent in giving the action to the knight in the first line so that he may remain an actor throughout these three stanzas, but with diminishing control over the action. Clearly the lady governs the action in the last two lines of stanza six and, in a broader sense, the action of the second line also, for the stanza states that the knight's seeing nothing else is the consequence of the lady's singing.

There is, then, a progressive shrinkage of the "I" as a power and a corresponding dominance of the "she," until in stanza seven, where the height of the pleasure thermometer is reached, the lady alone controls the entire action, and the knight passively yields to her. The consequence of ascending the pleasure thermometer, it will be recalled, is that one enters into the essences of progressive intensities, which are "Richer entanglements, enthralments far / More self-destroying." And proportionately as the knight ascends from nature to song to love, his active self is being absorbed into the ideal, which increasingly exercises control over his self. It is in this sense of empathic enthrallment that the knight is cautioned, "La Belle Dame sans Merci / Hath thee in *thrall*!" Once he has wilfully entered into sensuous essence and set up the lady as an ideal ("I set her on my pacing steed"), he has abandoned his selfhood; even the apparently wilfull act of looking at the fairy's child is the passive consequence of being so absorbed into the essence of song that he can perceive only ideality: "And nothing else saw all day long." Since those who have "a proper self" are "Men of Power," the retreat of the "I" and the emergence of the "she" as the sources of activity are the grammatical dramatization of the destruction of that power as the knight enters into greater and greater enthrallments.

At the tip-top of the humanly attainable scale is the "orbed drop / Of light, and that is love"; "Nor with aught else can our souls interknit / So wingedly." Consequently, in stanza seven, in which the lady expresses her love, she is the only power, and the knight is completely enthralled by essence, ready now to enter into the heaven's bourne of the elfin grot. Moreover, the inter-knitting of the soul with essence through love so elevates the soul that it may partake of the spiritual stuff of which it is itself made, and hence "Life's self is nourish'd by its proper pith, / And we are nurtured like a pelican brood." In other words, by the knight's entrance into essence through love the ideal nourishes him with the source of his own spiritual mystery—with "roots of relish sweet, / And honey wild, and manna dew."

The structural pattern of the main narrative stanzas (4–12) is, then, as precisely balanced as that of the "Ode on a Grecian Urn." In the ode the first two stanzas trace the ascent to a perception of the frieze as a timeless, spaceless, selfless realm of endless vitality; the last two, the descent from this realm, bring the poem back to the condition from which it started. And the central stanza both depicts the oxymoronic nature of this area and introduces the chemicals for its destruction Correspondingly, the firt four stanzas (4–7) of the main narrative in the ballad lead towards the oxymoronic elfin grot; the last four (9–12), away from it. And the central stanza (8) both admits the knight into the elfin grot and motivates the dissolution of the vision, for in this stanza the knight takes it upon himself to shut the "wild wild eyes" of the mistery. In the ode, the heaven's bourne of the frieze is dispelled by a force within the poet himself, the unavoidable recollection of the mortal world; in the ballad, a force within the mortal knight—not an act of the fairy's child—causes him to shut out the wild mystery of the ideal. The tug of mortality converts the timeless and spaceless, but vital, frieze into a physical activity in the ever-recurring journey from the town-world to the altar-heaven; the tug of mortality converts the inward mystery of the elfin grot into its outward and merely physical form, the cold hill side.

With the dissolution of heaven's bourne and of the knight's complete assimilation into essence in stanza seven, the grammatical controls in the poem retrieve his selfhood until once again he is wholly self-contained. The "stings of human neighbourhood" have envenomed all; and thus when "thoughts of self came on," he travels "The journey homeward to habitual self." Therefore the empathic order of stanzas four to seven is inverted. In stanza eight the lady governs the action of the first two lines, and the knight that of the last two, for it is the interfering power of his own mortal identity that shuts out the mystery. In the next stanza the lady controls only the action of the first line, and the knight that of the last three. And now at last the knight has fully emerged from the enthrallment, and his self is dominant in the remaining three stanzas. The empathic involvement and withdrawal that were enacted in the "Ode on a Grecian Urn" dramatic gesture and verbal moods are here enacted by overt dramatic action and by the gradual transfer of grammatical control from one actor to the other.

One of the remarkable features of the ballad is the intricate interlacing of the meaningfully balanced patterns we have been examining. In one sense the first three stanzas are introductory to the following narrative. Within this main narrative (4–12) the action is perfectly pivoted on the central stanza (8), the narrative, the symbols, and the grammatical controls symmetrically rising to and falling away from this central point. And in yet another sense, the first three stanzas (1–3) and the last three (10–12) are prologue and epilogue, the central six (4–9) being perfectly balanced by the distribution of the opening patterns, "I" and "she." Since we have seen a similar meaningful balance in the "Ode on a Grecian Urn," we might well suspect that Keats is far from being merely an associative poet whose only control over structure is the subjective pattern that his feelings spontaneously dictated to him. Quite to the contrary, Keats conceived of a poem as a perfectly ordered cosmos, an experience not only completed but also self-contained by reason of its circularity. And this perfect circularity—because of which he delighted in what he called the "rondeau"—not only is a control over the work of art as a poetic microcosm but also is itself a meaning functional to the poem. That this sense of the complete and organically meaningful architecture of a work of art was deep in Keats' poetic conceptions is clear from the second of his three axioms of poetry. The touches of beauty in poetry, he wrote,

> should never be half way thereby making the reader breathless instead of content: the rise, the progress, the setting of imagery should like the Sun come natural to him—shine over him and set soberly although in magnificence leaving him in the Luxury of twilight.

## IV

What emerges from this analysis is that "La Belle Dame Sans Merci" has grown out of the same body of conceptions, beliefs, and aspirations that motivate the "Ode on a Grecian Urn," and that it is shaped by the same mode of poetic perception. The major difference between the ode and the ballad is that the latter fails to attain the high consolation of the last stanza of the ode; but otherwise the ballad is the projection into myth of what was experienced in the ode as symbol. The increase in psychic distance gained by translating the drama within the consciousness of the poet into objective correlatives allows the poet to stretch out into the chronological span of a narrative a drama that he could express in the ode only as the evolving inward recognition of symbolic values. But the same sense of great harmonic control appears in both poems in their meaningfully pivoted structure and in the interweaving of patterns. And both are variant artistic intertextures of the three coexistent themes that dominate Keats' deepest meditations and profoundest system of values: the oxymoronic heaven's bourne towards which his spirit yearned; the pleasure thermometer which he conceived of as the spiritual path to that goal; and the self-annihilation that he understood to be the condition necessary for the journey. In this sense the ballad differs from the ode essentially in enacting this triune drama in a realm of space and time; and hence the self-conscious identity of the poet becomes the knight, the coexistent symbols of the thermometer are spread out into a context of time, and the journey heavenward is a passage through a spatial world.

Yet, because the ballad lacks the resolution of the ode, the differences are immense. In his discovery that art prefigures an attainable heaven where beauty will be truth, Keats spoke to man an Everlasting Yea; "La Belle Dame Sans Merci" is his Center of Indifference.

**Source:** Earl R. Wasserman, "La Belle Dame sans Merci," in *The Finer Tone: Keats' Major Poems*, Johns Hopkins University Press, 1953, pp. 65–83.

## Sources

Caine, T. Hall, "That Keats Was Maturing," in *Tinsley's Magazine*, Vol. XXI, August 1882, pp. 197–200.

de Reyes, Mary, "John Keats," in *Poetry Review*, Vol. III, No. 2, August 1913, pp. 72–82.

Ward, Aileen, *John Keats: The Making of a Poet*, The Viking Press, 1963, p. 273.

## Further Reading

Bostetter, Edward E., *Romantic Ventriloquists: Wordsworth, Coleridge, Keats, Shelley, Byron*, University of Washington Press, 1975.

> The method used here is primarily biographical with relationships drawn between the poet's life and the poem. Bostetter shows how Keats's mistress, Fanny Brawne, fit the love pattern he describes in this poem.

Evert, Walter H., *Aesthetic and Myth in the Poetry of Keats*, Princeton University Press, 1965.

> Evert analyzes the attempts of critics to determine the "source," or inspiration, of this poem. Examining different theories, he finds substantial evidence that the theme of "La Belle Dame sans Merci" was drawn from a sub-theme in his earlier work, *Endymion*.

Grant, John E., "Discovering 'La Belle Dame sans Merci,'" in *Approaches to Teaching Keats's Poetry*, edited by Walter H. Evert and Jack W. Rhodes, Modern Language Association of America, 1991, pp. 45–50.

> This brief analysis was written primarily to help instructors make the poem more understandable for students.

Harding, Anthony John, *The Reception of Myth in English Romanticism*, University of Missouri Press, 1995.

> Harding examines the myths and folk stories that romantic writers worked into their poetry, tracing source materials and noting the ways in which traditional stories were altered to fit the mood of the times.

Hirst, Wolf Z., *John Keats*, Twayne's English Authors Series, No. 334, Twayne Publishers, 1981.

> Hirst's analysis of the poem visualizes it in "three concentric dream circles," examining it in terms of the interrelationships among the encounter between two men, the encounter between two lovers, and the knight's encounter with the pale dream figures.

# The Blue Rim of Memory

**Denise Levertov**

**1978**

Some critics consider Denise Levertov's poem "The Blue Rim of Memory" one of the many written about her mother's death in Mexico that make up much of *Life in the Forest*, in which it first appeared in 1978. While this may well be the case, the poem could also reflect the poet's thoughts on any sorrowful occasion, as her mother is not specifically mentioned in it, and the images described would be as effective, regardless of the particular event. The poem is wholly metaphorical and divided into four primary images, each describing "the way sorrow enters the bone." Levertov turns to a historical reference—appropriate in discussing the concepts of memory—and to the natural world—specifically, fire, fish, and snow—to express the presence of sadness as it persists in the human mind, soul, and body. Both the message of the poem and its clarity depend on the beauty of language and the power of creating a sharp picture in the reader's mind to exemplify what sorrow feels like. In each of the four instances portrayed, the reader is offered a sensory experience to consider, a provocative image detailing how sorrow operates in memory.

"The Blue Rim of Memory" was also published in *Poems 1972–1982*, which compiles Levertov's books *The Freeing of the Dust* (1975), *Life in the Forest* (1978), and *Candles in Babylon* (1982). This book was released by Levertov's former publisher, New Directions Press, in 2001.

*Denise Levertov*

## Author Biography

Denise Levertov was born October 24, 1923, in Ilford, England. Her Russian-born father had converted from Judaism to become an Anglican priest in England, and her Welsh mother was artistically prolific as a singer, painter, and writer. Levertov and her older sister were schooled at home by their mother, and their upbringing in a highly intellectual, well-read family had a tremendous influence on their adult vocations. The parents were also political activists, protesting fascism in Spain and Germany and providing aid to political refugees during World War II. Their involvement in social justice issues gave direction to their daughters' involvement with similar causes later on.

As a teenager, Levertov took ballet, piano, and art lessons, and at nineteen she entered nurses' training and worked as a civilian nurse during World War II. During the war, Levertov met her future husband, American soldier Mitchell Goodman, who had studied at Harvard. They were married in 1947 and moved to New York City where their son was born two years later. Levertov had been writing and publishing poetry since she was a child, and her first collection, *The Double Image*, was published in 1946. However, being a wife and mother and adjusting to her new life in America occupied her for the next eleven years, and her second volume was not released until 1957. During this time, she continued to write and to publish single poems, and her former highly structured British style of writing underwent an American transition in both idiom and subject matter. Her major influences were William Carlos Williams and Wallace Stevens, as well as Black Mountain poets Robert Creeley and Charles Olson.

During the 1960s, Levertov went on reading tours, served as poetry advisor for the *Nation*, and taught at a variety of colleges and universities, such as City College of New York, Vassar College, and the University of California, Berkeley. Also during the 1960s and into the 1970s, Levertov became heavily involved in Vietnam War protests, and many of her poems reflected her political and social justice beliefs. Some of them were controversial, and she found herself both adored and hated by readers and scholars on either side of the issues. "The Blue Rim of Memory," which first appeared in her collection *Life in the Forest* (1978), was not among these political poems, for it expresses no political persuasion. In her later years, Levertov continued to teach, holding positions at Tufts University in the 1970s and Brandeis and Stanford Universities in the 1980s. Levertov and her husband divorced in the early 1970s, and she eventually moved alone to Seattle, where she died at the age of seventy-four on December 20, 1997.

Levertov is considered one of the most prominent and prolific poets of the twentieth century. She received a Guggenheim Fellowship, an American Academy and Institute of Arts and Letters grant, the Lenore Marshall Poetry Prize, and an NEA Senior Fellowship, among several other awards. Upon her death, Levertov left forty finished poems, which her literary executors published as *This Great Unknowing: Last Poems*, in 1999.

## Poem Text

The way sorrow enters the bone
is with stabs and hoverings.
From a torn page
a cabriolet
approaches over the crest of a hill,      5
first the nodding, straining head of the horse
then the blind lamps, peering;

the ladies within the insect eagerly
look from side to side awaiting the vista—
and quick as a knife                      10
are vanished. Who were they? Where is the hill?

Or from stoked fires of nevermore
a warmth constant as breathing hovers out
to surround you, a cloud of mist
becomes rain, becomes cloak, then skin.      15

The way sorrow enters the bone
is the way fish sink through dense lakes
raising smoke from the depth
and flashing sideways in bevelled
syncopations.                                 20
It's the way the snow
drains the light from day but then,
covering boundaries of road and sidewalk,
widens wondering streets
and stains the sky yellow                     25
to glow at midnight.

## Media Adaptations

- A video recording of Levertov reading from *Evening Train* and selected unpublished poems was produced by the Lannan Foundation in 1994. This is a VHS tape, titled simply as *Denise Levertov*, which runs sixty minutes.

- Go to the W. W. Norton web site at http://www.wwnorton.com/trade/multimedia.htm to hear Levertov read her poem "Tenebrae," which appeared in the *To Stay Alive* collection and is one of her protest poems about the Vietnam War.

## Poem Summary

### Lines 1–2

The first line of "The Blue Rim of Memory" sets up the premise for all the images and events that follow throughout the poem. Everything from this point on will be a description of "the way sorrow enters the bone," and the poet will rely on metaphors to get her point across. Line 2 generalizes the specific images that are about to come, suggesting that sorrow is sometimes felt quickly and can be as painful as the "stabs" of a knife. At other times, it seems to linger on the sidelines of a person's thoughts and emotions, an ever-present grief that permeates the memory.

### Lines 3–5

These lines open the first of four central metaphors in the poem, and the most extended one as well. "From a torn page" implies that this image is like one taken from a book, a moment alienated from the rest of the story. The scene described is reminiscent of eighteenth-century transportation. A "cabriolet" is a two-wheeled, one-horse carriage with room for two people and a top that folds down. Today, they are popular for sporting newlyweds around city streets as part of the wedding celebration, but in "The Blue Rim of Memory" the cabriolet is a strange, even haunting figure from long ago. Perhaps representing sorrow, it "approaches over the crest of a hill," more like a suspended, hovering entity than a quick, sharp stab.

### Lines 6–7

These two lines simply embellish the image of the cabriolet. Anyone who has seen a horse pulling a carriage can picture the animal's "nodding, straining head," and anyone who has seen a movie set in the eighteenth century or earlier, recognizes the "blind lamps, peering" from the darkness, apparently held out by the riders.

### Lines 8–9

The fact that there are "ladies" riding in the carriage (a cabriolet here resembles a humpy "insect" with long feelers up front) may be inconsequential, and the poem would work the same if the inhabitants were two men or a man and a woman. The only significant reason for placing two women here instead may fall in line with some critics' belief that this poem is Levertov's reflection on her relationship with her mother and her sorrow over the older woman's death, which occurred a year prior to the release of *Life in the Forest*. Line 9 suggests that the ladies are anxious about their surroundings and apparently unaware of what lies ahead, for they are "awaiting the vista," or distant view.

### Lines 10–11

These two lines close out the first metaphor and include an allusion to the general description in line 2 regarding the way sorrow "stabs" its victims. Here, the ladies, the horse, and the cabriolet all disappear "quick as a knife," much like some painful memories that creep into the mind and then evaporate when some other thought or action interrupts. The questions "Who were they? Where is the hill?" echo the elusiveness of memories that, like "torn pages," seem incomplete, having little purpose other than instigating grief as a person contemplates why they come and where they go.

### Lines 12–13

Line 12 is the beginning of the second central metaphor in "The Blue Rim of Memory." Notice that it begins with the word "Or," expanding on the dynamics of memory and sorrow set forth in lines 1–2. In other words, line 12 picks up where line 3 left off: "From a torn page . . . / Or from stoked fires of nevermore." But this time, instead of a horse and carriage approaching, it is "a warmth constant as breathing" that "hovers out." Note the correlation between "hoverings" in line 2 and "hovers" in line 13. The gist of these lines 12–13, then, is that the human mind is often like a land of "nevermore," of things forgotten or dormant until its "fires" are "stoked" and memory rushes back like a warm breath suddenly exhaled.

### Lines 14–15

These two lines finish the second metaphor and describe how the "warmth" in line 13, which represents sorrow or memory or both, surrounds the individual like a "cloud of mist." But the mist turns heavy and suffocating as it "becomes rain, becomes cloak, then skin." Sorrowful memories, it seems, may begin lightly and innocently enough, but they can gradually become so consuming that they feel as tight as one's own flesh, as though sorrow is a physical part of the human being.

### Lines 16–20

These five lines make up the third central metaphor in the poem. Line 16 is simply a repetition of line 1, but this time the way sorrow gets into the bone is compared to "the way fish sink through dense lakes." The "smoke" in line 18 is probably the cloud of sand or mud that rises when one touches the bottom of a body of water, and the image makes a nice tie-in with the smoky imagery of stoked fires and clouds of mist in the previous stanza. Like sorrow, fish do not often move in a direct line but shift back and forth in "beveled / syncopations," just as painful memories shift about in one's mind, never quite uniform or predictable.

### Lines 21–24

Line 21 is the beginning of the fourth and final central metaphor in "The Blue Rim of Memory." The idea of grief's heaviness and suffocating power comes up again here, as sorrow is now compared to snow that can turn daylight suddenly dim with thick clouds and blinding precipitation. Once the ground is covered in a blanket of white, one can no longer distinguish the "boundaries of road and sidewalk," or anything else for that matter.

### Lines 25–26

The final two lines of the poem complete the fourth metaphor and offer at least a glimmer of hope from beneath the smothering snow. Since boundaries have disappeared, once narrow streets now seem wider, and the sky that went dark during the daytime now appears bright in the nighttime because of the reflecting snow. Anyone who has witnessed a heavy snowfall knows how the outdoors appears "to glow at midnight," and, in keeping with the metaphorical allusion, perhaps this image suggests that the sorrow that has entered the bone is not necessarily as dark and debilitating as what may at first have been presumed.

## Themes

### The Impersonal as Personal

In the introductory note to *Life in the Forest*, Levertov discusses the influence that the work of Italian poet and novelist Cesare Pavese had on her own poems in this collection. Addressing his 1936 publication of *Lavorare Stanca* (Hard Labor), Levertov notes that "Pavese's beautiful poems are about various persons other than himself; though he is a presence in them also, their focus is definitely not autobiographical and egocentric." She admires Pavese's "concept of suggesting a narrative through the depiction of a scene, a landscape, rather than through direct recounting of events as such," and she admits wanting to accomplish the same in her current work. "The Blue Rim of Memory" is a testimony to her success in this endeavor.

There is no "I" in this poem, nor is there a "you" or any indication that a specific person is being addressed. Yet, there is an intensely personal *feel* to the poem, something that draws one in and allows a reader to identify with the circumstances it describes. What may usually be considered an element of style, then, becomes a thematic issue in this poem. Levertov's message depends strictly on third person, seemingly impartial depictions of landscapes and nature—the eerie presence of a hill crest over which a cabriolet approaches, a cloud of mist and rainfall, snow-covered streets, and fish

## Topics for Further Study

- Which do you prefer—poems like "The Blue Rim of Memory" that are strictly objective, third-person descriptions or more personal, autobiographical poems that seem to tell a story? Tell why you like one over the other and explain the advantages and disadvantages of each.

- Why do you think the scene with the cabriolet is effective in this poem? What does it say about the time period in which these carriages were popular, and how does evoking something historical relate to sorrow?

- Metaphor is one of the most common ways that people use to describe their feelings or to make someone understand how a thing may look, sound, taste, and so forth. What would be the effect on communication if metaphor did not exist? How may it change the way you try to tell someone your feelings?

- Write a poem based on "The Blue Rim of Memory" in which you come up with four *more* ways that "sorrow enters the bone." Remember: use third-person descriptions only—no I, me, we, or you.

### Sorrow

The most obvious theme in "The Blue Rim of Memory" is the human response to sorrow. In this case, the response is more indirect than blunt, as made clear in the use of metaphors to express it. But whether one makes a candid statement about mourning a loss or implies grief by describing a cloud of mist that becomes rain that becomes a cloak that becomes skin, the message is arguably the same. Sorrow is painful, often suffocating the spirit and emotions. Sometimes it is only a dull, lingering discomfort, but it has the potential to suddenly and sharply overwhelm like a knife wound inflicted by memory.

The title of this poem suggests that the sorrow that it addresses is not based on something that has just happened or that has happened very recently. Instead, it is *memory* that evokes sadness and *memory* in which the sorrow resides. Perhaps the concept of sorrow immured in memory elicits the dichotomy of soft, pervasive and instant, intense sorrow that is depicted in the poetic metaphors. Time and distance work in the poem to both buffer initial pain, represented in the uneasy stillness of certain imagery, and create the potential for the piercing sorrow of memories suddenly recalled. Sorrow, then, sits at the "blue rim" of memory, just on the edge, where its presence is felt, but is not always intrusive. Many humans may experience grief in this way, especially after the passage of time when reflection and contemplation have replaced shock, anger, or depression. Levertov's take on it is not only beautifully poetic but realistic, as well.

sinking into dense lakes. But the underlying meaning is not impartial at all. Perhaps an autobiographical factor comes in if this poem is about the death of the poet's mother, but, even if a specific event is not at the heart of it, the sentiment is just as strong, just as intimate as if it were. Levertov's imagery is vivid and provocative, touching on scenes and encounters that most everyone has witnessed or experienced firsthand. By using four very different yet very powerful metaphors to portray the same emotion, she shows how connections can be made between the personal and the impersonal through graphic depictions instead of diary-like narrative. Like Pavese, she accomplishes heartfelt meaning with objective representations. Though her own grief—whatever its source—is not directly proclaimed in this poem, its overwhelming presence is unmistakable.

## Style

### Lyric Poetry

As noted previously, Levertov's attempt in *Life in the Forest* was to write in the objective, third-person style of Cesare Pavese, omitting sentimentality, emotionalism, and autobiography. Not all the poems in this collection reflect any success with her ambition, but "The Blue Rim of Memory" does. It is considered a lyric poem because it is still personal without being obviously autobiographical, and it still offers a heartfelt contemplation of its subject without lapsing into pathos. The poem is presented in third person, start to finish, and contains no rhyme nor contrived meter or rhythm. The language, however, is strongly *poetic*, not lending itself to being turned into prose by simply writing it in paragraph form. Many contemporary lyric poems can stand that test, reading like passages from a book as well as poems. But Levertov's later work maintained some of the earlier, more stylized poetry she produced while living in England. The language in "The Blue Rim of Memory" may not be quite as stiff as early-twentieth-century poetry or certainly anything from the Victorian period, yet it is chock-full of carefully selected, tight images and intentional connections between metaphors with the repetition of specific words or allusions. For instance, "hoverings" as a noun in line 2 compares to "hovers" as a verb in line 13, and the "stoked fires" of line 12 shift nicely into "raising smoke" in line 18, even though the latter image is actually a description of sand in a lake bed. The reference to the horse-drawn cabriolet and the "blind lamps" gives this poem a historical feel and adds to its restrained poetics. That restraint is softened by the lushness of the metaphors and the easily pictured events that they represent.

## Historical Context

On a small scale, the decade of the 1970s was a time of personal change in the subject matter of Levertov's poetry, and, on a large scale, these were years of sometimes odd, sometimes benign change. In America, the 1960s were unprecedented in their all-encompassing antiwar, free-love, politically radical themes, and some of that carried over into the 1970s. But by the middle of the decade—after the Vietnam War had ended, Richard Nixon had resigned, the Watergate scandal finished its media blitz, and the rock-and-roll sounds of Vanilla Fudge and the Rolling Stones gave way to the disco beat of the Bee Gees and Donna Summer—many Americans were left disillusioned by their own government's clandestine activities and doubtful that the fiery, high-minded social missions of the previous decade held any real value for the doubting, unenthusiastic members of this generation. As a result, many social activist flames were snuffed, and political writers like Levertov turned to more personal, less volatile issues to create their work. The decade of the 1970s, however, was not without at least a few of its own themes, though most generally get credited back to the 1960s or cast forward to the more memorable 1980s.

The social and political liberalism that dominated the country beginning in the early 1960s was fueled primarily by many people's belief that an American presence in Vietnam was unjustified and, ultimately, futile. Along with antiwar protests, other causes spurred citizens into action: from Civil Rights to the Women's Movement, ecology to cosmology, politicians, students, housewives, farmers, and university professors all found a reason to have their voices heard in a very clamorous society. After the war, many of those issues remained just as vital, but many of their supporters seemed to run out of steam. Vietnam veterans returned home bitter and emotionally shattered, not only because of the horrors of war they had experienced but also because of the less-than-warm welcome they received from the folks back home had protested the war. Hippies got older and got jobs. By the mid- to late-1970s, many of them had traded in their love beads and bell-bottomed jeans for leisure suits and offices in corporate America. Some former left-wing radicals even softened their liberal views, turning more toward the conservative, family-oriented values that would dominate the country in the 1980s. The decade of the 1970s, it seems, was one of transition more than anything else.

However, the shift to conservatism in the latter part of the 1970s is not likely due to the fact that radicals had grown up but was spurred mainly by political foreign policies and the economy at home. The rising American economy of the previous decade was assumed to go hand-in-hand with making the improvements in society that people were in the streets carrying placards to support. This type of economy was also believed to enhance expanding overseas markets, including opening doors to trade with communist or socialist states typically considered unlikely partners in trade. Many Americans were still under the illusion that post-World War II prosperity was so great that it could support new social programs at home, expand foreign markets, and still maintain an anticommunist crusade, at least in theory, if not in practical economics. Unfortunately, they were wrong. By the end of the decade, the U.S. economy was faltering, overseas expansion was coming to a halt, and domestic reforms were all but over. As a result, disillusionment in previous high ideals caused some Americans to reevaluate their political stances, essentially paving the way for the Reagan years of the 1980s.

On a lighter note, the 1970s are remembered for spawning some of the shortest-lived music, dance, and dress fads in modern America. While many hardliners never gave up their Levi's and rock-and-roll, a trendier set climbed into platform shoes, glittery dresses, and wide-lapel, polyester suits and danced all night to the highly rhythmic,

# Compare & Contrast

- **1970s:** The last American troops leave Vietnam as North Vietnamese troops complete their Communist takeover of South Vietnam. The unpopular, largely unsupported conflict costs more than 56,000 American lives and sharply divides the country at home.

   **Today:** American troops in Afghanistan and other hotbeds of terrorism throughout the world are greatly supported by their own nation and many others, as countries across the globe unite in the war on terrorism.

- **1970s:** The world's last known case of smallpox appears in Somalia, and the deadly disease is considered eradicated when it does not appear for two more years.

   **Today:** Pharmaceutical researchers scramble to create smallpox vaccines to protect Americans from the threat of biological terrorism in the wake of the September 11, 2001, attacks on the World Trade Center and the Pentagon and subsequent cases of anthrax poisonings.

- **1970s:** In a sorrowful and bizarre religious cult display, Jim Jones and over nine hundred followers drink Kool-Aid spiked with cyanide and die in a mass suicide in Jonestown, Guyana.

   **Today:** Suicide bombers and suicide hijackers spread terror throughout the world under the guise of martyrdom and religious fundamentalism.

---

drum-and-bass-centered sounds of disco. When *Saturday Night Fever* hit movie theaters in 1977, disco's popularity soared, and John Travolta's signature dance-king stance—legs spread wide, one arm up, one arm down, a finger pointing triumphantly skyward—became the fastest copied pose of "fever fans" across the country. Like most pop-up fads, however, the thrill soon waned, and by the early 1980s, disco music and leisure suits were little more than the butt of late-night TV comedians' jokes. Unfortunately, many events of this decade wound up with the same dubious honor, but the same case could surely be made for years prior to and after the infamous 1970s.

## Critical Overview

From her early, tightly-structured poetry written in England to her more Americanized verse, which spanned the latter half of her life in the United States, Levertov's creative work is some of the most well respected, highly praised to come out of the twentieth century in both countries. While some critics cast doubts about her liberal delving into political poetry in the 1960s and early 1970s, even this work grabbed attention, if more so for its controversial subjects and accusatory tones than pure poetics. In the final two decades of her life, Levertov settled into quieter, more spiritual themes, essentially bringing to the front the religious beliefs and contemplations on God that many critics saw lurking in the background of her earlier work as well. Her "middle" collections—those published in the late 1970s and early 1980s—are transitional, revealing the mellower tone and meditative spirituality, yet they are not wholly religious in nature. *Life in the Forest* is one of those transitional books, and it was met with praise when it came out in 1978. Writing for the *National Review*, critic N. E. Condini says that in Levertov's poetry "there's an insistence on the need to watch nature as it incessantly recreates life.... This concept is taken up again in *Life in the Forest*, where the two main themes of the previous collection—mother and the forest symbol—stand for the inevitability of death and the permanence of creation." Also picking up on the nature-life death theme, critic and poet Diane Wakoski, writing in *Contemporary Poets*, notes that

> this worldliness is the source of a belief in some primal deep reality, or other-worldliness, underlying her materialism.... [In *Life in the Forest*] she reveals her vision of a jungle world which is always out there,

ready to reassert itself as soon as the ephemeral hand of civilization relaxes.

Over the nearly fifty years of Levertov's writing career, critics have spent more time studying, analyzing, and contemplating the poet's themes, metaphors, and styles rather than just criticizing them. This by itself is a testament to the truly evocative work Levertov continued to produce from the 1940s through the 1990s. Not many poets publish even half the number of volumes that Levertov did, and very few of those who do manage to retain the interest of critics and readers, book after book after book. Levertov was—and still is—an exception.

## Criticism

### Pamela Steed Hill

*Hill is the author of a poetry collection, has published widely in literary journals, and is an editor for a university publications department. In the following essay, Hill makes a case for Levertov's poem being honored with the title of the "perfect" poem—keeping the dubiousness of that word in mind.*

Rarely does one find a poem about which there is nothing negative to say. That is, most poems can stand some criticism that offers viable suggestions for improvement: stronger clarity, less verbiage, more descriptive language, not so much didactic finger-pointing. These are common grounds for complaints from critics, and poets have simply learned to live with them and decided individually whether to heed any outside advice. Although Levertov was undeniably one of the most respected poets throughout her poetic career, her work has had its share of negative comments, particularly those generated by the more volatile poems she published during the Vietnam War. Controversy makes good fodder for leveling opinions about opinions. Most levelers consider their own beliefs and theories *right*, giving a poem little chance of being left alone as it was written. "The Blue Rim of Memory" is a rare poem for these reasons. It is not controversial nor didactic nor full of unnecessary words. One could hardly ask for more descriptive language, and it takes only a careful reading and some term definitions to make its message effectively clear. In short, this poem is as close to perfect as one can get.

The three primary aspects of "The Blue Rim of Memory" that make the poem work so well are its strong vocabulary, its cohesiveness, and the ability of its overall meaning to make a reader contemplate it for some time. Metaphors, similes, and various other figures of speech are all common, useful ways of enhancing any kind of writing, and they are especially effective in poetry where much can be said in a small amount of space. Vocabulary is the key to communication, and Levertov demonstrates a beautiful mastery of it in this poem. With highly descriptive language, she comes at her topic—sorrow—from four different angles, each expressing what sorrow feels like from the remote perspective of things that do not even experience the emotion. The mysterious scene she portrays with the cabriolet and unknown riders who peer from it with their lanterns extended does not need further explanation to make it applicable to the message. Sorrowfulness is implicit here—in the darkness, in the furtive glances, in the sudden disappearance of the entire scene. The speaker's questions of "Who were they? Where is the hill?" are merely rhetorical, for an answer need not be given to get the point across. Similarly, the second image carries its own air of mystery while still evoking sadness and one's inability to escape it. How "a warmth constant as breathing" gradually becomes suffocating does not need to be spelled out, for the words that describe the process are plain enough: "a cloud of mist / becomes rain, becomes cloak, then skin." These descriptors, in the order they are presented, summarize quite aptly the progression from looseness to confinement.

The final two images in "The Blue Rim of Memory" are just as precise and evocative as the first two, and they also rely on the power of figurative language to make an impact. Hardly could back-to-back images be more unalike than those of fish sinking into a lake and heavy snow disguising the "boundaries of road and sidewalk." But, as different as these scenarios are, they have something very poignant in common: both imply a kind of smothering, suffocating feeling. While fish do not drown in "dense lakes" and sidewalks do not die beneath deep snow, words like "sink," "raising smoke," "drains," and "stains" illuminate what sorrow—here portrayed as water and snow—can do to a human being. It "enters" stealthily, softly, hiding the true deadliness of its nature until the lake overtakes its victim, the snow buries the unsuspecting. These images are stark and satisfying. They need nothing more to express their sentiment.

"The Blue Rim of Memory" may contain diverse metaphors that seem worlds apart in the mental pictures they conjure, but they are held together by a verbal cohesiveness that gives the poem an overall *tight fit*. Levertov uses a remarkable manipulation of language to move from one image to another, sometimes even skipping over several lines and still providing a smooth transition between phrases. For instance, note how line 3 is tied directly to line 12: "From a torn page" is essentially continued with "Or from stoked fires of nevermore." More obviously, of course, is the repetition of line 1 in line 16 and the use of the words "hoverings" and "hovers" to create a bond between the two very different images in which each appears. Also, in each metaphor, there is a sense of mystery and things hidden or just beyond comprehension. The first scene, which appears to be straight out of the eighteenth century, offers no explanation for its enigmatic portrayal of two ladies riding in a cabriolet and their strange approach "over the crest of a hill." Most odd is that they suddenly disappear, along with the carriage, horse, and the hill itself. The reason for their presence remains unknown, but their initial *approach* implies that the purpose is there, but just out of reach.

The cryptic nature of the second metaphor is more subtle than the first, yet its premise is shrouded in the "cloud of mist" that it describes. The word "nevermore" is both archaic and foreboding, and the phrase "breathing hovers out" evokes a sense of apprehension and uneasiness. There is also a question of who the "you" is that becomes surrounded by breath, mist, rain, a cloak, and, finally, skin. Perhaps the reference is only generic, denoting any human being, or perhaps it is the reader or a specific person the poet has in mind. Maybe it is even herself, addressed in second person. Frankly, the identity is unimportant to the message. Regardless of who the "you" refers to, the situation in which the individual finds himself or herself is rather eerie and, again, just beyond total understanding.

The third and fourth metaphors in this poem deal with enigma in a slightly different manner, this time invoking scenes of the natural world, both animal and landscape. *Obscurity* plays the key role here. Imagine peering into a lake trying to see how deep it is or whether there are fish swimming in it. Visibility is usually very limited, but Levertov makes that point unmistakable by calling the lakes "dense" and having the fish raise "smoke" as it sinks to the sandy bottom. Obviously, one could not see anything in such conditions. Like dense water, heavy snowfall also affects visibility, and once it covers the ground, all that lies beneath it is hidden, obscuring natural boundaries. The mysteri-

> *"The perspective is not one-dimensional, but deepened, rather, into layers of viewpoints, stimulating the intellect as well as the emotions."*

ousness in this final metaphor is implied through the image of a yellowish sky glowing at midnight. It may be a common view on a snowy winter night, but there is an eeriness to the scene as well. The firmament appears too dark to be daytime and too bright to be nighttime, but lies somewhere in between, just out of the grasp of either. While each of the four metaphors in this poem portrays a sense of strangeness and incomprehension in various ways, the overall tie-in of the images makes it cohesive in its tone, presentation, and meaning.

Finally, it is the meaning that makes "The Blue Rim of Memory" leave a lasting impression in most readers' minds. Sorrow is one of the most common of human emotions and likely one of the most understood. One *knows* why people cry, why people become sad, regretful, and depressed: death, illness, loss of love, loss of a job, violations against human rights, famine, violence, loss of a pet, failure at achieving a goal, and the list could go on and on. Perhaps what one does not know is how to look at it from an angle other than dead-on. Sorrow seems to need no explanation except for its source to be named. Some critics believe Levertov's source for this poem was her mother's death, and perhaps that is true. But, it is never mentioned. Instead, the reader catches glimpses of the sad mental state in "bevelled / syncopations" like fish swimming sideways through water. The perspective is not one-dimensional, but deepened, rather, into layers of viewpoints, stimulating the intellect as well as the emotions. The poem may not leave one cheerful or warm, but neither does it leave one bored or disappointed. Instead, it makes the reader *think*—think about sorrow from a new angle, think about the mind's process of dealing with sadness, think about feelings that lurk somewhere inside, unable to rest or to go away. In short, the poem fascinates, in the strongest sense of the word.

> *For Levertov, a poem is a record of the moment-by-moment interaction between consciousness and natural phenomena, whether they be wholly inner experiences or encounters with the outer world of nature.*

"The Blue Rim of Memory" is not one of Levertov's most recognized poems, nor does it show up in anthologies of great American or English literature. In fact, it is safe to assume that very few people are familiar with it at all. This is unfortunate, for—at the risk of seeming doting and fatuous—this poem could make those who read poetry only by force perhaps give the genre a fairer chance, and it could, of course, validate the love of the craft some academics and nonacademics already feel for it. So is this poem perfect? Admittedly, *perfect* is a chancy word, and not much lives up to it. The contention here is that "The Blue Rim of Memory" has a fighting chance, if anything does.

**Source:** Pamela Steed Hill, Critical Essay on "The Blue Rim of Memory," in *Poetry for Students*, The Gale Group, 2003.

## Marjorie Partch

*Partch is a Jungian astrologer, writer, and graphic designer. In this essay, Partch considers the mystical orientation that Levertov brings to the discipline of poetry.*

In "The Blue Rim of Memory," Denise Levertov wastes no time in building subtly to her point and little or no interpretation is required in even the first reading of the poem. By the third word of the first line, the reader knows exactly what this poem is about: sorrow.

The poem proceeds in a manner where it zeros in on the sensation of sorrow, while simultaneously distances from any accompanying emotion. Because of this duality, the poem never quite yields its detachment to the point of sympathy or detaches to the point of total abstraction.

Levertov brings the phenomenon of sorrow, as it is in and of itself, into such sharp relief that the particulars become irrelevant. Such narrative questions as, what sorrow? Which sorrow? Whose sorrow? Sorrow over what? Who caused the sorrow? The source is not important and neither is the context.

This close, disciplined cropping of the frame forces a more intimate look at the specific experience of sorrow, as a distinctly human experience—as universal, natural, and inevitable as breathing. The close focus suspends judgement or rationalization mid-sentence. Left in the astonished state of recognition, the reader is invited to consider how sorrow, once within the realm of experience, informs life from that point forward. Does it, as Levertov suggests in her final image of falling snow, make day darker and night lighter? Does this particular loss of innocence perhaps dampen joy and simultaneously lighten subsequent sorrows? Is this what it means to move out of childhood's bliss?

These are the questions left to consider, beyond the particularization of the experience. Levertov is more concerned with evoking the distinct sensation of sorrow than explaining or even describing it, let alone answering the ultimate burning question of why. The images employed are neither sad nor personal. They reach beyond sentiment, beyond emotion even, and beyond interpersonal relations and situations. There is no protest against human action or fate, no cry of injustice or remorse. There is just the simple fact of this experience entering the bone, a condition as eternal as day passing into night.

Levertov's poem offers only the strictest attention to the sensation of the knowing of sorrow, sorrow that is here to stay. Levertov does not proffer the hope that it will season and temper its host like fine wine, if one is very good or wise or lucky; nor does she warn that it may char or curdle if not. Readers have entered a realm beyond the solace of comprehension or redemption. This is a realm of pure phenomenon, of pure experience, beyond the reach of reason. Where reason leaves off is where faith picks up, if one can push through that stubborn membrane. This is where Levertov is taking her readers, through the borderline of rationality, across the threshold of the intellect, and through the void of despair on the other side.

This kind of detachment, from personal identity and context, often tends toward dissociation altogether into the surreal, into completely disembodied abstraction. But this poem permits only one lapse in this direction, in the second stanza, where the image of a cabriolet suddenly veers off the page, into a Edward Gorey-grotesque cartoon landscape, and readers glimpse "the ladies within the insect."

This one exception contrasts Levertov's otherwise consistent use of concrete imagery from nature. Here, readers can recognize the mind's tendency in moments of crisis and severe shock to juxtapose the absurdly comic with horror. For the most part, however, the concreteness and simplicity of the poem's imagistic analogies mitigate against floating off into the surreal dissociation of the bizarre, and the poem's evoked recognitions are very much anchored in the real—nearly in the physical body itself.

There is a certain acceptance of the naturalness of sorrow in its very inevitability. There is no conditional *if*; there is only the ineluctable *when*. However, this acceptance does not constitute a lesson or a moral or embody an attitude. It is simply acknowledging a fact of life, a fact of unalterable natural law, honoring its existence by painting its portrait as vividly as possible, with words calling forth images that form familiar but startling analogies.

This matter-of-fact acceptance of experience has come to strike the modern Western sensibility as rather "Zen" in its detached, compassionate examination. Is this quality not a legitimate claim to the poet's natural place? While Levertov's mature personal spirituality reclothed itself in the Christian traditions of her youth, her work seems to transcend categorization. One can see traces here and there in her work of various traditions; here a little Buddhism, there a little Kabbalah, here a Gnostic streak. Indeed, as Levertov's path at various points in her life has wandered through each of these gardens, it has gathered their various hues and shades and depths along the way.

As the function of the mystic is not to seek analysis or conclusion but to deepen the sense of mystery, this poem may raise more questions than it answers, which, in this tradition would definitely be seen as a good thing.

The first two lines describe the workings of the poem: "The way sorrow enters the bone / is with stabs and hoverings."

The poem itself brings sudden moments of startled, piercing awareness, intermixed with its more oblique, subtler realizations: "a cloud of mist / becomes rain, becomes cloak, then skin."

# What Do I Read Next?

- Editor Christopher MacGowan collected *The Letters of Denise Levertov and William Carlos Williams* and published them in 1998. The correspondences cover Levertov's first few years in New York City and her two years in Mexico, and they reveal a coming-of-age as she grows from a worshipful student writing to her mentor into Williams's self-confident colleague in the field of poetry.

- Upon her death, Levertov left a notebook containing forty finished poems that show the poet's creative genius active right up until the end. *This Great Unknowing: Last Poems* was collected by her literary executors—who left the poems in the same chronological order in which they found them—and was published by New Directions Books in 1999.

- The recent publication by Susan Roos called *Chronic Sorrow: A Living Loss* (2002) explores the natural grief reaction to losses that are not final but continue to be present in the life of the griever. The book addresses feelings of sorrow from a lifelong perspective and discusses its effects on those who see no end to their grief.

- The second edition of editor Andrew Ortony's *Metaphor and Thought* (1993) expands this collection of stimulating essays on the function of metaphor in human language and thought. Most discussions are very readable to the non-philosopher and non-psychologist, and the overall sentiment is that using metaphor to describe reality is a vital part of the human ability to communicate and to understand.

So it is with sorrow as well. It comes quickly *and* slowly; in sharp increments penetrating to the core *and* in gradual layerings over time. Sorrow becomes a part of one's being and a part of one's *experiencing* from that point forward. Perhaps the blue rim (memory) is the lens through which experience must from now on filter as it penetrates and ultimately becomes self.

Knife and mist are alchemically combined in the final stanza:

> fish sink through dense lakes
> raising smoke from the depth
> and flashing sideways in bevelled syncopations.

It is the startling use of familiar, everyday, and otherwise innocuous images against the field of the subject of sorrow that creates the confluence of content and form and a sense of awe-inspiring mystery. It could be thought of as a higher order of onomatopoeia, almost like a pun between image and meaning, which sets the mystical imagistic poets apart from their more sentimental or prosaic cousins. Levertov's colleague Robert Creeley asserted in Levertov's *The Poet in the World* that "Form is never more than an extension of content," to which Levertov added (also quoted in *The Poet in the World*, "Form is never more than a *revelation* of content."

Some might say it is the function of any art to join the life of the inner self with the inner life of the outer world, but it is without question the task of Levertov's poetic tradition. As she put it so succinctly herself in her "Appreciation" of H. D.'s work, Levertov is concerned with "the interplay of psychic and material life." For Levertov, a poem is a record of the moment-by-moment interaction between consciousness and natural phenomena, whether they be wholly inner experiences or encounters with the outer world of nature.

In "The Blue Rim of Memory," readers see a master at work, confidently and quietly sculpting, summoning the very mystery of existence into being. People may never know the why of any of it—why people are alive, why people feel, why people love, why people gain, why people lose—but the fact that people are alive and do experience at all is miracle enough, as Denise Levertov reminds us in this stabbing and hovering meditation on the human experience of sorrow.

**Source:** Marjorie Partch, Critical Essay on "The Blue Rim of Memory," in *Poetry for Students*, The Gale Group, 2003.

## Sources

Condini, N. E., "Embracing Old Gods," in *National Review*, Vol. XXXII, No. 6, March 21, 1980, pp. 360–61.

Levertov, Denise, *Life in the Forest*, New Directions Books, 1978.

———, "Some Notes on Form," in *The Poet in the World*, New Directions, 1973.

Wakoski, Diane, "Levertov, Denise," in *Contemporary Poets*, 5th ed., edited by Tracy Chevalier, St. James Press, 1991, pp. 554–56.

## Further Reading

Levertov, Denise, *Poems 1972–1982*, New Directions Books, 2001.

> This book collects three of Levertov's volumes that were published in succession during the ten-year period mentioned. They include *The Freeing of the Dust* (1975), *Life in the Forest* (1978), and *Candles in Babylon* (1982). It is interesting to read the poems that Levertov wrote for the collections that appeared on each side of *Life in the Forest* and to compare their use of metaphor to that of "The Blue Rim of Memory."

Marten, Harry, *Understanding Denise Levertov*, University of South Carolina Press, 1988.

> This book is part of the *Understanding Contemporary American Literature* series, written for both students and nonacademic readers. It provides an insightful look at Levertov and her work in chapters such as "The Poet in the World: Private Vision and Public Voice" and "Deciphering the Spirit—People, Places, Prayers." The latter includes a discussion of *Life in the Forest*.

O'Connell, Nicholas, *At Field's End: Interviews with 22 Pacific Northwest Writers*, University of Washington Press, 1998.

> This collection contains Denise Levertov's final interview before her death in 1997. In it, she discusses the egotism that pervades much modern poetry, her feelings on the sacredness of writing, and what she sees as the spiritual hunger of an American society that depends so heavily on technology.

Rodgers, Audrey T., *Denise Levertov: The Poetry of Engagement*, Fairleigh Dickinson University Press, 1993.

> This book is a beautifully written exploration of Levertov's work, taking the reader through her early "English" poetry, through the turbulent 1960s, and on to the more contemplative, spiritual poems of the 1970s and 1980s. This is an excellent read for anyone interested in Levertov's work.

# The Cobweb

## Raymond Carver
## 1986

"The Cobweb" appears in Raymond Carver's 1986 collection of poems, *Ultramarine*, for which he received *Poetry* magazine's Levinson Award. The title of the collection comes from the book's epigraph, lines from Irish poet Derek Mahon's poem, "Mt. Gabriel," included in his collection, *Antarctica*:

> Sick with exile, they yearn homeward now,
> their eyes
> Turned to the ultramarine, first-star-pierced dark
> Reflected on the dark, incoming waves.

"Ultramarine Blue" is also a color listed under the section titled "Palette" in the second poem of the book, "What You Need for Painting." The title underscores the importance of both sky and sea as symbolic images appearing throughout the collection.

Carver is known for his storytelling, and he tells a story in this poem, albeit a short one. Carver's speaker, a thinly veiled version of Carver the author, recounts an experience in which he walks into a cobweb and then brings it back into his house, where he muses about it and reflects on how it, like life, is fragile. It is a brief poem, only thirteen lines, and written in short, choppy sentences, with a rhythm closer to prose than poetry. A meditation on his death and his own mortality, the poem is significant, for it was written only a few years before Carver succumbed to cancer in 1988. More than likely the poem was written in Port Angeles, Washington, at Sky House, the home of his future wife, Tess Gallagher. Carver spent a good deal of time there during the mid-1980s writing poems and stories.

*Ramond Carver*

## Author Biography

Raymond Carver was born May 25, 1938, to Clevie Raymond Carver and Ella Beatrice Casey in the tiny logging town of Clatskanie, Oregon, population seven hundred. Carver's parents were working-class poor and often struggled to make ends meet. His father, an alcoholic saw filer in a sawmill, had a nervous breakdown in 1957, the same year that Raymond married sixteen-year-old Maryann Burk and they had their first child. Carver's adult life eerily mirrored that of his father's: he drank heavily, worked at a series of menial, low-paying jobs, including one in a sawmill, and moved his family from city to city, always hunting for better opportunities. His impoverished and often desperate circumstances, however, also provided Carver with the subject matter for his poems and stories. Apart from his family and his own experience, Carver credits novelist John Gardner, with whom Carver studied at Chico State College in 1959, as the most important influence on his writing. Gardner showed a keen interest in Carver's work and encouraged him to be more disciplined in his writing. Carver also claims Ernest Hemingway, Leo Tolstoy, Gustav Flaubert, and especially Anton Chekhov as literary influences.

Carver graduated in 1963 with a degree in English from Humboldt State University in California and then moved his family to Iowa City to begin graduate work in the Iowa Writer's Workshop. Although Carver was famous for his short stories, his early success as a writer came from his poetry. In 1970, he was awarded a National Endowment for the Arts Discovery Award for poetry and his first book, *Winter Insomnia*, was published. In 1977, the year Carver stopped drinking, Carver met Tess Gallagher, a poet and fiction writer, who eventually became his second wife. Gallagher's encouragement helped Carver stay sober, and the next ten years proved to be the most productive writing years of his life. In addition to the short-story collection, *Will You Please Be Quiet, Please?* (1976), which was nominated for a National Book Award, Carver published *Furious Seasons and Other Stories* (1977); *What We Talk About When We Talk About Love* (1981); *Cathedral* (1983), nominated for the National Book Critics Circle Award and runner-up for the Pulitzer Prize; and *Where I'm Calling From* (1988). His poetry collections include *Ultramarine* (1986) and *Where Water Comes Together With Other Water* (1985), as well as the posthumously published *All of Us* (1998) and *A New Path to the Waterfall* (1989).

In 1983, the American Academy and Institute of Arts and Letters granted Carver one of its first Mildred and Harold Strauss "Living" awards, freeing him from teaching so he could concentrate on his writing. Carver produced some of his finest writing during the next few years, including the haunting poem, "The Cobweb," and a short story about Chekhov's death, "The Errand," his last published piece. In 1987, Carver experienced pulmonary hemorrhages and had two-thirds of his cancerous left lung removed. In 1988, the cancer resurfaced, and on August 2, Carver died in the new house he and Gallagher had bought just east of Port Angeles, Washington.

## Poem Text

A few minutes ago, I stepped onto the deck
of the house. From there I could see and hear the
　　　water,
and everything that's happened to me all these
　　　years.
It was hot and still. The tide was out.
No birds sang. As I leaned against the railing　　　5
a cobweb touched my forehead.

It caught in my hair. No one can blame me that I
    turned
and went inside. There was no wind. The sea
was dead calm. I hung the cobweb from the
    lampshade.
Where I watch it shudder now and then when my      10
    breath
touches it. A fine thread. Intricate.
Before long, before anyone realizes,
I'll be gone from here.

## Poem Summary

### Lines 1–3

"The Cobweb" is a disarmingly simple poem written in free verse. Carver relies on the rhythm of sentences, rather than any fixed meter or rhyme scheme. Because Carver's poems, especially his later ones, carry a good deal of autobiographical information in them, knowledge of his life increases a reader's appreciation of the poem. The poem could be set anywhere near water, but from Carver and Gallagher's essays, letters, and other writings released after his death, Carver fans know that the poems were written in Port Angeles, Washington, in a house near the water. When the speaker steps onto the deck and says, "From there I could see and hear the water, / and everything that's happened to me all these years," readers understand that he's referring to the difficult and painful life he had while a struggling writer and an alcoholic. Carver is using "seeing" in this instance figuratively. This means that he cannot literally see his past but that the setting and the time that has passed have provided him a perspective from which he can better understand how far he has come and how much he has changed.

### Lines 4–6

In these lines, Carver employs short, declarative sentences describing the weather. The "hot and still" air and the quiet evoke a feeling of emptiness and calm, suggesting the speaker's own reflective state of mind. Leaning into a cobweb underscores the fact that he is paying more attention to what is happening inside of him than outside. Cobwebs can be symbolic of confusion, of being caught in something from which one cannot escape. Once the image is introduced, readers expect more information about it.

### Lines 7–9

In these lines, the speaker moves inside, itself symbolic of the attention he is paying to the incident's effect on his own inner emotional life and memory. This is highlighted in the odd statement, "No one can blame me that I turned / and went inside." Who would blame him? There does not appear to be anyone around watching him. Something else is happening to the speaker that he leaves unsaid. If it is perfectly natural to go inside to untangle the spider web, why even mention it?

Once inside, the speaker focuses on the stillness of the day, how windless and calm it is, "dead calm." It would have to be calm in order for a cobweb to remain intact. Mentioning the weather again is odd, given that the speaker is now indoors. Doing so suggests that the speaker is using the description of the weather to actually comment on his "internal weather," that is, his emotional state.

The gesture of hanging the cobweb from the lampshade befits a man who is tender and thoughtful. He is not saving a spider; rather, he is using the cobweb as an object on which he can meditate and which can be used as a symbol for his own life.

### Lines 10–13

In these lines, the speaker is inside the house, breathing on the cobweb, studying how it responds to his breath. That the web "shudders" tells readers he must be pretty close to it. Again, Carver uses short sentences, fragments, to describe the cobweb. By using longer and shorter sentences, Carver creates a rhythm suggestive of the sea's tides, his breath, and the physical composition of the web

## Media Adaptations

- Director Robert Altman adapted a number of Carver's stories for the screen in the motion picture *Short Cuts* (1993), available in most video stores and many libraries.

- PBS Seattle television station KCTS has released a documentary of Carver's life called *To Write and Keep Kind*.

- In 1983, American Audio Prose Library released an audio cassette of Carver reading his stories, including "Nobody Said Anything" and "Fat."

## Topics for Further Study

- Complete this exercise in small groups. Assume you have only two years to live. Write your own obituary and then have each group member also write an obituary for you. What differences do you notice between your description of your life and your group members' descriptions? Explain what this tells you about how you see yourself and how others see you?

- Write an essay about how you would live the last two years of your life if you knew you had only two years to live. Read the essay to your class.

- Make a timeline of your life's most significant events, both bad and good, and then show the timeline to family members or close friends. Do any of the events surprise them? Do they have suggestions to include?

- Write a short essay arguing for how Carver's poem might be read as an expression of regret.

- In groups, compose a poster of one or more themes that "The Cobweb" addresses. Use any materials, including paint, markers, cutout images from magazines, and so forth. However, do not include an image of a human being or an image of a cobweb in the poster. Present your poster to your class, explaining why it looks the way it does.

- Make a list of all the poems in *Ultramarine* about mortality and then rank each poem according to how closely it expresses your own feelings about the subject. Share your rankings with other students. Are there poems you included that they did not? Make a case for your own choices.

itself. Its fragility and intricacy also suggest the fragility and intricacy of human life. This comparison is subtly underlined in the poem's last two lines when the speaker states, "Before long, before anyone realizes, / I'll be gone from here." This rumination on death became reality just two years after the publication of the collection in which the poem appears. Carver's obsession with his own mortality is evident not only in "The Cobweb" but in many of the other poems in *Ultramarine*.

## Themes

### Mortality

Many writers and artists often claim that their work can give them a kind of immortality. The poems in *Ultramarine*, written in a short period of time, just a few years before Carver's own death, all evoke the speaker's awareness of his inevitable death. There's nothing subtle about this awareness in "The Cobweb." Human beings die. Everyone knows this. What is startling, however, is the suddenness with which the speaker acknowledges his own impending death, after what seems an innocent description of a rather mundane experience with a cobweb. When the speaker announces, "Before long, before anyone realizes, / I'll be gone from here," readers understand that he's not referring to leaving on a vacation, but to dying. The poem has gained an added poignancy since Carver's death in 1988, making it seem prophetic. If Carver were still alive, readers would consider it just one more poetic musing on the brevity of life.

### Nostalgia

Nostalgia is a kind of homesickness for the past, a mood thick with feelings of melancholy, longing, and often regret. Carver expresses nostalgia when he refers to "everything that's happened to me all these years." Readers are not told what these "things" are, but they feel the speaker's reflective mood and can infer that these "things" are significant. The calmness of the water and the absence of wind form an appropriate setting for the speaker's reflection, as he does not have to contend with the elements but, instead, can focus on his memories and his response to them.

The speaker's nostalgia is also tinged with regret. Carver illustrates this when the speaker says, "No one can blame me that I turned / and went inside." As the speaker is alone, the only person watching him is himself. This split consciousness, of the self watching the self, suggests that a part of the speaker feels remorse or guilt for "everything that's happened to me all these years."

### Romanticism

Humanity's difference from and similarity to the natural world is a familiar theme in much poetry, especially romantic poetry. For romantics, nature is the source of inspiration and goodness. Romantic poets such as William Wordsworth often used observations of nature as occasion for reflecting on the human condition and the subjective experience of the individual "self." Carver's poem is written in this tradition, as his speaker uses his encounter with nature—represented by the water, the sea, and the cobweb—as an opportunity to dwell on his past and his own mortality. Romantics also privilege the idea of spontaneity in composition, which Carver's poem embodies in its casual opening, conversational tone, and "surprise ending."

## Style

### Symbol

Symbols are things or actions that suggest or stand for something else. The "something else" is often a range of interrelated attitudes, emotions, or ideas. Symbols can also be private or public. Public symbols have a range of associations accessible to many readers. Most Western readers understand, for example, that a rose can signify love, lust, passion, and beauty. Private symbols are often peculiar to a particular writer and so are not as accessible, especially for readers unfamiliar with that writer's work. Carver's spider web and the sea are public symbols. The cobweb is often associated with ideas of both creation (spinning a web) and death, how a spider traps its prey, while the sea has a wide range of symbolic associations, chief among them are ideas of life and death. The sea, like life, is constantly in flux, at once changing and the same. The ocean sustains much life and is often referred to as "the mother of life." To return to the sea is to return to the mother and to that which one was before life.

### Anecdote

An anecdote is a short, informal story that relates an event or idea. Many of Carver's poems are anecdotal in that he tells stories that also carry a moral punch or an emotional weight beyond their surface description. Critics sometimes fault contemporary poetry for being *too* anecdotal and for not distinguishing itself enough as poetry. Other prominent late-twentieth-century poets who use an anecdotal style include Charles Bukowski, Stephen Dunn, Louis Simpson, and Sharon Olds.

### Understatement

Writers use understatement to suggest, rather than to explicitly express, an idea or emotion. They often accomplish this through the use of images and remarks that appear to be casual or off-handed but that hint at something deeper. Carver's speaker never comes out and says that he is experiencing an overwhelming sense of loss and foreboding, but that is what the images in the poem suggest, as does the leap, an unexpected concept or phrase, embodied in the last two lines. Understatement is the opposite of hyperbole, which is a form of exaggeration and embellishment.

## Historical Context

### 1980s

In 1983, Carver published *Cathedral*, his best-known collection of short stories, which was nominated for the Pulitzer Prize. That same year the American Academy and Institute of Arts and Letters awarded Carver its first Mildred and Harold Strauss Living Award, freeing him from having to teach for a living. Carver quit his job at Syracuse University and moved to Port Angeles, Washington, and at the beginning of 1984, he wrote the collection of poems *Where Water Comes Together with Other Water*. Carver wrote the poems in *Ultramarine* between September 1984 and March 1985 in an unexpected burst of creative energy, after he and Gallagher returned from Brazil and Argentina on a trip sponsored by the United States Information Service. Carver had clearly established himself as a leading voice in American fiction, and his style of writing was widely imitated. Critics often lumped Carver's fiction in with that of other writers such as Bobbie Ann Mason, Ann Beattie, Tobias Wolfe, Frederick Barthelme, and Mary Robison, pejoratively calling their "brand" of fiction "Kmart realism," to denote the writers' emphasis on characters who struggled economically, smoked and drank, ate fast food, and shopped at discount stores in lower-middle-class suburbs. These writers also often sprinkled their prose with brand names of consumer products, emphasizing not only the tastes of their characters but the consumer culture in which they are locked.

The political landscape of America during this period was dominated by President Ronald Reagan's conservative fiscal and social policies. The Economic Recovery Act of 1981 reduced taxes by 23 percent and pegged tax rates to inflation. Between 1981 and 1986, corporations saved almost $150 billion in tax reductions. Social critics dubbed the 1980s the "Me Generation" because of

## Compare & Contrast

- **1980s:** In 1983, smoker Rose Cipollone, dying of lung cancer, sues the Liggett Group for not warning her that their products were dangerous. She wins a $400,000 judgment against the company, but it is overturned on appeal.

    **Today:** In 2000, a jury orders the tobacco industry to pay $145 billion in punitive damages to sick Florida smokers, a record-setting verdict.

- **1980s:** In 1986, the life expectancy for white males in the United States is 71.9 years.

    **Today:** In 1997, the life expectancy for white males in the United States is 74.3 years.

- **1980s:** In 1981, to address a deepening economic recession, the House passes the Economic Recovery Act, reducing taxes by 23 percent and pegging tax rates to inflation.

    **Today:** In 2001, to address a deepening economic recession, the House passes an eleven-year $1.35 trillion tax cut, reducing tax rates and the marriage penalty.

- **1980s:** The largest stock-market drop in Wall Street history occurs on "Black Monday"—October 19, 1987, when the Dow Jones Industrial Average plunges 508.32 points, losing 22.6 percent of its total value.

    **Today:** The great bull market of the 1980s and 1990s comes to an end, as technology stocks lead the markets lower and the United States sinks into a recession. Analysts place much of the blame on the "bubble" (i.e., inflated prices) on the public's infatuation with technology stocks and on the rise of Internet stock trading.

---

Americans' (especially baby boomers') emphasis on making money and acquiring brand-name goods and the media's emphasis on corporate culture celebrities such as Donald Trump, Leona Helmsley, and Ivan Boesky.

Reagan's cold war rhetoric during the 1980s no doubt contributed to the popularity of espionage writers such as Ken Follett, Robert Ludlum, Frederick Forsyth, Martin Cruz Smith, Tom Clancy, and John le Carre, all considered writers of "popular" rather than "literary" fiction like Carver's. Other well-known novelists of the decade include Stephen King, Danielle Steele, Tom Wolfe, Toni Morrison, Larry McMurtry, James Michener, John Irving, and Alice Walker. In poetry, the 1980s witnessed the re-emergence of narrative and formal poetry on one hand and the increasing practice of what has been labeled language poetry on the other hand. Regarding the former, presses such as Story Line Press, founded by maverick poet and critic Robert McDowell, published and promoted works by writers such as Louis Simpson, Donald Hall, and Weldon Kees, offering their work as accessible alternatives to what McDowell sees as the dominant influence of the insular and claustrophobic lyric, the kind of poem most practiced and published by graduates of creative writing programs. Language poetry, which some see as a natural extension of the rise of literary theory (especially French literary theory) in the academy in the 1970s, questioned the notion that language could ever be anything but self-referential. Language poets such as Charles Bernstein, Ron Silliman, and Bob Perleman treat language as a material substance, much like cotton or wood, and compose poems that often baffle readers unfamiliar with the theoretical assumptions underpinning their poems and challenge the idea that language could ever be transparent.

## Critical Overview

*Ultramarine* was widely praised when it was released in 1986. Reviewing the collection for the *New York Times Book Review* in 1987, Patricia Hampl wrote, "This book is a treasure, one to return to. No one's brevity is as rich, as complete, as Raymond Carver's." Although academic criticism of Carver's writing focuses on his fiction rather than his poetry, a few critics have addressed the poems in *Ultramarine*, and interest is likely to increase over time. In his study of Carver's writing, *Raymond Carver*, Adam Meyer calls Carver "a poet of considerable skill" and argues that "The Cobweb" is a projection of his own death. "Carver produced poems that are deserving of much more attention than they have received to date," Meyer writes, noting that critical interest in Carver's poetry is "primarily for its similarities to and difference from his fiction." In his own study of Carver's writing, *Reading Raymond Carver*, Randolph Paul Runyon calls the poems in *Ultramarine* "metafictional," meaning that they comment on themselves as much as the world outside. Runyon argues that many of the poems are about Carver's willing himself to focus on the here and now and not the past. Runyon writes:

> *Ultramarine* has the kind of unity one would expect from a collection of poems written in a short space of time and meant to appear together in a sequence.... it has an integration that rivals that of the three major story collections [Carver has written].

In a 1986 interview with Roxanne Lawler, "Carver's World," Carver says about *Ultramarine*: "I feel like I haven't written any better poems."

## Criticism

### Chris Semansky

*Semansky is an instructor of literature and composition. In this essay, Semansky considers the idea of vision in Carver's poem.*

Like many of Carver's poems and stories, "The Cobweb" uses visual imagery to suggest the emotional depth of its main character. Through his encounter with the cobweb, the speaker moves from sight to insight, undergoing a transformation in which he recognizes the complexity, yet brevity, of his own life. By using the physical world to evoke the unseen world of the heart, Carver achieves what his best work always has: a vision of the smallness of the self in relation to the processes of nature and time.

It is Carver's voice, more than anything, that reaches readers, convinces them of the truth in his observations. This is in large part because of the casual way that Carver's speaker recounts his experience: it is as if he is at a party or having coffee with a friend. He creates intimacy and wins readers' trust by detailing the experience, rather than speaking about it in general terms. It occurred

> "*This relationship between indoors and outdoors in the poem parallels the relationships between sight and insight, the physical and the emotional, self and other.*"

"a few minutes ago" on "the deck / of the house." He then retreats into a generalization when he says, "From there I could see and hear the water, / and everything that's happened to me all these years." This is the rhythm of conversation, the way people talk in the course of their everyday lives, unconsciously moving between observation and reflection. It is not fancy or poetic or pretending to be full of hidden meaning. The "everything" could, in fact, be anything. Readers not familiar with Carver's personal life can fill in the blank and imagine what that "everything" might be, using their own experiences. That is the beauty of Carver's poem: what he leaves unsaid.

In an interview with Nicholas O'Connell, Carver said before he began writing the poems that constitute *When Water Comes Together with Other Water* and *Ultramarine*, that he believed he would never write poetry again, but

> they [the poems] allowed me to satisfy my storytelling instinct; most of the poems in there have a narrative line to them. And it was wonderful to write them; there was just nothing else like it. And I did it because I wanted to, which is the best reason for doing anything.

That is Carver the realist speaking, the plain-speaking hunter and fisherman who had little time for the "why" of writing and was more interested in the "what" and the "how." In another interview, this one with John Alton, Carver says that his poems never start with ideas. "I always see something," he says:

> I start with an image, a cigarette being put out in a jar of mustard, for instance, or the remains, the wreckage, of a dinner left on the table. Pop cans in the fireplace, that sort of thing.

The examples Carver gives Alton are all domestic images, indoor things. It is significant that

## What Do I Read Next?

- Frederick Barthelme's 1983 short story collection, *Moon Deluxe*, features characters from the Deep South who live alienated suburban lives spent shopping and drifting aimlessly. Barthelme, like Carver, has been labeled a minimalist and practitioner of "Kmart realism."

- *Carver Country: The World of Raymond Carver* (1990), with photographs by Bob Adelman, presents photographs of places where Carver grew up and lived, accompanied by text from Carver's poems and stories.

- Some of Carver's best-known short stories are collected in *Cathedral*, published in 1983.

- Some critics believe Carver's 1985 collection of poems, *Where Water Comes Together with Other Water*, is his strongest collection.

- *No Heroics Please*, published in 1991, collects Carver's unpublished stories, reviews, and other uncollected prose.

- Tess Gallagher's 1996 collection of poems, *Portable Kisses*, is a collection of fine love poems, many of them inspired by her relationship with Carver.

- Another practitioner of "Kmart realism" is Bobbie Ann Mason, whose short-story collection, *Shiloh and Other Stories* won the 1982 PEN/Hemingway Award for Fiction and was a finalist for the National Book Critics Circle Award, the American Book Award, and the PEN/Faulkner Award.

- Arthur Saltzman's 1988 book, *Understanding Raymond Carver*, though brief, is the first full-length study of Carver's writing and remains a useful introduction to his work.

---

Carver sets many of his poems and stories indoors rather than outdoors, though he considered himself a lover of the great outdoors. Even the cobweb, which he encounters on the "deck / of the house," must come indoors before it can cause a change in the consciousness of the poem's speaker. This relationship between indoors and outdoors in the poem parallels the relationships between sight and insight, the physical and the emotional, self and other. Although Carver prides himself on "fundamental accuracy of statement," what Ezra Pound claimed is "the ONE sole morality of writing," his statements are not void of figurative language or suggestion; his words mean more than what they describe. For example, Carver uses a list of outdoor images to evoke emptiness and a kind of existential void: "It was hot and still. The tide was out. / No birds sang." And, after becoming entangled with the web, the speaker says: "There was no wind. The sea / was dead calm." However, rather than commenting on the idea of nothingness and death that the images suggest, the speaker takes action, hanging the web from a lampshade and watching "it shudder now and then when my breath / touches it. A fine thread. Intricate." These descriptions are both literal, that is, they accurately describe the physical attributes of the web and the speaker's actions, and figurative, in that they also describe the nature of human life. But Carver does not use metaphor to accomplish this; he does not write, "My life is a cobweb, fine and intricate." Rather, he employs a stacking strategy, letting the images accrue meaning as he places them near one another. In this way, the images become symbolic; even though the surface of Carver's poem is realistic, the undercurrent resonates with other meaning. In his essay "On Writing," in *Fires*, Carver writes:

> It's possible, in a poem or a short story, to write about commonplace things and objects using commonplace but precise language, and to endow those things—a chair, a window curtain, a fork, a stone, a woman's earring—with immense, even startling power.

Although it is what Carver does not say that makes "The Cobweb" successful, it is also what he *does* say, particularly in the last two lines of the poem, that makes the poem poignant. For whereas the description of the speaker's encounter with the cobweb is a relatively commonplace occurrence, the speaker's realization of his own impending death is surprising. It is this leap between the description of the event and the insight it engenders that is so characteristic of Carver's style and vision. The last image, of the speaker breathing on the web under the light, is a perfect lead-in to the last two lines, as it employs the symbolic imagery of light and breath to underscore the fragility of life.

In his essay "On Bobber and Other Poems," included in his collection of uncollected prose and fiction, *Call If You Need Me*, Carver writes that he remembers the occasion surrounding the writing of his poems better than those surrounding his stories:

> I feel the poems are closer to me, more special, more of a gift received than my other work, even though I know, for sure, that the stories are no less a gift. It could be that I put a more intimate value finally on the poems than I do the stories.

Carver acknowledges, as do many other writers about their own work, that although there are autobiographical elements in his poems and that they spring from specific occasions, they are not literal renderings of those occasions. Rather, he takes the raw material from which the poem arises and shapes it to fit the emotional truth from which it springs. Carver's "vision" is deeply tied to his notions of poetry's purpose. "They are always about something," he writes, adding that when he reads over his poems, he is "looking back over a rough, but true map of my past." Carver's poems, however, are more than simply chronicles of his own past; they also comment on the human condition, on how one person's life and pain illustrate many people's lives and pain.

**Source:** Chris Semansky, Critical Essay on "The Cobweb," in *Poetry for Students*, The Gale Group, 2003.

## Carey Wallace

*Wallace is a freelance writer and poet. In this essay, Wallace details Carver's use of seemingly meaningless details to reveal emotional truth as he attempts to take in the scope of a troubled life.*

Carver was a man with much to celebrate and much to regret. Perhaps more than any other American writer since Hemingway, his life story is legendary: born in an Oregon mining town, Carver grew up in a blue-collar family in the American West, with big dreams of making it as an author. But, marriage at age nineteen, and the birth of his first daughter six months later, put those dreams on hold. By the time he was 20, Carver was a father of two and struggling to support his family while beginning his education as a freshman at California's Chico State University. His course of study in creative writing did pay off, with a number of early publications in small but significant "little magazines" and a growing literary reputation. By the time his first book of stories appeared in 1976, alcoholism had largely destroyed both his fifteen-year marriage and his writing.

Unlike so many stories with similar openings, Carver's does not end there, but continues, with both personal and professional redemption. In

> *The shift may constitute an admission on the speaker's part that, while he wishes the past were something he could remain detached from, it is actually far more like the cobweb: unavoidable, clinging."*

1977, spurred on by the offer of a book contract from McGraw-Hill, Carver quit drinking, for good. Five months later, at a writer's conference, he met Tess Gallagher, a poet who would be a life companion and a significant stabilizing influence for the next ten years—and, finally, his second wife.

Sober, Carver set to work on a body of short stories that established him as a master of that craft in the second half of the twentieth century. Although his poems are less well known than his short stories, he also devoted a great deal of energy to them. In fact, his first published book was not of short stories, but poems, and he joked once that it would be enough for him if, on his gravestone, his loved ones simply engraved "Poet." Carver's stories are known for their spare focus on one perfectly-drawn subject, but his poems, while they share simplicity of language with his prose, were more clearly autobiographical, often with somewhat larger scope. In "The Cobweb," which was published originally in *Ultramarine* (1986), a book that Carver completed after a trip to South America with Gallagher, he looks back on his life.

One of the distinctive points of Carver's prose is the indirect nature with which he approaches his subjects; in Carver's work, revelation tends to sneak up on both characters and reader from nowhere, often when they least expect it. The same thing is true in "The Cobweb." In the poem, the speaker has gone out "onto the deck / of the house," where he can see and hear "the water," which he might expect. But, the next line changes the stakes dramatically, adding that, along with the water, the speaker can also see "everything that's happened to me all these years." This line has a powerful effect on the reader, operating very much like the memories that sometimes rush in on people when they least expect them—often in quiet moments like the one that the speaker has been describing. It is not clear from the poem whether the speaker is surprised. The first three lines leave room for interpretation: the memories may have come unbidden, or the speaker may have gone out of the house looking for them, intentionally. One possible reading, in light of Carver's recent trip to South America, which strongly influenced other parts of *Ultramarine*, is that Carver's distance from his homeland (for which stepping "onto the deck of the house" might be a metaphor) allowed him a new vantage point from which to write about someone looking back over his life.

Whether the speaker is surprised or has sought the vision deliberately, he holds steady, avoiding directly describing the very thing that the reader now wants to see: the "everything" of his life that has spread out before him. The general sense of the description he does give is of loss and helplessness: "It was hot and still. The tide was out. / No birds sang." In these lines, the tide and birds, the only two physical objects that Carver mentions, are both absent; they are things that used to be there, and now are not. Both are also forces of nature that are notoriously outside of man's control. Behind them, they have left nothing but silence. In this landscape of water and memory, the speaker is the only thing moving, and only barely, as if trying to make it out of the room without waking anybody. If he is careful, he might make it out clean.

But that is not to be. As the speaker leans against the railing (perhaps for support, perhaps to get a better look), a cobweb touches his forehead—the first action by anything other than the speaker in the entire poem to this point. The cobweb is a familiar symbol—from high art to Halloween decorations, it appears as a sign of things forgotten or left behind. In its association with spiders, the cobweb is somewhat threatening. The one the speaker brushes against is inescapable: no sooner has it touched his forehead than it becomes caught in his hair.

The past that the speaker has been gazing out upon has suddenly crept up onto the deck, and quite literally, caught the speaker in its web. In response, Carver offers the first statement of opinion in a poem which, until this point, has been entirely description. "No one can blame me," he says, "that I turned and went inside." In his denial of anyone's right to blame him, the speaker implies that someone might, admitting at least the possibility of his guilt in turning away. Carver adds two more lines of description, as if to give the speaker a defense, further images of absence and silence: "There was no wind. The sea / was dead calm." There was nothing, really, out there to see, Carver seems to say. Why should anyone blame the speaker for turning away?

By this point, however, caught by the cobweb, the speaker cannot escape. The two lines of description in the speaker's defense also serve to point out the fact that, even after he goes inside, nothing changes. His past, in the form of the cobweb, has followed him in. In fact, the shift between Carver's initial description of the speaker's life as something he can look down on from the deck, and its later incarnation as the cobweb may be significant. The shift may constitute an admission on the speaker's part that, while he wishes the past were something he could remain detached from, it is actually far more like the cobweb: unavoidable, clinging.

The fact that the speaker cannot loose himself from the cobweb forces him, finally, to look directly at it. Deliberately, he settles the cobweb on the lampshade, where he will "watch it shudder" under his breath as if it has some life of its own—as opposed to the "everything that's happened to me" of the early part of the poem, which the speaker can only "see." Again, even inside, the speaker is the only thing that is moving, and again, his movements are minimal. They have a profound effect on the cobweb, which "shudders" now and then, when the speaker's breath "touches it." Interestingly, in a poem in which both movement and word choice are extremely constrained, Carver uses "touch" again, linking the current action of the speaker's breath against the cobweb back to the initial contact of the cobweb against the speaker's forehead: the pattern of his life has affected him, seemingly without his permission, but he also can affect it. On an even deeper level, Carver may be commenting on the role memory plays in reshaping the events of a person's life as they appear in his mind. The cobweb—which now represents everything that has happened to the speaker—does not come to pieces, but the speaker's presence does disturb it.

In fact, the cobweb as a symbol of the past even offers some hope for the future. Although Carver begins the poem with profound feelings of emptiness and stasis associated with the past, by the end, after it touches the speaker (whether the speaker allows it or it clings to him unbidden), he is able to remove it from his person, looking clearly at it, and in that way he still affects it. In carrying the cobweb, the speaker succeeds in preserving his history, and therefore his essence, even as he crosses boundaries from one space or phase of life to the next. Finally, although the cobweb at first made him turn away from the view of his life that he commanded from the deck, Carver pronounces his judgement of the cobweb as positive: "A fine thread. Intricate."

Then, jarringly, Carver closes the poem with what sounds like a threat: "Before long, before anyone realizes / I'll be gone from here." Is the speaker unhappy with the life he has created? Is he simply unable, despite the steps he has taken over the course of the poem, to really look directly at "everything that's happened" for long? Or, is he predicting yet another transformation in his life, one so profound that he will leave the emptiness and silence of his past life behind for another life completely? Good arguments could be made for any of these interpretations, but the most obvious, and probably best reading of the final lines of "The Cobweb" is that, in them, the speaker predicts his own death.

Along with the warning that he will be gone soon, Carver offers a final lesson, the same one that he teaches again and again through the indirect way he reveals truth in both his poems and prose. When truth arrives in Carver's work, it is revealed indirectly, when least expected. With the line "before anyone realizes / I'll be gone from here," he contends that death will not be any different. It will arrive just like a sudden rush of memories and will be as impossible to escape as an unnoticed cobweb, which first brushes against one's forehead, then catches in one's hair.

Still, Carver's poem is not hopeless. In the lines just before the final lines, he has pronounced the pattern of the speaker's life, in the form of the cobweb to be, in his estimation, "fine" and "intricate." The final sense of "The Cobweb" is that the speaker, although deeply ambivalent about some of his past, is pleased with the entire pattern.

**Source:** Carey Wallace, Critical Essay on "The Cobweb," in *Poetry for Students*, The Gale Group, 2003.

### Tamara Sakuda

*Sakuda holds a bachelor of arts degree in communications and is an independent writer. In this essay, Sakuda discusses how Carver's description of common objects and everyday events invites the reader to explore life's deeper meanings.*

Carver is perhaps more known for his collections of short stories rather than his poems. However, his third volume of poetry, *Ultramarine* was

> *"The simple elements of water, a cobweb, a lampshade, and a human breath are woven together to create a thoughtful poem about the complexities of life, death, and human relationships."*

published in 1986 and received critical acclaim. This anthology conveys themes of love, nature, gratitude, and death using free verse poems about seemingly simple objects and moments in time. While the volume contains vibrant, rich, and healing poems, "The Cobweb" illustrates Carver reflecting on his imminent death. Instead of sadness, "The Cobweb" conveys a meditative quality. Carver's style of using few words to convey a depth of meaning keeps the poem from sounding morbid or melancholy. Critics often describe Carver as a minimalist who creates art out of everyday experiences. Adam Meyer notes in his book, *Raymond Carver*, that Carver learned to use the language of common people and to eliminate unnecessary verbiage early in his career. Carver uses the poem "The Cobweb" as an invitation to reflect on one's life. The poem is also an example of Carver's unique writing style. While sparse, Carver's writing is not unsophisticated. Roxanne Lawler's article, "Carver's World," in *Conversations with Raymond Carver*, quotes Carver describing his writing this way, "I place a high premium on clarity and simplicity, not simple-mindedness—which is quite different."

Carver was born in 1938 in Clatskanie, Oregon to working class parents. During Carver's formative years, the family moved frequently and worked hard just to make ends meet. The situation was made worse by Carver's father's addiction to alcohol. At nineteen, Carver married his sixteen-year-old, pregnant, high school sweetheart, Maryann Burk. By the time he was 20, Carver was supporting his wife and two children, finishing college, and finding work as a writer. Financial hardships and marital strife took their toll on Carver and he soon followed in his father's footsteps of alcohol abuse. Despite these setbacks, Carver continued to write and was critically acclaimed for both his poetry and short stories. He also continued to drink heavily, and he was hospitalized several times for acute alcoholism. Carver and his wife separated several times and eventually divorced.

On June 2, 1977, Carver took his last drink. In the days leading up to his decision to quit drinking, Carver felt he had hit rock–bottom. Bruce Weber's article, "Raymond Carver: A Chronicler of Blue Collar Despair," in, *Conversations with Raymond Carver*, edited by Marshall Bruce Gentry and William Stull, quotes Carver as saying,

> For all intents and purposes, I was finished as a writer and as a viable, functioning male. It was over for me. That's why I can speak of two lives, that life and this life.

Carver saw that June day as a dividing line between his two very different lives, lives that were separate but entwined—much like a cobweb is made of entwined, silken fibers. Carver did not forget his earlier, alcoholic life; he overcame it. Later in 1979, Carver began living with the poet Tess Gallagher. They married in 1988. Unfortunately, Carver's happiness was short-lived. He died of lung cancer in 1988.

It was during Carver's second life that he was able to write the poems in *Ultramarine*. "These poems expressed, among other things, a thankfulness even for his trials, and for having been delivered into a life he considered happy," says Tess Gallagher in the forward to *All of Us*. While the poems in *Ultramarine* are more upbeat than in previous collections, Carver's style of employing common objects and everyday situations to explain deeper meanings is still evident. The simple elements of water, a cobweb, a lampshade, and a human breath are woven together to create a thoughtful poem about the complexities of life, death, and human relationships.

Written before he was diagnosed with cancer, Carver uses the poem "The Cobweb" to ponder life and his own eventual death. The speaker of the poem steps out to the deck of his house to: "see and hear the water, / and everything that's happened to me all these years." This unassuming moment of watching water is infused with the significance of reflection on one's life. Carver goes on to simply describe what the speaker sees and feels and hears: "It was hot and still. The tide was out. / No birds sang." Through his spare, but descriptive text, Carver invites the reader to stop and enter this moment of time on a hot, still, quiet day, a calm moment where there is no movement. A moment made for reflection. As Stephen Dobyns writes in Randolph Runyon's book *Reading Raymond Carver*

> "I can think of no contemporary American poet who could locate this sort of small yet intensely emotional moment as well as Ray could. They are the moments we mostly don't have time for. Unfortunately, they are also the moments that give life its significance."

Carver goes on to tell the reader: "As I leaned against the railing / a cobweb touched my forehead. It caught my hair." Cobwebs are the stuff of spiders, dirt and decay. Now, one is stuck in the speaker's hair. Readers are mesmerized. Carver uses this cobweb to bring tension to the poem. It gives the reader a vivid and ironic picture of the speaker standing on a windless day overlooking a "dead calm" sea with a cobweb on his hair. As Michael Schumacher writes in his article, "After the Fire, Into the Fire: An Interview with Raymond Carver" in *Conversations with Raymond Carver*, edited by Marshall Bruce Gentry and William Stull, "Carver's poems are dynamic and compressed, with each word a carefully chosen tool used to stretch tension to near-breaking point."

Instead of brushing the cobweb from his head, the speaker welcomes it. He does not shy away from this dusty, dirty bundle as it clings to his hair. Instead, he carefully walks inside and hangs the cobweb from a lampshade, "Where [he] watch[es] it shudder now and then when [his] breath touches it." Carver turns this simple cobweb into a metaphor for the speaker's life. While a cobweb is often seen as a distasteful thing, like drinking, the speaker does not destroy it. He gently moves it to a place of safety; a place where he continues to reflect on this cobweb of his life. Carver often spoke of his two separate lives, and while he found happiness in his second life, he never shied away from the memories of his first life. He carried those experiences with him and used them to shape his later poems and short stories. In her *New York Times Book Review* of *Ultramarine*, Patricia Hampl writes of Carver, "He has the astonished, chastened voice of a person who has survived a wreck, as surprised that he had a life before as that he has a life afterward; willing to remember both sides."

A cobweb entangles, obscures, or confuses. In his poem, Carver describes the cobweb as "A fine thread. Intricate." Again, Carver gives us another view of this seemingly simple cobweb. No longer does the reader see this as a dusty, decaying bundle, but as a complex weaving of delicate strands. People's lives are like that—woven over time. Delicate strands link people to experiences and relationships. Through his description of the cobweb, Carver illustrates how tenuous these connections are that link people to relationships with others. These relationships can confuse and entangle. People can get caught up in the cobwebs of their own lives.

The last lines of "The Cobweb" are direct and get to the heart of this poem: "Before long, before anyone realizes, / I'll be gone from here." The speaker is contemplating his own death. While dramatic, these lines do not convey a sense of dread or of panic. They have a meditative quality. Carver's unaffected words are calming as the speaker reflects on his life in this quiet moment. "He was the celebrator of those small occasions of fragile contentment, of time lived instead of time passing," says Stephen Dobyns in Runyon's *Reading Raymond Carver*. Even though this poem speaks of death, Carver's use of language imparts an air of solemnity, not sadness. Carver invites the reader to reflect on the complexities of life as the speaker's breath expands and contracts the fragile cobweb.

Carver's direct but descriptive language and subject matter invite readers of all backgrounds to examine his poems. He writes of everyday things: going to get groceries, his car, mail, and getting cobwebs caught in one's hair, but the meditative quality of these poems invites the reader to examine their deeper meaning. Again, Stephen Dobyns reflects on Carver's poems in Runyon's *Reading Raymond Carver*: "They are not a critic's poems. They are not decorative. They need no one to interpret them. They are a reader's poems. They exist to define moments of emotion and wonder." Through its simple phrasing and modest descriptions, "The Cobweb" shows the reader a wonderful snapshot of Carver's unaffected style. A style that appears simple on the surface but is never simple-minded in its depth of meaning.

**Source:** Tamara Sakuda, Critical Essay on "The Cobweb," in *Poetry for Students*, The Gale Group, 2003.

## Sources

Alton, John, "What We Talk about When We Talk about Literature: An Interview with Raymond Carver," in *Conversations with Raymond Carver*, edited by Marshall Bruce Gentry and William Stull, University Press of Mississippi, 1990, pp. 151–68.

Carver, Raymond, *Fires*, Capra, 1983, pp. 13–19.

———, "Introduction," *All of Us*, edited by William Stull, Alfred A. Knopf, 1999, pp. xxviii.

———, *No Heroics, Please*, Knopf, 1992, pp. 190–93.

———, "On Bobber and Other Poems," in *Call If You Need Me: The Uncollected Fiction and Other Prose*, Vintage Books, 2001.

———, *Ultramarine*, Vintage, 1986.

Gentry, Marshall Bruce, and William Stull, eds., *Conversations with Raymond Carver*, University Press of Mississippi, 1990, pp. 88–89, 172, 216.

Hampl, Patricia, "Surviving a Life in the Present," in *New York Times Book Review*, Vol. 92, June 7, 1987, p. 15.

Lawler, Roxanne, "Carver's World," in *Conversations with Raymond Carver*, edited by Marshall Bruce Gentry and William Stull, University Press of Mississippi, 1990, pp. 169–76.

Mahon, Derek, *Antarctica*, Gallery Press, 1985.

Meyer, Adam, *Raymond Carver*, Twayne, 1995, pp. 5, 163–70.

O'Connell, Nicholas, Interview with Raymond Carver, in *Conversations with Raymond Carver*, edited by Marshall Bruce Gentry and William Stull, University Press of Mississippi, 1990, pp. 133–50.

Runyon, Randolph, *Reading Raymond Carver*, Syracuse University Press, 1992, pp. xii, 207–16.

## Further Reading

Gentry, Marshall Bruce, and William L. Stull, eds., *Conversations with Raymond Carver*, University Press of Mississippi, 1990.
   This is the most comprehensive collection of interviews with Carver. In them, Carver discusses his life before and after alcohol, his craft, and his writing habits.

Halpert, Sam, ed., *What We Talk about When We Talk about Raymond Carver*, Gibbs Smith, 1991.
   Halpert collects interviews with those who were closest to Carver. Halpert's book remains one of the best sources of biographical and critical information about Carver and his writing.

Meyer, Adam, *Raymond Carver*, Twayne, 1995.
   Meyer provides a thorough and useful introduction to Carver's work, though he focuses, like most Carver critics, on his stories rather than his poems.

Stull, William L., and Maureen P. Carroll, eds., *Remembering Ray: A Composite Biography of Raymond Carver*, Capra, 1993.
   This volume collects useful comments and anecdotes about Carver by friends, editors, and readers.

# Driving to Town Late to Mail a Letter

*Robert Bly*

*1962*

"Driving to Town Late to Mail a Letter" appears in Robert Bly's 1962 collection of poems, *Silence in the Snowy Fields*. Like many of Bly's poems, it is short—only five lines. It appears midway through the second section of the collection titled "Awakening." The first section is "Eleven Poems of Solitude," and the last section is "Silence on the Roads." Bly, who was born and has lived most of his life in rural Minnesota, describes driving to town on a cold and snowy night to mail a letter and recounts the revelation he has during the event. It's easy to see why Bly placed it in the "Awakenings" section, as it details the speaker's sudden recognition of how the meaningful can be found in the mundane. Like many of Bly's poems, "Driving to Town Late to Mail a Letter" is quite accessible. It uses a few well-placed and well-drawn images to evoke the feelings of solitude and wonder from the natural world, and it contains the kind of "leaping image" for which Bly's poetry has been celebrated, and criticized. There are other poems for which Bly is better known, but "Driving to Town Late to Mail a Letter" is significant because it is typical of the kind of poems Bly wrote during the early 1960s.

## Author Biography

For a twenty-first-century poet, Robert Bly is an anomaly in that he does not make his living teaching at a university or college. Instead, Bly earns his keep writing, not only poetry but nonfiction as well, on subjects such as the men's movement and the family. He has made a career out of his own spiritual and political preoccupations, a feat very few poets have accomplished. Born in Madison, Minnesota, on December 23, 1926, to farmer Jacob Thomas Bly and his wife, Alice, Bly attended a one-room schoolhouse in Lac Qui Parle County in the western part of the state. While in the navy during World War II, his literary interests blossomed thanks to shipmates Marcus Eisenstein and Warren Ramshaw, who encouraged him to write and read as much as he could, especially poets Carl Sandburg and Walt Whitman. Bly transferred to Harvard after studying writing at St. Olaf College in Northfield, Minnesota. At Harvard, he met poets Adrienne Rich, Kenneth Koch, John Ashbery, and Donald Hall, who has remained a lifelong supporter and friend, and his future wife, Carolyn McLean.

After taking a master of fine arts degree in creative writing at the University of Iowa, he traveled to Norway on a Fulbright grant to translate Norwegian poetry. While in Norway, Bly read the poetry of Latin American surrealist poets such as Pablo Neruda and European surrealists such as Georg Trakl, Tomas Transtroemer, and Juan Ramon Jiminez. The writing of these poets inspired Bly to rethink his own poetics, and he began composing a kind of verse that used the image to evoke a complicated range of emotion and thought. Bly's interest in myth, evolutionary neurology, and Jungian psychology burgeoned and formed the basis for his theory of the image, which he outlines in *Leaping Poetry: An Idea with Poems and Translations*. Such an image makes connections between the human mind/brain and the external world, which can be intuited but not explained. "Leaping images" appear in many of the poems in Bly's first collection, *Silence in the Snowy Fields* (1962), including "Driving to Town Late to Mail a Letter" and "Driving Toward the Lac Qui Parle River." Exploring the ways in which imagery, both verbal and iconic, forms a bridge between inner and outer worlds has been a thematic constant in Bly's work.

In the early part of his career, Bly protested against United States involvement in Vietnam, and many of his poems addressed explicitly political subjects; but, in the latter half of his career, he has become more interested in gender and masculinity. In 1990, he published *Iron John: A Book about Men*, one of the seminal books of the men's movement, and he continues to lecture and write on men's issues, Jungian psychology, and European mythology. Bly is a heavily decorated poet. His awards include

*Robert Bly*

the National Book Award in 1968 for *The Light Around the Body*, a Fulbright grant (1956–1957), the Amy Lowell traveling fellowship (1964), a Guggenheim fellowship (1964), and a Rockefeller Foundation fellowship (1967). He has written, edited, and translated scores of books. Some of his most recent titles include *Eating the Honey of Words: New and Selected Poems* (1999) and *Morning Poems* (1997), in which Bly pays homage to his friend and mentor, poet William Stafford.

## Poem Text

It is a cold and snowy night. The main street is deserted.
The only things moving are swirls of snow.
As I lift the mailbox door, I feel its cold iron.
There is a privacy I love in this snowy night.
Driving around, I will waste more time.     5

## Poem Summary

### First line

The first line of "Driving to Town Late to Mail a Letter" elaborates on the action of the poem's title, setting the scene. Two simple declarative

# Media Adaptations

- In 1983, Dolphin Tapes released *Robert Bly: Poetry Reading—an Ancient Tradition*, in which Bly discusses the oral tradition in poetry. Dolphin Tapes can be reached at P.O. Box 71, Esalen Hot Springs, Big Sur, California 93920.

- An audiocassette of Bly reading his poems has been produced by Everett/Edwards. It is titled, *Contemporary American Poets Read Their Work: Robert Bly.*

- Bly appears on the recordings *Today's Poets 5*, by Folkways, and *For the Stomach: Selected Poems*, produced by Watershed Tapes in 1974. Watershed Tapes are distributed by Inland Book Company, P.O. Box 120261, East Haven, Connecticut 06512.

- Bly's positions on the men's movement can be found on the video *A Gathering of Men* (1991), with Bill Moyers, available from Mystic Fire Video, P.O. Box 9323, South Burlington, Vermont 05407.

- Brockport Writers Forum and the State University of New York at Brockport's English Department produced a videotape titled *Robert Bly: Interviews and Readings.*

- *A Man Writes to a Part of Himself* (1978), a videotape of Bly reading and lecturing, is available from Intermedia Arts, 425 Ontario St. SE, Minneapolis, Minnesota 55414.

- Sound Horizons distributes a recording of Bly reading poetry. It is titled *Robert Bly: An Evening of Poetry*. The company can be reached at 250 West 57th Street, Suite 1517, New York, New York 10107.

- In an audiocassette produced and distributed by Ally Press in 1987 called *Robert Bly: Fairy Tales for Men and Women*, Bly reads poems and applies psychoanalysis to them. Ally Press can be reached at 524 Orleans Street, St. Paul, Minnesota 55107.

---

sentences create the image of emptiness. The cold and the snow evoke the season and, for readers familiar with Bly's work, the upper Midwest where Bly lives and where many of his poems are set. The deserted main street evokes solitude and, perhaps, the presence of death. The fact that it is a "town" and not a city suggests that the speaker is driving in from a rural setting.

### Second line

This image focuses the reader's attention on the swirling snow and emphasizes the utter desolation of the street. It matters little whether or not one is familiar with snowy nights in the upper Midwest. A tumbleweed could just as easily stand in for the "swirls of snow." What's important here is the speaker's attention to the only thing moving, as it figuratively "freezes" the reader's imagination for an instant.

### Third line

Like the speaker, readers too feel the "cold iron" of the door. By bringing the sense of touch to the poem, Bly emphasizes the "embodiedness" of the speaker, even as he evokes his self-consciousness in other parts of the poem. This is typical of much Bly poetry.

Bly's epigraph to *Silence in the Snowy Fields* is a quotation from the sixteenth-century German mystic, Jacob Boehme: "We are all asleep in the outward man." Boehme's writing heavily influences Bly and appears frequently in the poet's work as both epigraph and inspiration. The following Boehme quotation, which appears in Bly's second collection of poems *The Light Around the Body* (1967), helps to explain the first quotation and is a key concept from which much of Bly's poetry is generated:

For according to the outward man, we are in this world, and according to the inward man, we are in the inward world.... Since then we are generated out of both worlds, we speak in two languages, and we must be understood also by two languages.

Touching the "cold iron" of the mailbox jolts the speaker from the inner world of his thoughts and perceptions into the outer world of sensation.

### Fourth line

The poem's tone changes in this line, as the speaker describes his emotional response to his perceptions for the first time. The "privacy" is akin to anonymity, as the street is deserted and the snowy scene forces the speaker inside of himself, where he can have such a thought as that contained in this line.

### Fifth line

Like the previous four lines, this one is end-stopped. An end-stopped line is a line of verse that completes a grammatical unit, usually with a mark of punctuation at its end. Each line, then, is a self-contained unit of meaning and does not rely on the preceding or succeeding line to make sense. The series of end-stopped lines in this poem give it a filmic feel, as if each line were a separate shot.

This last line is an example of the "leaping" that occurs in so much Bly poetry. The leap, a manifestation of unconscious desire, occurs when something happens or an image appears that is frequently the opposite of what the reader expects. In this case, readers expect that the speaker will comment on the natural world or the idea that life is short. Rather, he says, "Driving around, I will waste more time." This sentiment belies the tone of the previous description, which suggests that watching the snow fall on the deserted street is an invaluable experience. But this line is ironic; the speaker does not really believe he is "wasting time," at least not in the conventional sense of the term. Rather, he assigns value to "driving around" doing nothing but more of what he has already done: basking in the privacy of his inner world while enjoying the austere winter beauty.

## Themes

### Human Condition

Conventional wisdom has it that human beings are different from animals in that they have language and are aware of their mortality. This awareness, which occurs more frequently in some people than in others, causes people to act in ways they otherwise might not. For example, in a well-known poem, "Lying in a Hammock at William Duffy's Farm in Pine Island, Minnesota," by Bly's friend James Wright, the speaker is enraptured by the assorted wonders of nature he sees, such as butterflies, "a field of sunlight between two pines," and a chicken hawk, and yet he concludes: "I have wasted my life." Bly's speaker, on the other hand, though also captivated by the (snowy) natural world—albeit from the driver's seat of a car rather than a hammock—comes to a different conclusion: that he will "waste more time" by "driving around." These two starkly different responses to experiences that led the speakers from the outer to the inner world imply things about the their respective attitudes towards the value of their own pasts and of their current lives. Another famous poem that follows the same emotional trajectory as the Bly and Wright poems is Ranier Maria Rilke's "Archaic Torso of Apollo," only Rilke lovingly details the statue of Apollo, rather than nature, before coming to the conclusion: "You must change your life."

### City and Country

Since the Industrial Revolution, the differences between city life and rural life have frequently been a theme in literature, with the country variously representing agrarian ideals, naiveté, simplicity, and wide-open spaces, and the city representing opportunity, sophistication, and a more hurried pace. Bly implies distinctions between the two in the title of his poem, though he never explicitly addresses features of either. However, by describing the town's "main street" as "deserted," he does turn expectations on their head, as readers usually associate a town's main street with people. That he has to drive to town to mail a letter suggests that he lives in a remote part of the state. He also counters expectations for what one does in the city, in the last line of the poem when he writes, "Driving around, I will waste more time." Cities are often places of activity and culture, where one could "waste time" doing a variety of things such as shopping, eating, and so forth.

### Consciousness

Consciousness always has an object; it is conscious of something. Bly's speaker is conscious of the emptiness around him as he drives into town and mails a letter. He emphasizes this in the word "deserted" and the phrase "the only things moving." The "privacy" he feels stems from this sense

## Topics For Further Study

- Write a short poem that uses the kind of "leaping image" that Bly uses in his poem and then read it to your class. Discuss whether or not the image is successful in evading a reader's cliché expectations without foreshadowing that evasion.

- Write a parody of Bly's poem and then compose a short essay explaining how your poem is a parody. Hold a poetry slam in your class, competing to see whose parody is best.

- Would Bly's poem be successful if he described emailing a letter as opposed to "snail mailing" one? Discuss in groups and report your findings to the class.

- Research other "deep image" poets such as Louis Simpson, W. S. Merwin, and James Wright. How do they compare to Bly? Read representative poems of the poets and then have classmates vote on their favorite, defending their choices.

- Make a list of what you would do if told that you had only six months to live. Compare this list to that of your classmates and discuss similarities and differences. Would you "waste time" delightfully as Bly's narrator does, or do you think your perspective of wasted time would change in the face of your mortality? How might Bly react to that same situation, especially considering the possibility that death is, perhaps, suggested in the poem?

- Bly contends that human beings have at least two selves, the spiritual, internal self and the political, external self. Make a list of features describing how you understand these two selves. Write a short dialogue exploring how they would converse with each other.

- Divide the class into groups. Each group finds as many "driving" poems as possible and brings them to class to read. Discuss how the act of driving is used in the various poems. Is it used symbolically? Metaphorically? Discuss the themes of the poems and then hold a class vote to determine which poem is most popular.

---

of emptiness, brought on by the snowy winter weather and the absence of people. Curiously, he finds pleasure in this emptiness, as it directs his attention inward at his emotions. In the poem's last line, he has an epiphany, or revelation, of just how much he loves the privacy and wants it to continue.

## Style

### Tone

Tone refers to the attitude of the speaker towards his subject. In "Driving to Town Late to Mail a Letter," Bly evokes feelings of contentment through his description of a deserted city street scene, the simple action of mailing a letter, the "privacy" of his solitude, and the desire to prolong the experience, expressed in the line, "Driving around, I will waste more time."

### Image

At its simplest level, an image is a mental picture created in a reader's mind by the writer's words. Images, however, can also relate to senses other than vision. Bly uses visual imagery for describing the setting of the town and tactile imagery in describing the action of mailing the letter, when the speaker feels the "cold iron" of the mailbox door. The concluding image, of the speaker "driving around," is a kind of "leaping image" for which Bly's writing has become known. Leaping images, according to Bly, are meant to evoke a reality beyond that which we see. These images "leap" back and forth between the conscious and the unconscious mind and often evoke feelings or thoughts surprising to even the writer himself.

## Compare & Contrast

- **1960s:** The United States Post Office begins widespread implementation of mechanized letter-sorting machines and high-speed optical character readers.

    **Today:** After a few postal workers die and others fall sick from inhaling the deadly spore-forming bacterium Bacillus anthracis (anthrax) sent in letters, the postal service implements a process for irradiating the mail to destroy the presence of any biohazardous material.

- **1960s:** Sixty percent of the world's automobiles are in the United States.

    **Today:** Ford and rival General Motors Corporation, two of the world's largest automobile producers, predict that United States vehicle sales will drop about 10 percent in 2002 from the previous year's near-record high.

- **1960s:** The life expectancy for American males is 66.6 and for females 73.1.

    **Today:** The life expectancy for American males is 74.3 and for females 79.1.

---

### Irony

The last line of the poem contains an example of verbal irony. A statement can be verbally ironic when it implies a meaning sharply different from what it expresses. In this case, Bly is winking at readers when he states, "I will waste more time," as the obvious joy he experiences belies the idea that time is being wasted.

## Historical Context

### The Early 1960s

When Bly published this poem in the early 1960s, a number of poets were using what poet-critic Robert Kelley in 1961 called the "deep image." Kelley used this term to describe a type of image that could fuse the experience of the poet's inner self and his outer world. Bly had been experimenting with this image in the late 1950s in poems he wrote for various journals and magazines. During his Fulbright year in Norway in 1956–1957, Bly began reading European and Latin American surrealist poets such as Georg Trakl, Pablo Neruda, and Caesar Vallejo, and he quickly embraced their use of the image to probe the unconscious mind. His translation of their work in his and William Duffy's literary magazine, *The Fifties*—renamed *The Sixties* and *The Seventies* in subsequent decades—helped introduce these poets to American readers. Bly considered these writers practitioners of the "new imagination" and their use of the image dramatically different from how poets such as Ezra Pound and William Carlos Williams used it—to describe the empirical world of things as accurately as possible. Other well-known contemporary poets of the deep image include James Wright, W. S. Merwin, Galway Kinnell, William Stafford, and Diane Wakowski.

Bly's magazine was part of the explosion of small press literary journals in the late 1950s and early 1960s. Writing in the late 1970s, critic Charles Molesworth claims, "No literary history of the last twenty years would be complete without reference to Bly's magazine, *The Sixties*." Other small press magazines of the time include Charles Olson's *Black Mountain Review*, John Logan's *Choice*, Jerome Rothenberg's *Poems from the Floating World*, Cid Corman and Robert Creeley's *Origin*, and Kelley's own *Trobar*. In 1958, when Bly was settling down in a Minnesota farmhouse with his first wife, Carolyn McLean, and putting together the first issue of his magazine, an important poetry anthology was published. *New Poets of England and America*, edited by Donald Hall, Robert Pack, and Louis Simpson, showcased the work of poets under forty, most of whom adhered to the formal, rational, and often irony-laden verse favored by the New Critics. Two years later, in 1960, Donald Allen's ground-breaking anthology, *New American Poetry 1945–1960*, championed poets descended from the poetic traditions established by Pound, William Carlos Williams, and Wallace Stevens. These poets, including beat writers such as Jack Kerouac, Gregory Corso, and Allen Ginsberg; New York school poets such as Frank O'Hara; and Black Mountain poets such as Robert Creeley and Charles Olson saw form as organic, arising from the subject of the poem itself, not something imposed on it from the outside. For the most part, they rejected the aesthetics of the poets in Hall's anthology, considering them academic and removed from the real world. Bly, who had yet to publish a collection of his own poems, made his first appearance in a major anthology in 1969, in *Naked Poetry*, which contained some of the same poets from Allen's anthology but also included newer voices, most prominently confessional poets such as Anne Sexton, John Berryman, and Sylvia Plath.

## Critical Overview

"Driving to Town Late to Mail a Letter" is a small poem and mostly overlooked by critics who reviewed *Silence in the Snowy Fields* or who study Bly's poetry. William V. Davis in *Understanding Robert Bly* contends that Bly's voice is most "authentic" in this collection and for that reason it is his "most important book." In noting that most reviewers praised the collection, Richard P. Sugg, in his introduction to Bly's prose and poetry *Robert Bly*, claims that the book contains what he calls "the enduring basis of Bly's work[:] . . . . the psychological theme of man's inward life and the act of perception/discovery necessary to connect with and develop it." Ronald Moran and George S. Lensing, in their study of Bly and his peers, *Four Poets and the Emotive Imagination: Robert Bly, James Wright, Louis Simpson, and William Stafford*, conclude, "The poems of *Silence in the Snowy Fields* are very much of a world" in their treatment of landscape and the small moments in a person's life. Noting the "bare statements" of "Driving to Town Late to Mail a Letter," and poems like it in the collection, Howard Nelson, in *Robert Bly: An Introduction*, speculates that a first reading of the book is "likely to be a mysterious or mystifying experience" for readers. Nelson points out some of the reservations critics have with the poems, most notably their lack of sophistication and "intellectual density." However, he argues:

> While it is the simplicity and quiet of *Silence in the Snowy Fields* that first strike the reader, the book was a key contribution to that period of great restlessness, energy, and originality in American poetry that began in the 1950s and continued through the 1960s.

*Silence in the Snowy Fields* remains one of the best-selling poetry titles in Wesleyan University Press's catalogue, forty years after its publication.

## Criticism

### Chris Semansky

*Semansky is an instructor of literature and composition. In this essay, Semansky considers the image of driving in Bly's poem.*

The image of driving permeates much American literature of the twentieth century. Think of Jack Kerouac's *On the Road* or William Least Heat Moon's *Blue Highways*. In these works and countless others, driving is symbolic of the quest for meaning. The act of putting hands to wheel is a metaphor for life's journey. Driving is both a means and an end in itself, signifying the relentless passing of time. Given the country's wide-open spaces and Americans' love of freedom and travel, America's infatuation with the automobile makes sense, especially for writers of prose. Driving often appears as image and theme in poetry, most surprisingly in the work of Bly, a poet most often associated with the natural world. Images of cars and driving appear in numerous Bly poems including "Three Kinds of Pleasure," "Driving Toward the Lac Qui Parle River," "Driving My Parents Home at Christmas," and many others. "Driving to Town Late to Mail a Letter," one of Bly's first "driving" poems, is significant in that it foreshadows many of the themes that occupy his later work.

Although Bly has developed the reputation as a poet whose material is grounded in myth and psychology, it should not be surprising that cars show up so frequently in his writing. For someone who has made his living writing and giving readings, workshops, and lectures, it is only natural that he would drive so much and that so much of his remembered experience would be of events that occurred while he was in a car, usually alone. Driving is often a solitary activity, with drivers given to reflection, fantasizing, bouts of nostalgia and regret. Driving long distances in the Midwest, as Bly does, would give one the opportunity to engage in these meditative activities more than most. Bly does not fetishize the car, however; most of the time, he does not detail its make or model or, indeed, provide any specifics other than the fact that he is in transit, being in one place and going another. In this way, then, driving becomes a metaphor for journeying, though Bly's journeys in these poems, at least on the surface, are usually fairly prosaic: mailing a letter, for example.

Literal journeys are integral to myth, symbolic of the process of self-exploration and discovery. Odysseus, for example, endured trials and tribulations through his journeys on Earth and in the underworld before he won the right to come home. Bly's speakers are not nearly as adventurous as Odysseus. They do not fend off monsters or speak with the dead or have themselves strapped to the masts of ships to resist the temptations of sirens. They are modern men who go about their daily business unheroically and whose "adventures" more often than not consist of sudden bursts of awareness of their own emotions, their own mortality.

Life, like driving and like the mail, involves movement and destination, travel. Cars, like mailboxes, are metal containers that shield their contents from the weather and provide them with a degree of anonymity. The "cold iron" of the mailbox door, however, also evokes the coldness of the coffin, another container, this one for goods that have reached their destination. Bly's speaker makes a trip into town to mail a letter, which itself expresses a desire to communicate with another human being. But, in taking in his surroundings, in paying them attention, he is also communicating with a deeper part of himself, a part that cannot be expressed in any rational way but that takes joy in its singleness, its "privacy." In *The Incorporative Consciousness of Robert Bly*, Victoria Frenkel Harris notes that Bly opens *Silence in the Snowy Fields* with a driving poem, which becomes a metaphor for Bly's deeper journey into self:

> The physical journey is of course a developmental extension of the more important psychic journey recorded in the entirety of Bly's work. Whereas the physical journey is linear and may be completed, the psychic journey has no destination. It is a journey of individuation, continual becoming. As the incorporative consciousness grows, inner and outer energies gradually intermingle, the subjective moment expands, and fixed boundaries give way to energy vibrations in a surrounding, fluctuating world. The identification of separate things is replaced by reciprocal motion whereby the world is internalized, and

> "The speaker's response to the sudden awareness of his mortality is also a response to his awareness of eternity, itself paradoxically embodied in the feeling of emptiness that he evokes in his images of the winter landscape."

each centripetal motion enlarges the poet so that his works spring from an increasingly greater psychic reservoir.

Bly's epiphany while mailing his letter, then, adds to that reservoir, while simultaneously springing from it. His is a transcendent poem in the tradition of other driving poems such as Emily Dickinson's "Because I could not stop for Death." Like Bly's speaker, Dickinson's speaker journeys in a vehicle—a horse-drawn carriage—while describing the natural landscape in symbolic imagery, but unlike Bly's poem, Dickinson's ends with the grave. The speaker in Bly's poem, however, although recognizing that the grave awaits, chooses to "waste" his time "driving around." Of course, he is not really wasting his time, but savoring the joy he is experiencing by extending it.

The speaker's response to the sudden awareness of his mortality is also a response to his awareness of eternity, itself paradoxically embodied in the feeling of emptiness that he evokes in his images of the winter landscape. Rather than becoming anxious that life is short and he should spend what time he has left pursuing worldly gains or "intense" experience, Bly's speaker opts to stay in the moment as long as he can.

That Bly's poems inevitably employ the present tense indicates his desire to embrace the now of living. Driving, especially driving long distances, is an act that often feels automatic and outside time. By using an image such as driving, Bly can employ other poetic techniques such as a speaker who catalogues what he sees as he drives by. This is the approach he uses in "Driving

## What Do I Read Next?

- Bly's national best-seller, *Iron John: A Book about Men* (1990), details the poet's thoughts about and experiences with the emotional lives of men. For those interested in men's issues and the men's movement, this is a good book to read.

- *Talking All Morning* (1980) is Bly's first collection of interviews. Material covers the late 1960s and the 1970s and reflects the subjects that inform Bly's writing, such as brain physiology, political poetry, and the ancient "Great Mother" spirituality.

- *Silence in the Snowy Fields* (1962) is Bly's first full-length collection of poems and contains "Driving to Town Late to Mail a Letter."

- In *The Sibling Society* (1996), Bly argues that Americans live in a "fatherless" society in which adults do not mature but continue to behave as siblings, arguing and fighting with one another. Bly uses mythology, legends, and poetry to tell his story.

- Bly won the National Book Award for *The Light Around the Body* (1967). It contains some of his most frequently anthologized poems and is more explicitly political in tone and subject matter than his previous work.

- Those interested in Bly's poetic theories, many based on evolutionary psychology, physical anthropology, and the structure of the human brain, will want to read *Leaping Poetry: An Idea with Poems and Translations*, published in 1975 by Beacon Press.

- Ronald Moran and George Lensing's book entitled *Four Poets and the Emotive Imagination: Robert Bly, James Wright, Louis Simpson, and William Stafford* (1976) presents Bly's work with three other prominent poets associated with the deep image.

---

Toward the Lac Qui Parle River." In three sections, the speaker locates himself in the geography of western Minnesota and then lists what he sees and hears: "The stubble field catch[ing] the last growth of sun / The soybeans . . . breathing on all sides," and so forth. In this poem, he also leaps between the outer and inner worlds, drawing attention to "This solitude covered with iron" that "Plunges through the deep fields of the night." In characteristic Bly fashion, the register of images heads further and further into the self, so that by the end of the poem the speaker announces: "When I reach the river, the full moon covers it; / A few people are talking low in a boat." By this point in the poem, readers are inside and outside the car at the same time, just as the speaker finds an image that both describes the things of the world and evokes the world of the unconscious. Howard Nelson claims that the organizational strategy of this poem is similar to the strategy Bly uses throughout *Silence in the Snowy Fields*: "The poem . . . expresses movements that are fundamental to *Snowy Fields*: movements towards the earth and into what lies beyond the rational, well-lit parts of the mind."

The movement "towards the earth" is also a movement deeper into the brain for Bly, who links the associative leaps in his poems to the leaps human thinking takes among the three parts of the brain: the reptilian, the mammalian, and the human. In his book, *Leaping Poetry: An Idea with Poems and Translations*, Bly writes, "We do not spend the whole day inside one brain, but we flip perhaps a thousand times a day from one brain to the other." Bly concludes that because "there is no central organization to the brain . . . . it means there is no 'I.'" This lack of "I"-ness, of individual identity, is illustrated in the final "leap" of many Bly poems, including "Driving to Town Late to Mail a Letter," in which the speaker's epiphany, or revelation, is an image rooted in one part of the brain "talking" to another part.

**Source:** Chris Semansky, Critical Essay on "Driving to Town Late to Mail a Letter," in *Poetry for Students*, The Gale Group, 2003.

## Adrian Blevins

*Blevins has published essays and poems in many magazines, journals, and anthologies and teaches writing at Roanoke College. In this essay, Blevins considers the risks of the lack of music, rhythm, and metaphor in Bly's poem.*

Bly's "Driving to Town Late to Mail a Letter" is like most classic lyric poems in that it manipulates the private meditations of a single speaker to explore a single theme or motif. But, Bly's poem is unlike the classic lyric in that it avoids overt lyricism. The lack of musical devices in "Driving to Town Late to Mail a Letter" is an example of the tendency of many poets of the contemporary American period to privilege clarity and accessibility over sound-play. Linguists and other students of language have generally held that lyricism obscures meaning. In *The Rhetoric of the Other Literature*, the linguist W. Ross Winterowd states

> As poets have always known, it is possible to increase the difficulty of a text—i.e., decrease its readability or accessibility—by creating features that call attention to the language system, namely, rhyme and alliteration. Insofar as attention is diverted from meaning to sound, reading is more difficult.

Poets interested in subverting the elitism of the complicated language systems of the modernists often work in the plain-style, relying on the strategy of speech rather than the lyricism of song to produce and emulate human thought and feeling.

In general, plain-style poems avoid musical flourish by using the common, everyday diction of a conversational speaker. Although some plain-style poems may replace the musicality achieved by sound-play with images and in this way become image-driven, some plain-style poems avoid image to emphasize conversational or speech-like diction to articulate emotion. In this age in which free verse has proven itself to be a more-than-valid means of writing memorable poems, it is important to ask what the risks of a lack of rhythm and music might be. Bly's poem fails to move not because it is a free verse poem, but because it does not counteract its lack of music with metaphor or the use of original images.

Poets generally agree that the musicality of traditional lyrics helped bards in antiquity remember the verses they were required to recite without the aid of printed text. The rise of the plain-style is attributed in some ways to the invention of the printing press. The more poetry was written down, the less it needed to rhyme sounds and words. Yet other, more archetypally-inclined critics have sug-

> *Bly's poem fails to move not because it is a free verse poem, but because it does not counteract its lack of music with metaphor or the use of original images."*

gested that the rhyming of sounds and words served psychological as well as technical purposes, suggesting, for example, that life patterns (such as the death of the harvest season each winter giving away to its own re-birth each spring) can be mimicked or emulated in the forms language takes. That is, a poem that produces a sound in its first line will remind people of the comforts of a returning season by repeating that sound in later lines.

Bly's "Driving to Town Late to Mail a Letter" explores the relationship between self and nature and the pleasures of privacy and peace by presenting a speaker who wants to "waste more time" by driving around in a snowstorm. Although Bly's poem attempts to be ironic by wishing to violate the cultural clichés that suggest that humans are happiest when they are in non-threatening (i.e., warm and comforting) weather, this intention is not achieved since Bly's speaker is not actually in the snowstorm, but rather inside his warm and comforting car. In other words, although Bly's speaker attempts to articulate pleasure in the landscape the poem describes, and thus attempts to surprise by suggesting that all of nature is wondrous on some level, the fact that the speaker is in a car, rather than inside the snowstorm itself, undercuts the poem's message. The form Bly has chosen for this observation also undercuts the poem's power.

"Driving to Town Late to Mail a Letter" is constructed of five end-stopped lines. The marriage of plain-style diction with statement or assertion produces a matter-of-fact tone. That is, the declarative sentences "It is a cold and snowy night" and "The main street is deserted" both describe nothing more or less than the bare facts of the speaker's situation. These lines are notably about the exterior world, rather than the interior world of the speaker. The poem's second line reinforces its first line's plainly-spoken claim with one of the poem's few images: the speaker states that "The only things moving are swirls of snow." The poem's third line places the speaker in a human activity; he tells us that he is lifting "a mailbox door." Coupled with the title, this line suggests that the speaker is mailing a letter. The poem's last two lines articulate a shift from a description of landscape and activity to a statement about the speaker's feelings—he tells readers that because "there is a privacy [he loves] in this snowy night," he will "[drive] around [and] waste more time."

Although Bly's speaker seeks to immerse a reader inside the natural world and make a statement about the possibility of even coldness and darkness producing pleasure by allowing for "privacy" or solitude, the poem's technique undercuts the poem's ability to move readers because it does not rise above its plain approach. That is, although a simple description of plainness could potentially articulate the kind of peacefulness and solitude Bly seeks to describe, the poem fails because its technical plainness is far too plain. Although it is possible to say that the repetition of the pronoun "I" in the poem is a kind of rhyme, the sound of the word is not its purpose. This fact is made clear by the fact that the word is not emphasized by its placement. Although the word "snowy" is repeated in the poem twice, the telling nature of the adjective undercuts lyricality, and may even seem lazyily inarticulate. Images, in comparison, are not often explicit or overtly obvious in meaning. Instead, the meaning of an image is suggested by the way a poet manipulates its presentation—the language, the format, and the subject matter of an image, and poem at large, can all be clues the poet uses to convey a point. The repetition of the sibilant 's' sound in "swirls of snow" in the poem's second line does produce a kind of pleasure, but this pleasure, too, is undercut by the fact that the description is cliché.

Bly's use of adjectives also does not help the poem to move readers. For example, the speaker states that the night is "cold" and "snowy." Although these words help describe the landscape of the poem, the use of comparison would have helped the speaker compare the night to something else in the world that is "cold" and "snowy." In other words, adjectives in general can undercut a poet's ability to imagine, since, unlike images, they do not require the imaginative leaps that linking unlike things together requires. It is not very difficult, that is, to say that a winter night is "cold" or that snow looks "snowy." The same can be said for the adjective "deserted." Hearing that "The main street is deserted" presents the loose picture of a street void of other people, but it does not depict the speaker's specific street. It does not describe the speaker's landscape in such a way as to distinguish it from all landscapes that could be said to be "deserted." The adjectives in "Driving to Town Late to Mail a Letter" thus make the speaker seem lazy or inarticulate.

Poets writing in the plain-style sometimes counter their use of conversational or speech-like diction with images, replacing the formal artifice of sound-play with the imaginative force of suggesting that one object or feeling in the world is like another object or feeling in the world. By these means, poets and other writers create pictures, making the essentially abstract nature of language more discernible and concrete. Yet, the only two images in "Driving to Town Late to Mail a Letter" are clichés. Bly's suggestion that "The only things moving are swirls of snow" in the poem's second line is the poem's first image, and his suggestion that the "mailbox" door in the poem's third line is like "cold iron" is his second. Although these images could have potentially counteracted the plain-style mode of this poem, they are clichés. It is too often said that snow "swirls," and maybe even more too often said that hard metals are "cold" and like "iron." Although it might be said that the ultimate point of poetry is to articulate feelings that cannot really be articulated, meaning in poetry, and in most forms of imaginative writing, is inherently tied to style or method. An original observation cannot be felt fully if it is articulated in unoriginal language or terms.

Since "Driving to Town Late to Mail a Letter" focuses on the landscape of a snowstorm, its descriptive power or lack thereof becomes central. That is, the vast majority of the poem seeks to describe "a cold and snowy night" so that the speaker might explain the importance and beauty of privacy and solitude. But the poem's refusal to counter a lack of interest in rhythm with sound play and image—as well as its reliance on clichéd descriptions—undercuts Bly's ability to articulate this message memorably.

As William H. Gass writes in "The Soul of the Sentence" in *The Habitations of the Word*, "art should not produce a feeling of ... gloom or dismay, but of energy, wholeness, perfection, joy." Although Bly seeks in "Driving to Town Late to Mail a Letter" to produce a moment of "energy, wholeness, perfection, [and] joy," he fails because he does not sufficiently counter the frank, declarative statement of the plain-style with sound-devices, metaphors, and images.

**Source:** Adrian Blevins, Critical Essay on "Driving to Town Late to Mail a Letter," in *Poetry for Students*, The Gale Group, 2003.

## Sources

Bly, Robert, *Leaping Poetry: An Idea with Poems and Translations*, Beacon Press, 1975, 1–6.

———, *The Light around the Body*, Harper & Row, 1967, p. 38.

———, *Silence in the Snowy Fields*, Wesleyan University Press, 1962, p. 37.

Davis, William V., *Understanding Robert Bly*, University of South Carolina Press, 1988, 17–43.

Gass, William H. *The Habitations of the Word*, Simon & Schuster, 1984, p. 136.

Harris, Victoria Frenkel, *The Incorporative Consciousness of Robert Bly*, Southern Illinois University Press, 32–59.

Molesworth, Charles, *The Fierce Embrace: A Study of Contemporary American Poetry*, University of Missouri Press, 1979, 112–139.

Moran, Ronald, and George Lensing, *Four Poets and the Emotive Imagination: Robert Bly, James Wright, Louis Simpson, and William Stafford*, Louisiana State University Press, 1976.

Nelson, Howard, *Robert Bly: An Introduction to the Poetry*, Columbia University Press, 1984, pp. 31–32.

Sugg, Richard P., *Robert Bly*, Twayne, 1986, pp. 18–37.

Winterowd, W. Ross, *The Rhetoric of the "Other" Literature*, Southern Illinois University Press, 1990, p. 17.

## Further Reading

Davis, William V., *Understanding Robert Bly*, University of South Carolina Press, 1988.

> Davis provides a thoughtful and accessible assessment of Bly's work from his first volume through his 1986 volume, *Loving a Woman in Two Worlds*.

Kay, Jane Holtz, *Asphalt Nation: How the Automobile Took Over America and How We Can Take It Back*, University of California Press, 1998.

> Kay, a planning critic for the *Nation*, uses her background to discuss the history of the automobile and its political, architectural, personal, social, geographic, and economic impact.

Peseroff, Joyce, ed., *Robert Bly*, University of Michigan Press, 1984.

> This critical anthology, part of the University of Michigan Press "Under Discussion" series, is packed with essays by Charles Molesworth, Charles Altieri, James F. Mersmann, Victoria Harris, and Wayne Dodd, all major voices in contemporary poetry criticism.

Zielinski, Sue, and Gordon Laird, *Beyond the Car: Essays on the Auto Culture*, Steel Rail Publishing, 1995.

> This anthology contains essays by writers such as Jane Jacobs, Michael Replogle, Joyce Nelson, and Marcia Lowe who examine car culture, the auto economy, urban planning, international development, and alternatives to the automobile.

# Early in the Morning

*Li-Young Lee*

*1986*

Li-Young Lee's "Early in the Morning," was published in *The American Poetry Review* and later included in Lee's first collection of poems, *Rose* (1986). It is a four-stanza, free-verse poem written from the point of view of an adult looking back on his adolescence or late childhood and, like many of the collection's poems, reflects on Lee's complex relationship with his parents and his past. It is the sixth poem in the collection, coming right after "Dreaming of Hair," and contains many subjects and images typical of Lee's poetry, such as parent-child relationships, the importance of food, family rituals, and the act of watching. Like many of Lee's poems, it is told in the first person. Although the first two stanzas of the poem describe Lee's mother's ritual of combing her hair, in the second two stanzas the speaker zeroes in on the significance of the act to his father. Lee's father, a powerful, authoritarian, emotionally distant, and, at times, tender man, died in 1980, and Lee's early poems can be seen as an attempt to come to peace with his memories of him. Lee's voice is soft, almost sad, and his language direct and accessible. This poem serves as a useful introduction to Lee's work, as it describes an experience with which most people are familiar: watching and learning from their parents.

## Author Biography

Li-Young Lee is one of the leading poetic voices of the Chinese diaspora writing in America. Lee was born August 19, 1957, in Jakarta, Indonesia, to Richard K. Y. Lee and Joice Yuan Jiaying, the granddaughter of China's provisional president, Yuan Shikai, elected in 1912 during the country's transition from monarchy to republic. Before moving to Indonesia, Lee's father was China communist leader Mao Zedong's personal physician. In 1959, the Lees left Indonesia after President Sukarno, for whom Lee's father had been a medical advisor, began openly persecuting the country's Chinese population. After wandering through the Far East for five years, the family immigrated to the United States, settling in Pennsylvania. Lee attended Kiski Area High School in Vandergrift, Pennsylvania; the Universities of Pittsburgh (1975–1979) and Arizona (1979–1980); and the State University of New York at Brockport (1980–1981). With publication of his first collection of poems, *Rose*, in 1986, Lee garnered widespread attention from critics, who were moved by the mix of tenderness, fear, and longing in his portraits of his family, especially his father. In poems such as "Early in the Morning," Lee evokes a child's wonder at the mysteries of adulthood and his parents' daily rituals. *Rose*, for which Lee received New York University's Delmore Schwartz Memorial Poetry Award, was followed in 1990 by *The City in Which I Love You*, which was the 1990 Lamont Poetry Selection of the Academy of American Poets. Lee has also received grants, awards, and fellowships from the Illinois Arts Council, the Commonwealth of Pennsylvania, the Pennsylvania Council on the Arts, the National Endowment for the Arts, the Ludwig Vogelstein Foundation, the Whiting Foundation, and the Guggenheim Foundation. In addition to the two titles mentioned above, Lee has written a critically acclaimed memoir, *The Winged Seed* (1995), which reads like an extended prose poem. His most recent collection of poems is *The Book of My Nights* (2001). Lee lives in Chicago, Illinois, with his wife and two children.

## Poem Text

While the long grain is softening
in the water, gurgling
over a low stove flame, before
the salted Winter Vegetable is sliced
for breakfast, before the birds, 5
my mother glides an ivory comb
through her hair, heavy
and black as calligrapher's ink.

She sits at the foot of the bed.
My father watches, listens for 10
the music of comb
against hair.

My mother combs,
pulls her hair back
tight, rolls it 15
around two fingers, pins it
in a bun to the back of her head.
For half a hundred years she has done this.
My father likes to see it like this.
He says it is kempt. 20

But I know
it is because of the way
my mother's hair falls
when he pulls the pins out.
Easily, like the curtains 25
when they untie them in the evening.

## Poem Summary

### Stanza One

Lee uses the title as the setting of the poem, the first stanza of "Early in the Morning" describing what happens at that time of day. He is very precise in locating the time when his mother combs her hair. It is "while the 'long grain' is softening" but "before / the salted Winter Vegetable is sliced." The "long grain" is most likely rice, a breakfast staple for many Asian cultures. It softens when cooked. The winter vegetable could possibly be a cucumber or a pickled whole radish with garlic. These are often heavily salted and served in a kind of gruel called congee. This is very early morning, as it is also "before the birds" appear. The precision with which Lee details when his mother combs her hair suggests an organized and efficiently run household, one in which such simple rituals carry meaning beyond their appearance. The fact that she uses a comb made of ivory, an expensive material, adds symbolic weight to the act and also provides visual contrast to the mother's black hair.

Lee uses a simile when he describes his mother's hair as "heavy / and black as calligrapher's ink." Similes are comparisons using "like" or "as" to underscore similarities between dissimilar things. Calligraphy refers to stylized writing or lettering, and Chinese calligraphy is comparable to painting in its ability to evoke emotion through a rich variety of form and design. It is both abstract art and, from a practical point of view, written language. By comparing his mother's hair to "calligrapher's ink," Lee evokes his knowledge and love of Chinese culture.

## Media Adaptations

- Lee has appeared with Bill Moyers in Public Broadcasting System's series *The Power of the Word*. This video is available at many public libraries.

- Lee reads poems from his collection *The City in Which I Love You* in a 1990 cassette distributed by New Letters on the Air, located at the University of Missouri at Kansas City, 5100 Rockhill Road, Kansas City, Missouri 64110.

- Acorn Media distributes the video series *A Movable Feast* (1991), which is hosted by Tom Vitale and profiles eight contemporary writers, including Lee. Acorn Media can be reached at 7910 Woodmont Avenue, Suite 350, Bethesda, Maryland 20814.

### Stanza Two

In this stanza, Lee locates his mother in space. The speaker not only watches his mother but his father as well, who is also watching the mother. The boy's attention now is on the father's observation of the hair-combing ritual. The boy watches his father watching. The sound of the combing is so beautiful that the speaker imagines it is "music" to his father's ears. Such subtle music could not be heard, however, without utter silence, and it is this silence that pervades this poem and acts as backdrop to the speaker's observations and thoughts.

### Stanza Three

In this stanza, the speaker describes the mother's actions step by step. It almost reads like an instruction manual for proper hair hygiene. Putting one's hair up often signifies that there is work to be done. It is not unlike "rolling up your sleeves." You do both to make sure your hair, or your sleeves, don't get dirty. The mother has been doing this for most of her life, as illustrated in the line, "For half a hundred years she has done this." Assuming she began combing her hair when she was a child, this makes Lee as speaker a late adolescent or young adult. As with the previous stanza, in the last lines of this one, the speaker's attention gravitates to the father, who likes his wife's hair back because "He says it is kempt." "Kempt" means neat and tidy. This line underscores both a primary value of the father's—neatness—and the mother's desire to please her husband.

### Stanza Four

For the last two stanzas, the speaker has described his mother's morning ritual of doing her hair and the father's response to it, and in the last line of the third stanza, the speaker says his father likes his mother's hair pulled back because it is "kempt." In this stanza, the speaker questions the father's explanation, saying that the reason he likes his wife's hair pulled back is that it means that he can undo it at the end of the day. Lee releases this information as carefully and as slowly as his father "pulls the pins out" of his mother's hair. He uses a simile for the way her hair falls, comparing it to how the curtains fall "when they untie them in the evening." This evening ritual, a bookend to the morning ritual, is also suggestive of sexual intimacy, as "letting one's hair down" can be an erotic act. The curtains close, admitting no more light to the observer, just as the poem closes.

## Themes

### Ritual

Rituals are acts or series of acts that are repeated at particular times for particular reasons, sometimes religious, sometimes secular. By detailing his mother's ritual of combing her hair, Lee emphasizes the importance of this act in his own life as well as his parents'. Family rituals are the glue that bonds members to one another, giving them both meaning and identity. Simple acts such as combing one's hair, or watching a mother comb her hair, accrue meaning for family members as time passes, as the very repetition of the act cements the image of the ritual in one's mind. This image can become the dominant memory a family member has for another. Lee's own memory of this ritual includes not only watching his mother comb her hair but watching his father watch her.

By presuming to know his father's "real" reason for liking his mother's hair pinned back, Lee provides an added dimension to his memory of the

# Topics For Further Study

- With classmates, brainstorm a list of daily rituals in which you engage and then discuss their origins. Are they rooted in family history? In necessity? Are they common among other people in your racial or ethnic group? Discuss what, if any, wider significance they may have.

- Write a short essay recounting your earliest memories of your parents. Are you a participant or an observer? Discuss the significance of the memories of your relationship with your parents.

- Conventional wisdom has it that children grow up to become just like their parents. In what ways are you most like your parents? Do you consider these similarities positive or regrettable? Discuss your responses with your class and with your parents.

- Lee's speaker claims to know something about his father that his father does not know. In your journal, describe something that you know about a family member and a friend that you think they do not know about themselves. What would be the benefits and drawbacks of sharing this information with them?

- In groups, represent this poem as a collage of images that you take from popular magazines. It cannot be a literal representation. That is, you cannot simply use images of a woman combing her hair. Rather, try to capture the tone or theme of the poem. Be prepared to discuss your collage with the rest of your class.

- Rewrite this poem from the point of view of the mother. Read the resulting poems aloud and discuss how point of view shapes the content of the poem.

- List all of the poems in which the image of hair appears in Lee's poems, and then, as a class, discuss the significance of this image.

---

ritual: it is an opportunity for Lee, the son, to feel superior to his father, who remains unaware of his own desires. In this way, Lee's own description of the ritual becomes a chance for him to show his love for his father and how, through time, he has come to understand him.

## *Gender*

Sociologists maintain that gender roles are learned rather than prescribed by one's genetic makeup. The mother in Lee's poem fulfills the conventional expectations of female behavior. She cooks for her family and shapes her physical appearance to please her husband, whose role it is to appreciate her beauty. Even when she is engaged in such a seemingly mundane act as combing her hair, her husband is there to watch, to savor "the music of comb / against hair." In the evening, it is the father who "pulls the pins out" of his wife's hair, adhering to his own gendered role of initiator, the one who acts upon the female.

## *Memory*

Some evolutionary psychologists claim that the memories that stay with human beings are of incidents and events that help them to survive. By choosing this memory of his mother's morning ritual to describe, Lee suggests that it remains somehow significant for him in the present, that it is formative to the way in which he sees himself and thinks of his parents. The absence of interaction between child and parents in the poem and the focus on the father's endorsement of his mother's ritual suggest a rather formal relationship among the three. However, the tenderness with which Lee describes his mother's actions and his father's obvious pleasure and love for his wife also illustrates a deep emotional bond. It is not surprising that in other poems in the collection, Lee weaves memories of his parents and childhood with descriptions of his own children, highlighting how memory contributes to shaping his own behavior.

## Style

### Imagery

Concrete imagery refers to images born of the senses. They include seeing, hearing, taste, touch, and sound. Lee describes his memory of his mother combing her hair by using a detailed set of images to present a clear description to readers. Following is a list of images and the sense to which each corresponds: "the music of comb / against hair": sound; "salted Winter Vegetable": taste; "black as calligrapher's ink": sight; "my mother glides an ivory comb / through her hair": touch. Images, such as the latter, can also be dynamic; that is, they can describe actions.

### Point of View

Point of view refers to the eyes and sensibility through which the poem is presented. Lee's poem is told from the first person point of view, meaning that he uses the "I" to structure his description. Short, first-person poems characterized by the expression of the speaker's private thoughts are known as lyrics and are the most popular kind of poetry written today. The term comes from the Greek for "lyre," a musical instrument played while a poem was being sung. Other well-known lyric poets include Emily Dickinson, Sara Teasdale, and Philip Larkin.

## Historical Context

### Asian-American Literature in the 1980s

The year during which Lee's poem is set is not given, nor is it important, for the poem expresses ideas and evokes emotions that are timeless. Lee's publication of *Rose* in 1986 was part of a tidal wave of literature published by Asian-American writers during the 1980s. This tidal wave, however, began as a ripple during the 1970s with the publication of three anthologies, *Asian-American Authors* (1972), *Asian-American Heritage* (1974), and *Aiiieeeee!* (1975). These anthologies, however, include work mostly by male Chinese and Japanese Americans. The popularity of Chinese-American Maxine Hong Kingston's novel *The Woman Warrior* in 1978 sparked increased interest in Asian-American women writers, which blossomed in the 1980s with works such as Filipina-American Jessica Hagedorn's *Pet Food and Tropical Apparitions*, which received the American Book Award in 1981, Chinese-American Cathy Song's lyrical and haunting first collection of poems, *Picture Bride*, which received the Yale Series of Younger Poets Award in 1982, and Chinese-American Amy Tan's first novel, *The Joy Luck Club*, which won the National Book Award and the L.A. Times Book Award in 1989. Anthologies such as *Home to Stay: Asian-American Women's Fiction* (1990) and *Our Feet Walk the Sky: Women of the South Asian Diaspora* (1993) collect many of the major Asian-American women's voices of the 1970s and 1980s.

Apart from Song and Lee, many other Asian-American poets launched their careers in the 1980s. Varied in approach, subject matter, and style, Asian-American poetry draws on sources from Zen Buddhism to American cartoons. Garret Hongo, a Hawaiian-born American of Japanese descent, won widespread acclaim for his collections, *Yellow Light* (1982) and *The River of Heaven* (1988), which received the Lamont Poetry Selection of the Academy of American Poets Prize and was nominated for the Pulitzer Prize. Hongo's poems address the search for cultural identity by those like himself who are estranged from their ethnic roots. Hongo, who teaches in the creative writing program at the University of Oregon, has also edited a collection of Asian-American poetry called *The Open Boat: Poems from Asian America* (1993). More recently, anthologies that target poets from particular ethnic groups have appeared, underscoring the differences among various groups and the traditions from which they spring. For example, in 1998, *Watermark: Vietnamese American Poetry & Prose*, was published, edited by Barbara Tran, Monique T. D. Truong, and Luu Truong Khoi. This collection signals a break with the idea that all Vietnamese-American poetry focuses on the all-too-expected theme of war. In 1996, *Flippin': Filipinos on America*, edited by Luis H. Francia and Eric Gamalinda, appeared. This anthology gathers writing from both Filipino and Filipino-American writers, who tell stories of their complicated relationship to country and self. Another important recent collection of Asian-American writing is *Black Lightning: Poetry in Progress* (1998), edited by Eileen Tabios, which traces the development of particular poems by some of the country's leading Asian-American poets, including Meena Alexander, Indran Amirthanay-agam, Mei-mei Berssenbrugge, Luis Cabalquinto, Marilyn Chin, Sesshu Foster, Jessica Hagedorn, Kimiko Hahn, Hongo, Timothy Liu, and Lee.

## Compare & Contrast

- **1980s:** With the opening to the outside world and the steady improvement in standards of living in the late 1970s and 1980s, Chinese women again attach great importance to their hairstyles. They begin to put waves and curls into their hair, and some even have permanents.

  **Today:** Chinese women can wear their hair in whatever style they like, give it the color they prefer, wear a wig, or even have their heads shaved. Most Chinese women style their hair because they want to improve the quality of their lives and show respect for themselves.

- **1980s:** Asian/Pacific Americans, according to the United States Census Bureau, number 3.5 million, or 1.5 percent of the total U.S. population, double the 1970 figure.

  **Today:** In 1999, Asian/Pacific Americans, according to the United States Census Bureau, number almost 11 million, or 4 percent of the total U.S. population.

- **1980s:** In 1982, Chinese-American Cathy Song's first collection of poems, *Picture Bride*, receives the Yale Series of Younger Poets Award; in 1989, Chinese-American Amy Tan's first novel, *The Joy Luck Club*, wins the National Book Award and the L.A. Times Book Award.

  **Today:** The readership for Asian-American literature continues to expand as Americans become more interested in learning about the Far East and the Asian-American population increases.

## Critical Overview

Reviewers were unanimous in their praise of *Rose*, though because Lee is such a young poet and has written relatively little, there is scant criticism on his work. Reviewing the collection for the *Nation*, Jessica Greenbaum writes, "*Rose* announces Lee's obsessions but also bears the innate triumph of ordering language." One of those obsessions is Lee's father, who appears throughout the book as a spectral presence Lee grapples to understand. Lee's mentor at the University of Pittsburgh, poet Gerald Stern, writes in the collection's foreword: "What characterizes Lee's poetry is a certain humility, a kind of cunning, a love of plain speech." Stern adds: "The father is the critical event, the critical "myth" in Lee's poetry." Ruth Y. Hsu, in the *Dictionary of Literary Biography*, ties Lee's passion for his family to his ethnic heritage, noting, "In *Rose* Lee reveals a diasporic consciousness that is frequently inextricably woven into the memories and feelings he holds for his father and the rest of the family." Hsu continues, "The sense of uprootedness, loss, the vague yearning for a return to some lost existence is sometimes the overt topic of his poetry." Reviewing the collection for *Prairie Schooner*, Roger Mitchell writes: "I don't think Lee set out to write a book about the loss of his father . . . but the dead father enters almost all of these poems like a half-bidden ghost." Chinese scholar Zhou Xiaojing takes issue with critics who focus on Lee's ethnicity. In his essay, "Inheritance and Invention in Li-Young Lee's Poetry," Xiaojing argues:

> Ethnocentric readings of Lee's poems . . . are not only misleading, but also reductive of the rich cross-cultural sources of influence on Lee's work and of the creative experiment in his poetry. Their readings presuppose a misconception that a pure and fixed Chinese culture has been inherited and maintained by Chinese immigrants and their descendants in America.

Xiaojing looks instead to the Bible and to Western philosophy for influences on Lee's poetry.

## Criticism

### Chris Semansky

*Semansky is an instructor of literature and composition. In this essay, Semansky considers Lee's voice.*

> *As a poet of ritual and memory, Lee honors the past but, in doing so, risks postponing the future."*

When critics discuss a writer's voice, they are using the term figuratively. They do not literally mean the way a writer might sound if his or her poem were read aloud. Voice, rather, refers to the writer's relationship to audience and subject matter and to the purpose he or she has for writing. Lee's voice in "Early in the Morning" is typical of the voice he uses throughout his work. It is sad and wistful and full of loss, and it expresses a self grappling with memory to make sense of the present.

Consisting of a list of concrete nouns that economically build a scene, the poem's first stanza is obsessed with time, with getting things just right. What difference does it make if the speaker's mother combs her hair before or after the water boils? By being precise with his list of what happens and when, the speaker establishes authority for himself. Readers trust him because they could not believe that anyone would be so detailed in making up something. This attention to seemingly mundane details of everyday life is a common feature of realistic writing and explains Lee's reputation as a poet of the possible.

Lee also wins readers' trust because he is writing about his family. People are often closer to members of their family than anyone else, and parents, especially in Chinese culture, are revered. By making readers privy to a morning ritual between his parents, Lee risks offending the sensibilities of readers who might see his poem as a betrayal of trust. However, Lee's tender attitude in describing the scene works to mitigate any misgivings some readers might have. He is, after all, highlighting the love his parents feel for each other and the love he feels for them. It is this tenderness, more than any other quality, that allows readers to imagine the person writing the words. In *Developing a Written Voice*, Dona J. Hickey writes this about the relationship among the reader, the writer, and voice:

> As we read, we are the audience to the voice we hear. Not only do we take in information about the world, but we also meet the person delivering information.

In all but purely technical or scientific writing, we hear not only what the writer knows but also who he or she is. The personality we hear determines the level at which we respond as one interested, sympathetic human being to another.

It is easy to confuse the living, breathing author of a poem with its speaker. Authors may or may not be writing about themselves, and the speaker is just one of the many tools of the writer's craft, the sensibility through which the writer presents the subject matter. Lee is an author who does write about his own lived experience, though he shapes it to fit the poem. In interviews and in his memoir, *The Winged Seed*, he recounts the experiences of his family as they wandered through the Far East on their way to the United States. In this way, his verse echoes information he has provided in nonfictional venues and has a kind of confessional feel to it. Because of Lee's accessibility, many readers who might otherwise not be readers of modern poetry find it easy to sympathize with him, as they like to believe themselves capable of noble sentiments and tenderness towards their parents.

All of Lee's work addresses memories of his family, in one way or another, and especially of his father, a man who, even in his absence, was at the center of Lee's life. As such, his poems are elegies of a sort, paying homage to the past. Elegies are poems or songs expressing sorrow for one who has died. Lee's sorrow is muted, less direct than that in conventional elegies, as he celebrates as much as mourns his father's life. The bulk of the poems in *Rose* were written in the early 1980s, shortly after Lee's father died and, taken as a whole, detail a portrait of a writer who is obsessed with the memory of his father and with searching for the meaning of his life. In his foreword to the collection, Gerald Stern writes that Lee's search emphasizes

> a willingness to let the sublime enter his field of concentration and take over, a devotion to language, a belief in its holiness, a pursuit of certain Chinese ideas, or Chinese memories, without any self-conscious ethnocentricity, and a moving personal search for redemption, which takes the form of understanding and coming to peace with a powerful, stubborn, remote, passionate, and loving father.

This desire, this longing to understand the father is evident in "Early in the Morning," as the speaker experiences his mother's ritual through his father's eyes, watching his father as his father watches his mother combing her hair. The desire to inhabit the position of witness to his father's desire as well as his own suggests a yearning to fathom a man whom Lee represents in other poems and prose as emotionally distant. In the penultimate stanza, Lee presents his father as someone with stereotypical Chinese tastes: for example, he likes his wife's hair tied back because it is "kempt." Lee, however, presents himself as a son who knows his father's desires even better than does the father. He insists that the real reason his father likes his mother's hair tied back is that it affords him an opportunity to let it down at night. By comparing how "[his] mother's hair falls / when he pulls the pins out" to "the curtains / when they untie them in the evening," Lee evokes the intimacy between his mother and father, an intimacy that Lee will articulate, even if his father will not or cannot. In her essay, "Beyond Lot's Wife: The Immigration Poems of Marilyn Chin, Garrett Hongo, Li-Young Lee, and David Mura," critic Mary Slowik claims that Lee's voice has a "declarative and documentary force." Slowik writes:

> Li-Young Lee is ... reverent towards his parents ... even brash, in evoking his father's life as a way of understanding his own. His writing is insistently in the present tense, where past experience and future promise are fused in the confusion of the present moment, intensely and immediately experienced.

Lee's voice, then, fights against itself. In attempting to document his past, he must rely on the only tool he has: his memory. But, memory is obstacle as well as tool for self-understanding, as it prevents him from moving forward. The personality behind the voice that Hickey writes about is of someone who is spinning his wheels, but for whom traction remains impossible. It is of someone who needs to relive his past to live in the present, which, ironically, is but another version of the past. In another poem, "Braiding," Lee describes brushing his daughter's hair, recalling that his father did the same thing for his mother and realizing that, in the future, one of them, Lee or his daughter, will have to imagine and remember this ritual. The ritual described in "Early in the Morning" is but one of many that Lee describes in *Rose*, poems such as "Eating Together," "The Weight of Sweetness," and "Braiding." As a poet of ritual and memory, Lee honors the past but, in doing so, risks postponing the future.

**Source:** Chris Semansky, Critical Essay on "Early in the Morning," in *Poetry for Students*, The Gale Group, 2003.

## Erika Taibl

*Taibl is an English instructor and writer. In this essay, Taibl examines Lee's poem in relationship to an Asian-American poetic tradition.*

> *In other words, his is not a poetry of specific images and specific stories but of universal spirit."*

Asian-American poetry developed as an institutionalized category of literature from the 1970s to the 1990s as the first anthologies of Asian-American poetry were received into the literary marketplace. The category emerged along with the work of other marginalized minority writers and, like the work of these writers, has been defined by several specific, observable poetic characteristics, including its use of a personal lyric voice using the "I" pronoun—the lyric "I"—to claim the poet's story. At the same time as many minority writers' voices were emerging, many white male heterosexual writers were involved in the Language Poetry movement, whose goals were opposite to many minority writers' goals. The Language Poets, according to Timothy Yu, in his *Contemporary Literature* article, "Form and Identity in Language Poetry and Asian American Poetry," strove to avoid the personal, lyric voice and shunned the lyric "I" in their work. Yu observes that the choices of minority writers, especially Asian-American poets, to claim their personal history through their work are a result of having been "'objects' rather than 'subjects' of American history." The subjugation of their identity through many decades of American writing created a "need to make their voices heard.... for these 'stories' have not yet been told." Li-Young Lee's work fits, in many ways, into this definition of Asian-American poetry. Whereas the Language Poets strove to undermine their personal voices in their work, the Asian-American poets, like Lee, along with other minority writers, embraced the personal lyric form as a way to claim a place in the American poetic tradition, a place they had never occupied before.

Many of the elements in Lee's "Early in the Morning" embody the tenets set out in the definition of Asian-American poetry mentioned above. Lee's story is personal and he uses the lyric "I" to tell his story. He also uses images that most readers would consider distinctly ethnic, specifically Asian, to tie the poem to his unique experience. In

## What Do I Read Next?

- *The City in Which I Love You* (1990) is Lee's second collection of poems and has been warmly received by critics and reviewers.

- In his most recent collection of poems, *Book of My Nights* (2001), Lee continues to explore his memories of his father and other family members.

- Essays in *An Interethnic Companion to Asian American Literature* (1997), edited by King-Kok Cheung, provide a useful introduction to the authors and themes of Asian-American writers, including Lee.

- Cynthia Sau-Ling Wong has also written *Reading Asian-American Literature* (1993), a more comprehensive approach to Asian-American literature.

- For readers who want to sample Asian-American fiction, the following anthologies offer a range of voices and subject matter: *The Big Aiiieeeee!: An Anthology of Chinese American and Japanese American Literature* (1991), edited by Jeffery Paul Chan et al., and *Charlie Chan Is Dead: An Anthology of Contemporary Asian American Fiction*, edited by Jessica Hagedorn (1993).

the poem, there are "Winter Vegetable" and cooking rice, distinct eastern foodstuffs. The mother's long black hair is "black as calligrapher's ink." Calligraphy, artistic, stylized, or elegant handwriting or lettering, is popular in Asian cultures. The eastern images, or ethnic markers, serve as ways to place the poem within the poet's unique story and ethnic identity.

Interestingly, Lee rejects taking a stance as an Asian-American writer, which he says, in a *Kenyon Review* interview with Tod Marshall, is "a question about one's dialogue with cultural significance." Lee claims to have no dialogue with cultural significance; his interest is in "spiritual lineage," the way poets are connected across the ages through theme, language, and spiritual motivation. In other words, his is not a poetry of specific images and specific stories but of universal spirit. Lee tells Marshall that he views himself in relationship to poets whose concrete "line of poetry says one thing, but . . . also says many other things." He cites T. S. Eliot, John Donne, and Pablo Neruda among his influences and implies that though his own images are specific and ethnic, the story they tell is not. The story is rooted in the universality of the spirit. Poetry, for Lee, is ultimately a dialogue with a poet's self, which he tells Marshall is "so essential to his being, to his self, that it is no longer cultural or canonical." The ethnic specificity in a poem, whether portrayed through images or through a story that is particular to a poet's identity, can be difficult for readers, who may find the "Winter Vegetable" and "calligrapher's ink" too personal to be relevant to their own experience. This is one challenge of Lee's poem, that the specific images and ethnic markers make it difficult for non-Asian-American readers to experience a deeper connection to the work. But, as Lee posits, the poem is about more than images, ethnic or otherwise. The poem is about spirit, though to assist the readers' translation of the poem, Lee offers one, central image from which to dissect and interpret underlying themes and messages.

The use of the central image—in this poem, the hair—is a common tool of Lee's. As critic Zhou Xiaojing, in his *MELUS* article, "Inheritance and Invention in Li-Young Lee's Poetry," says, "To deal with his cross-cultural experience and to show culturally conditioned ways of perception in his poetry, Lee employs and develops a major technique which relies on a central image as the organizing principle for both the subject matter and structure of the poem." Lee said of this technique, in a 2001 interview with Amy Pence in *Poets & Writers* that, "The image is a revelation of sorts, therefore apocalyptic as opposed to ecliptic. While eclipses cover, an apocalypse is an uncovering." The central image as Lee writes it is apocalyptic because it uncovers several layers of meaning that transcend his particular ethnic experience. In this poem, the image is the tying up of the mother's hair. This simple, daily act becomes metaphor, or symbol, for other revelations about history, family, and personal identity.

The hair is compared to ink, the medium through which a story is written. It is not simply ink, but calligrapher's ink. A calligrapher in the Asian tradition is artist, storyteller, and poet, who writes in an ancient Asian form. The hair as ink connects the mother to her Asian identity and suggests a written or recorded history. The hair also sings through the comb, which suggests the passage of stories through oral history. So, the hair represents a history and identity that is older than writing. The darkness of the hair is juxtaposed, or set against, the "ivory" of the comb. The contrast between dark and light suggests that the mother's identity is plain to see. She looks Asian; her hair sets her apart. Though her son shares much of the same ethnic identity, his identity is a bit more ambiguous. He watches his mother tie up her hair, which is an action that he has come to associate strongly with his mother's identity. He also watches his father watching his mother. His share in the moment is from the periphery. He is an observer, not an actor, and therefore, the story is not so much his as it is his parents,' which raises questions about the lyric "I's" identity and where he might locate himself in relation to his parents, their ethnicity, and his own experience.

Like the images of dark and light that begin to uncover the complexities of the relationship the son has with his parents, there are many other dichotomies, or opposites, presented in the poem that work to tell a story that goes beyond the moment of the hair. There is a temporal dichotomy. Early in the morning, the mother ties her hair into a bun. At night, it comes down. There is distinction between what is "kempt," or tidy, and what is messy. There is a suggestion of public propriety when the hair is pulled up and a private freedom when the hair is released and free. There is an opposition between youth and age, between parent and the child, and there is a suggested opposition in the cultural difference that stems from generational gaps and cultural gaps when Asian parents raise a son in America.

The mother's hair is the immediate link for all of the poem's dichotomies. In the hair, there is familial lineage. There is a suggestion that the father, mother, and son are connected through extensions of time, place, physical likeness, and culture. There are parts of this connection that are tidy and kempt, just as the hair is tidy and kempt during the day, and there are times when that history and identity is untidy, when the ethnic and relational ties are blurry. As the son grows up in America—on a symbolic level, as he lives from the early morning of his life toward the evening—these ties and connections become even blurrier. As an observer of the scene, the son must step back to reconcile the dichotomies that make him who he is. The poem is the place in which he does this.

Like the mother's hair in a bun, the Asian-American poetic tradition can be viewed as a tidy category with the distinct characteristics mentioned in the opening of this essay, or it can be more free and uncertain than that, which is what Lee suggests is his preferred outlook. Just as critics make tidy definitions of poetry, the father claims to like the tidiness of the mother's hair. In truth, the father revels in its evening fall, just as Lee seems to revel in the complexities of his poetic identity, the spirit of the poem rather than its technical and ethnic characteristics and manifestations. The son's understanding of his father's preference for the free hair is the revelatory moment in the poem, the moment in which the son sees the complexities of the familial and cultural relationship. In this moment, the poem transcends ethnic markers and enters the world of the spiritual and universal.

The poem ends with an image of curtains falling in the evening, which is a comparison to the hair's fall when the father pulls out the pins. Depending on the side on which you stand when a curtain falls, the curtain either retains the private stories that occur behind it or prevents the outsider from entering into a private scene. Both of these distinctions are supported in the poem. As an observer, the son is prevented from understanding the complexities of his parents' relationship and identity. He cannot see behind the curtain of their relationship. There is something mysterious, something "easy" left between the couple that does not translate to those outside of their relationship. Similarly, the non-Asian-American reader is prevented, just as the son is prevented from knowing his Asian parents, from fully understanding the Asian identity presented in the poem. For the mother and father, the curtain protects identity and keeps some aspects of their life together and the history they share private. Similarly, the Asian-American poem portrays enough of the complex Asian-American identity for the reader to know it just a bit. The revelation in the poem is knowing that there are things that simply cannot be known and finding in them, despite the curtain, something to appreciate beyond the specific.

In his interview with Pence, Lee claims that what he is trying to do now in his work "is to embody my twofold nature." This twofold nature manifests itself in all the dichotomies established in the poem. Lee has also suggested, in his conversation with Marshall, that the poet's job is not to witness the visible acts of life but the invisible, to write the spirit. Writing the spirit, the invisible, is what leads to a more universally accessible poetry in which cultural and ethnic markers are simply the beginning of understanding. In this poem, Lee is witness to the visible, his mother's hair, his father's observation of his mother, and the complexities of their relationship and identity in the context of his own ethnicity. In a broader context, and one that allows a connection with a more general audience, he is also witness to the invisible history of relationships between man and woman, parent and child, and what resides between them that is unutterable in every culture except through a suggestion of what lay beyond the curtain that separates these apparent opposites. The central image allows for apocalypse, or the revelation of the complex that, in rare and precious moments, reveals a person's physical and spiritual place in the world. For the reader who reads beyond the specificities of image and ethnic markers in Lee's poetry, a richer story than the personal history of one poet, is revealed, a story that can offer any reader an insight into identity, a story in which the lyric "I" may become the readers' as well as the poet's.

**Source:** Erika Taibl, Critical Essay on "Early in the Morning," in *Poetry for Students*, The Gale Group, 2003.

## Sources

Greenbaum, Jessica, "Memory's Citizen," in the *Nation*, Vol. 253, Issue 11, October 7, 1991, pp. 416–19.

Hickey, Dona J., *Developing a Written Voice*, Mayfield Publishing, 1993, 1–4.

Hsu, Ruth Y., "Li-Young Lee," in *Dictionary of Literary Biography*, Vol. 165: *American Poets Since World War II, Fourth Series*, edited by Joseph Conte, Gale Research, 1996, pp. 139–46.

Lee, Li-Young, *Rose*, BOA Editions, 1986, p. 25.

———, *The Winged Seed*, Simon & Schuster, 1995, p. 63.

Marshall, Tod, "To Witness the Invisible," in the *Kenyon Review*, Vol. 22, No. 1, Winter 2000, pp. 143–47.

Mitchell, Roger, Review of *Rose*, in *Prairie Schooner*, Vol. 63, Fall 1989, pp. 129–39.

Pence, Amy, "Poems from God: A Conversation with Li-Young Lee," in *Poets & Writers*, November–December 2001, pp. 22–27.

Slowik, Mary, "Beyond Lot's Wife: The Immigration Poems of Marilyn Chin, Garrett Hongo, Li-Young Lee, and David Mura," in *MELUS*, Fall–Winter 2000, p. 221.

Stern, Gerald, Foreword, in *Rose*, by Li-Young Lee, BOA Editions, 1986, pp. 8–10.

Xiaojing, Zhou, "Inheritance and Invention in Li-Young Lee's Poetry," in *MELUS*, Vol. 21, Issue 1, Spring 1996, pp. 113–33.

Yu, Timothy, "Form and Identity in Language Poetry and Asian American Poetry," in *Contemporary Literature*, Vol. 41, No. 1, Spring 2000, pp. 422–61.

## Further Reading

Lee, Li-Young, *The Winged Seed*, Simon & Schuster, 1995.
Lee's memoir of his family's life in China and Indonesia reads at times like a prose poem. This is a fine introduction to many of the characters that populate Lee's poems.

Maira, Sunaina, and Rajini Srikanth, eds., *Contours of the Heart: South Asians Map North America*, Temple University Press, 1996.
Winner of the 1997 American Book Award from the Before Columbus Foundation, this anthology critically explores the family tension about the concept of home for South Asians who have immigrated to America. It includes fiction, poetry, essays, and photography.

Miller, Matt, "Darkness Visible," in *Far Eastern Economic Review*, Vol. 159, Issue 22, pp. 34–37.
This short essay describes Lee's family's migration to the United States after leaving Indonesia, Lee's emergence as a poet, and his kinship to classic Chinese poets Li Bo and Tu Fu of the Tang dynasty.

Wong, Cynthia Sau-Ling, *Reading Asian-American Literature: From Necessity to Extravagance*, Princeton University Press, 1993.
Wong's examination of Asian-American literature has become a classic in its short time in print and an indispensable resource for students just beginning their research and for seasoned critics seeking new perspectives.

Xiaojing, Zhou, "Inheritance and Invention in Li-Young Lee's Poetry," in *MELUS*, Vol. 21, Issue 1, Spring 1996, pp. 113–33.
Xiaojing discusses the ideas of inheritance and invention in Lee's poetry and how Lee has fashioned himself as an immigrant in America and as a poet.

# For Jennifer, 6, on the Teton

## Richard Hugo
## 1975

"For Jennifer, 6, on the Teton" is included in Richard Hugo's 1975 collection, *What Thou Lovest Well, Remains American*, which was nominated for the National Book Award and reprinted in *Making Certain It Goes On: The Collected Poems of Richard Hugo* (1983). Hugo often wrote poems to lovers, students, and sometimes children of friends and lovers, and this is one of the latter. Hugo addresses the child, Jennifer, throughout the poem, making comparisons between her life and the Teton River, which inspired the poem. Historically, poets have used the river as a symbol of time, life, and change, and Hugo draws on this tradition in the poem. The form of the poem, though not a letter, has much in common with the poems in Hugo's next collection, *31 Letters and 13 Dreams* (1977), many of which he addresses to friends and acquaintances.

In five stanzas, the speaker, acting as sage, makes observations about childhood, nature, ageing, language, and death, providing the child with an idea of what life has in store for her. Hugo's language in the poem, like the language of one of his primary literary influences, Wallace Stevens, is highly elliptical. This means he leaves much unsaid, and his comparisons can be difficult to grasp upon first reading. However, as with good poems that stand the test of time, Hugo's poem offers something new upon each rereading.

## Author Biography

Richard Franklin Hogan was born December 21, 1923, to Esther Clara Monk Hogan and Franklin James Hogan in White Center, a poor working-class neighborhood on the south side of Seattle, Washington. Hugo's father abandoned his family, and Hugo's mother left the child with his grandparents, who raised Hugo in what he describes as a loveless and often mean environment. Esther Hogan married Herbert F. Hugo in 1927 but never reclaimed her son. Nevertheless, Hugo took his stepfather's name in 1942. After serving in the United States Army Air Forces from 1943 to 1945, where he received the Distinguished Flying Cross and Air Medal, Hugo attended the University of Washington, receiving both his bachelor's and master's degrees in English on the G.I. Bill, while taking poetry classes with Theodore Roethke. Between 1951 and 1963, Hugo worked as a technical writer for Boeing.

At the age of forty and after publishing his first collection of poems, *A Run of Jacks* (1961), Hugo took a position as visiting lecturer of English at the University of Montana, and a few years later, he was running the master of fine arts program in creative writing. Hugo's hard-luck childhood, his sense of wonder at the natural world, his difficulties with women, and his relentless need for approval define his intensely emotional poetry. Place is integral to Hugo's poetry, and he readily owned up to being a regional writer. Frequently exploring the relationship of the past to a landscape's present, Hugo's poems tie the particular to the universal, the emotions to the land. In poems such as "For Jennifer, 6, on the Teton," included in his National Book Award nominated collection, *What Thou Lovest Well, Remains American* (1975), Hugo connects the fate of the individual to that of the natural world.

In addition to his poetry collections, which include *Good Luck in Cracked Italian* (1969), *The Lady in Kicking Horse Reservoir* (1973), *31 Letters and 13 Dreams* (1977), and *White Center* (1980), Hugo has also published prose. For his Pulitzer Prize-nominated novel, *Death and the Good Life*, published in 1981, he was awarded an Academy of American Poets Fellowship, and his collection of essays on craft, *The Triggering Town: Lectures and Essays on Poetry and Writing* (1979), has become a classic for teachers of poetry writing and lovers of poetry. After Hugo died of leukemia in 1982, a few other collections of his writing were published, including *Making Certain It Goes On: The Collected Poems of Richard Hugo* (1984), *Last Judgment* (1988), and *The Real West Marginal Way: A Poet's Autobiography* (1986).

## Poem Text

These open years, the river
sings 'Jennifer Jennifer.'
Riverbeds are where we run to learn
laws of bounce and run.
You know moon. You know your name is silver.     5

The thought of water locked tight in a sieve
brings out the beaver's greed.
See how violent opaque runoff moves.
Jennifer, believe
by summer streams come clean for good.     10

Swirl, jump, dash and delirious veer
become the bright way home
for little girl and otter
far from the punishing sun,
games from organized games.     15

This river is a small part of a bigger.
That, another.
We get bigger and our naming song gets lost.
An awful ghost
sings at the river mouth, off key.     20

When you are old and nearing the sea,
if you say this poem
it will speak your name.
When rivers gray,
deep in the deepest one, tributaries burn.     25

## Poem Summary

### Stanza One

In the first stanza of "For Jennifer, 6, on the Teton," "These open years" refers to the childhood of Jennifer, the six-year-old child of the poem's title and the person the speaker is addressing. The first lines introduce the image of the river, which Hugo develops as a metaphor in the rest of the poem. The Teton River flows 110 miles east out of the Lewis and Clark National Forest across Teton and Choteau counties, joining the Missouri River just outside of Loma, Montana. The river is home to native Yellowstone cutthroat trout, as well as hatchery brook and rainbow trout. Hugo, an avid fisherman, was most likely inspired by an actual—as opposed to an imagined—occurrence with Jennifer, while either fishing or canoeing the river.

The speaker compares the girl's childhood to a riverbed, "where we run to learn / laws of bounce and run." Both childhood and riverbeds are foundations upon which bigger things are built (i.e., selfhood and river). "Laws of bounce and run" suggest laws of physics, why things work the way they do. In the last line, the speaker explicitly addresses the child, pointing out what she already knows. She understands the concept of the moon, and she knows her "name is silver." This last statement alludes to the history of the girl's name. "Jennifer" is a derivative of the Celtic *Gwenhwyvar* (Guinevere), usually translated as "white wave," though "white skin" or "white shoulders" is also possible.

### Stanza Two

In this stanza, the speaker adopts the persona of a teacher describing the river to Jennifer. The first line refers to the river ("water locked tight in a sieve"); it makes beavers "greedy" because beavers love rivers, building their homes there. In the third line, the speaker points out "how violent opaque runoff moves." "Opaque runoff" suggests that Hugo is describing the Lower Teton, which cuts huge banks through rich topsoil, creating heavy sedimentation. The water running down from the Rockies cleanses the river by summer. These lines also refer to the time in life when circumstances or prospects might seem bad. However, the speaker seeks to assure the child that bad times pass, when he writes, "Jennifer, believe / by summer streams come clean for good."

### Stanza Three

In this stanza, the speaker lists actions that apply to both child and otter. "Swirl, jump, dash and delirious veer" evoke a child and an otter's playfulness, as well as the movements of the river. The words suggest that being playful and taking action are also ways to lead one's life, rather than always calculating behavior according to risk. This comparison is echoed in the last line, "games from organized games," which underscores the difference between good kinds of games (i.e., playful, spontaneous) and the "bad" kind (i.e., "organized" with predetermined rules).

### Stanza Four

In this stanza, the speaker illustrates the interconnectedness of all things, pointing out, "This river is part of a bigger [river]. / That, another [river]." He also introduces the theme of language's relationship to human identity in the line "We get bigger and our naming song gets lost." Here, the speaker

## Media Adaptations

- New Letters on the Air distributes *Richard Hugo* (1980), an audiocassette of Hugo reading poems from his 1979 collection *White Center*. The tape includes comments made by poet William Stafford in 1983 after Hugo's death.

- The Media Project distributes a 16 MM film about Hugo, *Kicking the Loose Gravel Home* (1976), directed by Annick Smith.

refers to the capacity of language to order the world. Getting bigger suggests growing older and losing the childlike awe and wonder for the world (i.e., "our naming song"). The "awful ghost" singing off key suggests an adult who has lost her way in life.

### Stanza Five

The speaker again directly addresses Jennifer, advising her to "say this poem" when she is "old and nearing the sea," a reference to when death will approach. Just as the river sings her name during her childhood, so will it sing her name during her old age. He presents the poem as a prayer of sorts, with the power to heal, or at least to remind the girl that human life is temporary and human identity illusory. The last two lines compare rivers with human life and underscore the idea that life exists inside of life. "Tributary" has two meanings: the first denotes a stream that feeds a larger stream or body of water, and the other means "paid or owed as tribute." Both meanings are present in the last line, as the speaker pays tribute to the child and her youth while urging her to pay tribute to the earth from which she came and to which she will return.

## Themes

### Nature

Nature has long been a source of inspiration to poets and writers, many of them finding in it meaning and purpose. By setting his poem on the Teton

## Topics for Further Study

- Read Hugo's collection of poems *31 Letters and 13 Dreams* and then write a "letter-poem" to a young child, offering him or her advice on life and on what the future holds. Read your poem to your class.

- Research the Teton River, paying particular attention to the wildlife the river supports, and present your research to your class.

- Hugo's language in the poem would be impossible for a six-year-old child to understand. Assume that you have a six-year-old child in front of you and you want to convey Hugo's ideas to her. What images would you use? What figures of speech?

- In the third paragraph, Hugo mentions "games from organized games." To what is he referring? Do you believe that life can be described as a series of games or as a game? Support your response with examples.

- Hugo admired Wallace Stevens, and many of his poems allude to Stevens's work. Compare "For Jennifer, 6, on the Teton" with Stevens's poem "The Idea of Order at Key West," focusing on what each poem says about the nature of language and poetry. Then, write a short essay comparing and contrasting the poems.

River, Hugo demonstrates his connection to and respect for the natural world, and by using the river as his central symbolic image, he pays tribute to the tradition of poets and thinkers who have similarly found in rivers insight into the human condition and lessons for living. Greek philosopher Heraclitus, for example, famous for saying that one can never step in the same river twice, saw in the continuous flow of the river a symbol for eternal change and renewal. Hugo's advice to Jennifer illustrates this idea and how it relates to her life, writing, "The river is a small part of a bigger. / That, another." Implicit in this statement is that individual identity is transitory and that death is a necessary and unavoidable part of life.

### Language

"For Jennifer, 6, on the Teton" is as much about the act of writing poetry as it is about change and the human condition. Hugo's attention to the sound of his words, his use of symbolic images with wide-ranging associations, and his focus on the river's ability to name all draw readers' attention to the role of language in the poem. A traditional role of poets is naming the world in such a way that others can see and experience it differently. Hugo accomplishes this by comparing rivers to the stages of human life and by giving the river the capacity to talk as it "sings 'Jennifer Jennifer.'"

As the speaker describes how life is like a river, he also points out to Jennifer what she knows: the word *moon* and that her "name is silver." He re-emphasizes the importance of naming again in the fourth stanza, writing, "We get bigger and our naming song gets lost," and in the last stanza he writes:

> When you are old and nearing the sea,
> if you say this poem
> it will speak your name.

By describing the poem as a kind of talisman, the speaker foregrounds the tradition of poet as visionary and language itself as magical, the thing that distinguishes human beings from their environment as it simultaneously fuses them to it.

### Education

By using a speaker who writes of life with wisdom and authority, drawing on the natural world for examples and illustrations, Hugo draws on poetry's didactic tradition. Didactic poetry aims to impart theoretical or practical knowledge to its audience. For example, the Roman poet Lucretius's "On the Nature of Things" expounds on naturalistic philosophy and ethics, and Virgil's "Georgics" explains how to run a farm. Hugo's poem, though highly imaginative in its description of the stages of human life, is didactic in that its purpose is, literally, to show Jennifer what life is like.

## Style

### Personification

Personification is the act of assigning human qualities to inanimate things. By giving the river the capacity to "sing," Hugo personifies it, making it a character in its own right, with human attributes. He also personifies the beaver when he writes, "The thought of water locked tight in a sieve / brings out the beaver's greed." Greed is a human construct and an idea not known to animals. By personifying the river, the speaker is better able to draw comparisons between it and Jennifer, as he does in the opening stanza.

### Sound

Hugo uses a variety of sonic devices in his poem to underscore the action of the river and the role of language as a subject in his poem. These devices include, but are not limited to, consonance, assonance, and alliteration. Consonance denotes the repetition of two or more consonants, as with the "r" in the line "Riverbeds are where we run to learn." Assonance denotes the repetition of vowel sounds in a line or lines of poetry, as with the "e" in "Riverbeds are where we run to learn." When a poet uses alliteration, he or she repeats a speech sound, usually a consonant, in a sequence of words, and usually at the beginning of a word. For example, Hugo uses both alliteration and assonance in the line "brings out the beaver's greed," emphasizing the "b" sound and the "e."

### Audience

Audience refers to the actual or purported person or people for whom the poet writes. Readers know from the title and from lines in the poem that the speaker is addressing a young girl named Jennifer. However, the real audience, of course, is the people who will read the poem. Jennifer is a tactic, a kind of trick, to create a scene in readers' minds. From the tone and the sometimes difficult language the speaker uses, the poem appears to be *written* to Jennifer, as opposed to being a representation of a conversation—real or imagined—between the two. An explicit address to someone not present is called an apostrophe. Well-known poems that apostrophize their subject include John Keats's "Ode on a Grecian Urn" and Samuel Taylor Coleridge's "Recollections of Love."

## Historical Context

### 1970s

In the early 1970s, when Hugo wrote "For Jennifer, 6, On the Teton," many of the rivers and lakes in the United States were heavily polluted. Lake Erie was dying, algae blooms choked the Potomac River, threatening public health, and authorities estimated wetlands losses at more than 400,000 acres annually. Dead fish regularly appeared on shorelines, and two-thirds of America's waters were unsafe for fishing and swimming. Just a few years before, in 1969, the Cuyahoga River in Cleveland, Ohio, was so polluted that it caught fire. The sight of the burning river on evening newscasts mobilized the nation and became a rallying point for passage of the Clean Water Act in 1972. Although the Federal Water Pollution Control Act of 1948 provided state and local governments with funds to address water pollution problems, the federal government viewed water pollution as primarily a state and local problem and did not issue goals or guidelines for reducing it. It was not until 1965 that the federal government required states to set standards for interstate waters that would be used to determine actual pollution levels. The Clean Water Act of 1972 increased federal assistance for municipal treatment plant construction, while expanding federal oversight of pollution control measures, in addition to requiring states to treat all municipal and industrial wastewater before discharging it into waterways. The ultimate goal of the CWA was the restoration and maintenance of the nation's waters.

In Montana, where Hugo worked and fished, the state legislature passed the Montana Environmental Policy Act in 1971. MEPA was patterned after the National Environmental Policy Act of 1969 and established Montana's environmental policy. The Act encourages Montanans to participate in state decisions affecting their environment and promotes efforts that prevent damage to the environment while maintaining the health and welfare of citizens. According to John Mundinger and Todd Everts in *A Guide to the Montana Environmental Policy Act*, "MEPA further acknowledges that each generation of Montanans has a custodial responsibility concerning the use of the environment. . . . Montanans are trustees for future generations." Hugo identified with the natural world in general and the West in particular, even though he grew up in inner-city Seattle.

Water was not the only thing polluted in the early 1970s. This was also the Watergate era, when Americans became increasingly disillusioned with politics and politicians. In 1973, amid charges of corruption and income tax evasion, Vice President Spiro Agnew resigned from office. The next year, President Richard Nixon, facing impeachment charges over what he knew about the burglary of the Democratic Party's National Committee offices in 1972 and when he knew it, was forced to resign. Nixon's resignation, and President Ford's pardoning of any crimes he may have committed, along with subsequent revelations about Nixon's

## Compare & Contrast

- **1970s:** The floppy disc appears in 1970, and the next year, Intel introduces the microprocessor, the "computer on a chip." Also, the first test-tube baby is "born." These technological events inaugurate a change in humanity's relationship with nature.

    **Today:** With the advent of genetic engineering and the increasing reliance on the Internet for work and entertainment, Americans continue to reshape the ways in which they interact with nature and other cultures.

- **1970s:** Before the Clean Water Act of 1972 is passed, only a third of America's water is safe for fishing and swimming, wetlands losses are estimated at more than 4,600,000 acres annually, and sewage treatment plants serve only 85 million people.

    **Today:** Two-thirds of America's waters are safe for fishing and swimming, wetlands losses are estimated at about 70,000 to 90,000 acres, and wastewater treatment facilities serve 173 million people.

- **1970s:** In 1970, on April 22, the first "Earth Day" is celebrated, effectively launching the environmental movement.

    **Today:** The battles between environmentalists and developers continue. The most recent manifestation of this battle is the Bush administration's proposal to open Alaska's Arctic National Wildlife Refuge to oil exploration and the opposition it has generated, both in Congress and with the public.

---

involvement in the Watergate cover-up, all contributed to citizens' growing cynicism with government. During this time, however, Hugo was experiencing a renaissance in his own life. In 1971, he was named full professor and director of the creative writing program at the University of Montana, and in 1973 his collection of poems, *The Lady in Kicking Horse Reservoir*, was nominated for the National Book Award. In 1973, he also met Ripley Schemm Hansen, whom he would marry in 1974. Hugo acknowledges that these events contributed to his growing self-esteem and his belief that he had wisdom to offer other people. They also no doubt contributed to the wise voice of the speaker in "For Jennifer, 6, On the Teton."

### Critical Overview

Critics have not paid much attention to "For Jennifer, 6, on the Teton," but they have addressed *What Thou Lovest Well, Remains American*. In *The Dictionary of Literary Biography*, Bob Group notes the book's organization into three parts, arguing the "sections roughly conform to the poet's boyhood past, his recent experiences, and speculations on the future, as if the author is codifying and organizing his perceptions in preparation for some new departure." Other critics develop Group's point. Donna Gerstenberger, in her study, *Richard Hugo*, while praising the collection, sees it as Hugo's "exploration toward the acceptance of the self that is." Michael Allen agrees. In his critical study, *We Are Called Human: The Poetry of Richard Hugo*, Allen calls *What Thou Lovest Well, Remains American* a "crucial" book, writing that the primary theme of the poems

> is the working out of, and the working against, regression, that psychological dynamic that yearns for what is past and builds, nostalgically, a glow around events gone by, and that ultimately creates visions of 'the good ole days,' the Golden Age, and unfallen Eden.

In *Landscapes of the Self: The Development of Richard Hugo's Poetry*, Jonathan Holden writes that the poems in the collection "dramatize Hugo's struggle with the future of his art, a struggle linked ... with his own survival." Holden claims that Hugo

*The Teton River in South Dakota*

had come to a crossroads, where he had to decide whether or not "to accept his 'true' heritage, his 'real' self in place of his persona."

Other critics were less specific in their response to the collection. Writing in *Survey of Contemporary Literature*, Leon V. Driskell, states, "This book confirms Hugo's importance as a poet, both through the sheer excellence of individual poems and through the larger interconnectedness of the whole."

## Criticism

### Chris Semansky

*Semansky is an instructor of literature and composition. In this essay, Semansky considers how Hugo's poem locates the writer's identity.*

In his essay "The Triggering Town," Hugo writes: "Your way of writing locates, even creates, your inner life." However, Hugo was no confessionalist. Hugo considers a writer's work an index for identity because he sees language itself as a constitutive part of a person's emotional life. For Hugo, writing poetry was both a way to negotiate the confusing demands of a self that he had given to him and a way to reshape that self. Hugo had his share of emotional pain, publicly talking and writing about his troubled childhood, his difficulty with women, his divorce, his battle with alcohol, and his psychoanalysis. His poem "For Jennifer, 6, on the Teton," an "advice" poem, can be read as a primer of sorts on what Hugo has learned from his experiences.

If writing locates the "inner life," as Hugo has written, his own was balanced between order and chaos and, like the processes of nature, subject to chance. Hugo begins the poem by describing childhood as a time of possibility, when the entire world seems to exist solely for the child. "These are open years," he tells the child, when "the river / sings 'Jennifer Jennifer.'" Describing childhood this way, as a time of learning and possibilities, when the self has yet to consolidate into a collection of habits and preconceived ways of interpreting experience, shows how far Hugo has recovered from his own childhood. In his essay "The Real West Marginal Way," Hugo writes of his childhood: "I was subjected to gratuitous beatings and distorted, intense but, by any conventional standards, undemonstrated affection by my grandmother, who, I was convinced years later, had not been right in the head."

> "Hugo still plumbed memory and imagination with his new persona-in-the-making, and there remains the weariness, the darkness of the old Hugo, but now there is also hope and acceptance."

Hugo's speakers are always approximations of Hugo the author. This is not to say they are the same person, only that his speakers embody the emotional truth of the poet, whether that truth exists before the writing of the poem or comes about during its conception. Holden, writing in *Landscapes of the Self: The Development of Richard Hugo's Poetry*, claims that *What Thou Lovest Well, Remains American*, Hugo's fifth collection, marks a watershed for the poet, as it came after the poet had exhausted the "artistic possibilities" for "the myth of personal failure" that Hugo had touted in his previous books. Poems such as "For Jennifer, 6, on the Teton," though certainly bleak in parts, are, in the end, an affirmation of the notion that people can re-invent themselves and, for Hugo, that process of re-invention necessarily takes place in language.

Although the speaker is ostensibly addressing a six-year-old girl, she is a poetic convenience for Hugo to explore the new persona he was crafting in the wake of his nervous breakdown in Iowa City in 1971 and the subsequent emergence of a more honest, robust self-image. Hugo still plumbed memory and imagination with his new persona-in-the-making, and there remains the weariness, the darkness of the old Hugo, but now there is also hope and acceptance. He can warn Jennifer about the "violent opaque runoff" inevitable in life, the sudden, inscrutable events that can emotionally sink a person, but he can also console her, assuring her, "by summer streams come clean for good." The belief that life works itself out like a river, however, is not sentimental or naive but a hard-won insight that has taken Hugo half a century to understand.

Hugo achieves that understanding through his poetry, for not only does his speaker use the exemplum of the river to describe life's twists and turns, but he also uses it to describe the processes of poetry itself, the writing of which creates and recreates the author. Thus, when the speaker uses the metaphor of "water locked tight in a sieve" to describe a river, he is also using it to describe poetry. "Water," in this case, might be emotions or experience or some combination of the two, and the "sieve," the form the poem takes. In his essay "Writing off the Subject," Hugo argues:

> A poem can be said to have two subjects, the initiating or triggering subject, which starts the poem or 'causes' the poem to be written, and the real or generated subject, which the poem comes to say or mean and which is generated or discovered in the poem during the writing.

It is hard to know the triggering subject of "For Jennifer, 6, on the Teton," though readers can infer the poem might have sprung from an actual event of fishing or canoeing or playing with Jennifer, who might have been a daughter of a friend or a lover. The "real" subject, however, is the relationship between language and emotional growth, a relationship Hugo uses the figure of Jennifer to articulate. The third stanza describes—as it embodies—the playful act of writing poems, as much as it shows the importance of risk-taking and following instinct:

> Swirl, jump, dash, and delirious veer
> become the bright way home
> for little girl and otter
> far from the punishing sun,
> games from organized games.

Hugo's advice to poets in his essay "Nuts and Bolts" is to make up rules for their writing. "If they are working," he says, "they should lead you to better writing. If they don't, you've made up the wrong rules." In "Writing off the Subject," Hugo notes that aspiring poets frequently feel wedded to the initiating subject of their poem, finding it difficult to free themselves. The advice he gives them about writing echoes the same advice he gives Jennifer about life:

> Don't be afraid to jump ahead. There are a few people who become more interesting the longer they stay on a single subject. But most people are like me, I find. The longer they talk about one subject, the duller they get. Make the subject of the next sentence different from the subject you just put down. Depend on rhythm, tonality, and the music of language to hold things together. It is impossible to write meaningless sequences. In a sense the next thing always belongs. In the world of imagination, all things be-

long. If you take that on faith, you may be foolish, but foolish like a trout.

Poetry is part of language, just as "[The Teton] river is a small part of a bigger [river]." For Hugo, human beings carve out their place among other creatures and landscapes through language. However, as one ages, the sense of wonderment and awe at the world the speaker describes in the opening stanza diminishes: "We get bigger and our naming song gets lost." That "naming song" refers to human beings' capacity not just to put words to experience but also to experience the world anew. The "awful ghost / . . . at the river mouth" singing off key seems to suggest someone whose eyes as well as tongue have grown weary. But, approaching death, for the new Hugo, does not spell imminent doom and the loss of self-worth. Poetry itself offers a way of being in the world. The final lines of the poem offer hope: "When rivers gray, / deep in the deepest one, tributaries burn." When all seems lost, something remains. Those burning tributaries suggest qualities that sustain people as they age: memory, friends, a life's work. They also undergird a self now confident of its worth to others, and its place in the world of things. In writing a poem to a six-year-old girl, Hugo was actually writing a poem to himself, re-inventing a self-pitying persona into one full of grace, confidence, and acceptance.

**Source:** Chris Semansky, Critical Essay on "For Jennifer, 6, on the Teton," in *Poetry for Students*, The Gale Group, 2003.

## Adrian Blevins

*Blevins has published essays and poems in many magazines, journals, and anthologies and teaches writing at Roanoke College. In this essay, Blevins suggests the success of Hugo's poem can be attributed to the way in which Hugo uses the lyric speaker to invent a character of ethos.*

Recent books of important criticism on American poetry have sought to evaluate the work of contemporary poets in terms of Aristotle's "ethos" (from *The Rhetoric*), which relates the value of a text to its speaker's ability to persuade, which is then related to the text's ability to present a speaker as a person of character. Carl Dennis's *Poetry as Persuasion* suggests that the speakers of poems can only be authentic if they are inclusive, discriminating, passionate, and generous. In other words, a poem can only work if its speaker reveals himself or herself to be a person readers can care about. In *The Old Formalism: Character in Contemporary American Poetry*, the American poet and critic

> "Yet, Hugo's speaker comforts Jennifer (and all his eavesdropping readers) by suggesting that this disappointment can be countered by the beauty of the kind of poetry that can sing a young girl's name even beyond death."

Jonathan Holden sounds much like Dennis when, quoting part of a poem by the American poet Naomi Shihab Nye, he says, "The achieved poem of ethos will affirm love in spite of 'the hundred disappointments.' It will be oriented to the future. It will risk sentimentality but overcome it. Most significant, it will be generous, focused not on the poet's self, but on other people."

Holden gives an entire chapter to Hugo's work in *The Old Formalism: Character in Contemporary American Poetry* partly in an attempt to reveal the ways in which Hugo's autobiographical or confessional inclinations do not undercut his ability to present speakers or personas of ethos. A close look at Hugo's "For Jennifer, 6, on the Teton" will also reveal the ways in which poems can succeed by using the conventions of the lyric, which presents a single person meditating on a single theme or motif and sometimes can thus seem self-serving and/or self-interested, to speak toward and about others, rather than just the lyric self. In other words, because Hugo's speaker in "For Jennifer, 6, on the Teton" is "focused not on the *poet's* self, but on other people," Hugo is able to use the isolated nature of the lyric speaker for what might be called "the greater good." The success of "For Jennifer, 6, on the Teton" can be attributed to many other virtues—Hugo's fresh metaphorical imagination, free verse rhythm, and original images are possible attributes—but the way Hugo uses the lyric speaker to invent a character of ethos can be said to be the poem's predominate virtue. Understanding the ethos of Hugo's speaker in this poem can provide readers with a fresh means of evaluating the success of lyric poems in general.

## What Do I Read Next?

- Rick Bass, a Mississippi-born writer now living in Montana's remote Yaak Valley, writes stories about the landscapes and people of Montana. Bass's books include *In the Loyal Mountains: Stories* (1995) and *The Roadless Yaak: Reflections and Observations about One of Our Last Great Wilderness Areas* (2002).

- Hugo was friends with Raymond Carver, another great writer from the American West. (Both were born in the Pacific Northwest.) Carver's 1983 collection of short stories, *Cathedral*, a classic work of contemporary fiction, was nominated for the National Book Critics Circle Award and was a runner-up for the Pulitzer Prize.

- For students interested in the development of Hugo's poetry, his posthumously published *Making Certain It Goes On: The Collected Poems of Richard Hugo* (1983), is indispensable.

- Hugo's 1979 collection of essays on writing, *The Triggering Town: Lectures and Essays on Poetry and Writing*, has become a classic text for teachers of poetry writing. The volume contains essays on topics such as the relevance of creative writing classes and "How Poets Make a Living."

---

As many poets and critics have said, Hugo is a poet of the landscape—his themes often involve or describe the exterior world of his native Pacific Northwest. Yet Hugo is not a pastoral poet; he does not use the landscape for the purposes of merely depicting or describing the landscape as phenomenon. Instead, he locates his emotions and observations within the landscape to speak about or toward the world of people. "For Jennifer, 6, on the Teton" is located in the place of the river Teton (in Montana), but the poem itself is about issues much larger than just this place. Although the celebration of childhood and bittersweet lament on its loss can be said to be directed toward the child, Jennifer, in the poem, Hugo's interest in humankind in general—manifested in his use of the plural first person "we" as well as a use of metaphor to link Jennifer's playing in the river to the behavior of all rivers across all spaces of time—makes the poem universal, or plural.

The poem begins when the unspecified speaker states that "These open years, the river / sings 'Jennifer, Jennifer.'" Because "For Jennifer, 6, on the Teton" opens metaphorically, suggesting that a river can sing a young girl's name, it leans toward the emotional world, rather than the world of depiction or description. The phrase "these open years" is also noteworthy since it qualifies or limits the river's ability to sing Jennifer's name. That is, by suggesting that the river Teton can sing Jennifer's name because the years are "open," the speaker has implied that a future is coming in which the river will no longer sing her name. This method helps Hugo foreshadow the expanse into larger time in the poem's last stanza or makes it possible for him to imbue the poem's opening sentence with a sorrow large enough to cast a shadow across the rest of the poem. This strategy helps Hugo weave celebration with lament. Since the marriage of celebration to lament is necessary for Hugo's theme about the inevitable passing of time, this strategy is essential to the poem's complexity and beauty.

In the poem's third and fourth lines, the speaker continues his metaphorical approach, tying Jennifer's experience as a child playing in a river to all humankind by stating that "Riverbeds are where we run to learn / laws of bounce and run." In other words, in the poem's first few lines, Hugo ties his celebration of the child Jennifer playing in a river to the larger observation that all children—"we"—learn "the laws of bounce and run" from such activity. Thus, though it is safe to say that although "For Jennifer, 6, on the Teton" focuses on a single child in a single moment in time, it is directed beyond a single person and time. The poem thus becomes inclusive; it locates narrowly for the purposes of being concrete but spreads outward to the larger world of all children and thus can be said to be more about the nature of childhood than the momentary experience of a single child.

Hugo's point of view shift in the poem's first stanza is also notable. The speaker moves from speaking in the third person ("These open years, the river / sings 'Jennifer, Jennifer.'") to the plural first person ("Riverbeds are where we run to learn / laws of bounce and run") to the second person, or point of view of direct address ("You know the moon. You know your name is silver.") This gradual and almost seamless shifting from the most distant point of view choice to the most intimate point of view choice mimics the movement of typical thought process. It duplicates the way the mind will think in generalities until it finds a point of focus. Of course, since much of the poem shifts between lines of direct address and more general, third person statements, this strategy also foreshadows the poem's entire approach, and so seems to anticipate what it is going to say before the saying is said. Such a technique solidifies the poet's authority over his subject matter. The speaker of "For Jennifer, 6, on the Teton" subtly reveals that he is not making random choices but carefully laying out the map for the poem's movement. Such a method also speaks, technically, toward the virtue of inclusivity since it includes and even embodies more than one point of view.

In his second stanza, Hugo focuses on describing the behavior of the river and the creatures who make their homes there. He says that "The thought of water locked tight in a sieve / brings out the beaver's greed." Although it is not clear at first that this metaphor is meant to suggest that childhood is also like "water locked tight in a sieve," the speaker's image of the river water being "violent opaque runoff" and moving, coupled with the command, "Jennifer, believe / by summer streams come clean for good," implies that the beaver's dam will unravel or come done. In this stanza, Hugo describes the temporary nature of childhood by marrying it to the temporary nature of the beaver's dam. The lines in this stanza about water moving also anticipate the poem's final last line in which "tributaries" (or small streams feeding in larger streams or lakes) "burn," and so reinforce the speaker's authority or supreme control over his subject matter.

The poem's fourth stanza details the "swirl, jump, dash and delirious veer . . . for little girl and otter." This stanza moves away from its future orientation to focus on the moment at hand. That is, Jennifer is being linked to the otter in the experience of play, and aside from making a comment about other forms of childhood play in the lines about Jennifer being "far from the punishing sun / games from organized games," the speaker refrains from being editorial in this part of the poem. He abstains from commenting on the fact that Jennifer's play is temporary and thus does not qualify or corrupt the idea of play. For this reason, stanza four in the poem is quite clear in its intention to celebrate the beauty of childhood.

The poem's fifth stanza breaks the celebration of play by moving out of the descriptive mode. It is, in other words, far more editorial, or about the speaker's feelings or observations, rather than the child herself. In this stanza, the speaker ties river and childhood together more overtly, and so begins the speaker's lament. The speaker moves away from addressing Jennifer directly to speaking in the plural first person again when he says, "We get bigger and our naming song gets lost." In other words, in stanza five, the speaker tells us that "swirl, jump, dash and delirious veer" of childhood will turn, in time, into "an awful ghost / ["singing" ] at the river mouth, off key." Although it is hard to say decisively what this "awful ghost" is, the context of the poem makes it clear that the lines mean to describe the reverse of the childhood joy depicted in earlier lines.

Yet the poem does not end on this sad note. Instead, "For Jennifer, 6, on the Teton" moves from the landscape of the river and Jennifer's childhood to the time when she "is old and nearing the sea." In this sense, "For Jennifer, 6, on the Teton" is oriented quite literally to the future. Although it focuses on the moment of Jennifer playing in the river Teton and celebrates the beauty of that moment, it is also wise enough or inclusive enough to lament the temporary nature of Jennifer's play. The poem is not content to do this much; it feels the need to move further outward toward the future where it can offer Jennifer itself. The speaker says, "When you are old and nearing the sea, / if you say this poem / it will speak your name." In other words, although Jennifer must move out of childhood and into a time in which "we get bigger and our naming . . . gets lost," Hugo offers the comfort of his poem, which, like the river Teton, quite literally "sings Jennifer, Jennifer." This last move in the poem reveals the generosity of Hugo's speaker. That is, by moving between celebration and lament to the final and most generous act of giving the gift of articulation to the child Jennifer, Hugo depicts his speaker as a man of character.

Although it is possible to evaluate the merits of any poem by any number of means, the American contemporary period tends to be speaker-centered; poets today tend to rely heavily on "voice" and "tone." Word choice, lineation, sound play, and the use of image and other figures of speech combine to produce a speaker's voice or tone. But, too little has been said until recently about a speaker's ability to reveal himself or herself to be worth listening to. Thus, critics interested in ethos, or the ability of a speaker to portray his or her personal virtues, have a new window by which to accurately measure the success of the poetry of their own time. "For Jennifer, 6, on the

Teton" continues to be studied and will not be forgotten because its speaker is inclusive and generous. To use Holden's terms again, it "[affirms] love despite the hundred disappointments." Since the leap from childhood into adulthood anticipates the leap from life into death, certainly it is a generally disappointing transformation. Yet, Hugo's speaker comforts Jennifer (and all his eavesdropping readers) by suggesting that this disappointment can be countered by the beauty of the kind of poetry that can sing a young girl's name even beyond death. What a gift—what an act of bigheartedness—this poem, thus, is.

**Source:** Adrian Blevins, Critical Essay on "For Jennifer, 6, on the Teton," in *Poetry for Students*, The Gale Group, 2003.

## Sources

Allen, Michael S., *We Are Called Human: The Poetry of Richard Hugo*, University of Arkansas Press, 1982, pp. 92–113.

Dennis, Carl, *Poetry as Persuasion*, University of Georgia Press, 2001.

Driskell, Leon V., "What Thou Lovest Well, Remains American," in *Survey of Contemporary Literature*, Vol. 12, edited by Frank N. Magill, Salem Press, 1975, pp. 8205–208.

Gerstenberger, Donna, *Richard Hugo*, Boise State University Press, 1983, pp. 30–34.

Group, Bob, "Richard Hugo," in *Dictionary of Literary Biography*, Vol. 5: *American Poets Since World War II, First Series*, edited by Donald J. Greiner, Gale Research, 1980, pp. 369–74.

Holden, Jonathan, *Landscapes of the Self: The Development of Richard Hugo's Poetry*, Associated Faculty Press, 1986, pp. 113–34.

———, *The Old Formalism: Character in Contemporary American Poetry*, University of Arkansas Press, 1999, p. 7.

Hugo, Richard, "Nuts and Bolts," in *The Triggering Town: Lectures and Essays on Poetry and Writing*, W. W. Norton & Company, 1979, pp. 37–53.

———, "The Real West Marginal Way," in *The Real West Marginal Way: A Poet's Autobiography*, W. W. Norton, 1992, pp. 3–19.

———, "The Triggering Town," in *The Triggering Town: Lectures and Essays on Poetry and Writing*, W. W. Norton & Company, 1979, pp. 11–19.

———, "Writing off the Subject," in *The Triggering Town: Lectures and Essays on Poetry and Writing*, W. W. Norton & Company, 1979, pp. 3–11.

Mundinger, John, and Todd Everts, *A Guide to the Montana Environmental Policy Act*, Legislative Environmental Policy Office and the Environmental Quality Council, 1998, pp. 1–10.

## Further Reading

Gerstenberger, Donna, *Richard Hugo*, Boise State University Press, 1983.

> Gerstenberger's pamphlet on Hugo's writing is a good introductory resource for students who want a quick overview of Hugo's poetry. Gerstenberger also includes a useful bibliography of secondary sources.

Hugo, Richard, *The Real West Marginal Way: A Poet's Autobiography*, W. W. Norton, 1992.

> *The Real West Marginal Way: A Poet's Autobiography* is not a conventional autobiography but a collection of essays that Hugo wrote over his life, addressing topics such as his trip to Italy, how he never met Eudora Welty, and his history of drinking and self-loathing.

Morris, Patrick, *Anaconda Montana: Copper Smelting Boom Town on the Western Frontier*, Swann Publishing, 1997.

> Hugo loved to visit and write about the small, often abandoned towns of rural Montana. Morris's social history of Anaconda, Montana chronicles the founding and growth of this smelting town in Montana's Deer Lodge Valley. Among other topics, Morris focuses on the industrial development of the town, examining it in relation to the labor movement in the western United States.

Simic, Charles, "The Bombardier and His Target: Two Poets and a Powerful Coincidence," in *Chronicle of Higher Education*, Vol. 47, Issue 10, November 3, 2000, pp. 12–14.

> Simic, a noted poet and friend of Hugo, recounts a poem Hugo wrote to him, acknowledging that he bombed Simic's town while in the air force during World War II.

Young, William, "Traveling through the Dark: The Wilderness Surrealism of the Far West," in *Midwest Quarterly*, Vol. 39, Issue 2, Winter 1998, pp. 187–202.

> Young analyzes the writings of Western poets Richard Hugo, Gregory Corso, and William Stafford, exploring how 1960s literary surrealism influenced their representations of the American West.

# Having it Out with Melancholy

## Jane Kenyon
## 1993

Jane Kenyon's "Having it Out with Melancholy" was first published in her 1993 collection *Constance*. The poem also appears in the posthumous collection *Otherwise: New and Selected Poems* (1996) and, more recently, on the Academy of American Poets web site at www.poets.org. *Constance* contains several poems that address issues of physical and mental illness, but probably none so disclosing of Kenyon's own life as "Having it Out with Melancholy." While it is rarely a good idea to assume that every word of a seemingly autobiographical poem is an actual account of the poet's "real" experiences and thoughts, one may safely assume that this one is based on Kenyon's own life. Her battle with chronic depression has been well documented—by herself, her husband, and critics—and the speaker of this poem faces the same fight.

"Having it Out with Melancholy" is a lengthy poem, with its one hundred lines broken into nine sections, each with an appropriate title. The parts are arranged chronologically, beginning with the speaker's first encounter with melancholy as an infant, continuing through her young adulthood into her thirties, and concluding at a later age. Throughout the poem, the voice remains calm and matter-of-fact, avoiding the painful emotionalism the speaker feels. The language is cool and spare, as Kenyon does an excellent job of describing a tortured life with non-torturing words.

## Author Biography

Jane Kenyon was born May 23, 1947, in Ann Arbor, Michigan. Kenyon eventually attended her hometown university, the University of Michigan, earning a bachelor's degree in 1970 and a master's in 1972. While at Michigan, she was a student of renowned poet, editor, and teacher Donald Hall, with whom she developed a personal relationship throughout the course of her studies. Kenyon and Hall married the same year she received her master's degree.

Her marriage and subsequent move to Eagle Pond Farm in New Hampshire—owned by the Hall family for generations—were the impetus behind Kenyon becoming a published poet. Her first book of poems, *From Room to Room*, published in 1978, chronicles the experience of living in her new home, and many of the poems reflect a speaker alone in the house, staring out a window, trying to write. Her work in this volume is primarily domestic and pastoral, although the intriguing imagery for which she would later become recognized is already evident here. Kenyon's second and third books, *The Boat of Quiet Hours* (1986) and *Let Evening Come* (1990), explore darker themes, most significantly, death, illness, and depression. During the period these poems were penned, her husband was diagnosed with cancer (which he survived) and she was in the midst of her own battle with severe depression. The fourth and final book of poems published during her lifetime, *Constance* (1993) contains even more references to disease and sadness and includes one of her most personally revealing poems, "Having it Out with Melancholy." After her death from leukemia in 1995, a fifth volume titled *Otherwise: New and Selected Poems* (1996) was published containing twenty poems written just prior to her death, along with several from her earlier works.

Kenyon's poetry was well received by critics and readers from her first publication onward. Although none of her books won specific awards, she herself was the recipient of several, including the Avery and Julie Hopwood Award for Poetry from the University of Michigan, and fellowships from the National Endowment for the Arts (1981), the New Hampshire Commission on the Arts (1984), and the Guggenheim Foundation (1992–1993). Kenyon died April 23, 1995, in Wilmot, New Hampshire, one month short of her forty-eighth birthday. She is survived by her husband and two step-children.

## Poem Text

1. FROM THE NURSERY

When I was born, you waited
behind a pile of linen in the nursery,
and when we were alone, you lay down
on top of me, pressing
the bile of desolation into every pore.      5

And from that day on
everything under the sun and moon
made me sad—even the yellow
wooden beads that slid and spun
along a spindle on my crib.      10

You taught me to exist without gratitude.
You ruined my manners toward God:
"We're here simply to wait for death;
the pleasures of earth are overrated."

I only appeared to belong to my mother,      15
to live among blocks and cotton undershirts
with snaps; among red tin lunch boxes
and report cards in ugly brown slipcases.
I was already yours—the anti-urge,
the mutilator of souls.      20

2. BOTTLES

Elavil, Ludiomil, Doxepin,
Norpramin, Prozac, Lithium, Xanax,
Wellbutrin, Parnate, Nardil, Zoloft.
The coated ones smell sweet or have
no smell; the powdery ones smell      25
like the chemistry lab at school
that made me hold my breath.

3. SUGGESTION FROM A FRIEND

You wouldn't be so depressed
if you really believed in God.

4. OFTEN

Often I go to bed as soon after dinner      30
as seems adult
(I mean I try to wait for dark)
in order to push away
from the massive pain in sleep's
frail wicker coracle.      35

5. ONCE THERE WAS LIGHT

Once, in my early thirties, I saw
that I was a speck of light in the great
river of light that undulates through time.

I was floating with the whole
human family. We were all colors—those      40
who are living now, those who have died,
those who are not yet born. For a few

moments I floated, completely calm,
and I no longer hated having to exist.

Like a crow who smells hot blood      45
you came flying to pull me out
of the glowing stream.
"I'll hold you up. I never let my dear
ones drown!" After that, I wept for days.

### 6. IN AND OUT

The dog searches until he finds me
upstairs, lies down with a clatter
of elbows, puts his head on my foot.

Sometimes the sound of his breathing
saves my life—in and out, in
and out; a pause, a long sigh....

### 7. PARDON

A piece of burned meat
wears my clothes, speaks
in my voice, dispatches obligations
haltingly, or not at all.
It is tired of trying
to be stouthearted, tired
beyond measure.

We move on to the monoamine
oxidase inhibitors. Day and night
I feel as if I had drunk six cups
of coffee, but the pain stops
abruptly. With the wonder
and bitterness of someone pardoned
for a crime she did not commit
I come back to marriage and friends,
to pink fringed hollyhocks; come back
to my desk, books, and chair.

### 8. CREDO

Pharmaceutical wonders are at work
but I believe only in this moment
of well-being. Unholy ghost,
you are certain to come again.

Coarse, mean, you'll put your feet
on the coffee table, lean back,
and turn me into someone who can't
take the trouble to speak; someone
who can't sleep, or who does nothing
but sleep; can't read, or call
for an appointment for help.

There is nothing I can do
against your coming.
*When I awake, I am still with thee.*

### 9. WOOD THRUSH

High on Nardil and June light
I wake at four,
waiting greedily for the first
note of the wood thrush. Easeful air
presses through the screen
with the wild, complex song
of the bird, and I am overcome

by ordinary contentment.
What hurt me so terribly
all my life until this moment?
How I love the small, swiftly
beating heart of the bird
singing in the great maples;
its bright, unequivocal eye.

## Poem Summary

### Lines 1–5

The epigraph appearing at the start of "Having it Out with Melancholy" sounds a rather foreboding note. The quote from Russian playwright Anton Chekhov's *The Cherry Orchard* not only implies pessimism and hopelessness with its certainty that an "illness has no cure," but also sets the stage for an upcoming section of the poem in which the speaker lists her own "many remedies" that have been prescribed for her sickness.

The poem moves from the epigraph to the title of the first section, "From the Nursery," which lets the reader know right away that the speaker is going back in time to her infancy, a time when the human mind cannot really remember events that occurred. But, in the poem, she speaks clearly of what she saw and felt from her crib as though the memories are real, and she personifies her illness in order to talk to it and about it as she would a human foe.

Apparently the speaker believes she was born with melancholia, for she claims that it "waited / behind a pile of linen in the nursery" when she was first brought home after birth. Melancholia does not expose itself until she is alone, at which time she describes it as an intruder come to suffocate her with "the bile of desolation" pressing "into every pore." These lines imply that, from the very beginning, she is helpless against the sadness and lifelessness that remained with her into adulthood.

### Lines 6–10

These lines reinforce the notion that depression, or at least the tendency for it, is something with which one is born and against which one is therefore defenseless. She states that "from that day on / everything under the sun and moon / made me sad"—quite an assertion by itself, made even more startling by the example of what "everything" entails. Even the simple "wooden beads" often seen on baby cribs meant to stimulate or entertain the child had just the opposite effect on the speaker. They, too, made her feel depressed.

### Lines 11–14

In these lines, the speaker gives a voice to the personified melancholy. First, she blames it for the fact that she is not even grateful to be alive and that she does not have a good relationship with a Supreme Being. This reference to God is reiterated later in the poem and is a matter that

## Media Adaptations

- Journalist Bill Moyers hosted a film called *A Life Together: Donald Hall and Jane Kenyon*. It was first broadcast on PBS in December 1993. The tape, recorded by Films for Humanities, Inc., won an Emmy award in 1994 and features a discussion with Hall and Kenyon. In the film, Kenyon reads parts of "Having it Out with Melancholy" and other poems.

- An audiocassette simply called "Jane Kenyon" was recorded in 1987 by the University of Missouri. The twenty-seven-minute tape features Kenyon reading poems from *The Boat of Quiet Hours*, as well as an interview recorded at her home in New Hampshire.

weighs heavily on the speaker's mind. The voice of melancholy appears in lines 13 and 14, in which it spouts a belief that runs contrary to what most "normal" human beings want to hear. Depression tells the speaker that "the pleasures of earth" are useless, and that she was placed on earth "simply to wait for death." The fact that these dismal thoughts are still within the "From the Nursery" section of this poem emphasizes the contention that even the very young may struggle with mental illness.

### Lines 15–20

The final six lines of the first part drive home the point that the speaker's illness began in early childhood. The illness has such a strong hold on her that she feels she belongs to it more so than to her mother. While she had all the material objects typical of a little girl growing up in the 1950s— "blocks and cotton undershirts . . . red tin lunch boxes / and report cards in ugly brown slipcases"— what she also had was a battle going on in her mind with a silent, horrifying enemy whom she calls a "mutilator of souls." She also refers to her melancholy as "the anti-urge," indicating the illness's ability to zap all human drive, passion, and determination from her very depths.

### Lines 21–23

The second section is called "Bottles," an appropriate title as the first three lines consist simply of a list of medications that come in these containers. Calling out the names of the eleven types of antidepressant medications, she tries to emphasize just how acute and chronic her illness is. All these drugs are commonly prescribed for depression and similar mental ailments, but it may not be so common for one individual to have sampled them all. The point here is that the speaker's melancholia is so deep that nothing seems to relieve it.

### Lines 24–27

The last four lines of the brief "Bottles" section imply the speaker's personal connection to her medication. She describes their textures and odors the way someone might talk about different foods or other necessities. The reference to the "chemistry lab at school" is a reminder that the troubled speaker is still a very young woman, young enough to recall vividly the smell of science experiments in high school or college.

### Lines 28–29

These two lines make up the shortest stanza in the poem. The section title, "Suggestion from a Friend," is indicative of the speaker's inability to explain her problems to others, even close friends. The "suggestion" here is almost accusatory, with the "friend" seeming to blame the speaker for her own depression. The implication is that if the ill individual only had faith in God's existence, then she would be cured. Since she apparently does not have that faith, the depression must be her own fault. As the speaker herself has already admitted that her "manners toward God" were "ruined," she may be struggling with feelings of guilt, resulting in a misinterpretation of the friend's suggestion.

### Lines 30–35

The fourth section, titled "Often," comes closest to pathos in this poem, particularly the first three lines. The speaker lets the reader know she wants to be "adult" and "try to wait for dark" to go to bed when apparently she feels like going to bed much sooner. However, she is rescued from total self-pity in the final three lines, if by no other means than a nice metaphor. Sleep is a sanctuary for the speaker and she likens it to a "coracle," or a small boat made of waterproof material stretched over a wicker or wooden frame. In the coracle she can "push away / from the massive pain" of mental illness the same way one would push a small craft away from a troubling shore.

## Lines 36–38

Line 36 moves the poem forward in time simply by revealing the speaker's age during the events of the fifth stanza. She is now in her "early thirties," and, as the title of this section ("Once There Was Light") suggests, experiences a moment of reprieve or "light." This section is one of the most highly imagistic sections of the entire piece, as it extends the metaphor of light to represent the speaker and all of humanity, and introduces a crow to represent depression. In lines 37 and 38, the speaker realizes she is a "speck of light in the great / river of light" that persists timelessly in a smooth, wavelike motion. This is the first time in the poem the speaker has anything positive to say about her position in the world or about the world in general.

## Lines 39–44

These lines describe the comfort and peace of mind the speaker feels during her break from depression. She does not explicitly state how long the break lasts, but the phrase "For a few / moments I floated, completely calm" is a good indication. No matter the length of time, what is most important is the kinship she feels with "the whole / human family." She even overcomes her typical drab, gray sadness long enough to announce that "We were all colors." Line 44 provides the best insight into the speaker's sense of euphoria; for once in her life she "no longer hated having to exist."

## Lines 45–49

The last stanza of "Once There Was Light" describes the speaker's return to melancholia in a very gripping metaphorical scene. She likens her depression to "a crow who smells hot blood" and hungrily rushes to retrieve her from her moments of peace in the "glowing stream" of light. Lines 48 and 49 make effective use of irony in the words melancholy uses to defend its actions. It seems the illness must *save* its human host from drowning in a sea of good health, and her response, understandably, is to weep "for days."

## Lines 50–55

These six lines in the sixth section (titled "In and Out") serve to calm the poem. The domestic scene of a dog consoling its owner by simply being near is actually a pleasant one, if considered outside the melancholic premise surrounding it. One can picture the loyal canine searching the house until he finds his loving master upstairs where the dog lies down with his head touching her foot. The dog's rhythmic breathing is a comfort to the woman and she describes it with a low-key tone and soothing words: "in and out, in / and out; a pause, a long sigh." In this stanza, what the dog accomplishes for its master is what the poet accomplishes for the reader—a moment of peace and quiet in the middle of a personal storm.

## Lines 56–62

In the first stanza of part seven (titled "Pardon"), the speaker returns to her dismal outlook for herself and an admission of her weariness with feigned hopefulness. She calls her body "a piece of burned meat," and then distances her *self* from what her physical being does, as though she is literally separated into warring parts. She refers to her own body as an "it," claiming that it "speaks / in my voice, dispatches obligations / haltingly, or not at all." The last three lines confess that "it" is "tired / beyond measure" of pretending that its heart is strong enough to continue.

## Lines 63–66

Few words are less poetic than "monoamine oxidase inhibitors," but in this poem they work quite well. These types of medication are sometimes called the antidepressants of last resort, and the speaker's dull announcement that "We move on" to them is further indication that her struggle continues and is, perhaps, worsening. Note that she uses the plural "we" instead of "I" in the opening line of this stanza. Apparently she still feels a separation from her *self*, as implied in the previous lines, but then suddenly in line 65, she returns to addressing herself as one being: "I feel as if I had drunk six cups / of coffee, but the pain stops / abruptly." The new drugs seem to ease her depression, although they also make her feel wired.

## Lines 67–72

In these lines, the speaker compares herself to a falsely-accused prisoner who suddenly finds herself pardoned and set free. One can imagine the joy of being released from jail, but one can also imagine the anger and resentment for having been wrongly locked up in the first place. The speaker's "prison" is her melancholia, and when the new antidepressants free her from it—at least for a while—she is able to return to the things in life she was forced to neglect, from her "marriage and friends" to her "desk, books, and chair."

## Lines 73–76

The uplifting end of the seventh part is shattered by the beginning of the poem's eighth part,

"Credo." As its title implies, the lines reveal a statement of belief, but, unlike formal credos, the faith asserted here is not a typical religious one. In fact, it is quite the opposite. The speaker believes "only in this moment / of well-being." The allusion to religious faith comes in her comparison of mental depression to an "Unholy ghost" that she knows is "certain to come again." The "pharmaceutical wonders" are *expected* to work only temporarily.

### Lines 77–83

In these lines, the speaker accuses the illness of being a "coarse, mean" individual who will come into her home and behave like a rude visitor, plopping his feet on the coffee table and leaning casually back on the couch. Just as casually, he will take away her ability to perform simple, daily functions such as speaking, sleeping, reading, and picking up the telephone to call her doctor.

### Lines 84–86

The last three lines of "Credo" sum up the speaker's feelings of complete futility and utter helplessness against the disease that has plagued her all her life. She believes there is nothing she can do to prevent it from returning over and over, and line 86 eerily suggests a sacred attachment to the disease. "*When I wake, I am still with thee*" reverberates with the haunting tone of a follower addressing her god.

### Lines 87–93

The title of the final section, "Wood Thrush," provides evidence of what may be the speaker's only savior. After all she has experienced, it is a simple bird that catches her most acute attention. At the outset of this stanza, she admits she is still "high" on drugs, this time naming Nardil specifically, but she also claims to be high on something else: "June light." This is unusual for someone who has never been able to enjoy the uncomplicated beauty of nature, and, even though her own state may not be so "natural," she still has cause to celebrate. While the "bile of desolation" pressed into her every pore at the beginning of the poem, it is now "easeful air" at her window that "presses through the screen," bringing the song of the wood thrush to her ears. The final phrase of line 93 clearly expresses the speaker's refreshed frame of mind as she listens to the bird singing: "I am overcome."

### Lines 94–96

Precisely what has caused the speaker to be "overcome" is not as obvious as it first seems. The softness of the June morning, the joyfulness of the bird's song, or witnessing such beauties of nature coming together while many people are still asleep are all likely candidates for the speaker's sudden elation, but it is actually more—or perhaps *less*—than that. Line 94 reveals that she is overcome "by ordinary contentment." All the common things of life most people take for granted have eluded her because of the illness. This one moment of peace that comes from listening to a bird's song may appear exaggerated, but it is indeed so important to the speaker that she must ask herself, "What hurt me so terribly / all my life until this moment?" It seems the simple song of the wood thrush has miraculously erased decades of pain, frustration, and hopelessness.

### Lines 97–100

The final four lines continue the nature theme that appears only in the last ten of the 100-line poem. For the first time, the speaker uses the word "love," and it expresses her feeling for the "small, swiftly / beating heart" of the wood thrush. Even the mention of the "great maples" is a positive turnabout for the speaker, for until this point she seemed incapable of noticing, much less appreciating, the grandeur of something as ordinary and as magnificent as a tree. The last line refers to something else she loves about the bird, "its bright, unequivocal eye." The selection of the word *unequivocal* is an interesting one. Its basic meaning of something that is completely clear and unambiguous, leaving no room for doubt or misunderstanding, is likely how she would "love" to feel about her own mind, or her own *self*. Many critics and readers claim the ending of the poem is a happy one. There is probably much room for debate on that matter.

## Themes

### Hope and Hopelessness

Poems with subjects laid bare before the reader and with language as plain as casual conversation tend to have fairly obvious themes. "Having it Out with Melancholy" is no exception, although its premise is a little unusual. As the title suggests, there is an argument occurring between the speaker and her own mental illness, which she personifies as "melancholy." Like most quarrels, this one involves give and take, and there is a constant flux of feelings. Essentially, the speaker fluctuates be-

## Topics For Further Study

- Which of the nine numbered sections of "Having it Out with Melancholy" do you think is the strongest in terms of poetic value and in conveying the poet's message? Give specific reasons and examples from the section to support your choice.

- Do you think this poem has a happy ending? Why or why not?

- Research the symptoms and treatment of clinical depression and manic depression? How do people suffering from clinical depression differ from those suffering from manic depression? How does treatment differ, if at all?

- Give examples of "ordinary contentment" that you have experienced and explain why simplicity is sometimes hard to come by in contemporary American life.

- Kenyon came to rely on monoamine oxidase inhibitors to help ease the severity of her depression. What do these drugs do to the human brain?

- After the events of September 11, 2001, many Americans and people throughout the world claim to be more depressed and anxious, including those who say they have not had those feelings before to any abnormal extent. What is the difference between this kind of depression and that which is diagnosed as "clinical?" Which is more prevalent and why?

- How might one reconcile the dilemma presented in the statement, "You wouldn't be so depressed if you really believed in God?" Would people of various faiths respond differently? Give some examples of how two or three different religions might approach the issue of believing in God and still suffering from a chronic malady. Conduct research to support your findings.

---

tween hope and hopelessness—a theme, as well as a condition, that lies at the very core of clinical depression.

The poem's first four stanzas are shrouded with the dismal prospect of going from birth to death without ever having a truly good moment. The speaker literally comes out of her mother's womb already depressed. The disease lurks in her nursery, follows her through school, and acts as a wedge between her and a friend who blames the speaker's mental problems on her lack of religious faith. From melancholy's point of view, people are on earth simply to "wait for death," and the speaker just needs to accept that. Even the list of all the medications she has tried serves only as a reminder of how desperate she is to find the relief that is apparently not coming. But then, about a third of the way through the poem, she admits there was a brief time in her early thirties when she found a "light," so to speak. She herself was a "speck of light" and all humanity made up a "great / river of light," and the speaker "no longer hated having to exist." But, for the depression sufferer, hope is short-lived. Like clockwork, melancholy returns to keep the speaker from drowning in hope and happiness.

This theme of hope and hopelessness plays throughout the remainder of the poem, with the speaker eking out small reprieves from her pain, sometimes just from the steady sound of the dog's breathing. Her next brush with hopefulness comes in an artificial form, as the "pharmaceutical wonders" to which she clings allow her both time and desire to find hope in a common, yet unlikely place for someone used to only dreariness and despair: the simple song of a bird and its "bright, unequivocal eye." Concluding the poem on this note seems to grant it a happy ending, the speaker having won the argument with melancholy and triumphed over its debilitating hold on her. However, the seesaw quarrel that dominates the entire poem may indeed swing back the other way if only a few more lines are added.

## Simple Pleasures

If there is a single main message in this poem, it is not revealed until the final stanza. The feeling of "ordinary contentment" is so unusual for the speaker that she claims she is "overcome" with it. After all she has endured, it is the simple pleasures—things most people take for granted—that astound her the most. Common occurrences like birds singing in the early morning are often overlooked by people at the start of a busy day. Instead of appreciating the daily, ordinary wonders of nature, many people spend their time waiting for a major event to occur—whether a positive event such as a raise at work, marriage, or graduation, or a negative event such as illness, loss of a job, or death. Because the speaker in this poem is so akin to negative things, she is suddenly overwhelmed by one of the most benign, commonplace happenings on the planet. She would likely trade "what hurt [her] so terribly" for a lifetime of simple contentment.

# Style

## Contemporary Lyric Poetry

Generally, lyric poetry expresses subjective thoughts and feelings, most often those based on deeply personal emotions or observations. Kenyon is recognized as a contemporary lyric poet, for her work is subjective and tends to address contemporary, everyday life. "Having it Out with Melancholy" is an example.

There is no rhyme in this poem and no cadence in the line formations of "Having it Out with Melancholy." Stanza lengths are uneven, with lines containing some alliteration. The language is straightforward and conversational. One could easily type the words into prose paragraphs and read them without missing anything and without having them sound too poetic. The most intentional formatting is in balancing each section's subject with its length. Some sections require more elaboration, as in the first, fifth, seventh, eighth, and ninth parts. In these, the poet tends to explain more, to use more vivid imagery to convey her messages. The fourth and sixth sections each contain six lines and one brief, striking image.

The poem's second section, "Bottles," is unique in the poem because nearly half of it consists of a list of antidepressant medications. Presenting a run-down of pharmaceutical names helps the speaker make a point about her dependency and desperation. It also maintains the very contemporary aspects of the poem. The third section, "Suggestion from a Friend," speaks for itself. The briefest part, it may also be the most poignant. Apparently, Kenyon felt no further explanation was needed for this section.

# Historical Context

The first half of the 1990s in the United States was marked by social and political volatility, from the heavily televised Gulf War and dramatic reporting from the front lines to the election of Bill Clinton as president, and the onslaught of public scandals brought to light by media exposing high-profile people in less-than-favorable circumstances. President Clinton himself was at the center of one of the most publicized sex scandals in political history when the Monica Lewinski fiasco hit the news later in the decade. Overall, the 1990s reflected the concerns of a society blessed with a period of strong economic growth and an optimism for financial gains, while at the same time besieged with doubts and cynicism toward American values that appeared to be withering into sensationalism, melodrama, and "acceptable" violence.

Although the war in Vietnam was the first conflict to be viewed in American living rooms via television, it was the 1991 Gulf War that inundated the airwaves with live broadcasts and blow-by-blow accounts of the battle from newscasters who became as much a part of the drama as military personnel. People tuned in to watch the action unfold between the United States and Iraq just the same as if they were watching a major sporting event or an evening soap opera. While the question of ethics did arise in the minds of some Americans who felt the horrors of war were being overshadowed by the excitement of seeing it from a safe distance, enough people kept watching to make television news one of the biggest, most profitable "entertainment" venues of the decade.

Public officials also provided fuel for the scandal-seeking media, mostly with sexual content. In 1991, Clarence Thomas was a nominee for the United States Supreme Court when allegations he had sexually harassed employees in the Equal Employment Opportunity Commission (EEOC) became public. Anita Hill, a former coworker of Clarence Thomas, accused the former head of the EEOC of making unwanted sexual advances, and when a judiciary committee convened for hearings on the case, it turned into a media circus. Congress had its own share of sexual harassment cases, as Senators Brock Adams and Robert Packwood and Representative Mel Reynolds were all accused of making improper advances toward women in the early 1990s. Again, the media gave these stories high priority, adding fuel to the disillusionment and emotional tensions many Americans were experiencing in the final decade of the twentieth century.

More sobering media coverage came from an amateur cameraman who in 1992 recorded the beating of a black motorist, Rodney King, by four white police officers in Los Angeles, California. The tape was broadcast over and over again on national television, enraging much of the public and kindling nationwide charges of racism against the Los Angeles Police Department. When the four officers were acquitted, rioting broke out in Los Angeles and fifty-two people died as a result. The riots were captured in graphic details on the evening news. A year later, a federal court re-tried the Rodney King case, and two of the four officers were convicted and given jail terms.

Perhaps no high-profile criminal case of the decade was as sensational and exploited as the O. J. Simpson murder trial, in which Simpson was accused of killing his ex-wife Nicole Simpson and her friend Ron Goldman. From live-action filming of the low-speed police pursuit of Simpson on a California freeway to a courtroom battle that ran through most of 1994, every moment of the trial, no matter how tedious, was broadcast on television. Attorneys on both sides became celebrities, and even their lives outside the courtroom became fair game for media attention and scrutiny. In the end, Simpson, who is black, was found not guilty, and public opinion tended to be divided along racial lines. Regardless of the race issue, however, few could deny that the overall carnival atmosphere of the trial served only to make a mockery of the American judicial system.

Along with the in-your-face broadcasting of political scandals and real-life police action during the early 1990s, Americans also endured coverage of increased violence in schools, anti-government survivalist groups that spawned the "Unabomber" and cult leader David Koresh, the bombing of the New York City World Trade Center in 1993, and the bombing of a federal building in Oklahoma City in 1995. Such social turmoil may have a connection to the rise in prescription drug abuse during this decade. More people began using pain relievers and tranquilizers for non-medical purposes, with increases of more than 100 percent from 1980 to 1990. While it is unlikely that publicized violence and graphic details of unscrupulous behavior can exacerbate true cases of clinical depression, perhaps it is not far-fetched to assume a connection between social upheaval and emotional stress. This is not to suggest that living in more peaceful times would have had any effect on Kenyon's—or anyone else's—struggle with mental illness. It could, however, foster fewer tendencies to turn to drugs for personal good when the world outside seems hopelessly bad.

## Critical Overview

Kenyon published only four volumes of poetry in her lifetime, but each book has been well received by critics and readers in general who find her work both provocative and accessible. Most critics applaud her ability to present both everyday subjects, such as pets or New England landscapes, and serious topics, such as terminal illness and depression, in a manner that justifies their presence in the poem. "Having it Out with Melancholy" has been used as an example by more than one reviewer, and the book in which it was first published, *Constance*, was one of her most highly acclaimed. Writing for *American Poetry Review*, critic Robin Becker claims that "Kenyon writes with a spare authority, her collection peppered with the language of hymn, psalm, and prayer.... [Her] intimacy with rural New England provides stunning and consoling imagery, even as she writes of illness and the death of loved ones." A review of *Constance* in *Publishers Weekly* states that "The cumulative effect of these quiet, unassuming poems lingers long after this slim volume is closed.... [Kenyon] writes, in addition to illness, of sleep, insomnia and death. She interacts with the insects, birds and flowers in her New Hampshire landscape, relying on their fragility to teach her of her own." Even prior to her final volume, Kenyon was already producing work that achieved the same "cumulative effect" that critics recognized in *Constance*. Writing about her 1990 collection, *Let Evening Come*, critic Robin Latimer discusses a poem in which a "contemplative but disciplined speaker" who has just learned of a loved one's cancer "retains the capacity to 'snap the blue leash onto the D-ring / of the dog's collar,' to attend to 'that part of life / [which] is intact.'" Latimer goes on to note that the act of dog-walking is used as a "simple image of coping, of the mind strolling with itself as it waits for what the speaker dreads." Just as in section 6 of "Having it Out with Melancholy," the simple pleasure of taking care of a pet is both commonplace and vital to this poet, and critics acknowledge the repetition of similar images in Kenyon's work as much as self-induced therapy as a signature theme. Ultimately, it is Kenyon's mixture of soft language and tough topics that attracts both critics and readers and sets her apart from other poets who tend to lapse into sentimentality or anger when addressing such personal problems.

## Criticism

### Pamela Steed Hill

*Hill is the author of a poetry collection, has published widely in literary journals, and is an editor for a university publications department. In the following essay, Hill suggests that religious faith and personal spirituality play a much greater role in this poem than is obvious on its surface or in the speaker's actual statements.*

The issue of religion in "Having it Out with Melancholy" appears minor in comparison to the overriding descriptions of and meditations on what life is like for a woman suffering from severe depression. By far, the themes in this poem center on the speaker's desperate attempt to be *normal*, to go through a day without sadness and dread, a day without hopelessness and drugs that sometimes work and sometimes do not. Her consideration of religious faith seems fleeting, at best, even cynical, as she bluntly announces her friend's opinion that she "wouldn't be so depressed" if only she believed in God. She allows this reprimand only two lines, then dismisses it to return to further lamentation on her own misery. Perhaps this summation is too hasty and based only on the poem's surface, or on what the speaker says instead of what she implies. A closer look may reveal that these two lines are the most powerful in the entire work and that spirituality is actually a primary concern of the woman's, as evidenced by the religious imagery and innuendoes she scatters throughout this story of her tragic life.

It seems that, since birth, the cards of gloom have been stacked against this speaker who claims she belonged more to depression's "anti-urge" than to her mother as an infant. The entire first section hangs on the notion that memories from the crib really do exist and that some are so strong, so torturous, that the grown-up can recall them vividly even at the distance of middle age. Also, in this first part, the speaker sneaks in the first allusion to religious piety, professing that her "manners toward God" were "ruined" in childhood and blaming depression for destroying them. What *manners* does she mean? It is an odd term to apply to one's relationship with a supreme being, but, in the sense that this is a child's relationship, the word likely implies a little girl's obedience and good behavior toward such things as saying her prayers or not giggling in church or in believing Heaven is a beautiful, gilded city somewhere above the clouds. Because her manners are ruined, she does not believe in anything other than sadness, despair, and eventual death. At least, that is what she would have her readers presume.

The speaker makes no more mention of God or religious faith until the two little lines that make up section three of the poem. The message in them comes as somewhat a shock for its abrupt, almost brutal context, but here again the speaker implies, through the words of her friend, that she has no faith in God. Then, the subject is dropped as quickly as it arises, but that may be misleading. The speaker returns to the subject—if not specifically, then emblematically—by the end of her story. So, too, will this writing.

First, it is interesting to take a look at other religious allusions that appear in the poem, such as in the fifth section in which the speaker employs symbols of light and darkness, peace and violence to describe a time of welcomed reprieve in her ongoing battle with mental illness. She imagines herself "a speck of light in the great / river of light," a metaphor seemingly built around images of God or Christ whose presence glows, emanating upon human beings who are faithful followers. Her moment in the light of a supreme being is cut short by the return of melancholy, represented this time by a "crow who smells hot blood." Crows, of course, are black, and they often symbolize the dark presence of evil or some lurking terror. The speaker's peace of mind, then, is wrenched from her the way a demonic creature may yank a helpless victim from the godlike "glowing stream" in which she finally feels secure. Even the words she attributes to melancholy—"'I'll hold you up. I never let my dear / ones drown!'"—sound as though they could come from the mouth of God in a modern interpretation of the Bible. The irony, of course, is that this time the savior is more like Satan.

Other than section three, the strongest suggestions regarding religion and spirituality in this poem appear in section eight, the very name of which may be a direct reference to the Apostles of Christ. One definition of "credo" is simply "creed," which usually implies a formal statement of religious belief or an open confession of faith. But, "Credo," when capitalized, refers to the "Apostle's Creed," or the Christian system of belief as ascribed to the twelve Apostles and often used in some church services today. The statements that make up this section may be seen as the speaker's confession of what she believes in, and she appears forthright about it: "I believe only in this moment / of well-being." The defiance in these words is unmistakable. Believing only in the moment at hand directly conflicts with the Christian notion of having faith in eternity, but the speaker explains her reasoning just as candidly as she states her creed: "Unholy ghost, / you are certain to come again." Notice the explicit allusion to spirituality here, as the woman compares her illness to the anti-Christ, or the polar opposite of the Holy Ghost. She accuses depression of being like a demonic force, able to possess her and turn her "into someone who can't / take the trouble to speak; someone / who can't sleep, or who does nothing / but sleep." In other words, she is completely helpless against this demon that has taken over her mind and, apparently, her soul. She plucks language and tone straight from the Bible in her final resigning line: "*When I awake, I am still with thee.*"

"Having it Out with Melancholy" may end on a more positive note than it begins, but the continuous roller coaster ride of clinical depression makes it clear that a downhill dip is just around the corner. The speaker must find something beyond her own physical being, beyond the chemical make-up of her brain in order, simply, to live. This brings readers back to section three—that tiny part of the poem that holds the weight of its message. The suggestion from a friend obviously implies that the speaker does not really believe in God, but the contention of this essay is that she really *does*. She spends too much time in the poem making references to religious entities and spiritual needs not to have them count for something—for quite a lot, actually. Section three is brief for a reason: it says it all. It encompasses what is at the heart of the speaker's most basic concern and her most dire need: finding comfort in a world of personal torture, reaching a spiritual heaven in spite of her physical and

> *It encompasses what is at the heart of the speaker's most basic concern and her most dire need: finding comfort in a world of personal torture, reaching a spiritual heaven in spite of her physical and mental hell.*

mental hell. So, this section is ultimately ironic. If she did not believe in God, she would not waste time agonizing over the gulf that the illness has created between her *real* self—the happy, content, and spiritual individual she wants to be—and the tired, disillusioned woman she sees in the mirror most every day. If she did not believe in God, then bringing up the subject, from childhood through adulthood, would not be necessary. But, the memories she describes and the thoughts she confesses clearly indicate that the subjects of God and personal spirituality are foremost in this speaker's troubled mind.

Looking at "Having it Out with Melancholy" from the religious perspective provides a possible alternative to a context that seems overburdened with one sad detail after another of the speaker's life and her battle with depression. Without an underlying theme, the poem may falter into a somber diary of a woman's chronic problems, as benign and defeating as the list of prescription drugs that makes up half of section two. But, much more is going on in this poem, and the main theme of how important it is to recognize the beauty and peacefulness in something as natural and simple as a bird's song is complemented well by the role that personal faith may play in that recognition. It is, after all, the *unequivocal* eye of the wood thrush that the speaker claims to love, and this notion of having no doubts, no ambiguities, must be one she would love to apply to her *self* as well.

**Source:** Pamela Steed Hill, Critical Essay on "Having it Out with Melancholy," in *Poetry for Students*, The Gale Group, 2003.

## What Do I Read Next?

- Kenyon's first poetry collection, *From Room to Room*, was published in 1978. It is interesting to contrast the poems in this early volume to the much darker, despairing ones in her later work. Themes in this collection center on the beauty of nature, the tranquility of country life, and gardening, instead of depression, illness, and death.

- Maxine Kumin's collection of poems entitled *The Long Marriage* (2002) addresses her relationship with her husband of more than fifty years along with her "marriage" to poetry and her "marriage" to nature. Like Kenyon, Kumin has spent much of her life in rural New Hampshire. Her poems also deal with personal tragedy but in a remarkably different way from Kenyon's poems.

- First-time author Jeffrey Smith's candid memoir called *Where the Roots Reach for Water: A Personal and Natural History of Melancholia* (1999) is a provocative examination of melancholia. When one antidepressant after another fails to relieve his symptoms, Smith decides to try to live with his depression, and this book is a fascinating account of the results of that decision.

- Dr. Kay Redfield Jamison, professor of medicine, is a world-renowned expert on manic depression. In her 1995 publication *An Unquiet Mind*, she provides a personal testimony of her own struggle since adolescence with the disease and how it has shaped her life. Jamison writes with vivid prose, wit, and even humor, making this highly complex and misunderstood subject accessible to anyone who wants to learn more about it.

### Kate Covintree

*Covintree is a graduate of Randolph-Macon Women's College with a degree in English. In this essay, Covintree examines the connection between faith and mental illness discussed in the poem, focusing primarily on Kenyon's choice of three section titles.*

Carefully divided into nine sections, Jane Kenyon's poem, "Having it Out with Melancholy," from her 1993 collection entitled *Constance*, is a personal and detailed account of living with depression. Throughout the poem, Kenyon marries this struggle with concepts that surround the understanding of faith. Kenyon writes that depression and faith are linked and connected. However, she appears to be unclear in her conclusions about this connection. Does she believe, as the third section suggests through its one couplet, that one's strong faith can heal depression? Is Kenyon's point that treasuring the simple moments during depression, like following the dog's breathy rhythm found in section six, brings greater peace than any ritual of faith? Or, is it her main purpose to show depression and faith as almost synonymous forces at work in one's life since, as the first section states, birth? Instead of focusing on one possibility, she introduces various relationships. In this way, the emphasis is not on the cause and effect of these two almost intangibles, but the fact that both faith and mental illness can be connected in any number of ways. Kenyon makes this deliberate connection to show the mystery both hold within the experience of living. One way she does this is through the titles of her sections. Three of the nine sections are titled with religious terminology. By titling one third of her sections with terms commonly used in religious circles, Kenyon demonstrates the connection of faith and depression as a strong emphasis in the poem.

The first section with a title of religious inference is section 5. Kenyon titles this section, "Once There Was Light," preparing the reader for an experience of creation or epiphany. Perhaps her story will be like the one told in Genesis in the Bible and surely with the light will come a revelation. What does come with this section is Kenyon's most upbeat and optimistic of all her nine sections. The light that she is writing about is a moment of amazing clarity, where she is removed from her mental illness and connected to every other being. Here, she is removed from her melancholy and brought to "the great / river of light that undulates through time."

What she then describes in this river could be seen as an image of Heaven:

> I was floating with the whole
> human family. We were all colors—those
> who are living now, those who have died,
> those who are not yet born.

In her enlightened state, she can see those who came before her and those who will follow. She can see her place in the picture of creation and the beauty of the shared experience of life and faith. In addition, she is "completely calm" in this experience and "no longer hate[s] having to exist." Kenyon is writing of a perfect experience, in many ways an experience of Heaven. In the first three stanzas of the poem, she is removed from struggle and granted peace.

This section was based on a true experience for Kenyon. As she said to Bill Moyers in a 1993 interview that can be found in her book *A Hundred White Daffodils*, "I really had a vision of that once.... I relaxed into existence in a way that I never had before." This heaven-like vision allowed her the opportunity to appreciate the world in which she lived and remove herself from the confines of depression. In the Bill Moyers interview, she continues to clarify the image by saying that "after having this wave of buoyant emotion, my understanding was changed fundamentally." Yet, even with this changed understanding and her image of an euphoric heaven, Kenyon ends this fifth section with an abrupt removal out of the experience.

According to the Bill Moyers interview in *A Hundred White Daffodils*, Kenyon herself supposed that this change was due to a bad crash following an episode of mania. Still, Kenyon leaves this final stanza in this section and compares her illness to a black crow pulling her out of her few moments of clarity. She personifies depression as a crow "who smells hot blood," and then talks with the crow as if they have a personal relationship. Kenyon shows herself to have a personal relationship to depression and not, as the third section advised, with God. It appears in this stanza that depression has become the unknown force in which Kenyon is forced to believe. The crow acts as a savior, rescuing the speaker from "the glowing stream" and reasons to the speaker that he is saving her from drowning, "'I'll hold you up. I never let my dear / ones drown!'" Yet, neither the reader nor the speaker wants to be pulled away or saved by this force because this rescue removes the peace and reinstates melancholy. Though Kenyon has been given a life-altering experience and a glimpse at Heaven, she has been brought by her illness back to a state of despair.

It is in this despair that Kenyon begins her first stanza of the section titled "Pardon." Thus titled, the reader awaits the absolution, forgiveness, and perhaps penance. Before the pardon, the speaker must confess to what pains her or perhaps, one could say, her "sins." Sin can be viewed as separation from God. Kenyon shows depression to be

> "This well-being is brief and unpredictable, but it is where Kenyon maintains her faith."

a separation from self. While depressed, the speaker sees herself as "[a] piece of burned meat" who is "tired of trying / to be stouthearted, tired / beyond measure." This is Kenyon's confession to the debilitating effect that this illness places on her and her life. This first stanza reiterates the speaker's struggle with her separation from self (and from God) that is shown throughout the first four sections of this poem. By placing the pardon in the second half of the poem (and the second half of this section), she begins to bring relief.

As a condition of the pardon, her penance is in the form of the "monoamine oxidase inhibitors." As in the poem's second section, the speaker is again at the mercy of prescribed cures for her illness. By placing these drugs in the section called "Pardon," Kenyon parallels the day to day use of drugs to a minister's advice for removing oneself from sinful behavior. These prescriptions remove the pain and the sin "[of] a crime she did not commit." Kenyon is grateful for the relief the penance of drugs brings. Yet, she views this pardon as partially undeserved, resenting the way depression removed her from life without her consent or permission.

She has been isolated, and now with the assistance of drugs, can return to the normalcy of life. With this, forgiveness comes. The speaker finds solace in the common parts of life. Forgiveness comes in the small and detailed portions; "marriage and friends ... pink fringed hollyhocks ... desk, books, and chair."

Once in drug therapy, she can see clearly what it is she believes in, and so her next section begins. Kenyon titles section 8 "Credo," and with this, a Christian reader might await a litany of what Kenyon believes, like creeds found in so many churches. What Kenyon gives, however is not a list of several beliefs, but belief in one thing "this moment / of well being." In making her belief compromise the second line and part of the third of the first stanza in the section, Kenyon gives the reader her belief for only a moment. It is obviously the moment that is so important to her. In section 5, Kenyon's calm comes only "[f]or a few / moments." In section 9, the moment will return as "ordinary contentment." This well-being is brief and unpredictable, but it is where Kenyon maintains her faith.

Kenyon begins to resign herself to the constancy of her depression and to the brief moments of release she will have from it. In her "An Interview with Bill Moyers" found in *A Hundred White Daffodils*, Kenyon connects her belief in the moment with her belief in God. In this interview she says, "[w]hen you get to be my age and you've lived with depression for a number of years, you begin to have a context for believing that you will feel better at some point." In this way, she resolves herself to her illness and to God's presence in this. In the same Moyers interview, Kenyon states that when depressed she can think about faith by calling out to God, and these moments of being better or even the belief that she will feel better eventually become the answer from God. In this way, Kenyon reveals to the reader "a God who, if you ask, forgives you no matter how far down in the well you are." This is the God she tells Moyers in the interview she was introduced to in her later years.

These moments of absolution must sustain her through her illness, because as the section suggests, depression becomes the "[u]nholy ghost ... certain to come again." Kenyon shows there is nothing redeemable about depression. She personifies depression as "[c]oarse, mean" and immobilizing. Depression is ever present. The speaker says "[t]here is nothing I can do / against your coming." Yet, by titling the section "Credo," Kenyon shifts the focus from the paralysis of depression to the possibility of clarity in the future. The illness is not a punishment from God but something that God will help her overcome.

"Having it Out with Melancholy" is an intensely intimate observation of Kenyon's relationship to mental illness. Her carefully crafted language describes the various conflicts and connections between mental illness, traditional beliefs, and personal experience. Though personal to her, these nine sections provide universal insights into the struggles of the mentally ill. In the process, she offers hope through her keen attention to the simple details like, God, dogs, and a wood thrush, hope that can help every person survive.

**Source:** Kate Covintree, Critical Essay on "Having it Out with Melancholy," in *Poetry for Students*, The Gale Group, 2003.

## Sources

Becker, Robin, "*Constance* (book reviews)," in *American Poetry Review*, Vol. 23, No. 6, November–December 1994, p. 23.

Kenyon, Jane, *Constance*, Graywolf Press, 1993.

———, "An Interview with Bill Moyers," in *A Hundred White Daffodils*, Graywolf Press, 1999, pp. 145–71

Latimer, Robin M., "Jane Kenyon," in *Dictionary of Literary Biography*, Vol. 120: *American Poets Since World War II, Third Series*, edited by R. S. Gwynn, Gale Research, 1992, pp. 172–75.

Review of *Constance*, in *Publishers Weekly*, Vol. 240, No. 28, July 12, 1993, p. 75.

## Further Reading

Hall, Donald, *Without: Poems*, Mariner Books, 1999.
Published after the death of his wife (Kenyon), the poems in this Donald Hall collection are all dedicated to the memory of Kenyon and their life together. Poem titles include "Her Long Illness," "Last Days," "Letter after a Year," and "Weeds and Peonies."

Hornback, Bert G., ed., *"Bright Unequivocal Eye": Poems, Papers, and Remembrances from the First Jane Kenyon Conference*, Peter Lang, 2000.
This book contains a collection of writings by poets and teachers who attended a 1998 conference held in honor of Kenyon in Louisville, Kentucky. The essays include such topics as "Our Lady of Sorrows: Some Thoughts on Jane Kenyon," "Affective Disorders: The Treatment of Emotion in Jane Kenyon's Poetry," and "The Interior Garden in Jane Kenyon's Poetry." The title of this book is derived from the last line of "Having it Out with Melancholy."

Kenyon, Jane, *A Hundred White Daffodils: Essays, the Akhmatova Translations, Newspaper Columns, Notes, Interviews, and One Poem*, Graywolf Press, 1999.
As the title suggests, this posthumous collection contains a miscellany of Kenyon's writing, including essays about her small country community, working in her garden, and a candid examination of what it is like to live with a terminal illness. There are also translations of some of the works of Russian poet Anna Akhmatova, and one of Kenyon's own unfinished poems.

———, *Otherwise: New and Selected Poems*, Graywolf Press, 1996.
The poems for this collection were selected in 1995 by Kenyon on her deathbed, with the assistance of her husband (poet Donald Hall). It includes poems from her first four books, as well as twenty previously uncollected poems.

# I Go Back to May 1937

## Sharon Olds
## 1987

Sharon Olds's poem "I Go Back to May 1937" is included in her collection *The Gold Cell*, published in 1987. Like much of Olds's poetry, "I Go Back to May 1937" is concerned with exploring the relationship between wife and husband, parents and children. In this poem the speaker travels back to a time just before her parents' marriage so that she might warn them of the mistake they are about to make. Although the speaker knows her parents will face pain, she cannot stop their union, since to do so would deny her own existence. She wants to live and so these people must be permitted to marry.

Olds has been unwilling to provide information to critics and readers about her personal life, including information about her parents. Many critics search her poems hoping to find some autobiographical truth about her, but Olds has made clear that she is trying to separate her life into two spheres, what she calls "the life of art and the life of life." Accordingly, it is difficult to know exactly what inspires the content of this poem. Is it the speaker's own unhappy childhood or is she responding from the experience of a child of divorce? The reader cannot know and is instead forced to find meaning in the words, separate from finding meaning in the poet's autobiography.

For her readers, Olds's poems seem very personal, including "I Go Back to May 1937." Many of her poems are concerned with the speaker's relationship with her father, as she seeks to understand his alcoholism, his abandonment of his family through divorce, and his painful death. The

*Sharon Olds*

exploration of her parents' marriage—beginning as this poem does, just prior to their wedding—presents the essential paradox. The speaker wishes her parents had never married, had never made one another's lives so miserable. She wishes her own childhood had been spared the torment of her parents' unhappiness, and yet to eliminate their marriage would be to eliminate the speaker. This paradox gives the poem a unique tension.

## Author Biography

Sharon Olds was born November 19, 1942, in San Francisco, California. She received a bachelor's degree from Stanford University (1964) and a Ph.D. from Columbia University (1972). Many years ago, Olds decided she would not speak about her family, and so little is known about her personal life. For instance, Olds's poetry focuses on relationships, especially the relationship between father and daughter, but there is no information about Olds's parents, such as who they are, if they are still alive, or what her childhood was like.

Olds's poem "I Go Back to May 1937" explores the meeting of two people, whom the speaker would rather stay apart. Readers may assume the poem is about Olds's parents, though Olds has eliminated such easy analysis of her work by limiting public knowledge of her family life. What is known is that Olds married and that her two children were born while she was still a student at Columbia. Olds has also spoken frankly about the influence of religion on her life, noting that she was brought up to be a Calvinist Christian, with strong beliefs in punishment and hell.

Although Olds began writing poetry while still in her twenties, she was thirty-seven before her first collection of poems, *Satan Says* (1980), was published. This collection won the 1981 San Francisco Poetry Center Award. Her next collection of poems, *The Dead and the Living* (1984), was a 1984 Lamont Poetry selection of the Academy of American Poets and won a 1985 National Book Critics Circle Award. Two more collections of poetry followed in 1987, *The Gold Cell* and *The Matter of This World*. Olds's poetry collection *The Father* was shortlisted for the T. S. Eliot Prize in England and was a finalist for a National Book Critics Circle Award. *The Wellspring: Poems* (1996) and *Blood, Tin, Straw* (1999) were also well received. *The Unswept Room* is due for publication in September 2002.

Olds's work has also been published in several anthologies, including *The Norton Anthology of Poetry* (2001), *Maverick Poets: An Anthology* (1988), *The Heath Introduction to Poetry* (2000), *The Bedford Introduction to Literature* (2001), and *The Longman Anthology of American Poetry* (1992). In addition, Olds's work has been included in *The Pushcart Prize: Best of the Small Presses* on six occasions. *The Pushcart Prize* collections are considered prestigious anthologies, featuring the best of American literature each year.

Olds teaches poetry for the graduate creative writing program at New York University in New York City. She was selected to be the New York State poet laureate from 1998 to 2000. Augmenting her professional accomplishments, Olds gives back to the community as the founding director of the New York University workshop program for the physically challenged at Goldwater Hospital in New York.

## Poem Text

I see them standing at the formal gates of their
    colleges,

I see my father strolling out
under the ochre sandscone arch, the
red tiles glinting like bent
plates of blood behind his head, I                          5
see my mother with a few light books at her hip
standing at the pillar made of tiny bricks with the
wrought-iron gate still open behind her, its
sword-tips black in the May air,
they are about to graduate, they are about to get           10
    married,
they are kids, they are dumb, all they know is they
    are
innocent, they would never hurt anybody.
I want to go up to them and say Stop,
don't do it—she's the wrong woman,
he's the wrong man, you are going to do things              15
you cannot imagine you would ever do,
you are going to do bad things to children,
you are going to suffer in ways you never heard of,
you are going to want to die. I want to go
up to them there in the late May sunlight and say           20
    it,
her hungry pretty blank face turning to me,
her pitiful beautiful untouched body,
his arrogant handsome blind face turning to me,
his pitiful beautiful untouched body,
but I don't do it. I want to live. I                        25
take them up like the male and female
paper dolls and bang them together
at the hips like chips of flint as if to
strike sparks from them, I say
Do what you are going to do, I will tell about it.          30

## Poem Summary

### Lines 1–9

In the first line, the speaker refers to "gates" and "colleges." The plural form of these words signals there are differences between the two adults being described. They are distinctly separate people, each coming from a different background and location. In the second and third lines the man emerges from under an ochre sandstone arch, which creates an earthy image of clay walls, tinted dark yellow or reddish brown, in the reader's mind. Combine the image of the sandstone arch with the "red tiles glinting like bent plates of blood," and an image of the southwestern United States emerges. Red ceramic tile roofs are a common architectural feature of Arizona and southern California, as are earthy brown walls. The "glinting" tiles suggest the sun's glare off the roof, which could also indicate the Southwest, a region known for its sunny, warm climate.

In contrast to the man's location, the woman stands at a "pillar made of tiny bricks," her books carried against her hip. A wrought-iron gate is behind her. While the man emerges from his college by passing under an arch, the woman must pass through the gate to begin her new life. The bricks and wrought-iron gate suggest a different location than that of the man's. The woman's college may be in the northeastern United States, perhaps New England. Her location, then, would be the opposite of the man's. And while she emerges with books, he is empty-handed.

## Media Adaptations

- *Sharon Olds: The Lannon Literary Series* is available on VHS. This 1991 production is sixty minutes long and includes Olds reading from *The Dead and the Living* and *The Gold Cell* as well as from unpublished work. This video also includes an interview with Olds by Lewis MacAdams.

- *The Power of the Word* with Bill Moyers, is a six-part, 1989 Public Broadcasting series, with a running time of 360 minutes. It includes interviews with many contemporary poets, including Sharon Olds. This series is available on VHS.

- *The Best of NPR: Writers on Writing* is a ninety-minute audiocassette with contemporary writers, including Sharon Olds, talking about their work.

- *Poets in Person* (1991) is a fourteen-part audio series featuring more than a dozen contemporary American writers discussing their poetry and how they composed some of their favorite poems. Sharon Olds talks about turning real life into poetry. Each cassette is thirty minutes in length.

- *In Their Own Voices: A Century of Recorded Poetry* (1996) is a four-CD boxed set featuring poets reading their own work. Many of the selections included are old recordings, some from as early as the nineteenth century, but this set also includes many contemporary poets reading their work. Sharon Olds reads her poem "Wonder."

These basic differences alert the reader to the divisions that separate the man and woman. They are not only separated by gender, but by location and culture as well. And although he leaves the books of academia behind; she still grasps her books to her body.

### Lines 10–12

The speaker now establishes the man's and woman's innocence. She tells her reader that the couple is about to graduate from college, and so the reader imagines the man and woman are young, probably in their early twenties. To reinforce the image of youth and inexperience, the speaker relates, "they are kids, they are dumb." The speaker also says they would "never hurt anybody." They are so innocent that the man and woman fail to see that their wedding might someday lead to pain. They see only the movement from their single college days into a new married existence. They are too young to consider their marriage might be a mistake. But the speaker is aware of the disaster awaiting the couple. She writes from the future, having seen the past, and knows that the couple stands on the precipice of a serious action, one that will affect others.

### Lines 13–19

The speaker considers the actions she might take to prevent this tragedy from occurring. She considers stopping the man and the woman. She wants to "go up to them and say Stop." The capital letter at the beginning of "Stop" suggests the red sign along the road, an absolute message for any driver. The speaker wants the couple's movement toward marriage to be blocked, and so she adds the imperative "don't do it" to emphasize her need to stop the marriage. The speaker does not tell them they are too young. Instead she says, "she's the wrong woman," and "he's the wrong man." The speaker warns that because they are wrong for one another, they will do things they cannot imagine. To strengthen her emphasis, the speaker continues, "you are going to do bad things to children." The reminder here is of the pain an unhappy marriage can cause children. The next lines make clear that not only the children will suffer, but the man and woman will suffer as well "in ways you never heard of." The reader is informed the misery is going to be particularly extreme, so severe that the man and woman "are going to want to die." The picture painted in these few lines is one of great unhappiness, a marriage so destructive that the children will carry the scars for a lifetime and the parents will find solace in wishing for death.

### Lines 20–25

These lines suggest the depth of the speaker's anguish. The speaker tells the reader how she would like to have warned the man and woman, how she might have tried to stop their marriage, but that she could not do so. Once again the speaker speaks from the future. She has the omniscience of a god, having seen the end result of this couple's union. As she did in the first line, the speaker again establishes the time: at graduation in late May. It is another reminder, two-thirds of the way through the poem, of the couple's youth, of their innocence that day in 1937 when they emerged from college. The woman's face is "hungry," ready to seize upon new desires and opportunities, but the blankness of her face also suggests she is unable to comprehend the risk she is taking. The blankness may also suggest the lack of experience with which the woman greets the world; nothing is written upon her brow, and her eyes lack the knowledge that pain will soon bring.

In contrast, the man is described as "arrogant," a clear allusion to his unwarranted pride, which was emphasized earlier when "he strolled out" and away from his college. The man did not simply "walk," he "strolled," suggesting the sort of leisurely walk of a supremely confident individual. The man's "blind face," however, tells the reader the man is as limited and unable to see as the woman.

The parallelism and repetition of the lines, "pitiful beautiful untouched body," suggest the emptiness of the marriage, but these are words that also hint at great loneliness and loss. These bodies have not known great passion and intimacy. The repetition of the lines is separated slightly, just as the man and woman are separated. She is beautiful and he is handsome, but their attractiveness has not brought them together. The speaker sees all these things: their beauty, their aloneness, their loneliness, and their blindness, and she wants to say, "Stop, / don't do it."

### Lines 26–30

The final lines of the poem relate the speaker's acceptance of her parents' fate and of her inability to alter the past. As she tells the reader in line 25, "I don't do it," she does not stop her parents from marrying. The speaker acknowledges she wants to live. To prevent the marriage and all the misery that flows from it is to prevent her existence. So, in a final effort, the speaker imagines she can force her parents to love one another. She tries to create a spark and ignite a passion between them by imagining her parents are paper dolls she can force together. The speaker says she will "bang" the two together. The word "bang" suggests the force with which the speaker hits the two together, but also suggests sexual intercourse (in vulgar slang), a meaning that works well for this poem. In lines 22 and 24, the speaker has made clear that passion has left this couple untouched. Now in banging the paper dolls together, the speaker would create intimacy where none has existed. Like "chips of flint" the speaker tries to ignite a flame that will consume the couple and melt them together.

In the last line, the speaker seems to acknowledge and accept the futility of her attempts. She cannot change the past, nor can she force a connection that never existed. With the words, "Do what you are going to do, and I will tell about it," the speaker signals her resignation. All that remains is to tell the story of this disastrous union.

## Themes

### Grief and Loss

This poem reveals the speaker's grief and anger at the misery her parents' marriage has created. The speaker establishes her grief and pain through her choice of language to describe her parents. She describes them as "kids" who are "dumb." While they would never deliberately hurt anyone, the speaker admits they did cause a great deal of pain. The speaker's loss is most acutely felt when she describes their innocence. She tells the reader, "they would never hurt anybody." That they do hurt somebody is evident in the lines that follow, which describe the bad things done to the children. But perhaps the most grief is signaled by the lines, "you are going to suffer in ways you never heard of, / you are going to want to die." This marriage has created so much pain and misery that the child of this union recognizes her parents' desire to die. In the final line of the poem, the speaker tells the reader her parents should "do what you are going to do." These words reveal her resignation and her acceptance of her inability to change her parents or heal the breech. Instead she will "tell about it," and in doing so she can experience a movement toward catharsis and perhaps find healing for herself.

### Loneliness and Isolation

Olds creates an image of her parents' loneliness and isolation with a few words in lines 22 and

# Topics for Further Study

- Olds's poem is about a marriage and the effect it has on the couple's child. Write a poem about your parents. Or, if you are unable to express how you feel about your own parents, write a poem that explores the parent-child relationship in either its ideal state or in the context of what you have observed in other families.

- Research the rate of divorce in the United States during the past twenty years. Does the rate seem to be increasing or is it holding steady? If it has changed, what factors might be responsible for that change?

- Poetry should create images and pictures in the reader's mind. Draw or illustrate one of the images her poem creates.

- Artists are often inspired by poets to create art. For instance, William Blake was inspired by John Milton's poetry to create illustrations of the poet's finest work. Spend some time looking through art books in the library and try to select a picture or illustration that you feel best illustrates Olds's poem. Then, in a carefully worded essay, compare the art that you have selected to Olds's poem, noting both the similarities and the differences.

- Olds's poem was composed early in the 1980s. Research and write about the economic status of single-parent homes during this period. Consider what kinds of employment were available for divorced mothers and how easy or difficult it was for single families to manage on just one income.

24. The speaker describes her mother's "pitiful untouched body." Two lines later she describes her father in exactly the same words. The language used carefully conveys the man's and woman's loneliness, even in marriage. Their bodies are "pitiful," in stark contrast to the next descriptive word, "beautiful." The paradox is that these two beautiful people can be deserving of pity and compassion

at the same time. Beauty is not often perceived as representing pity, but in this case there is no joy in their beauty, since it is empty of happiness. This couple has never known the true beauty of one another's bodies. No passion has touched them. A few brief words convey the emptiness of their marriage and the loneliness of their lives.

### Parent and Child

This poem relates the speaker's efforts to imagine a way to fix what cannot be fixed: her parents' unhappy lives. By moving back in time to a period just before her parents' marriage, the speaker explores the fundamental differences between her mother and father. American society often paints a picture of the ideal family, with parents, children, and pets living out their ideal lives in happy bliss. The reality is often very different, and when families are not happy, children may need to understand why this unhappiness exists. In this poem the speaker is on a journey to understand her parents' unhappiness and her own unhappy childhood, and she does so by returning to 1937 and the period before their marriage. The speaker describes this marriage as one that resulted in the parents doing "bad things to children." These words reveal the depth of pain that these parents caused for this child. The speaker is the child of this disastrous union, a fact she makes clear when she states she wants to stop the marriage but cannot because "I want to live." This man and woman are wrong for one another; the speaker knows this, but if she stops this marriage, she also stops her own creation.

## Style

### Analogy

Analogy is a common element used in poetry, and suggests a similarity between things that appear, on the surface, to be dissimilar. For example, Olds uses the initial image of the college gates as analogous commentary on her parents. The speaker describes each college gate individually to suggest differences, and perhaps incompatibility. The father's gate is ochre sandstone covered in red tile, whereas the mother emerges from wrought iron and bricks. The use of architectural details represents the differences between the two people, while serving as an analogy of the parents' movement from college to marriage. The use of analogy in Olds's poem is very subtle, so the reader needs to review the poem carefully to understand all the allusions.

### Catharsis

Catharsis is the purging or release of unwanted emotions, often through the use of poetry or drama. The speaker in Olds's poem uses the poem to work through the pain and grief caused by her parents' unhappy marriage. At the beginning of the poem the speaker imagines she can journey to a time before her parents' marriage and stop the wedding. She relates her parents' unhappiness and the destructiveness of their union with its disastrous effects on their children. By the conclusion of the poem, however, the speaker is resigned to a past she could not change, the narrating of the events having functioned as a sort of catharsis. Rather than prevent the marriage, the speaker decides instead to write about it. She uses language and expression as one means to stop the pain, even if she cannot return to the past to stop the events themselves from occurring.

### Imagery

Imagery refers to the use of figurative or expressive language to represent objects, actions, or ideas. The relationships between images can suggest important meanings in a poem. For instance, in Olds's poem the speaker describes her father in language that suggests the type of person he was, painting an unflattering picture of him. The father is described as "arrogant handsome blind." Each of these words suggests a different image. Arrogant denotes a sense of self-importance or exaggerated sense of pride. Handsome seems easy—maybe the speaker means that her father is attractive or pleasing to her sight—but handsome can also mean impressive in appearance, as in large. Blind suggests an inability to see, but it may also denote an unwillingness to notice what occurs or even an ability to disregard what he knows is true. Thus these three words create an image of the speaker's father that is far more extensive than the space the words themselves occupy on the page.

### Lyric Poetry

Lyric poetry describes poems that are strongly associated with emotion, imagination, and a song-like resonance, especially when associated with an individual speaker. Since lyric poetry is so very individual and emotional in its content, it is by its very nature also subjective. Lyric poetry is also the most common form of poetry, and its attributes are common to many other forms of poetry. Olds's poem makes effective use of both imagination and emotion, and since it presents only the speaker's point of view, it is also highly subjective. The reader does not hear the voices of the speaker's parents; instead, we hear their story through their child's perspective, a subjective voice filled with pain and grief.

### Narrative Poem

A narrative poem is a poem that tells a story. Olds's poem imagines that the speaker might travel back in time to a period before her parents' marriage. The details of the poem tell of her parents' unhappiness, of the unhappiness of their children, and of the destruction their marriage wrought on all concerned. The story ends with the speaker's recognition that she cannot change the past, but that she can tell her parents' story, and perhaps find healing in that act.

### Parallelism

Parallelism refers to repetition in style or words within the poem. This stylistic device is a means to express several ideas of similar importance in a similar manner. For example, Olds uses parallelism to describe her parents: "her hungry pretty blank face turning to me" is balanced with "his arrogant handsome blind face turning to me." Another example occurs in lines 17 through 19, and the repetitive use of "you are going to." Parallelism focuses the reader's attention on these lines and signifies they are important elements of the poem.

## Historical Context

### Economics and Politics in the 1980s

Although Sharon Olds did not publish *The Gold Cell* until 1987, the poems contained in this collection were written in the early 1980s, a time marked by such international crises as the war between Iraq and Iran, the western boycott of the Olympics in Russia, and the assassination of President Anwar al-Sadat of Egypt. In the United States, Ronald Reagan was elected president; *Dallas* was the most popular show on television; and Sally Ride, the country's first female astronaut, entered space aboard the *Challenger* space shuttle.

Also at this time, many social conflicts consumed American life. Unemployment was high and rising inflation made those who were employed feel they were losing money with each passing day. America became more fragmented, with widening divisions based on gender, race, ethnicity, sexual orientation, and wealth. Individuals who enjoyed economic success during the 1980s were predominately well-educated white males, while women and people of color lost ground in the movement toward economic success.

While on the surface, Reagan's America appeared to be white, male, and Christian, underneath the surface, America was replete with change. Increases in immigration changed the ethnic mix of America, leading to an increased need for schooling and health care. The need for improved social programs added to the fight for fewer federal tax dollars. Tax cuts, combined with huge military expenditures, did away with many social programs and led to a major recession and a budget deficit so large it would take more than twenty years to eliminate it. Unemployment, at about 10 percent, was the highest since before World War II. The poverty rate was increasing, particularly among children, and the AIDS epidemic soared.

### The Social World

The 1980s brought huge changes to America's social fabric. Sandra Day O'Connor became the first female justice on the United States Supreme Court. In fact many women were now working outside the home. By the early 1980s it is estimated that 50 percent of all women held jobs outside the home, though few of them achieved the kind of success that O'Connor attained. Most women held low-paying, entry-level positions, often making so little money that they needed two jobs to support a family.

Equal rights for women, and especially equal pay, had been the objective of the Equal Rights Amendment (ERA) when it was passed by Congress in 1972; but by 1982 the amendment was defeated when an insufficient number of states failed to ratify it. In spite of this setback, the ideas behind the ERA helped change American life. As a result of the attention paid to the failure of the amendment to pass, more people began to examine the conventional ideas that governed male and female roles. The idea that girls studied home economics in school and boys took shop was one of the first traditions to be examined. It seemed reasonable that both boys and girls might find it useful to learn to cook and repair or build small items. The feminist movement began with just that kind of small questioning and change. The changes brought by feminism, and they were hard-fought changes that came very slowly, eventually led to similar activism by other groups. Blacks and environmentalists learned lessons from the feminists and discovered that protests, especially when well organized and attended by the media, could change

## Compare & Contrast

- **1980s:** This decade begins with the "perfect" marriage between an English princess and prince. The marriage of Lady Diana Spenser and Charles, the Prince of Wales, suggests the sort of fairy-tale marriage that many women still want for themselves, in spite of the feminist movement that began at the end of the preceding decade. The fantasy appeal of the wedding for women is represented by the 700 million people who watched the wedding on television.

    **Today:** Within fifteen years, the Prince and Princess of Wales are divorced. A year later, Diana is killed in an automobile accident. The divorced Prince of Wales is left a single father of two boys. In the United States, the number of single parents is rising as well, often as a result of divorce—the outcome in approximately fifty percent of all marriages.

- **1980s:** Steven Spielberg's *ET: The Extra-Terrestrial* is only one example of a wave of new films enhanced by the elaborate use of special effects often supplied by computers. One important feature of this film, though, does not involve special effects; it is the inclusion of divorce. The children who befriend ET live in a single parent household. This film's popularity is so great that it remains the top grossing film for eleven years.

    **Today:** Movies are still an important element in American life. The development of more elaborate computers continues to contribute to special effects in film, with each new film more elaborate than its preceding competition. *ET: The Extra-Terrestrial* is updated with additional special effects and is re-released in movie theatres in celebration of its twentieth anniversary.

- **1980s:** In 1982, in Chicago, the first cellular phones are introduced for common use, at a cost of $3000 each for the purchase price and $150 a month for service. New transmitters make mobile phone use available in more areas.

    **Today:** Statistics suggest that fifty percent of all households own and use a cellular phone. A reduction in cost and competition among suppliers helps increase the number of users.

- **1980s:** The United States President for most of this decade is Ronald Reagan, a former Hollywood actor. Reagan wins the presidency using his acting talents, including an adept use of television and film to promote his ideas. Reagan's presidency illustrates the fascination Americans have with film stars and the willingness of the population to ignore experience in favor of performance.

    **Today:** The public's fascination with Hollywood and film stars continues. Although no actor since Reagan has been elected to the nation's highest office, a significant part of the election process focuses on the media coverage and celebrity surrounding a candidate. In many ways, this movement suggests a superficiality about the American public, with less emphasis on the content of the message, and more emphasis on the delivery.

the world. In the end, the early 1980s became a period of great social change.

## Critical Overview

"I Go Back to May 1937" is included in Olds's collection *The Gold Cell*. Reception of Olds's poems is often mixed, including reception for *The Gold Cell*. While individual poems from a collection are rarely singled out for comment in a review of the book, Terri Brown-Davidson does comment specifically on "I Go Back to May 1937" in a review of *The Gold Cell* for the *Hollins Critic*. Brown-Davidson refers to the first dozen lines of the poem as "disturbing," not because of the poem's intensity or topic, but because the critic finds the poem "formulaic." Brown-Davidson suggests that Olds is not taking chances with her poetry, and is instead refusing "to push beyond the boundaries to grow and keep growing." The critic argues that Olds's poetry is "belabored" and "overdramatic," and that "I Go Back to May 1937" is "fossilized." Brown-Davidson's primary criticism focuses on what the critic perceives as the sameness of Olds's work. According to Brown-Davidson, Olds has not grown as poet and has not been willing to try new approaches to her poetry.

However, one critic finds much to praise about *The Gold Cell*. Peter Harris, writing for the *Virginia Quarterly Review*, states, "Olds treats both the present and the past with a make-you-squirm explicitness that's buffered only by an ingenuous honesty about her relationship to the events she describes." These are poems that Harris labels as "confessional" and "gripping." Harris also cites Olds as having the "voice of a peculiarly exuberant survivor who speaks with gusto." In responding to criticism that Olds's poems have a sameness to them, Harris argues that this sameness "should not obscure the fact that she writes with great flair and often shows a resonant dramatic intelligence in searching out the contexts, or the frameworks of implication." Harris also cites Olds's "fertile metaphoric imagination" and her "analogical imagination" as strengths that provide insight into her poems. Harris concludes by stating, "*The Gold Cell* is saner and more full of love than anyone could reasonably expect."

A slightly more mixed reaction is offered by Christian McEwen, writing for the *Nation*. In a review of *The Gold Cell*, McEwen states that the political poems contained in the beginning of Olds's collection are "thrilling with imaginative sympathy." McEwen suggests that while other poets have attempted this style of poetry, none have managed to convey the images so well. McEwen also singles out the family poems in this book, which display the author's "fierce rhetorical skill." Although McEwen acknowledges that Olds's poems are not without fault, his critique singles out only a few individual poems as lacking the overall strength of the other poems. In spite of some small concerns, McEwen's endorsement of Olds's work is very favorable.

## Criticism

### Sheri E. Metzger

*Metzger has a doctorate in English Renaissance literature. She teaches literature and drama at the University of New Mexico, where she is a lecturer in the English department and an adjunct professor in the university's honors program. In this essay, Metzger discusses the depiction of the mother character in Olds's poem and explores the influences of Olds's own admitted childhood Calvinist indoctrination on her poetry.*

Olds's poems often focus on the parent-child relationship, especially the relationship between the poem's speaker and her father. A study of Olds's poems about the father reveals a cruel man who drank too much bourbon, terrorized his children and wife, and whose love, even in death, the speaker craves. Olds's poems expose the speaker's childhood, opening up a life filled with painful memories, where her abusive father dominates the landscape. The mother, when she appears, is cowed by the superior strength and meanness of her husband. She offers no rescue for the speaker or her two siblings, and indeed, in many of Olds's poems, it is the mother who looks to her children for rescue, thus reversing the traditional image of parent as a symbol of strength. Olds has suggested that her early childhood, which she describes as "very Calvinist, very Hell oriented," influenced the rhythm in her poems. Olds is speaking of the church hymns that she sang as a child and how those rhythms are responsible for the singsong nature of her poetic lines. But, the church influences more than the movement of the line; it also permeates the content of her work. Olds's poems contain the self-righteousness of biblical text. The speaker suffers as Job suffered and is righteous in that suffering. When asked to forgive, the speaker knows she must accede to that request, however reluctant she may be, because the bible teaches forgiveness of others. The speaker does not want to forgive, but the lessons of childhood, especially those on the forgiveness of God for his sinners, have not been lost on the speaker. There is a self-righteousness in agreeing to forgive that appeals to the speaker, even as she is reluctant to put away a lifetime of anger and blame.

Although much of the emotion of Olds's poetry is directed toward the speaker's father, whom she often blames for her childhood misery, the poems that explore the mother's role in this misery are also worth close examination. The poems that focus on Olds's mother, in which the speaker must forgive her mother, present the speaker as conflicted and unwilling to let go of a lifetime of reproach. Forgiveness, as Olds no doubt learned as a child in church, is much more difficult to achieve

> *The poems that focus on Olds's mother, in which the speaker must forgive her mother, present the speaker as conflicted and unwilling to let go of a lifetime of reproach.*

than the sermons promised. It would be easier to simply assuage the anger of her childhood without letting go completely, as the speaker in the poems about the mother would admit. Three of Olds's poems—"I Go Back to May 1937," "Why My Mother Made Me," and "After 37 Years My Mother Apologizes For My Childhood"—all taken from *The Gold Cell*, reveal the speaker's inner conflict as she moves among blaming her mother, pitying her, and acknowledging that, by forgiving her, the speaker is forced to redefine meaning in her own life.

If the reader assumes that the poems in *The Gold Cell* are arranged in chronological order, then "I Go Back to May 1937" is the earliest poem of the three to be discussed here. In this poem, the speaker imagines herself back in time, at a period just before her parents' wedding. At first, she contemplates warning her parents of the misery that their future holds, but when she realizes that she cannot stop the wedding, since to do so would be to prevent her own life, she imagines that she can force her parents to find happiness together. To do this, the speaker imagines that her parents are two paper dolls. She uses these toys of childhood to create what is missing in her life. Rather than the reality of divorce, the speaker can use the dolls as surrogate parents. She can "bang them together" and force them to unite, as she could not do in reality. The forcefulness of the "bang" suggests the depth of anger that the speaker feels as she tries to force her parents to feel a passion and a connection that was missing in their lives. This is an angry movement, revealing the speaker's defiance and rejection of her past. In forcing these two paper dolls together, the speaker also attempts to forge a union that divorce has now rendered in two. By the end of the poem, the speaker acknowledges that she cannot prevent nor repair her parents' lives, and so the poem ends on a note of resignation. The speaker cannot change their lives, but she can write of their lives. There is a melodramatic note evident in the last lines of the poem:

> I want to live. I
> take them up like the male and female
> paper dolls and bang them together
> at the hips like chips of flint as if to
> strike sparks from them, I say
> Do what you are going to do, and I will tell about it.

There is an emotional extravagance to these lines, an exaggerated sense of conflict, followed by an equally exaggerated sense of resignation and acceptance. In an interview published in the *Poetry Society of America Newsletter*, Olds suggests that it is her religious upbringing that is responsible for the melodrama present in much of her work. She also credits biblical influences for the tone of self-righteousness and the desperation of her characters, who are defined by extremes of good or bad. Those biblical influences also stand out in this poem. The man and the woman lack a complexity; they are "going to do bad things"; they are going to "suffer." The woman is "hungry pretty blank" and "pitiful beautiful." The man is "arrogant handsome blind" and "pitiful beautiful." Real parents are more complex than this man and woman; but then, the speaker is holding paper dolls, which are one-dimensional. If the speaker can maintain this lack of depth, she is not forced to confront her parents, nor deal with the anger that momentarily has escaped as she bangs the two dolls together. Instead, Olds can fall back on biblical teaching to create characters who are either obedient or not, righteous or not, but such characters need not reveal any complexity.

In the second of Olds's poems, "Why My Mother Made Me," the speaker moves forward in her examination of her parents' marriage to the creation of the child, herself. She sees herself as fulfilling her mother's need. As a child, she is what her mother wanted: "my father as a woman." Once again, there is a sense of melodrama and desperation in these words. Later in the poem, the speaker describes her parents' creation of her in words that are very different from the Bible's instructions in Genesis 2:24 that a husband and wife "become one flesh." While the words are different, the image is very much the same. The speaker describes how her mother,

> pressed the clear soft
> ball of herself like a stick of beaten cream
> against his stained sour steel grater
> until I came out the other side of his body.

The joining of the speaker's parents is methodical, lacking passion. In many ways, this joining creates an image of function, not so very different than all those biblical men and women who "knew" one another, and so the next generation is created. After her birth, the speaker imagines that her mother gazes at her with the same pride that the "maker of a sword gazes at his face in the / steel of the blade." This is not a depiction of motherly love, but one of pride and triumph. Once again, these words suggest the speaker's sense of self-righteous judgment of her mother. There is no attempt at mediation or an effort to admit that her mother might be more complex than these words suggest. The speaker can only see practical reasons for her creation: her mother's need to recreate someone in her father's image, the opportunity for the mother to recreate herself as she wished to be, or the pride of ownership that being a parent conveys. The speaker does not ask, "Where is the love?" Although unspoken, the question still hangs at the end of the poem. Virtually every book in the Bible defines God's love for his creation. It is a godly pattern that parents are expected to imitate for their own children. Olds knows this from her own childhood, and the speaker, who is Olds's creation, knows of this expectation as well. So, the poem ends without an affirmation of the mother's love for her infant. It cannot be otherwise. To affirm the mother's love would be to negate the anger that the speaker feels. The only way to maintain her anger is to increase the sense of righteousness and melodrama in the poem. Love would disperse those elements and leave the poem without a focus.

This lack of love again emerges in the third poem under consideration, "After 37 Years My Mother Apologizes for My Childhood." Love is the one important element missing from this poem, in which the speaker's mother finally apologizes to the speaker for having subjected her to the father's drunken violence. The speaker acknowledges her mother's physical efforts to force an image of sincerity into her apology:

> your
> tiny face glittered as if with
> shattered crystal, with true regret, the
> regret of the body.

The final line, "the / regret of the body," suggests that while her mother is using her body to create an image of sincerity, the speaker recognizes that this is only performance. The regret is all in the body and not in her mind. The mother may feel regret at that moment, but the speaker doubts its authenticity. However, the mother's apology forces the child to respond, "I said *It's all right, / don't cry, it's all right.*" The parent-child role has been reversed, and the child is forced to comfort the parent. The mother has never spoken of love, only of justification: *"Where else could I turn? Who else did I have?"* The mother's tears and her pleas are too much for the child to ignore, and so the speaker is compelled to accept the apology. How reluctant she is to do so is revealed in the final lines: "I hardly knew what I / said or who I would be now that I had forgiven you." The speaker has invested so much of her life in blaming her mother that the forced forgiveness leaves her with no real sense of her own identity. Who is the speaker if she cannot hate her mother? She cannot imagine what she will do with the rest of her life. Once again, as she did in the early two poems, Olds turns to melodrama to convey her ideas. The images are ones of desperation and overwrought emotion. These are the very images that Olds admits were conveyed during her Sundays in church. Forgiving the mother permits the speaker to achieve a kind of biblical self-righteousness that would appeal to the Calvinist orientation that formed Olds's childhood.

Just as Job has come to symbolize the image of the long-suffering and willing believer, the speaker in Olds's poems imagines herself as a self-righteous sufferer who has been forced to endure much pain. Because Olds has refused to divulge details about her own life, there is a temptation to see the author in her texts. That, of course, would be a mistake. Although there is no personal information to inform the readings of Olds's poems, her own admittance of the importance of the Bible on her childhood can be used to help define her characters' lives. Writers use what is familiar in life to create depth in their creations. And so, it is reasonable to assume that Olds has borrowed from her own experience with religion to help create a reality for her characters. As a result, the three mother-daughter poems included here are laden with self-righteousness and melodrama. The characters reveal a desperation but without the depth that the reader would hope to see. Olds does an effective job of capturing the Calvinist spirit in her poems, but she leaves the readers still wondering about the truth of the mother's identity.

**Source:** Sheri E. Metzger, Critical Essay on "I Go Back to May 1937," in *Poetry for Students*, The Gale Group, 2003.

## Dwight Garner

*In the following interview, Olds discusses her books of poetry and the way she approaches writing.*

## What Do I Read Next?

- Olds's *The Father* (1992) is a collection of poems on the death of the speaker's father. This book continues many of the father-daughter themes touched upon in Olds's earlier books.

- Olds's *The Unswept Room* is a new collection of poems to be published in September 2002 by Knopf.

- *The Pushcart Prize: Best of the Small Presses*, published every year since 1977, contains the editor's annual selections for the best contemporary poetry and fiction. A study of the poems in this book provides readers with contemporary poets of Olds's caliber.

- *Otherwise: New and Selected Poems* by Jane Kenyon is a collection of the author's work. Published in 1997, two years after Kenyon's death, this work offers a glimpse at another female contemporary poet.

- *Womanifestos*, published in 2000 by the Women's Writing Circle, is an anthology of women's poetry, containing feminist and Latina poetry. While Olds is not Latina, many of these poems explore issues that are similar to Olds's work: the relationship between parents and children, and a woman's role in the world.

- *The Longman Anthology of American Poetry*, published in 1992, is an anthology of American poetry that includes poetry from several different time periods. This book provides a compilation of poetry that allows students to visualize Olds's poetry within a context of other American poets and to understand how Olds fulfills or deviates from the poetic traditions that influenced her work.

- *The Heath Introduction to Poetry*, with a fifth edition published in 2000, is an anthology of poetry that includes poems from the earliest poets through contemporary poetry. Selections are drawn from around the world. A study of the history of poetry can assist the reader in understanding how American poets fit into a worldview.

---

Domesticity, death, erotic love—the stark simplicity of Sharon Olds' subjects, and of her plain-spoken language, can sometimes make her seem like the brooding Earth Mother of American poetry. ("I have learned to get pleasure," Olds wrote in her last book, "from speaking of pain.") In photographs she tends to look somewhat dark and remote, too; there's a sense of brewing drama. She seems a natural heir to such melancholy talents as Ann Sexton and Sylvia Plath.

It's a happy surprise, then, to discover that the 54-year-old Olds is anything but withdrawn and more-serious-than-thou. In fact, she comes across as a bundle of nervous energy, slightly neurotic, a bit like an intellectual Julie Haggerty. It's the end of the semester at New York University, where Olds has taught in the Graduate Creative Writing Program for the last 12 years, and the atmosphere outside her small office is chaotic. Olds herself arrives a few minutes late, looking slightly harried, and apologizes profusely while pulling two paper cups of tea from a brown bag—one for herself, one for a visitor.

It's hard to blame her for seeming a little breathless. In addition to her multiple duties at NYU, Olds runs the poetry workshop she founded in 1984 at New York's Goldwater Hospital for the severely disabled, and she reads at numerous speaking engagements. What's more, she claims to have such a backlog of poetry that when she does find the time to issue a new book—such as *The Wellspring* (Knopf), published earlier this year—it is generally made up of work written more than a decade earlier.

Born in San Francisco and educated at Stanford and Columbia, Olds arrived as a poet somewhat late: her first collection, *Satan Says*, was published when she was 37. Over the course of five books, however, she has quickly become one of America's most highly regarded poets; her readings attract overflow audiences, and her volume *The Dead and the Living* won the 1983 National Book Critics Circle Award.

Olds' new book, which follows on the heels of *The Father* (1992), a harrowing series of poems about the death of the narrator's alcoholic father, is comprised largely of poems on somewhat more accessible themes—family life, parenthood, romantic love. But as Olds' many readers have learned over the years, her work's apparent simplicity can't hide the scalding honesty of her observations. As Michael Ondaatje put it recently, her poems "are pure fire in the hands." Like each of her previous books, *The Wellspring* leaves an emotional afterburn.

Olds spoke with *Salon* for nearly two hours, on topics ranging from poetic inspiration and bad reviews to the problem with reading the morning's *New York Times*.

*Thanks for the tea. Which reminds me that I once read somewhere that you don't smoke or drink coffee, and that you consume very little alcohol. Why is that?*

Well, one thing I'm really interested in, when I'm writing, is being accurate. If I am trying to describe something, I'd like to be able to get it right. Of course, what's "right" is different for every person. Sometimes what's accurate might be kind of mysterious. So I don't just mean mathematically accurate. But to get it right according to my vision. I think this is true for all artists. My senses are very important to me. I want to be able to describe accurately what I see and hear and smell. And what they say about those things not being good for one's longevity makes an impression on me also. So I did quit coffee and I did quit smoking. But I haven't managed that with drinking!

*So many poets are associated with alcohol and other kinds of excess.*

There are some fine books and essays about that. Lewis Hyde has written about alcoholism and poets and the role that society gives its writers—encouraging them to die [laughs]. And Donald Hall has wonderful, sobering stories about many of these poets. But I don't think anyone believes anymore that drugs and alcohol are good for writing, do they? I'm probably so out of it at my age that I don't know what people think. But I think that exercise and as much good health as one can enjoy is the best thing for writing.

> *The opportunities for offense and failure are always aplenty. They lie all around us."*

*I was even more surprised to read that you don't take a newspaper or watch television.*

It's true, but it's kind of a different issue. At one point I took on a new job, and I just didn't have time to do anything but work. [Olds was the Director of the Graduate Creative Writing Program at NYU from 1989–91.] So I figured that for a year, just for the first year of this job, I would not watch TV, I wouldn't read a newspaper, I wouldn't read a book, I wouldn't go hear any music, I wouldn't do any of that kind of thing. Just so I'd have enough time. I was very afraid that I wouldn't be able to do this job well. And the time never came back. But there are problems connected with this—with keeping informed about what's happening in the world. So I try to look at the front page whenever I'm walking by a newsstand. And people talk about what's happening, so I get a certain amount of information that way. It might be a bad thing, not to know what's going on in the world. I can't say I really approve of it.

*Is this paring down an attempt to get back to basic things, in your life as well as your work?*

I'm not sure that the benefit—as a writer and as a citizen—that I would get from reading at least the front page of the *Times* every day or every other day would outweigh the depression. Learning about so many things that we can't do anything about. The amount of horror one used to hear about in one village could be quite extreme. But one might not have heard about all the other villages' horrors at the same time. I just don't have a big mind, I don't have a big picture, I am very limited.

*Yet didn't some of your earlier, somewhat political poems take their inspiration from things you'd read in newspapers?*

Yes, and they still do. I wish I wrote more about the world at more distance from myself. I think that for any of us to be able to imagine another person's life, if we could do that really well, would be wonderful.

*There is only one in* The Wellspring, *your new book. It's a poem titled "Japanese-American Farmhouse, California, 1942."*

Well, *The Wellspring* was written from 1983 to 1986. And it had a section in the beginning that was poems that began from others' experience. But the book just insisted on having this more domestic shape—against my wishful thinking.

*I didn't realize that the "new" poems were so old.*

That's why I didn't have time to go to the movies and read the paper and drink coffee [laughs]—because I'm very far behind in terms of putting books together.

*Can you put this new book into place for me, then, in terms of your chronology?*

*The Gold Cell* was published in 1987, and the poems in it were written in 1980, 1981 and 1982. Half of *The Father* [published in 1992] was written in '83 and '84. The second half was composed of one or two poems each from 1984, '85, '86, '87, '88, '89. So for *The Wellspring* I went back to where *The Gold Cell* left off, which was work written through 1982. So *The Wellspring* goes through 1986. The book I'm working on now will be made of poems written in '87, '88 and '89. The next one will be from 1990, '91 and '92.

*I find that fascinating. Do many poets work that way?*

I don't think so. I got behind in putting books together.

*How hard is putting a book together? It would seem like the hard part would be writing the poems in the first place.*

Well, you just need time. When I quit all these things and said I didn't have any time, I meant I didn't have *any* time. So the teaching, the writing of first drafts, the traveling, the reading, and whatever else might be in the life—that was all I had time for. I didn't have time to sit down and look at the work of a year and choose what to type. And then choose, among what gets typed, what to work on. And then among what's worked on what to *keep* working on until lots of poems become just the ones that seem the best. Or the least worst!

*Why do you keep yourself so busy with things that don't pertain directly to writing? Is it because you love these other jobs, or is it because you've had to take them?*

It's a combination of both. The teaching is very rewarding, and very time-consuming, and very exhausting. But it's wonderful. The community here at NYU is very precious to me. And the traveling and reading is rewarding in a different way, and it's an honor to be asked. It's hard to say no, when one is asked.

*People who know your work well might be surprised to know that you have such a vigorous public life. Because your work is very focused and often kind of quiet. It's hard to imagine the narrator of one of your poems fending off multiple phone calls.*

But don't you think that every single one of us is leading a harried life? We're all taking on too much, we're all asking too much of ourselves. We're all wishing we could do more, and therefore just doing more. So I don't think my life is different from anybody else's. Every poet I know—although there may be some I don't know who lead very different lives, who maybe live in the country and don't teach—tends to be just like the rest of us: just really busy, really overcommitted. We wouldn't necessarily see it in their poems. Because a poem is not written while running or while answering the phone. It's written in whatever minutes one has. Sometimes you have half an hour.

*Can you write a poem in half an hour?*

Forty-five minutes is much better [laughs]. Many, many poets whose work I love, they take longer than I do to write a first draft. In a way, it doesn't matter how long it takes, if we can each just find the right way to do it. Everyone is so different. I sometimes wish I wrote in a different way. You know, that feeling of: So-and-so writes slowly, if only I wrote slowly. But it's just the way I work. I feel a very strong wish, when a poem does come to me, to write it and get to the end of it.

*So you don't sit down every morning at 9 a.m. and say: Now I'm going to write a poem.*

No. I don't know if there are many poets who do that. I think that there are fiction writers for whom that works well. I could never do it. I feel as if, by the time I see that it's a poem, it's almost written in my head somewhere. It's as if there's someone inside of me who perceives order and beauty—and disorder. And who wants to make little copies. Who wants to put together something that will bear some relationship to the vision or memory or experience or story or idea or dream or whatever. Whatever starts things out.

*What did you mean when you once said that your poetry comes out of your lungs?*

[Laughs] Well, you know, it's curious where different people think their mind is. I guess a lot of people believe that their mind is in their brain, in their head. To me, the mind seems to be spread out in the whole body—the senses are part of the brain. I guess they're not where the thinking is done. But poetry is so physical, the music of it and the movement of thought. Maybe we can use a metaphor for it, out of dance. I think for many years I was aware of the need, in dance and in life, to breathe deeply and to take in more air than we usually take in. I find a tendency in myself not to breathe very much. And certainly I have noticed, over the years, when dancing or when running, that ideas will come to my mind with the oxygen. Suddenly you're remembering something that you haven't thought of for years.

*Your last book,* The Father, *was an unflinching account of your father's—or at least the narrator's father's—death from cancer. Your new book deals with more domestic themes, and while it's not lightweight, it doesn't have that sense of darkness that hung over* The Father. *Did you find that writing these poems was refreshing, a kind of release?*

The decision for me was whether to have *The Father* be a book that told a story—from the point of view of this speaker, the daughter—without, as in the earlier books, then having a section on something else and a section on something else. At first I thought it would not be a good idea to have a book all on one theme. I also didn't know if I had enough poems on the subject that I liked well enough to make a book of them. But it turned out that I did. And it just seemed true to make a story that was all of itself. It pleased me to do so, and it still does. I've never had regrets that I went that way with *The Father*. The fact that there was a lot of anger and sorrow and a sense of connection to destructive feelings in *The Father* doesn't bother me. For me, the subject kind of makes its demands. And I don't write books. I just write poems. And then I put together books. Many poets write books. They'll tell you: Well, I've got my next book, but there are two poems I need to write, one about x, one about y. This is a wonder to me. But I think in another way I am like these poets: we like to get in the art's way as little as possible.

*That's an interesting phrase, not getting in art's way. Is that why you write your poems in a style that's somewhat accessible?*

I think that it's a little different from that for me. I think that my work is easy to understand because I am not a thinker, I am not a…How can I put it? I write the way I perceive, I guess. It's not really simple, I don't think, but it's about ordinary things—feeling about things, about people. I'm not an intellectual, I'm not an abstract thinker. And I'm interested in ordinary life. So I think that our writing reflects us.

I was recently reading in Des Moines with Yusef Komunyakaa and Philip Levine. You listen to them and you're hearing a world-view, a body-view, you're hearing a spirit of a person, and mind, and heart, and soul. Their work is completely distinctive; you know you're hearing a Komunyakaa poem immediately. And I don't think they are trying to sound one way or another—it doesn't seem to me to be something that comes from a conscious decision. Their spirits and their visions are embodied in their craft. And so is mine. It's not Jane Saw Puff. But the clarity of Jane Saw Puff is precious to me. What was the other part of your question?

*Well, I was wondering what you meant about not getting in art's way.*

There are some things that have to do with art that we can't control. This creature of the poem may assemble itself into a being with its own centrifugal force. That's what I'm thinking about when I'm trying to get out of art's way. Not trying to look good, if a poem's about me. Not trying to look bad. Not asking a poem to carry a lot of rocks in its pockets. But just being an ordinary observer and liver and feeler and letting the experience get through you onto the notebook with the pen, through the arm, out of the body, onto the page, without distortion. And there are so many ways I could distort. If I wrote in a sonnet form, I would be distorting. Or if I had some great new idea for line breaks and I used it in a poem, but it's really not right for that poem, but I wanted it, that would be distorting. It's kind of like ego in a way, egotism or narcissism. Where the self is too active.

*Your poems often seem, on the surface anyway, somewhat more autobiographical than most—not that the "I" in your work is necessarily you. Do people try to read your life into them?*

I don't know if it would feel accurate to me to say that I put myself into my poems. I don't know if that would describe what was happening in a poem that I wrote and that I liked. Someone is seeing, someone is thinking, dreaming, wondering, and remembering, in everybody's poems. Whether there's a speaker that has an explicit "I" or not, there is some kind of self or spirit or personality. We think of Lucille Clifton's poems, and they don't have to have an "I" in them for the spirit of the poet, a person, to be felt. I wouldn't say she was putting herself in, but the qualities of her being come through. She's not leaving herself, her wisdom and experience and music out. That's partly what craft is, I think. The body of the poem is the spirit of the poem. But I do sometimes make an effort to use the word "I" as little as possible. I would not have chosen to have that word appear so much in my poems. *My* poems—I don't even like the sound of that, in a way. Not that anyone else wrote them. But we know that only people who are really close to us care about our personal experience. Art is something else. It has something to do with wanting to be accurate about what we think and feel. To me the difference between the paper world and the flesh world is so great that I don't think we could put ourselves in our poems even if we wanted to.

*Do you ever wonder what one of your children will think when he or she reads one of your poems that might be, at least in some small way, about them? Or do you wonder about what insight they will have into their mother's life through your work?*

It's a wonderful question, and it's not one I can answer, really. Ten years ago I made a vow not to talk about my life. Obviously, the apparently very personal nature of my writing made this seem to me like maybe a good idea, for both sides of the equation—both for the muses and for the writer. But it's a wonderful and important question. I think the thing that's most important to me about it is this idea that every writer has to decide these things for themselves, and we learn by making mistakes. We learn by finding out, five years later, what we wish we hadn't done. I've worked out this thing I've called "the spectrum of loyalty and betrayal." Which is also the spectrum of silence and song. And at either end, we're in a dangerous state, either to the self, or to others. We all try to fall in the right place in the middle.

*As accessible as your poetry can seem to be, there also seems to be an almost brutally direct emotional quality sometimes. There are some tough images.*

I think that I am slowly improving in my ability to not be too melodramatic, to help the images have the right tenor. My first book came out when I was 37, so when I was finally able to speak as a writer my wish to not be silent was, in my early work, extreme. It's like someone, in baseball, who thinks that the ball is being thrown by a very strong arm from the outfield, and so she can't just land on home, she has to try to run way past it, practically into the dugout. Reading some of my earlier work, I get that sense of the need for too big a head of steam to be built up. It seems extreme to me at times, some of the imagery. That's part of why I'm not so sorry I'm a little behind in putting books together, because some of those rather crude images I can now maybe correct. It also might be that maybe I've used an image that is too mild, and I'll correct in the other direction. I don't want to imply that it's always going the other way. But my tendency was to be a little over the mark. And so I just really love now the possibility of getting it right.

*Your new book contains several poems that are quite realistic in terms of their descriptions of sex. Is it difficult writing poetry about sex, not to fall into language that might seem cliched?*

I don't think that sex has been written about a lot in poetry. And I want to be able to write about any subject. There is a failure rate—there are subjects that are probably a lot harder to write about than others. I think that love is almost the hardest thing to write about. Not a general state of being in love, but a particular love for a particular person. Just one's taste for that one. And if you look at all the love poetry in our tradition, there isn't much that helps us know why that one. I'm just interested in human stuff like hate, love, sexual love and sex. I don't see why not. It just seems to me if writers can assemble, in language, something that bears any relation to experience—especially important experience, experience we care about, moving and powerful experience—then it is worth trying. The opportunities for offense and failure are always aplenty. They lie all around us.

*Your poetry isn't necessarily known for its comic aspects. But I'm wondering about your wonderful poem "The Pope's Penis," from* The Gold Cell, *where that came from and if it has proven controversial.*

Life has a lot of sorrow in it, but also has a lot of funny things in it, so it makes sense to me to have that range. So many poets whose work I love are funny now and then. We're just funny creatures, human beings. But that particular poem—I am careful where I read it, not wishing to give maximum offense. It's a poem I didn't get for a long time. I didn't ask myself: Why do you feel okay about teasing this stranger? Why do you think that's okay? I was just so startled when I noticed that this particular Pope was also a man. And I thought: Well, that means ... [trails off]. And I just began musing on The Other, in a way.

And I wasn't thinking, "I must not write anything about a religion that is not mine because I have no business doing so." I'm sure there are a lot of people who feel that way, that we can write well only about what we deeply know and have known all our lives—that we can't write about very different experiences. I don't think that's necessarily always true. I grew up in what I now call a hellfire Episcopalian religion—I think that phrase communicates the atmosphere—and I didn't feel light years away from understanding the male hierarchy of power leading up toward the male God.

But I didn't understand, until years later, that this poem was kind of a return gesture. This man, the Pope, seemed to feel that he knew a lot about women and could make decisions for us—various decisions about whether we could be priests or not, and who would decide whether we could have an abortion or not. He had crossed our line so far—this is according to my outsider's point of view—that hey, what's a little flirtatious poem that went across his line somewhat?

It looks like a young poem now. It mixes its metaphors. So I don't tend to read that poem, but I don't wish I hadn't written it. I don't want to take it out of the book. And unlike maybe three other poems in that book that I've rewritten—in the latest printing they are different from what they were—it's okay enough for me that I don't feel like I have to, or could, rewrite it. If I tried to fix the images it would just fall apart.

*Many of the poems in your new book, certainly unlike that poem about the Pope's penis, take their inspiration from very simple domestic things—a kid blowing bubbles in milk, a pair of blue jeans, a sick child.*

Why is it, do you suppose, that you have two people in two different apartments, and they are surrounded by all the same stuff, and one of them will write about blue jeans and bubbles in milk, and the other will write about something less ordinary, or something with more ideas connected to it? How we perceive is just very different.

*You published your first book of poems somewhat late, at 37. Can you tell me a bit about why that was?*

That sure seemed old then, and it sure seems young to me now. It seemed old because I knew of all these amazing people who had done amazing work in their 20s. Of course, anyone who ever can do anything is lucky. It means that there has been enough education, enough peace, enough time, enough whatever, that somebody can sit down and write. Many lives don't allow that, the good fortune of being able to work at it, and try, and keep trying.

*Can you imagine your life if you hadn't become a writer? Do you feel lucky?*

No, I certainly can't imagine my life not being a writer. Lucky? Um-hmm. It's hard to believe—it's like this is a dream. I need to write, and I need to write a lot. And I've been very lucky to be able to make the time, have the time given me, depending on what stage of my life I'm thinking of. Yes, luck. Luck. "Sometimes a crumb falls / From the tables of joy, / Sometimes a bone / Is flung. / To some people / Love is given, / To others / Only heaven." That's Langston Hughes' poem "Luck." It's one of the poems on the subways.

*Have you ever learned anything from a review of your work?*

Oh sure. Sometimes I feel like warning signs are thrown up. As long as one doesn't get too discouraged.

*I haven't seen many—or any, actually—negative reviews of your work. Maybe it's because I see so few poetry reviews. But do bad ones get to you?*

Yeah. Sure. I think there have been plenty of them [laughs]. You were looking in a different direction. And they have differed a lot from each other in their amount of thoughtfulness, their amount of bad feeling. But we put our boat in the stream. By putting one's work out there, one is asking to be considered as a part of the world. If the world feels very powerfully that this work should not have been written, it will say so. That seems quite fair. But then I think of the great things I have read, great stuff describing other people's work that a critic likes or loves. Criticism can be so enriching, it can add to the pleasure we take in the poetry.

**Source:** Dwight Garner, "Sharon Olds," in *Salon.com*, http://www.salon.com/weekly/interview960701.html, July 1, 1996.

## Alicia Ostriker

*In the following review excerpt, Ostriker, praises Olds's diverse themes in her poetry collection* The Gold Cell.

The opening section of Sharon Olds's *The Gold Cell* contains some of her most haunting poems. A white woman faces a black youth with the "casual cold look of a mugger" on the subway and considers how deeply they are in each other's power. Some policemen coax a suicide from his parapet on a hot night, and they light cigarettes whose "red, glowing ends burned like the / tiny campfires we lit at night / back at the beginning of the world." Some Ugandan villagers during a drought are beating to death a food-thief whose headwounds are "ripe and wet as a / rich furrow cut back and cut back at / plough-time to farrow a trench for the seed." A 12-year-old girl who has been raped and has watched her best friend raped and stabbed to death lives on to go to high school where she works hard at math and becomes a cheerleader, "and she does a cartwheel, the splits, she shakes the / shredded pom-poms in her fists." Olds's characteristic note is a clear unsentimental compassion; her characteristic imagery is laid on thick, wet, and warm as bodies.

The book's three remaining sections return to themes powerfully treated in her earlier volumes, *Satan Says* and *The Dead and the Living*: father and mother, sexuality, son and daughter. In "I Go Back to May 1937," the poet pictures her parents on the brink of their marriage and is tempted to warn them to stop:

> but I don't do it. I want to live. I
> take them up like the male and female
> paper dolls and bang them together
> at the hips like chips of flint as if to
> strike sparks from them, I say
> Do what you are going to do, and I will tell about it.

Tell she does, sparing neither parent—father another Saturn eating his young, mother rolling over daughter like a tongue of lava—while the stunningly awful details, by their very intimacy and physicality, make anger impossible. These people are the poet, she is they. When Olds writes of sex, she sinks into voluptuous metaphors of food, predatory animals, satiety, birth. Writing of her children, she concentrates on their living and imperilled flesh, which we see as it were suspended in the amber of the poet's locutions and her love. While she neither philosophizes nor moralizes explicitly, Olds's refusal to establish any conventional poetic distance from her subjects amounts to a tacit moral imperative: that we affirm as intensely as possible our biological existence and the attachments to others it implies, and that we hold life as absolutely precious. "The gold cell" as a figure for life's primary unit implies both entrapment (we cannot escape our parents, our children, our sexuality, our bodies) and pure treasure.

Olds's poems here are longer and slightly less taut than her earlier work. I'm puzzled at times by her lineation (e.g., many lines ending in "the" or "a" for no apparent reason other than a general preference for run-on). But the grace, the ease, the American casualness of her phrasing, along with the rich and precise tactility of her imagery, make a perfect combination. I found many of these poems no less than breathtaking.

**Source:** Alicia Ostriker, "Comment: The Tune of Crisis," in *Poetry*, Vol. CXLIX, No. 4, January 1987, pp. 231–37.

## Sources

Anonymous, "Three Poets on Poetry: Carolyn Forche, Sharon Olds & Alicia Ostriker," in *Poetry Society of America Newsletter*, Vol. 31, Fall 1989, pp. 1, 4–8.

Brown-Davidson, Terri, "The Belabored Scene, The Subtlest Detail: How Craft Affects Heat in the Poetry of Sharon Olds and Sandra McPherson," in *Hollins Critic*, Vol. 29, No. 1, February 1992, pp. 1–10.

Harris, Peter, "Four Salvers Salvaging: New Work by Voigt, Olds, Dove, and McHugh," in *Virginia Quarterly Review*, Vol. 64, No. 2, Spring 1988, pp. 262–76.

McEwen, Christian, "Soul Substance," in *Nation*, Vol. 244, No. 14, April 11, 1987, pp. 472–75.

Olds, Sharon, *The Gold Cell*, Alfred A. Knopf, 1987, pp. 33, 43.

Spalding, Esta, "The Earthly Matter: A Conversation with Sharon Olds," in *Brick*, Vol. 67, Spring 2001, pp. 85–92.

## Further Reading

Dacey, Philip, and David Jauss, eds., *Strong Measures: Contemporary American Poetry in Traditional Forms*, Addison-Wesley, 1986.

    This collection of poetry provides the reader with a large selection of poems that demonstrates the many different poetic forms used.

Mullaney, Janet Palmer, ed., *Truthtellers of the Times: Interviews with Contemporary Women Poets*, University of Michigan Press, 1998.

    This book is a collection of interviews with fourteen contemporary poets. Although an interview with Olds is not part of this book, the text does provide a glimpse into the creative world of some of Olds's contemporaries.

Pinsky, Robert, *The Sounds of Poetry: A Brief Guide*, Farrar, Straus & Giroux, 1999.

    An easy to read primer on how to read and understand poetry, in which Pinsky discusses line, syntax, meter, rhyme, and the art of poetry.

Schaller, Michael, *Reckoning with Reagan: America and Its President in the 1980s*, Oxford University Press, 1984.

    This book provides a comprehensive overview of the Reagan years. The author focuses on Reagan's politics, the economy, the social world, and the diplomatic world of the 1980s.

Slansky, Paul, *The Clothes Have No Emperor: A Chronicle of the American Eighties*, Fireside, 1989.

    Slansky provides a humorous look at the 1980s and an often cutting assessment of the Reagan presidency. This text is largely non-partisan.

Strand, Mark, and Eavan Boland, eds., *The Making of a Poem: A Norton Anthology of Poetic Forms*, W. W. Norton & Company, 2001.

    An excellent guide to how to read poetry, this text offers help to the reader who is trying to understand poetic form. It includes an anthology of poems that illustrate the various concepts discussed.

# Knoxville, Tennessee

*Nikki Giovanni*
*1968*

Originally published in the 1968 poetry collection *Black Judgement*, Nikki Giovanni's poem "Knoxville, Tennessee" has had many incarnations. In 1994, it was published as a children's book complete with full-color illustrations by Larry Johnson. A delightful and nostalgic visit to a summertime memory, the poem evokes the voice of a child in the midst of this reverie. The poem is generally not complicated by literary references or stodgy style but leans heavily upon an innate rhythm that seems to rise from the child's own heartbeat. Originally written for an adult, African-American audience, the poem has found a much wider readership. Its simplicity draws readers into a world where the most important decision to make is whether to have more "barbecue" or keep some room for the "homemade ice-cream."

## Author Biography

Giovanni was born in Knoxville, Tennessee, in 1943, but she grew up in Lincoln Heights, Ohio, a predominantly black community. Her happy childhood, spent partly with her grandparents in Tennessee, became a major theme of her poetry. "Nikki Rosa," which recounts Giovanni's contented childhood, is often considered her signature poem. Giovanni received her bachelor's degree in history from Fisk University in 1967. While at Fisk, Giovanni was strongly influenced

*Nikki Giovanni*

by a creative writing workshop taught by novelist John Oliver Killens. She also rejected her formerly conservative views in favor of the radicalism she encountered in fellow classmates. *Black Judgement* and *Black Feeling, Black Talk*, her first two volumes of poetry, reflect the anger and enthusiasm of the community of writers and political activists with whom Giovanni became involved. Adopting a revolutionary stance, Giovanni advocated open violence and expressed her impatience for change. In 1969, Giovanni took a teaching position at Rutgers University and gave birth to her son Thomas. During the mid-1970s, her work became more domestic and less angry, alienating her from some of her earlier supporters, though other critics praised her introspection and personal development. In 1971, Giovanni began to experiment with sound recordings of her poetry, and her first album, *Truth Is on Its Way*, was the best selling spoken-word record that year, greatly contributing to her nationwide fame. Although subsequent publications, such as *Cotton Candy on a Rainy Day* (1978) and *Those Who Ride the Night Winds* (1983), depart from her previous stylistic and thematic structures, Giovanni continues to receive the admiration of critics as an important voice in contemporary poetry.

## Media Adaptations

- "Knoxville, Tennessee" is included on a 1976 LP record issued by Folkways Smithsonian Records called *Legacies: The Poetry of Nikki Giovanni*. It was reissued on compact disc in 1997.

- The Poetry Center of San Francisco released a videocassette of Nikki Giovanni reading at San Francisco State University in 1984. The title is *Nikki Giovanni*, and it was released on video in 1984.

- A videocassette of Nikki Giovanni reading her poetry was released in 1988 by Direct Cinema Limited. It is entitled *Spirit to Spirit* and was produced and directed by Mirra Bank.

- Giovanni is one of the poets featured in the four-videocassette series *Furious Flower: African American Poetry, 1960–1995*. This collection of conversations with poets was released in 1998 by California Newsreel. Joanne Gabbin was the executive producer, and Judith McCray was the director.

## Poem Summary

### Lines 1–2

In each line of this poem, the speaker identifies something about summer. It is clear by the simplicity of language and affections that this speaker is not an adult but perhaps a child. It seems to be told from the point of view of a young person who is both nostalgic about a past summer spent and also looking forward to the return of summer's delights.

### Lines 3–12

In these lines, the speaker focuses on the taste sensations of summer and the quality of abundance. The presence of the family patriarch is perhaps the only slightly political statement in the whole poem. This poem can be determined as political if one considers the times in which the author was writing this poem and the feeling that black men were under siege. Otherwise, having a "daddy" who has a "garden" could not be more natural to a child's memories.

### Lines 13–17

Now, the speaker evokes a higher sensation, perhaps an almost spiritual quality to the memory by asking the reader to consider the "gospel music" and the tight-knit community centered on the "church." The fact that these lines fall in the center of the poem suggests that perhaps this is the heart and soul of the speaker's memory. The importance of this vision of a "homecoming" cannot be overlooked and can perhaps tell the reader that the speaker is not always in this earthly paradise.

### Lines 18–24

Finally, the speaker makes the connection to the place itself. The place is identified by "mountains," which often represent truth or vision. That the speaker goes to this place with a grandmother re-enforces the idea that wisdom is somehow shared by osmosis. The way that the speaker connects to the time and place is like the feeling of a good dream and perhaps that is why the reader is taken to the end of the day, to "sleep."

## Themes

### Simple Life

"Knoxville, Tennessee" was written at a time when many writers and social critics identified the experience of black Americans with urban problems such as poverty, crime, and race riots. This poem presents a sense of nostalgia for happier and simpler times, which are all related to summer in the mind of the poem's speaker. The first half of the poem centers on vegetables that are eaten in the same place they are grown, cutting away the chain of producers and handlers that comes between most city and suburban dwellers and the vegetables they consume. This phase of the poem gives way to another phase, represented by foods that are only slightly altered from their natural ingredients, such as barbecue, buttermilk, and homemade ice cream. All of these products are common, but their processed versions are far from the simple pleasures that the natural versions evoke in this poem's speaker. In a similar way, gospel music is a type of religious experience that invites participants to involve themselves directly in religion, rather than

## Topics for Further Study

- When this poem was first published in 1969, racial tensions in America were at their height. Explain how you think a white author would have handled the situation described in this poem differently.

- The reference to going "to the mountains" in line 18 refers to old spiritual songs. Research African-American spiritual music and find some songs that refer to mountains. Then, explain the significance of this symbol.

- The foods that Giovanni lists in this poem are traditional Southern foods. Make a list of things that the poem's speaker would remember fondly if she had spent her childhood summers in some other part of the country.

- Write a response poem, using the same voice and style used here, that explains what this poem's speaker does during the winter.

filtering religion through abstract philosophical thoughts.

### Food

Giovanni uses food to represent life in Knoxville for two reasons. For one thing, it is a powerful cultural indicator. The foods that this poem's speaker associates with Knoxville give readers a clear sense of the people who are discussed here. For instance, "fresh corn" implies that this poem takes place in the country, but not exactly on a farm, since the fresh corn in the poem comes from a garden. "Home made ice cream" similarly implies a rural setting. Several specific vegetables, such as okra and especially greens, are found in the southern part of the country and are strongly associated with the South's culinary tradition. Even though the poem's title makes it possible for readers to locate its setting on a map, these foods help readers experience the culture being discussed.

Frequently mentioning food also makes the poem a powerful experience for readers by appealing to their sense of taste. Poets often try to help readers experience the reality of the world about which they are writing by using images that affect the five senses. As the sense that is least often used in poems, taste is particularly effective in drawing readers into a situation, making them feel reality as the poem's speaker feels it. This poem uses words to remind readers of foods and their particular tastes, rendering the experience of summer in the South.

## Home

The church event mentioned in the poem is not just any gathering: it is referred to in line 17 as a "homecoming." This one word extends the meaning of the church beyond its natural religious function to a social function, welcoming people back to the community after they have gone on to live in different places. They may attend religious services wherever they move, but, regardless of where they have gone or how long they have been gone, this church identifies Knoxville as their home.

The sense of "home" that runs through "Knoxville, Tennessee" is emphasized even more by the attention given to family. A father is mentioned early, in line 4; traditionally, the father is the head of the family and, in this case, he lives up to tradition by providing nourishment with vegetables he has raised. The addition of a grandmother in line 19 establishes a home that is open beyond the narrowest definitions, a home that includes members of the extended family.

But, the aspect of the poem that most clearly identifies this situation as "home" is the speaker's familiarity with the routine that occurs there. The speaker uses the present tense to speak of eating and listening to music and going to the mountains, indicating that she has done these things often and expects to do them again and again.

## Security and Insecurity

The use of the word "daddy" in line 4 establishes the poem's point of view as that of a child, or at the very least as someone who finds comfort and security in speaking of her father. Throughout the poem there is a tone of security in the rituals and familiar foods the speaker finds in Knoxville. This culminates in the final lines, which identify Knoxville in the summer as a place where one can "be warm / all the time / not only when you go to bed / and sleep." This warmth can literally be the warmth of summer days, in contrast to cold winter days, but warmth can also be used to symbolize a sense of safety, implying that the poem's speaker no longer feels the need to be guarded most of the day.

Using "warmth" as a symbol for security in this poem leads readers to wonder why the poem's speaker sometimes feels insecure. If she only feels secure in her bed or during the summers, when she can wander in nature, then the implication seems to be that insecurity occurs when dealing with other people in society. If such is the case, then "Knoxville, Tennessee" is a true reflection of the experience of many Americans who moved from farms to cities but who only feel comfortable when they return to a country environment.

# Style

Minimally constructed, "Knoxville, Tennessee" depends on the simplicity of its language and rhythm to evoke the language and memories of a child. Giovanni relies on the simple device of singling out phrases and images in each line to crystallize the whole movement of the poem into a tangible time and place. Reading it, one can easily imagine the words spilling from the mouth of a young girl remembering her favorite place on earth.

# Historical Context

## Black Identity

Although "Knoxville, Tennessee" does not address any specific issues regarding race, it was published at a time when Giovanni's writing was very much concerned with the question of black identity. Other selections in *Black Judgement*, the volume in which this poem was first published, make affirmative statements about being black (such as "Beautiful Black Men") and about mocking the white males who held political power (such as "Ugly Honkies, or The Election Game and How to Win It"). A prose poem titled "Reflections on April 4, 1968," about the assassination of Martin Luther King Jr., begins with the line "What can I, a poor Black woman, do to destroy America?" It goes on to state, "[t]he assassination of Martin Luther King is an act of war. President Johnson, your unfriendly candidate, has declared war on Black people." This book was published during the Civil Rights Movement, a time when black-American writers were struggling to use words to affirm the cultural identity of their people.

## Compare & Contrast

- **1969:** In the wake of the assassination of Reverend Martin Luther King the year before, dozens of cities across the country—including Chicago, New York, Baltimore, Boston, Newark, Kansas City, and Washington, D.C.—experience race riots. Some black communities are completely devastated by the riots.

   **Today:** Racial tensions seldom boil over into riots. The last major spate of race riots occurred in 1992, after the verdict was handed down in the trial of the Los Angeles police officers who arrested Rodney King.

- **1969:** Americans look nostalgically toward the wholesomeness of country life as an antidote for the violence and corruption of inner city life.

   **Today:** "Urban sprawl" has pushed Americans beyond the crowded city into the semi-rural comforts of the suburbs.

- **1969:** Only a few black actors are offered recurring roles on network television, most notably Bill Cosby in *I Spy*, Diahann Carroll in *Julia*, and Nichelle Nichols in *Star Trek*.

   **Today:** The color lines on television are not as marked as in previous decades. However, there are still fewer leading roles for black actors than white actors, particularly on the major networks.

- **1969:** A growing number of Americans oppose America's military involvement in Vietnam.

   **Today:** After the destruction of the New York City World Trade Center and an attack on the Pentagon in 2001, Americans are largely supportive of the U.S. military's operations in Afghanistan.

- **1969:** Growing awareness of the earth's ecological balance and of humanity's potential to destroy the environment lead to the first International Earth Day in 1970.

   **Today:** Earth Day is still celebrated annually. Environment-friendly ideas that once seemed strange, such as emissions testing and recycling programs, are common parts of daily life.

---

Historically, blacks in America have met resistance to attempts to form a cultural identity. From the time the first Africans were brought to the new world as slaves in 1501 to the fall of the Confederacy in 1864, it was in the interest of mainstream culture to view blacks as subhuman, lacking in the mental and emotional capacity to form authentic, significant cultural ties. After the end of the Civil War, it was in the interest of whites, especially those on the lower end of the social strata, to promote the myth that held blacks to be too incompetent to control their own fate through property ownership and voting. Laws were passed to keep the races separate and to keep blacks out of the political process, assuring that organized black voters would not be able to change oppressive laws. These laws, referred to collectively as "Jim Crow laws" (after a foolish black character in minstrel comedies), claimed to offer blacks "separate but equal" facilities, such as schooling and public transportation. In reality, the facilities provided for black citizens were not equal to, rather far worse than, those provided for whites.

The struggle against racial discrimination in America made great strides in the 1950s and early 1960s. In 1954, the United States Supreme Court found the "separate but equal" doctrine to be unconstitutional while ruling on the case of *Brown v. the Board of Education of Topeka, Kansas*. While the case specifically discussed the issue of integrating public schools, its basic principle came to be used to tear down racial barriers in all areas of society. In 1955, Rosa Parks, a Montgomery, Alabama resident, refused to sit in the back of a public bus, as blacks were required to do by law. Her arrest and a subsequent boycott of the Montgomery bus system by blacks served to change the law and showed blacks the power of presenting a united front. In 1963, President John F. Kennedy proposed far-reaching legislation to ensure the rights of black citizens a hundred years after President Lincoln had abolished slavery in America with the Emancipation Proclamation.

The Black Pride movement was both a cause and an effect of the push for civil rights. A major psychological barrier was breached as black Americans became increasingly aware throughout the twentieth century of their own rich culture and of the artificial standards of mainstream culture that associated black traditions and physical characteristics with shame and ugliness. During the mid-1960s, authors and social critics made a point of emphasizing the beauty of black life. "Black is beautiful" became a popular slogan in the movement for racial equality, along with "Black Power." In this context, Giovanni's inflamed condemnation of the traditionally white power structure in *Black Judgement* was a fairly common claim for the legitimacy blacks had been denied for hundreds of years.

"Knoxville, Tennessee" is not written from a perspective of anger; instead, it affirms black traditions by showing the joy of the speaker, who remembers how much she loved growing up in her situation. The fact that the speaker is black is not mentioned openly, which in itself makes a political point. At a time when black Americans were struggling to show both whites and blacks that black traditions were positive and supportive, Giovanni chose to deemphasize the race of the speaker of the poem, showing readers that black children experience the world in much the same way that white children do. At a time when the black experience was just emerging into the public consciousness, this point would have been much more significant than it would be today.

## Critical Overview

Giovanni first garnered attention as a revolutionary poet with her book *Black Judgement* in 1968. Known then primarily for her angry verse, Giovanni's critics and supporters alike paid more attention to her themes of revolution than her larger themes of family and love. In 1971, Don L. Lee commented in his *Dynamite Voices*, "Nikki writes about the familiar: what she knows, sees, experiences. It is clear why she conveys such urgency in expressing the need for Black awareness, unity, solidarity. She knows how it was. She knows how it is. She knows also that a change can be affected."

Giovanni early on seems to have departed from her political stance with her poem "Knoxville, Tennessee." One senses that beneath the revolutionary is a woman truly at peace with herself and her past. Suzanne Juhasz commented in *Naked and Fiery Forms: Modern American Poetry by Women, A New Tradition* that "power and love are what are at issue in Nikki Giovanni's poetry and life. In her earlier poems (1968–1970), these issues are for the most part separate. She writes of personal love in poems of private life; of black power and a public love in political poems."

In her later work, Giovanni more fully embraces the politics of personal life. Giovanni is perhaps her own most interesting critic and seems to understand very well what she does with her art form. In an interview by Claudia Tate in 1983, Giovanni states of her process, "A poem is a way of capturing a moment. I don't do a lot of revisions because I think if you have to do that then you've got problems with the poem. Rather than polish the words, I take the time to polish the poem."

## Criticism

### David Kelly

*Kelly is an instructor of creative writing and literature at Oakton Community College. In this essay, Kelly discusses the childlike voice and nostalgic tone that make Giovanni's poem a work to which people from different societies can relate.*

At the time that "Knoxville, Tennessee" was published in the late 1960s, Nikki Giovanni was gaining public attention for writing angry political poems that contained racial slurs and calls for violence. Other poems from her collection *Black Feeling, Black Talk / Black Judgement* have not withstood the test of time. Lines of poetry like "Blessed be machine guns in Black hands" from her poem "A Litany for Peppe" or her advice to black children to "grow a natural [afro] and practice radicalism" from "Poem for Black Boys" catapulted her to stardom in her twenties, but their significance has faded as the spirit of revolution has, for better or worse, faded from the racial dialog in America. But, for more than thirty years, "Knoxville, Tennessee" has endured, quietly proving itself more powerful than the poems with heated rhetoric and inflammatory ideas. Speaking simply about a simple subject, the poem has insight to offer people across racial, age, and cultural differences.

Often readers who think they are praising a poem by saying they can "relate to it" are actually

> *Giovanni provides specific details that readers find meaningful because the poem's speaker finds them meaningful."*

disrespecting the poet's skill without even knowing it. To say that many people understand something might just mean it is superficial enough to be appreciated without much thought. The most common way to produce something thousands of unrelated strangers will be able to understand would be to offer something that has very little substance. Millions of people relate to television shows that make a point of leaving out anything that might alienate anybody, and critics generally agree that television has less artistic merit than poetry, which alienates just about everyone. Even though there are poems that gain popularity by being shallow, there are also works like "Knoxville, Tennessee," which are able to speak to a wide audience without having to water down its message because it understands the common threads of human existence and is able to address them directly. This poem succeeds because it does not shy away from the task of showing readers one specific situation and relating this situation to something they may have experienced.

One way this poem is able to reach so many readers is its narrative perspective. Giovanni renders this poem in the persona of a child, but subtly, without any condescension. This is a key factor in the reader's ability to relate to the situation she describes because each reader was a child once. Although she makes this narrative stance seem easy, a technique like this is actually a true test of a poet's skill. There is much that could go wrong when writing in a child's voice. The particular details a child would focus on are not the ones that an adult sees, and the language a child would use limits the poet. The poet trying to write in a child's voice risks failure with each line.

Giovanni does not make any pointed reference to the speaker's age; instead, she reveals it through sublime methods, leaving it for the reader to discern. For instance, she works in references to other family members who are older. The fourth line's reference to "daddy" is a clear clue that the speaker at least feels like a child in reference to her father. The later mention of "grandmother" gives an even stronger sense of the speaker's age, establishing her as young enough to have two living generations around. These two words are probably the most direct indicators that this poem is being told from a young person's perspective.

But, they are only clues and do not, in and of themselves, provide enough evidence to know the poem's speaker. The sense of familiarity that most readers get from this poem comes from Giovanni's ability to write convincingly in a child's voice without making a big issue of the fact that she is doing so. It is a child's voice, but it is not childish. The poem consists of words that are simple, but not too simple, arranged in short lines that generally run for no more than four or five words each. The narrowness of the lines gives the poem's rhythm a jerky, breathless quality, with ideas chopped into short phrases the way they would be by a child who is overenthusiastic, as if the speaker is impatient and finding that words come too slowly. By contrast, a poem with wide, flowing lines that stretch from one side of the page to the other would indicate a speaker who is a smooth and polished orator. The narrator of "Knoxville, Tennessee" seems to be in a rush to discuss all of the things she likes about her favorite season of the year, so impatient to get all of the images in that she can find no better way to express herself than using the simplest connective word: of twenty-four lines in the poem, eleven start with the word "and." This is the way that children tell stories, before they learn more sophisticated methods of tying thoughts together with logical reasoning.

One other stylistic technique worth noting is the poem's use of the word "you." Many contemporary poems use "you," but usually when they do so they create a specific, recognizable character. These poems use "you" often, because each time they do helps readers build a profile of the character being described. Giovanni uses the word in a different way. It does not appear often enough in "Knoxville, Tennessee" to think it is meant to describe a specific "you" character. The few times it is slipped into the poem—in lines 3 and 23, and in line 19 as "your"—read like minor grammatical slips by a speaker who is too unsophisticated to write formally. "You" appears in complex poetry, but it is also a young or simple person's way of telling a story.

While the simple voice of "Knoxville, Tennessee" encourages readers to think like children again, the poem also has a nostalgic tone that serves to remind its readers of all that is lost as one grows. As with the childlike voice, the nostalgic tone could easily, if handled incorrectly, become an embarrassment for the poet, inviting readers' resentment if they feel that the author is trying to manipulate them.

To make the nostalgic experience have the greatest impact on a majority of readers, Giovanni avoids the easy path, which would be to oversimplify everything being discussed and speak in vague terms instead of giving concrete examples. Giovanni provides specific details that readers find meaningful because the poem's speaker finds them meaningful. The title itself, for example, names the place where Giovanni spent her childhood summers, and this invites readers to reflect upon their own lives. Similarly, readers who have never experienced okra, greens, or buttermilk, or who have tried them and do not like them, can share the fondness this poem's speaker has when thinking about the things of her childhood, and they can relate it to the way they look at their own childhood.

Near the end of the poem, the childlike perspective and nostalgic tone come together in one image, that of being barefooted. Being barefooted, in short, represents the simple life that is the poem's focus, as if it is the sum of all that came before. As much as being barefooted reflects the early part of the poem, it can also be considered a jumping-off point for the poem's last movement, where the good life that Giovanni describes is slightly shaded with the hint of danger.

In the poem's last two lines, there is an insinuation of troubled times. Giovanni steers clear of giving a specific description of what it is like to be warm only when one is in bed, sleeping. Readers are left to imagine a place that is never heated properly in the winter, or a life that is so bad that a child can only find peace or warmth by sleeping. This sinister life is not as important as the fact that the poem manages to mention it at all. Without any acknowledgement of the difficulty of the speaker's life outside of Knoxville, the whole poem would be too kind-hearted to be believed. It is an unfortunate fact that most nostalgic reminiscences of childhood make readers feel happy only by ignoring the problems associated with growing up. In "Knoxville, Tennessee," Giovanni uses restraint to avoid saying much about the scary side of childhood, but she does at least recognize that aspect, to round out the poem.

"Knoxville, Tennessee" is a daring poem that could have gone wrong in any number of ways, but does not. It shows more restraint than Giovanni's other poems of the time, which were full of flash but burned out quickly. It also shows more substance than other poems that pretend to offer warmhearted looks at childhood. Through the use of specific imagery and a good understanding, or memory, of how a young person would talk about the situation, Giovanni is able to make readers from all different backgrounds feel how her poem's narrator feels. It is a triumph of quiet restraint, and a good example of what poetry can do at its best.

**Source:** David Kelly, Critical Essay on "Knoxville, Tennessee," in *Poetry for Students*, The Gale Group, 2003.

## Carol Dell'Amico

*Dell'Amico is a college instructor of English literature and composition. In this essay, Dell'Amico reads Giovanni's poem as a work about a typical childhood experience of summer and, more particularly, as a poem about Giovanni's own childhood summers in Knoxville, Tennessee.*

The distinguished U.S. poet Nikki Giovanni came of age, as a poet, during the Civil Rights era in U.S. history, publishing her first volume of poems in 1968. She is known as a central voice in African-American letters, a poet who has dedicated her career to expressing and documenting the aspirations and cultures of African-American peoples. However, her poetry also addresses topics apart from strictly African-American ones, as well as topics that encompass African-American and other, overlapping concerns simultaneously. For example, Giovanni may write from the point of someone in love, from the point of view of a woman, or from the point of view of a woman who is also an African American. Or, as in the poem "Knoxville, Tennessee," she is writing from the points of view of an individual (or a child), an African-American and Southern child in particular, and *any* child enjoying his or her long, delicious summer holiday.

"Knoxville, Tennessee" is both a personal and a public poem. It is personal in the sense that Giovanni spent most of her childhood summers in Knoxville, and so she is in part remembering her own particular history in this poem (Giovanni was born in Tennessee, moved with her family to Ohio when she was an infant, but, thereafter, returned regularly to her grandparents' home in Knoxville to spend summer vacations and other holidays). In addition to this personal, autobiographical

> "The combination of accessibility and social commitment that characterizes Giovanni's poetry has led many to call her a 'poet of the people,' as she demonstrates in these ways that it is necessary and possible to write politically relevant but non-alienating and non-elitist works."

dimension, the poem has a public, broader significance, in that it captures any child's experience of summer. The poem's personal-public doubleness can be seen in the following lines: "you can eat fresh corn / from daddy's garden." The "you" in this first line gestures toward all readers who enjoyed summers like Giovanni's while the words "daddy's garden" points to how Giovanni is thinking of her own childhood in particular, a childhood graced, in part, by a private family garden plot.

The language employed in Giovanni's poem is characteristic of the language employed in her poetry throughout her career. Giovanni favors everyday words, language that is broadly accessible or capable of being understood and enjoyed by any North-American reader, regardless of the reader's education and experience. The combination of accessibility and social commitment that characterizes Giovanni's poetry has led many to call her a "poet of the people," as she demonstrates in these ways that it is necessary and possible to write politically relevant but non-alienating and non-elitist works. It is important to note, in this regard, that Giovanni's employment of everyday words and speech patterns does not mean that the poems are simple or shallow in sense or meaning. On the contrary, Giovanni's poems are as admired by critics as those by poets who prefer more adorned language; Giovanni simply has perfected a means of complex poetic expression that does require rare or unusual words to communicate.

"Knoxville, Tennessee" is an affectionate ode to childhood and childhood summers, the sort of childhood summers enjoyed by children who can be safely let loose during the summer months to freely roam their neighborhoods or the countryside surrounding the city or town in which they live. This wild freedom is in direct contrast to the rules and regulations under which children live during the school year, when they must follow a strict schedule, obey their teachers in addition to their parents, and fulfill all the tasks that being a student entails. Hence, as the child speaker of this poem asserts—in a typically childish way—she likes summer, of all seasons, "best."

Summer is so wonderful to this poem's child because she is not only free of school-year restrictions, but also because summer is so rich in delights, so full of favorite treats and activities. During the summer months she eats "fresh corn" straight from "daddy's garden," and "okra / and greens / and cabbage / and lots of / barbecue / and buttermilk / and homemade ice-cream." These foods and treats are, clearly, among the child's favorites—but, then again, which child would turn down "homemade ice-cream" or succulent "barbecue"? Indeed, of the poem's twenty-four lines, eleven begin with the word "and," and so the reader understands that wonderful delights are many during summer; they pile up; there is, seemingly, a never-ending supply of them ("lots of" them, as the childish speaker hints).

This poem's very short lines convey the excitement and jam-packed days of summer, days in which one wonderful activity is followed immediately by another. These lines, which can be so rapidly read, which seem to tumble down the page, suggest the headlong progress of busy days during which children are free to run about as much and as wildly as they please. This is an outdoor life, most children's favorite kind of life, as one of the isolated words of poem makes clear: "outside." Further, the poem's middle portion, beginning with the line "at the church picnic," is, essentially, a list of the types of special summer events so enjoyed by children: church picnics, other special church events (the "church / homecoming"), hikes to the "mountains" with one's "grandmother," and running around "barefooted." Although it is understood that special events such as church "picnics" and "homecomings" do not happen on the same day, the idea that summer days are full of any number of wonderful activities is nevertheless conveyed by the length and variety of this list, as well as by Giovanni's choos-

## What Do I Read Next?

- *Black Feeling, Black Talk* (Giovanni's first collection of poems) and *Black Judgement* (in which "Knoxville, Tennessee" was published) were combined into one book called *Black Feeling, Black Talk / Black Judgement* in 1970 by the William Morrow Company.

- In 1994, the poem "Knoxville, Tennessee" was adapted to a children's book of the same title as the poem, with original illustrations by Larry Johnson. *Knoxville, Tennessee* is published by Scholastic, Inc.

- Written around the same time that "Knoxville, Tennessee" was published, Giovanni's book *Gemini* bears the subtitle "An Extended Autobiographical Statement on My First Twenty-Five Years of Being a Black Poet." In it, she describes her life and the state of race relations in America at the time and clearly outlines her views of both. This book was published in 1971 by the Bobbs-Merrill Company.

- Poet Gwendolyn Brooks has praised Giovanni's poetry. Many of Brooks's best works can be found in her *Selected Poems*, published in 1999 by HarperCollins.

- In 1971, author James Baldwin appeared with Giovanni on a British television program. Their conversation, with slight editing, was transcribed into a book called *A Dialogue: James Baldwin and Nikki Giovanni*. It was published in 1973 by J. B. Lippincott Company.

- In 1972 and 1973, Giovanni had a series of conversations with esteemed African-American poet Margaret Walker. Their talks were taped, transcribed, and printed in the book *A Poetic Equation: Conversations between Nikki Giovanni and Margaret Walker*. This book was published in 1974 by Howard University Press.

- Giovanni wrote the introduction for *The Rose That Grew from Concrete*, a posthumous collection of poems by recording artist Tupac Shakur written between 1989 and 1991, before he became famous. It was published in 1999 by MTV Books.

- The sense of displacement and determination that appears in Giovanni's powerful work from the 1960s is evident in the poetry of Naomi Shihab Nye, a Palestinian American living in Texas. Her poems can be found in *Words under the Words: Selected Poems*, which was published in 1995 by Eighth Mountain Press.

- One of the most distinctive African-American voices of 1960s literature was that of Amiri Baraka, the poet who formerly went by the name Leroi Jones. His forty-year career as a poet, essayist, playwright, and fiction writer is surveyed in *The Leroi Jones/Amiri Baraka Reader*, published in 1999 by Thunder's Mouth Press.

- Giovanni's *Racism 101* (1985) is a collection of essays she has written concerning what it is like to be a "Black American." These essays discuss a wide-range of topics and give a good perspective on Giovanni's personal feelings about race and race relations in America.

---

ing to end the poem with the word "sleep." Since each day is full of so much running around and socializing, each summer day's end finds the child happily, thoroughly exhausted, thoroughly ready for rest. The poem's headlong, tumbling rush, then, mimics the exiting pace of a child's typical summer day, a day that will end in deep, satisfied "sleep."

In addition to this idea of summer plenty (whether plenty of favorite foods or activities), this poem conveys the idea that summers are special to children also because they are closely ensconced within the warm embrace of family during this time. Giovanni refers specifically to a "daddy" and a "grandmother" in the poem and speaks of the "warm" weather of summer to suggest how children appreciate not having to leave their family circle for the public space of school during the holiday months. This is a safe, cozy feeling, like snuggling in bed: "and be warm / all the time / not only when you go to bed."

A sense of solid, comforting community is also reinforced by the poem's mention of church events, as one's church community is in some sense an extension of one's immediate family. That Giovanni mentions a "church / homecoming" in particular supports these ideas of an extended church-family, as well as how children feel as if they are, for all their roaming about, comfortably at *home* for the duration of the summer vacation. This mention of a church homecoming also suggests that, even as Giovanni lived most of her life outside of Tennessee, Tennessee is somehow her first and most special home, either because she was born there or perhaps because she was so close to her grandparents, particularly her grandmother, Emma Louvenia Watson.

At the same time that any reader who enjoyed summers like Giovanni's will relate to this poem, the poem presents a picture of summers as they are experienced by many Southern and African-American children in particular. Words such as "fresh corn" and "okra" conjure the U.S. South, as these are regional Southern specialties. A specifically African-American Southern culture is suggested by Giovanni's focus on church events, especially "gospel music," as gospel music is an art form of central importance within U.S. African-American cultures, cultures that have their roots in the South. Further, church events and socials are, both historically and still today, central components of African-American community and public life.

The Civil Rights era in the United States was a fraught time during which many pitched battles were fought. Schools and other public institutions had to be integrated, and African Americans fought for equal opportunity in all areas of contemporary life. For this reason, many of Giovanni's poems, especially from the earlier collections, convey trenchant protest, although some work toward African-American equality simply by documenting the specificity and particularity of African-American lives and cultures. (That is, by documenting the lives and cultures of African Americans, Giovanni writes these ways of living into being and social significance.) However, as Giovanni has made clear—and as she makes clear in "Knoxville, Tennessee"—being political and sometimes angry does not mean being unhappy. As she writes in

the autobiographical poem "Nikki-Rosa," for example, (which, like "Knoxville, Tennessee," is from Giovanni's first published collection, the 1968 volume entitled *Black Feeling Black Talk / Black Judgement*),

and I really hope no white person ever has cause
to write about me
because they never understand
Black love is Black wealth and they'll
probably talk about my hard childhood
and never understand that
all the while I was quite happy.

"Knoxville, Tennessee" is a testament to Giovanni's happy childhood, and this and other poems in the poet's long, distinguished career are testaments to the fact that being outraged over inequality and fighting for one's rights is not necessarily an occasion for unhappiness. Being political, Giovanni's writing suggests, is being a complete human, a person not wholly enwrapped in a small bubble of private concerns but also involved in the events of the larger, surrounding, public world.

**Source:** Carol Dell'Amico, Critical Essay on "Knoxville, Tennessee," in *Poetry for Students*, The Gale Group, 2003.

## Martha Cook

*In the following excerpt, Cook explores the scope of Giovanni's poetry and her presence as a Southern poet.*

In her first collection of poems, Giovanni expresses themes anticipated by the title *Black Feeling, Black Talk*. But already she demonstrates occasionally her gift for the original, individual image, for example, as she evokes the days and places of childhood in "Poem (For BMC No. 2)":

There were fields where once we walked
Among the clover and crab grass and those
Funny little things that look like cotton candy

There were liquids expanding and contracting
In which we swam with amoebas and other Afro-Americans

This poem is a striking contrast to the best-known poem from this volume, "The True Import of Present Dialogue, Black vs. Negro (For Peppe, Who Will Ultimately Judge Our Efforts)," with its repetition of the lines "Nigger / Can you kill." Like "Nikki-Rosa" and "Knoxville, Tennessee" from her next volume, "Poem (For BMC No. 2)" recalls a time and place that endure in memory, even in the face of violence and hatred.

One of Giovanni's finest poems is set in this homeland of the past. "Knoxville, Tennessee," written at the height of the unrest of the civil rights movement of the 1960s, develops a theme of security, of belonging, through simple yet highly effective images of nature, of family, of religion. Although it is almost imagistic, it builds to an explicit thematic statement:

> I always like summer
> best
> you can eat fresh corn
> from daddy's garden
> and okra
> and greens
> and cabbage
> and lots of
> barbecue
> ...
> and be warm
> all the time
> not only when you go to bed
> and sleep

The simple diction, the soothing alliteration, the short lines to emphasize each word, all create a feeling of love for this place and these people that transcends topical issues.

Giovanni later wrote a prose description of Christmas in Knoxville using images of winter rather than summer, yet conveying the same feeling of warmth: "Christmas in Knoxville was the smell of turnip greens and fatback, perfume blending with good Kentucky bourbon, cigars and cigarettes, bread rising on the new electric stove, the inexplicable smell of meat hanging in the smokehouse (though we owned no smokehouse), and, somehow, the sweet taste of tasteless snow." As Roger Whitlow notes, though, this kind of warmth is "rare" in Giovanni's early work. Still, Giovanni's use of this Southern place from her past speaks to the same aspects of Southern life as poems by James Dickey or prose by Eudora Welty.

Most of the poems in *Black Judgement* are militant in subject and theme; one of the most effective is "Adulthood (For Claudia)," in which Giovanni catalogs the violence of the decade, the deaths of leaders from Patrice Lumumba to John F. Kennedy to Martin Luther King, Jr., and of lesser-known civil rights workers such as Viola Liuzzo. In another poem from this volume, "For Saundra," Giovanni seems to explain why poems of political rhetoric dominate her first two volumes. The persona speaks of the difficulty of composing poems in revolutionary times; for example,

> so i thought
> i'll write a beautiful green tree poem
> peeked from my window
> to check the image
> noticed the schoolyard was covered

> *The simple diction, the soothing alliteration, the short lines to emphasize each word, all create a feeling of love for this place and these people that transcends topical issues.*

> with asphalt
> no green—no trees grow
> in manhattan

She concludes that "perhaps these are not poetic / times / at all." Although the thrust of the poem is toward the civil rights strife of the late 1960s, the reader also senses something of the alienation and displacement of a Southerner in the urban North.

Giovanni uses the South and its people to develop the specific theme of the past in "Alabama Poem" from her next collection, *Re: Creation*. A student at Tuskegee Institute meets an old black man and then an old black woman whose remarks indicate that knowledge must be gained through experience, must be inherited from the past. The persona speculates in conclusion: "if trees would talk / wonder what they'd tell me." Her words do not seem ironic; rather she seems to have learned a valuable lesson in her walk along this Southern country road. Though the images in this poem are sparse, the rural place and its people are seen to be of vital significance to one who seeks knowledge. The theme of the necessity of learning from the past what one needs to live in the present links this poem by Nikki Giovanni to a rich tradition in Southern writing, especially from the Fugitive poets of the 1920s to the present.

A more challenging use of the concreteness of place and the thematic significance of the past can be seen in the complex, ironic poem "Walking Down Park," also from *Re:Creation*. Speculating about the history of New York City, the speaker wonders what a street such as Park Avenue looked like "before it was an avenue," "what grass was like before / they rolled it / into a ball and called / it central park." She even thinks:

ever look south
on a clear day and not see
time's squares but see
tall birch trees with sycamores
touching hands

Questioning why men destroy their environment, she returns to days of the past, musing, "probably so we would forget / the Iroquois, Algonquin / and Mohicans who could caress / the earth." Possibly this relationship with nature, which characterized the Indians of an earlier time, can be recaptured:

ever think what Harlem would be
like if our herbs and roots and elephant ears
grew sending
a cacophony of sound to us

Here through a complex set of images Giovanni connects the situation of blacks in contemporary America with the past of the American Indian, another oppressed minority group, as well as with their African heritage. "Walking Down Park" thus becomes a statement of a longing for happiness, related in the mind of the speaker not only to life in the past, which allowed for a closeness to nature lost in contemporary urban life, but also to a specific place from the past—Africa.

One of the most important examples of the ways Giovanni employs places in her poetry is her use of houses, both literal and metaphorical, from the past and in the present. In "Housecleaning," another poem from *Re:Creation*, the persona speaks first of her pleasure in ordinary chores essential to maintaining a house, then turns tidying up into a metaphor to describe aptly the chores necessary in human relationships as well. The growing sense of independence and identity in this poem anticipates the major themes of Giovanni's next volume, *My House*.

At this point, in the early 1970s, Giovanni is still using the lowercase "i," which R. Roderick Palmer identifies as a common device in revolutionary poetry, more than the uppercase. Perhaps she intends to symbolize the concept she has often invoked, that one retains qualities of childhood, even when striving for maturity. She uses this device in a poem from *My House* set, as is "Knoxville, Tennessee," in a place that now exists only in memory. In "Mothers," Giovanni depicts a woman remembering her mother sitting in a kitchen at night:

she was sitting on a chair
the room was bathed in moonlight diffused through
those thousands of panes landlords who rented
to people with children were prone to put in windows

Recalling a poem her mother taught her on this particular night, the persona determines to teach the same poem to her son, to establish with him the relationship she had with her mother. This relationship is re-created for the reader in the simple description of a place remembered, especially in the quality of light Giovanni uses as the central image of the poem.

In the title poem, Giovanni uses homes and houses to represent the movement toward maturity, symbolized by the movement away from the places, homes, of one's childhood toward establishing a home for oneself, or an identity as a mature person. Like Giovanni's poems about childhood, "My House" is characterized by images of warmth and security, emphasizing that in her house the speaker is in complete control:

i mean it's my house
and i want to fry pork chops
and bake sweet potatoes
and call them yams
cause i run the kitchen
and i can stand the heat
…
and my windows might be dirty
but it's my house
and if i can't see out sometimes
they can't see in either

As Suzanne Juhasz emphasizes, the woman speaker "orders experience and controls it… She controls not only through need and desire, but through strength, ability…" In contrast to the child persona of "Knoxville, Tennessee," the "i" here has discovered that she is an autonomous being who can shape at least the smaller places of her world to suit her own needs and desires; at the same time, the "i" is willing to take responsibility for her actions, to pay the price for such control…

These examples from Nikki Giovanni's poetry—and her prose as well—demonstrate that, for her, place is more than an image, more than a surface used to develop a narrative or a theme, just as place functions in the best poetry of the Southern tradition lying behind her work. Further, the changing sense of place in these poems can be seen to reveal Giovanni's developing sense of herself as a woman and as a poet. Suzanne Juhasz, Anna T. Robinson, and Erlene Stetson all emphasize in their recent critical discussions the growing feminist consciousness they find in Giovanni's work. Her use of place is broader than simply a feminist symbol, though, just as her poetry has developed beyond purely racial themes. The relationships of people to places and the ways people have responded to and tried to control places are important themes for Giovanni, as are the ways places sometimes control people. Greatest in thematic significance are the need to belong to a place or in a place and the necessity of moving beyond physical places to spiritual or metaphysical ones.

Looking at Giovanni's poetry in the context of Southern literature expands rather than limits the possibilities for interpretation and analysis. In fact, this approach reveals that within the body of her work lies a solid core of poems that do not rely on political or personal situations for their success. Rather, they develop universal themes, such as coming to terms with the past and with the present so that one may move into the future—again, themes that have been and continue to be of particular significance in Southern poetry. These themes mark her work as a contribution to the canon not just of Southern poetry, of black poetry, of feminist poetry, but also of contemporary American poetry. However, Giovanni's response to any generalization, any categorization, would probably echo the closing line of her poem "Categories," from *My House*. Emphasizing her uniqueness as an individual, she might well proclaim, "i'm bored with categories."

**Source:** Martha Cook, "Nikki Giovanni: Place and Sense of Place in Her Poetry," in *Southern Women Writers: The New Generation*, University of Alabama Press, 1990, pp. 279–300.

## Sources

Giovanni, Nikki, "A Litany for Peppe," in *Black Feeling, Black Talk / Black Judgement*, William Morrow & Company, Inc., 1970 p. 57.

———, "Nikki-Rosa," in *Black Feeling, Black Talk / Black Judgement*, William Morrow & Company, Inc., 1970.

———, "Poem for Black Boys," in *Black Feeling, Black Talk / Black Judgement*, William Morrow & Company, Inc., 1970, pp. 50–51.

———, "Reflections on April 4, 1968," in *Black Feeling, Black Talk / Black Judgement*, William Morrow & Company, Inc., 1970, pp. 54–55.

Giovanni, Nikki, and Claudia Tate, Interview, in *Black Women Writers at Work*, edited by Claudia Tate, Continuum, 1983, pp. 60–78.

Juhasz, Suzanne, "'A Sweet Inspiration . . . of My People': The Poetry of Gwendolyn Brooks and Nikki Giovanni," in *Naked and Fiery Forms: Modern American Poetry by Women, A New Tradition*, Harper Colophon Books, 1976, pp. 144–76.

Lee, Don L., "Nikki Giovanni," in *Dynamite Voices*, Broadside Press, 1971, pp. 68–74.

## Further Reading

Fowler, Virginia C., *Nikki Giovanni*, Twayne's United States Authors Series, No. 613, Twayne Publishers, 1992.

   Fowler, who has been a collaborator with Giovanni (she provided the forward for Giovanni's book *Racism 101*), gives a synopsis of the rise of the poet's career.

Franklin, V. P., *Living Our Stories, Telling Our Truth: Autobiography and the Making of the African-American Intellectual Tradition*, Oxford University Press, 1996.

   Franklin examines how the willingness to use their own experience as subject matter enabled important black writers to change the racial dialogue in America.

Jago, Carol, *Nikki Giovanni in the Classroom*, National Council of Teachers of English, 1999.

   Jago's book is a slim guide, suggesting ways to introduce students to Giovanni and her work.

Josephson, Judith Pinkerton, *Nikki Giovanni: Poet of the People*, Enslow Publishers, Inc., 2000.

   A biography written for students, this book has an entire chapter devoted to Giovanni's childhood in Knoxville and the relationship between her life and the poem.

# Mind

### Jorie Graham
### 1980

Jorie Graham's "Mind" first appeared in the literary journal *Water Table*, and is included in her first collection of poems titled *Hybrids of Plants and of Ghosts* (1980). The title for the collection comes from German philosopher Friedrich Nietzsche's book *Thus Spake Zarathustra*. The poem appears in the fourth section of the collection, following "The Nature of Evidence," a poem about the speaker's ability to apprehend reality. Comprised of thirty-nine short lines, "Mind" tackles a similar theme and is more accessible than many of Graham's poems. However, it still requires rereading for full appreciation.

Graham is known for abstraction in her poems, which means she is as interested in ideas and argument as she is in presenting striking images. Many of her poems are informed by her reading in history, science, art, and philosophy. In "Mind," Graham uses a series of metaphors to describe the idea of the mind and the thinking process. Her poem embodies, as much as depicts, thinking. By comparing processes of nature with the ways in which the human mind makes sense of perception, Graham draws on the romantic tradition in poetry from Samuel Taylor Coleridge through Wallace Stevens, particularly in the ways these poets describe the relationships between imagination and reality, nature and humanity, and the self and other.

## Author Biography

Jorie Graham was born May 9, 1951, in New York City, the daughter of journalist Curtis Bill and sculptor Beverly (Stoll) Pepper. She was raised in Italy, as her father worked as *Newsweek's* bureau chief in Rome. As a teenager, she haunted old churches and watched Michelangelo Antonioni films, soaking up Italy's history and culture. After being expelled from the Sorbonne in Paris for participating in student protests, Graham transferred to New York University, where she studied film with Haig Manoogian and Martin Scorsese. Graham began publishing poems in literary journals and magazines regularly during her twenties and published her first book, *Hybrids of Plants and of Ghosts*, in 1980, with Princeton University Press. In poems such as "Mind," critics recognized Graham's metaphysical leanings and her ability to synthesize disparate material from the sciences, philosophy, literature, art, and history. Her primary influences, however, are modern poets such as William Butler Yeats, Wallace Stevens, T. S. Eliot, and John Berryman.

Upon earning a bachelor of fine arts degree from New York University in 1973, Graham enrolled in the writing workshops at the University of Iowa, receiving her master of fine arts degree in 1978. She has spent almost her entire adult life in academia, teaching at institutions such as Murray State University in Murray, Kentucky; Humboldt State University in Arcata, California; Columbia University in New York City; and the University of Iowa in Iowa City. In 1999, Graham was named Boylston Professor of Rhetoric and Oratory at Harvard University, succeeding Irish poet Seamus Heaney. She was the first woman to hold this professorship.

Graham's passion for teaching has not stifled her passion for writing. Her numerous collections include *Erosion* (1983); *The End of Beauty* (1987); *Region of Unlikeness* (1991); *The Dream of the Unified Field: Selected Poems, 1974–1994* (1995), for which she received a Pulitzer Prize (1996); *The Errancy* (1998); *Swarm* (1999); and *Never* (2002). In addition to the Pulitzer Prize, Graham has been awarded numerous fellowships and grants, including a 1979 Discovery/*The Nation* award, and a MacArthur "genius" grant. She has also received awards from the Guggenheim Foundation, the National Endowment for the Arts, and the Whiting Foundation. In 1997, she was named a chancellor of the Academy of American Poets.

*Jorie Graham*

## Poem Text

The slow overture of rain,
each drop breaking
without breaking into
the next, describes
the unrelenting, syncopated     5
mind. Not unlike
the hummingbirds
imagining their wings
to be their heart, and swallows
believing the horizon     10
to be a line they lift
and drop. What is it
they cast for? The poplars,
advancing or retreating,
lose their stature     15
equally, and yet stand firm,
making arrangements
in order to become
imaginary. The city
draws the mind in streets,     20
and streets compel it
from their intersections
where a little
belongs to no one. It is
what is driven through     25
all stationary portions
of the world, gravity's
stake in things. The leaves,
pressed against the dank
window of November     30
soil, remain unwelcome

till transformed, parts
of a puzzle unsolvable
till the edges give a bit
and soften. See how                                  35
then the picture becomes clear,
the mind entering the ground
more easily in pieces,
and all the richer for it.

## Poem Summary

### Lines 1–6

In the first lines of "Mind," the speaker offers a metaphor for the mind, comparing it to "the slow overture of rain." Overture in this context denotes an orchestral introduction to a musical dramatic work. The speaker compares the way the mind moves from one perception to the next, one thought to the next, with the way an overture leads into the musical work itself. The mind is "unrelenting" because it never stops. It is "syncopated" (also a musical term) because, as in an overture, there is a shift to something else, maybe another perception, another subject, or another way of thinking. These lines comment both on the workings of the mind and the workings of this poem, which also shifts subjects.

### Lines 7–13

The speaker continues comparing the mind with natural phenomena. The speaker imagines that the hummingbird and the swallow perceive the world in ways that make sense to them. The hummingbird, for example, mistakes its wings for its heart because its wings are its most strategic asset. Hummingbirds flap their wings from fifty to two hundred times per second and can lift from perches without pushing off. Swallows, which dip and dive dramatically, could easily confuse how the horizon appears to them in flight for what they are doing to it (i.e., lifting and dropping it). This connection between the birds' misunderstanding of the world and themselves and the human mind suggests that human beings also delude themselves into thinking they know what is real and what is imaginary. When the speaker asks, "What is it / they cast for?," she anthropomorphizes them. This means that she projects onto them human attributes, in particular the attribute of desire. "Casting" suggests fishing, a familiar enough activity for birds.

### Lines 14–19

The speaker continues her comparisons, noting the swallows' perception of poplars, quick-growing trees of the willow family found in North America. The speaker describes how their appearance changes depending on the swallows' perception of them. In describing them as "making arrangements," the speaker personifies them, just as she had the swallows and hummingbirds. "Arrangement" is also a musical term meaning an adaptation of a musical composition by rescoring.

### Lines 20–24

The speaker reverses the subject and object of perception. Whereas in the previous descriptions she shows how birds perceive the physical world, in this description she positions the city as the subject drawing "the mind in streets." This reversal gives credit to the phenomenal, material world in constructing reality. The streets "compel" the mind "from their intersections," meaning from where lines connect. The relationship between subject and object, perceiver and perceived, dissolves here.

### Lines 25–28

The speaker depicts the mind as an active force that is nonetheless "driven" (though by what readers are not told). These lines are typical of the heavily abstract statements for which Graham is known,

## Media Adaptations

- On May 20, 1999, Graham read and talked with Michael Silverblatt, producer and host of the literary interview program "Bookworm," broadcast on public radio stations nationwide. In 2001, the Lannan Foundation released a video of the reading and talk, *Jorie Graham*. Tapes can be ordered by writing to The Lannan Foundation, 313 Read Street, Santa Fe, New Mexico 87501-2628.

- Audio Literature has published an audiocassette on which Graham and other women poets read poems from *The Muse in the Body: Love Poems by Women*, edited by Catherine Bartlett. Tapes can be ordered by writing to Audio Literature, 370 W. San Bruno Ave., Ste. F, San Bruno, CA 94066.

statements that are difficult to translate or paraphrase. Gravity has a stake in "all stationary portions / of the world." These "portions" are stationary because gravity keeps them that way (unlike, for example, hummingbirds or swallows, which can defy gravity with their ability to fly).

### Lines 29–35

The speaker uses the symbolic image of leaves in the November soil to suggest decay and fragmentation. When the "edges give a bit / and soften" they lose their definition and become part of their environment. This blurring of a thing (i.e., leaves) with the larger body to which it belongs (i.e., soil) echoes the way in which the mind also blurs as it changes from subject to subject, perception to perception.

### Lines 36–39

The speaker implicitly compares the leaves to the mind, suggesting that in time both fragment and come to rest in the ground, where they are "all the richer for it." This last image suggests a picture of a compost heap where the leaves return to the soil from which they came, and the mind returns to a state in which it no longer differentiates the particularities of the physical world, and is no longer aware of itself as a perceiving entity.

## Themes

### Nature

Nature has long been a source of inspiration and an object of inquiry for writers and scientists. Graham employs images of nature to underscore humanity's connection to it. By describing the mind in terms of rain, hummingbirds, swallows, leaves, and soil, the speaker shows how human beings are part of the processes of nature. She links these processes to human acts of perception and imagination. The first lines of the poem, for example, liken "The slow overture of rain" to "the unrelenting, syncopated / mind." By comparing the mind with natural processes, Graham binds the mind inextricably to them. The mind functions in an organic way and, like nature, is subject to and defined by all that surrounds it. Like the leaves described in the latter part of the poem, the mind also dies "in pieces." For Graham that is more a reason for celebration than mourning.

### Imagination

"Mind" explores the interplay between imagination and reality, suggesting that subjective ex-

## Topics for Further Study

- Draw a picture of *how* you think (not what you think). What image or images would best represent your thinking processes? Compare your picture with others in your class and discuss differences and similarities.

- Set aside a particular time at the end of each day to meditate on your thinking. Reflect on what subjects have occupied your mind for the day and describe these subjects and your responses to them in a notebook. At the end of two weeks, read through your entries and write a short essay describing any patterns you might see in your descriptions.

- In groups, discuss the differences between the brain and the mind. What points, if any, does the class agree on and how do you account for any disagreements?

- Some critics note similarities between Graham's poetry and that of John Ashbery and James Tate. After reading a few poems from Ashbery and Tate, discuss the similarities and differences among the three.

- Read the rest of the poems in Graham's collection *Hybrids of Ghosts and of Plants*, taking notes on her statements about identity, perception, and language. Then, write a short essay describing Graham's worldview based on the poems in this book.

- In "Mind," Graham describes the mind as "unrelenting." With your classmates, brainstorm a list of other adjectives you would use to describe the mind. Discuss as a class and be prepared to defend your choices.

perience colors perception of the world. Graham uses the hummingbird and the swallow as examples of beings that believe something about nature that human beings, with their scientific understanding of the world, do not. However, the birds' reality is no less real because their beliefs are different than the beliefs of human beings. In exploring the realm of the imagination, Graham writes from the tradition of romantic poets such as William Wordsworth and Samuel Taylor Coleridge, who developed their own styles instead of imitating other writers, and who privileged individual expression. For romantics, the imagination is also the seat of creativity, from which poetry itself springs. By making the subject of her poem the mind and how it apprehends reality, Graham emphasizes her debt to the romantic tradition.

### Reality and Appearances

"Mind" attempts to do two things. First, through a series of comparisons, it attempts to figuratively describe what the mind is. Second, it asks readers to question their understanding of reality by paying attention to *how* their own minds work. By using a series of images connected by abstract statements, Graham forces the reader to participate in the meaning-making process, rather than merely passively consuming her images. This strategy of presenting images and then showing how they are not what they appear to be calls to mind Plato's *Allegory of the Cave*, a text in which the Greek philosopher argues for the existence of a higher reality than the one human beings experience with their senses. The ultimate reality of "Mind" is, paradoxically, earthbound and unresolved.

## Style

### Imagery

Writers create pictures in readers' minds through images utilizing the five senses. Graham employs aural imagery when describing "the slow overture of rain," visual imagery when describing "hummingbirds / imagining their wings," and tactile imagery when describing "the dank . . . soil." With the exception of the city and its streets, all the images in her poem come from nature.

### Abstraction

Abstraction refers to ideas or qualities as opposed to things. Graham mixes abstract statements with her imagery, often using them to comment on the imagery. For example, in the following lines from the middle of the poem, she comments on the mind, using an abstract statement:

> It is
> what is driven through
> all stationary portions
> of the world, gravity's
> stake in things.

Graham's abstractions make her poem difficult while also making it intriguing. She has attributed her propensity for abstraction to her schooling in France.

### Enjambment

Enjambment, also know as run-on lines, occurs when the syntactic unit, or sentence, runs over onto the next line for completion. It is the opposite of an end-stopped line, in which the syntactic unit or sentence ends with the line. Graham employs enjambment throughout "Mind," each line depending on the next to complete its meaning. In this way, the form of the poem dictates the way it is read. The poem is both a description of mind *and* an illustration of how the mind works during the reading process.

## Historical Context

### 1970s and 1980s

Graham wrote "Mind" in the late 1970s and it appears in her 1980 collection *Hybrids of Plants and of Ghosts*. Like many of her poems, "Mind" is not set in any identifiable time or place. Rather, it is a meditation on an idea, the idea of mind. During the 1970s and 1980s, Graham was both a student and a professor in various departments of English, where post-structural literary theories were becoming a regular part of the curriculum. Post-structuralism refers to a set of approaches or attitudes towards texts rather than any codified body of knowledge, and is a response to structuralist theories of knowledge. Some of the features post-structuralist theories share include a rejection of ideas such as essentialism and foundationalism, which inform structuralism. Essentialism suggests there is a reality beyond language, unmediated by how human beings name the world and invest it with significance. Plato, for example, was an essentialist in his belief that ideal forms of ideas and things existed outside of how human beings saw them. Foundationalism refers to the notion that systems of thought can accurately reflect the world and how it works. The ideas of post-structuralist thinkers such as Jacques Derrida and Michel Foucault, both of whom question conventional ways in which critics interpret texts, became both celebrated and hated in English departments. The antihumanist theories of Derrida and Foucault were a source of contention *and* an inspiration for scholars and students alike, and contribute in no small

# Compare & Contrast

- **1980s:** A 1980 study by the American Council on Education shows that college freshmen are more interested in status, power, and money than at any time during the past fifteen years. Business management is the most popular major.

   **Today:** Students continue to enroll in business programs and classes. However, because of the downturn in the economy, a master of business administration degree no longer carries the same clout that it did in 1980.

- **1980s:** Columbia University, the last all male Ivy League school, begins accepting women in 1983.

   **Today:** Like hundreds of other colleges and universities, Columbia University now offers classes and degrees online, making it possible for students to receive a degree without physically attending class.

- **1980s:** In 1985, scientists confirm a hole had opened in the ozone layer surrounding the earth, posing considerable potential health risks for humans.

   **Today:** In 1999, scientists announce that warming temperatures in the Antarctic have caused two ice shelves to break up and melt faster than anyone expected, posing potential danger to human welfare if sea levels rise too quickly.

---

part to the ongoing factionalism in humanities departments today.

The anti-war protests of students in American universities in the 1960s and 1970s helped foster an attitude of rebellion that created an intellectual space for new ideas. This rebellion reached a violent apex in 1970 when Ohio National Guardsmen opened fire on students during a noontime demonstration at Kent State University in Ohio, killing four people and wounding nine others. The protests of the 1970s carried over into curricular reforms in the university itself, as previously ignored groups battled for representation in courses and departments. During the 1970s and 1980s, for example, a number of women's studies programs were formed, as well as programs explicitly addressing the history and culture of groups such as African and Asian Americans. The 1970s and 1980s also saw a dramatic increase in the number of master of fine arts programs in creative writing offered in American universities. Graham herself studied in such a program at the University of Iowa. Thousands of students enroll in these programs each year to hone their writing skills, hoping to land jobs teaching in higher education or to win fame with a blockbuster novel or screenplay.

Outside the academy during these decades, writers explored humanity's increasing alienation from society and one another. Toni Morrison's novels *Song of Solomon* (1977), *Tar Baby* (1981), and *Beloved* (1987), for example, examined the plights of African Americans in a society violently hostile towards them. David Mamet's plays *Glengarry Glen Ross* (1984) and *Speed the Plow* (1988) chronicled the declining morality of the real estate and show business industries respectively. John Updike continued his detailed examination of the spiritual emptiness of middle-class suburban white men in novels such as *Rabbit is Rich* (1981).

## Critical Overview

Graham was well supported in writing the poems for *Hybrids of Plants and of Ghosts*. Poems included in the work had been accepted by quality literary journals such as *American Poetry Review*, *Iowa Review*, and the *New Yorker*, and she received a grant from the Paul Mellon Fund of Princeton University Press to help publish the collection.

Because she is still a relatively young poet whose work has just begun to be addressed by critics, there is no criticism as yet explicitly addressing "Mind." However, some critics have written glowingly about *Hybrids of Plants and of Ghosts*.

In *American Poetry Review*, Dave Smith writes that the collection is "as promising a first book as any recently published." In his essay "About Jorie Graham" for *Ploughshares*, Robert Casper praises Graham's ability and calls her poems "crystalline in their concision." In the *Dictionary of Literary Biography*, Peyton Brien points out the influences of artists and poets on Graham's work, including Paul Eluard, Voltaire, Paul Cézanne, and Mark Rothko, all of whom are subjects of individual poems by Graham. Noting the brevity of many of the collection's poems, Brien argues, "Graham's formal strategies in the book are relatively simple and well designed to enhance the intellectual searching of a neophyte poet." Margaret Gibson, who reviewed the collection for *Library Journal*, emphasizes the abstract quality of the poems, writing, "These are distanced poems, whose difficult language catches and moves us with its beauty." Gibson, herself a noted poet, calls Graham's poems a "mixture of wisdom and discord, desire and faith."

Unlike the critics above, Askold Melnyczuk does not find Graham's first book inspiring, calling it "apprentice work." In "The Mind of the Matter: CAT Scanning a Scat Singer," written for *Parnassus*, Melnyczuk claims, "The work in this first book leaves this reader annoyed and disappointed. Graham seems to be testing out ways of making poems that will support a content yet to surface."

## Criticism

### Chris Semansky

*Semansky is an instructor of literature and composition. In this essay, Semansky considers the philosophy of Graham's poem.*

In the introduction to *The Best American Poetry 1990*, Graham says about poetry: "Each poem is ... an act of the mind that tries ... to clean the language of its current lies, to make it capable of connecting us to the world." However, her own poems often belie this very claim, as they suggest that language is incapable of such an act, and that humanity's separation from the world and human beings' separation from one another are inevitable. "Mind" shows how lying forms an inescapable part of human experience, and how self-delusion is unavoidable.

The very act of writing a poem called "Mind," which attempts to describe in a universal fashion how the mind works, is in keeping with Graham's metaphysical tendencies. Metaphysics, derived from the Greek *meta ta physika* ("after the things of nature"), refers to a branch of philosophy that pursues knowledge that cannot be gleaned from human sense perception. It is conceptual and abstract in nature, terms critics also use to describe Graham's poetry. More specifically, Graham's poem addresses questions of epistemology (that area of metaphysics concerned with how human beings know what they know) and ontology (that area concerned with the nature and relations of being, or things that exist). Metaphysics by its very nature, however, is speculative. Attempting to describe any subject outside of historical or cultural context dooms one to accusations of universalizing. It is an accusation, however, with which Graham is willing to live.

One of the first "lies" of "Mind" is its use of figurative language. In comparing how the mind works with how nature works, the speaker employs metaphors. However, the very act of using metaphor as a means of description demands lying, in that comparisons are always necessarily approximations of the thing described, and part of a system of knowing. In his essay "Figurative Language," Thomas McLaughlin argues, "If figures tell us anything, it's that meaning is up for grabs, that the world can be shaped in an endless variety of forms, that language is a battleground of value systems." "The slow overture of rain" does not accurately describe "the unrelenting, syncopated / mind" because, after all, the mind is not an overture or rain, but "like" them. Furthermore, the comparison of the mind's working with how hummingbirds mistake "their wings / to be their hearts" and how swallows mistake the horizon to be a fishing line underscores the idea that knowledge of the outside world is impossible, or at least unsatisfying, and that what remains is the imagination.

For Graham, as for Wallace Stevens, the imagination is what animates human knowledge, and the faculty that gives the world meaning. However, the imagination itself is an inherently unstable category, and so different for each person as to make shared experience impossible. Some thinkers, in fact, claim that the category of the imagination itself is innately misleading. For example, in his study *Literary Theory*, Terry Eagleton argues that, historically, the imagination, "offered the writer a comfortingly absolute alternative to history itself." Eagleton notes that the imagination became emphasized as a transcendent realm during the late eighteenth and early nineteenth centuries when the function of poets and artists in society had changed, and their work was now seen as "product." Eagleton writes, "The whole point of 'creative' writing was that it was gloriously useless, an 'end in itself' loftily removed from any sordid social purpose." In the last two decades, this notion of the imagination as a transcendent space from which writers can comment on humanity's condition has only solidified.

Rather than "social purpose," the aim of poems such as "Mind" undermines the idea of a common language, adding credence to the notion that poetry is only for other poets, and that real communication, the kind that can "connect people to the world," is impossible. How else to make sense of lines such as the following:

> The city
> draws the mind in streets,
> and streets compel it
> from their intersections
> where a little
> belongs to no one. It is
> what is driven through
> all stationary portions
> of the world, gravity's
> stake in things.

Graham's abstractions here make it difficult to know to just what she is referring, and even if readers are able to "decode" the references, their reaction is more likely to be "so what" than "wow!" or "hmmmm." Askold Melnyczuk, writing in *Parnassus*, writes of Graham's collection that: "Only rarely does the voice speak from an urgency deep enough to justify breaking that cardinal rule of the Pythagoreans: be silent, or say something better than silence."

The poem's final image, that of the mind like leaves in November soil disintegrating into so much compost ("and all the richer for it") is an image of the mind's instability, its refusal to be anchored to the world, yet the inevitability that it will be. This image suggests a more materialist philosophy of mind than a romantic one and is more consistent with post-structural theories of the mind than it is with Graham's notion of the imagination as a place of salvation and comfort, and poetry as a practice that can bring people together. Post-structural theorists question the very possibility of transcendence and transparent communication. Theorists such as Foucault write about "subjects" rather than individuals, and locate the mind in relation to the material phenomena of culture and history. Since "subjects" are embodied in the world, their thinking is social and they take their identities from the groups to which they belong. Reading "Mind" one is hard pressed to "imagine" a body behind the words or a society in which the speaker makes her observations. Yet, the very ideas about the mind that Graham's poem implies are rooted in the twentieth century, and in philosophical and literary discourse.

> "Rather than 'social purpose,' the aim of poems such as 'Mind' undermines the idea of a common language, adding credence to the notion that poetry is only for other poets, and that real communication, the kind that can 'connect people to the world,' is impossible."

It is not that Graham is naïve or unaware of the contradictions inherent in her statements about poetry and her poems themselves. In an interview with Mark Wunderlich, Graham offers her wish for poetry's future:

> If I have a wish, it is that the body's (the heart's) knowledge be trusted again, that the fear of the body—certainly understandable in the age of AIDS and the plague-like virulence of our instant information technologies—decrease, and that the senses be used again in our poetry, that real images be felt, written, and most importantly, understood for the knowledge they contain.

Understanding "real images ... for the knowledge they contain" is an odd desire, coming from one whose own poems appear to question the possibility that the real can ever be known, and whose abstractions dilute the impact of her own images. But then, Graham has made her reputation *writing* poetry, not *talking* about it.

**Source:** Chris Semansky, Critical Essay on "Mind," in *Poetry for Students*, The Gale Group, 2003.

### Michelle Prebilic

*Prebilic is an independent author who writes and analyzes children's literature. She holds degrees*

> *Graham invites readers to reflect on her prose and hopes that they acquire the belief that they perceive things in ways that meet their needs and that create safety."*

*in psychology and business. In this essay, Prebilic discusses how Graham's poem considers the normally weak proclivity of the human phenomenological mind.*

Graham published her first collection, *Hybrids of Plants and Of Ghosts*, in 1980. Graham admired the work of Friedrich Nietzsche, a renowned philosopher, and based the title on his characterization of human beings. Graham bases her collection on the themes of death and change. This collection gained recognition for Graham; subsequently, critics learned to both admire and condemn her poetic prose.

According to Bonnie Costello in *Contemporary Literature*:

> Graham emerged in the 1980s as a major poet, distinguished for her philosophical depth, her sensuous vision, the grandeur of her style and themes. . . . In her first book, *Hybrids of Plants and of Ghosts*, Graham limited her meditation primarily to tentative reflections based on natural objects.

Graham's associations with the art forms of nature bring beauty and style to her work. As Dave Smith says in *The American Poetry Review*, "Hers is an intricately shaped poetry that is as given to decorum as to discipline." Graham uses her good taste and precision to lure readers into a proactive participation. Whether she poses a question or presents an idea in a new way, Graham's words compel readers to grasp humanness. She presents her ideas succinctly and without pretense. Her style encourages readers to search for a deeper meaning in life and to make sense of things around them.

"Mind," a thirty-nine line poem about change, fits in well into *Hybrids of Plants and of Ghosts*. According to Costello in *Contemporary Literature*, Graham limited her "meditation to individual objects of nature or art around which her thoughts could circle to form twisting, elegant designs." This meditation describes "Mind"; Graham implements this twisting, elegant design superbly by using nature's concrete beauty around which her thoughts can take shape: rain, hummingbirds, swallows, and poplars. As the verse meanders down the page, "Mind" contends with the weakness of the human phenomenological mind. She seeks to convince readers that their minds resist transformation. Graham successfully suggests that the truth of peoples' minds consists of objects and events as people perceive them and not of anything independent to them.

Graham opens "Mind" by immediately introducing an element of nature. She infers a metaphysical connection between the rain and the mind, which swiftly presents the human mind in a way that lures readers into reflection: "The slow overture of rain, / each drop breaking / without breaking into / the next, describes / the unrelenting, syncopated / mind."

The words in Graham's poem fall like an overture: the unhurried, introductory aspect of rain. Her words have formed like raindrops: condensed over time from vapor in the atmosphere and spread systematically onto the page. They stand alone with meaning, each drop gently taking its path without spilling into the next one. Graham's language coaxes readers to broaden their perspectives; some of the words, "overture" and "syncopated," may create a desire to pull out the dictionary and to learn more. This desire starts the search for a deeper meaning.

Graham requests that readers believe that the brain is unrelenting, yet weak. She begins this presentation like the beginning of a rainstorm. At first, readers notice the raindrops, yet they do not foresee the storm's intensity. This engaging metaphor alludes to the idea that people's minds often fail to connect the information that dribbles in, especially at the beginning of an experience. As readers enter her poem, they notice nature, yet do not foresee the journey that comes more intensely as the poem develops.

As Graham's reflections circle around the natural objects, her ruminative process formulates her images and germinates her concept of the mind's weakness. Readers experience this as Graham continues her poem: "Not unlike / the hummingbirds / imagining their wings / to be their heart, and swallows / believing the horizon / to be a line they lift / and drop." The hummingbirds, with brilliant iridescent plumage and long, slender bills, form an image in their mind's eye that their wings are their hearts. In addition, the graceful swift-flying passerine swallows believe that the perceptible intersection of the earth and the sky can only be a line that they lift and then drop. Although from a human perspective, one knows that these perceptions do not hold truth; it does not change the imagination of the hummingbirds or the belief of the swallows. According to Costello in *Contemporary Literature*, Graham "celebrated the spiritual and metaphysical reach of art" by painting these pictures with her words. Graham invites readers to reflect on her prose and hopes that they acquire the belief that they perceive things in ways that meet their needs and that create safety.

"What is it / they cast for?" Graham's interactive technique, a question, gently asks readers to join in her meditative journey and experience the philosophical and spiritual moment she has presented. Readers cannot easily answer this question in the same way they would describe the color of the sky or the characteristics of a horse. It is more like describing the shape of a jewel whose light radiates from within. The answer requires interpretation. Interpretation comes from within one's mind. It also comes with vulnerability as one identifies and expresses one's beliefs.

Graham continues this inward journey as she introduces the poplars: "The poplars, / advancing or retreating, / lose their stature / equally, and yet stand firm, / making arrangements / in order to become / imaginary." These fast-growing deciduous trees have unisexual flowers densely crowded with catkins. Perhaps the density of their weeping flowers distinguishes them: they lose and gain, advance or retreat, their beauty based on the season or the soil's health. Graham suggests that the trees, like all living things, have an undeniable status or achievement level that they have gained and lost regularly. As the season's change and events occur around them, these trees stand firm. Perhaps this quality mimics the weak, unrelenting nature of people's minds. As events occur and achievements come and go, the mind holds onto its beliefs, its imagination, and its unreality.

The mind forms the perceptions it needs, and needs what it creates: "The city / draws the mind in streets, / and streets compel it / from their intersections / where a little / belongs to no one." People believe that the people, animals, and wildlife that reside in a city, created it. When looked at in a new way, could it be that the city created the mind? Do the streets define people instead of peo-

## What Do I Read Next?

- Graham's 1995 collection *The Dream of the Unified Field: Selected Poems 1974–1994* includes poems from her five previous volumes of poetry, including *Erosion* and *Hybrids of Plants and of Ghosts*. This collection received the 1996 Pulitzer Prize for poetry.

- *The Best American Poetry 1990*, edited by Graham and David Lehman, was published in 1991. Graham penned the introduction, in which she elaborates on her ideas of what makes good poetry.

- John Ashbery writes many of the blurbs for Graham's books, and she for his. Like Graham, Ashbery has been influenced by many nineteenth- and early twentieth-century French poets. His comic novel *A Nest of Ninnies*, co-written with poet James Schuyler, was published in 1976.

- Graham derived the title of *Hybrids of Plants and of Ghosts* from German philosopher Friedrich Nietzsche's characterization of human beings in his treatise *Thus Spake Zarathustra*. Walter Kaufmann's 1995 Modern Library translation of *Thus Spake Zarathustra* is considered one of the best translations available.

- Steven Pinker's 1997 study *How the Mind Works* explains what the mind is, how it evolved, and how it allows people to sense the world around them. Pinker is an M.I.T. psychologist whose research interests include evolutionary biology.

- Critic Helen Vendler has been one of Graham's chief admirers, writing about her poetry in her 1995 study *The Breaking of Style: Hopkins, Heaney, Graham*.

ple defining the streets? What forms the intersections, a locus of points where the streets cross, or the street pavers laying the material and posting a stop sign? As Graham reverses the common beliefs, she argues that people's minds create the views that suit them best. It asks the age-old question: Which came first, the chicken or the egg? Graham surmises that the city may be a place where a little belongs to no one. This verse in the poem requires that readers step aside from a literal interpretation and begin to meditate on the deeper value to be gained.

Graham continues: "It is / what is driven through / all stationary portions / of the world, gravity's / stake in things." Gravity draws matter towards its center. It is the natural force of attraction exerted by earth upon objects at or near its surface. Graham concedes that gravity pushes, propels, or presses itself onward forcibly through all fixed parts of the earth. It is the way of things; it exists and influences all things just because they are near its power. In the same way, Graham contends that people's minds claim their power over their world. It is the way of people's minds. People's experiences filter through this mind's eye and perceptions form. They emerge as reality. Only if one allows one's mind's eye to shift focus will one allow for transformation.

As the poem winds towards resolution, Graham sums up her underlying principle: "The leaves, / pressed against the dank / window of November / soil, remain unwelcome / till transformed, parts / of a puzzle unsolvable / till the edges give a bit / and soften." Looking at experiences in a new way encourages transformation. Using the vivid metaphor of a window, Graham begins to persuade readers that transformation does occur.

The word "window" originated from Scandinavian invaders and settlers of England in the early Middle Ages. Related to Old Norse *vindauga*, this compound word summarized the ideas of wind and of eye. At one time, windows contained no glass. So, the "Window of November," as Graham defines it, ties in directly with her concept of seeing things without a filter. The wind caresses the eye of change, the dank leads to a discomfort that encourages discovery, and November sits on the heels of an unwelcome winter season. These things do not feel good. They are unwelcome. They propel people to see things differently. Perhaps people allow their new knowledge to transform them. Graham concludes that if people can look at the unsolvable parts of the puzzle in new ways, the edges of the problem will begin to resolve. When problems seem less rigid, solutions present themselves more fully. The shifts in attitudes allow people to change the nature, function, or condition of something. People can convert their experiences and attitudes of their mind to a new, richer awareness.

Graham presupposes that readers accept her idea when she says: "See how / then the picture becomes clear, / the mind entering the ground / more easily in pieces, / and all the richer for it." People allow their experiences to change them for the better. Through new choices, people can seek out and experience things in ways they never thought possible. When people allow this change to take place in small doses, like pieces of a puzzle they finally link, the picture of their experience becomes clear in a new way. One's mind becomes grounded in true reality. The dank no longer feels unwelcome but becomes an accepted and appreciated part of one's life. People know the dank leads to a window that defines an opportunity. It becomes part of life's cyclical nature. Graham believes that this realization transforms people; their lives contain more meaning and significance.

"Mind" invites readers to take an inward journey to discover its gem. It is not didactic, yet offers an opportunity to learn. Expressive words encourage readers to gain knowledge of new terminology. Associations with nature allow readers to view Graham's theory of transformation in a new way. Although not clear-cut, her poem imparts a straightforward idea: people see life through their mind's filter. Yet, people can change their filter. The ultimate picture comes from a puzzle whose pieces fit together as one meditates. Whether or not a reader agrees with Graham's idea that the mind's truth consists of objects and events as people perceive them, one thing is certain: her meditative poetry draws readers into the mind of Graham, and Graham into the minds of her readers.

**Source:** Michelle Prebilic, Critical Essay on "Mind," in *Poetry for Students*, The Gale Group, 2003.

## Marjorie Partch

*Partch is a Jungian astrologer, writer, and graphic designer. In this essay, Partch considers the validity of Jorie Graham's use of poetry as a "medium for spiritual undertaking."*

While there are many excellent poets who are fully accessible through a single glance at a single poem, Graham is not a poet whose work can be understood or appreciated in isolation.

Some critics may object to the need for any special "preparation," lobbying for the democracy of immediacy. But how many uninitiates can truly appreciate a Jackson Pollock painting, say, without some introduction? To the casual or innocent eye, his work looks like the careless splatterings of a child or a madman, and indeed these comparisons have been made. With a little guidance, it becomes apparent that Pollock was attempting not at all to make pretty pictures but to portray movement in time. Beyond that, he sought to challenge the whole conceptual framework of reality—to bend space and time. With this perspective, his "action paintings" can be appreciated as delayed-shutter portraits of his dance, more like capturing the motion of writing with a penlight in the dark than snapshots of a posed static scene.

Graham is an enthusiastic fan of Pollock's work and shares similar aims of evoking process in her own work. Rather than the body's dance through the fields of space and time, she seeks to simulate, and then to stimulate, perception and thought isolation, to extend this motion beyond the limits of language, the static "poetic moment" and the printed page, into the reader's ongoing experience. Graham seeks in her poetry to create for herself and recreate for the reader moments of opening, of beginning, rather than endings. Her poems may not always succeed on these grounds, but they must be judged as moving collages rather than failed still life snapshots, or the neatly wrapped-up happy ending will always appear to be missing. The open-ended lack of resolution is deliberate, not accidental. The suspended non-ending is intended to invite the reader's participation.

Many of Graham's detractors, such as Sven Birkerts, writing in the *New York Times Book Review*, question "the viability of poetry as an instrument of philosophy." Birkerts is also bewildered by "the onward march of mind and spirit searching for some arrival, some consummation, some end to all of this tending toward." But who is to say what is a suitable theme for poetic experience and expression: only matters of the heart? Can the processes of the mind really be declared off-limits? Apart from the aesthetic values normally applied to poetry (and here Graham's work must speak for itself), surely the realm of experience to be explored is no less a matter of poetic license than experiments in form. Some would have it that the immediately accessible realm of the senses and emotions, with some kind of conclusive *point*, constitutes the only "appropriate" terrain for "the poetic impulse." How can one really reserve the poetic endeavor for such touchy-feely subjects as love, loss, and memory? It could even be said that the whole crux of the poetic moment lies in the collision between consciousness and experience—reality. Poets, even the ancients, have always explored this synaptic leap of faith between the so-called objective and the subjective, between outer fact and inner response. Mo-

> *Moments of sublime realization, however ambivalent or complex, cannot be disqualified as too intellectual if the entire question of mind is the very landscape of the poet's (perhaps deeply emotional) experience."*

ments of sublime realization, however ambivalent or complex, cannot be disqualified as too intellectual if the entire question of mind is the very landscape of the poet's (perhaps deeply emotional) experience. The postmodern view has shown once and for all that the very notions of self, identity, experience, other, object, etc., are nothing if not conceptual.

The mind can be said to be the heroic subject of a great deal of Graham's enormous body of work, and "Mind" can by no means be considered an exhaustive portrait. But she does here achieve the elusive goal of transcendence, going beyond the individual personal mind. The poem reaches beyond even the projected divine mind to the more mystical concept of the phenomenon of mind underlying and pervading reality on a subatomic level. For mystics of every tradition, mind inhabits and vivifies the infinite spaces between things and is the governing principle behind thingness—the very ground out of which subject and object emerge. In keeping with the model of modern physics, the perspective of modern phenomenology maps the activity of the mind as more of a field of consciousness than a linear progression of thoughts. The mind is seen as but one phenomenon within the universe, which is a field of interwoven and interacting forces, rather than a simple progression of causally related events.

The opening lines of "Mind" evoke and mimic the atmospheric affect of this nonlinear percolation:

The slow overture of rain,
each drop breaking
without breaking into
the next, describes
the unrelenting, syncopated
mind.

Everyday thoughts may seem to unfold one into the next, in an orderly single-file procession of cause and effect. However, Graham points out that in actuality, thoughts are often more random and chaotic than one might like to think, more like popcorn popping or rain drops falling than links in a chain. Sometimes thoughts come one after the other, sometimes simultaneously—but one thought may no more arise with any causality or logic from its predecessor than one rock following another in an avalanche.

Graham both imitates and mocks this common misconception of the inherent orderliness of the mind's associative processes in the shape of the poem—a neat, narrow column of no more than five words on a line—and the poem's uninterrupted flow, coming on in a downpour of images, ideas, and words. But in the end the poem does resolve itself, not with the decisive closing of a door but with a beckoning to a window, where it tells the reader to "See."

The second group of lines following the lines above portray the mind's tendency to project the patterns of its own workings onto what it perceives:

> Not unlike
> the hummingbirds
> imagining their wings
> to be their heart, and swallows
> believing the horizon
> to be a line they lift
> and drop. What is it
> they cast for?

Later in the poem, Graham subtly shifts the ground of what readers think of as cause and effect:

> The city
> draws the mind in streets,
> and streets compel it
> from their intersections
> where a little
> belongs to no one.

Thoughts tend to follow their routes, once established, as obediently as falling rocks yield to "gravity's stake in things." So, the question arises, does the mind arise from thought and not the other way around? Can the mind exist without language? Is there mind without thinking? Descartes would have it that being itself is dependent on thought, while spiritual teachers of the East and the West would have it precisely the other way around— being begins when thinking stops. Only when the continual chatter of the mind is silenced, when its relentless busy-bee buzzing is stilled, can consciousness truly interact with reality. This is what is meant by pure mind. Pure mind is the intersection toward which Graham is ever striving—the intersection between not only reality and consciousness but between being and doing, between experience and expression. Graham is continually striving to write from this place of clarity of pure being and to evoke those gem-like moments for the reader.

Like Pollock's attempt to explode the boundaries of his canvas, Graham seeks to speak from silence, to arrive at a place beyond words, by using language to delineate the contours of the ineffable.

It is only when the sharp edges of the "puzzle pieces," the random shards of Mind (thoughts), soften a bit that readers can see how

> the picture becomes clear,
> the mind entering the ground
> more easily in pieces,
> and all the richer for it.

The unity of the whole emerges from the fragmentation of the habitual mental processes of the mind, into the fertile ground of the universal mind from which all phenomena, within nature and human consciousness, arise. When the edges are sharp and rigid, overly defined, the edges cannot penetrate the ground of their own being and the puzzle remains unsolvable. It is only when the thoughts' hard edges "give a bit" that they can return to their source.

In a 1992 interview with Thomas Gardner in the *Denver Quarterly*, Graham commented, "Poetry is an extraordinary medium for spiritual undertaking." The immediate and unceasing appreciation and recognition that her work has received—including a Pulitzer Prize in 1996—attest to the validity and viability of her endeavor. The more one knows about poetry and spirituality, the more one will appreciate the risks Graham has taken in her bold experiments in both her content and its necessary form, as well as her task and her achievement. As to the appropriateness of her "use" of poetry for philosophical or spiritual purposes, one might even ask, what else? Are they not one and the same?

The ambitious thoughts represented in "Mind" are not so shabby, coming from the precocious mind of a twenty-something-year-old poet in the late 1970s, a self-confessed hybrid of Whitman's lyricism on the one hand and Nietzsche's philosophy on the other.

Graham's early musings inscribe an arc with a promising trajectory; a promise duly fulfilled in the ongoing experiments and mature work of this highly complex, philosophical, and intellectual—

and also beautifully musical—poet of the postmodern mind.

**Source:** Marjorie Partch, Critical Essay on "Mind," in *Poetry for Students*, The Gale Group, 2003.

## Sources

Birkerts, Sven, "States of Being," in the *New York Times Book Review*, May 19, 2002.

Brien, Peyton, "Jorie Graham," in *Dictionary of Literary Biography*, Vol. 120: *American Poets Since World War II, Third Series*, edited by R. S. Gwynn, Gale Research, 1992, pp. 96–101.

Casper, Robert, "About Jorie Graham," in *Ploughshares*, Vol. 27, Issue 4, Winter 2001, pp. 189–94.

Costello, Bonnie, "Jorie Graham: Art and Erosion," in *Contemporary Literature*, Vol. 33, No. 2, Summer 1992, pp. 373–95.

Eagleton, Terry, *Literary Theory*, University of Minnesota Press, 1983, pp. 20–21.

Gardner, Thomas, "An Interview with Jorie Graham," *Denver Quarterly*, 1992.

Gibson, Margaret, Review of *Hybrids of Ghosts and of Plants*, in *Library Journal*, May 15, 1980, p. 1170.

Graham, Jorie, *Hybrids of Ghosts and of Plants*, Princeton University Press, 1980, p. 61.

———, ed., *The Best American Poetry 1990*, Scribners, 1991, pp. xiii–xviii.

McLaughlin, Thomas, "Figurative Language," in *Critical Terms for Literary Study*, edited by Frank Lentricchia and Thomas McLaughlin, University of Chicago Press, 1995, pp. 80–90.

Melnyczuk, Askold, "The Mind of the Matter: CAT Scanning a Scat Singer," in *Parnassus*, Vols. 12–13, Nos. 1–2, Spring–Summer and Fall–Winter 1985, pp. 588–601.

Smith, Dave, Review of *Hybrids of Ghosts and of Plants*, in *American Poetry Review*, January–February 1982, pp. 36–46.

Wunderlich, Mark, "Interview: The Glorious Thing," in *American Poet*, Fall 1996.

## Further Reading

Bottoms, David, and Dave Smith, eds., *The Morrow Anthology of Younger American Poets*, William Morrow & Co., 1985.
   This is one of the first major anthologies in which Graham's work appeared.

Furniss, Tom, and Michael Bath, *Reading Poetry: An Introduction to Theories, Histories, and Conventions*, Prentice Hall, 1996.
   Furniss and Bath provide an introduction to the ideas and techniques that can help students critically analyze poetry. This study shows how various and contemporary strands of literary theory can be applied to difficult poetry such as Graham's.

Holden, Jonathan, *Style and Authenticity in Postmodern Poetry*, University of Missouri Press, 1986.
   Holden analyzes Graham's work and that of her contemporaries in this critical study.

McDowell, Robert, ed., *Poetry after Modernism*, Story Line Press, 1991.
   This collection of essays by poets and critics examines the various aspects of postmodern poetry such as formalism, the relationship between business and poetry, politics and poetry, and psychoanalysis and creativity.

# On His Having Arrived at the Age of Twenty-Three

*John Milton*

*c. 1632*

"On His Having Arrived at the Age of Twenty-Three," which exists in manuscript and was printed twice during Milton's lifetime (in the *Poems* of 1645 and 1673), was most likely written in 1632 at a crucial time in Milton's life, just after his graduation from Cambridge. Milton here acknowledges that he may not seem as mature as some of his contemporaries but expresses a desire to use his talents well and his trust in God's will for him over time. One thing to understand about Milton's sonnets is their topical range. Not a writer of love sonnets in English (although the sonnets he wrote in Italian are love sonnets), Milton writes political sonnets, occasional sonnets, elegiac sonnets, and sonnets of personal meditation, like this one.

## Author Biography

Milton was born in Cheapside, London, in 1608, the son of John Milton, Sr., a prosperous scrivener, notary, and composer, and Sara Jeffrey Milton. Because of the family's financial standing, Milton received an excellent education in Greek, Latin, Hebrew, French, and Italian. Music and literature were particular favorites with the boy, and Milton began composing his own poetry at a young age. From 1618 to 1620, he was privately tutored at the family home. He then attended St. Paul's School before moving on to Christ's College, Cambridge, at the age of sixteen. At first unpopular, Milton

eventually made a name for himself as a rhetorician and public speaker. Upon leaving the university in 1632 with a master's degree, Milton retired to Hammersmith for three years and later to Horton, Buckinghamshire, where he devoted himself to intense study and writing. In May of 1638, Milton embarked on an Italian journey that was to last nearly fifteen months. The experience, which he described in *Pro populo anglicano defensio secunda* (*Second Defence of the People of England*, 1654), brought him into contact with the leading men of letters in Florence, Rome, and Naples, including Giovanni Battista Manso, Marquis of Villa, who had been an intimate of the epic poet Torquato Tasso. Scholars view the Italian tour as seminal in Milton's literary development; a new self-confidence emerged in the letters he wrote during his travels, and it was in Italy that Milton first proposed to write a great epic.

With the coming of the English Civil War and the Commonwealth, Milton's life changed completely as his attentions shifted from private to public concerns. Abruptly, Milton left off writing poetry for prose, pouring out pamphlets during the early 1640s in which he opposed what he considered rampant Episcopal tyranny. Milton declared his Puritan allegiance in tracts in which he argued the need to purge the Church of England of all vestiges of Roman Catholicism and restore the simplicity of the apostolic church. In 1642, he married his first wife, Mary Powell, who left him shortly after the wedding (but returned to him three years later; paradoxically, though Milton was to marry two more times, he was never divorced). With the execution of Charles I in 1649, Milton entered the political fray with *The Tenure of Kings and Magistrates*, an assertion of the right of a people to depose or execute a ruling tyrant. This view constituted a complete about-face for Milton, who had written as a good monarchist in his early works. Henceforth, Milton was permanently on the political left. He accepted an invitation to become Cromwell's Latin secretary for foreign affairs and issued a number of tracts on church and state issues. The restoration of the monarchy in 1660 left Milton disillusioned and hastened his departure from public life; as a former member of the Commonwealth, he lived for a time in peril, but for reasons not entirely clear, he was spared harsh punishment.

The remaining fourteen years of Milton's life were spent in relatively peaceful retirement in and around London. Completely blind since 1652, he increasingly devoted his time to poetry. Amanuenses, assisted sometimes by Milton's two nephews and his daughter Deborah, were employed to take dictation, correct copy, and read aloud, and Milton made rapid progress on projects he had put off many years before. During the writing of *Paradise Lost*, Milton spent mornings dictating passages he had composed in his head at night. *Paradise Lost* was published in 1667, followed in 1671 by *Paradise Regained*. "Samson Agonistes," a verse tragedy, appeared in the same volume as *Paradise Regained*. He died in November 1674, apparently of complications arising from gout.

*John Milton*

## Poem Text

How soon hath Time, the subtle thief of youth,
Stol'n on his wing my three-and-twentieth year!
My hasting days fly on with full career,
But my late spring no bud or blossom shew'th.

Perhaps my semblance might deceive the truth        5
That I to manhood am arrived so near;
And inward ripeness doth much less appear,
That some more timely-happy spirits endu'th.

Yet be it less or more, or soon or slow,
It shall be still in strictest measure even          10
To that same lot, however mean or high,
Toward which Time leads me, and the will of
    Heaven;

All is, if I have grace to use it so,
As ever in my great Task-Master's eye.

## Poem Summary

### Lines 1–2

These lines introduce the poem's theme and create a metaphor of Time as a bird flying away with ("stol'n on his wing") Milton's youth.

### Line 3

Here, the poet expresses his sense of how quickly time passes: "hasting days" and "full career."

### Line 4

The poet here uses a seasonal metaphor to express that his time of life is a "late spring" but that so far, it has not shown any "bud or blossom," in other words any promise of fruit or achievements in his life.

### Lines 5–6

The poet remarks that he does not seem as old as he is (his look "deceive[s]" the truth that he is practically a man).

### Lines 7–8

"Inward ripeness" continues the natural metaphor of "bud" and "blossom" in line 4; the poet has more maturity or ripeness inside than he shows outside, and more than some other young people, the "more timely-happy spirits" have. But, note the various possibilities in the word "endur'th." The lines are grammatically inverted and could be paraphrased, "and inward ripeness, that imbues / clothes some others, appears less in me." The phrase "timely-happy spirits" can be understood to refer to those who are more comfortable with their age or whose age reflects more happily their inner being.

### Lines 9–12

"It" may refer to the appearance of inward ripeness of line 7; whether ripeness appears less or more, now or later, it shall be just right according to his destiny, the "lot . . . / Toward which Time leads" him. Where the octave found dissonance between his inner and outward states of maturity, the sestet's answer is that time and the will of heaven will even things out according to plan. Note the multiple puns in this line: "measure" could mean a musical measure or a line of verse; "even" may be an adjective modifying "measure" or may lead the reader into the next line, "even to that same lot." Milton often places adjectives both before and after nouns, and he likewise often lets the word at the end of a line work in two different ways in each line.

### Lines 13–14

Critics have differed as to the precise interpretation of these lines, but, in general, they suggest that whatever the outcome of the speaker's life, it will be with God's knowledge and in accordance with His world. The "great Task-Master" is God.

## Themes

### Crisis of Faith

The crisis created by Milton's awareness of the passage of time is one that can be resolved by the poet's choice to put his future in God's hands. In the first eight lines of the poem, Milton worries that time has passed too quickly. He has been at Cambridge studying, but has had little time to fulfill what he sees as his destiny. Milton is aware he is a talented poet, but instead of writing poetry, he has been studying. This precipitates a crisis of faith for the poet, who worries he has wasted precious time. But maybe the poet's talent, which "be it less or more," will be less when he is mature. He worries, although he is still confident of his future. In the final six lines of the sonnet, Milton acknowledges that time, whether "soon or slow," will still inevitably lead him to God. This is the same future that all men will face, "however mean or high." Time will lead Milton to God, if he can accept the limitations of earthly time. In these final lines, Milton finds the answer to his problem in giving control over his life to God and, as a result, his crisis of faith is resolved.

### Journey

Milton uses this sonnet to symbolize the poet's journey from doubt to self-discovery. He feels guilty about his time spent studying when he has not published anything. He is slow to mature, and by "late spring no bud or blossom shew'th." But, in line 9, the pronoun "it," whose antecedent is unclear, but which is usually thought to refer to the poet's maturity, might suggest that the poet's talents will ripen with maturity, that rather than having wasted his youth, the poet has been marking time until he is mature enough to create the kind of poetry he feels destined to create. As he nears age twenty-four, the poet feels he is at the border between youth and manhood, a time to which he has "arrived so near." He worries that when he reaches maturity his talent may be less, rather than more. Although worried, he is confident in his own abilities, and so the sonnet moves the poet from the hesitation and questioning of youth to the realization that perhaps he will achieve all he wishes. The sestet is filled with obscure references: it, more, less, soon, slow. There are contradictions and uncertainties, all of which indicate that the journey will not always be clear. Ultimately, the poet feels the journey will bring him success. His intent is to please God and use his abilities as best he can. The journey is to reaffirm the poet's faith in God and to find his place in the world.

## Passage of Time

Milton's sonnet explores the idea of time as a guide to his destiny. Milton calls time "the subtle thief of youth" because time steals without awareness. This sonnet is written sometime after Milton's twenty-third birthday, and already the poet is thinking about the approach of his twenty-fourth birthday. He sees the ways in which time steals the days away from him, and he is not even aware of each day passing. The poet notes how he has planned to accomplish so many things, yet instead feels he has spent too much time studying and learning. What he considers the promise of his youth has come to no fruition, "no bud or blossom shew'th." In lines 5 through 8, the poet suggests that time can deceive others, since he still appears to be young; but Milton knows the truth, that time has stolen his youth. In the final six lines of the poem, Milton changes direction and the sestet responds to the problem expressed in the octave: time which steals his youth is also bringing him closer to God. This religious interpretation of time expresses the Renaissance notion that the passage of time will bring mankind closer to a final meeting with God. Milton justifies his use of time because, regardless of how he spends it, in the end time is on his side, bringing him closer to his God.

## Predestination and Free Will

This poem makes clear that Milton is incorporating both Calvinist ideas of predestination and the Anglican Church's emphasis on free will into his poem. The poem's octave, the first eight lines, focuses on the problem of free will. Milton has chosen his course of study, and as a result he has neglected his own talents, his poetry. This time spent on academics has flourished and flown, as he acknowledges in line 3: "My hasting days fly on." But now, as he readies himself to leave Cambridge,

# Topics for Further Study

- Milton's poem is really a journey from questioning to knowledge. Write an essay that explores a personal journey you have made from questioning a choice to the acknowledgement of understanding that your choice was a correct one for you.

- William Blake used art to interpret many of Milton's poems. Use whatever artistic format that fits your talents to create an artistic interpretation of this poem on the passing of time.

- Milton uses his poem to explore what he thinks is his destiny. Write a poem that explores your future.

- Religion was an important part of early seventeenth-century English life. The idea of God's plan for mankind was especially important. Research the early seventeenth century and write an essay discussing the role of religious thought in how men and women in this period planned their futures.

- Research the education system in place for both males and females in seventeenth-century England. What kinds of careers could boys plan to pursue? Compare these to the options available for girls.

he must face the awareness of lost time. In the poem's sestet, Milton moves toward resolution, which he finds in embracing both the Calvinist idea of predestination and the Anglican promise of free will. He can reconcile his wasted youth if he gives the choice to God. His youth has not been wasted, since it moves him closer to God; this is "the will of Heaven." At the same time, the next line, "if I have grace to use it so," takes the poem back to free will. His talents will grow and develop if Milton chooses to do so. As a result of Milton's playing with this opposition, he creates a tension in his poem. Human effort and divine will are partners in Milton's future. The resolution to Milton's dilemma is in recognizing this fact.

## Style

In its form, "On His Having Arrived at the Age of Twenty-Three" is an Italian sonnet (also known as a Petrarchan sonnet), written, like most sonnets, in iambic pentameter. Its thematic organization closely follows the structure of the form, with two well-developed movements corresponding to the eight-line octave and the six-line sestet. The octave follows the conventional Petrarchan rhyme scheme of *abbaabba*, while the sestet rhymes *cdcdee*, one of several conventional patterns. The octave breaks conventionally into two shorter movements, each consisting of a quatrain rhyming *abba*. The beginning of the sestet, where the rhyme scheme changes, is known as the turn of the sonnet because at this point an Italian sonnet's theme or tone usually shifts. In the case of "On His Having Arrived at the Age of Twenty-Three" the transitional "But" signals a change from the impatient arrogance of the octave into the humbler prayer of the sestet.

## Historical Context

### Seventeenth Century

The years between 1576 and 1642 are often described as the golden age of English poetry, drama, and theatre, although the period was not golden for those who lived through it. For one hundred years, farmers had been displaced by enclosure acts that fenced off agricultural land for pastures, resulting in inflation and unemployment in the countryside. Crop failures, the threat of war abroad, and the sometimes brutal religious strife that enveloped the country, had shaken English society by the time Elizabeth assumed the throne in 1558. The Elizabethan regimen produced relative stability, but the queen's failure to name a successor brought discontent and the threat of civil war even before her death. Initially, James I's rule was greeted with enthusiasm, but religious, class, and political divisions intensified with time. Rural unemployment drove many people to London, making it the largest city in Europe. Civil problems led to widespread disorder, while the establishment of a capitalistic economy took the place of the feudal agrarian social order. Disorder and conflict led writers to grapple with new ideas about science, philosophy, religion, and politics. There was a new emphasis on individual thought, action, and responsibility. In spite of this turmoil, or perhaps because of it, the most important drama in Western history was produced.

### A Period of Change

The period in which John Milton was writing is one marked by enormous changes. After nearly fifty years as queen, Elizabeth I died in 1603. James IV of Scotland became the new English king, James I. While Elizabeth had encouraged a degree of individualism, James believed in absolute monarchy based on the divine right of kings. Although Elizabeth had reinstated the Protestant church, with herself as the official head of the Church of England, she was also more tolerant of religious choice than her predecessor Mary I had been. While the people still mistrusted and barely tolerated the Roman Catholic Church, which was associated with papal corruption and intolerance, Elizabeth managed to keep these religious issues subdued. With Elizabeth's death, the movement toward religious tolerance changed, and religion became a problem for public debate once again.

One issue was the marriage of James's son Charles, the new heir, to the French princess, a Roman Catholic. The debates about religion, however, involved more than just the opposition of Protestant and Catholic. The Anglicans, who argued for free will governing men's actions, opposed the Calvinists, who argued for predestination. There were debates about the use of prayer books and the designation of church officials. This controversy and debate heavily influenced the poetry of this period. Consider, for example, Milton's sonnet, "On His Having Arrived at the Age of Twenty-Three," which creates tension in the opposition between predestination and free will.

### Puritan Intolerance

Another religious group whose actions would have lasting impact were the Puritans. Both James and Charles encouraged Sunday festivals and sporting contests. The Puritans thought these activities were the work of the devil or, at the very least, an embracing of the pagan past. James and Charles were also big patrons of the theatre. Charles, in particular, supported huge theatrical productions called masques. These were often very elaborate and very expensive, a cost born by the public in the form of additional taxes. The Puritans opposed the burgeoning theatre and thought actors were sinful and displayed substandard morals. In part this view of the theatre was based on the social environment of the playhouse, which was libertine. Puritan opposition to theatre was based on a philosophical ar-

# Compare & Contrast

- **1630s:** An epidemic of the plague killed more than 40,000 people in London only a few years earlier, and it continues to kill thousands more in the years that follow. As a result, government and much of London social life is suspended during the peak months of plague each summer. The wealthy move to summer houses, while the poor, with no place to go, remain in London to battle the plague on their own. This escape of the wealthy from the plague further establishes the privileges of the wealthy and helps lead to revolution.

  **Today:** Society is not as clearly divided between the rich and poor as was the case during the seventeenth century, and the plague no longer decimates the population every year. However, in spite of some advances in equality now evident in England, English society is still somewhat stratified, with divisions based on social rank and income.

- **1630s:** The new interest in science is very important to Englishmen. One of the newest discoveries is a published account by William Harvey, who posits that the heart is a muscle and it pushes blood throughout the body. Harvey cannot explain the creation of blood. While many of the new scientists endorse Harvey's viewpoints, others dispute this claim, believing instead that the liver is the organ of circulation. New scientific discoveries influence the poets of the period, who incorporate tension produced by scientific disovery into their poetry.

  **Today:** Harvey's hypothesis has long since been proven true, and today, both heart transplants and artificial hearts are common. One thing has not changed, however, and that is the skepticism that often greets new ideas in medicine. New ideas about medicine often undergo laborious tests to prove their validity. It is predominantly journalists and not poets, however, who discuss new scientific ideas.

- **1630s:** Puritan William Prynne attacks the London theatre as lewd and as a haven for prostitutes. Because the wife of King Charles I has participated in performances at court, Prynne's attack is viewed as a slander on the queen, and he is thrown into prison after being branded and having his ears cut off. By 1642, the Puritans succeed in having all the theatres in London closed.

  **Today:** While film is often condemned for excessive violence and sexual content, theatres are rarely the object of protest.

- **1630s:** Galileo is tried in Rome for endorsing an earlier scientific theory that the sun is the center of the universe and the earth only a rotating planet. Galileo's ideas violate Church teachings that God created mankind, and so the earth, on which man resides, must be more important than all other planets and it must be the center of the universe. Because he is threatened with torture, Galileo eventually retracts his proposition and is confined to his villa for the rest of his life.

  **Today:** Galileo was eventually proven correct, and while it took the Church in Rome nearly 400 years to admit Galileo was right, eventually the Church cleared Galileo of heresy and retracted his excommunication.

- **1630s:** Religion continues to divide the English. When the House of Commons petitions King James I to prevent a Catholic marriage for his son Charles, James I rebukes the Commons for meddling in foreign affairs. The Commons responds that the marriage, religion, and birthright of a king is a suitable subject for the Commons to debate. Eventually, Charles is deposed and beheaded, and Milton serves as Secretary of Letters for Cromwell's government.

  **Today:** Rules governing marriage of the royal family are still an important topic in England. In the twentieth century, Edward VIII abdicated when he was not allowed to marry a divorced American woman, and heirs to the English throne are still not permitted to marry Roman Catholics. Because of a tumultuous past, with vicious attacks against both Catholics and Protestants, the English continue to govern the religious choices of the royal family.

gument: acting is lying, role-playing. Plays also brought large numbers of people together, thus increasing crime and disease, and they enticed people away from their jobs and so affected trade. As a result, city officials often sided with Puritans in wanting theatres closed or moved outside town. Eventually Puritan opposition led to revolution and the beheading of King Charles I. Milton later allied himself with the rebellion and Oliver Cromwell, and so religion emerged as an important focal point of Milton's life and of this period.

## Critical Overview

Milton is regarded as one of the greatest and most influential English poets, ranking with Chaucer and Shakespeare. He wrote both poetry and prose, and in poetry wrote pastoral, elegy, epic, drama, sonnet, and other kinds of verse. His most famous and influential work is the epic *Paradise Lost*, which has been at the center of English literary criticism since Milton's day. His sonnets have received less critical attention. Lord Macaulay, in his essay "Milton" published in 1860, differed from most critics in that he valued the sonnets highly. He found that "traces ... of the peculiar character of Milton may be found in all of his works; but it is most strongly displayed in the Sonnets. Those remarkable poems have been undervalued." Macaulay links the sonnets firmly to Milton's life and character, a view that seems especially true of "On His Having Arrived at the Age of Twenty-Three."

"On His Having Arrived at the Age of Twenty-Three" is fairly straightforward until the last three lines. Many explications of this section have been attempted. K. Svendsen, in *The Explicator*, offers three interpretations, but prefers the following: "All that matters is whether I have grace to use my ripeness in accordance with the will of God as one ever in his sight." D. C. Dorian, writing in another issue of *The Explicator*, differs, thinking that "ever" can mean "eternity" and paraphrases the section this way: "All time is, if I have grace to use it so, as eternity in God's sight."

Another way to interpret these lines is with recourse to the manuscript, which has no punctuation. Instead of reading line 12 as if it had two subjects (toward which Time and the will of heaven lead me) one can read "will of heaven" as the subject of "is" (the will of heaven is all). In that case, line 14 could variously take as antecedent "I" (the will of heaven is all, if I, being watched by God as always, have grace to treat it as if it is all) or more loosely the using of his lot (the will of heaven is all, if I have grace to act as if that is so, remaining in God's sight). Other interpretations are of course possible; several are noted in *A Variorum Commentary on the Poems of John Milton* by A. S. P. Woodhouse and Douglas Bush.

## Criticism

### Sheri E. Metzger

*Metzger has a doctorate in English Renaissance literature. She teaches literature and drama at the University of New Mexico, where she is a lecturer in the English department and an adjunct professor in the university's honors program. In this essay, Metzger discusses Milton's reworking of the sonnet format in his poem and explores the influences of earlier and contemporary English poets on Milton and the development of the sonnet format.*

In England, the sixteenth and seventeenth centuries were marked by a phenomenal outpouring of poetic talent. The poets of this era often took older established formulas and rewrote and revised the formulas to express new, often controversial, ideas about their world. These poems were not published until many years after their composition. Instead, the poems were copied and circulated among other poets. This circulation of poems led to a competitiveness between poets, with each successive poet "playing" with the formula and content to create a new kind of poem, one that he would then pass on to his friends. This was especially true of the poetic form known as the sonnet. For instance, in John Milton's sonnet "On His Having Arrived at the Age of Twenty-Three," the poet uses the sonnet format to explore the passing of time and to question if he is fulfilling God's plan or if he is wasting precious time in study that might be better devoted to writing. In using the sonnet form for such questioning, Milton is only the most recent of the Renaissance poets to appropriate and revise the traditional sonnet to serve a purpose that is very different from its traditional intent. In a sense, Milton's use of the sonnet serves as the culmination of a creative period that saw the use of the sonnet transformed from a simple vehicle to express a lover's lament to an elaborate and complex formula that could be used to express religious fervor, personal anguish, and the poet's fears about life.

When Sir Thomas Wyatt introduced the Italian sonnet to England early in the sixteenth century, he was importing a well-defined poetic formula that illustrated certain carefully crafted ideas. The Italian sonnet probably developed in Italy in the thirteenth century but was adapted by Petrarch a century later to express a lover's lament. The formula is simple, and few poets deviated from either the Italian rhyme scheme or the Petrarchan content. The rhyme consists of fourteen lines, with the first eight lines forming an octave, *abbaabba*, that presents either a narrative or raises a question. The octave is followed by a sestet, *efgefg*, that either makes an abstract comment upon the narrative or offers a solution for the problem. The traditional devices included elaborate conceits and exaggerated comparisons that expressed a lover's beauty and charm and her cruelty to her lover. These sonnets always emphasized the suffering of the forlorn lover at the hands of his cruel mistress. Wyatt's "The Long Love That in My Thought Doth Harbor" (1540) is typical of this style. In this poem, love is compared to war, and the lover is cold and distant. In another Wyatt poem, "Whoso List to Hunt" (1540), the object of the hunt is a woman, thought to be Anne Boleyn, one of King Henry the VIII's wives. The woman is even more objectified than normal and is diminished in her role as prey. Of course, she is also unavailable and thus cold to his pleas, and so the poet is even more dejected and rejected than usual.

Initially, these Italian sonnets were used to express an abject suitor's desire or love for a reluctant woman. Love was often painful and explored through elaborate conceits. A favorite comparison was love as a battle or war, or as illness or pain. But, it did not take very long for English Renaissance poets to deviate from this formula. For example, William Shakespeare avoids the traditional Italian pattern in *Romeo and Juliet* (1595). In act I, scene v, lines 90 to 103, Shakespeare's conceit involves saints and the kissing of palms as lips. Instead of the typical Petrarchan declaration of how hopeless his love and how cold his lover, Shakespeare uses logic and reason in his argument. This sonnet also provides for two speakers. Romeo speaks the first four lines, Juliet the next four, and then the two lovers alternate the next six lines. This deviation from typical sonnet style and content was not unusual for Shakespeare. Many of his sonnets deal with topics other than love and desire. He also explores issues such as time and death, in which he presents solutions such as immortalizing oneself in verse or in the creation of children to outwit death.

> *The pinnacle of this adaption of the traditional sonnet is reached with Milton, who finds the sonnet a useful vehicle for exploring time, politics, and his own personal pain, as well as to reaffirm his belief that God has not abandoned him.*

Of course, Shakespeare also wrote of the pain of love in sonnets, but he addressed many of his sonnets to a young man, a departure from sixteenth century norms in which a woman was typically both the subject and the audience for a sonnet. By the end of the sixteenth century, a new English sonnet had been created to join the more familiar Italian format. The English sonnet contained three quatrains, *abab cdcd efef*, and ended with a couplet, *gg*, instead of the octave and sestet found in the Italian sonnet. However, the end of the sixteenth century does not mark the end of the modification of the sonnet. It took the efforts of several other poets to complete the transformation of the sonnet from a vehicle to express lament for a mistress to a complex piece of poetry capable of using rhyme to enhance a theme that has little to do with a woman's love.

Early in the seventeenth century, the sonnet was transfigured into a way to worship God, and a whole new wave of poets, including John Donne, George Herbert, and John Milton, took this new format in a completely different direction. Donne uses the sonnet format to question God or, more correctly, demand of God the means to his salvation. As with Herbert, Donne is also concerned with his soul. In "Sonnet X," Donne demands that God "Batter my heart." The poet asks for God to ravish him and save him from Satan. This is a more violent poem than either Herbert or Milton write. The jaggedness and choppiness of the verse suggest the emotion of the content. For Donne, salvation is brought through a more violent questioning, rather than through

## What Do I Read Next?

- *John Milton*, published in 1991 by Oxford University Press, is a complete edition of Milton's poetry and prose works, with extensive textual notes.

- *The Complete Poems*, published in 1999 by Penguin Classics, contains all of Milton's poems in a fully annotated edition.

- *A Preface to Milton*, by Lois Potter, with a revised edition published in 2000 by Longman, is a slim book that provides background information on Milton and the period in which he lived.

- *George Herbert and the Seventeenth-Century Religious Poets* (1990), edited by Mario A. Di Cesare and published by W. W. Norton & Company, contains poems by Milton's contemporaries. This text also includes critical essays on these poets.

- *John Donne*, published in 1990 by Oxford University Press, is a complete edition of Donne's work. A contemporary of Milton, Donne composed both secular and religious poetry, also manipulating and occasionally inventing variations on the traditional forms of poetry.

- *Sir Thomas Browne: Selected Writings* (1995) is edited by Claire Preston and published by Carcanet Press, Limited. Browne, one of Milton's contemporaries, is best known for his essays and treatises that explore religion and melancholy, important issues in seventeenth-century thought.

---

praise. Donne implores God to defeat their common enemy, Satan. He foresees salvation only if God imprisons him within his grace. In his less angry poems, Donne substitutes images for demands, but he still holds back from simple praise. In "Sonnet IX," Donne calls forth an image of the crucifixion and uses a meditative format to find his way to God: Donne calls forth the image, analyzes the image, and then prays to God. This method, while different from the one that Herbert uses, is still focused on finding a way to salvation. Donne plays with the sonnet's rhyme scheme by blending the English and the Italian sonnet and creating his own format, one that Herbert also uses. The first two quatrains of the sonnet maintain the English formula, *abab cdcd*, but the final quatrain is changed from the English formula, *efef*, to the Italian formula, *effe*, and an English couplet, *gg*, is added to complete the sonnet. By modifying both content and rhyme, Donne alters the traditional formulas, moving his sonnets away from both the early incarnation by Wyatt and the later reincarnation by Shakespeare, and into a format by which the poet can dialogue with God. Herbert's use of the sonnet differs slightly from that of Donne. Herbert also demands answers from God, although he is not as strident in his demands. In "Prayer (I)," Herbert uses the sonnet as a prayer to God, but one notable difference from Donne's format is that Herbert removes the division between octave and sestet. There is no posing of a question in the first two quatrains, nor is there a response in the sestet. Herbert does not use verbs in his sonnet/prayer; instead, the poem is a series of noun phrases, which mirror the content: a demand for answers from God.

The changes that Shakespeare, Donne, and Herbert make in the sonnet establish the poets' authority to play with or to manipulate the traditional format of the sonnet. As Donne and Herbert did in their sonnets, Milton also sets up a dialogue with God in "When I Consider How My Light Is Spent," his poem on his blindness. Like Herbert, Milton is also wondering about his ability to serve God. Half his days are gone and he thinks he has not fulfilled all that his talent had predicted. Now he is blind, and in response, Milton questions how he can accomplish what he was sure God intended him to accomplish. The poet is discussing the most difficult moment of his life and wondering if he will be unable to reach his goals. The first part of the sonnet, the octave, is focused on Milton's questioning of how best to serve God if he is blind; the sestet is the voice of patience, of God, who provides the answer just as he did for Herbert. Milton is told that "They also serve who only stand and wait." By standing, of course, the poet has not fallen to sin/Satan. But, in patience, rather than in despair, God provides the answer and reassurance. Milton departs from Herbert's use of praise and instead seeks his salvation through questioning. Although he is chastised by patience to "prevent that murmur," the idea of questioning God is a tactic also used by Donne. Finally, the poem ends on a note of hope, as with Herbert's sonnet. Milton uses the form and the theme of the sonnet to suit his purpose. He uses the Italian format in the octave, *abbaabba*, but varies the sestet in composition. In this sonnet, the sestet's rhyme is the traditional Italian, *cdecde*, but in "On His Having Arrived at the Age of Twenty-Three," Milton varies the sestet's rhyme to *cdedce*. In this case, the complicated rhyme of the sestet reflects the complicated theme, the problem of time. The resolution of the octave's problem is in the production of the sestet: the poet has produced his poem in spite of the restrictions of time. In another sonnet, "To The Lord General Cromwell," Milton responds to a political problem. The army wants to name Cromwell king, but Milton is asking Cromwell not to accept this offer. The octave flatters Cromwell, but the change in the sonnet's direction comes in the sestet and the more subtle movement to a request that is signified with the use of the word "yet." The rhyme of the sestet changes also. Instead of the traditional Italian form, the sestet *cddcee* ends in a couplet, which reflects the pairings also found in the poem: "war and detractions" in line 2, and "faith" and "fortitude" in line 3.

Although Milton is composing sonnets in the seventeenth century, his sonnets reflect both the style and content, though modified, of the typical sixteenth-century sonnet. Shakespeare altered the form and the content slightly to reflect his own needs and objectives, and Milton altered it again to reflect the needs of his poetry. Milton takes what he wishes from the Italian sonnet, largely the octave's rhyme, but he creates a sestet that reflects his own themes. Content, too, is open to modification. Where Shakespeare used the sonnet to explore a variety of secular ideas, the poets who followed in the early seventeenth century turned to religion, especially as a dialogue with God. The pinnacle of this adaption of the traditional sonnet is reached with Milton, who finds the sonnet a useful vehicle for exploring time, politics, and his own personal pain, as well as to reaffirm his belief that God has not abandoned him.

**Source:** Sheri E. Metzger, Critical Essay on "On His Having Arrived at the Age of Twenty-Three," in *Poetry for Students*, The Gale Group, 2003.

## Carol Dell'Amico

*Dell'Amico is a college instructor of English literature and composition. In this essay, Dell'Amico considers Milton's poem within the contexts of the poet's career, his influence on other poets, and the nature of his religious beliefs.*

> *Milton's regret over his advancing age (mortal time) and belated development pales in significance once the rule and time of Heaven and God is considered."*

Poems that are not given titles by their writers, such as this one by Milton, tend to be identified by their first line ("How soon hath Time, the subtle thief of youth"). About fifty years after Milton's death, however, this poem was dubbed "On His Having Arrived at the Age of Twenty-Three." This title was immediately popular and has endured, even if some scholars of Milton wonder whether in saying that "Time" has "Stol'n" his "three-and-twentieth year" Milton is actually saying that he is commemorating in this poem his *twenty-fourth* and not his twenty-third birthday (in this case, what has been "Stol'n" is not really his twenty-third year of life, but rather that year which begins with the poet already at the age of twenty-three).

While this matter of the precise date of this poem is interesting (1631 or 1632?), it is, nevertheless, a minor point in the criticism, as Milton does not change radically as a writer in between his twenty-third and twenty-fourth years. Rather, scholars tend to divide Milton's career into three phases: a first period that ends around 1640 (during which time he wrote "On His Having Arrived at the Age of Twenty-Three"), a second period during which he devoted himself to political, reformist writing (1640–1660), and a third period in which he returns to poetry and writes his greatest works, most notably the epic poem *Paradise Lost*.

More significant than the precise year of the poem's composition, then, are matters such as its sentiments and form, specifically the way in which the pious Christian sentiments of the poem presage the mood and concerns of Milton's later poetry and the way in which its form proved to be so influential. "On His Having Arrived at the Age of Twenty-Three" is a sonnet, which is a particular type of poem, and it is a sonnet organized in a manner that had yet to be tried in English literature. Following Milton's adoption of this different sonnet form, his poetic contemporaries began writing sonnets in the same way, and they emulated, as well, his writing of sonnets on subjects other than love (sonnets written in English before Milton were usually love poems).

Sonnets were first written in England in the sixteenth century and had fallen out of fashion by the time Milton began writing them. They were (and always are) written according to strict rules and conventions, and the sonnet form preferred by Milton's predecessors tended to be fourteen line sonnets divided up into three quatrains and one couplet (a quatrain is a set of four lines; a couplet is a set of two lines).

What readers and other poets particularly appreciated about Milton's different sonnets was his use of a wholly different line arrangement, namely an octave (a set of eight lines as two linked quatrains), followed by a sestet (a set of six lines as two tercets, or two groupings of three lines). Although Milton, as in this poem, occasionally added an extra line or two to this major two-part arrangement, this different sonnet form is nevertheless characterized by its primary, central octave and sestet.

What this type of two-part sonnet encourages are poetic meditations that first introduce or set up a problem in the octave and then resolve or reflect upon the problem in the sestet. This problem-resolution structure allowed Milton and the poets who emulated him to address more mundane topics than love in their sonnets, topics in politics, for example, or, as in this poem, topical subjects. What "On His Having Arrived at the Age of Twenty-Three" considers, specifically, is the problem of the poet's belated creative maturity. Milton already knew by this time that he wished to be a great writer, and his problem is that he is growing older but still has not produced the sort and amount of work that might be expected of one with such ambitions: "My hasting days fly on with full career / But my late spring no bud or blossom shew'th." In these lines, Milton complains that his years are advancing but he has little to show for them; no real "bud or blossom" is in evidence.

Milton's poem exemplifies the problem-solution organization of the octave-sestet sonnet form. The poet has no sooner stated that he sees "no bud or blossom" to show for his years than he states that he even looks younger than his age: "Perhaps my semblance might deceive the truth / That I to manhood am arrived so near." Milton's "semblance" was deceptive in his early twenties, scholars say, because his delicate, feminine facial features made him appear much younger than he really was.

Moving on from the matter of his outward appearance, Milton returns in the octave's next lines to the problem of his professional belatedness. He points to some "more timely-happy spirits" who have achieved feats commensurate with their age, persons whose "ripeness" would seem to accord with their stage in life: "And inward ripeness doth much less appear, / That some more timely-happy spirits endu'th." Critics suggest that Milton had in mind close friends who, like himself, had chosen writing as their profession, but who, unlike Milton, had already published substantially by their early twenties.

The octave's focus is, therefore, quite clear. The poet is wondering whether his tardiness to mature might mean that he will never mature at all, whether his ambition to become a writer of renown may never come to be. This would be a catastrophe for Milton, for he had set himself by this time a strict course of reading and study, all to the end of becoming a master of English letters. Indeed, Milton is said to have gone blind in 1651 owing to his prodigious reading during these years of apprenticeship; he is said to have read, in his early manhood, everything of note written in English, Latin, Italian, and Greek.

The sestet and final, extra line of Milton's sonnet solves the problem put forth in the octave by re-conceiving time and ambition. Milton subordinates his own, individual ambitions to God's will in the sestet, and he substitutes God's eternal time for mortal, human time. Milton has thus decided by the end of this poem that his own ambitions are secondary to God's plans for him, that he will submit to God's will, and that in submitting to God's will in this way he no longer feels keenly the possibility of any personal disappointment. Milton's regret over his advancing age (mortal time) and belated development pales in significance once the rule and time of Heaven and God is considered.

Thus, where time is that which is "hasting" or accumulating rapidly in the octave, "Time" is that which is meaningful only in terms of "the will of Heaven" in the sestet. As critic R. F. Hall noted in *The Cambridge Companion to Milton*, edited by Dennis Danielson, time in the poem seems to "slow down" in the sestet, so that by the

> end of the poem, it is as if movement has become an irrelevance under the divine eye which gazes in eternal stasis at the poet (and us), yet provides the grace

Milton in the octave is a worried, ambitious young man who is comparing himself to friends and wondering when he will produce the creative work he so desires to compose. In the sestet, to the contrary, youthful worry and ambition dissolves as God's will is embraced.

This change of mood and perspective is evident in the very first line of the sestet: "Yet be it less or more, or soon or slow." Instead of anxious concern over his development ("it"), this line expresses a sanguine acceptance of whatever the poet's personal pace and capabilities turn out to be. A creative output minor or major—"less" or "more"—is acceptable; a development "slow" or quick ("soon") is likewise acceptable:

> Yet be it less or more, or soon or slow,
> It shall be still in strictest measure even
> To that same lot, however mean or high,
> Toward which Time leads me, and the will of Heaven;

This attitude of acceptance comes about because Milton in the sestet is not conceiving of himself as an individual, but rather as a servant and subject of the Christian Almighty, God. What he as an individual wants, he realizes, might not be what God has in store for him. Regardless of his own wishes, his progress is determined, ultimately, in "strictest measure," by the Almighty. His "lot" will be that which God decides, and whether it is "mean" (low) or "high," he will embrace it as "the will of Heaven."

Yet, even as the sestet of the poem replaces worldly, mortal time and ambition with God's eternal time and will, there are, still, glimmerings of the youthful, hopeful Milton in the poem's last lines: "As ever in my great Task-Master's eye. / The "great Task-Master" is God." As critic E. A. J. Honigmann suggests in *Milton's Sonnets*, "Milton borrowed the word [Task-Master] not to complain of a harsh overseer but to suggest that he himself may have a special task, as a poet." Milton subordinates his life to God's will, but he is still hoping, at the poem's end, that God's "grace" portends what he especially longs for, namely greatness as a poet.

The mix of Christian humility and proud individualism in this poem is characteristic of much of Milton's writing, including his last works, and it says a great deal about both the nature of Milton's religiosity and of Christian belief in general at the time. What this period in Britain is known for are the many Christian reform movements that contested the hierarchical and elitist composition of the Church. Of particular importance to reformers was a new way of conceiving the status of the individual Christian in relation to priests, parsons, and other official church representatives. These reformers insisted that the individual Christian did not need an official church representative to be an intermediary in between him or herself and God. Rather, to the reformers, any Christian was, in God's eyes, as privileged as the next, and all Christians, regardless of their station in life, should consider themselves as godly as the next person, no matter that this person was a priest, bishop, and so on. What this teaching points to, on the one hand, is the deep piety of the reformers: they were propagating a version of Christianity that encouraged direct and constant communication with God. On the other hand, this teaching elevates the individual, as any person is deemed godly enough to commune with God directly. This suggests both the populism (a belief in the equality of persons) and individualism (the belief in the importance of the individual) of the movements, in that any and each individual on the planet was considered good enough to communicate directly with the greatest of beings himself, God Almighty. Milton and these other reformers were, then, pious populists and individualists of sorts.

The force of this Christian reform movement in England was immense, as its populism intersected with equally populist political movements, movements designed to replace England's monarchy with a republican (elected) form of government. These various reform movements led, in fact, to a Civil War, an upheaval in which Milton played an important role and whose major event was the deposing and execution, in 1649, of the King of England, Charles I. In 1660, however, monarchy was restored, and since Milton had been a vigorous and prolific writer in defense and support of the reformers, he was incarcerated at this time. Yet, thanks to the intervention of powerful friends, he was soon freed. He then settled into his final period of literary output, his greatest period in which he produced the poems for which he is most especially admired (*Paradise Lost*, *Paradise Regained*, and "Samson Agonistes.")

**Source:** Carol Dell'Amico, Critical Essay on "On His Having Arrived at the Age of Twenty-Three," in *Poetry for Students*, The Gale Group, 2003.

## Carey Wallace

*Wallace is a freelance writer and poet. In this essay, Wallace explores Milton's use of biblical imagery in his youthful discussion of his own destiny.*

> "For the young Milton, then, bearing fruit would not mean just a matter of personal success—it was a matter of spiritual life or death."

When a young John Milton penned "On His Having Arrived at the Age of Twenty-Three," he was still a student at Cambridge University, working towards a master of arts degree, which he would receive the next year, at the age of twenty-four. Milton had been writing poems since the age of fifteen, and by the time he left Cambridge, he had accumulated a significant body of poetry: Latin elegies, translations of biblical psalms, and many pages of English verse.

He would wait almost another ten years before he began to publish widely, and even then the works he put his name to would be political or theological arguments, not poetry. Not until fourteen years later, at the age of thirty-seven, would his first volume of poems appear. His literary reputation would not be solidified until just before his sixtieth birthday, with the publication of his epic masterpiece, *Paradise Lost*.

In the meantime, Milton would live through some of the greatest upheaval in Western history. The Renaissance, with its new emphasis on the dignity of humanity, and its amazing scientific and artistic accomplishments, was still a recent memory, which led, both directly and indirectly, to great political and social upheaval. During Milton's lifetime, an English king would be deposed by his own people and replaced by Oliver Cromwell's socially-conservative Protectorate, which would itself be replaced by another member of the royal family.

Milton underwent enormous personal turmoil: a famously fragile first marriage, the deaths of two children, public censure for his liberal opinions on divorce, political reversals as the English government shifted beneath his feet—and, perhaps most significantly, his own blindness, which struck him at the age of forty-four, sixteen years before *Paradise Lost* was completed.

Modern readers approaching "On His Having Arrived at the Age of Twenty-Three" know something even Milton did not know about the poem at the time: the end of the story—both the events of Milton's life and eventual death and the place he has taken in history. Since, in the poem, Milton looks forward over his life and wonders what he might turn out to be, the details of his personal life, and secondarily of the history he lived through, take on a special meaning. For many modern readers attempting to make sense of this early sonnet, the most salient detail of all may be that it was written in 1631.

In 1631, Milton was writing in modern English, but just barely. In fact, that date places him closer on the historical timeline to Chaucer's Middle English than to the English spoken by today's modern readers. That means that, for the average reader, Milton's language may initially seem difficult. But, a close examination reveals a sonnet that is actually quite beautiful in its simplicity—one in which a young man ponders on the universal theme of destiny and what he might turn out to be.

Milton opens the poem by describing time as a winged thief, one who has "stol'n" his "three-and-twentieth year"—playing with a theme that is still common today, the sense that time often passes too quickly, with milestones appearing far before people believe they are ready. Not only has his twenty-third birthday arrived too quickly for Milton, but winged time shows no signs of slowing down: his "hasting days fly on with full career." In this phrase, "career" takes an archaic meaning indicating high velocity.

Although the days of Milton's life speed by, young Milton tells the reader that he is not sure what he has to show for himself, with the line "But my late spring no bud or blossom shew'th." Milton's mention of "late spring" is a reference to the season of life he considers himself to be in: still in early adulthood, he is not yet in the "summer" of his life, but there are not, for him, many more days of springtime. Although spring usually brings with it the signs of the summer to come in the form of buds and blossoms that will yield summer flowers and fruit, Milton says that his life, as yet, shows no such concrete potential—no buds or blossom from which to guess the shape of things to come or even prove that he may ever be fruitful.

There might be several reasons for this, Milton goes on to say. It could be simply that he does not look as old as he actually is: "Perhaps my semblance might deceive the truth / That I to manhood am arrived so near." But, the lack of outward proof of his maturity is not just an illusion, Milton admits. In fact, he finds his entire character still not as mature as other people of his age, a fact that he describes by continuing his blossom metaphor and comparing himself to unripe fruit: "And inward ripeness doth much less appear, / That some more timely-happy spirits endu'th."

For Milton, as a student of the New Testament, this description of himself as a possibly barren plant must have had special resonance: it is highly unlikely that he could have chosen the metaphor without conscious awareness of its resemblance to a metaphor that Christ used during his famous encounter with a barren fig tree. In that story, Christ curses the tree for not bearing fruit in season and tells a parable that ends with Christ commanding that every tree that does not produce good fruit be cut down and thrown into the fire. For the young Milton, then, bearing fruit would not mean just a matter of personal success—it was a matter of spiritual life or death.

In the next lines, however, Milton softens his judgment of himself with hope for the future, in language that echoes St. Paul's well-known statement on the love of God, in which he affirms that "neither death nor life, neither angels nor demons, neither the present nor the future, nor any powers, neither height nor depth, nor anything else in all creation, will be able to separate us from the love of God that is in Christ Jesus our Lord." (Romans 8:38-39) Milton's next phrases, while not identical, are very similar to St. Paul's cadence, and take a similar stand of hope in God in spite of any circumstance: "Yet be it [inward ripeness] less or more, or soon or slow, / It shall be still in strictest measure even / To that same lot, however mean or high, / Toward which Time leads me, and the will of Heaven." Milton even imitates St. Paul's slightly asymmetrical listing, interrupting himself with the long phrase "It shall be still in strictest measure even / To that same lot," before continuing his list of circumstances with "however mean or high." In these lines, the archaic use of "even" roughly substitutes for the modern "equal." Whether he matures more or less, or quickly or slowly, Milton says, his maturity will exactly equal the life, however small or great, which God has planned for him.

Milton's closing lines paraphrase another statement of St. Paul, also in Romans 8, in perhaps the saint's most powerful teaching on the working of God in human destiny, when he says that "In all things God works for the good of those who love him, who have been called according to his purpose" (Romans 8:28). Although Milton has yet to bud or flower, he remains certain of God's attention and care: "All is, if I have grace to use it so, / As ever in my great Task-Master's eye." As he makes this claim, even time, which Milton initially figured as a somewhat hostile winged thief, becomes part of the pattern of "all things" in which, Milton and St. Paul assert, God works. By the end of the sonnet, time is no longer working against Milton, stealing his youth, but a partner (and implicitly a servant) of the "Will of Heaven," leading Milton inexorably toward his destiny.

Throughout the poem, Milton achieves a delicate balance in the age-old tension between free will and predestination. His reference to Christ and the unproductive fig tree and his meditations on his own achievements reveal a deep sense of his own responsibility—but he is also aware that the forces that will shape his character, and his destiny, are finally in God's hands, not his own. Even as he finds a measure of peace through his argument for belief in the providence of God, he acknowledges that he must still act well within the circumstances time and Heaven give him, that he must "have the grace to use it so."

To modern readers looking back, Milton's poem may seem almost prophetic. Milton knew himself well when he wrote that he was not yet inwardly ripe at twenty-three. Even after graduation at twenty-four, he would return to his parents' home to continue his private studies for almost eight years before he began publishing in earnest. He would not solidly establish himself as one of the brightest stars in the English literary constellation for another forty years. But, his sense of destiny, of the finger of God on his life, proved to be no lie. No generation of readers since has been able to ignore Milton: his work has been widely reprinted, and read, in every century since his death, and many critics place him secondary only to Shakespeare among English poets. Even his prose works continued to affect the destinies of humanity long after his death: his writings against tyranny formed part of the framework for revolution in both America and France, and "Areopagitica," his 1644 defense of free speech, has even figured in modern United States court decisions.

Although "On His Having Arrived at the Age of Twenty-Three" is profoundly interesting given Milton's historical context, Milton's true genius is revealed in the fact that, even if he had never become the towering literary figure he did, the poem would stand alone as a universal document of human experience. In it, Milton captures the essence of the moment at which a young person stands on the cusp of adulthood, looking both forward and back, and asking themselves the same questions that every young person, at some point, asks: What have I accomplished here, yet? What do I have to show for it? What should I do next? How do my plans intersect with a future I can barely see? Which way is my destiny? What is going to happen? What does Time hold, what does Heaven have planned?

In the midst of all these questions, Milton's poem offers comfort to the reader—not because Milton finally succeeded, but because, as he and St. Paul both assert, despite any circumstance, destiny lies finally in God's great hands.

**Source:** Carey Wallace, Critical Essay on "On His Having Arrived at the Age of Twenty-Three," in *Poetry for Students*, The Gale Group, 2003.

## Sources

Dorian, D. C., in the *Explicator*, Vol. 8, Item 10, 1949–1950

Hall, R. F., "Milton's Sonnets and His Contemporaries," in *The Cambridge Companion to Milton*, Cambridge University Press, 1999.

Honigmann, E. A. J., *Milton's Sonnets*, St. Martin's Press, 1966.

Macaulay, Thomas Babington, Lord, "Milton," in *Critical, Historical, and Miscellaneous Essays,* Vol. I, Sheldon and Company, 1860, pp. 202–66.

Shakespeare, William, *Romeo and Juliet*, in *The Norton Shakespeare: Tragedies*, edited by Stephen Greenblatt, W. W. Norton & Company, 1997, p. 166.

Svendsen, K., in the *Explicator*, Vol. 7, Item 53, 1948–1949.

Woodhouse, A. S. P., and Douglas Bush, *A Variorum Commentary on the Poems of John Milton*, Columbia University Press, 1972, II.2.372–73.

## Further Reading

Bradford, Richard, *The Complete Critical Guide to John Milton*, Routledge, 2001.

Bradford's work is a guide to Milton's work that provides a discussion of his life and the period in which he was writing, while making connections to the texts that Milton wrote. This book provides a context for the study of Milton's work.

Danielson, Dennis, *The Cambridge Companion to Milton*, Cambridge University Press, 1999.

This book includes information on Milton's works and the period in which they were written, while also summarizing the critical approaches to Milton studies.

Fish, Stanley, *How Milton Works*, Harvard University Press, 2001.

Offering a comprehensive look at Milton's texts, Fish focuses on Milton's use of language and a close reading of the text, ignoring the more common cultural and historically based readings of the poet's work.

Lake, Peter, and Michael C. Questier, *The Anti-Christ's Lewd Hat: Protestants, Papists and Players in Post-Reformation England*, Yale University Press, 2002.

This book looks at the production of pamphlets in early sixteenth- and seventeenth-century England and how the competing religious communities used those pamphlets to further their agendas.

Lewalski, Barbara Kiefer, *The Life of John Milton: A Critical Biography*, Blackwell Publishers, 2001.

Lewalski provides a thorough examination of Milton's life. The author uses Milton's works and a meticulous study of the period to create a comprehensive guide to Milton's life and works.

# Poetry

## Marianne Moore
## 1919

The poem "Poetry" was first published in a literary journal in 1919. Later, it was included in three of Moore's books: *Observations*, *Collected Poems*, and *Complete Poems*. The poem varies in length with each publication, changing from thirteen lines to almost forty lines, and then to three lines, respectively. In "Poetry," the speaker opens the poem by claiming that she "dislikes ... all this fiddle"—meaning poetry. In a tone that is both authoritative and witty, the speaker then goes on to develop her argument, carefully cataloging many of poetry's shortcomings. Occasionally, she illustrates her logic by using carefully chosen images. The speaker says that one of poetry's biggest flaws occurs when it lacks genuineness. She insists that poetry should combine both imagination and reality. She illustrates this point by saying that true poetry is able to present "imaginary gardens with real toads in them." This metaphor has become one of the most widely cited metaphors for poetry. Ironically, through the speaker's exploration of what is "derivative" and "unintelligible" in poetry, this poem proves the merits of poetry. It offers the very model of what "genuine" poetry is, and it exemplifies how valuable good poetry can be.

*Marianne Moore*

## Author Biography

Marianne Moore was born to John Milton Moore and Mary Warner Moore on November 15, 1887, in Kirkwood, Missouri. Moore never knew her father, who had been committed to an asylum some months before her birth; she lived near St. Louis with her mother, brother, and grandfather until the age of seven. The family then moved to Carlisle, Pennsylvania, where her mother taught English at the Metzger Institute for Girls. Moore attended Metzger Institute as a girl, later attending Bryn Mawr College, where she took a bachelor's degree in biology and histology in 1909.

Moore's early poetry was published in the literary magazine of Bryn Mawr College. She also first became aware of new trends in the arts through the influence of Goddard King, a Bryn Mawr lecturer in comparative literature and art history who was among the early champions of Picasso and other modern European painters. After graduating from Bryn Mawr in 1909, Moore completed a business course at Carlisle Commercial College before taking a European vacation with her mother, visiting France and England. When she returned to the United States, Moore began a career as a teacher of English and business subjects at the United States Industrial Indian School in her hometown of Carlisle.

Although she had published a few poems in college publications, Moore first caught the attention of a wider audience in 1915, when several of her poems appeared in such prominent literary magazines of the time as the *Egoist*. Moore moved to Chatham, New Jersey, in 1916, when her brother Warner Moore, recently ordained a Presbyterian minister and appointed to a church there, invited her and her mother to join him. In 1918, the two women moved to a basement apartment in Greenwich Village, and Moore found work as a secretary and a girls' school tutor. She later became an assistant at the Hudson Park branch of the New York Public Library.

During the early 1920s, Moore published her first three collections of poems. In 1924, she received an award of $2,000 from the Dial Press for her contributions to literature, an award that raised some controversy in literary circles. In 1925, Moore became editor of *The Dial*, a position that brought her into contact with many of the noted literary and artistic figures of the time, including T. S. Eliot, Conrad Aiken, William Butler Yeats, Ezra Pound, and Malcolm Cowley. When the magazine ceased publication in 1929, Moore was well enough established that she was able to support herself and her mother by writing essays and reviews for magazines. The two women moved to Brooklyn in 1929 to be near Moore's brother, who was now in the Navy and stationed at the Brooklyn Naval Yard. Moore was to live in Brooklyn until 1966 when the neighborhood finally became too unsafe and she returned to Manhattan. Except for brief teaching assignments at the Cummington School in Massachusetts in 1941 and at Bryn Mawr in 1953, Moore earned her living as a freelance writer until her death in 1972.

Moore's literary contributions were recognized with a host of awards and honors, including the Poetry Society of America's Gold Medal for Distinguished Development, the National Medal for Literature, and an honorary doctorate from Harvard University. Today, such noted poets and commentators as Grace Schulman and Tess Gallagher continue to praise Moore's verse, hailing the poet as one of the most important in modern literature.

## Poem Summary

### Line 1

The poem begins with its speaker making a rather ironic statement about her distaste for poetry. The statement is contradictory because, while she does not prefer poetry, the speaker nevertheless expresses herself through the medium of a poem. The reason the speaker dislikes poetry may be inferred from the use of the word "fiddle." Apparently the speaker believes that poetry can be trifling, or that the poetry-writing process involves too much petty tampering. The speaker's conversational opening of the poem allows for a tone that seems casual, yet it is one that is marked by a witty intelligence.

### Lines 2–3

These lines contain a statement that argues with the one given in line 1 and line 2. Here the speaker admits that although one may think oneself perfectly justified in despising the triviality of poetry, through poetry one also might find that which is real and honest. The beginning lines of the poem thus establish the dialectic that will be elaborated upon in the rest of the poem.

### Lines 4–7

In these lines, the speaker gives specific examples of things that are "genuine," and then she explains exactly how and why those things strike her as being original and sincere. The syntax of this sentence places the images of grasping hands, dilating eyes, and rising hair as close as possible to the word "genuine" from the previous sentence. Because Moore claims to have hated "connectives," she relies on this syntactical proximity to imply a connection. Having made that connection, the sentence then progresses the logic of the argument. It states that functioning hands and eyes and hair are significant not because critics can deduct lofty conclusions about them but because they each serve a distinct purpose. The poem may be suggesting that, in good poetry, every detail must be functional rather than merely academic or ornamental.

### Lines 8–11

The pronoun "they" in line 8 refers, in part, to the hands, eyes, and hair mentioned in line 4. On another level, the pronoun "they" also refers to any significant objects included in any poem. This section echoes the earlier suggestion that every detail within a poem should serve a purpose. These lines imply that if the meaning of an object within a poem is so obscure that it cannot be understood, then the poem will be confusing to its reader. The reader will not appreciate what she or he does not comprehend. Another possible interpretation of lines 8–11 is as a warning against the use of enigmatic symbolism in poetry.

## Media Adaptations

- Moore reads her poems on *Caedmon Treasury of Modern Poets Reading Their Own Poetry*, released by Caedmon/HarperAudio. Their address is P.O. Box 588, Dunmore, Pennsylvania 18512.

- Caedmon/HarperAudio also carries *Marianne Moore Reading Her Poems & Fables from La Fontaine*.

- In 1965, Audio-Forum released an audiocassete of Moore reading her poems, *Marianne Moore Reads Her Poetry*. Audio-Forum is part of Jeffrey Norton Publishers, 96 Broad St., Guilford, Connecticut 06437.

- In 1987, The Annenberg/CPB Project produced *Voices and Visions*, a series of documentaries on modern American poetry that appeared on public television. A segment is devoted to Moore entitled *Marianne Moore: In Her Own Image*. Many libraries and video stores carry this series.

### Lines 12–19

These lines offer a catalog of the different types of "important phenomena" that are sometimes included in poetry but whose meanings are not necessarily understood as they should be. Moore frequently uses animals in her poetry to draw a connection between art and the natural world. Here, she provides images of a sleeping bat, "elephants pushing," "a wild horse taking a roll," and "a tireless wolf under / a tree." The poem offers these creatures as examples of a kind of genuineness that is often misrepresented and misunderstood in poetry. However, the poem does not "discriminate" against the human kingdom, either: these lines acknowledge that poetry often concerns itself with the significant "phenomena" of the critic, the statistician, the baseball fan, business documents, and schoolbooks. Line 18 acknowledges that all such considerations are, indeed, significant.

The speaker's tone becomes cautioning, even didactic, as she again qualifies one of her previous statements. Although she says in line 18 that the "phenomena" she mentions are important, she now warns against the use of such phenomena by "half poets." The phrase "dragged into prominence" shows that the speaker believes that some poets force emphasis upon certain details within their poems. The speaker seems to think that certain subjects in poems are exploited, and when they are, "the result is / not poetry." These lines serve to remind poets and readers alike of the dangers of superficiality in poetry.

### Lines 20–24

Here, the speaker urges poets to strive to be "'literalists of / the imagination.'" This phrase is a quote taken from W. B. Yeats. Moore often includes quotes from other literature within her own work as a way of responding to the ideas of other writers. In doing this, she demonstrates her belief that the ideas presented in literature should be so important as to be open to lively, ongoing response. Apparently, Moore believes that good writing integrates other literature.

The phrase "'literalists of / the imagination'" contains a paradox. This phrase calls upon poets to be literalists, which means that they ought to present what they imagine word for word, without embellishment, and in such a way as to adhere to reality. Of course, such a task is nearly impossible when one is presenting that which is a product of the imagination. If something is imagined, then, by definition, it has no reality, no actuality. Undoubtedly, Moore recognizes the contradiction of this paradox. Perhaps she includes it here as a way of acknowledging the near impossibility poets face in using words to reconcile that which is imagined with that which is actual. Nevertheless, the paradox seems to serve as the ultimate standard toward which poets ought to strive in their representation of what is "genuine."

Lines 22–24 then describe literalist poets as those that rise above arrogance and pettines, avoiding the tendency of half-poets, defined in line 19, to force pointless emphasis on an unnecessary subject. The word "triviality" echoes the word "fiddle" from line 2 and repeats the suggestion that sometimes poetry is not as vital as it could be.

The phrase "'imaginary gardens with real toads in them'" is a paradox that provides a visual complement to the paradox given in line 21 and line 22. (Although this paradox also is surrounded by quotations marks, its original source has never been found; therefore, it is generally attributed to Moore.) Through the example of real toads in imaginary gardens, the speaker shows the reader what she means by saying that poets must be "'literalists of the imagination.'" Here, the poem suggests that good poetry is the "imaginary garden" in which "real toads"—or anything that is genuine—may reside. The speaker implies that only when a poet uses imagination to present reality in an honest way is a poem created.

### Lines 25–29

These lines repeat the notion that poetry is created from a combination of imagination ("raw materials") and reality ("that which is on the other hand / genuine"). The word "demand" indicates that the speaker thinks one must hold poetry to high standards. Although she acknowledges that much poetry does not yet meet these high expectations, the speaker admits that, in the meantime, it is still possible for one to be "interested" in poetry. The poem concludes with this resolution of the dialectic that was established in the poem's opening lines.

## Themes

### Nature

Nature was a popular subject for romantic poets who found in it their inspiration, energy, and, often, their reason for being. Modernist poets enlarged their conception of subject matter and of nature itself. Moore, even though she described the natural world with an almost scientific eye for detail, using decidedly unromantic language, nonetheless considered it a place of beauty and mystery. She underscores this attitude in the third stanza when she uses the odd behavior of animals as examples of what the human mind "cannot understand." But like poetry, these behaviors should be embraced rather than ignored, as they embody the very "raw material" of life itself, which cannot be reduced to mean this or that, as critics would have it.

### Modernism

Modern poetry has often been criticized for its obscurity and elitism, with some writers claiming that it shows a deliberate attempt to alienate general readers. Moore addresses this in her opening line when she claims about poetry: "I, too, dislike it." What she implies here is that she dislikes the popular conception of modern poetry as writing that has nothing to do with the real world, and is often abstract. However, in the rest of her poem she

# Topics For Further Study

- Work in pairs: One person play the role of Moore and the other person play the role of a critic interviewing Moore about the meaning of her poem. Write up a transcript of the interview and exchange this with other students, comparing the variety of ways Moore is presented.

- Write Moore's poem in paragraphs instead of lines. Does this change the meaning or the effect of the poem? What is lost and what is gained in the new version, and what does this have to say about the nature of poetry itself? Report your findings to your class.

- Write a poem about a term that many people disagree on. In the poem, try to define this term. Then, read the poem to your class and discuss your responses.

- Research the behavior of the animals that Moore describes. Is this behavior, in fact, unexplainable? Do you agree with her statement that "we do not admire what / we cannot understand?" Why or why not? Discuss your responses in groups.

- If Moore were writing today, what examples would she use to describe behavior than cannot be explained? Work in groups and then list your ideas on the board.

- Moore makes a number of claims for the idea of the "genuine." As a class, brainstorm definitions of this term and then work to come up with one on which the entire class can agree.

- Work in groups: Make two lists and compare what Moore suggests about critics in "Poetry" with what she suggests about them in her poem "Critics and Connoisseurs." Discuss the lists as a class.

- Compare the 1919 version of "Poetry" to the 1967 version, in which Moore cut the poem down to three lines. Which is more effective and why? Would including the earliest version in the footnotes for the final edition provide a helpful context for reading the poem? Discuss as a class whether or not footnotes alienate or inform a reader, and whether or not imagist poets might prefer an intertextual reading of Moore's poem versus a reading of the final three-line version as it stands.

---

utilizes explicitly modernist techniques, such as irony, allusion, paradox, quoting others, and incorporating footnotes—techniques that often invite the very accusation of elitism. In this way, she shows herself to be a true modernist, interested in process as much as product and embracing contradiction and abstraction while appearing to endorse unequivocal statements about the real world.

## *Imagination*

Poets have paid homage to the idea of the imagination ever since romantics such as Samuel Taylor Coleridge and William Wordsworth championed its powers, naming it as a crucial part in the poetic process. Coleridge, for example, distinguished between imagination and "fancy," terms that previously had been used synonymously, by giving imagination a more important role. Whereas fancy merely reassembles sense impressions, the imagination synthesizes disparate impressions, ideas, etc. into a unified whole, a whole greater than its parts. Moore's "Poetry" endorses this view as well, although she claims the imagination can only be effective if applied to stuff of the real world, that is, the "genuine." This is one reason why Moore attacks critics, as they are champions of "understanding" more interested in analyzing than re-seeing the world and accepting its contradictions and mysteries, which are indicative of the reality and of poetry itself.

## *Poetry*

Categorizing writing into genres such as poetry, fiction, drama, non-fiction, and the like is often a vexing matter not only for bookstores and marketers but for poets and critics as well. Moore was particularly notorious for her ambivalence about labeling what she did, noting once that her writing is called poetry only because no one else knew what to call it. "Poetry" is ironic partly because of its name and the fact that its argument about poetry's definition is never resolved. Moore's writing resembles poetry the most in its physical appearance, as she makes innovative use of line breaks and indentation. However, her choppy rhythms, use of multi-claused sentences, quotations, and footnotes all give her writing the appearance of prose. Partly, this approach to poetry stems from Moore's affinity with the Imagist movement, members of which argued that, to rejuvenate poetry, meter should be replaced by the rhythms of colloquial speech and conventionally poetic diction should be replaced by contemporary language and phrasing.

## Style

"Poetry" is constructed in syllabic verse, which is a sub-category of free verse. Free verse means that the poem does not follow a regular pattern of rhyme and meter. Meter refers to units of stressed and unstressed syllables. Instead, the poem loosely relies on "syllabics," which refers to the number of syllables per line. In syllabic verse, the number of syllables in any given line in a stanza is the same as the number of syllables of the same given line in the other stanzas. For example, you will notice that the final lines of each stanza in "Poetry" all contain thirteen syllables. Although Moore varies her syllabics, if one counts the syllables throughout the poem, one will notice a rough pattern emerging. By relying on syllabics instead of rhythm and meter, Moore is able to create a poem that more closely follows the patterns of natural speech.

Moore varies the typography of this poem. "Typography" refers to the way in which the poem is typed on the page. Moore often uses equal indentation to signify lines that rhyme. For example, the final words in line 4 and line 5 both rhyme ("eyes" and "rise"), and both lines are indented the same amount of spaces. The same may be said of line 27 and line 28 ("and" and "hand"). Not all of Moore's rhymes appear at the end of the lines, nor are they necessarily true rhymes. Rather, some are slant rhymes, also known as off rhymes, which means that they are close in sound, but do not exactly rhyme. An example of an off rhyme is the "baseball fan" and the "statistician" in line 15.

Rather than overwhelming her reader with blatant rhymes, Moore mutes them so that her reader may experience the pleasure of hearing similar sounds in the way they subtly occur in natural speech.

## Historical Context

### Literature and Art of the 1920s

In 1919, when the first version of "Poetry" was published in the journal *Others*, people were still figuratively—and some literally—shell-shocked from World War I, which ended the preceding year. In literature, poets and novelists experimented with form and subject matter, trying to craft work that embodied the uncertainty, fear, and anxiety that consumed people. T. S. Eliot's poems in his collections *Prufrock and Other Observations* (1917), *Poems* (1920), and *The Wasteland* (1922) accomplished this through use of fragmentation, allusion, irony, myth, and symbolism. Ezra Pound, an important influence on many modernist poets, exhorted poets to "make it new" and claimed the image as the cornerstone of his poetics. In addition to publishing and translating works such as *The Sonnets and Ballate of Guido Cavalcanti* (1912), *Hugh Selwyn Mauberly* (1920), and *Personae* (1926), Pound mentored numerous writers including Eliot, William Carlos Williams, and James Joyce, and supported new literary magazines including *Poetry* and *The Little Review*. In his poem "Hugh Selwyn Mauberly," Pound called the carnage of World War I "wastage as never before" and described the "disillusions as never told in the old days." Moore, who corresponded with Pound, Eliot, Williams, Wallace Stevens, and a host of other influential poets, eschewed emotionalism in her writing and embraced a poetry that attempted to describe the physical world with precise and detailed images, often couched in argument. She also borrowed from other texts, sprinkling her verse liberally with quotations. Moore developed her reputation as both poet and critic largely through publishing in smaller, newer journals such as *Poetry*, established in 1912, *The Egoist*, a magazine of imagist verse, and *Others*, and as an editor of *The Dial*, a prestigious literary journal of the 1920s.

Moore's concern for the "genuine" in poetry is also a concern that early twentieth-century painters held. However, their approach towards subject matter was less concrete than Moore's, and instead of precision in representation, they experimented with abstract depictions of ideas and things.

# Compare & Contrast

- **1920s:** The Roaring Twenties in America was a time of prosperity and pleasure seeking, as people sought to recover from the changes wrought by World War I.

  **Today:** Seeking to recover from a terrorist attack on New York City, Americans flaunt their patriotism and temper their spending. Millions of American flags are sold across the country.

- **1920s:** Though some schools teach poetry and fiction writing, no one American college or university offers a degree in creative writing.

  **Today:** Hundreds of American colleges and universities offer undergraduate and graduate degrees in creative writing. Many people holding these degrees take jobs teaching in universities.

- **1920s:** The 19th Amendment gives American women the right to vote.

  **Today:** Though women are better represented in industry and government than eighty years ago, they are still paid less than men in similar jobs.

- **1920s:** There is a small boom in literary journals and magazines to showcase the work of experimental writers such as Ezra Pound, e. e. cummings, and Moore.

  **Today:** The World Wide Web has made publishing easier and cheaper than ever. Literally thousands of "e-zines" featuring some very good and some very bad writing have debuted in the last decade, and more come online every day.

---

Cubists such as Pablo Picasso and Georges Braque broke down their subject matter, analyzed it, and then reconstructed it in abstract form. Picasso's painting *Les Demoiselles d'Avignon*, considered by many to be the first Cubist painting, depicted five nude women in an angular and distorted way, destroying the continuity of the human body and creating an almost three-dimensional effect. A raft of other art movements including surrealism, futurism, imagism, and dadaism sought during this time to provoke viewers and readers to see and experience the world anew. In addition to the war, events such as Albert Einstein's publication of the theory of relativity, the popularization of the automobile and the radio, Daylight Savings Time in America, and the women's vote contributed to reconfiguring the ways in which people thought about and perceived their world and one another.

After the war, many American writers fled to Europe, where it was possible to live well inexpensively. Seeking new ideas and to revive their flagging spirits, writers such as Malcolm Cowley, Ezra Pound, Archibald MacLeish, and Ernest Hemingway moved to France, Spain, and Italy. Many of these expatriates gathered around Gertrude Stein, a wealthy American art collector and writer who sponsored "salons" at her apartment at 27, rue de Fleurus in Paris, that attracted artists, writers, and musicians like F. Scott Fitzgerald, Henri Matisse, Pablo Picasso, Virgil Thompson, and scores of others who helped to create and define the modernist tradition. Noting their restlessness and the fact that many of the American writers who gathered around her during this time were morally and spiritually adrift, Stein referred to the group as "a lost generation." Though she had traveled to Europe before the war, Moore stayed in the States during and after it, living with her mother in Manhattan.

## Critical Overview

Because many of Moore's poems rely upon the careful presentation of visual imagery to convey intellectual and emotional ideas, she is sometimes linked to the imagists, a school of writers popular in the 1920s. On the other hand, her poetry also demonstrates an experimental arrangement on the page, a preoccupation with science and technology, a certain intellectualism, and the kind of emotional distance that is often found in modernist poetry. Still others claim Moore's writing is so unique that it does not fit into any one particular school of poetry. In any case, almost all critics would agree with the following conviction asserted by T. S. Eliot in an introduction to Moore's *Selected Poems*: "Miss Moore's poems form part of the small body of durable poetry written in our time ... in which an original sensibility and alert intelligence and deep feeling have been engaged in maintaining the life of the English language."

Although "Poetry" was written early in Moore's career, it generally is regarded as one of Moore's most accomplished poems. In the poem, the speaker expresses a "dislike" for poetry, arguing that it often lacks "that which is ... genuine." Through her argument, the speaker ends up exemplifying all that is valuable about poetry. As Sven Birkerts says in *The Electric Life: Essays on Modern Poetry*, "The poem is, in fact, a kind of anthology of the attributes and techniques that readers have most cherished in Moore." One of those cherished techniques is the use of paradox, particularly the paradox that the speaker supplies when she says poems should be like "'imaginary gardens with real toads in them.'" In his book *Marianne Moore*, Bernard F. Engel praises Moore's use of this paradox. He says,

> Fascination with paradox is the most immediately striking aspect of the verse of Moore. This interest in the seemingly contradictory is often witty and, at times, playful.... But it is also profound. Paradox is of the essence of her work because she wishes to advocate a set of values.

Paradox is only one aspect of Moore's poems that make them valuable to their readers. As poet James Dickey writes in *Babel to Byzantium*, "Every poem of hers lifts us toward our own discovery-prone lives. It does not state, in effect, that I am more intelligent than you, more creative because I found this item and used it and you didn't. It seems to say, rather, that I found this, and what did you find? Or better, what *can* you find."

## Criticism

### Chris Semansky

*Semansky is an instructor of literature and composition. In this essay, Semansky considers the question of definition in Moore's poem.*

Coming up with an adequate definition of the term "poetry" has obsessed critics, poets, and philosophers since Plato, who wanted to banish them for misrepresenting the truth. Some link the term to formal features of writing, while others focus on the composing process or the attitude or qualities of the writer. Some believe that poetry does not necessarily even have to use words, but rather is a matter of perception. Moore's poem tackles the "problem" of defining poetry by creating a hierarchy of degree separating "genuine" poetry from bad poetry, and by linking "genuine" poetry to a specific purpose.

By titling her poem "Poetry," Moore creates expectations that the ensuing lines will describe or explain the phenomenon. However, her first line disarms readers when she claims, "I, too, dislike it: there are things that are important beyond all this fiddle." In *Marianne Moore: The Cage and the Animal*, Donald Hall writes that the "fiddle" Moore refers to is "a kind of poetry that is neither honest nor sincere but that has found fashionable approval by virtue of its very obscurity." The "things that are important beyond all this fiddle" are obviously related to "hands that can grasp, eyes / that can dilate, hair that can rise," which, Moore tells readers, are "useful." But how are they useful, and what do they have to do with poetry?

They are useful in that they are fodder for the imagination. They are the stuff of the real, physical, concrete world. Moore represents the world of the senses in her list of images and underscores two things: the importance of concrete imagery in poetry, and the appropriate use of these images by the imagination. These criteria have been staple features in definitions of good poetry since the romantics. Moore also makes a dig at critics in her claim that these things are important "not because a / high-sounding interpretation can be put upon them." Rather, their mere existence is reason enough for their importance, for they give human beings themselves definition.

Moore further differentiates between "fiddle" and the "genuine" in the second stanza, saying that the former is derivative, while the latter is what poetry should be all about. Moore critic Elizabeth Joyce writes that genuine poetry for Moore is about the here and now, and that "its reason for existence is entrenched in its ability to capture a sincere response to life's experiences, those that accurately reflect the social context of the poet." Of course, one person's idea of accuracy is another person's idea of sloppy thinking, and sincerity itself has become a suspect term for much of modern poetry. Moore's genius is that by implicitly espousing such a modest purpose for poetry she stands to gain more readers, as she acknowledges poetry's diminished status in modern society while also attempting to salvage a place for it. She wants to give meaning back to poetry, to rescue it from the posers, but the more she elaborates her desire the more muddied her ideas become.

The third stanza provides the very element that Moore claims makes up genuine poetry: the use of concrete images in the service of the imagination. Animal behavior that appears incomprehensible to human beings is like poetry in that people attempt to explain it, though it appears unfathomable. She slips in yet another dig at critics by including them in the list of odd animal facts: "the immovable critic twitching his skin / like a horse that feels a flea." All of these descriptions, however mundane, contribute to the variety of the natural and the human world and present readers with material things in a new way. Joyce elaborates on the connection between these items and abstract poetry itself:

> Even though abstract poetry is obscure, Moore poses, it is worth our attention because it is no more difficult to understand than anything else around us: it remains a reflection of the changes in our culture.

The notion of abstraction is especially important for modern poetry, and for Moore's own writing, which, like T. S. Eliot's and Wallace Stevens's, is dense with allusions and requires readers to be active participants in the meaning-making process. In this sense, the poem is validation, justification, and an example of the very ideas it espouses. Unlike concrete images, which provide a mental picture of the material world and evoke its sensuous qualities, abstractions denote qualities or attributes of things and are based in the world of ideas. In the early part of the twentieth century when Moore wrote this poem, abstraction was becoming more and more fashionable in the arts and in poetry. In painting, artists such as Pablo Picasso and Wassily Kandinsky composed wholly abstract paintings based upon ideas and theories rather than what they saw with their eyes, and in theater dramatists such as Eugene O'Neill and Frank Wedekind wrote plays that featured representative types rather than particular people with distinct personalities.

The genuine, for Moore, then, did not mean *just* the real or the original, at least not in any surface-level way. The writing of others was as important to her own work as her perceptions of worldy things. This is evident in her allusions to Leo Tolstoy and William Butler Yeats to make her argument. Tolstoy struggled to say where poetry ended and prose began, and Yeats argued that William Blake was a "literalist of the imagination"

> *Moore's poem, then, an example itself of the genuine, achieves its effects not only through its concrete and detailed imagery but also by referring readers to other writers. In this way, she draws on tradition while simultaneously helping to reshape it.*

in his belief that figures conjured by the imagination had real observable properties. Moore's poem, then, an example itself of the genuine, achieves its effects not only through its concrete and detailed imagery but also by referring readers to other writers. In this way, she draws on tradition while simultaneously helping to reshape it. Quoting and alluding to other writing is a key feature of intertextuality, the notion that all texts are related and ultimately depend upon one another for their meaning. In *Marianne Moore: Imaginary Possessions*, Bonnie Costello argues that Moore's strategy in quoting others is part of her broader strategy of evasion, of scrupulously examining something—an object, an animal, an idea—but never defining it precisely, a strategy seemingly at odds with her own reputation for precision and accuracy. Costello writes that in "Poetry," Moore

> posits an ideal in which the genuine is absorbed into form, reference into poem, the real into the imaginary. In the meantime poetry turns out to be a magic trick that does not quite succeed, but which absorbs us in its dazzling sleight-of-hand, in which we think we glimpse the genuine before it turns into the poet once again.

For Costello, then, Moore is an illusionist, which means that Costello, as critic, is the one who "unmasks" her tricks. This is an intriguing reading of the poem, given Moore's own description of critics in this poem and others. It is interesting that Moore revised "Poetry" a number of times, and that her last revision, published in her *Complete Poems*

## What Do I Read Next?

- T. S. Eliot published his first collection of verse, *Prufrock and Other Observations* in 1917. Eliot was the major poetic voice in America during the first half of the twentieth century.

- In 1925, F. Scott Fitzgerald wrote *The Great Gatsby*, widely considered to be the great American novel. This was just a few years after Moore published "Poetry."

- Moore's collection of essays *Predilections*, published in 1955, contains essays on major poets such as Wallace Stevens, William Carlos Williams, and Ezra Pound, and Moore's own idiosyncratic views on poetry and nature.

- Moore alludes to William Butler Yeats's 1903 book, *Ideas of Good and Evil*, which contains essays on the poets Percy Bysshe Shelley and William Blake as well as essays on magic and mysticism.

---

(1967) consisted of just three lines, thereby giving critics paradoxically both more *and* less to work with. It is more because critics can now focus on Moore's practice of revision and the evolution of her thinking about poetry, and it is less because three lines is fewer than twenty-nine.

Critics have paid more attention to her numerous revisions of the poem than the poem itself. Bonnie Honigsblum, for example, in "Marianne Moore's Revisions of 'Poetry,'" argues that Moore revised her poem through the years because she was influenced by other writers, and that Moore's idea of the possibility of poetry itself evolved. Focusing on Moore's notes to the poem, what literary theorists sometimes refer to as its "paratextuality," Honigsblum claims that what Moore left out in terms of explanatory notes, rather than what she included, tells readers more about her reasons for revision than the revisions themselves. It is in this extra-literary material that researchers have looked for clues to Moore's intentions and meanings. This is fitting, considering that Moore considered her writing part of the world-as-text around her, instead of merely an expression of individual genius, as other poets might claim. The clearest expression of what she meant by the "genuine" in poetry is best summed up by her own words, written in a letter to a college student (reprinted in *The Marianne Moore Newsletter*), Thomas P. Murphy, who had asked her what she meant by the term.

> I meant by the genuine, a core of value—expressed in whatever way the writer can best express it. Like you, I prefer rhyme to free verse; I like a tune and I feel that one should be as clear as one's natural reticence allows one to be. The maximum efficiency of expression in poetry should be at least as great as it could be in prose; certainly, one should be natural. The reversed order of words seems to me poetic suicide.

**Source:** Chris Semansky, Critical Essay on "Poetry," in *Poetry for Students*, The Gale Group, 2003.

### Bernard F. Engle

*In the following excerpt, Engle writes about Moore's treatment of the subject of poetry in her poems.*

It is a truism that all poems are "about" poetry. At least the next nine pieces in *Complete Poems* are more or less direct treatments of poetry itself and of the poet and his critics. In "Poetry" Moore stated something of her own artistic creed; in "Pedantic Literalist," "Critics and Connoisseurs," and "The Monkeys," she commented upon criticism; in "In the Days of Prismatic Color," "Peter," "Picking and Choosing," "England," and "When I Buy Pictures," she presented particular aspects of her aesthetics.

In its complete form "Poetry" contains Moore's most comprehensive reflections on her art. Since she customarily made decisions for artistic reasons, it is most likely that she became dissatisfied with the poem's views or with the way it expresses them. It is also possible that she was tired of the endless rehashing of the poem by critics. Whatever her motive, in her last revision she retained only two and a half of the first three lines of the 1951 version. The resulting fragment amounts to an abstract summary of her position, lacking the detail that made the position vividly comprehensible. The editors of the 1981 collection complied with her wishes by publishing the abbreviated version in the text; fortunately, in the view of most readers, they gave the full version in the notes. I will discuss this version. The beginning assertion that "I, too, dislike it" is sometimes quoted as evidence that Moore was a good sophisticate who did not take her art seriously, that under the skin she was essentially a middle-class intellectual without unmodish convictions. But to so read her is to read quite wrongly. Though the remark is on the face of it ironic, it is more than a simple comment of obvious indirection. She was declaring her disgust with the common view of poetry as a way of prettifying standard opinions, usually those of intellectual liberalism. The critics who read her as having contempt for all poetry are thus hoisted on their own petard: the kind of poetry she disliked is, or includes, that which they commonly prefer. What she liked is "the genuine"; the rest of "Poetry" is an effort at explanation of this quality.

Her speaker declares, in lines reminiscent of T.S. Eliot's "The Hollow Men," that vivid presentation of the specific details of a subject is important not because it may lead to "high-sounding interpretation" but because it is "useful": because it can lead to the "genuine." But if these details are only "derivative," removed from the actuality of the experience, none of us will admire them. The "us" is delightfully and pointedly represented as creatures engaged in a variety of activities; the passage deftly scores the "immovable critic" as a horse to whom the work of art is a flea. No one, the poem is saying, is likely to be diverted from his usual concerns by anything other than the accurately presented. All the "us" are possible subjects; even the business and schoolroom documents sometimes excluded from the canon of literary material may be used for poetry.

Yet, as these inclusions would indicate, the mere thing in itself is not a poem: "half poets" who celebrate the humdrum detail for its own sake do not thereby make poetry. What is important is that the poet be true ultimately, not to fact but to his imagination; poets must be "literalists of the imagination," above the insolence of expecting presentation of the trivial to be poetry. The poet must give "'imaginary gardens with real toads in them'"—a populace of real objects that, taken together, will produce an imagined experience. Perhaps no one at present has achieved such art; meanwhile, one may qualify as being "interested in poetry" if he demands fulfillment of the objectivist paradox that "rawness," the accurate presentation of the thing itself, must be the basis for, the material of, a "genuine" garden that is more than the sum of its physical components.

This theory is, of course, ultimately a neoromantic one; for it requires something more than realism of observation. It does insist, however, that one start from the accurately realized object. In

> "... Moore was a good sophisticate who did not take her art seriously, that under the skin she was essentially a middle-class intellectual without unmodish convictions."

Moore's creed, poetry must climb to heights beyond realism, but it must begin its ascent on a stairway of fact. The enameled kylin of "Nine Nectarines" was a better object of art than the painted fruit, though delineated with perhaps equal inaccuracy because his creator perceived the spirit within him.

In rhetorical form "Poetry" follows one of Moore's common patterns; moving from an artfully casual beginning to a climax of feeling in the next-to-last stanza, it then ends almost off-handedly with a final, fairly direct comment upon what has been presented. As a work of art, it is its own exemplification. Though it deals more directly with an abstract subject than most of her work, it is grounded on a sufficient quota of such specificities as "hair that can rise," a bat upside down, a "wild horse taking a roll." Because it is provided with these concrete details, it is much more successful than "In This Age of Hard Trying, Nonchalance..." in which the subject is equally abstract but the incident the poem is based upon is not clearly delineated.

Each of the remaining eight poems on poetry works through a particular object or set of circumstances. The injunction in "Poetry" that one must be a "literalist of the imagination" does not, of course, mean approval of the "Pedantic Literalist" who is disparaged in the poem of this title. The chief error of the mundanely minded is illustrated as deceptiveness: his failure to perform what he seems to promise. Such a literalist is termed in the opening line a "Prince Rupert's drop" (a blob of glass so treated that it appears attractive but flies apart when handled) and a "paper muslin ghost," a spurious spirit that would crumple if embraced. A further comparison is to a heart that, failing to give warning of its weakness, caused its owner's death. The result of long practice at deception—perhaps of trying vainly and unimaginatively to make poetry out of the merely literal—is that the spontaneity with which even the "literalist" is born turns into wood.

The "hardihood" that resists spontaneities is the topic of "Critics and Connoisseurs," a poem opening with the somewhat resounding remark that there is "a great amount of poetry in unconscious/fastidiousness." Certain "products" of conscious fastidiousness are "well enough in their way," the poem continues, but such spontaneous attempts at careful procedure as a child's efforts to right a toy and to feed a puppy are better acts of art because they are unforced. Another example of overdone fastidiousness is a swan remembered as reluctant to give up its "disbelief," its false dignity, in order to eat food thrown to it. In the third stanza the poem turns to "you," the critics and connoisseurs who, like the swan, have "ambition without understanding." An illustration of the fault is furnished by the behavior of an ant that foolishly continued attempts to find a use for burdens that could contribute nothing to ant goals. The poem ends with an inquiry: of what use are such ambitions as those of the swan and the ant, ambitions to maintain an impenetrable reserve or to demonstrate that one has struggled for a useless trophy? Remembering the comment in "Poetry" that objects are good if in some sense useful, we may deduce that critics, like the swan, and connoisseurs, like the ant, are guilty of adopting attitudes and of choosing goals that could be valuable if intended to serve some useful purpose but are often clung to without understanding. The poem is recommending more attention to the spirit, less to the letter.

"The Monkeys" makes it clear that, though the artist is to find a "spirit" in the object his enterprise is not to be an expedition into the "arcanic." The poem, which begins with comments upon sights observed during a long-past trip to a menagerie (or a parliament of literary critics?) remarks on the difficulty of recalling in detail the reasons for the impression of "magnificence" that remains. But one creature will not be forgotten, a large, kingly cat who perhaps represents those described at the end of "Poetry" as "interested in poetry." He, it seems, gave the indignant speech of the last two stanzas of "The Monkeys," a protest against critics' imposition of "inarticulate frenzy" and their insistence on almost "malignant" depths in poetry. Moore, an impressionist in her own criticism, was again arguing for the spontaneous rather than the codified and pseudo-profound that she apparently believed typical of the "immovable" critic of "Poetry," the "consciously fastidious" interpreter of "Critics and Connoisseurs."

The ease with which she had a cat deliver a comment, almost a diatribe, on literary criticism demonstrates the art in the seemingly casual beginning and an ending that give a rightness to the choice of a feline spokesman. Having an animal convey the message provides a neat irony; the poem's original title, "My Apish Cousins," made somewhat more obvious the ironic comparison of human and animal.

(The unimaginative literalist was again a target in "Melanchthon," a work printed in 1951 but omitted from the 1981 book. It closes with a question that amounts to an assertion of the belief that the depth of a life and of a poet's work will not be perceived by one who fails to sense the "unreason" or mystery that Moore believed to lie behind all experience.)

Yet though the poet is not be "consciously fastidious" and is to see an "unreason," he is nevertheless to be clear. "In the Days of Prismatic Colour" declares that early in creation color was "fine" or exact, not because of art but because of its closeness to its origins. Even "obliqueness," indirection, was apparent and understandable, not hidden. But now the oblique is no longer accessible, and color no longer holds its purity; original simplicity has been replaced by "complexity." Though there is nothing wrong with complexity when it reflects actual perception, it is wrong when indulged in to the point that it obscures. And it is especially wrong when made an end in itself, when a poet values the vehemence instead of the worth of what he is saying, and insists that all truth must be dark. Such insistence, being "principally throat," is a "sophistication" that is the direct opposite to truth.

Sophisticates, it appears, view the truth as something like a monster of Greek myth, crawling, gurgling, and darksome. "To what purpose!," she exclaims, are the perverse misunderstandings that see truth as complex and even as monstrous. Truth is "no Apollo / Belvedere, no formal thing": it is, we gather, spontaneous and unconscious. Though complexity may appear in it, not this but courage and endurance are its chief characteristics. The "wave" of critical fashion, of philosophical challenge, may roll over it; but, like the cliff in "The Fish," it will survive.

The virtue of being "natural," of doing without pretense or alibi what one is designed to do, is celebrated with appropriate playfulness in "Peter," a presentation of a cat belonging to two of Moore's women friends and a demonstration of her ability to exemplify in a poem the virtues she was meditating upon in the process of writing it. The observations of Peter that she sets down are those identified with what might be called his cat-ness: complete relaxation, narrowed eyes, obvious nightmares, and lack of concern with judgment that would condemn him for possessing the claws and tail he was born with. Emphasis is upon his animality, his unself-conscious turning from the coddled to the clawing and back again. The poem has been read as an attack on Catholicism, the cat representing the church that claims to have been founded by the apostle Peter and that to some Protestants has appeared as both lethargic and rapacious. The poem has even been read as a feminis attack on Catholicism's failure to ordain women. But it takes a considerable stretch to read into the piece an attack on another Christian church: the focus is on the cat in his cat-ness, not on use of him as a symbol, and when the poem appeared in 1924 neither Moore's own Presbyterian church nor other mainline denominations were ordaining women. Remaining unabashed by the "published fact"—his obvious animality—and willing "to purloin, to pursue" as instinct bids him, Peter the cat is a living example of natural behavior.

That naturalness is essential for the literary critic, who should see literature as "a phase of life," is the assertion of "Picking and Choosing." The advice is, as in "In the Days of Prismatic Colour," that we should not approach literature with fearful reverence. And, as in the passage in "Poetry" dismissing "half poets," we must not come to it as though it were merely commonplace. In his statement the critic must use the "true" word, avoiding the murky and the faked. As examples of the kind of "fact" that critcs should give, the speaker presents capsule comments on Shaw and Henry James that mention flaws in their work but also point to virtues. (The comment on James has changed several times. The first version said flatly that James "is not profound"; later versions say that James is all that he is said to be "if feeling is profound"; the 1981 book reads "James / is all that has been said of him".)

Moore concludes the passage with lines observing that Thomas Hardy, for example, should be seen not primarily as either novelist or poet but as a writer conforming to a dictum like T. S. Eliot's assertion that one should interpret life through "the medium of the emotions." "The Monkeys" shows Moore's own preference for criticism that has an emotional basis and her scorn for merely intellectual methods. She did in "Picking and Choosing" concede that, if the critic must have an opinion, he may be permitted to "know what he likes." The next lines admit Gordon Craig and Kenneth Burke to the rank of good critic, both apparently having impressed Moore as knowing what they like.

Thought of Burke brings up the phrase *summa diligentia*, which Moore translated (in the essay "Humility, Concentration, and Gusto") as "with all speed." These words remind the speaker of the schoolboy mistranslation of the Latin as meaning "on top of the diligence," an example of one kind of bad literary criticism. In a tone of reasonableness the poem then comments that "We are not daft about the meaning but that the "familiarity" critics exhibit with "wrong meanings" is puzzling. The next several lines address those who exhibit such familiarity, adjuring them that, for example, the simple candle should not be seen as an electrified mechanism.

The last six lines ostensibly are addressed to a dog yapping to the world at large his daydream that he has caught a badger. He is told that he should remember that, even if he had really accomplished the feat, he would scarcely need to make such a clamor about it. The moral is that the critic should give hints, a few spontaneous reactions, not mystification and not boasts of imagined retrievals. The poet is recommending the process named in her title: the "picking and choosing" that she considered to be primarily a task for the emotions, not for powers of abstraction and analysis. We may note that Moore could be reasonably impersonal in her opinions of critics, for her work had been praised since the 1920s by Yvor Winters, R. P. Blackmur, Kenneth Burke, Eliot, Stevens, and Williams—a range including "new critics," impressionists, and eclectics.

**Source:** Bernard F. Engle, "The Armored Self: Selected Poems," in *Marianne Moore*, rev. ed., Twayne's United States Authors Series, Twayne, 1989.

## Sven Birkerts

*In the following excerpt, Birkerts looks into the craft of Moore's poetry and the differences between her two versions of "Poetry."*

Marianne Moore's decision to cut her well-known anthology piece "Poetry" down to an unremarkable three-liner bearing the same title has baffled readers and critics alike. Such a histrionic, exhibitionistic gesture—like a woman taking scissors and roughly shearing off an admired head of

> "Moore was imprisoned—by disposition, by sensibility—in a condition of ironic self-consciousness."

hair. (No sexism intended here—I'm referring to a celluloid archetype.) Clearly it was an act of some kind of loathing, a deed perpetrated against the self. My guess is that Moore wished to inflict a symbolic injury upon a sensibility that could produce poetry only of a certain kind. Never mind that it was a poetry that had won for her a near-universal adulation. It was as if she knew in her heart wherein lay the real soul of poetry—in the *genuine*—and she knew that her own work could never get there. The disfiguring truncation of one of her best-loved poems was her way of incising the recognition directly into the body of that work.

From the *Selected Poems* of 1935, as preserved in *The Complete Poems of Marianne Moore*, we can cull a rather interesting set of aesthetic statements:

> "Taller by the length of
> a conversation of five hundred years than all
> the others," there was one, whose tales
> of what could never have been actual—
> were better than the haggish, uncompanionable
> drawl
> of certitude; his by-
> play was more terrible in its effectiveness
> than the fiercest frontal attack.
> The staff, the bag, the feigned inconsequence
> of manner, best bespeak that weapon, self-
> protectiveness.
> —from "In This Age of Hard Trying, Nonchalance Is Good and"

> Prince Rupert's drop, paper muslin ghost,
> white torch—"with power to say unkind
> things with kindness, and the most
> irritating things in the midst of love and
> tears," you invite destruction.
> —from "Pedantic Literalist"

> There is a great amount of poetry in unconcious fastidiousness. Certain Ming
> products, imperial floor-coverings of coach wheel yellow, are well enough in their way but I have seen
> something
> that I like better—a
> mere childish attempt to make an imperfectly ballasted animal stand up,
> similar determination to make a pup
> eat his meat from the plate.
> —from "Critics and Connoisseurs"

> complexity is not a crime, but carry
> it to the point of murkiness
> and nothing is plain. Complexity,
> moreover, that has been committed to darkness, instead of
> granting itself to be the pestilence that it is, moves all a-
> bout as if to bewilder us with the dismal fallacy that insistence
> is the measure of achievement and that all
> truth must be dark. Principally throat, sophistication is as it al-
> ways has been—at the antipodes from the
> initial great truths.
> —from "In the Days of Prismatic Color"

> Small dog, going over the lawn nipping the linen and saying
> that you have a badger—remember Xenophon;
> only rudimentary behavior is necessary to put us on the scent.
> "A right good salvo of barks," a few strong wrinkles puckering
> the skin between the ears, is all we ask.
> —from "Picking and Choosing"

> —a collection of little objects—
> sapphires set with emeralds, and pearls with a moonstone,
> made fine
> with enamel in gray, yellow, and dragon-fly blue;
> a lemon, a pear
> and three bunches of grapes tied with silver: your dress a
> magnificent square
> cathedral tower of uniform
> and at the same time diverse appearance—a
> species of vertical vineyard rustling in the storm
> of conventional opinion. Are they weapons or scalpels?
> Whetted to brilliance
> by the hard majesty of that sophistication which is superior to
> opportunity,
> these things are rich instruments with which to experiment.
> But why dissect destiny with instruments
> more highly specialized than components of
> destiny itself?
> —from "Those Various Scalpels"

> Perceiving that in the masked ball
> attitude, there is a hollowness
> that beauty's light momentum can't redeem;
> since disproportionate satisfaction anywhere
> lacks a proportionate air,
> he let us know without offense
> by his hands' denunciatory
> upheaval, that he despised the fashion

of curing us with an ape—making it his care
to smother us with fresh air.
—from "Nothing Will Cure the Sick Lion but to
Eat an Ape"

I could go on citing passages. Indeed, I could argue—some probably have—that the whole of Moore's *oeuvre* is an aesthetics, a careful establishing through example and commentary of both what is seemly for human conduct and what is essential for true artistic expression. It is the latter that interests me here, especially since Moore appears to propose values that are at odds with her own poetic performance.

"Are they weapons or scalpels?" she asks of the hypertrophied refinements of civilization. We may well ask the same about her own lines. The first citation, from "In This Age of Hard Trying, Nonchalance Is Good and," would suggest weapons, but of a defensive, not a first-strike, variety. Moore praises the power of indirection over the "haggish, uncompanionable drawl / of certitude," but then she mitigates that praise somewhat by tracing the origin of that power back to "self-protectiveness" and revealing it, ultimately, as a by-product of vulnerability. But this is nothing more than the age-old view of art as compensation.

Weapons or scalpels? Scalpels they assuredly are not. For the scalpel is an instrument designed to cut through surfaces; its purpose is to get the user *inside*. And Moore's art is anything but interior. She is a taxonomist, a gleaner, a weaver. The most thrilling feature of her poetry is its attentiveness and deliberation—the way she ranges over the intricate surfaces of the material and textual worlds, drawing forth what she needs with an avian fastidiousness. Moore's poems are not written from within; they are appliquéd. She subjects what she has elicited from the near-infinite plenitude of the *out there* to the stringent ordering system of her syntax. She produces her effects through shocks of precision and shocks of juxtaposition. Our diffuse imaging of the world collides with her insistently accurate ordering of things. If she strikes an occasional depth, if she produces what appears to be a penetration, it is not by virtue of any probing action of her own. This comes about, rather, because we, as readers, are forced to make an inference out of certain bits of adjacent information. *We* make the sequences yield sense—*we* do the penetrating.

How odd it is, then, that Moore should on so many occasions adumbrate artistic values that her own craft belies. Reading over these quotations, we can abstract a clear preference for frankness over duplicity, simplicity over ornamentation and needless complexity, directness over sophistication, and "unconscious" naturalness over the straining for effect that is artifice. A preference, in short, for the genuine. But Moore's own poetry is nothing if not ironic and oblique. Her detailings are almost blindingly precise, but their accumulation produces a sly indirection. Moore is ornamental and deliberately disproportionate. When she inspects destiny, she does so with instruments more specialized than destiny itself. She is, herself, "principally throat"—and in this resides her idiosyncratic magic.

The tension between her beliefs—or, to use a Moore word, "preferences"—and her practice is immediately evident in these quoted passages. It manifests itself as a pervasive irony. Listen as she militates against complexity in a series of lines that are themselves semantically, syntactically, and prosodically complex:

Complexity,
moreover, that has been committed to darkness, instead of
granting itself to be the pestilence that it is, moves all
about as if to bewilder us with the dismal
fallacy that insistence
is the measure of all achievement and that all
truth must be dark.

What is this self-reflexive rhetorical stratagem but an effort to distance and disarm a truth that she is compelled to iterate?

There is a second, even more obvious sign of her tension, her peculiar entrapment between preference and practice. Moore relies heavily on displacement. She speaks with a domino held in front of her features. She assigns the burden of speaking the truth to some creature (a cat, for instance, in a poem I did not cite here—"The Monkeys"), or to some incorporated literary source, like Xenophon. When she does use her own voice, as in "Critics and Connoisseurs" or "Those Various Scalpels," the linguistic screen—complexity—is securely in place. For Moore could not turn her recognitions directly upon herself without thereby negating her sensibility and her poetic mode—the work could not survive.

And yet this is precisely what she has done in her one act of self-mutilation. She has pronounced her truth directly, in the first person, and the second version shows us what results when the poet abides by her own strictures. The piece might make more sense if it were called "My Poetry." . . .

If the original version of "Poetry" was the symbolic site of Moore's aesthetic assault upon herself, then we may reasonably regard it as representing the poetic sensibility that a part of her despised.

The poem is, in fact, a kind of anthology of the attributes and techniques that readers have most cherished in Moore—the very ones that made her the revolutionist she was. The original is prosy, prosodically sprawling; it is syntactically complex, to the point of near unintelligibility in places; it shows off Moore's taxonomic fetish, her delight in drawing together creatures from the various phyla of the natural and human worlds ("a tireless wolf … the baseball fan"); it incorporates textual material from other sources (Tolstoy and A. H. Bullen on Yeats)—thereby sabotaging self-containment, and opening the poem out to the continuum of the printed word; it is rhetorically strategic, in the way that so many of her poems are, starting with a straightforward assertion, building and cantilevering sense outward until it almost evaporates (e.g., the sentence that begins, "When they become so derivative …"), then rounding to some clear assertion; it encloses, here more fully than elsewhere, an aesthetic formulation: a justification of what is now fashionably called framing.

The revised "Poetry" has eliminated everything but the prosiness. A short poem that is a shaved-down version of a well-known longer poem is not the same thing as an independent short poem—that should be obvious. Moore's second "Poetry" cannot be read except against the original text. It makes no declaration of independence. Indeed, Moore saw fit to include the first "Poetry" in the notes to her *Complete Poems*. We are asked to read her gesture, to puzzle out her reasons for disapproving of the original.

There are two ways of looking at the matter—unless, of course, we ascribe her move to pure whimsy. If we think of the second version as a rewrite, then the poem has to be seen as a replacement, effectively canceling the first version. But then Moore would not have included it in her *Complete Poems* even as a note. More tellingly, the modifications made are not those of a rewrite, but an edit. She did not alter a single word. The words (most of them) have been struck out; only punctuation and spacing have been altered. We are compelled, therefore, to regard the second "Poetry" as an operation performed upon the first. A cut, an erasure—our choice of words here carries large implications, determines whether we regard her action as one of subliminal violence, or some mere agitated impatience....

If the short poem *is* an edit, then what interpretation can we make? One benign possibility is that Moore recognized, as an editor might, a prolixity; she saw "Poetry" as verbose and she moved to rectify the matter. She made her cuts in a spirit of "Enough said!" But this does not get rid of the larger symbolic statement. For according to that criterion, the bulk of Moore's work is marred by a similar abundance. It is her very method: to harvest and arrange. Trim one detail and you are soon throwing everything out the window.

The other possibility, to which I incline, is that Moore was deliberately repudiating everything that followed the first two sentences. Not just verbal superfluity, but manner and tone as well. The word "genuine" is placed for maximum impact. Moore was henceforth connecting genuineness with simple, direct, unsophisticated utterance. She was establishing it as the primary moving force of all real poetry. So much the worse that she could not attain it in her own work.

At the core of the issue is irony. Moore's poetry—and her "Poetry"—is the apotheosis of ironic discourse. It belongs to "civilization" as opposed to "culture," which means, according to the Spenglerian definition I'm using, that it represents vital forces embalmed, order and intellection set above instinct and energy. All ironic usage implies self-consciousness on the part of the speaker. An ironic statement does not fully coincide with itself—it incorporates a play between what is said and the underlying intention, between utterance and implication, between the content and the means. The etymology of the word gives us, from the Greek, "dissimulation" and "feigning"; an ironist is one who "says less than he thinks or means" (Skeat). Irony is, to put it bluntly, the inverse of the genuine.

We have Moore's statements on the matter. Using the image of the "drop," or concealing cloth, in "Pedantic Literalist," she asserts in no uncertain terms that duplicity—seen here as the gulf between affect and true feeling—is seen as inviting "destruction." In "Nothing Will Cure the Sick Lion," she strikes against the "masked ball attitude." Examples could be multiplied. And while in neither case is she addressing irony *per se*, she might as well be. Irony, like duplicity, depends upon a distance between feeling and expression; the difference between them is merely one of degree.

Irony, then, is the opposite of the "unconscious fastidiousness" that Moore celebrates in the child's attempt to prop the faltering pet (children, of course, are notoriously incapable of dissimulation). It shares nothing in common with the dog's reaction, the "few strong wrinkles puckering the skin between the ears," that she fastens upon in "Picking and Choosing." In poem after poem, as it turns out, she aligns herself with the *naïfs*, simple creatures and beings that coincide with themselves, that bear no taint of self-consciousness.

We can change what we do, but we cannot really change what we are. Moore was imprisoned—by disposition, by sensibility—in a condition of ironic self-consciousness. She could fully comprehend its limitations, but she was powerless to achieve the poetic simplicity and force she admired. Consciousness moves along a unidirectional path—it can strive to evolve, but it cannot undo previous evolutionary attainments. Moore was stuck.

Moore was not, however, a two-face. She did not say one thing while meaning another. No, her distinctive irony was the product of a disjunction between means and ends. Her technique, which we can see as her effort to come to terms with the gap between her belief and her natural endowment, was to render up the mind's motion, its progress toward some realization or certainty—even though, *especially though*, that realization finally argued against the hesitant discursiveness of the process. Moore set out after simplicity along the only route she could take: that of complexity. She stalked unsophisticated truths in a sophisticated manner. She could not help herself. But when her eye beheld what her hand had done, she had to cry out against it. The mere tension between expression and content was not enough. One time, and one time only, she excised as superfluous the manneristic approach to truth and gave just the truth itself. The truth she gave—her recognition of the genuine—reflected directly on her deed. And vice versa: The deed was the warranty for the words.

Considered by itself, without the ghost-text of the original, the short version of "Poetry" is Moore's worst poem. We should be happy that she did not thereafter insist that *Dichtung* and *Wahrheit* are always the same thing. She continued to spin out her delightful and sublimely ironic poems for a good many years. Though she had cut off all of her beautiful hair, it did grow back again.

**Source:** Sven Birkerts, "Marianne Moore's 'Poetry': She Disliked It, She Did," in *The Electric Life*, William Morrow, 1989, pp. 127–37.

## Sources

Birkerts, Sven, "Marianne Moore's 'Poetry': She Disliked It, She Did," in *The Electric Life: Essays on Modern Poetry,* William Morrow and Co., 1989, pp. 127–37.

Costello, Bonnie, *Marianne Moore: Imaginary Possessions*, Harvard University Press, 1981, p. 20.

Dickey, James, "Marianne Moore," in *Babel to Byzantium*, Farrar, Straus & Giroux, 1968, pp. 156–63.

Eliot, T. S., "Introduction," in *Selected Poems by Marianne Moore*, Macmillan Publishing Co., 1935, pp. vii–xiv.

Engel, Bernard F., *Marianne Moore*, Twayne, 1989, p. 160.

Hall, Donald, *Marianne Moore: The Cage and the Animal*, Pegasus, 1970, pp. 40–42.

Honigsblum, Bonnie, "Marianne Moore's Revisions of 'Poetry,'" in *Marianne Moore: Woman and Poet*, edited by Patricia C. Willis, National Poetry Foundation, 1990.

Joyce, Elizabeth W., *Cultural Critique and Abstraction: Marianne Moore and the Avant-Garde*, Bucknell University Press, 1998, pp. 33–37.

Moore, Marianne, *The Complete Poems of Marianne Moore*, Macmillan, 1967, p. 36.

———, "The Genuine in 'Poetry': A Letter from Marianne Moore," in the *Marianne Moore Newsletter*, No. 5, Fall 1981, pp. 14–15.

## Further Reading

Abbott, Craig S., *Marianne Moore: A Descriptive Bibliography*, University of Pittsburgh Press, 1977.

Abbott lists primary and secondary material on Moore. This is an excellent research resource, though it stops at 1975.

Allen, Frederick Lewis, *Only Yesterday: An Informal History of the 1920s*, Harper Perennial Library, 2000.

Originally published in 1931, *Only Yesterday* traces the rise of post–World War I prosperity up to the Wall Street crash of 1929. It is set against the backdrop of flappers, prohibition, and the rise of the women's suffrage movement.

Molesworth, Charles, *Marianne Moore: A Literary Life*, Atheneum, 1990.

Molesworth's biography is the best so far on Moore's life. Using Moore's correspondence and diaries, he deftly makes connections between the poet's work and her life.

Stapleton, Laurence, *Marianne Moore: The Poet's Advance*, Princeton University Press, 1978.

Stapleton's accessible critical study of Moore's poetry contains a good deal of biographical information and makes connections between her work, other poets and poetry.

# The Rhodora

**Ralph Waldo Emerson**

**1847**

"The Rhodora" was published in 1847 in *Poems*, the first of Emerson's two volumes of poetry. In this response to a question, Emerson finds an opportunity to celebrate a flower simply for "being." A deeper look, however, reveals that the poem is in keeping with Emerson's transcendentalist beliefs about the mystical unity of God's love throughout all nature. He comes to an appreciation of the Rhodora, a relatively common New England flowering shrub, by seeing it in its own context—by visiting it at home—and he offers that appreciation as a model for contemplating all of nature.

Readers might compare this to an earlier poem of William Wordsworth's, "I Wandered Lonely as a Cloud," which also concerns the effect of an encounter with flowers in the wild. Wordsworth was a literary idol of Emerson, and his work profoundly influenced Emerson. For a more contemporary yet similar approach, readers might also investigate some of the work of e. e. cummings, whom many considered a modern transcendentalist.

## Author Biography

Emerson was born in Boston in 1803. He was the son of Ruth Haskins Emerson and William Emerson, a Unitarian minister who died when his son was eight. Emerson attended Boston Public Latin School and then enrolled in Harvard College at the age of fourteen. After graduation, he briefly tried teaching

but soon returned to Harvard to attend divinity school. He was ordained a minister in 1829. That same year, he married Ellen Tucker, who died of tuberculosis only a year and a half later. Experiencing doubts about Christianity and the validity of organized religion, Emerson resigned his ministry in 1832. He spent the next several months traveling in Europe. While visiting a Paris botanical exhibition, Emerson had a vision of the intimate connection between humans and nature, and he resolved to be a naturalist. In Great Britain, Emerson met several of his literary idols, including Samuel Taylor Coleridge, William Wordsworth, and Thomas Carlyle, who became a lifelong friend. Upon returning to the United States in 1833, Emerson began a career as a public lecturer, speaking on various topics, including science, biography, literature, and travel. Emerson married Lydia Jackson in 1835 and settled in Concord, Massachusetts, where, except for regular trips in America and abroad, he resided for the rest of his life. In Concord, Emerson became the center of a discussion group called the Transcendentalist Club, which met to discuss religious and philosophical issues. Emerson and the other members of the group developed the theory of transcendentalism, which holds that humanity and nature are in essence the same, are merely different manifestations of the divine spirit. Transcendentalism has been one of the most influential ideas in American literary history. Emerson's first book, *Nature*, an important statement of his transcendentalist views, was published in 1836. The succeeding decade was the most productive period in Emerson's career, in which he continued to deliver lectures while publishing collections of his philosophical essays and poetry, as well as serving as editor of the *Dial*, a publication of the transcendentalist movement. During the 1850s and 1860s, Emerson was an outspoken opponent of slavery and actively campaigned for abolition. By the end of the 1860s, however, his memory began to fail, and he gradually slipped into senility. He died at home in Concord in 1882.

*Ralph Waldo Emerson*

## Poem Text

*On Being Asked, Whence is the Flower?*

In May, when sea-winds pierced our solitudes,
I found the fresh Rhodora in the woods,
Spreading its leafless blooms in a damp nook,
To please the desert and the sluggish brook.
The purple petals fallen in the pool,                    5
Made the black water with their beauty gay;
Here might the red-bird come his plumes to cool,
And court the flower that cheapens his array.
Rhodora! if the sages ask thee why
This charm is wasted on the earth and sky,               10
Tell them, dear, that if eyes were made for seeing,
Then Beauty is its own excuse for being:
Why thou wert there, O rival of the rose!
I never thought to ask, I never knew;
But, in my simple ignorance, suppose                     15
The self-same Power that brought me there brought you.

## Poem Summary

In the heading, "Whence" does not mean when, but from what place, or from what origin or source. Thus, the heading of the poem implies that someone asked the speaker where the flower came from. Which might be another way of asking, what is so special or important about this ordinary flowering shrub?

### Lines 1–4

The speaker begins by noting the season and the general weather. It is May, when flowers are just beginning to bloom; an off-shore breeze has inspired him (and, noting the plural use of "solitudes," possibly a companion) to take a walk. He then describes coming upon the rhodora and its immediate surroundings, which seem to indicate that the plant is alone in an otherwise none too thrilling spot: it is a damp nook or corner; the brook is not babbling happily, but sluggishly. He even uses the word "desert," which seems oddly misplaced for this part of the world, especially given the description of the nook. However, the New England spring comes notoriously late, following several months of very muddy conditions, so perhaps it is the desert of mud—with no other blooms in sight—that Emerson is referring to. As line 3 reveals, the rhodora is a shrub that blooms before its leaves appear, meaning that the petals stand out in stark relief.

### Lines 5–6

With the alliterative "P's" in line 5, Emerson uses the most musical line in the poem to describe the flower itself. Notice, though, that the petals have fallen into a pool of black water, which might mean that it is really more of a stagnant puddle, an image that is consistent with the sluggish brook of line 4. Perhaps the speaker was particularly struck by the purple blooms because they were in such an otherwise unattractive water, just as the water brought a special beauty to the otherwise simple petals.

### Lines 7–8

Emerson continues to add colors, as "red-bird" joins the purple petals and black water. The bird's plumes will be outdone, says the speaker, by the flower's color. He also uses the word "court," which hints at the fertility of spring.

### Lines 9–10

As the second half of the poem starts, the speaker shifts and addresses the flower, rather than the companion whose question inspired the poem. He even uses an exclamation point to add a celebratory verve to the line. The rest of this couplet, and the two lines that follow, have an implication of Emerson's impatience with those who would elevate Man above Nature. Readers might even hear a certain sarcasm for the so-called sages who fail to appreciate the flower's charm or beauty, as well as the majesty of the earth and sky.

### Lines 11–12

The use of the affectionate term "dear" personalizes the flower even more. The speaker also cleverly plays off those who would ask, and have asked, "what's the purpose of this flower?" by pointedly remarking that the purpose of one's eyes is to appreciate beauty for its own sake, without asking the flower to justify its existence.

### Lines 13–14

Continuing the thought of the previous lines, the speaker declares that it never even occurred to him to ask the simple rhodora what purpose it served. Furthermore, he considers it the rival of the rose, the most poetically celebrated flower of all.

### Lines 15–16

The "simple ignorance" is probably written with a dash of irony since the rest of the poem seems to argue that the speaker's view is more knowledgeable, or at least more encompassing and tolerant, than that of those who question the flower's purpose. The last line openly suggests that since the rhodora was made by God as surely and as expertly as He made Man, the flower—and by extension all living things—should be granted a deserved respect and honor. The flower might just as easily have asked, and have a God-given right to ask, whence is this man? For Emerson, the answer to both questions might be that man and flower both came from the self-same Power—the Creator—and that power brought each of them to this meeting as equals.

To better understand this final point, it is helpful to consider what Emerson said of himself as a poet, in an 1862 entry in his journal: "I am a bard because I stand near them [flowers, rocks, trees, etc.], and apprehend all they utter, and with pure joy hear that which I also would say." In other words, Emerson and nature not only speak the same language, but they speak for each other.

## Themes

### Divinity

The speaker's belief in a divine power that guides the events of the world is evident in the final two lines: "But, in my simple ignorance, suppose / The self-same Power that brought me there brought you." The speaker is responding to the question of why the rhodora is in such a secluded place. He is satisfied with the answer that God guides the flower's place in the world, just as He guides the speaker's. This conclusion reveals a belief that the world is ordered according to a divine plan, and the speaker's role is merely to accept his place in that plan. He is appreciative of the lessons he learns from nature; presumably, he seeks the wisdom of nature because of his belief that it is ordered by God.

The speaker is subtle in his spiritual assertions; the poet does not use the word "God." Instead, he capitalizes "Power" to let the reader know that he means a divine power. The speaker also capitalizes "Beauty," indicating that the beauty is of divine origin. When the speaker says "Beauty is its own excuse for being," he makes the claim that the beauty to which he refers requires no justification nor does it need a forum in which to be appreciated. That it is divine makes it inherently significant, even unseen in the middle of the woods. By extension, the speaker has the same significance, because he, too, is divinely directed.

### Beauty

The speaker happens upon a "fresh" rhodora as he walks through the woods. He is immediately moved to describe it in the context of its bland surroundings. The rhodora seems to bring vibrancy and beauty to an otherwise dull landscape. The speaker describes the setting as a "damp nook" near a "sluggish brook" of "black water." There are no birds; the speaker only imagines that a bird might be drawn to the area because of the rhodora. He writes, "Here might the red-bird come his plumes to cool, / And court the flower that cheapens his array." To the speaker, an image as beautiful and lively as a redbird is no match for the beauty of the rhodora, and even the bird knows it.

The speaker is so moved by the rhodora's beauty that he anticipates wise people ("sages") wondering why such a flower is growing in a desolate area where it might never be seen. The response is that beauty is worthwhile in its very existence, not just in being admired. Given that the speaker capitalizes the word "Beauty," the reader can expand the idea to include anything that is fundamentally good or divine. The reader can assume, therefore, that virtues (such as honesty, loyalty, and compassion), acts of kindness, prayers, and any other examples of fundamental goodness are worthwhile whether anyone notices or admires them.

### Surprise Inspiration

The poet is surprised to be so inspired by the rhodora. He does not expect to be struck with a profound insight as he casually walks through the woods, yet he is. His description of the rhodora's surroundings indicates that the rhodora seems out of place, so the speaker is surprised to find it there. In line nine, the speaker has a surprising revelation when he exclaims, "Rhodora!" At this point, he comments that the sages would not understand what he is realizing at that very moment—that the beauty of the rhodora has inherent value apart from being admired by human eyes. In line thirteen, the speaker

## Topics for Further Study

- Many scholars consider the poet e. e. cummings a transcendentalist, even though he is a more modern poet than Emerson and his contemporaries. Review cummings's work, along with his background, his views on poetry, and criticism of his work. Stage a debate with a classmate in which one of you claims that cummings is a transcendentalist and the other claims that he is not.

- The English poet Matthew Arnold accused Emerson of being overly vague in his poetry. He claimed that Emerson left too much to the reader, forcing him or her to guess at the meanings of symbols and allusions. Write a position paper in which you use "The Rhodora" either to support or to counter Arnold's criticism.

- The rhodora is a native shrub in New England. Choose a plant or flower native to your part of the country and compose a poem about it. You may adopt the transcendentalist point of view or you may choose another way of interpreting the plant's significance.

- Examine Emerson's use of color in the poem. Find a work of art that you would use in a textbook to illustrate the poem. Create a one-page layout, including the poem and its title, the illustration, and a caption.

addresses the rhodora as the "rival of the rose." Perhaps no other flower has been the subject of as much poetry as the rose, yet here the speaker claims that the rhodora is its rival. The rhodora is a native flowering shrub in New England. It is not rare or unexpected, so it is somewhat surprising that it should be the inspiration of a poem.

## Style

In "The Rhodora," Emerson uses a familiar rhyme scheme of two paired couplets, followed by four lines of alternating rhymes. For instance, lines 9–16 end with the following sounds:

why—sky / seeing—being / rose—knew suppose—you.

Each eight-line section constitutes one half of the sixteen-line poem, resulting in a unified and balanced feel to the piece. The rhyme scheme provides an additional surrounding structure to the iambic pentameter Emerson uses for this poem. "Iambic" refers to a segment of two syllables where the emphasis, or stress, falls on the second syllable. It is "pentameter" (*penta* meaning *five*) because each line has five two-syllable pairs. An example of this is in line 5:

The pur / ple pet / als fal / len in / the pool.

The stresses on the second syllables emphasize the alliteration of purple, petals, and pool by falling on the "P's."

The observant reader might note that the final line of the poem, line 16, has eleven syllables, not ten. Whenever an iambic line has an extra unstressed syllable, it is said to have a "female ending," because it ends softly. Emerson's use of this device only at the end of the poem is similar to a soft final chord in a song, as opposed to a heavy or abrupt one, that gently fades away. In addition, because the last unstressed syllable is the word "you," meaning the rhodora, it creates an open and lingering sound that both literally echoes and also thematically echoes Emerson's celebration of the flower itself.

## Historical Context

### Transcendentalism

Transcendentalism was a philosophical movement in Europe, based heavily on the writings of Immanuel Kant. When it reached the United States, however, the movement grew to encompass literature. Most scholars acknowledge Emerson as the writer who had the strongest influence on the movement's development in New England. Its early formation came from meetings of a small group of people interested in discussing new philosophies. Central to their discussions was the idea that there was a personal and intuitive force that transcended the material world. This force revealed itself to people under certain circumstances, making it possible to learn from nature and to acquire wisdom.

Transcendentalism claims that nature has a wealth of knowledge and wisdom available to those committed to learning from it. Henry David Thoreau took this belief very seriously, and his *Walden* is the result of his commitment to live alone in nature to learn what it had to teach him. Transcendentalists also praised manual labor and intellectual fellowship. They strove to support one another's spiritual lives, which focused on personal growth through individual relationships with God rather than membership in an organized church. Their adherence to the values of democracy, individualism, and self-reliance explains why so many transcendentalists were involved in social reform. They were especially interested in abolishing slavery and gaining equality for women.

Two events were important to the rise of transcendentalism in New England. First was the launch, in 1840, of the *Dial*, a magazine dedicated to transcendentalist thought. Among its contributors were Emerson, Thoreau, and Margaret Fuller. The magazine was published until 1844. The second event was the founding of Brook Farm, a utopian community sponsored by the Transcendentalist Club of Boston. Its objective was to provide for everyone's basic needs so that they would have the opportunity to develop themselves intellectually and spiritually. Brook Farm was planned as a self-sustaining farm where members would rotate duties. Started in 1841, Brook Farm only lasted until 1846, when various factors, including dissension and poor soil, brought about its closing.

### Women's Rights

During the first half of the nineteenth century, social changes were slowly improving conditions for women. In 1821, Emma Willard established America's first school for girls, Troy Female Seminary. In 1824, the first public school for girls opened in Worcester, Massachusetts. Oberlin College awarded the first college degree to a woman in 1841. These milestones were important because educated girls expected to be full participants in society and to have opportunities to use their educations. Finding few such opportunities, they began to organize to seek social reform. Many girls, such as Margaret Fuller, received their early education at home before attending educational institutions. Fuller went on to be an outspoken women's rights advocate and the first editor of the transcendentalist magazine the *Dial*, established in 1840.

Sarah Grimke and her sister, Angelina, wrote persuasive pamphlets in the mid-1830s denouncing the oppression of blacks and women. These pamphlets include *An Appeal to the Christian Women of the South*, *Address to Free Colored Americans*, and *Appeal to the Women of the Nominally Free States*. Sarah also wrote a longer work entitled *Letters on the Equality of the Sexes and the Condition*

# Compare & Contrast

- **1800s:** A growing women's movement is working for equal rights, including the right to vote. Activist and social reformer Sarah Grimke publishes her *Letters on the Equality of the Sexes and the Conditions of Woman*. Margaret Fuller establishes discussion groups for women in Boston. Activists such as Elizabeth Cady Stanton praise Fuller for supporting women's right to full participation in society.

  **Today:** As a result of the tireless efforts of early advocates for women's rights, women today have the right to vote, own property independently, own and operate businesses, hold public office, and advance in the work place. While there are still areas of disparity (such as national pay averages), women have strong legal foundations for asserting their rights.

- **1800s:** Transcendentalism, which borrows some elements of Eastern philosophies and religions, takes hold in Massachusetts and influences many American intellectuals and writers.

  **Today:** Yoga is increasingly popular throughout the United States. Yoga, the Sanskrit word for "union," is a philosophy that was first systematized by the Indian sage Patanjali. The various schools of yoga taught today have some commonalities with transcendentalism, such as the beliefs that each individual soul is directly linked to God and that truth is everywhere present in creation and that truth can be experienced intuitively, rather than rationally. While millions of Americans practice only one element of yoga—its regimen of physical postures and exercises—a growing number are adopting the broader philosophy and its more mystical practices, such as meditation.

- **1800s:** Transcendentalist poetry presents challenging new ideas but adheres to certain traditions of form and content. Emerson, for example, writes with a rhyme scheme and often draws on nature for inspiration and themes.

  **Today:** Stephen Dunn wins the 2001 Pulitzer Prize for poetry for his collection entitled *Different Hours*. Dunn writes in free verse, using familiar imagery from everyday life. Still, his poetry can be difficult to interpret because the themes are very subtle.

---

*of Woman* in 1838. The Grimke sisters were outraged by the legislated powerlessness of women. They believed that women should be given the same rights and opportunities as men, including the right to vote and own land. Through their actions, they challenged social assumptions about the appropriate position of women in society. Although they encouraged women to excel at their domestic duties, they also expected women to be taken seriously in the public domain as writers and speakers.

## Critical Overview

John Jay Chapman, whose admiration of Emerson did not prevent him from offering unflattering criticism of his poetry, nonetheless considered "The Rhodora" to be among "that class of poetry which . . . is poetry because it is the perfection of statement." Whether or not one agrees with the poet's sentiment is irrelevant, Chapman appears to say; the piece itself is so finely composed and its argument so convincingly made, that it must be admired. This poem is also a fine example of what Chapman was referring to when he said,

> [Emerson's] worship of the New England landscape amounts to a religion. His poems do that most wonderful thing, make us feel that we are alone in the fields and with the trees,—not English fields nor French lanes, but New England meadows and uplands.

Bliss Perry, in his 1931 essay titled "The Mystic and the Poet," notes that "The Rhodora" is one of a number of Emerson's works that deals with a chance encounter in nature. "In such poems," he writes "there is little attempt to generalize or to enforce any doctrine." Perry notes that Matthew Arnold failed to understand a similar poem of Emerson's ("The Titmouse") simply because Arnold had never seen such an animal himself, and a similar response could be made to those who do not appreciate Emerson's celebration of a common New England shrub in this poem.

Arnold, an Englishman, while a great admirer of Emerson's overall contribution to American letters, was a harsh critic of his poetry, especially his Nature poems. In his essay in *Macmillan's Magazine* of May 1884, Arnold explained that he considered Emerson a failure as a poet because his meaning was often unclear, leaving the reader to guess at it. According to Arnold, "a failure of this kind goes through almost all [Emerson's] verse, keeps him amid symbolism and allusion and the fringes of things, and, in spite of his spiritual power, deeply impairs his poetic value."

Char Mollison and Charles C. Walcutt, on the other hand, note in a 1981 essay in *Arizona Quarterly* that before one criticizes Emerson's ability as a poet, one must make certain assumptions about his use of language: "(1) Words are signs of natural facts; (2) Particular natural facts are symbols of particular spiritual facts; (3) Nature is the symbol of spirit." They argue that, for Emerson, man's perceptions are forever linked to natural reality "because nature's laws and the laws of human perception are identical." Keep this thought especially in mind while reading the last six lines of this poem.

Mollison and Walcutt also refer to Emerson's description, in his famous essay "Nature," of the optimum condition for poetry: "Man in nature, alone in the woods." Elsewhere in "Nature," Emerson writes that "the beauty of Nature reforms itself in the mind, and not for barren contemplation, but for new creation." It is easy to see how this would apply to "The Rhodora." That single, simple plant that Emerson viewed one day lives on in his poem and is recreated in the minds of those who read it.

## Criticism

### Jennifer Bussey

*Bussey holds a master's degree in interdisciplinary studies and a bachelor's degree in English literature. She is an independent writer specializing in literature. In the following essay, Bussey uses Ralph Waldo Emerson's poem and William Wordsworth's "I Wandered Lonely as a Cloud" to contrast transcendentalism with romanticism.*

Emerson is as strongly associated with transcendentalism as the English poet William Wordsworth is associated with romanticism. Romanticism in England began in 1798, and the style did not dominate American literature until 1830. Transcendentalism began as a philosophical movement in Europe but blossomed into a literary movement in the United States. These two movements share a few basic ideas and beliefs, but they diverge in important areas. Comparing Emerson's "The Rhodora" and Wordsworth's "I Wandered Lonely as a Cloud" affords the opportunity to examine the differences because the poems are similar in their occasions and subjects. In both cases, the speaker is wandering alone, enjoying nature, when he happens upon a flower that inspires a poetic impulse. From these very similar experiences and impulses, the two poets diverge in a way that illustrates the differences between the movements to which they belong.

In both poems, the speaker is moved by something he sees in nature. He is open to what nature has to teach and, as a result, he gains something from the experience. The theme of nature as a teacher is a traditional one in poetry, so it is not surprising that two accomplished poets such as Emerson and Wordsworth would find inspiration in nature and in the tradition of nature in poetry. Similarly, it is not surprising that both poems occur in the spring, which is another hallmark of nature poetry. But, beyond these few basic similarities, the poems are quite different from each other. Contrasting the two reveals the fundamental differences between the literary movements with which they are associated.

First, the specific subjects of the poems—the flowers—are different. Emerson writes about the rhodora, a flowering shrub native to New England. It produces multiple blooms, which appear before the shrub's leaves do. The daffodil grows from a bulb and is native to northern Europe. It produces a single flower, whose bud emerges with the leaves. Despite the fact that the daffodil only produces a single bloom, Wordsworth expands its presence by describing a "host" of them. While Emerson focuses on a single shrub, Wordsworth focuses on a field of daffodils that blanket areas beside the lake, under the trees, and beyond. Each flower is native to the poet's country.

Second, the ways in which the poets portray the flowers are altogether different, and their portrayals reveal how the poets see themselves in relation to the flowers. Emerson observes the rhodora in its natural state. He sees it in a realistic context, appreciating the beauty of its contrast to the dark, muddy surroundings. He imagines a bird coming and challenging the rhodora for outshining its red plumage. In the end, he addresses the rhodora, telling it how to answer the sages that question its hidden location. The way Emerson perceives the rhodora is consistent with the transcendentalist perspective because he seeks wisdom in nature and relies on his intuition to bring him closer to God.

In contrast, Wordsworth employs a great deal of personification in describing the daffodils. It is not a realistic depiction of the flowers as they truly are but a portrait of them as they exist in the poet's mind. They are a "crowd" and a "host" (like angels), "tossing their heads in sprightly dance." Wordsworth assigns emotion to them, describing their glee. The speaker becomes engaged with the daffodils through sharing their perceived delight. Wordsworth writes, "A poet could not but be gay, / In such a jocund company." At the end, he writes that when he is alone, he often sees the daffodils in his mind's eye, which again brings him pleasure. The speaker has joined the daffodils and, together, they enjoy nature. Wordsworth's poem reveals the romantic imagination and reliance on emotion. He allows himself to be carried away by the moment, and he is drawn by the wildness of the daffodils rather than by the serenity that attracts Emerson to the rhodora.

Third, Emerson's experience is anchored in the past, but Wordsworth's experience encompasses the past, present, and future. For Emerson, the revelation he had through the rhodora was an intense moment that engaged his intellect. He describes what happened as he walked through the woods that day, and it is evident that he recalls the moment in the past but preserves the lesson in the present. This reflects the transcendentalist emphasis on building a deep relationship with God on a personal level. Wordsworth, however, not only recalls the experience in the past but also preserves the actual experience of joining the daffodils in the present. Further, the last stanza suggests that he plans to continue to do so in the future. After all, he will again be on his couch in a pensive mood. When he recalls the effect the daffodils had on him, his language is vibrant, bringing the reader into the experience. The speaker tells that when he is alone on his couch (in other words, indoors and far re-

> "'I Wandered Lonely as a Cloud' represents the romantic ideal of experiencing with the heart, or emotions, while 'The Rhodora' represents the transcendentalist ideal of experiencing with the mind in order to feed the spirit."

moved from the daffodils' landscape), he revisits his experience with his "inward eye" and again "dances with the daffodils." For Wordsworth, it is the feeling, not the lesson, that is most important. This emphasis is consistent with the romantic notion of immersing oneself in life and freeing the imagination and emotions. "I Wandered Lonely as a Cloud" represents the romantic ideal of experiencing with the heart, or emotions, while "The Rhodora" represents the transcendentalist ideal of experiencing with the mind in order to feed the spirit.

The conclusions of the two poems emphasize what their respective literary movements value most. "The Rhodora" concludes with a spiritual insight that is both humble and pious. Emerson attributes the occasion of the poem, and his reaction to the flower, to God. He sees himself as being guided by a divine force, just as the rhodora grows in that particular spot because of God's will. It is a contemplative conclusion, and it is one that presumably brings the speaker to a deeper understanding of the divine realm and his role in it. On the other hand, Wordsworth concludes with a comment about himself among the flowers. While Emerson claims that it is by God's design that he has seen the rhodora, Wordsworth claims that he goes to the daffodils of his own will by using his imagination. The emotional focus of the romantics is evident in Wordsworth's claim that his "heart with pleasure fills, / And dances with daffodils." It is his heart that directs his experience, not his spirit. And, despite the similar occasions of the two poems and the similarities of their subjects, in the end the two poems diverge sharply. Emerson comes to a contemplative,

## What Do I Read Next?

- Emerson's "Self-Reliance" in his *Essays* (1841) is considered one of the most important works to come out of the transcendentalist movement. In this essay, Emerson extols the virtues of solitude and independent thinking.

- Richard Geldard's *God in Concord: Ralph Waldo Emerson's Awakening to the Infinite* (1998) presents Emerson's spiritual journals to demonstrate how his understanding of God and spirituality changed as he matured. Geldard sets out to show how Emerson came to be regarded as a spiritual leader.

- Edited by Joel Myerson, *Transcendentalism: A Reader* (2000), is an anthology of key transcendentalist writings reflecting the ideology of the movement and its presence in New England society. Readers will find essays, poems, correspondence, and book excerpts by well-known and lesser-known writers.

- Henry David Thoreau's *Walden* (1854) is a classic transcendentalist work. This book records the author's time at Walden Pond, where he went to be alone and to live simply and deliberately. The book includes both philosophical writing and minute details about Thoreau's daily life.

---

intuitive conclusion, and Wordsworth comes to an imaginative, emotional one. Wordsworth's experience enables him to return to feelings of glee, delight, and carefree abandon. In fact, the daffodils seem to save him from just the sort of thought process that Emerson values. Wordsworth writes that when he is "in vacant or in pensive mood," the daffodils return to carry his heart away. As a transcendentalist, Emerson draws from his encounter affirmation that God is ordering the world, from a common shrub to a man seeking wisdom in nature. As a romantic, Wordsworth draws from his encounter a memory to which he can escape into pure feeling.

**Source:** Jennifer Bussey, Critical Essay on "The Rhodora," in *Poetry for Students*, The Gale Group, 2003.

### Michelle Prebilic

*Prebilic is an independent author who writes and analyzes children's literature. She holds degrees in psychology and business. In this essay, Prebilic discusses how Emerson's poem embodies his spiritual fundamentals of awakening, transformation, and introspection.*

Ralph Waldo Emerson published "The Rhodora" in *Poems*, the first of two volumes of poetry, in 1847. Well known for his ideas about nature's beauty, influence, and power, Emerson invokes, awakens, and transforms readers to a richer perspective. In fact, this theme of nature as a transforming agent is among the most fundamental concepts of Emerson's works. As Robert Richardson, Jr. explains in *Dictionary of Literary Biography*, Emerson believed that "the aim and effort of literature . . . give[s] voice to the whole of spiritual nature . . . to record in words the whole life of the world."

The foundation for "The Rhodora" lies in Emerson's belief that nature is a transforming agent. He crafts this meditative poem with precision and purpose. To fully appreciate its depth, readers can gain insight into the poem's essence by understanding Emerson.

Emerson emerged in the nineteenth century as one of the most prolific and chief influential writers and intellectuals of the era. He zealously affirmed that humans must see the beauty in nature and respect its inherent power. According to Donald Avery in the *Dictionary of Literary Biography*, Emerson believed that "everything in nature corresponds to some state of mind." Emerson believed that nature connected the person to the all–knowing source. During a tumultuous time when states declared independence, women sought more rights, new inventions increased farm productivity, Indians lost their land, and the anti-slavery movement thrived, perhaps Emerson sought to broaden America's consciousness through a connection with nature. Whatever his motivations, Emerson cultivated these concepts not only as a lecturer and civic philosopher, but also as editor and publisher of the *Dial*, a transcendentalist journal. Emerson crafted innumerable essays, poems, and articles based on his beliefs, including "The Rhodora."

Many critics and supporters alike believe that Emerson's first work, *Nature*, formed the basis for most of his later works, including his poems. Some people dismissed *Nature*, hastily believing that it represented a doctrine identifying the divine being with the universe. However, countless others believed that his work ushered in a new era of American literature, particularly transcendentalism, a philosophical and religious movement. Some believed that "The Rhodora" gives a beautiful example of the romanticism of transcendental poetry: a poetry style that suggests an intuitive source of knowledge independent of experience. Whether one agrees with Emerson, the work itself is so beautifully written and its line of reasoning so believable, that readers cannot help but admire it.

Emerson declared in *Nature* that "Words are signs of natural facts. Particular natural facts are symbols of particular spiritual facts. Nature is the symbol of spirit." "The Rhodora," Emerson's sixteen-line poem, flows down the page employing natural facts: the description of this flower, its place in the woods, and its relationship to its surroundings. He wants readers to get its deeper meaning: the spiritual fundamentals of awareness, transformation, and reflection. He argues that this beauty is the art of a life-force common to both humans and nature, reaffirming that "nature is the symbol of spirit."

The poem's essence lies behind the 136 words, starting with Emerson's subtitle: "On Being Asked, Whence is the Flower?" This question convinces readers that its answer will not be simple. As he explains in *Nature*, "we have no questions ... which are unanswerable. We must trust the perfection of the creation ... as to believe that whatever curiosity the order of things has awakened in our minds, the order of things can satisfy." Like the curiosity that the flower awakens in one's mind, readers must trust that the order of things can satisfy.

The poem's introduction reflects on the origin of the flower. "Whence," an introspective word inquiring about origin, prompts a meditative journey. The use of whence has evoked conflict for centuries, although Emerson may not have known the full extent of its debate in his day. Since the fourteenth century, reputable writers used "from whence," especially in biblical writing. In the eighteenth century, intellectuals criticized "from whence" as redundant. By the nineteenth century, perhaps Emerson employed whence to create redundancy. This repetition, something critics have noted in Emerson's writing, may have pierced his ideas into readers' attentiveness.

Emerson opens "The Rhodora" by describing an awakening to the beauty of nature: "In May, when sea-winds pierced our solitudes, / I found the fresh Rhodora in the woods, / Spreading its leafless blooms in a damp nook, / To please the desert and the sluggish brook." In Emerson's New England home, this deciduous shrub grows about three feet tall and produces delicate rose–purple, two–lipped flowers that bloom in the spring before or with its leaves. A natural, unplanned wind penetrates the symbolic solitude of winter. It announces the eruption of spring. As Emerson describes in *Nature*, "to go into solitude, a man needs to retire as much from his chamber as from society." As the poet lets the sea-winds pierce the consciousness and its chamber, spring jolts the poet into a new awareness. The poet sees the fresh flowers in the woods. The attentiveness rouses the soul.

> "Whether one agrees with Emerson, the work itself is so beautifully written and its line of reasoning so believable, that readers cannot help but admire it."

As the poet examines the shrub, the awakening intensifies. The leafless blooms spread in a damp nook; Emerson alludes to the idea that this location pleases both the desert and the brook. It symbolizes a fitting in, a desire to belong, much like the way new people gently settle into an established neighborhood. The people, like the flowers, seek the basic elements to live comfortably and yearn for a place to grow. They nudge at the existing hierarchy to establish their roots and hope to make new friends. This awakening to the new place represents the first of Emerson's spiritual fundamentals.

Emerson could best illustrate transformation, his second spiritual fundamental, if he allowed himself to experience it. Emerson's surroundings gave him the courage to transform. As Richardson notes, Emerson "was at the center of much that was new, exciting, and vital in American cultural life" in the 1830s, 1840s, and 1850s. Richardson also observes that "in religion, in philosophy, and in literature, the group around Emerson was liberal, learned, forward-looking and reform-minded." Surrounded by an encouraging community and devoted family,

Emerson allowed new ideas to enter his mind and he created the words to express them. As a result, he impacted the world with his ideals and left a living legacy. This foundation gave him the fundamentals that he needed to welcome and seek transformation. Once he could transform himself, he could share his experience with others in his writing.

The next verse develops this concept of transformation: "The purple petals fallen in the pool, / Made the black water with their beauty gay; / Here might the red-bird come his plumes to cool, / And court the flower that cheapens his array." Awakened to nature's beauty, the poet notices things previously unseen. The beautiful petals transform the appearance of the small body of still water, the pool. This deep or still place in the stream serves as the background for the purple petals, creating an unexpectedly brilliant and colorful scene. The male red-bird, with its bright red body, black wings and tail, usually draws the attention of the observer. Yet, its spectacular array fades next to the purple flowers. The red-bird at the pool no longer contains the same influence that it did before. The natural facts have led to a spiritual fact; these new events have changed the observer's perception.

To Emerson, beauty exists for pleasure. Emerson believed, as he expresses in "Nature," "a nobler want of man is served by nature, namely, the love of beauty." He saw beauty as the "constitution of all things ... the primary forms, as the sky, the mountain, the tree, the animal, give us a delight in and for themselves; a pleasure arising from outline, color, motion, and grouping." Emerson draws on this core belief in the next verse: "Rhodora! if the sages ask thee why / This charm is wasted on the earth and sky, / Tell them, dear, that if eyes were made for seeing, / Then Beauty is its own excuse for being."

When sages, people respected for experience, judgment, and wisdom, ask the rhodora why beautiful flowers squander their delightfulness only to be seen by earth and sky, Emerson answers. He asserts that just as human beings use eyes to see, beauty is there to be seen. The harmony of form or color, truthfulness, and originality serve as the excuse. Emerson holds the beauty of nature so reverently, that he applies the term dear when conversing with the rhodora. Dear identifies the flower as highly valued, something he is fond of, like a sweetheart.

The culmination of the poem shows the natural introspection that follows a transformation: "Why thou wert there, O rival of the rose! / I never thought to ask, I never knew; / But, in my simple ignorance, suppose / The self-same Power that brought me there brought you." For the first time, the poet wonders why the rhodora appeared in that place and at that time. With reflection and with the want of knowledge, the poet assumes that precisely the same strength or force that brought the rhodora brought the poet. Many critics assume that this last verse references a deity. Perhaps. Yet, as Robert Richardson Jr. describes in *Dictionary of Literary Biography*, Emerson, a deeply religious man, believed that one should "not turn to God, not to the state, not to society or to history ... but to nature" for an understanding of spirit. Emerson alludes that because the poet knows no newer knowledge and that the self-same power brought both to be there. Whether the identical power comes from a religious affiliation or a doctrine that a deity does not exist, Emerson believes that nature is the symbol of spirit. Through introspection, the third of Emerson's spiritual fundamentals, the question gets answered for each individual.

In this simple poem, Emerson gave readers a multifaceted illustration of his three spiritual principles: awareness, transformation, and introspection. Yet, he could only do that if he achieved these principles in his life. Much like the elements of nature, the soil, water, sun, and shade that nurtured the rhodora to blossom, Emerson created his own foundation. As Wilfred McClay observes in *First Things: A Monthly Journal of Religion and Public Life*, "no man is an island.... Emerson's brand of heroic individualism silently ... took utterly for granted ... a wide range of social, institutional, cultural, and moral supports provided by the family and community life" in which he lived. The social resources that Emerson relied upon allowed him not only to become the man people study today, but also the quiet soul that transformed his language into magnificent poetry, a legacy of which "The Rhodora" takes part.

**Source:** Michelle Prebilic, Critical Essay on "The Rhodora," in *Poetry for Students*, The Gale Group, 2003.

### R. A. Yoder

*In the following excerpt, Yoder divulges Emerson's poetic influences and discusses themes within "The Rhodora" that are echoed in his essays.*

An exhaustive study would show how Emerson moved from an undergraduate's imitation of Augustan couplets to a variety of less polished and less constraining verse forms—ballads, epigrammatic quatrains, Wordsworthian blank verse in 1827, and the extraordinary if ungainly "Gnothi Seauton" of 1831, lines that are as unorthodox in form as they are in doctrine, and that prefigure Emerson's settled practices of a decade later. Emerson was not, however, consciously preparing himself for a poetic career. The role of his journal poetry is unquestionably self-expression, dialogue with oneself—moving away from the style of performance toward a means of formulating one's private convictions, or, as Leslie Fiedler has suggested, toward "the speech of a man urging himself on, rather than appealing to a crowd." To summarize these early experiments we may say that Emerson sought a mode of expression appropriate to the essentially meditative aim of this writing. Not surprisingly, he turned finally to Wordsworth, whose star was just rising on this side of the Atlantic in the late 1820's, and to the Metaphysical tradition of meditative verse, especially to the poetry of George Herbert.

"The River," dated June 1827 in the Centenary Edition, and the following lines from Emerson's journal are unmistakably Wordsworthian in setting and cadence:

> He is a man who tho' he told it not
> Mourned in the hour of manhood, while he saw
> The rich imagination that had tinged
> Each earthly thing with hues from paradise
> /Abandoning/ /Forsake/ forever his instructed eye.
> ...
> But he was poor & proud & solitary
> He would walk forth at moonlight, for the moon
> And quick eyed stars do sympathize with all
> Who suffer ...
> When thy soul
> Is filled with a just image fear not thou
> Lest halting rhymes or unharmonious verse
> Cripple the fair Conception. Leave the heart
> Alone to find its language. In all tongues
> It hath a sovereign instinct that doth teach
> An eloquence which rules can never give.

Associated with Wordsworth's rural solitary is a language sincere and unpretentious, that comes spontaneously from the heart. Emerson's admiration for Herbert over a period of at least seven years culminates in the 1835 lectures, where Herbert is placed foremost among English poets: "I should cite Herbert as a striking example of the power of exalted thought to melt and bend language to its fit expression." Undoubtedly in Herbert—in the "Jordan" poems, for example— Emerson also found an ideal of simple, heartfelt poetry. Herbert's contribution is larger, however, for Herbert provided a model, not merely for simplicity of speech and imagery, but for combining

> "*The rhodora needs no reasoned argument, no 'excuse' for its existence.*"

that simplicity with architectonic skill, with the concentrated and integrated organization that distinguishes the seventeenth-century meditative style, just as it distinguishes Emerson's poetry of 1834 from the prosaic, discursive blank verse and free verse that dots his journals between 1827 and 1832. "Each and All," "The Rhodora," and "The Snow-Storm" are among the most admired of Emerson's poems. What they owe to Herbert is not explicit, but the debt is clear enough in another poem probably written about this time and later taken for Herbert's own work.

> "Grace"
> How much, preventing God, how much I owe
> To the defences thou hast round me set;
> Example, custom, fear, occasion slow,—
> These scorned bondmen were my parapet.
> I dare not peep over this parapet
> To gauge with glance the roaring gulf below,
> The depths of sin to which I had descended,
> Had not these me against myself defended.

Here, as John Broderick has shown, is a direct parallel with the first line of Herbert's "Sinne," "Lord! with what care hast thou begirt us round," Moreover, the retard effected by the naming or cataloging device in the third line is characteristic of Herbert and may also have been taken over from the catalog somewhat more extended in "Sinne" (though cataloging is a common enough technique among seventeenth-century poets, and Emerson may have found precedents in Milton, Herrick, or even the American William Bradford). Personification of the defenses as "scorned bondmen" calls to mind Herbert's specific recommendation that "things of ordinary use" ought to illustrate "Heavenly Truths." This advice Emerson never forgot; the bondmen of "Grace" reappear constantly in his poetry, importing truths well above their station. The "drudge in dusty frock" who appears in "Art" has been compared to Herbert's servant in "The Elixir," a poem that Emerson especially admired, and the stooped crones who sweep and scour the poet's cottage in "Saadi" are suddenly transformed into gods. Thus there is no doubt about Herbert's influence. More generally—and here I think we can include the poems of 1834 as having the same qualities—Emerson learned from Herbert, and perhaps from some of his contemporaries, the art of "neatness": the way to structure a poem on a single metaphor or situation, the way "Grace" is based on the figure of a fortress; the smoothness of tone and rhythm, conversational but always melodic, never jagged but sufficiently pointed and varied to gain the quality of speech, as in the catalog or in the stressed pronouns ("these me") which give the last line of "Grace" a peak before it falls off to the diminished feminine ending.

"The Rhodora", one of the 1834 poems, displays the same neat structure and rhythm as "Grace," again modulated by a feminine rhyme that sets off the gnomic couplet, and by the deliberateness of the last line with its hyphenated adjective, monosyllabic parallelism, and pointed pronouns. "The Rhodora" conveys, too, the humility and intense dedication that Emerson and Herbert shared. One might go further to argue that Emerson's poem deploys the formal structure of seventeenth-century meditation, beginning with the composition or focusing upon a concrete situation and proposing or the spiritual problem therein dramatized; following with an analysis of the problem; and ending in the colloquy, an intimate conversation and union between the poet and the object of his spiritual exercise. But here I think the essential difference between Emerson and the Metaphysicals is evident: whereas the meditative formula is triadic, the structure of "The Rhodora" is clearly binary, two sets of eight lines each. In the first, the situation is posed and the question implied (actually stated already in the subtitle of the poem); in the second, an answer is given immediately, without any deliberation, and the answer itself eschews analysis:

> Rhodora! if the sages ask thee why
> This charm is wasted on the earth and sky,
> Tell them, dear, that if eyes were made for seeing,
> Then Beauty is its own excuse for being:
> Why thou wert there, O rival of the rose!
> I never thought to ask, I never knew:
> But, in my simple ignorance, suppose
> The self-same Power that brought me there brought you.

The rhodora needs no reasoned argument, no "excuse" for its existence. In terms of the meditative formula, we have only "composition" and "colloquy," two parts subtly intertwined. The first part of the poem portrays the rhodora as a humble, self-sacrificing flower which, though equal to the celebrated rose, prefers obscure service to worldly fame. Sacrifice and service are implied, almost to the point of martyrdom, in the fallen petals. In the last eight lines the poet identifies himself with the same Christian virtues: his "simple ignorance" is faith, if not in Providence, certainly in a wise and sensitive Creator; the worshipful humility which the poet and the flower share explains their intimate rapport. The philosophical sages, on the other hand, are shut out; as the flower leans toward Christian sacrifice, the sages are associated with self-seeking, utilitarian interests, perhaps even cavalier interests, who see the flower's charm as "wasted." Thus a dramatic undercurrent—the subtle alliance of poet and flower against the sages—helps to create a mood of religious dedication that excludes the inquiring, analytical mind, and at the same time militates against a narrowly esthetic, "beauty for beauty's sake" interpretation of the poem.

In a number of ways "The Rhodora" is consonant with Emerson's achievement in *Nature* (1836). Both works illustrate the attention to structure, the eye for neatness and symmetry, that Emerson cultivated during these years. Herbert, probably Emerson's chief model for the poetry of 1834, is also one of the inspiring spirits of *Nature*, where a large portion of "Man" is quoted. There is a well-known passage concluding the section of *Nature* on "Beauty" that bears out the message of "The Rhodora": "This element [Beauty] I call an ultimate end. No reason can be asked or given why the soul seeks beauty. Beauty, in its largest and profoundest sense, is one expression for the universe. God is the all-fair." Finally, the binary structure of the poem reflects, in its omission of any extended analysis, Emerson's attack on the Understanding in *Nature*.

More generally, the binary form is a model for Emerson's philosophical inquiry and for the dramatic situation he used to symbolize it. The "Introduction" to *Nature* defines the terms of his inquiry: "Philosophically considered, the universe is composed of Nature and the Soul." Emerson took as a starting point the post-Kantian idealists' distinction between consciousness and otherness, the ME and the NOT ME, and this initial dualism colors all of his writings. Nature or the NOT ME, taken as a whole, is conceived as a problem to be solved, and in 1836, at least, Emerson expressed utter confidence that the solution is at hand:

> Undoubtedly we have no questions to ask which are unanswerable. We must trust the perfection of the creation so far as to believe that whatever curiosity the order of things has awakened in our minds, the order of things can satisfy. Every man's condition is a solution in hieroglyphic to those inquiries he would put. He acts it as life, before he apprehends it as truth. In like manner, nature is already, in its forms and tendencies, describing its own design.

Confidence in the "order of things," and faith in the "like manner" that bridges the gap between man and nature: here, in an incipient version, is the doctrine of correspondence that supports Emerson's early Romanticism. This correspondence is the hidden alliance between the poet and the rhodora, which makes them both responsive to sentiments of beauty and sacrifice. Much of Emerson's poetry thus resolves itself into a binary, question-and-answer form, often dramatized as an wencounter between the poet and Nature personified as a whole or symbolized by a single object, a tree, stream, or mountain. According to Emerson's early faith, the poet needs only to put the question and Nature will awaken in him the answer. He does not analyze, nor does he require any formal discipline of meditation—he "apprehends," in an instant he grasps the truth of what he has already acted out. The spontaneity of true insight is one of Emerson's Romantic axioms:

> A man should learn to detect and watch that gleam of light which flashes across his mind from within, more than the lustre of the firmament of bards and sages. ("Self-Reliance")

> The only mode of obtaining an answer to these questions of the senses is to forego all low curiosity, and, accepting the tide of being which floats us into the secret of nature, work and live, work and live, and all unawares the advancing soul has built and forged for itself a new condition, and the question and the answer are one. ("The Over-Soul,")

**Source:** R. A. Yoder, "Toward the 'Titmouse Dimension': The Development of Emerson's Poetic Style," in *PMLA*, Vol. 87, No. 2, March 1972, pp. 255–70.

## Sources

Arnold, Matthew, "Emerson," in *Discourses in America*, Macmillan, 1924, pp. 138–208, originally published in *Macmillan's Magazine*, Vol. L, No. 295, May 1884.

Avery, Donald, "Ralph Waldo Emerson," in *Dictionary of Literary Biography*, Vol. 73: *American Magazine Journalists, 1741–1850*, edited by Sam G. Riley, Gale Research, 1988, pp. 85–92.

Chapman, John Jay, "Emerson," in *Emerson: And Other Essays*, Charles Scribner's Sons, 1898, pp. 3–108, originally published as "Emerson, Sixty Years After," in the *Atlantic Monthly*, Vol. 79, January–February 1897.

Emerson, Ralph Waldo, *Nature*, James Munroe, 1836.

McClay, Wilfred M., "Mr. Emerson's Tombstone," in *First Things: A Monthly Journal of Religion and Public Life*, No. 83, Institute on Religion and Public Life, May 1998, pp. 16–22.

Mollison, Char, and Charles C. Walcutt, "The Emersonian Key to Whitman's 'Out of the Cradle Endlessly Rocking,'" in *Arizona Quarterly*, Vol. 37, No. 1, Spring 1981, pp. 5–9.

Perry, Bliss, "The Mystic and Poet," in *Emerson Today*, Princeton University Press, 1931, pp. 85–97.

Richardson, Robert D., Jr., University of Colorado, "Ralph Waldo Emerson," in *Dictionary of Literary Biography*, Vol. 59: *American Literary Critics and Scholars, 1800–1850*, edited by John W. Rathburn and Monica M. Grecu, Gale Research, 1987, pp. 108–29.

## Further Reading

Heilmeyer, Marina, *The Language of Flowers: Symbols and Myths*, Prestel, 2001.

> Heilmeyer considers thirty-five different flowers, describing their historical importance, their symbolic meanings to different people and cultures, and their presence in literature. The book includes more than one hundred illustrations to enhance the text.

Myerson, Joel, ed., *A Historical Guide to Ralph Waldo Emerson*, Historical Guides to American Authors series, Oxford University Press, 1999.

> In addition to extensive biographical information, this book includes essays by various authors exploring Emerson's philosophies, views on society, and beliefs about literature. Readers will also find information about the historical and social context for Emerson's life in New England.

Porte, Joel, and Saundra Morris, eds., *The Cambridge Companion to Ralph Waldo Emerson*, Cambridge University Press, 1999.

> This volume is a good critical introduction to Emerson's wide-ranging work. Contributors evaluate Emerson's poetry, essays, and articles, providing a variety of viewpoints on the works themselves and on how they influenced the literary world. The editors include a chronology and a bibliography.

Rowe, John Carlos, *At Emerson's Tomb: The Politics of Classic American Literature*, Columbia University Press, 1996.

> Beginning with Emerson, Rowe examines the political positions held by many of America's most prominent literary figures. Rowe focuses on abolition and women's rights, as these were the dominant political issues of the nineteenth century. Rowe writes about Emerson, Herman Melville, Edgar Allan Poe, Frederick Douglass, Walt Whitman, and Mark Twain.

# The Singer's House

## Seamus Heaney
## 1979

Seamus Heaney's poem, "The Singer's House" was first published in his 1979 volume of poetry, *Field Work*, which was published in both England and America that year. The volume marked a departure from Heaney's earlier poetry volumes, most of which had addressed the modern conflict between Protestants and Catholics in Northern Ireland—often referred to as the Troubles—in an indirect way. However, many of the poems in the new volume, which were written during a period of self-exile from Northern Ireland, demonstrated Heaney's more concentrated attempts to define his role in the Irish conflict. For this reason, many critics singled out *Field Work* as the transitional point in Heaney's poetry career.

In "The Singer's House," Heaney uses his poetic abilities to appeal to another artist—his singer friend, David Hammond. The poem was written after Hammond canceled a recording session, following a terrorist bombing. Heaney wanted to encourage Hammond that his voice counts, and that it was important for Hammond to inspire his fellow Irish countrymen and -women with his songs. Heaney was hoping to inspire a revival in Irish language and literature, which had been largely replaced over the centuries by the language and culture of British colonizers. A current copy of the poem can be found in *Opened Ground: Selected Poems 1966–1996*, which was published by Farrar, Straus and Giroux in 1999. This collection also includes the lecture that Heancy gave after receiving the Nobel Prize for Literature in 1995.

# Author Biography

Seamus Heaney was born in Mossbawn, in County Derry, in Northern Ireland on April 13, 1939, the same year that Irish poet William Butler Yeats died. This coincidence has been noted by many critics, who often compare Heaney's poetry with that of Yeats. Although he was born Catholic in predominantly Protestant Northern Ireland, the 1947 Education Act gave Heaney—along with other Northern Catholics—the opportunity to pursue secondary education that had been previously closed to them. When he was eleven years old, Heaney received a scholarship to study at Saint Columb's College in Derry (also known as Londonderry). In 1957, Heaney attended Queen's University in Belfast, where he received a bachelor of arts degree in 1961—with First Class Honors in English. The following year, after a year of postgraduate study, Heaney was awarded his teaching certificate from the St. Joseph's College of Education in Belfast.

While he was in college, Heaney contributed his first poems to his university literary magazines, under a pseudonym. Later, during his first years of teaching at St. Thomas's Secondary School in Ballymurphy, Belfast (1962–1963) and St. Joseph's College (1963–1966), Heaney had a number of his poems published in various periodicals. His poetry attracted the attention of Faber and Faber, a British publisher, and the one who would end up producing many of Heaney's volumes. Heaney's first major volume of poetry, *Death of a Naturalist*, was published in 1966, and received overall good reviews. In 1969, two months after his second volume of poetry, *Door Into the Dark*, was published, fighting erupted between the Catholics and Protestants in Northern Ireland. The increasing strife affected Heaney's writing, and subsequent volumes, such as 1972's *Wintering Out*, began to address the situation. In 1972, Heaney moved from his home in Belfast to a cottage in Glanmore, outside of Dublin, in the Republic of Ireland.

The move was seen by some as a betrayal of Heaney's Northern Irish heritage, and Heaney himself struggled with his self-imposed exile. However, the distance from the strife in Northern Ireland gave him the clarity he needed to write about it. Heaney produced two volumes of poetry while at Glanmore—*North* (1975) and *Field Work* (1979), the latter of which contained the poem, "The Singer's House." Since then, Heaney has produced several other volumes of poetry, including 1996's *The Spirit Level* and 2001's *Electric Light*.

*Seamus Heaney*

Heaney has also been involved in the translation of classic stories, including a best-selling translation of the epic poem, *Beowulf* (2000). The translation also won Heaney Britain's prestigious Whitbread Award for poetry as well as book of the year. Heaney has won numerous other awards for his poetry, including Whitbread Awards in 1987 for *The Haw Lantern* and in 1997 for *The Spirit Level*. He was awarded the Nobel Prize for Literature in 1995.

# Poem Text

When they said *Carrickfergus* I could hear
the frosty echo of saltminers' picks.
I imagined it, chambered and glinting,
a township built of light.

What do we say any more                5
to conjure the salt of our earth?
So much comes and is gone
that should be crystal and kept,

and amicable weathers
that bring up the grain of things,      10
their tang of season and store,
are all the packing we'll get.

So I say to myself *Gweebarra*
and its music hits off the place
                                        15

like water hitting off granite.
I see the glittering sound

framed in your window,
knives and forks set on oilcloth,
and the seals' heads, suddenly outlined,
scanning everything.                                    20

People here used to believe
that drowned souls lived in the seals.
At spring tides they might change shape.
They loved music and swam in for a singer

who might stand at the end of summer                    25
in the mouth of a whitewashed turf-shed,
his shoulder to the jamb, his song
a rowboat far out in evening.

When I came here first you were always singing,
a hint of the clip of the pick                          30
in your winnowing climb and attack.
Raise it again, man. We still believe what we hear.

## Poem Summary

### Stanza One

"The Singer's House" starts out with the reaction of the speaker, Heaney, to the reference of an outside group—the unidentified, "they." This group has spoken of Carrickfergus, a medieval city in County Antrim, on the eastern coast of Northern Ireland. Carrickfergus is known for its rich deposit of rock salt that was mined extensively from the 1850s until the early part of this century. When Heaney was writing the poem in the 1970s, many of the salt mines in Carrickfergus had already been abandoned. However, in one of his explanatory footnotes to the poem in the 1991 reprint of *Field Work*, Heaney makes no mention of this, saying only that: "There are salt-mines at the town of Carrickfergus in Co. Antrim." Instead, the reader must infer from the poem that the salt mines are mainly an item from the past.

This idea is emphasized by "the frosty echo of saltminers' picks," a phrase that hearkens back to a time in Ireland's history when the salt mines were active. Heaney may be considering this echo "frosty" for a couple of reasons. As part of Northern Ireland, Carrickfergus is subject to the same winter climate as the rest of northern Europe. Also, because the echo is from the past, it is only a memory of a heritage that has grown cold. In any case, Heaney continues his reconstruction of this past, giving the sound of the saltminers' picks a physical form in his imagination, as it becomes "chambered and glinting," a reference to the crystalline nature of rock salt. The poet continues sketching out the image in his mind, and the sound becomes "a township built of light." The image of light in poetry is often used to denote goodness or happiness. Collectively, this stanza invokes a nostalgic image of a mystical, happy society.

### Stanza Two

In this stanza, Heaney's pleasant memory of the saltminers is abruptly terminated, as he comes back into the present, the 1970s, when he is writing the poem during his self-imposed exile from Northern Ireland. Heaney uses the idea of salt mining as a transition between the past and the present, asking: "What do we say any more / to conjure the salt of our earth?" This sentence works on two levels. Literally, the sentence laments the loss of the salt mines in Carrickfergus. However, the subtext—or hidden meaning—of the sentence offers a lament for the increasing loss of Irish language and culture as a result of England's colonization of Ireland. Up until this point, the use of Irish Gaelic had been preserved mainly by "the salt of our earth." The salt of the earth is a common phrase used to indicate the working classes that help to provide an economic and cultural foundation in a society. As Heaney notes in the next two lines, "So much comes and is gone / that should be crystal and kept." The rate of deterioration of Irish language and culture is rapid. Once again, there is a double meaning on the word, "crystal," which invokes the image of the rock salt once again, but which also implies something valuable—Irish traditions—that should be saved.

### Stanza Three

In this stanza, Heaney builds on the theme of change. The first two lines—"and amicable weathers / that bring up the grain of things"—offer a contrast to the "frosty echo" from the first stanza. Amicable, or friendly, weather usually implies sunny days, which in this case helps to raise grains. However, the words "bring up," an odd choice for talking about the growth of crops, serve a deeper meaning. They invoke an image of bringing up, or raising, a family—the "grain" of society. But this is not a positive connotation, as the next two lines indicate: "their tang of season and store, / are all the packing we'll get." The way these two lines are written, it produces an image of monotony. In British-controlled Northern Ireland, where Irish language and culture have been continuously suppressed, the years go by blandly, the only "tang," or spice, being the passing seasons—as marked by the crops that are continually grown and stored. These things "are all" that Heaney and others who are living in Northern Ireland have for "packing," a word that is in itself very telling. Grain and other crops are usually stored in tightly packed containers such as silos. The word's inclusion in the last line of this stanza gives it a greater meaning. Packing also denotes travel, underscoring the fact that many Irish nationalists, especially Catholics, have left Northern Ireland, like Heaney has done.

## Stanza Four

At the beginning of this stanza, Heaney has moved, and more importantly, is resolving to move on. Since the northern city of Carrickfergus is no longer a possible home for many Irish nationalists, Heaney says to himself, "Gweebarra." In the same footnote mentioned above in the 1991 reprint edition of *Field Work*, Heaney notes that "Gweebarra is the name of a river and a bay in Co. Donegal." Once again, Heaney offers little explanation as to why he contrasts "Carrickfergus" with "Gweebarra" in the poem, but his intentions can be inferred by geographical divisions in the northern half of Ireland. County Donegal is one of three counties in the northern portion of Ireland that is not included in the official, British province of Northern Ireland. Just as Heaney is in a self-imposed physical exile in a cottage in the Republic of Ireland, many other Irish nationalists have experienced a similar physical, and cultural, exile. But if he is going to leave his home, Heaney will try to find a way to recreate the Irish culture in his new home.

Heaney notes that when he says "Gweebarra," "its music hits off the place / like water hitting off granite." Gweebarra has a beauty of its own, and in his mind, he once again reconstructs an image, like the "township built of light" from the first stanza. Instead of a saltminer's pick hitting salt, however, the image is one more suited to Gweebarra Bay, which features a number of granite cliffs. Nevertheless, the "glittering sound" created from the sea spray hitting the cliffs in this new location, mimics the "chambered and glinting" sound from the first stanza. In the process, Heaney shows that the Irish people can begin to reclaim their lost heritage, by letting memories of Northern Ireland fade, while accepting the lands that they have in the Republic and re-creating their heritage there.

## Stanza Five

In this stanza, Heaney carries over the "glittering sound" from the last stanza, saying that he can see it "framed in your window." The "your" who Heaney refers to is his friend, David Hammond, a singer. Heaney wrote this poem for Hammond, following an incident one night. The two were setting up to record some songs and poems for a radio show, when they were interrupted by the sound of a number of explosions, followed by sirens—signs of the ongoing sectarian, or politically extreme, violence in Northern Ireland. Hammond felt that his songs were powerless against this type of violence and that it was offensive to the victims, and canceled the recording session as a result. At this point in the poem, Heaney is drawing Hammond into his image of a healed society that hearkens back to the past. He imagines himself at Hammond's house, looking out the window. The poet describes "knives and forks set on oilcloth," a highly civilized picture that contrasts sharply with the other earthy images of salt, grain, and sea spray. This noticeable difference once again points to the loss of traditional Irish culture for the more "civilized" English culture. However, Heaney quickly draws Hammond, and his readers, outside once again, into nature, where "the seals' heads, suddenly outlined," are "scanning everything."

## Stanza Six

Heaney now begins to speak in nostalgic terms once more, as he did in the beginning, saying that: "People here used to believe / that drowned souls lived in the seals." Heaney's use of seals references the Celtic legend of the Selchies, gray Atlantic seals who could turn into humans—and vice versa. This legend was particularly popular in Gweebarra and other coastal areas of County Donegal, where people's lives were tied to the sea. However, this myth, like many Irish myths, began to die out in the twentieth century when the educational system in Ireland pressured children to speak in English. At the same time, many of the younger generations had no desire to adhere to old traditions, preferring more modern radio broadcasts. These combined circumstances helped to supplant the traditional storytelling that had been used to pass the Selchie stories from generation to generation.

The legend of the Selchies is further examined by Heaney's next line: "At spring tides they might change shape." Here, Heaney is using his ability as a poet and storyteller to try to invoke the legend once again. The use of the word "spring" is particularly noticeable, since poets often use spring and springtime as a symbol for a rebirth. In the natural cycle, spring is the season of growth that follows the cold death of winter. In the poem, "the frosty echo" of the saltminers' picks, words that invoke an image of winter, is dead. However, in the rebirth of spring, things have the potential to change. Just as the Selchies have the ability to change shape, Hammond has the ability to take up his traditional songs once again for the cause of renewing Irish language and culture. The final line in the stanza emphasizes this, saying of the seals that "They loved music and swam in for a singer." The drowned souls of the Irish, who have been flooded by the massive assimilation of English language and culture, can be recovered if an Irish singer—Hammond—will sing his songs to them once again.

### Stanza Seven

This possibility for change is emphasized in the next line, when Heaney says the singer "might stand at the end of summer." The "might" implies that Hammond has the option to take a "stand," by singing his songs once again. Heaney also changes the season from spring in the last sentence to summer in this sentence. This is telling, since summer symbolizes the natural progression of growth that happens after the rebirth of spring. Heaney is saying that if Hammond takes a stand and raises his voice in song once again, Irish culture will one day grow strong again. The next image, Hammond standing "in the mouth of a whitewashed turfshed," invokes the image of a clean, "whitewashed," start that is based on Irish traditions. In America, turf generally refers to grass. However, Heaney's use of the word, "turf," refers to peat—a spongy energy source that is found in the many bogs in Ireland. The harvesting of peat into blocks that can be dried out and burned is an established tradition in Ireland. Heaney uses this earthy and recognizable image to contrast with the British modern convenience of "knives and forks set on oilcloth" in the fifth stanza. The poet continues the transformation of Hammond in his poem, as he places the singer with "his shoulder to the jamb, his song / a rowboat far out in evening." The image of the singer is one of support, helping to shoulder the load of reviving Irish culture. Hammond does this by sending his song out on a journey, a cultural rowboat that will presumably help to spread the influence of traditional Irish culture.

### Stanza Eight

In the last stanza, Heaney sums up his appeal to Hammond by referencing how Hammond used to sing—"When I came here first you were always singing," implying that he does not sing any longer. Heaney says that Hammond's Irish songs, sung in the harsh sounds of Gaelic, echo the "clip of the pick" from the first stanza. Heaney uses the style of Hammond's singing, "your winnowing climb and attack," as a means for telling him that he needs to fight for Irish language and culture. This will be a difficult "climb," and the use of the word "attack" suggests that it could be dangerous. Irish nationalists who were vocal during the Troubles often got threatened or killed. Heaney asks Hammond to "Raise it again, man," signifying that Hammond should use his "pick," his singing voice, again, in the old style. Heaney's last sentence, "We still believe what we hear," implies that if Hammond will sing his Irish music again, he can help to resurrect Irish beliefs, which are not dead yet. "The singer's house" referred to by the title is ultimately the one that Hammond can help provide for his Irish people, who have been physically and culturally displaced from their traditional homes by the influence of English language and culture. Through the healing and reviving powers of poetry and song, however, Heaney and Hammond can help to revive the lost Irish traditions, a loss that has been magnified by the strife in Northern Ireland.

## Themes

### Irish Culture and Mythology

Heaney's primary goal in the poem is to inspire a rebirth in the native culture of Ireland. Heaney laments the loss of old traditions such as the salt mining in Carrickfergus, noting that this way of life is nothing but a "frosty echo." Using Carrickfergus as a springboard, Heaney illustrates that the salt mines are not the only abandoned tradition. Many Irish nationalists lack a cultural identity. Some of them, having been driven out of Northern Ireland, either by force or by choice, as in the case of Heaney's own self-exile, do not have anywhere to call their cultural home. Much of the Irish way of life throughout the island has been transformed. Like the "drowned souls" that live in the seals, many Irish men and women have had their identities drowned by the influence of English language and tradition. These influences have transformed Irish life into a routine, much like that of the farming seasons, which lack the "tang," or spice of the old Irish ways. Heaney invokes one Irish legend in particular, the legend of the Selchies, when he notes that "People here used to believe / that drowned souls lived in the seals."

### Artistic Responsibility

With this poem, Heaney is acknowledging the artist's responsibility to help resurrect and maintain

## Topics for Further Study

- Read one of the many stories associated with the legend of the Selchies, then read a story from the mythology of a different seafaring culture. Compare the two stories.

- The Irish Republican Army (IRA) has been involved in many of the conflicts in Northern Ireland, although since 1998, they have been observing a cease-fire. Research the current state of the IRA and discuss what you think the future holds for this organization. Use details from your research to support your claims.

- Pick another culture outside of the United Kingdom that has been affected by colonization. Write a profile of this culture, including a short history, the primary language spoken, and any legends or myths. Discuss any ways that this society has been changed by the colonization.

- Research the life of David Hammond, the singer in the poem, and write a short biography about him. Be sure to discuss the relationship between Hammond and Heaney, and include Hammond's reaction to "The Singer's House," if any, as well as any effect the poem may have had on Hammond's life.

- Research the life of William Butler Yeats, including his upbringing, writing style, and political beliefs. Imagine that Yeats has read Heaney's poetry and is time-travelling to our time to talk about it. Write a short script that describes what a potential encounter between Heaney and Yeats might be like.

---

a national identity. Heaney issues a challenge to Hammond, and to himself, in the second stanza, asking "What do we say any more / to conjure the salt of our earth?" This poem is Heaney's response for himself. He is using his poetic abilities to address the issue, and enlist help, mainly from Hammond. Heaney details the situation in detail for Hammond, explaining that if they are not careful, the Irish identity could slip away forever, instead of being "crystal and kept." The displaced Irish men and women, symbolized in the seals, need Hammond's help. In the last stanza, Heaney is more direct with this request, saying that "When I came here first you were always singing." In other words, Heaney is trying to remind Hammond that he has a duty to do, as he has done in the past. However, now the situation is more dangerous, and music has become an "attack," a fight to save the last remnant of Irish identity and build it up again. As Heaney notes in the last line, "We still believe what we hear." If Hammond follows his artistic responsibility and sings his Irish songs once again, Heaney tells him he will help to inspire a movement among the culturally displaced Irish citizens.

### Cultural Healing

Although Heaney ends the poem with some combative language, emphasizing the "attack," the poem is for the most part a peaceful attempt at resurrecting and rebuilding the national Irish identity. Heaney does not want to fight in the literal sense, as there has been enough violence in Northern Ireland already. In fact, it was this violence that caused Hammond to put down his guitar and stop singing, so Heaney takes a different approach with this plea to pick it up again. He recognizes that what Ireland needs is healing, not more fighting. As a result, even though he is nostalgic about Carrickfergus, he puts aside these memories from his life in Northern Ireland and sets about trying to affect a change where he can—by rescuing the language and culture.

## Style

### Setting

As in most of Heaney's poetry, and Irish culture for that matter, setting is an important issue. In this poem, setting becomes an equally important technique. Although Heaney takes the reader on a journey through his mind, offering imagery of different places from the past, present, and potential future, he anchors the poem with the discussion of two cities, *Carrickfergus* and *Gweebarra*. The italics help denote that somebody is speaking these two words, but they also serve to underscore the stability of these two places as the actual settings of the poem. Heaney uses Carrickfergus to represent a nostalgic view of Ireland's past, incorporating the salt mines—formerly one of Carrickfergus's booming industries—to bring the past back to life in his mind. Heaney uses Gweebarra, on the other hand, to discuss Ireland's future. While he is wistful in the beginning about losing the salt mines and other memories about former ways of Irish life, Heaney pushes these issues aside three stanzas into the poem to focus on Gweebarra. Carrickfergus is dead, a lost cause, while Gweebarra represents an opportunity. It is here, in one of the areas of the Republic of Ireland, that Heaney stages his appeal to Hammond to send out his song once more, and help Heaney to revive Ireland's cultural identity.

## Symbol

"The Singer's House" is saturated with symbolism. From the very beginning of the poem, the reader is let inside Heaney's mind, and shown images that often exist on two levels—the literal and the symbolic. When Heaney poses the question, "What do we say any more / to conjure the salt of our earth?" he could be talking about actual salt, especially since he has mentioned saltminers in the previous stanza. However, given the context of the poem, it is obvious that Heaney is referring to the working classes of Ireland for centuries, the salt of the earth folk who have provided a foundation for the island. Heaney implies that he does not know what to say to "conjure," or summon, these people. In other words, he wants to wake his people up and get them to embrace a unified Irish identity, but they are lost, unable to be enchanted—another meaning of the word, "conjure." The symbolism throughout the rest of the poem supports this idea. The Irish identity that "comes and is gone" is equated to a "crystal," which should be saved. In the fourth stanza, Heaney works on doing this, as he begins building up his argument to Hammond. The "knives and forks set on oilcloth" symbolize civilization, especially British sensibilities, an idea that is contrasted sharply with the symbol of the Irish masses, the "seals' heads." These masses, the "salt of our earth" referenced in the second stanza, "might change shape," back into their native Irish form, if Hammond will sing to them in his Irish voice.

## Imagery

In addition to relying on symbols to point out the subtext of the poem, Heaney also creates a number of images, most of which are generated in his mind. The reader follows Heaney on this journey through his memory and thoughts of the present and future, starting with the first reference to "Carrickfergus." Heaney tells the reader that a past conversation involving the city made him imagine the "frosty echo of saltminers' picks." During this first stanza, Heaney gives the sound of these picks a physical form, shaping it into an image of "a town-

ship built of light," words that are meant to evoke a positive image in the reader's mind. Heaney's mental images reach a higher level of detail after he says "Gweebarra." In this new place, in the present, he formulates his argument to Hammond to sing again. Heaney pulls Hammond—and the reader—into an increasingly complex image, each line adding another detail. Like the first stanza, it starts with a sound, "water hitting off granite." From there, Heaney follows the physical manifestation of this "glittering sound" as it travels to a window, then down to the beach where the "seals' heads, suddenly outlined" are "scanning everything." Finally, in the future that Heaney imagines could take place if Hammond sings again, the singer stands "in the mouth of a whitewashed turf-shed," sending his song out like "a rowboat far out in evening," two vivid images.

# Historical Context

## Establishment of the Irish Free State

Although the poem takes place in the 1970s, Heaney refers either directly or indirectly to a number of other items of historical interest from Ireland's past. The most notable of these is the ongoing conflict between Britain and certain groups in Northern Ireland who are opposed to Britain's control—a situation that is present in some form in most of Heaney's poetry. While England has been involved in the colonization of many of the world's lands, the struggle in Ireland—one of its closest neighbors—has been particularly bitter. The issue of Britain's domination of Ireland is a centuries-old conflict, dating back to the first English invasion of Ireland in the twelfth century. An uneasy peace was eventually reached in 1922, with the establishment of the Irish Free State, known today as the Republic of Ireland. The Republic of Ireland consists of twenty-six of Ireland's thirty-two counties. The remaining six counties, situated on the northeastern portion of Ireland, were named Northern Ireland—with the capital city of Belfast—and were put under the auspices of the United Kingdom.

## Conflicts among Catholics, Protestants, and Other Groups

However, the geographic division of Ireland did not solve the conflict. In the new province of Northern Ireland, also known as Ulster, people who followed the Protestant, English faith were the ma-

# Compare & Contrast

- **Late 1960s–Early 1970s:** Although Gaelic is technically the official language of the Republic of Ireland, it is hardly used, and faces the possibility of dying out entirely, being displaced by English language and culture. This is true for other aspects of Irish culture and mythology.

  **Today:** Irish culture, including the myths and legends of the ancient Celtic peoples, comprise a major industry worldwide. Vendors sell everything from Celtic crosses to traditional Irish folk music, and Irish movies like *The Secret of Roan Inish* (1995) and *Dancing at Lughnasa* (1998) are two of the many recent films that explore Irish legends and culture.

- **Late 1960s–Early 1970s:** The Troubles, the most recent wave of sectarian violence in Northern Ireland, begin, and many people—Protestants, Catholics, paramilitary groups on each side, British military, and British citizens—die in a sustained campaign of violence. Bloody Sunday, the killing of thirteen unarmed Catholic protesters on January 30, 1972, inspires a backlash bombing by the Irish Republican Army and escalates the violence.

  **Today:** Following a cease-fire in 1998, residents in Northern Ireland observe an uneasy peace. Having belonged to divided camps for so many years, many find it hard to put aside differences, and, as a result, sectarian violence continues to flare up sporadically in Northern Ireland.

- **Late 1960s–Early 1970s:** Northern Ireland is not the only area in the world that is torn by civil war. In Vietnam, America and other nations go to war in an effort to stop the spread of Communism in Indochina. In the long war, many Americans lose their lives as they support South Vietnam's attempt to establish democratic independence from Communist North Vietnam. The United States does not achieve its goals in the war, which was not widely supported on the American home front.

  **Today:** Following terrorist bombings in New York and Washington, America is one of many nations that devotes itself to stopping the spread of international terrorism. The resulting military campaign in Afghanistan and other areas of the Middle East is widely supported on the American home front.

- **Late 1960s–Early 1970s:** A new salt mine is opened at Kilroot in Northern Ireland in 1967. Northern Ireland's 1969 Mineral Development Act gives the Department of Enterprise, Trade & Investment responsibility for abandoned mines, including salt mines.

  **Today:** Most salt mines in Carrickfergus and the surrounding area are abandoned. Following the collapse of an abandoned salt mine in Carrickfergus, the Department of Enterprise, Trade & Investment issues a press release informing the public to keep their children away from the abandoned salt mines—many of which are supported by pillars of rock salt that can dissolve over time. The Department lists about two thousand abandoned mines in Northern Ireland, which they continue to monitor for structural problems.

---

jority, and the division suited them, since they preferred to be ruled by England. But in Northern Ireland, there was a strong minority of Irish Catholics, who maintained the belief that the entire island of Ireland should be a unified, self-governing state. Unionist (meaning loyal to the English crown) Protestants often discriminated against Irish nationalist Catholics, refusing to hire them or provide them with necessary educational or social services. While some Catholics emigrated to the Republic of Ireland or to other countries to avoid this treatment, others did not want to leave their homes, or the good economy, in Northern Ireland. Catholics in Northern Ireland fought back against the discrimination by forming groups such as the Irish Republican Army (formed in 1919), or IRA, a militant guerilla group that devoted itself to unifying all of Ireland as a free state. Meanwhile, Protestants formed corresponding paramilitary groups, which were often aided by British forces. In this highly sectarian climate, violence was a way of life, although it reached a head in the mid-1960s, with the outbreak of a particularly violent bout of sectarian violence dubbed the Troubles. On January 30, 1972, in an event known worldwide as Bloody Sunday, British forces in Northern Ireland massacred thirteen civil-rights demonstrators in Derry (called Londonderry by the British), prompting the IRA to escalate its terrorist campaign of violence—adding targets in England.

### The British Influence on Ireland's Language and Culture

Over the many centuries of English colonization in Ireland, English language and culture slowly began to replace much of the Irish language and culture—a common effect of colonization. By the end of the nineteenth century, Gaelic was almost a dead language. However, in 1891, William Butler Yeats, an Irish poet, founded the Irish Literary Society. Along with his friend, Lady Augusta Gregory, Yeats helped to inspire a movement in Irish literature. In his own poetry and prose writings, Yeats helped to resurrect old Celtic myths and present them to the world again. Despite these and other efforts—including the establishment of Gaelic as the official language of the Republic of Ireland in 1937—throughout the twentieth century, Irish culture and language were steadily replaced by British culture and language. As a result of this loss, writer David Thomson set out in the late 1940s to document and preserve one aspect of Irish mythology in particular, the legend of the Selchies—seals who can change into human form and vice versa. Other writers, including Heaney, also lamented the loss of Irish culture, mythology, and language, and expressed a desire to both recapture lost heritage and remain distinct from Britain.

### The Field Day Theatre Company

In 1980, one year after Heaney published *Field Work*, the Irish playwright, Brian Friel, and the Irish actor, Stephen Rea, formed the Field Day Theatre Company. The same year, with their first production of Friel's play, *Translations*, in Derry, they offered an artistic, peaceful arena that they hoped would transcend the violence in Northern Ireland. Heaney, Hammond, Seamus Deane, and Tom Paulin—all prominent Irish artists—quickly joined Field Day as members of the Board of Directors. The success of their plays propelled Field Day's board into politically motivated publishing in 1983, with the publication of essays by Paulin, Heaney, and Deane. These essays were printed in individual pamphlets, all of which addressed the issues of Irish language and culture, especially as it had been affected by British colonization and influence. In Heaney's essay, "An open letter," he objected to his 1982 inclusion in the *Penguin Book of Contemporary British Poetry*, on the grounds that he was Irish, not British. Heaney's essay illuminated the greater issue, that Ireland did not have a national identity, much less a body of literature that it could call its own. As a result, Field Day's Board of Directors set about compiling a massive and definitive anthology of Irish writing. The three-volume collection, edited by Deane, was published in 1990.

## Critical Overview

Although Heaney's reputation was already strong by the time *Field Work* was published in 1979, the new volume was hailed by most critics as a powerful and impressive departure from his first four volumes of poetry. Says Ian Hamilton, in a 1987 review of Heaney's *The Haw Lantern* for the *London Review of Books*: "It was with his fifth book, *Field Work*, that Heaney found a voice that is neither bleakly antiquarian nor awkwardly portentous." Still, not everybody liked *Field Work*, or Heaney, for that matter. In his 1979 review for *Parnassus*, critic Calvin Bedient notes that Heaney's strong reputation "is astonishing in view of his modest ambition and tone." This negative view of Heaney is by far the minority opinion. In fact, as Helen Vendler says in her 2000 book, *Seamus Heaney*, much of the negative criticism of Heaney is politically motivated: "Heaney's adversary critics read the poems as statements of a political position, with which they quarrel."

Several critics have commented on the structure of *Field Work*. Says Daniel Tobin in his 1999 book, *Passage to the Center: Imagination and the Sacred in the Poetry of Seamus Heaney*: "Unlike *North* and *Wintering Out*, *Field Work* composes a seamless structure." Tobin further notes that this structure is "symmetrical. It forms a whole that integrates the subject matter of the earlier volumes."

Several critics have also commented on the influence that the American poet, Robert Lowell, has had on *Field Work*. While some see the influence as good, many others, such as Andrew Waterman, do not. In Waterman's 1992 essay, "'The Best Way Out Is Always Through,'" he notes that "it is worrying to see a poet of Heaney's maturity as overwhelmed by another's influence as is pervasively apparent in *Field Work*." For "The Singer's House" in particular, Waterman notes that the sentence—"What do we say any more / to conjure the salt of our earth?"—is an example of the types of tones that Lowell uses.

Still, most critics have had positive things to say about the volume. Although "The Singer's House" is rarely singled out for critical attention, the critics who have written about it have praised it. In his 1980 article for the *Times Literary Supplement*, "The Voice of Kinship," critic Harold Bloom names the poem as one of the most moving, saying that it practices "a rich negation, an art of excluded meanings, vowels of earth almost lost between guttural consonants of history." In *The Poetry of Seamus Heaney* (1998), editor and critic, Elmer Andrews, notes that "The Singer's House" is one of the poems in *Field Work* that celebrates "the kind of poetic 'release' Heaney writes about in *The Government of the Tongue*." Andrews quotes Heaney from "Nero, Chekhov's Cognac and a Knocker," a section of *The Government of the Tongue* that illustrates what Andrews means:

> The achievement of the poem is an experience of release ... The tongue, governed for so long in the social sphere by considerations of tact and fidelity, by nice obeisances to one's origin within the minority or the majority. This tongue is suddenly ungoverned. It gains access to a condition that is unconstrained.

In his essay, "A More Social Voice: 'Field Work,'" published in the 1994 book, *The Art of Seamus Heaney*, critic Tony Curtis notes of the poem that: "The belief that imagery and story can sway the imagination and alter the world is what drives every writer." Citing the final three stanzas, Curtis also remarks on the danger of raising one's voice in Northern Ireland: "But to sing you have to rise to your feet and getting noticed in Ulster may not be prudent." Similarly, in his 1994 book, *Questioning Tradition, Language, and Myth: The Poetry of Seamus Heaney*, critic Michael R. Molino notes the theme of artistic responsibility, saying that "even though the beliefs that once bonded the community have faded, the speaker senses something of value in the singer's raised voice." In his 1996 essay, "Seamus Heaney's Anti-Transcendental Corncrake," Jonathan Allison gives an interesting observation about the singer's voice itself. Allison notes that the harsh-sounding corncrake, a bird employed by many Irish poets, including Heaney, seems to be present in "The Singer's House." Says Allison, there is "something of the broken voice of the crake in Heaney's depiction of the voice of David Hammond."

## Criticism

### Ryan D. Poquette

*Poquette has a bachelor's degree in English and specializes in writing about literature. In the following essay, Poquette discusses Heaney's emphasis on sounds to underscore the power of David Hammond's songs in Heaney's poem.*

When one first looks at Heaney's poem, "The Singer's House," it may not appear to have a planned structure, other than the anchoring of the two place names, "*Carrickfergus*" and "*Gweebarra*." The poem references a number of separate ideas and creates images that may not make sense at first. However, upon further inspection, the poem is revealed to be a carefully designed effort to underscore the power of and need for David Hammond's contributions as a singer. This planning starts with the poem's overall structure, the organization of the stanzas. The poem is divided into eight stanzas, and both the first and the last stanza are self-contained units, which talk about "saltminers' picks" and "the pick" of Hammond's singing voice, respectively.

The use of the word, "pick," in both of these stanzas links them together and creates a circular effect—the last stanza brings the poem around full circle. The "picks" in the first stanza represent the tools that the saltminers used to mine the salt in Carrickfergus. However, the word also represents the picking sound that these tools make. When a word or phrase imitates the sound that it makes, it is known as onomatopoeia. Poets often use this technique when they want to achieve a special effect. In this case, Heaney is using sounds to emphasize the importance of sound. In the first line, after "they said *Carrickfergus*," the name of the place sparks an elaborate vision in Heaney's mind. Heaney's imagination goes back into his heritage and recreates the sound of the "saltminers' picks." This imaginary sound in turn leads Heaney to envision "a township built of light"—Carrickfergus, and Ireland, in its cultural heyday. Within the context of the poem, sound becomes a powerful force, an idea that is established in this first stanza.

> *Since Heaney has been able to create entire visions of communities in the past and present—based only on the uttering of placenames—Hammond's music will have even more power in helping to realize visions of future communities, like the one that Heaney creates in the poem.*

Following the first stanza, the next six stanzas are organized into blocks of two stanzas each, all of which end with a period—just like the first and last stanzas end with periods. In this way, the eight stanzas of the poem are broken down into five definitive blocks—the first stanza, the three two-stanza blocks in the middle, and the final stanza. While the first stanza of the poem invokes the past life of Carrickfergus, the next block (stanzas two and three) jumps to the present and talks about the current crisis in Ireland. In the first line of this block, the use of the words, "we say," mimics the use of the words, "they said," from the first line of the first stanza. This pattern is repeated in the first lines of the other blocks in the poem. For example, in the first line of the next block (stanzas four and five), Heaney uses the words "I say."

In the next block (stanzas six and seven), it would seem that Heaney breaks this pattern by saying, "People here used to believe," as opposed to saying "used to say." However, this is not the case. The traditional belief systems of Irish people, like many older cultures, have in the past been based on an oral tradition. Crucial cultural beliefs were passed on to the successive generations through stories and songs. Heaney knows this fact, as would Hammond, a singer himself. The use of the word "believe," which sticks out when compared to the other uses of the words "say" or "said," is therefore very telling. Finally, the first line in the last block (the final stanza), underscores this fact. "When I came here first you were always singing," Heaney says to Hammond, invoking both Hammond's status as singer—another reference to sound—and Hammond's responsibility to uphold the oral tradition of Ireland.

Given this obvious structural emphasis on sound, it becomes easier to see the other ways in which Heaney uses sounds within the poem. After Heaney has invoked the past life of Ireland in the first stanza, he changes his tactics somewhat in the next three blocks. In stanzas two and three, Heaney moves to the present, where Ireland is having problems maintaining its identity. Says Heaney: "What do we say any more / to conjure the salt of our earth?" The Irish masses who have formed the basis of the island's culture for hundreds of years are being changed by English influence and by the changing society. As Ireland enters the modern world, which is dominated by mass media, the oral tradition is falling off even more, and Heaney makes it seem like there is not much that anybody can "say" to stop it. Heaney laments this loss, saying that so much of the Irish identity, which "comes and is gone," is priceless. Once it is gone, there is no recovering it. As a result, it should be treated like "crystal and kept." The descriptions of a rural life that seems to lack "tang," or spice, without the Irish identity, underscore this devastating idea.

In stanzas five and six, Heaney moves on from the sorrow in the previous block, resolving not to dwell on Carrickfergus and the problems in Northern Ireland, but instead to try to get a fresh start. "So I say to myself *Gweebarra*" Heaney starts, indicating that he is ready to do his part. As in the first stanza, when the sound of the word, "*Carrickfergus*," inspired a vision from Heaney's Irish heritage, the sound of the word, "*Gweebarra*," inspires a new vision in Heaney's mind. This second vision also contains a number of distinct sounds, including the first reference to "music," which "hits off the place / like water hitting off granite." The music reference begins Heaney's attempt to inspire Hammond to sing again. The music, like the picks of the saltminers from the first stanza, inspires a greater vision, one with physical form—at least in Heaney's mind. The sea spray that hits off the granite cliffs of Gweebarra gives the image a sound and a presence. This presence is developed even more, as Heaney, and the reader, follow the music. As Heaney notes in the last line of stanza four, "I see the glittering sound," an idea that he carries over into stanza five with the words, "framed in your window," where he pulls Hammond into the poem.

## What Do I Read Next?

- *Beowulf*, an anonymous poem written in Old English, is believed to have been written sometime between the eighth and tenth centuries. It was losing favor in literary circles by the end of the twentieth century. In 2000, however, Heaney revitalized studies of the epic poem with his gritty and engaging translation. The translation, an unexpected best-seller, also caused controversy when it was awarded the Whitbread Award, one of Great Britain's top honors—normally awarded to an original work.

- Heaney is not the only writer who has discussed the problems generated by colonization efforts like the one in Ireland. In 1983, the Field Day Theatre Company in Derry began publishing essays from Heaney and others, as individual pamphlets. Three of these—Terry Eagleton's "Nationalism: Irony and Commitment," Fredric Jameson's "Modernism and Imperialism," and Edward Said's "Yeats and Decolonization"—all originally published in 1988, were collected and reprinted in *Nationalism, Colonialism and Literature*, in 1990.

- The Field Day Theatre Company was originally founded to host the plays of Irish playwright Brian Friel. Their first production, Friel's *Translations*, first published in 1981, is set in 1833, when the British authorities are remapping and renaming many old Irish towns. An English Lieutenant is sent to County Donegal, where he falls in love with an Irish woman who speaks only Gaelic. Their tragic love affair emphasizes the loss of cultural traditions and the division of Ireland that was in full force at the time of the play's production.

- Although Heaney is known mainly for his poetry, he has also written a variety of essays during his literary and teaching career. *The Redress of Poetry*, published in 1995, collects a number of these essays that are based on lectures Heaney gave as a professor at Oxford University. Heaney's opinions of poetry range from the work of individual poets in the literary canon to the meaning of poetry itself.

- In the poem "The Singer's House," Heaney references the seal legends from Celtic mythology, stories that were largely phased out by the widespread assimilation of English language and culture in the twentieth century. In his 1954 book entitled *The People of the Sea: A Journey in Search of the Seal Legend*, David Thomson attempts to document the stories of the seal legend and the culture in which these stories were told. In 2000, two years after Thomson's death, Heaney—a friend of Thomson's—was instrumental in getting the book reprinted. Heaney also provides an introduction in this new edition.

- Heaney has often been compared to an earlier Irish poet, William Butler Yeats, whose efforts in the early twentieth century helped to revive Irish legends and culture in a literary movement known as the Irish Renaissance. Yeats's poems are available in a variety of volumes, although *The Collected Poems of W. B. Yeats*, published in 1996, offers one of the most comprehensive anthologies available. The volume includes all of the poems that Yeats authorized for publication.

- In addition to his poetry, Yeats's extensive research into Irish tales resulted in a number of published essays, introductions, and sketches. *Writings on Irish Folklore, Legend and Myth*, published in 2002, collects all of these published prose works. Presented in chronological order, this diverse collection illustrates the evolving nature of Yeats's research and analysis.

---

Heaney notes the "knives and forks set on oilcloth" in Hammond's house, a reference to the type of civilized domestic products that English society introduced to Ireland and its people. Since this type of change has often come at the expense of old traditions, Heaney wants to get Hammond to focus on old Ireland, which he does by pointing out the seals—powerful figures in Ireland's legends.

Using the seals as a transition point, Heaney moves on to the next block (stanzas six and seven), where he invokes the specific legend of the Selchies. Says Heaney: "People here used to believe / that drowned souls lived in the seals." However, Heaney does more than invoke an old legend. Given the context of the rest of the poem, the "drowned souls," become those of the Irish masses, whose Irish identity has been drowned in the ravages of English colonization and modern society. Heaney says that these masses "loved music," again referencing Hammond's profession, and says that the seals "swam in for a singer." Although the words are in past tense, the use of the word "might" indicates that this past is possible again. Heaney now breaks once again from talk of past traditions and focuses on the future. He has already used Carrickfergus to create a vision of the past and Gweebarra to sketch out a vision of the present. Now, he paints a vision of a possible future, where Hammond, the singer, can "stand at the end of summer"—a period of growth in the national Irish identity. In this future scenario, Heaney has Hammond send out his traditional song, which becomes "a rowboat far out in evening."

The emphasis on sounds in Heaney's poem has, up until this point, provided a powerful example to Hammond. Since Heaney has been able to create entire visions of communities in the past and present—based only on the uttering of place-names—Hammond's music will have even more power in helping to realize visions of future communities, like the one that Heaney creates in the poem. In the final stanza, Heaney emphasizes this idea even more directly, addressing a challenge to Hammond:

> When I came here first you were always singing,
> a hint of the clip of the pick
> in your winnowing climb and attack.
> Raise it again, man. We still believe what we hear.

This last stanza, the one that critics seem to comment on the most, is the culmination of Heaney's efforts in the poem to indicate the artist's responsibility for preserving his or her own culture. As Tony Curtis notes of the poem in his 1994 book, *The Art of Seamus Heaney*: "The belief that imagery and story can sway the imagination and alter the world is what drives every writer." Similarly, in his 1994 book, *Questioning Tradition, Language, and Myth: The Poetry of Seamus Heaney*, critic Michael R. Molino notes Heaney's belief that Hammond can help to effect a change: "even though the beliefs that once bonded the community have faded, the speaker senses something of value in the singer's raised voice."

Heaney reminds Hammond of the value of his role by associating the "saltminers' picks" from the first stanza with Hammond's voice, which is "a hint of the clip of the pick." Hammond's singing voice signifies his Irish heritage, so by raising his voice he can also help to revive his heritage. The last line is particularly effective. This is the only place in the poem where Heaney includes two complete sentences in one line. These two short sentences, an abrupt departure from the flowing nature of the rest of the poem, force Hammond—and the reader—to sit up and take notice. The people will believe in their heritage again, Heaney says, if Hammond will help give them something to believe in.

**Source:** Ryan D. Poquette, Critical Essay on "The Singer's House," in *Poetry for Students*, The Gale Group, 2003.

### Frank Pool

*Pool has published poems and reviews in several journals and teaches advanced placement and international baccalaureate English. In this essay, Pool interprets Heaney's poem by close reading and by placing it in a variety of contexts.*

Seamus Heaney's poem "The Singer's House" presents several problems of interpretation. Unfamiliar place names, ambiguity of language, and the juxtaposition of the poet's personal life with the political situation of his native Ireland all establish initial uncertainties that can be overcome by placing the poem in biographical, religious, and most importantly, in artistic contexts. This poem uses imagery and indirectness masterfully.

At first reading, the poem presents a contrast between two places, Carrickfergus and Gweebarra. Carrickfergus is associated with salt miners, with their picks laboring away in the earth, and Gweebarra is associated with water and the enigmatic imagery of seals. The poet could hear Carrickfergus as "the frosty echo" and "imagined it, chambered and glinting / a township built of light." The picture is one of industry, of toiling laborers in their workplace underground, yet filled with light. Consistent with a poem about a singer, the auditory imagery is in the foreground and will be sustained throughout the poem until it is reprised in the onomatopoetic "hint of the clip of the pick" in the final stanza.

Immediately afterward, the poet shifts to a rhetorical question which is "one of Heaney's saddest generalized reflections," says Neil Corcoran in *A Student's Guide to Seamus Heaney*. "What do we say any more / to conjure the salt of our earth? /

So much comes and is gone / that should be crystal and kept, // and amicable weathers / that bring up the grain of things, / their tang of season and store, / are all the packing we'll get."

The expression "salt of the earth" is an allusion to Matthew 5:13: "Ye are the salt of the earth, but if the salt have lost his savour, wherewith shall it be salted? It is thenceforth good for nothing, but to be cast out, and to be trodden under foot of men." There is a subtle but inescapable reference to the Irish "Troubles," which obsessed Heaney early in his career, and additionally, "salt of the earth" is a colloquial expression that refers to trustworthy and honest people. Trust and the hope of reconciliation prove to be important to this poem.

The sense of hearing dominates the imagery in the poem, an auditory motif that Heaney extends as he turns to Gweebarra, where "its music hits off the place / water hitting off granite." Music is central to the poem's theme, as indicated by the title. That image is immediately contrasted with the "glittering sound," reminiscent of Carrickfergus, which is framed in the window of the unnamed person Heaney addresses in this poem. In the window is a most commonplace sight, knives and forks on a cloth, here joined with the striking and unusual image of seals' heads, "scanning everything." Once again, the poet moves from reality into the realm of imagination, noting that people of Gweebarra once believed that "drowned souls lived in the seals." These souls might change shape, and they would swim in to hear a singer Heaney imagines standing in the doorway of a "whitewashed turf-shed" singing a song that is "a rowboat far out in evening." There seems to be little about this imagery that is morbid or frightening; indeed, the seals that can change their shape seem somehow buoyant, and their love of music an encouraging sign.

In the last stanza, the poet addresses an unnamed person, apparently male, perhaps himself. His first three lines seem to refer to real events in his life and refer back to the salt miners of Carrickfergus. He concludes with an exhortation and a challenge for the singer to raise his voice, and he neatly concludes the motifs of hearing and singing and imagining and believing. He ends with a note of affirmation and hope. "When I came here first / you were always singing, / a hint of the clip of the pick / in your winnowing climb and attack. / Raise it again, man. We still believe what we hear."

Heaney's style is loose and informal. Meter, rhyme, and the slant rhyme so often employed by the poet are absent here. Form is subordinate to the

> *Imagery, indirectness, personal authenticity, love of country, and the tension between domestic satisfaction and the demands of art—these are highly tuned instruments of the poet singer."*

poem's meanings and gestures; the quatrains of this poem do not correspond to sentences or complete thought. The first and last stanzas form complete units of thought; most other units are eight lines, or two quatrains in length.

All these are observations gained from close reading of the poem. Some research into geography, history, politics, culture, and, indeed, into the poet's life and career is needed here. Carrickfergus is a seaport in County Antrim, Northern Ireland. Seamus Heaney was born in 1939 in Northern Ireland. He was a Catholic in Protestant-dominated Ulster and as such was a second-class citizen in his own country. Gweebarra is a town on the bay in County Donegal, in the Republic of Ireland, or Eire. The Heaneys moved to the South in the early 1970s. This poem is from a book called *Field Work*, which was composed after Heaney and his family left the urban center of Belfast and came to live in the rural Glanmore Cottage far from the Troubles. Much of what goes on in this poem can best be understood as a contrast between life in the North, which is industriously and symbolically mining something valuable but sterile, salt, and life in the South, which is simple and rustic and contains elements of myth and metamorphosis and a vague promise of personal transformation. Heaney takes the occasion to do something that distinguishes great poets from minor ones. He changes style and subject matter; he grows as a poet by changing his style and his subject matter. Helen Vendler, in her book *Seamus Heaney*, notes this phase of his career, saying "his poetry becomes recognizably that of an individual man engaged in ordinary domestic and social relations ... his poems visibly kept at a middle level of both genre and style."

Heaney had tried to avoid taking part in the sectarian violence of Northern Ireland, known there as the Troubles. Though unequivocally a member of the Catholic community, he had resisted the call to devote his talents to the services of Republican propaganda, and he had tried to dedicate himself to the requirements of his art, to delve deep into the history and prehistory of his country in ages long before the seventeenth-century split between Protestant and Catholic. His often-anthologized early works such as "Digging" and "The Tollund Man," the latter one of a series of poems about two-thousand year old corpses ritually murdered and preserved in the bogs of Ireland and Western Europe, demonstrate his turn away from contemporary political issues and his looking to the past for artistic and personal inspiration. Tony Curtis, in *The Art of Seamus Heaney*, notes that "Heaney is fond of the metaphor which leads him to dig into the Irish earth through layers of history, language, and tradition." By the 1970s, he had realized that he could no longer be silent about the struggle for Irish unification, but he resisted demands for him to turn his pen to mere propaganda. Heaney's ambivalence, his sense of guilt, his ambivalent childhood as Irish Catholic in a Protestant British culture, all have generated creative struggles that resulted in his distinctive poetic identity. Henry Hart, in *Seamus Heaney: Poet of Contrary Progressions*, says, "These contrary forces form the fundamental tension in Field Work, where marriage poems speak of tearing responsibilities toward spouse and art, and political poems speak of similar tearing responsibilities toward poetic freedom and tribal demands."

The poem still means what it meant upon its first reading, but an understanding of the contexts in which the work occurs gives evidence of what Heaney, in his Nobel Prize acceptance lecture, says is "poetry's gift for telling the truth but telling it slant." Research into place names, which the poet is fond of scattering through his works, the history of Ireland in the twentieth century, and into the poet's own career permit a deeper, fuller, more comprehensive interpretation of the poem. For example, in the "salt of our earth" passage quoted above, the poet is wistfully longing not only for personal friendship and companionship not to be trodden under the foot of men, but he is also longing for reconciliation between the religious communities in the North, where the people look alike, dress alike, speak with the same accent, but whose very names identify them. "Seamus," for instance, is a Catholic name, whereas "Shawn" is its Protestant cognate.

The ferocity and futility of the violent struggles between those communities works itself into the writings of Ireland's most esteemed poet. Readers see Heaney's political commitments, not just in the lines of this one poem, but also in the context of the collection of poems which includes "The Singer's Voice," and also in the context of developing issues throughout his distinguished career. Those seals transforming themselves seem upon further investigation to be a longed-for transformation of people whose love of music may in some way bring them the personal and the political reconciliation that the poet deeply desires. He writes other poems in *Field Work* and elsewhere in which animals stand in for humans, an approach that was probably influenced by his friend and fellow poet Ted Hughes, and the American poet Robert Lowell likely showed the way to a looser and more personal means of expression.

Heaney's poem "The Singer's House" is full of imagery. Even if one does not know where Carrickfergus is, the imagery of the salt mines, the clink of the pick, the preservation and packing (one vowel away from "picking") and preservation in salt, the tang of its flavor, the strange shape-changing seals, souls of the dead, and the specific picture of the singer himself, "who might stand at the end of summer / in the mouth of a whitewashed turf-shed / his shoulder to the jamb, his song / a rowboat far out in evening" are all strongly evocative images which move his readers in ways that bald declamation does not. This is a poem about a man and his country, but it avoids the temptation, common among lesser poets, simply to get to the point and make some kind of public preachment regarding the political situation in Ulster and in Eire. Instead, the poet is indirect, using images to carry his poem to levels where straightforward propaganda could never reach. Imagery, indirectness, personal authenticity, love of country, and the tension between domestic satisfaction and the demands of art—these are highly tuned instruments of the poet singer.

**Source:** Frank Pool, Critical Essay on "The Singer's House," in *Poetry for Students*, The Gale Group, 2003.

# Sources

Allison, Jonathan, "Seamus Heaney's Anti-Transcendental Corncrake," in *Seamus Heaney: The Shaping Spirit*, edited by Catharine Malloy and Phyllis Carey, University of Delaware Press, 1996, p. 76.

Andrews, Elmer, ed., "Powers of Earth and Visions of Air," in *The Poetry of Seamus Heaney*, Columbia University Press, 1998, p. 143.

Bedient, Calvin, "The Music of What Happens," in *Parnassus: Poetry in Review*, Vol. 8, No. 1, Fall-Winter 1979, pp. 109–122.

Bloom, Harold, "The Voice of Kinship," in the *Times Literary Supplement*, No. 4011, February 8, 1980, pp. 137–38.

Corcoran, Neil, *A Student's Guide to Seamus Heaney*, Faber and Faber, 1986, p. 149.

Curtis, Tony, "A More Social Voice: *Field Work*," in *The Art of Seamus Heaney*, edited by Tony Curtis, Dufour Editions Inc., 1994, pp. 108–09, 115–16.

Hamilton, Ian, "Excusez-moi," in *London Review of Books*, Vol. 9, No. 17, October 1, 1987, pp. 10–11.

Hart, Henry, *Seamus Heaney: Poet of Contrary Progressions*, Syracuse University Press, 1992, p. 122.

Heaney, Seamus, "Crediting Poetry: The Nobel Lecture," in *Opened Ground: Selected Poems 1966–1996*, Farrar, Straus and Giroux, 1998, p. 420.

———, "Nero, Chekhov's Cognac and a Knocker," in *The Government of the Tongue*, Faber, 1988, p. xxii.

———, "Notes," in *Field Work*, The Noonday Press, 1991, p. 65.

———, "The Singer's House," in *Field Work*, The Noonday Press, 1991, p. 27.

Molino, Michael R., *Questioning Tradition, Language, and Myth: The Poetry of Seamus Heaney*, Catholic University of America Press, 1994, p. 135.

Tobin, Daniel, *Passage to the Center: Imagination and the Sacred in the Poetry of Seamus Heaney*, University Press of Kentucky, 1999, p. 146.

Vendler, Helen, *Seamus Heaney*, Harvard University Press, 2000, pp. 9, 59.

Waterman, Andrew, "The Best Way Out Is Always Through," in *Seamus Heaney: A Collection of Critical Essays*, edited by Elmer Andrews, St. Martin's Press, 1992, p. 23.

## Further Reading

Ardagh, John, *Ireland and the Irish: Portrait of a Changing Society*, Hamish Hamilton, 1994.

> In this accessible book, Ardagh examines how the Irish Republic has undergone a tremendous transformation in the last half of the twentieth century, from a mainly rural society to one that embraces the modern world. Although the writer addresses the conflict in Northern Ireland, he is not limited by it, discussing a wide variety of topics—from life in the slums of Dublin to the massive success of the Irish rock band U2.

Burris, Sydney, *The Poetry of Resistance: Seamus Heaney and the Pastoral Tradition*, Ohio University Press, 1990.

> This critical overview of Heaney's poetry examines the same issue that Heaney explores in much of his poetry—the artist's responsibility of addressing the current problems of society in his or her work.

Conroy, John, *Belfast Diary: War as a Way of Life*, Beacon Press, 1987.

> Conroy, a Chicago journalist, won an award from the Alicia Patterson Foundation in 1979 to live in Belfast, documenting the effect that the violence in Northern Ireland had on residents. The resulting book offers an emotional look at what life was like for residents of Northern Ireland in the 1980s. The 1995 edition has a new afterword by the author.

Holland, Jack, *Hope against History: The Course of Conflict in Northern Ireland*, Henry Holt and Company, 1999.

> Holland gives a clear, concise historical overview of the complex conflict in Northern Ireland, which is often misunderstood. The writer is a native of Belfast who has mixed Catholic and Protestant heritage, giving him a rare perspective from which to view the conflict.

O'Donoghue, Bernard, *Seamus Heaney and the Language of Poetry*, Prentice Hall, 1995.

> O'Donoghue—a poet and critic—offers one of the first book-length, chronological studies of Heaney's exploration of language.

Parker, Michael, *Seamus Heaney: The Making of the Poet*, University of Iowa Press, 1993.

> Parker's detailed biography of Heaney describes the poet's Catholic upbringing in Protestant Northern Ireland and the effects that this life had on Heaney's development as a poet.

Richtarik, Marilynn J., *Acting between the Lines: The Field Day Theatre Company and Irish Cultural Politics, 1980–1984*, Catholic University of America Press, 1994.

> Heaney and singer David Hammond were two of several artists who joined the Field Day Theatre, as a means of transcending the violence in Northern Ireland through their productions. This book offers a thorough study of these individuals, as well as the circumstances that led to the founding of Field Day.

# Wild Swans

## Edna St. Vincent Millay
## 1921

In 1921, two volumes of Edna St. Vincent Millay's poetry were published in New York: *A Few Figs from Thistles* and *Second April*. The latter contains many poems about Millay's romantic disappointments and heartbreaks. These poems are sometimes passionate and sometimes subdued, but they are all intensely personal. Scholars often comment that Millay's poetry is feminine in its focus on emotions, but it also breaks from the feminine tradition in its raw honesty. "Wild Swans," which appears in *Second April*, is a good example of this phenomenon. The speaker expresses traditionally feminine feelings of heartache and despair, but she is less traditional in that she is harsh toward her own heart. Although she focuses on her feelings, she seeks a solution to her emotional upheaval by escaping domesticity.

In only eight lines, Millay describes an episode in which the speaker recalls observing the flight of wild swans and then longs for their return. The subject of birds in poetry about human emotion is a long-standing tradition, but Millay uses it in a unique way. In response to seeing the birds, the speaker essentially makes a choice between her "tiresome" heart and the swans, and she chooses the swans. Millay creates a subtle tension in the structure of the poem, which is both measured and spontaneous.

## Author Biography

Edna St. Vincent Millay was born in Rockland, Maine, on February 22, 1892. When Millay was eight, her parents divorced, and her mother reared her. Mrs. Millay encouraged the girl's independent spirit and interest in writing. As a result, Millay submitted some of her early poems for publication, and the children's magazine *St. Nicholas* published several of them. Millay first attracted widespread attention, however, at the age of nineteen, when her poem "Renascence" was published. In fact, the success of this poem was a major factor in Millay's earning a scholarship to Vassar College in 1914 after completing a semester at Barnard College.

Upon graduating in 1917, Millay went to live in New York's bohemian Greenwich Village. She lived on limited means, working with a theater troupe and writing poetry. In the free-spirited atmosphere of Greenwich Village, Millay was very open about her relationships with several literary men. During the 1920s, Millay was known as much for her hedonistic lifestyle as for her acclaimed poetry. Both reflected the changing attitudes and rebellion of post-World War I young adults. Despite her independent nature and her deepening cynicism about love relationships, Millay married a businessman and widower named Eugen Jan Boissevain on July 18, 1923.

Millay's first volume of poetry, *Renascence, and Other Poems*, was published in 1917 to critical and popular acclaim. Four years later, two more volumes were published: *A Few Figs from Thistles* and *Second April* (in which "Wild Swans" appeared). *Second April* contains many emotional poems about Millay's brief but intense affair with poet Arthur Davison Ficke. These poems convey despair and cynicism. In 1923, she received the prestigious Pulitzer Prize for Poetry for *The Ballad of the Harp-Weaver*. In the late 1920s, her attention turned toward social and political concerns, an interest that shaped her poetry into the early 1940s. Millay died of cardiac arrest on October 19, 1950, in Austerlitz, New York.

Millay's poetry is unique because she introduces nontraditional themes and subjects within traditional verse forms, most notably the sonnet. Scholars note the dichotomy between the unrestricted content and the disciplined forms Millay often chose. In addition to poetry, Millay wrote plays, essays, translations, and short stories. Critics disagree on Millay's significance among American poets. While some maintain that she was a talented lyricist who failed to live up to the promise she showed early in her career, others argue that her wit, lyrical gift, and mastery of the sonnet place her among the great literary figures of the century.

*Edna St. Vincent Millay*

## Poem Text

I looked in my heart while the wild swans went
    over.
And what did I see I had not seen before?
Only a question less or a question more;
Nothing to match the flight of wild birds flying.
Tiresome heart, forever living and dying,     5
House without air, I leave you and lock your door.
Wild swans, come over the town, come over
The town again, trailing your legs and crying!

## Poem Summary

"Wild Swans" is the speaker's recollection of watching swans fly overhead. She begins by explaining that seeing the swans made her look into her heart, apparently expecting to find something new. Instead, she merely saw what she had seen before. Any change in her heart was minimal

("Only a question less or a question more") and did not compare to the awesome spectacle of the swans in flight. She perceives the swans as untamed and free; every mention of them includes the word "wild." The swans embody freedom because they are in flight, literally liberated from the earth. The speaker marvels at their sense of direction and purpose, which stands in marked contrast to the uncertainty of her heart.

Lines five and six are introspective and personal, moving from observing the external world to evaluating the internal world. The speaker addresses her heart, calling it "tiresome" and referring to it as a "house without air." The tone is one of exasperation, and it is clear that the speaker longs to be free of her feelings because she has been through emotional turmoil. She decides to free herself by closing her heart and abandoning her emotions ("I leave you and lock your door").

Once she has detached herself from her emotional upheaval, she needs somewhere to go or someone to follow. At this moment, she recalls the swans and beckons them to come again. She is eager for them to return and repeats her plea: "Wild swans, come over the town, come over / The town again, trailing your legs and crying!" The last image reveals that the speaker identifies with the swans and sees herself in them.

## Themes

### Uncertainty

The speaker responds to the swans largely because they seem to fly with such direction and purpose. This direction contrasts with the speaker's uncertainty and confusion, as evident when she looks into her heart and finds "only a question less or a question more." Her heart has apparently been filled with questions for some time ("And what did I see I had not seen before?"), because she is nonchalant about finding nothing but questions there. She is emotionally uncertain, and she feels lost. In this state, she seeks guidance or reassurance, which is why she reacts to the swans so intensely. She sees in them the confidence and purpose she desires for herself.

That the birds are in flight is very significant to the speaker. She reiterates their action throughout the poem, and in line four, she mentions it twice: "Nothing to match the flight of wild birds flying." The act of flying requires certainty. A bird

## Topics for Further Study

- Compare the style of this poem to Victorian poetry, such as that by Robert Browning, Edward Lear, Matthew Arnold, or Alfred, Lord Tennyson. Consider differences in style, expression of emotion, and tone and write a Victorian version of Millay's poem.

- "Wild Swans" is one of many poems that associate human emotion with birds. Other examples include Gerard Manley Hopkins's "The Windhover," John Keats's "Ode to a Nightingale," Edgar Allan Poe's "The Raven," and William Butler Yeats's "The Wild Swans at Coole." Read at least three other poems about birds and write an essay explaining why poets often use bird imagery to explore or describe human emotion.

- Read Millay's "Renascence" or "The Ballad of the Harp-Weaver," which are considered her crowning achievements in poetry. Write a review of the poem expressing your opinion of it and using as many specific references to the poem as appropriate. Take a stand on whether you think, based on the poem, that Millay should be considered a major or a minor poet.

- Swans are considered among the most beautiful and graceful of all birds. Artists are often inspired to portray them. Find examples of swans in art and prepare a short presentation that discusses how swans are perceived by artists. Conclude your presentation with the example that best complements Millay's poem.

- Swans symbolize different things in different cultures and religions. Do research to learn about the significance of swans in Christianity, Hinduism, ancient Celtic religion, and others. Then, write a short poem about swans drawing on the tradition that you find most appealing.

cannot indulge in uncertainty while in flight because it requires constant effort. All the movements must be perfectly coordinated and directed toward an unwavering purpose. The speaker, however, is standing motionless and looking up at the sky. Standing in one place, she has the potential to go in any direction, but she does not know where to go until the end of the poem, when she calls for the swans to return.

### Emotional Exhaustion

The speaker's emotional exhaustion shapes her state of mind in the poem. She has been struggling with her emotions and wants peace so much that when she sees swans in flight, her impulse is to look into her heart. She seems to expect a vision or experience to bring about a change in her that will lead to emotional relief. Upon seeing the swans, however, she finds little change in her heart. It still offers only questions instead of insight or inspiration. She writes that when she looked into her heart, she found, "only a question less or a question more; / Nothing to match the flight of wild birds flying."

Finding no real change in her heart, she rebukes it. She writes, "Tiresome heart, forever living and dying," suggesting that the speaker is at the mercy of her emotions. Her constantly changing emotional state makes her tired and weary. In fact, having her emotions out of control is stifling, and she calls her heart a "House without air." Her exhaustion finally reaches the point at which she detaches herself from her emotions, imagining that her heart is an actual house that she can leave and lock behind her. She makes a decisive move to abandon her emotions and lock them away forever. The final line, however, in which she describes the swans as trailing their legs and crying, demonstrates that she cannot truly be free of her feelings. She sees her trials in the swans who previously represented carefree freedom.

### Freedom

The swans represent freedom and liberation. The speaker longs to be carefree and self-directed rather than steered by her emotions. The swans are in flight; they have physically removed themselves from the earth. Symbolically, they are above the cares of the world in their absolute freedom. They can flap their wings and change their surroundings. Because they are animals, they are not subject to the complex and vexing emotional difficulties endured by the speaker. Not only are they animals, but they are wild animals. The swans are untamed and untouched by the concerns of human life. They are physically and emotionally free, making them enviable to the speaker. She finds their freedom so magnificent that nothing, including her deepest pain, compares. She comments that the questions in her heart are "Nothing to match the flight of wild birds flying."

## Style

### Literary Devices

Although "Wild Swans" is only eight lines, Millay introduces a number of literary devices to add depth to the poem. The swans are symbolic of freedom and certainty; that the speaker describes them as wild emphasizes their totally unfettered existence and their instinctual sense of purpose. Millay employs synecdoche (using a part to represent the whole) by referring to the heart. The heart represents the speaker's entire emotional reality, including feelings past and present. Millay uses personification when she describes the heart as "tiresome." This implies that the heart is a separate entity that exhausts the powerless speaker. Millay also introduces a metaphor of a house to describe the heart. Line six reads, "House without air, I leave you and lock your door." The speaker regards her heart as a stifling house that lacks life-giving air. The metaphor extends as the speaker states that she is leaving the house and locking its door. In the final line, Millay employs anthropomorphism (assigning human characteristics or feelings to non-human beings) as she suggests that the swans are crying.

### Rhyme Scheme and Meter

Millay creates a subtle tension in the poem's structure. The rhyme scheme, for example (*abbc-cbac*), does not have a predictable pattern. The first five lines seem to follow a pattern, but the last three lines seem random. Examining the content of those three lines, however, reveals Millay's purpose. In the last three lines, the speaker undergoes a change as she decides to cut herself off from her emotions and seek the liberation enjoyed by the swans. The disrupted rhyme scheme reflects this change.

A similar approach is evident with the meter in the poem. Each of the first two lines has a single iambic foot (one unstressed syllable, one stressed) followed by three anapestic feet (two unstressed syllables, one stressed). The first line has a hanging unstressed syllable at the end, but this is a common poetic feature. Beginning with line three, however, there is no apparent rhythm for the rest of the poem. The rhythm becomes more like that of natural speech. The content of the third line describes the

# Compare & Contrast

- **1921:** In late January or early February, T. S. Eliot begins work on his opus "The Waste Land." Eliot works on the poem throughout the year and sees it published in 1922.

  **Today:** "The Waste Land" is among Eliot's crowning achievements and one of the greatest literary works to come out of the 1920s. Students of American literature study this poem as a matter of course in their high school, undergraduate, and graduate studies.

- **1921:** President Warren G. Harding is inaugurated after winning the first election in which women had the right to vote. The Nineteenth Amendment, granting women over the age of twenty-one the right to vote, was ratified in August, 1920. This enabled millions of women to cast their ballots for the first time in American history.

  **Today:** Voter turnout among women is low. Although more women vote than men (by a narrow margin), the percentage of voting-age women who vote in presidential elections hovers around 50 percent.

- **1921:** World War I has been over for three years, and America is in a period of high spirits, confidence, patriotism, and growth. Many people are optimistic that the end of this war marks the end of large-scale wars forever.

  **Today:** Having emerged victorious in World War II and smaller-scale wars such as the Persian Gulf War, Americans continue to feel confident in their nation's position as a world leader. American patriotism returns in earnest when terrorists crash planes into New York City's World Trade Center and into the Pentagon on September 11, 2001. In the wake of these events and President George W. Bush's "war on terrorism," Americans feel a renewed bond with one another.

---

speaker looking into her heart, which contains only uncertainty and turmoil. Logically, this is where measured rhythm would stop, and Millay conveys this by eliminating metrical consistency.

## Historical Context

### The Roaring Twenties

Victory in World War I and the economic boom that followed it brought about a period of carefree living and a sense of well-being in the United States. America underwent a cultural transformation, having solidly established itself as a major military and economic leader in the world. Advances in technology affected almost every aspect of society, from science to the family kitchen. The construction industry was busy with high demand for residential and commercial buildings, which included hotels, banks, and chain stores. Mass-produced items and improved household appliances made everyday life easier, and increased production of airplanes and automobiles added a decidedly modern aspect to American life.

Expanding industry offered increased work opportunities in cities. As a result, city populations soon surpassed rural populations. While this was good for businesses, it created new social challenges. Population density and diversity brought about conflicts over issues such as religion, prohibition of liquor, race relations, and immigration. Many of these contentious issues carried over into the depressed years of the 1930s.

Although the Eighteenth Amendment to the U.S. Constitution forbade the making, sale, and distribution of liquor, Americans who wanted liquor were able to find it. Organized crime groups ran clubs where people could buy drinks, dance, and listen to music. "Bootleggers" sold liquor to individuals who wanted to drink in their homes or at parties.

Women became more independent in the 1920s. Flappers were women who rejected convention, wore form-fitting dresses, and attended parties where they could drink and smoke. Women in the 1920s began to seek recognition of their abilities and were less likely to shy away from competition with men. As early as 1920, 25 percent of women were working outside the home. In the same year, women won the right to vote when the Nineteenth Amendment to the Constitution was ratified in time for the presidential election that year.

## Naturalistic and Symbolistic Period in American Literature

The naturalistic and symbolistic periods are often combined in discussions of American literary periods, but "Wild Swans" fits better with the symbolistic period. The symbolistic period began after World War I as writers' greater awareness of international events influenced their writing. For most writers during this period, this awareness led to an appreciation of European—particularly French—literature. Typical symbolistic writers became cynical of American idealism, and the Lost Generation of writers reacted by temporarily moving to Europe, satirizing American culture, or harking back to what they considered a better time in America's history. Those who moved to Europe became collectively known as the expatriates, and they included Ernest Hemingway, F. Scott Fitzgerald, e. e. cummings, and Sherwood Anderson.

The satirists were concentrated in New Haven, Connecticut; Cambridge, Massachusetts; and Greenwich Village in New York City. Although Millay lived in Greenwich Village and knew the work and attitudes of these writers, she was not a satirist. Millay did, however, have fundamental ideas in common with the symbolistic writers. She also sought a new social order and new forms of expression. She was independent and did as she pleased, with little regard for what was traditionally feminine. In her poetry, she disregarded the idea that writing in a new, contemporary style meant leaving everything traditional behind. Instead, Millay forged a new style by introducing new subjects in traditional poetic forms. Critics are particularly impressed with her work in developing the sonnet.

Millay's work also shares some of the naturalistic characteristics. The naturalists believed that biological and environmental forces shape human behavior. They looked to a character's experiences and innate drives to determine what he or she would do in a given situation. In "Wild Swans," the speaker reacts emotionally to a natural occurrence. Her experiences are painful, so she reacts accordingly. Her inborn drive is to escape pain, so she responds to the sight of the swans by longing to join them. It is not an intellectual response or a societal response; it is a personal response that comes from her experience.

## Critical Overview

Critics have repeatedly commented on Millay's multifaceted personality as it shaped her poetry. Reviewers regard her as a complex woman whose career blossomed in a unique time for American women. Paula L. Hart of *Dictionary of Literary Biography, Volume 45: American Poets, 1880–1945*, for example, observes that Millay should be "recognized for breaking through the boundaries of conventional subject matter for women writers, while showing the range and the depth of the feminine character." Millay's personal life was part of her mystique as a writer, and her readers and fellow writers were intrigued. Mary M. Colum in the *New Republic* comments on Millay's role as a high-profile nonconformist:

> Her reputation for unconventionality caused her to be discussed by people for whom her poetic expression was not of first interest. It also caused W. B. Yeats, who was not overly impressed by her poetry, and Thomas Hardy, who was, to be excitedly interested in her personality. When Edna Millay first began to be noticed, American women still could not smoke in restaurants or swim in such garb as the European *maillot* ... [Millay] seemed to be the standard-bearer for the breakdown of futile conventions and of taboos.

Although critics do not always agree on Millay's status among the great American poets, they agree that she was a poet of great vision and ability. Famed poet and critic John Crowe Ransom expresses his mixed reaction to Millay's poetry in the *Southern Review*:

> Miss Millay is an artist of considerable accomplishments. She is the best of the poets who are 'popular' and loved by Circles, Leagues, Lyceums, and Round Tables.... She can nearly always be cited for the virtues of clarity, firmness of outline, consistency of tone within the unit poem, and melodiousness. Her career has been one of dignity and poetic sincerity. She is an artist.... [Her weakness] is her lack of intellectual interest.... The formal, reflective, or 'literary' poems fall for the most part outside [the field of Millay's talent]. She is not a good conventional or formalist poet, and I think I have already suggested

*Swans flying overhead*

why: because she allows the forms to bother her and to push her into absurdities.

Other contemporaries, however, expected Millay to remain an important poet in American literature. Harriet Monroe of *Poetry* comments in a 1924 review:

> Wilful, moody, whimsical, loving, and forgetting, a creature of quick and keen emotions, she has followed her own way and sung her own songs. Taken as a whole, her poems present an utterly feminine personality of singular charm and power; and the best of them, a group of lyrics ineffably lovely, will probably be cherished as the richest, most precious gift of song which any woman since [the ancient Greek poet] Sappho has offered to the world.

In a 1925 essay, Sister Mary Madeleva remarks:

> Today Miss Millay looks important poetically. It may be that we are too near to her.... These things can be said for her: ... she has withstood unguessed temptations to be clever rather than true, and she has reached in a decade a poetic stature half a head above a goodly number of contemporary poets. Her weakness lies in her strength—she is versatile. She adapts herself too easily to the forms and moods of the day. She can be mystical, epigrammatic, flippant, serious, dramatic. She can be neat and sweet and beautiful, and she usually is.

While there is little specific critical commentary on "Wild Swans," critics praise the volume in which it appeared, *Second April*. Most critics characterize the volume as an improvement over her previous work. They find that it shows the poet maturing as a woman and an artist. Hart, for example, writes, "*Second April* showed a more honest approach to the already favorite Millay themes of death, love, and nature." Later in her essay, Hart adds, "Even in the familiar themes, there is a pervading sense of disenchantment in the volume." Although Hart recognizes growing cynicism in *Second April*, Louis Untermeyer of *American Poetry Since 1900* sees elation expressed in a more subdued tone than in Millay's previous work. He explains that

> [*Second April*] recaptures the earlier, concentrated ecstasy. There is little rhetoric here, no mere imitation of prettiness; the too-easy charm to which Miss Millay occasionally descends is replaced by a dignity, almost an austerity of emotion.... Hers is a voice that is both intellectually thrilling and emotionally moving.

## Criticism

### Jennifer Bussey

*Bussey holds a master's degree in interdisciplinary studies and a bachelor's degree in English* literature. She is an independent writer specializing in literature. In the following essay, Bussey evaluates the ways in which the speaker in Millay's poem projects her feelings and desires onto the swans.

In Millay's "Wild Swans," the speaker recalls being captivated by wild swans flying overhead. She admires them for their beauty, freedom, and sense of purpose, but the reason she has such an intense response to them is that she sees herself in them. Throughout most of the poem, she sees what she wants for herself in the swans, but at the end, she sees herself as she is in them. She projects both her ideal self and her actual self onto the wild birds. Because she sees her ideal self realized in the swans, the speaker finds hope in them. Having failed to find hope anywhere else, the speaker understandably responds intensely to this experience.

The speaker's self-absorption is apparent when, upon seeing swans flying across the sky, her immediate impulse is to look deep within herself. She seems to look into her heart hoping to find that some change or resolution has occurred, but she is disappointed that very little has changed. She seems to expect that swans that happen to fly across the sky will automatically affect her internal self. This is an unusual response to the beauty of nature. Most people observing birds in flight pause to appreciate the birds. Poets have long written about birds, and they usually write about the birds' ability to conquer gravity in flight, produce haunting or uplifting melodies, prey on other animals, or convey emotion. Very often, poets introduce birds as symbols of broad themes such as loneliness, determination, wisdom, or nurturing.

In "Wild Swans," however, the speaker sees swans in flight and is immediately moved to look at herself rather than at the birds. The reader knows that the speaker's response is immediate because the swans are still flying overhead when she looks into her heart, as she relates in the first line: "I looked in my heart while the wild swans went over." This response to the swans lets the reader know from the start that although the poem's title references the swans, and they captivate the speaker, the poem is actually about the speaker.

Millay sets up a contrast between the action of the swans and the inaction of the speaker. This contrast is important to the poem because the poem emphasizes the movement of flying. The inspiration for the opening moment of the poem is the swans' flight; the speaker comments that the uncertainty in her heart is nothing like the swans'

> *The self-absorption evident in the first line reappears at the end of the poem. To the speaker, the swans are admirable for what they offer her personally."*

flight. At the end, she pleads with the swans to fly over again. The speaker's fixation on flying turns the reader's focus to the image of the birds in flight. The speaker concentrates on this action because it is what she longs for in her own emotional life. She projects onto the swans, flying gracefully and with purpose, her desire to be free and moving forward. In fact, the speaker is so effective at showing the reader the excitement of the swans in flight that the speaker almost forgets to glance downward and see that she herself is motionless. She is the opposite of the swans because she is anchored to the earth, paralyzed by her emotions, and standing still. She is not moving toward or away from anything and feels so incapable of making a decision that she continues to stand in one place, beckoning the swans to come back to her. The only actions taken by the speaker are internal or passive ones: she looks into her heart, she abandons her tumultuous emotions, and she asks the swans to return.

The last two lines are significant because they indicate that she is prepared to take real action despite the pain and difficulty of doing so. The way Millay conveys this, however, is very subtle. The speaker exclaims, "Wild swans, come over the town, come over / The town again, trailing your legs and crying!" Prior to these lines, the speaker does not perceive the swans as having feelings, but now that she has turned away from her own feelings, she sees the swans crying. Rather than hold onto her hurt, she has cast it onto the swans. This suggests the speaker's willingness to take action because the swans embody action, and she now relates to them on a personal, emotional level. She can now join them because they are like her, and they share her pain. That their legs are trailing indicates the uselessness of their legs to them, just as her own legs seem useless to her. Her inaction in

## What Do I Read Next?

- Elizabeth Dodd's *The Veiled Mirror and the Woman Poet: H. D., Louise Bogan, Elizabeth Bishop, and Louise Gluck* (1992) explores the lives of four twentieth-century female poets. Dodd shows how each woman navigated her male-dominated environment to find her unique voice as a poet.

- Few novels capture the uninhibited consumption of the 1920s as well as F. Scott Fitzgerald's classic *The Great Gatsby* (1925). In a love story about Jay Gatsby and Daisy Buchanan, Fitzgerald depicts the high-spirited parties and materialism of the decade.

- Edited by Millay biographer Nancy Milford and published by Modern Library, *The Selected Poetry of Edna St. Vincent Millay (Modern Library)* (2001) includes the poet's early works, her most renowned poems, and many of her sonnets. The introduction provides a biographical context for the reader.

- Edited by June Skinner Sawyers, *The Greenwich Village Reader: Fiction, Poetry, and Reminiscences, 1872–2002* (2001) is a compilation of the work of some of the major writers who lived in and around Greenwich Village. Some of the selections are written about, as well as by, Greenwich Village literary figures.

---

the poem demonstrates that her legs are also trailing. If she can only take flight with the swans, her motionless legs will no longer matter.

The speaker also projects her uncontrolled emotions onto the swans by consistently calling them "wild." Every mention of the swans includes this word, so the swans' wildness is clearly important to the speaker. A typical reader would likely assume that swans are wild, yet the speaker makes a point of emphasizing this. The speaker's emotional state is characterized by uncertainty ("Only a question less or a question more") and turmoil ("Tiresome heart, forever living and dying"). She focuses completely on her emotions, and they are chaotic. Her heart is as untamed as any wild animal; her emotions are not controlled or disciplined by anyone else, just as wild animals are not domesticated nor under the control of an owner. She takes this painful and exasperating turmoil and projects it onto the swans.

The final characteristic the speaker projects onto the swans is the need for purpose and direction. Lines three and four show the contrast between the speaker's uncertainty and confusion and the swans' certainty and resolve. Line three reveals what the speaker finds in her heart, which is what she always finds: "Only a question less or a question more." Line four celebrates the swans' steady movement in a fixed direction: "Nothing to match the flight of wild birds flying." Twice she refers to flight, which to her represents movement with a purpose. The sharp distinction between herself and the swans is evident by her use of the word "nothing," which places a significant gap between the state of her heart and the state of the "wild birds flying." Her complete lack of direction brings her to the conclusion that any plan at all is suitable for her. When she beckons the swans back, she wants to join them in their flight and their purpose. Although she lacks a plan, she projects the necessity of a plan on the swans. As a result, she assumes that their direction is *her* direction. Wherever they are going and whatever they are going to do when they get there is right for her. Whether out of despair or laziness, the speaker latches on to the first creatures she sees that seem to be going somewhere and longs to join their quest. The self-absorption evident in the first line reappears at the end of the poem. To the speaker, the swans are admirable for what they offer her personally. She sees in them a possible solution to her problems, so she determines that she should join them. There is no mention of what she has to offer them or give back to them, and there is no indication that she will eventually decide to stand on her own.

From start to finish, the speaker reveals herself as being wholly absorbed in her problems: her inability to take action, her emotional chaos, and her lack of direction. Each of these is contrasted to the nature of the swans flying overhead. They represent her current predicament and her deepest desires. Because she has the ability to see her hopes realized in them, and because she longs to see them again, the speaker has the potential to resolve her problems. While she initially looked into her heart and saw no change, by the end of the poem, there has been a major change in her heart. She has opened herself up to hope and action. Rather than wait for peace to find her, she is ready to draw it to her. Still, the last word of the poem is "crying,' and it is in reference to the swans, her harbingers of optimism. This use of anthropomorphism in the last line indicates that ultimately, the speaker cannot run away and escape her feelings. She will have to resolve them before she can truly engage in the world, whether it is the swans' world or her own. While she perceives the world of the swans as one that is liberating, carefree, and light, she realizes at a deeper level that her own world can also be this way.

**Source:** Jennifer Bussey, Critical Essay on "Wild Swans," in *Poetry for Students*, The Gale Group, 2003.

## Carey Wallace

*Wallace is a freelance writer and poet. In this essay, Wallace explores Millays ambivalence about the tension between pure intellect and deep passion.*

The tensions are there for everyone: between mind and body, between reason and desire, between the purity of idealism and the complexities of reality. Humanity has always struggled with the push and pull between the animal and the soul which blend in human nature: ascetics have attempted to escape their flesh, and hedonists have tried to extinguish the intellect—both without much success. For writers, especially, the body-spirit division has been a favorite subject, perhaps because writers especially seem to suffer from it—their imagination and intelligence provide them with vivid intellectual visions, but, perhaps also more than others, they are susceptible to very human passions.

For Millay, one of the best-loved and most famously passionate poets of twentieth- century American letters, the tug of war between her body and her soul, her reason and her passion, was a lifelong obsession.

This obsession was partly because, as a woman who came of age in the early part of the twentieth century, she was a member of a generation in which the roles of women, as both intellectual beings and creatures of passion, were in dramatic flux. As Millay came of age in the 1920s, the women's suffrage movement had just won the right for the feminine half of American society to vote, giving women new power and new investment in public life and implicitly placing them on equal footing with men in the intellectual arena. At the same time, the Bohemian arts community in New York City, which Millay became a part of after her graduation from Vassar, was experimenting with ideals of free love, cutting loose the bonds of marital fidelity in which

> *Millay's judgment against her own heart in the first four lines may not be a simple rejection of intellectualism; it may be a hint at Millay's own limitations, a suggestion that she does not have the same capacity for passion as the swans."*

most women had previously expressed themselves as sexual beings. The ideals of intellectual achievement and the possibilities of unbridled passion lay at women's feet.

As daughters of a generation that had not had their opportunities, Millay and her fellow young countrywomen were uniquely aware that their choices could not be made without danger. In a world in which men still ruled almost every major institution, a woman who chose to achieve in intellectual spheres ran a strong risk of sacrificing a traditional domestic life. On the other hand, forty years before birth control became widely available, indulging in carnal passions posed great risks for liberated women.

For Millay, these very practical concerns were not even the central question. She was more concerned with issues of identity: was she primarily an ideal thinker, following some pure vision, or an earthly creature of passion? Was she a poet, or a lover? Or, as she suspected and dreaded, were the two inseparable sides of the same coin? Millay returned to these questions again and again, sometimes embracing and sometimes rejecting each identity. "Renasance," (1912) the poem with which Millay burst on the literary scene at age nineteen, details an extremely idealistic intellectual vision, in which the young poet's mind expands even to the reach of God's omniscience. In her following collection, *A Few Figs from Thistles*, (1920) Millay seems almost to repudiate "Renasance"'s pure intellectualism, reveling in modern wit, carnal love, and feminine freedom with a group of poems that solidified her literary reputation as a joyful hedonist. With *Second April*, (1921) a new group of poems that appeared a year later, Millay began to investigate the tensions between the two positions she had played with. In "Wild Swans," from *Second April*, she offers a complicated and conflicted meditation on the tug of war between them.

*Second April*, which still ranks among Millay's best-known and perhaps best-executed collections, is also famous for the sonnet series at its close, a series of idealized love poems to fellow poet Arthur Davidson Fricke, with whom Millay had had an affair. The rest of the poems in the collection, although not overtly addressed to Fricke, were written during the same period and were likely influenced by their relationship.

One obvious reading of "Wild Swans" then is through the lens of this relationship and in the context of the poems about Fricke that follow "Wild Swans" in *Second April*. In this reading, "Wild Swans" follows the simple story of a poet's rejection of solitude and intellectualism in favor of shared passion. The poet, alone, describes herself looking around her heart while wild swans fly over her. The poet, it is implied, misses her chance to glimpse the flight of the birds and also finds nothing of value in her search of her heart, only "a question less or a question more." In comparison, the wild swans offer each other, and the poet, companionship. In response, the poet shuts the door on her "tiresome heart," and begs the birds to return to her to give her a second chance to catch the sight of them she has just missed, and perhaps, to join them.

The reading of the swans as symbolic of the choice of shared passion over the solitary intellectual life is reinforced by the language Millay uses to describe her heart and the birds' flight. Millay uses almost no imagery whatsoever in describing her heart. She asks, rhetorically, what she sees there, but leaves the reader blind with the line "only a question less or a question more." The only concrete images of her heart in the entire poem appear after she has rejected it in favor of the swans, when she describes it as a "house without air," to which she "lock"s the "door." The swans, on the other hand, are always described lushly, with flowing lines like "the flight of wild birds flying." Their physicality becomes even more clear in the final line, when the poet begs them to return, "trailing your legs and crying!"

Throughout her life, Millay would use her current personal experiences to lend focus and imagery to her long-term obsessions. Although it is likely that her relationship with Fricke strongly influenced "Wild Swans," there is far more than a personal relationship at stake, beneath the surface of the poem. In fact, "Wild Swans" is a far more complex statement on the strain between Millay's desire for intellectual solitude and her wilder, more "natural" side—and one which, although it seems to contain a decisive moment, actually contains no easy answers.

In a deeper reading, the first four lines remain much the same: the poet, regrettably, misses the flight of the birds due to her introspection, is disappointed by what she finds, and judges it finally inferior to the graceful arc of the swans across the sky. One might assume from the opening that the poet will now make a decision to embrace the wildness and life of the swans instead of the sterile solitude of her heart. Even in anticipating this decision, the intellectual/natural dichotomy is thrown into question. Millay, after all, is not judging her mind inferior to the birds, but her heart. Traditionally, the heart is the location of the passion and freedom Millay sees in the swans. Millay's judgment against her own heart in the first four lines may not be a simple rejection of intellectualism; it may be a hint at Millay's own limitations, a suggestion that she does not have the same capacity for passion as the swans.

In the following lines, any hope of a simple division falls apart. For whatever reason, Millay, disappointed with her heart, accuses it of "forever living and dying." Again, this is not the kind of charge you would expect a poet to level if she were making a simple choice between the intellect and passion. If the swans represent life fully lived, then what crime has Millay's heart committed by "forever living and dying?" Actually, Millay's charge against her heart sounds more like the frustrated cry of an intellect that has become fed up with the vagaries of its emotional side, and would prefer a more reasoned, or stable, existence. If this is the case, then the symbolism of the swans themselves must be re-examined. Rather than freedom in passion and wildness, they may represent for Millay freedom from passion-flying high above daily trials, loves, and slights, unaffected by the "question less" or "question more," immune to "living and dying."

Millay, who had wrestled, and would wrestle, with these questions for the rest of her life, does not decide in "Wild Swans," although it is clear that she would like to. She implies that her heart has become unlivable by calling it a "house without air." She announces that she is leaving it, and for good measure, locking the door behind her. These lines, which seem so decisive, are actually rife with ambiguity. The major question is one of sheer possibility: can anyone, especially a poet, really leave his heart behind? It is not likely. Millay, who was both passionate and extremely bright, undoubtedly wrote these lines with a keen awareness of the futility of her announcement, even as she made it. She might wander the streets for a while, she implies, but she and her heart both know that she will be back later that evening.

In fact, the poem's two final lines, which seem to be an impassioned cry for the swans' return, further undermine Millay's declaration that she would leave her heart behind for them. Even as she repeats her plea for the swans to "come over the town, come over / The town again," she gives the reader the most complete description of the swans yet, adding that they will be "trailing" their "legs" and "crying." Both of these details suggest that the swans may not possess quite everything that Millay has imagined. Their perfect flight, whether it symbolizes purity of passion or of intellect, is marred by the description of their trailing legs, which complicate their silhouette. The trailing legs, which may seem useless in the sky but are absolutely necessary on the ground, remind the reader that it is impossible to leave some things (like the heart) behind and that even though the birds are now in flight, they must eventually land. The swans, as Millay suggests by mentioning their "trailing legs," may not be as free as they seem.

Finally, with the poem's last word, Millay tells the reader that the swans are "crying." In so doing, she strips away any last vestige of hope that the swans are truly living a better life than her own heart, with its incessant "living and dying." The swans, whether they stand for pure passion or lofty intellectual vision, suffer from the same pain and emotion as the poet. There are no simple decisions to be made amidst the age-old tensions. Although she stands outside her "locked" heart, claiming to call for the birds, the poem betrays that Millay recognizes the complexity of her nature.

Lover or visionary, passion or reason, social or solitary—the questions of identity Millay addresses in "Wild Swans" are too deep to be decided in eight short lines. But "Wild Swans," though brief, is a remarkably deep distillation of the tensions between body and soul, between the spiritual and the animal, that mankind has wrestled with throughout history and that would continue to haunt Millay for a lifetime.

**Source:** Carey Wallace, Critical Essay on "Wild Swans," in *Poetry for Students*, The Gale Group, 2003.

## Michelle Prebilic

*Prebilic is an independent author who writes and analyzes children's literature. She holds degrees in psychology and business. In this essay, Prebilic discusses how Millay uses universal emotional associations and symbolism in her poem to share her life's experiences.*

Millay published *Second April*, the strongly melancholic volume containing the poem "Wild Swans," in 1921. This anthology conveys the themes of love, nature, and death with free verse poems and passionate sonnets. Known for its spirited celebration of feminism and free love, this anthology mirrored the developing attitudes of an era of free choice. A number of critics believe that *Second April* captured the mood and atmosphere of Bohemian Greenwich Village in the glitzy post-World War I period. However, the poem "Wild Swans" shies away from the eccentric. Rather, it is a straightforward and intimate poem; an expression of a melancholy affair of the heart. It stays true to Millay's style of revealing a worldwide emotion, such as love, using a universal element and association with wild swans. Therefore, a complete interpretation of this lyrical poem requires a brief insight into Millay's background, as well as an understanding of swans.

Millay, commonly referred to as a feminist and an unconventional writer of her time, developed love relationships with both men and women. These experiences shaped her life and flavored her work. For example, like countless critics, Paula Hart in *Dictionary of Literary Biography* speculates that Millay's three-day love affair in 1918 with married poet Arthur Davison Ficke, "found direct expression in [Millay's] love letters . . . and indirectly in much of her other work." It is after this affair that Millay's collected works appeared in *Second April*. Whether the affair sparked this sorrowful poem, "Wild Swans," critics believe that her love for Ficke, and the subsequent loss, affected her for the rest of her life. Millay wove these intense experiences into her poems in a non-specific and musical way. By transforming her experiences into this style, she shared her wisdom and understanding. Millay's creative expression of these events gives *Second April* its acclaimed qualities.

> "Millay wrote about her life as she lived it and her wisdom as it came to her."

In *Poetry Criticism*, Harriet Monroe affirms it flawlessly when she observes:

> Indeed, though love and death and the swift passing of beauty have haunted this poet as much as others, she is rarely specific and descriptive. Her thought is transformed into imagery, into symbol, and it flashes back at us from the facets of a jewel. And this thing is so simply done.

For example, "Wild Swans" draws on nature to explain a tragedy of love. It flows effortlessly on the page. The swans function as a catalyst for Millay's realization that her heart cries out for something more. The imagery of a swan as a symbol begins in the opening line: "I looked in my heart while the wild swans went over." The swans noisy flight triggers Millay's reflection into herself. As Harriet Monroe observes about Millay's work: "in the lightest of her briefest lyrics there is always more than appears." This something more begins to form in Millay's delicate and well-implemented interplay of nature and emotion.

The depth of her poem is unveiled in the next words: "And what did I see I had not seen before?" Millay informs readers that she has thought about this experience many times. She alludes to an eternal hope that maybe this time she will see something new, something to fix what ails her heart. In reply to herself: "Only a question less or a question more; / Nothing to match the flight of wild birds flying." Immediately, readers understand that Millay continues to struggle with an unpleasant and dreaded reality. This tough reality cannot compare to the beauty of the swans flying overhead.

In considering Millay's piece, the beauty, determination, and stamina of the swan cannot be minimized. Weighing more than thirty pounds, and with wing spans eight feet from tip to tip, scientists consider swans the largest wildfowl. Swans grace this planet with supreme elegance, especially in flight. Anyone who has seen them cannot forget their beauty as they flap their wings furiously and methodically, legs tucked tightly behind them. Whether flying overhead or swimming across a lake, swans appear to be the classiest of the wildfowl. Although time and again romanticized in writing, these birds must work hard to survive.

When birds of this size begin to fly, they flap their wings and scoot along the water until they gain enough momentum to take off. This take-off sounds simple, yet it is not. It requires a long preparation that begins at birth and continues through a swan's lifetime. For instance, when a cygnet, or a baby swan, hatches from its egg, it spends its time eating, training, and exercising. It flaps its wings while bathing and when chasing other cygnets across the water in play. It takes many practice flights across the water, beating its newly feathered wings with all its power. These activities develop its strength and stamina, and train its flight muscles. It must be ready to migrate when the adult swans bob their heads and trumpet.

Millay discloses that she notices her: "tiresome heart, forever living and dying. / House without air, I leave you and lock your door." She has perceived the cycle of living and dying as the heart greets and says goodbye to love. Millay realizes that the events that brought her to this emotional place have not only caused her much heartache, but also have left her tired, depleted, and discouraged. She recognizes that she can choose to leave her situation and prevent herself from returning. From this sad and rejected place, Millay draws readers' awareness back to the swans by declaring: "Wild swans, come over the town, come over / the town again, trailing your legs and crying." Millay reveals her personal tragedy as she ends the poem by asking that the wild swans fly over the town repeatedly, "trailing your legs and crying." Perhaps Millay unveils that she wants the swans to do what she feels like doing—trailing her legs away from her situation that no longer provides nourishment and crying loudly in mourning for the loss of her dreams. Readers can sense the desperation Millay feels as she pleads with the graceful swans to come by again. Perhaps Millay finds comfort in the noise of their journey. She may find beauty and hope in the gracefulness of their wings in flight. Maybe the noise will drown out the tears that Millay will shed.

As Millay leaves her "House without air," she must realize the extensive preparation it will take, similar to the preparation of a swan before migration. Perhaps the preparation comes in the form of mental readiness and self-awareness. Possibly, it is directly correlated to finding a new place and, in time, a new person to love. Whatever it is, Millay must know that it takes a Herculean effort to survive wrenching away from a comfortable situation. However, unlike the swans that act on instinct without contemplation, criticism, or regret, Millay must face this departure with these emotions in tow. That realization makes the journey particularly difficult. Readers can almost feel firsthand the turmoil Millay experienced in wrenching herself away from her "House without air."

Millay chose her symbolism splendidly. Much like the endless tasks that encompass the daily life of a swan, Millay must work hard to understand her situation. She must have the courage to pursue a place with more nourishment. She must know that she can endure her journey, and that when she arrives at her destination, she can expect to find warmth, safety, and love. Her emotional survival depends on it. The cycle of living, learning, and loving for Millay will continue, with destinations shifting much like the cyclical migration of the swans. The swans express their voyage by trumpeting; Millay tells her journey through poetry. The result does not uncover how much preparation and tedium went into its creation and implementation. Observers only see the beauty or hear the call.

Millay wrote about her life as she lived it and her wisdom as it came to her. "Wild Swans" is no exception. Conceivably, Millay used her writing to clarify her life and give it meaning. Perhaps she wrote simply because she felt inspired to do it. Her ability to match wit and wisdom with imagery and symbolism may have been her spiritual gift. Nonetheless, she wrote about her experiences in an easy-to-read and comprehensible way. As Hildegarde Flanner remarks in *After the Genteel Tradition: American Writers since 1910*, "Millay is not to be classed among the 'makers' who have left language altered and disturbed by their experiments, ready for new forms and sensibilities.... She wrote in measures already possessing emotional associations for all readers." Her way of taking nature and applying its elegance to her life makes her poem seem simple and elegant.

Readers can identify with the universal experience of coming into a deeper awareness as a result of seeing a natural occurrence. How many times has one been distraught over a problem or situation, constantly questioning its meaning, only to come to peace with it one day through a simple yet profound revelation that seems to come from nowhere?

Millay's poetic approach remained uncomplicated yet universally meaningful throughout her life. Its straightforward and uncomplicated style defined her poetry and sonnets. As Amy Clampitt writes in *The New Republic*, Millay's style made "no real demand on her readers: an obscure word now and then, an occasional classical reference ... so one hardly feels obliged to look them up." Although poems from other authors may require attentiveness and speculation to fully understand their greatness, readers can readily grasp the experiences that Millay offers. This simplicity may be what inspires Millay's readers the most.

**Source:** Michelle Prebilic, Critical Essay on "Wild Swans," in *Poetry for Students*, The Gale Group, 2003.

## Sources

Clampitt, Amy, "Edna St. Vincent Millay, Selected Poems: The Centenary Edition," in the *New Republic*, Vol. 205, No. 28–29, January 6, 1992, pp. 44–47.

Colum, Mary M., "Edna Millay and Her Time," in the *New Republic*, Vol. 124, No. 11, March 12, 1951, pp. 17–18.

Flanner, Hildegarde, "Two Poets: Jeffers and Millay," in *After the Genteel Tradition: American Writers since 1910*, edited by Malcolm Cowley, Peter Smith, 1959, pp. 155–67.

Hart, Paula L., "Edna St. Vincent Millay," in *Dictionary of Literary Biography*, Vol. 45: *American Poets, 1880–1945*, edited by Peter Quartermain, Gale Research, 1986, pp. 264–76.

Madeleva, Sister M., "Where Are You Going, My Pretty Maid?" in *Chaucer's Nuns and Other Essays*, 1925, reprint, Kennikat Press, 1965, pp. 143–58.

Millay, Edna St. Vincent, "Wild Swans," in *On Wings of Song: Poems about Birds*, edited by J. D. McClatchy, Alfred A. Knopf, 2000, p. 155.

Monroe, Harriet, "Edna St. Vincent Millay," in *Poetry*, Vol. XXIV, No. 5, August 1924, pp. 260–67.

Ransom, John Crowe, "The Poet as Woman," in *The Southern Review*, Vol. 2, No. 4, Spring 1937, pp. 783–806.

Untermeyer, Louis, "The Lyricists—1," in *American Poetry since 1900*, Henry Holt and Company, 1923, pp. 205–33.

## Further Reading

Freedman, Diane P., *Millay at 100: A Critical Reappraisal*, Ad Feminam: Women and Literature series, Southern Illinois University Press, 1995.

 This collection of twelve essays addresses major themes in Millay's work and attempts to evaluate her stature in American literature. In addition to examining her poetry, critics include commentary on Millay's work in other genres.

Milford, Nancy, *Savage Beauty: The Life of Edna St. Vincent Millay*, Random House, 2001.

> Milford's biography is the first comprehensive telling of Millay's life story. Until this biography, Millay's sister kept letters and journals out of the public eye, but she decided to release them to Milford for her authoritative book.

Thesing, William B., *Critical Essays on Edna St. Vincent Millay*, Critical Essays on American Literature series, Macmillan Library Reference, 1993.

> Thesing's critical volume on Millay's work includes copies of reviews by her contemporaries and evaluations by modern critics. In addition to a thorough introduction, this book contains a fictional interview of Millay by Arthur Davison Ficke, a poet with whom Millay had a brief, intense affair.

Wukovits, John F., *The 1920s*, America's Decades series, Greenhaven Press, 2000.

> Wukovits provides a historical and cultural overview of the 1920s. By using an anthology format, he is able to offer the reader first-hand accounts of many of the decade's events in addition to various viewpoints on the decade as a whole.

# Glossary of Literary Terms

## A

**Abstract:** Used as a noun, the term refers to a short summary or outline of a longer work. As an adjective applied to writing or literary works, abstract refers to words or phrases that name things not knowable through the five senses.

**Accent:** The emphasis or stress placed on a syllable in poetry. Traditional poetry commonly uses patterns of accented and unaccented syllables (known as feet) that create distinct rhythms. Much modern poetry uses less formal arrangements that create a sense of freedom and spontaneity.

**Aestheticism:** A literary and artistic movement of the nineteenth century. Followers of the movement believed that art should not be mixed with social, political, or moral teaching. The statement "art for art's sake" is a good summary of aestheticism. The movement had its roots in France, but it gained widespread importance in England in the last half of the nineteenth century, where it helped change the Victorian practice of including moral lessons in literature.

**Affective Fallacy:** An error in judging the merits or faults of a work of literature. The "error" results from stressing the importance of the work's effect upon the reader—that is, how it makes a reader "feel" emotionally, what it does as a literary work—instead of stressing its inner qualities as a created object, or what it "is."

**Age of Johnson:** The period in English literature between 1750 and 1798, named after the most prominent literary figure of the age, Samuel Johnson. Works written during this time are noted for their emphasis on "sensibility," or emotional quality. These works formed a transition between the rational works of the Age of Reason, or Neoclassical period, and the emphasis on individual feelings and responses of the Romantic period.

**Age of Reason:** See *Neoclassicism*

**Age of Sensibility:** See *Age of Johnson*

**Agrarians:** A group of Southern American writers of the 1930s and 1940s who fostered an economic and cultural program for the South based on agriculture, in opposition to the industrial society of the North. The term can refer to any group that promotes the value of farm life and agricultural society.

**Alexandrine Meter:** See *Meter*

**Allegory:** A narrative technique in which characters representing things or abstract ideas are used to convey a message or teach a lesson. Allegory is typically used to teach moral, ethical, or religious lessons but is sometimes used for satiric or political purposes.

**Alliteration:** A poetic device where the first consonant sounds or any vowel sounds in words or syllables are repeated.

**Allusion:** A reference to a familiar literary or historical person or event, used to make an idea more easily understood.

**Amerind Literature:** The writing and oral traditions of Native Americans. Native American literature was originally passed on by word of mouth, so it consisted largely of stories and events that were easily memorized. Amerind prose is often rhythmic like poetry because it was recited to the beat of a ceremonial drum.

**Analogy:** A comparison of two things made to explain something unfamiliar through its similarities to something familiar, or to prove one point based on the acceptedness of another. Similes and metaphors are types of analogies.

**Anapest:** See *Foot*

**Angry Young Men:** A group of British writers of the 1950s whose work expressed bitterness and disillusionment with society. Common to their work is an antihero who rebels against a corrupt social order and strives for personal integrity.

**Anthropomorphism:** The presentation of animals or objects in human shape or with human characteristics. The term is derived from the Greek word for "human form."

**Antimasque:** See *Masque*

**Antithesis:** The antithesis of something is its direct opposite. In literature, the use of antithesis as a figure of speech results in two statements that show a contrast through the balancing of two opposite ideas. Technically, it is the second portion of the statement that is defined as the "antithesis"; the first portion is the "thesis."

**Apocrypha:** Writings tentatively attributed to an author but not proven or universally accepted to be their works. The term was originally applied to certain books of the Bible that were not considered inspired and so were not included in the "sacred canon."

**Apollonian and Dionysian:** The two impulses believed to guide authors of dramatic tragedy. The Apollonian impulse is named after Apollo, the Greek god of light and beauty and the symbol of intellectual order. The Dionysian impulse is named after Dionysus, the Greek god of wine and the symbol of the unrestrained forces of nature. The Apollonian impulse is to create a rational, harmonious world, while the Dionysian is to express the irrational forces of personality.

**Apostrophe:** A statement, question, or request addressed to an inanimate object or concept or to a nonexistent or absent person.

**Archetype:** The word archetype is commonly used to describe an original pattern or model from which all other things of the same kind are made. This term was introduced to literary criticism from the psychology of Carl Jung. It expresses Jung's theory that behind every person's "unconscious," or repressed memories of the past, lies the "collective unconscious" of the human race: memories of the countless typical experiences of our ancestors. These memories are said to prompt illogical associations that trigger powerful emotions in the reader. Often, the emotional process is primitive, even primordial. Archetypes are the literary images that grow out of the "collective unconscious." They appear in literature as incidents and plots that repeat basic patterns of life. They may also appear as stereotyped characters.

**Argument:** The argument of a work is the author's subject matter or principal idea.

**Art for Art's Sake:** See *Aestheticism*

**Assonance:** The repetition of similar vowel sounds in poetry.

**Audience:** The people for whom a piece of literature is written. Authors usually write with a certain audience in mind, for example, children, members of a religious or ethnic group, or colleagues in a professional field. The term "audience" also applies to the people who gather to see or hear any performance, including plays, poetry readings, speeches, and concerts.

**Automatic Writing:** Writing carried out without a preconceived plan in an effort to capture every random thought. Authors who engage in automatic writing typically do not revise their work, preferring instead to preserve the revealed truth and beauty of spontaneous expression.

***Avant-garde***: A French term meaning "vanguard." It is used in literary criticism to describe new writing that rejects traditional approaches to literature in favor of innovations in style or content.

# B

**Ballad:** A short poem that tells a simple story and has a repeated refrain. Ballads were originally intended to be sung. Early ballads, known as folk ballads, were passed down through generations, so their authors are often unknown. Later ballads composed by known authors are called literary ballads.

**Baroque:** A term used in literary criticism to describe literature that is complex or ornate in style or diction. Baroque works typically express tension, anxiety, and violent emotion. The term "Baroque Age" designates a period in Western European literature beginning in the late sixteenth century and ending about one hundred years later.

Works of this period often mirror the qualities of works more generally associated with the label "baroque" and sometimes feature elaborate conceits.

**Baroque Age:** See *Baroque*

**Baroque Period:** See *Baroque*

**Beat Generation:** See *Beat Movement*

**Beat Movement:** A period featuring a group of American poets and novelists of the 1950s and 1960s—including Jack Kerouac, Allen Ginsberg, Gregory Corso, William S. Burroughs, and Lawrence Ferlinghetti—who rejected established social and literary values. Using such techniques as stream-of-consciousness writing and jazz-influenced free verse and focusing on unusual or abnormal states of mind—generated by religious ecstasy or the use of drugs—the Beat writers aimed to create works that were unconventional in both form and subject matter.

**Beat Poets:** See *Beat Movement*

**Beats, The:** See *Beat Movement*

*Belles-lettres*: A French term meaning "fine letters" or "beautiful writing." It is often used as a synonym for literature, typically referring to imaginative and artistic rather than scientific or expository writing. Current usage sometimes restricts the meaning to light or humorous writing and appreciative essays about literature.

**Black Aesthetic Movement:** A period of artistic and literary development among African Americans in the 1960s and early 1970s. This was the first major African American artistic movement since the Harlem Renaissance and was closely paralleled by the civil rights and black power movements. The black aesthetic writers attempted to produce works of art that would be meaningful to the black masses. Key figures in black aesthetics included one of its founders, poet and playwright Amiri Baraka, formerly known as LeRoi Jones; poet and essayist Haki R. Madhubuti, formerly Don L. Lee; poet and playwright Sonia Sanchez; and dramatist Ed Bullins.

**Black Arts Movement:** See *Black Aesthetic Movement*

**Black Comedy:** See *Black Humor*

**Black Humor:** Writing that places grotesque elements side by side with humorous ones in an attempt to shock the reader, forcing him or her to laugh at the horrifying reality of a disordered world.

**Black Mountain School:** Black Mountain College and three of its instructors—Robert Creeley, Robert Duncan, and Charles Olson—were all influential in projective verse. Today poets working in projective verse are referred to as members of the Black Mountain school.

**Blank Verse:** Loosely, any unrhymed poetry, but more generally, unrhymed iambic pentameter verse (composed of lines of five two-syllable feet with the first syllable accented, the second unaccented). Blank verse has been used by poets since the Renaissance for its flexibility and its graceful, dignified tone.

**Bloomsbury Group:** A group of English writers, artists, and intellectuals who held informal artistic and philosophical discussions in Bloomsbury, a district of London, from around 1907 to the early 1930s. The Bloomsbury Group held no uniform philosophical beliefs but did commonly express an aversion to moral prudery and a desire for greater social tolerance.

*Bon Mot*: A French term meaning "good word." A *bon mot* is a witty remark or clever observation.

**Breath Verse:** See *Projective Verse*

**Burlesque:** Any literary work that uses exaggeration to make its subject appear ridiculous, either by treating a trivial subject with profound seriousness or by treating a dignified subject frivolously. The word "burlesque" may also be used as an adjective, as in "burlesque show," to mean "striptease act."

# C

**Cadence:** The natural rhythm of language caused by the alternation of accented and unaccented syllables. Much modern poetry—notably free verse—deliberately manipulates cadence to create complex rhythmic effects.

**Caesura:** A pause in a line of poetry, usually occurring near the middle. It typically corresponds to a break in the natural rhythm or sense of the line but is sometimes shifted to create special meanings or rhythmic effects.

*Canzone*: A short Italian or Provencal lyric poem, commonly about love and often set to music. The *canzone* has no set form but typically contains five or six stanzas made up of seven to twenty lines of eleven syllables each. A shorter, five- to ten-line "envoy," or concluding stanza, completes the poem.

*Carpe Diem*: A Latin term meaning "seize the day." This is a traditional theme of poetry, especially lyrics. A *carpe diem* poem advises the reader or the person it addresses to live for today and enjoy the pleasures of the moment.

**Catharsis:** The release or purging of unwanted emotions—specifically fear and pity—brought about by exposure to art. The term was first used by the Greek philosopher Aristotle in his *Poetics* to refer to the desired effect of tragedy on spectators.

**Celtic Renaissance:** A period of Irish literary and cultural history at the end of the nineteenth century. Followers of the movement aimed to create a romantic vision of Celtic myth and legend. The most significant works of the Celtic Renaissance typically present a dreamy, unreal world, usually in reaction against the reality of contemporary problems.

**Celtic Twilight:** See *Celtic Renaissance*

**Character:** Broadly speaking, a person in a literary work. The actions of characters are what constitute the plot of a story, novel, or poem. There are numerous types of characters, ranging from simple, stereotypical figures to intricate, multifaceted ones. In the techniques of anthropomorphism and personification, animals—and even places or things—can assume aspects of character. "Characterization" is the process by which an author creates vivid, believable characters in a work of art. This may be done in a variety of ways, including (1) direct description of the character by the narrator; (2) the direct presentation of the speech, thoughts, or actions of the character; and (3) the responses of other characters to the character. The term "character" also refers to a form originated by the ancient Greek writer Theophrastus that later became popular in the seventeenth and eighteenth centuries. It is a short essay or sketch of a person who prominently displays a specific attribute or quality, such as miserliness or ambition.

**Characterization:** See *Character*

**Classical:** In its strictest definition in literary criticism, classicism refers to works of ancient Greek or Roman literature. The term may also be used to describe a literary work of recognized importance (a "classic") from any time period or literature that exhibits the traits of classicism.

**Classicism:** A term used in literary criticism to describe critical doctrines that have their roots in ancient Greek and Roman literature, philosophy, and art. Works associated with classicism typically exhibit restraint on the part of the author, unity of design and purpose, clarity, simplicity, logical organization, and respect for tradition.

**Colloquialism:** A word, phrase, or form of pronunciation that is acceptable in casual conversation but not in formal, written communication. It is considered more acceptable than slang.

**Complaint:** A lyric poem, popular in the Renaissance, in which the speaker expresses sorrow about his or her condition. Typically, the speaker's sadness is caused by an unresponsive lover, but some complaints cite other sources of unhappiness, such as poverty or fate.

**Conceit:** A clever and fanciful metaphor, usually expressed through elaborate and extended comparison, that presents a striking parallel between two seemingly dissimilar things—for example, elaborately comparing a beautiful woman to an object like a garden or the sun. The conceit was a popular device throughout the Elizabethan Age and Baroque Age and was the principal technique of the seventeenth-century English metaphysical poets. This usage of the word conceit is unrelated to the best-known definition of conceit as an arrogant attitude or behavior.

**Concrete:** Concrete is the opposite of abstract, and refers to a thing that actually exists or a description that allows the reader to experience an object or concept with the senses.

**Concrete Poetry:** Poetry in which visual elements play a large part in the poetic effect. Punctuation marks, letters, or words are arranged on a page to form a visual design: a cross, for example, or a bumblebee.

**Confessional Poetry:** A form of poetry in which the poet reveals very personal, intimate, sometimes shocking information about himself or herself.

**Connotation:** The impression that a word gives beyond its defined meaning. Connotations may be universally understood or may be significant only to a certain group.

**Consonance:** Consonance occurs in poetry when words appearing at the ends of two or more verses have similar final consonant sounds but have final vowel sounds that differ, as with "stuff" and "off."

**Convention:** Any widely accepted literary device, style, or form.

*Corrido*: A Mexican ballad.

**Couplet:** Two lines of poetry with the same rhyme and meter, often expressing a complete and self-contained thought.

**Criticism:** The systematic study and evaluation of literary works, usually based on a specific method or set of principles. An important part of literary studies since ancient times, the practice of criticism has given rise to numerous theories, methods, and "schools," sometimes producing conflicting, even contradictory, interpretations of literature in general as well as of individual works. Even such basic issues as what constitutes a poem or a novel have been the subject of much criticism over the centuries.

# D

**Dactyl:** See *Foot*

**Dadaism:** A protest movement in art and literature founded by Tristan Tzara in 1916. Followers of the movement expressed their outrage at the destruction brought about by World War I by revolting against numerous forms of social convention. The Dadaists presented works marked by calculated madness and flamboyant nonsense. They stressed total freedom of expression, commonly through primitive displays of emotion and illogical, often senseless, poetry. The movement ended shortly after the war, when it was replaced by surrealism.

**Decadent:** See *Decadents*

**Decadents:** The followers of a nineteenth-century literary movement that had its beginnings in French aestheticism. Decadent literature displays a fascination with perverse and morbid states; a search for novelty and sensation—the "new thrill"; a preoccupation with mysticism; and a belief in the senselessness of human existence. The movement is closely associated with the doctrine Art for Art's Sake. The term "decadence" is sometimes used to denote a decline in the quality of art or literature following a period of greatness.

**Deconstruction:** A method of literary criticism developed by Jacques Derrida and characterized by multiple conflicting interpretations of a given work. Deconstructionists consider the impact of the language of a work and suggest that the true meaning of the work is not necessarily the meaning that the author intended.

**Deduction:** The process of reaching a conclusion through reasoning from general premises to a specific premise.

**Denotation:** The definition of a word, apart from the impressions or feelings it creates in the reader.

**Diction:** The selection and arrangement of words in a literary work. Either or both may vary depending on the desired effect. There are four general types of diction: "formal," used in scholarly or lofty writing; "informal," used in relaxed but educated conversation; "colloquial," used in everyday speech; and "slang," containing newly coined words and other terms not accepted in formal usage.

**Didactic:** A term used to describe works of literature that aim to teach some moral, religious, political, or practical lesson. Although didactic elements are often found in artistically pleasing works, the term "didactic" usually refers to literature in which the message is more important than the form. The term may also be used to criticize a work that the critic finds "overly didactic," that is, heavy-handed in its delivery of a lesson.

**Dimeter:** See *Meter*

**Dionysian:** See *Apollonian and Dionysian*

*Discordia concours:* A Latin phrase meaning "discord in harmony." The term was coined by the eighteenth-century English writer Samuel Johnson to describe "a combination of dissimilar images or discovery of occult resemblances in things apparently unlike." Johnson created the expression by reversing a phrase by the Latin poet Horace.

**Dissonance:** A combination of harsh or jarring sounds, especially in poetry. Although such combinations may be accidental, poets sometimes intentionally make them to achieve particular effects. Dissonance is also sometimes used to refer to close but not identical rhymes. When this is the case, the word functions as a synonym for consonance.

*Double Entendre:* A corruption of a French phrase meaning "double meaning." The term is used to indicate a word or phrase that is deliberately ambiguous, especially when one of the meanings is risque or improper.

**Draft:** Any preliminary version of a written work. An author may write dozens of drafts which are revised to form the final work, or he or she may write only one, with few or no revisions.

**Dramatic Monologue:** See *Monologue*

**Dramatic Poetry:** Any lyric work that employs elements of drama such as dialogue, conflict, or characterization, but excluding works that are intended for stage presentation.

**Dream Allegory:** See *Dream Vision*

**Dream Vision:** A literary convention, chiefly of the Middle Ages. In a dream vision a story is presented as a literal dream of the narrator. This device was commonly used to teach moral and religious lessons.

# E

**Eclogue:** In classical literature, a poem featuring rural themes and structured as a dialogue among shepherds. Eclogues often took specific poetic forms, such as elegies or love poems. Some were written as the soliloquy of a shepherd. In later centuries, "eclogue" came to refer to any poem that was in the pastoral tradition or that had a dialogue or monologue structure.

**Edwardian:** Describes cultural conventions identified with the period of the reign of Edward VII of England (1901–1910). Writers of the Edwardian Age typically displayed a strong reaction against the propriety and conservatism of the Victorian Age. Their work often exhibits distrust of authority in religion, politics, and art and expresses strong doubts about the soundness of conventional values.

**Edwardian Age:** See *Edwardian*

**Electra Complex:** A daughter's amorous obsession with her father.

**Elegy:** A lyric poem that laments the death of a person or the eventual death of all people. In a conventional elegy, set in a classical world, the poet and subject are spoken of as shepherds. In modern criticism, the word elegy is often used to refer to a poem that is melancholy or mournfully contemplative.

**Elizabethan Age:** A period of great economic growth, religious controversy, and nationalism closely associated with the reign of Elizabeth I of England (1558–1603). The Elizabethan Age is considered a part of the general renaissance—that is, the flowering of arts and literature—that took place in Europe during the fourteenth through sixteenth centuries. The era is considered the golden age of English literature. The most important dramas in English and a great deal of lyric poetry were produced during this period, and modern English criticism began around this time.

**Empathy:** A sense of shared experience, including emotional and physical feelings, with someone or something other than oneself. Empathy is often used to describe the response of a reader to a literary character.

**English Sonnet:** See *Sonnet*

**Enjambment:** The running over of the sense and structure of a line of verse or a couplet into the following verse or couplet.

**Enlightenment, The:** An eighteenth-century philosophical movement. It began in France but had a wide impact throughout Europe and America. Thinkers of the Enlightenment valued reason and believed that both the individual and society could achieve a state of perfection. Corresponding to this essentially humanist vision was a resistance to religious authority.

**Epic:** A long narrative poem about the adventures of a hero of great historic or legendary importance. The setting is vast and the action is often given cosmic significance through the intervention of supernatural forces such as gods, angels, or demons. Epics are typically written in a classical style of grand simplicity with elaborate metaphors and allusions that enhance the symbolic importance of a hero's adventures.

**Epic Simile:** See *Homeric Simile*

**Epigram:** A saying that makes the speaker's point quickly and concisely.

**Epilogue:** A concluding statement or section of a literary work. In dramas, particularly those of the seventeenth and eighteenth centuries, the epilogue is a closing speech, often in verse, delivered by an actor at the end of a play and spoken directly to the audience.

**Epiphany:** A sudden revelation of truth inspired by a seemingly trivial incident.

**Epitaph:** An inscription on a tomb or tombstone, or a verse written on the occasion of a person's death. Epitaphs may be serious or humorous.

**Epithalamion:** A song or poem written to honor and commemorate a marriage ceremony.

**Epithalamium:** See *Epithalamion*

**Epithet:** A word or phrase, often disparaging or abusive, that expresses a character trait of someone or something.

*Erziehungsroman:* See *Bildungsroman*

**Essay:** A prose composition with a focused subject of discussion. The term was coined by Michel de Montaigne to describe his 1580 collection of brief, informal reflections on himself and on various topics relating to human nature. An essay can also be a long, systematic discourse.

**Existentialism:** A predominantly twentieth-century philosophy concerned with the nature and perception of human existence. There are two major strains of existentialist thought: atheistic and Christian. Followers of atheistic existentialism believe that the individual is alone in a godless universe and that the basic human condition is one of suffering and loneliness. Nevertheless, because there are no fixed values, individuals can create their own characters—indeed, they can shape themselves—through the exercise of free will. The atheistic strain culminates in and is popularly associated with the works of Jean-Paul Sartre. The Christian existentialists, on the other hand, believe that only in God may people find freedom from life's anguish. The two strains hold certain beliefs in common: that existence cannot be fully understood or described through empirical effort; that anguish is a universal element of life; that individuals must bear responsibility for their actions; and that there is no common standard of behavior or perception for religious and ethical matters.

**Expatriates:** See *Expatriatism*

**Expatriatism:** The practice of leaving one's country to live for an extended period in another country.

**Exposition:** Writing intended to explain the nature of an idea, thing, or theme. Expository writing is often combined with description, narration, or argument. In dramatic writing, the exposition is the introductory material which presents the characters, setting, and tone of the play.

**Expressionism:** An indistinct literary term, originally used to describe an early twentieth-century school of German painting. The term applies to almost any mode of unconventional, highly subjective writing that distorts reality in some way.

**Extended Monologue:** See *Monologue*

# F

**Feet:** See *Foot*

**Feminine Rhyme:** See *Rhyme*

**Fiction:** Any story that is the product of imagination rather than a documentation of fact. Characters and events in such narratives may be based in real life but their ultimate form and configuration is a creation of the author.

**Figurative Language:** A technique in writing in which the author temporarily interrupts the order, construction, or meaning of the writing for a particular effect. This interruption takes the form of one or more figures of speech such as hyperbole, irony, or simile. Figurative language is the opposite of literal language, in which every word is truthful, accurate, and free of exaggeration or embellishment.

**Figures of Speech:** Writing that differs from customary conventions for construction, meaning, order, or significance for the purpose of a special meaning or effect. There are two major types of figures of speech: rhetorical figures, which do not make changes in the meaning of the words; and tropes, which do.

***Fin de siecle***: A French term meaning "end of the century." The term is used to denote the last decade of the nineteenth century, a transition period when writers and other artists abandoned old conventions and looked for new techniques and objectives.

**First Person:** See *Point of View*

**Folk Ballad:** See *Ballad*

**Folklore:** Traditions and myths preserved in a culture or group of people. Typically, these are passed on by word of mouth in various forms—such as legends, songs, and proverbs—or preserved in customs and ceremonies. This term was first used by W. J. Thoms in 1846.

**Folktale:** A story originating in oral tradition. Folktales fall into a variety of categories, including legends, ghost stories, fairy tales, fables, and anecdotes based on historical figures and events.

**Foot:** The smallest unit of rhythm in a line of poetry. In English-language poetry, a foot is typically one accented syllable combined with one or two unaccented syllables.

**Form:** The pattern or construction of a work which identifies its genre and distinguishes it from other genres.

**Formalism:** In literary criticism, the belief that literature should follow prescribed rules of construction, such as those that govern the sonnet form.

**Fourteener Meter:** See *Meter*

**Free Verse:** Poetry that lacks regular metrical and rhyme patterns but that tries to capture the cadences of everyday speech. The form allows a poet to exploit a variety of rhythmical effects within a single poem.

**Futurism:** A flamboyant literary and artistic movement that developed in France, Italy, and Russia from 1908 through the 1920s. Futurist theater and poetry abandoned traditional literary forms. In their place, followers of the movement attempted to achieve total freedom of expression through bizarre imagery and deformed or newly invented words. The Futurists were self-consciously modern artists who attempted to incorporate the appearances and sounds of modern life into their work.

# G

**Genre:** A category of literary work. In critical theory, genre may refer to both the content of a given work—tragedy, comedy, pastoral—and to its form, such as poetry, novel, or drama.

**Genteel Tradition:** A term coined by critic George Santayana to describe the literary practice of certain late nineteenth-century American writers, especially New Englanders. Followers of the Genteel

Tradition emphasized conventionality in social, religious, moral, and literary standards.

**Georgian Age:** See *Georgian Poets*

**Georgian Period:** See *Georgian Poets*

**Georgian Poets:** A loose grouping of English poets during the years 1912–1922. The Georgians reacted against certain literary schools and practices, especially Victorian wordiness, turn-of-the-century aestheticism, and contemporary urban realism. In their place, the Georgians embraced the nineteenth-century poetic practices of William Wordsworth and the other Lake Poets.

**Georgic:** A poem about farming and the farmer's way of life, named from Virgil's *Georgics*.

**Gilded Age:** A period in American history during the 1870s characterized by political corruption and materialism. A number of important novels of social and political criticism were written during this time.

**Gothic:** See *Gothicism*

**Gothicism:** In literary criticism, works characterized by a taste for the medieval or morbidly attractive. A gothic novel prominently features elements of horror, the supernatural, gloom, and violence: clanking chains, terror, charnel houses, ghosts, medieval castles, and mysteriously slamming doors. The term "gothic novel" is also applied to novels that lack elements of the traditional Gothic setting but that create a similar atmosphere of terror or dread.

**Graveyard School:** A group of eighteenth-century English poets who wrote long, picturesque meditations on death. Their works were designed to cause the reader to ponder immortality.

**Great Chain of Being:** The belief that all things and creatures in nature are organized in a hierarchy from inanimate objects at the bottom to God at the top. This system of belief was popular in the seventeenth and eighteenth centuries.

**Grotesque:** In literary criticism, the subject matter of a work or a style of expression characterized by exaggeration, deformity, freakishness, and disorder. The grotesque often includes an element of comic absurdity.

# H

*Haiku*: The shortest form of Japanese poetry, constructed in three lines of five, seven, and five syllables respectively. The message of a *haiku* poem usually centers on some aspect of spirituality and provokes an emotional response in the reader.

**Half Rhyme:** See *Consonance*

**Harlem Renaissance:** The Harlem Renaissance of the 1920s is generally considered the first significant movement of black writers and artists in the United States. During this period, new and established black writers published more fiction and poetry than ever before, the first influential black literary journals were established, and black authors and artists received their first widespread recognition and serious critical appraisal. Among the major writers associated with this period are Claude McKay, Jean Toomer, Countee Cullen, Langston Hughes, Arna Bontemps, Nella Larsen, and Zora Neale Hurston.

**Hellenism:** Imitation of ancient Greek thought or styles. Also, an approach to life that focuses on the growth and development of the intellect. "Hellenism" is sometimes used to refer to the belief that reason can be applied to examine all human experience.

**Heptameter:** See *Meter*

**Hero/Heroine:** The principal sympathetic character (male or female) in a literary work. Heroes and heroines typically exhibit admirable traits: idealism, courage, and integrity, for example.

**Heroic Couplet:** A rhyming couplet written in iambic pentameter (a verse with five iambic feet).

**Heroic Line:** The meter and length of a line of verse in epic or heroic poetry. This varies by language and time period.

**Heroine:** See *Hero/Heroine*

**Hexameter:** See *Meter*

**Historical Criticism:** The study of a work based on its impact on the world of the time period in which it was written.

*Hokku*: See *Haiku*

**Holocaust:** See *Holocaust Literature*

**Holocaust Literature:** Literature influenced by or written about the Holocaust of World War II. Such literature includes true stories of survival in concentration camps, escape, and life after the war, as well as fictional works and poetry.

**Homeric Simile:** An elaborate, detailed comparison written as a simile many lines in length.

**Horatian Satire:** See *Satire*

**Humanism:** A philosophy that places faith in the dignity of humankind and rejects the medieval perception of the individual as a weak, fallen creature. "Humanists" typically believe in the perfectibility of human nature and view reason and education as the means to that end.

**Humors:** Mentions of the humors refer to the ancient Greek theory that a person's health and personality were determined by the balance of four basic fluids in the body: blood, phlegm, yellow bile, and black bile. A dominance of any fluid would cause extremes in behavior. An excess of blood created a sanguine person who was joyful, aggressive, and passionate; a phlegmatic person was shy, fearful, and sluggish; too much yellow bile led to a choleric temperament characterized by impatience, anger, bitterness, and stubbornness; and excessive black bile created melancholy, a state of laziness, gluttony, and lack of motivation.

**Humours:** See *Humors*

**Hyperbole:** In literary criticism, deliberate exaggeration used to achieve an effect.

# I

**Iamb:** See *Foot*

**Idiom:** A word construction or verbal expression closely associated with a given language.

**Image:** A concrete representation of an object or sensory experience. Typically, such a representation helps evoke the feelings associated with the object or experience itself. Images are either "literal" or "figurative." Literal images are especially concrete and involve little or no extension of the obvious meaning of the words used to express them. Figurative images do not follow the literal meaning of the words exactly. Images in literature are usually visual, but the term "image" can also refer to the representation of any sensory experience.

**Imagery:** The array of images in a literary work. Also, figurative language.

**Imagism:** An English and American poetry movement that flourished between 1908 and 1917. The Imagists used precise, clearly presented images in their works. They also used common, everyday speech and aimed for conciseness, concrete imagery, and the creation of new rhythms.

*In medias res*: A Latin term meaning "in the middle of things." It refers to the technique of beginning a story at its midpoint and then using various flashback devices to reveal previous action.

**Induction:** The process of reaching a conclusion by reasoning from specific premises to form a general premise. Also, an introductory portion of a work of literature, especially a play.

**Intentional Fallacy:** The belief that judgments of a literary work based solely on an author's stated or implied intentions are false and misleading. Critics who believe in the concept of the intentional fallacy typically argue that the work itself is sufficient matter for interpretation, even though they may concede that an author's statement of purpose can be useful.

**Interior Monologue:** A narrative technique in which characters' thoughts are revealed in a way that appears to be uncontrolled by the author. The interior monologue typically aims to reveal the inner self of a character. It portrays emotional experiences as they occur at both a conscious and unconscious level. Images are often used to represent sensations or emotions.

**Internal Rhyme:** Rhyme that occurs within a single line of verse.

**Irish Literary Renaissance:** A late nineteenth- and early twentieth-century movement in Irish literature. Members of the movement aimed to reduce the influence of British culture in Ireland and create an Irish national literature.

**Irony:** In literary criticism, the effect of language in which the intended meaning is the opposite of what is stated.

**Italian Sonnet:** See *Sonnet*

# J

**Jacobean Age:** The period of the reign of James I of England (1603–1625). The early literature of this period reflected the worldview of the Elizabethan Age, but a darker, more cynical attitude steadily grew in the art and literature of the Jacobean Age. This was an important time for English drama and poetry.

**Jargon:** Language that is used or understood only by a select group of people. Jargon may refer to terminology used in a certain profession, such as computer jargon, or it may refer to any nonsensical language that is not understood by most people.

**Journalism:** Writing intended for publication in a newspaper or magazine, or for broadcast on a radio or television program featuring news, sports, entertainment, or other timely material.

# K

**Knickerbocker Group:** A somewhat indistinct group of New York writers of the first half of the nineteenth century. Members of the group were linked only by location and a common theme: New York life.

*Kunstlerroman*: See *Bildungsroman*

## L

*Lais:* See *Lay*

**Lake Poets:** See *Lake School*

**Lake School:** These poets all lived in the Lake District of England at the turn of the nineteenth century. As a group, they followed no single "school" of thought or literary practice, although their works were uniformly disparaged by the *Edinburgh Review.*

**Lay:** A song or simple narrative poem. The form originated in medieval France. Early French *lais* were often based on the Celtic legends and other tales sung by Breton minstrels—thus the name of the "Breton lay." In fourteenth-century England, the term "lay" was used to describe short narratives written in imitation of the Breton lays.

*Leitmotiv:* See *Motif*

**Literal Language:** An author uses literal language when he or she writes without exaggerating or embellishing the subject matter and without any tools of figurative language.

**Literary Ballad:** See *Ballad*

**Literature:** Literature is broadly defined as any written or spoken material, but the term most often refers to creative works.

**Lost Generation:** A term first used by Gertrude Stein to describe the post-World War I generation of American writers: men and women haunted by a sense of betrayal and emptiness brought about by the destructiveness of the war.

**Lyric Poetry:** A poem expressing the subjective feelings and personal emotions of the poet. Such poetry is melodic, since it was originally accompanied by a lyre in recitals. Most Western poetry in the twentieth century may be classified as lyrical.

## M

**Mannerism:** Exaggerated, artificial adherence to a literary manner or style. Also, a popular style of the visual arts of late sixteenth-century Europe that was marked by elongation of the human form and by intentional spatial distortion. Literary works that are self-consciously high-toned and artistic are often said to be "mannered."

**Masculine Rhyme:** See *Rhyme*

**Measure:** The foot, verse, or time sequence used in a literary work, especially a poem. Measure is often used somewhat incorrectly as a synonym for meter.

**Metaphor:** A figure of speech that expresses an idea through the image of another object. Metaphors suggest the essence of the first object by identifying it with certain qualities of the second object.

**Metaphysical Conceit:** See *Conceit*

**Metaphysical Poetry:** The body of poetry produced by a group of seventeenth-century English writers called the "Metaphysical Poets." The group includes John Donne and Andrew Marvell. The Metaphysical Poets made use of everyday speech, intellectual analysis, and unique imagery. They aimed to portray the ordinary conflicts and contradictions of life. Their poems often took the form of an argument, and many of them emphasize physical and religious love as well as the fleeting nature of life. Elaborate conceits are typical in metaphysical poetry.

**Metaphysical Poets:** See *Metaphysical Poetry*

**Meter:** In literary criticism, the repetition of sound patterns that creates a rhythm in poetry. The patterns are based on the number of syllables and the presence and absence of accents. The unit of rhythm in a line is called a foot. Types of meter are classified according to the number of feet in a line. These are the standard English lines: Monometer, one foot; Dimeter, two feet; Trimeter, three feet; Tetrameter, four feet; Pentameter, five feet; Hexameter, six feet (also called the Alexandrine); Heptameter, seven feet (also called the "Fourteener" when the feet are iambic).

**Modernism:** Modern literary practices. Also, the principles of a literary school that lasted from roughly the beginning of the twentieth century until the end of World War II. Modernism is defined by its rejection of the literary conventions of the nineteenth century and by its opposition to conventional morality, taste, traditions, and economic values.

**Monologue:** A composition, written or oral, by a single individual. More specifically, a speech given by a single individual in a drama or other public entertainment. It has no set length, although it is usually several or more lines long.

**Monometer:** See *Meter*

**Mood:** The prevailing emotions of a work or of the author in his or her creation of the work. The mood of a work is not always what might be expected based on its subject matter.

*Motif:* A theme, character type, image, metaphor, or other verbal element that recurs throughout a single work of literature or occurs in a number of different works over a period of time.

**Motiv:** See *Motif*

**Muckrakers:** An early twentieth-century group of American writers. Typically, their works exposed the wrongdoings of big business and government in the United States.

**Muses:** Nine Greek mythological goddesses, the daughters of Zeus and Mnemosyne (Memory). Each muse patronized a specific area of the liberal arts and sciences. Calliope presided over epic poetry, Clio over history, Erato over love poetry, Euterpe over music or lyric poetry, Melpomene over tragedy, Polyhymnia over hymns to the gods, Terpsichore over dance, Thalia over comedy, and Urania over astronomy. Poets and writers traditionally made appeals to the Muses for inspiration in their work.

**Myth:** An anonymous tale emerging from the traditional beliefs of a culture or social unit. Myths use supernatural explanations for natural phenomena. They may also explain cosmic issues like creation and death. Collections of myths, known as mythologies, are common to all cultures and nations, but the best-known myths belong to the Norse, Roman, and Greek mythologies.

# N

**Narration:** The telling of a series of events, real or invented. A narration may be either a simple narrative, in which the events are recounted chronologically, or a narrative with a plot, in which the account is given in a style reflecting the author's artistic concept of the story. Narration is sometimes used as a synonym for "storyline."

**Narrative:** A verse or prose accounting of an event or sequence of events, real or invented. The term is also used as an adjective in the sense "method of narration." For example, in literary criticism, the expression "narrative technique" usually refers to the way the author structures and presents his or her story.

**Narrative Poetry:** A nondramatic poem in which the author tells a story. Such poems may be of any length or level of complexity.

**Narrator:** The teller of a story. The narrator may be the author or a character in the story through whom the author speaks.

**Naturalism:** A literary movement of the late nineteenth and early twentieth centuries. The movement's major theorist, French novelist Emile Zola, envisioned a type of fiction that would examine human life with the objectivity of scientific inquiry. The Naturalists typically viewed human beings as either the products of "biological determinism," ruled by hereditary instincts and engaged in an endless struggle for survival, or as the products of "socioeconomic determinism," ruled by social and economic forces beyond their control. In their works, the Naturalists generally ignored the highest levels of society and focused on degradation: poverty, alcoholism, prostitution, insanity, and disease.

**Negritude:** A literary movement based on the concept of a shared cultural bond on the part of black Africans, wherever they may be in the world. It traces its origins to the former French colonies of Africa and the Caribbean. Negritude poets, novelists, and essayists generally stress four points in their writings: One, black alienation from traditional African culture can lead to feelings of inferiority. Two, European colonialism and Western education should be resisted. Three, black Africans should seek to affirm and define their own identity. Four, African culture can and should be reclaimed. Many Negritude writers also claim that blacks can make unique contributions to the world, based on a heightened appreciation of nature, rhythm, and human emotions—aspects of life they say are not so highly valued in the materialistic and rationalistic West.

**Negro Renaissance:** See *Harlem Renaissance*

**Neoclassical Period:** See *Neoclassicism*

**Neoclassicism:** In literary criticism, this term refers to the revival of the attitudes and styles of expression of classical literature. It is generally used to describe a period in European history beginning in the late seventeenth century and lasting until about 1800. In its purest form, Neoclassicism marked a return to order, proportion, restraint, logic, accuracy, and decorum. In England, where Neoclassicism perhaps was most popular, it reflected the influence of seventeenth-century French writers, especially dramatists. Neoclassical writers typically reacted against the intensity and enthusiasm of the Renaissance period. They wrote works that appealed to the intellect, using elevated language and classical literary forms such as satire and the ode. Neoclassical works were often governed by the classical goal of instruction.

**Neoclassicists:** See *Neoclassicism*

**New Criticism:** A movement in literary criticism, dating from the late 1920s, that stressed close textual analysis in the interpretation of works of literature. The New Critics saw little merit in historical and biographical analysis. Rather, they aimed to examine the text alone, free from the question of how external events—biographical or otherwise—may have helped shape it.

**New Journalism:** A type of writing in which the journalist presents factual information in a form usually used in fiction. New journalism emphasizes description, narration, and character development to bring readers closer to the human element of the story, and is often used in personality profiles and in-depth feature articles. It is not compatible with "straight" or "hard" newswriting, which is generally composed in a brief, fact-based style.

**New Journalists:** See *New Journalism*

**New Negro Movement:** See *Harlem Renaissance*

**Noble Savage:** The idea that primitive man is noble and good but becomes evil and corrupted as he becomes civilized. The concept of the noble savage originated in the Renaissance period but is more closely identified with such later writers as Jean-Jacques Rousseau and Aphra Behn.

# O

**Objective Correlative:** An outward set of objects, a situation, or a chain of events corresponding to an inward experience and evoking this experience in the reader. The term frequently appears in modern criticism in discussions of authors' intended effects on the emotional responses of readers.

**Objectivity:** A quality in writing characterized by the absence of the author's opinion or feeling about the subject matter. Objectivity is an important factor in criticism.

**Occasional Verse:** Poetry written on the occasion of a significant historical or personal event. *Vers de societe* is sometimes called occasional verse although it is of a less serious nature.

**Octave:** A poem or stanza composed of eight lines. The term octave most often represents the first eight lines of a Petrarchan sonnet.

**Ode:** Name given to an extended lyric poem characterized by exalted emotion and dignified style. An ode usually concerns a single, serious theme. Most odes, but not all, are addressed to an object or individual. Odes are distinguished from other lyric poetic forms by their complex rhythmic and stanzaic patterns.

**Oedipus Complex:** A son's amorous obsession with his mother. The phrase is derived from the story of the ancient Theban hero Oedipus, who unknowingly killed his father and married his mother.

**Omniscience:** See *Point of View*

**Onomatopoeia:** The use of words whose sounds express or suggest their meaning. In its simplest sense, onomatopoeia may be represented by words that mimic the sounds they denote such as "hiss" or "meow." At a more subtle level, the pattern and rhythm of sounds and rhymes of a line or poem may be onomatopoeic.

**Oral Tradition:** See *Oral Transmission*

**Oral Transmission:** A process by which songs, ballads, folklore, and other material are transmitted by word of mouth. The tradition of oral transmission predates the written record systems of literate society. Oral transmission preserves material sometimes over generations, although often with variations. Memory plays a large part in the recitation and preservation of orally transmitted material.

*Ottava Rima:* An eight-line stanza of poetry composed in iambic pentameter (a five-foot line in which each foot consists of an unaccented syllable followed by an accented syllable), following the *abababcc* rhyme scheme.

**Oxymoron:** A phrase combining two contradictory terms. Oxymorons may be intentional or unintentional.

# P

**Pantheism:** The idea that all things are both a manifestation or revelation of God and a part of God at the same time. Pantheism was a common attitude in the early societies of Egypt, India, and Greece—the term derives from the Greek *pan* meaning "all" and *theos* meaning "deity." It later became a significant part of the Christian faith.

**Parable:** A story intended to teach a moral lesson or answer an ethical question.

**Paradox:** A statement that appears illogical or contradictory at first, but may actually point to an underlying truth.

**Parallelism:** A method of comparison of two ideas in which each is developed in the same grammatical structure.

**Parnassianism:** A mid nineteenth-century movement in French literature. Followers of the movement stressed adherence to well-defined artistic forms as a reaction against the often chaotic expression of the artist's ego that dominated the work of the Romantics. The Parnassians also rejected the moral, ethical, and social themes exhibited in the works of French Romantics such as Victor Hugo. The aesthetic doctrines of the Parnassians strongly influenced the later symbolist and decadent movements.

**Parody:** In literary criticism, this term refers to an imitation of a serious literary work or the signature style of a particular author in a ridiculous manner. A typical parody adopts the style of the original and applies it to an inappropriate subject for humorous effect. Parody is a form of satire and could be considered the literary equivalent of a caricature or cartoon.

**Pastoral:** A term derived from the Latin word "pastor," meaning shepherd. A pastoral is a literary composition on a rural theme. The conventions of the pastoral were originated by the third-century Greek poet Theocritus, who wrote about the experiences, love affairs, and pastimes of Sicilian shepherds. In a pastoral, characters and language of a courtly nature are often placed in a simple setting. The term pastoral is also used to classify dramas, elegies, and lyrics that exhibit the use of country settings and shepherd characters.

**Pathetic Fallacy:** A term coined by English critic John Ruskin to identify writing that falsely endows nonhuman things with human intentions and feelings, such as "angry clouds" and "sad trees."

**Pen Name:** See *Pseudonym*

**Pentameter:** See *Meter*

***Persona***: A Latin term meaning "mask." *Personae* are the characters in a fictional work of literature. The *persona* generally functions as a mask through which the author tells a story in a voice other than his or her own. A *persona* is usually either a character in a story who acts as a narrator or an "implied author," a voice created by the author to act as the narrator for himself or herself.

***Personae***: See *Persona*

**Personal Point of View:** See *Point of View*

**Personification:** A figure of speech that gives human qualities to abstract ideas, animals, and inanimate objects.

**Petrarchan Sonnet:** See *Sonnet*

**Phenomenology:** A method of literary criticism based on the belief that things have no existence outside of human consciousness or awareness. Proponents of this theory believe that art is a process that takes place in the mind of the observer as he or she contemplates an object rather than a quality of the object itself.

**Plagiarism:** Claiming another person's written material as one's own. Plagiarism can take the form of direct, word-for-word copying or the theft of the substance or idea of the work.

**Platonic Criticism:** A form of criticism that stresses an artistic work's usefulness as an agent of social engineering rather than any quality or value of the work itself.

**Platonism:** The embracing of the doctrines of the philosopher Plato, popular among the poets of the Renaissance and the Romantic period. Platonism is more flexible than Aristotelian Criticism and places more emphasis on the supernatural and unknown aspects of life.

**Plot:** In literary criticism, this term refers to the pattern of events in a narrative or drama. In its simplest sense, the plot guides the author in composing the work and helps the reader follow the work. Typically, plots exhibit causality and unity and have a beginning, a middle, and an end. Sometimes, however, a plot may consist of a series of disconnected events, in which case it is known as an "episodic plot."

**Poem:** In its broadest sense, a composition utilizing rhyme, meter, concrete detail, and expressive language to create a literary experience with emotional and aesthetic appeal.

**Poet:** An author who writes poetry or verse. The term is also used to refer to an artist or writer who has an exceptional gift for expression, imagination, and energy in the making of art in any form.

**Poete maudit:** A term derived from Paul Verlaine's *Les poetes maudits* (*The Accursed Poets*), a collection of essays on the French symbolist writers Stephane Mallarme, Arthur Rimbaud, and Tristan Corbiere. In the sense intended by Verlaine, the poet is "accursed" for choosing to explore extremes of human experience outside of middle-class society.

**Poetic Fallacy:** See *Pathetic Fallacy*

**Poetic Justice:** An outcome in a literary work, not necessarily a poem, in which the good are rewarded and the evil are punished, especially in ways that particularly fit their virtues or crimes.

**Poetic License:** Distortions of fact and literary convention made by a writer—not always a poet—for the sake of the effect gained. Poetic license is closely related to the concept of "artistic freedom."

**Poetics:** This term has two closely related meanings. It denotes (1) an aesthetic theory in literary criticism about the essence of poetry or (2) rules prescribing the proper methods, content, style, or diction of poetry. The term poetics may also refer to theories about literature in general, not just poetry.

**Poetry:** In its broadest sense, writing that aims to present ideas and evoke an emotional experience in the reader through the use of meter, imagery, connotative and concrete words, and a carefully constructed structure based on rhythmic patterns. Poetry typically relies on words and expressions that have several layers of meaning. It also makes use of the effects of regular rhythm on the ear and may make a strong appeal to the senses through the use of imagery.

**Point of View:** The narrative perspective from which a literary work is presented to the reader. There are four traditional points of view. The "third person omniscient" gives the reader a "godlike" perspective, unrestricted by time or place, from which to see actions and look into the minds of characters. This allows the author to comment openly on characters and events in the work. The "third-person" point of view presents the events of the story from outside of any single character's perception, much like the omniscient point of view, but the reader must understand the action as it takes place and without any special insight into characters' minds or motivations. The "first person" or "personal" point of view relates events as they are perceived by a single character. The main character "tells" the story and may offer opinions about the action and characters which differ from those of the author. Much less common than omniscient, third person, and first person is the "second-person" point of view, wherein the author tells the story as if it is happening to the reader.

**Polemic:** A work in which the author takes a stand on a controversial subject, such as abortion or religion. Such works are often extremely argumentative or provocative.

**Pornography:** Writing intended to provoke feelings of lust in the reader. Such works are often condemned by critics and teachers, but those which can be shown to have literary value are viewed less harshly.

**Post-Aesthetic Movement:** An artistic response made by African Americans to the black aesthetic movement of the 1960s and early 1970s. Writers since that time have adopted a somewhat different tone in their work, with less emphasis placed on the disparity between black and white in the United States. In the words of post-aesthetic authors such as Toni Morrison, John Edgar Wideman, and Kristin Hunter, African Americans are portrayed as looking inward for answers to their own questions, rather than always looking to the outside world.

**Postmodernism:** Writing from the 1960s forward characterized by experimentation and continuing to apply some of the fundamentals of modernism, which included existentialism and alienation. Postmodernists have gone a step further in the rejection of tradition begun with the modernists by also rejecting traditional forms, preferring the antinovel over the novel and the antihero over the hero.

**Pre-Raphaelites:** A circle of writers and artists in mid nineteenth-century England. Valuing the pre-Renaissance artistic qualities of religious symbolism, lavish pictorialism, and natural sensuousness, the Pre-Raphaelites cultivated a sense of mystery and melancholy that influenced later writers associated with the Symbolist and Decadent movements.

**Primitivism:** The belief that primitive peoples were nobler and less flawed than civilized peoples because they had not been subjected to the corrupt influence of society.

**Projective Verse:** A form of free verse in which the poet's breathing pattern determines the lines of the poem. Poets who advocate projective verse are against all formal structures in writing, including meter and form.

**Prologue:** An introductory section of a literary work. It often contains information establishing the situation of the characters or presents information about the setting, time period, or action. In drama, the prologue is spoken by a chorus or by one of the principal characters.

**Prose:** A literary medium that attempts to mirror the language of everyday speech. It is distinguished from poetry by its use of unmetered, unrhymed language consisting of logically related sentences. Prose is usually grouped into paragraphs that form a cohesive whole such as an essay or a novel.

*Prosopopoeia*: See *Personification*

**Protagonist:** The central character of a story who serves as a focus for its themes and incidents and as the principal rationale for its development. The protagonist is sometimes referred to in discussions of modern literature as the hero or antihero.

**Proverb:** A brief, sage saying that expresses a truth about life in a striking manner.

**Pseudonym:** A name assumed by a writer, most often intended to prevent his or her identification as the author of a work. Two or more authors may work together under one pseudonym, or an author may use a different name for each genre he or she publishes in. Some publishing companies maintain "house pseudonyms," under which any number of authors may write installations in a series. Some authors also choose a pseudonym over their real names the way an actor may use a stage name.

**Pun:** A play on words that have similar sounds but different meanings.

**Pure Poetry:** poetry written without instructional intent or moral purpose that aims only to please a reader by its imagery or musical flow. The term pure poetry is used as the antonym of the term "didacticism."

# Q

**Quatrain:** A four-line stanza of a poem or an entire poem consisting of four lines.

# R

**Realism:** A nineteenth-century European literary movement that sought to portray familiar characters, situations, and settings in a realistic manner. This was done primarily by using an objective narrative point of view and through the buildup of accurate detail. The standard for success of any realistic work depends on how faithfully it transfers common experience into fictional forms. The realistic method may be altered or extended, as in stream of consciousness writing, to record highly subjective experience.

**Refrain:** A phrase repeated at intervals throughout a poem. A refrain may appear at the end of each stanza or at less regular intervals. It may be altered slightly at each appearance.

**Renaissance:** The period in European history that marked the end of the Middle Ages. It began in Italy in the late fourteenth century. In broad terms, it is usually seen as spanning the fourteenth, fifteenth, and sixteenth centuries, although it did not reach Great Britain, for example, until the 1480s or so. The Renaissance saw an awakening in almost every sphere of human activity, especially science, philosophy, and the arts. The period is best defined by the emergence of a general philosophy that emphasized the importance of the intellect, the individual, and world affairs. It contrasts strongly with the medieval worldview, characterized by the dominant concerns of faith, the social collective, and spiritual salvation.

*Repartee*: Conversation featuring snappy retorts and witticisms.

**Restoration:** See *Restoration Age*

**Restoration Age:** A period in English literature beginning with the crowning of Charles II in 1660 and running to about 1700. The era, which was characterized by a reaction against Puritanism, was the first great age of the comedy of manners. The finest literature of the era is typically witty and urbane, and often lewd.

**Rhetoric:** In literary criticism, this term denotes the art of ethical persuasion. In its strictest sense, rhetoric adheres to various principles developed since classical times for arranging facts and ideas in a clear, persuasive, appealing manner. The term is also used to refer to effective prose in general and theories of or methods for composing effective prose.

**Rhetorical Question:** A question intended to provoke thought, but not an expressed answer, in the reader. It is most commonly used in oratory and other persuasive genres.

**Rhyme:** When used as a noun in literary criticism, this term generally refers to a poem in which words sound identical or very similar and appear in parallel positions in two or more lines. Rhymes are classified into different types according to where they fall in a line or stanza or according to the degree of similarity they exhibit in their spellings and sounds. Some major types of rhyme are "masculine" rhyme, "feminine" rhyme, and "triple" rhyme. In a masculine rhyme, the rhyming sound falls in a single accented syllable, as with "heat" and "eat." Feminine rhyme is a rhyme of two syllables, one stressed and one unstressed, as with "merry" and "tarry." Triple rhyme matches the sound of the accented syllable and the two unaccented syllables that follow: "narrative" and "declarative."

**Rhyme Royal:** A stanza of seven lines composed in iambic pentameter and rhymed *ababbcc*. The name is said to be a tribute to King James I of Scotland, who made much use of the form in his poetry.

**Rhyme Scheme:** See *Rhyme*

**Rhythm:** A regular pattern of sound, time intervals, or events occurring in writing, most often and most discernably in poetry. Regular, reliable rhythm is known to be soothing to humans, while interrupted, unpredictable, or rapidly changing rhythm is disturbing. These effects are known to authors, who use them to produce a desired reaction in the reader.

*Rococo*: A style of European architecture that flourished in the eighteenth century, especially in

France. The most notable features of *rococo* are its extensive use of ornamentation and its themes of lightness, gaiety, and intimacy. In literary criticism, the term is often used disparagingly to refer to a decadent or overly ornamental style.

**Romance:**

**Romantic Age:** See *Romanticism*

**Romanticism:** This term has two widely accepted meanings. In historical criticism, it refers to a European intellectual and artistic movement of the late eighteenth and early nineteenth centuries that sought greater freedom of personal expression than that allowed by the strict rules of literary form and logic of the eighteenth-century Neoclassicists. The Romantics preferred emotional and imaginative expression to rational analysis. They considered the individual to be at the center of all experience and so placed him or her at the center of their art. The Romantics believed that the creative imagination reveals nobler truths—unique feelings and attitudes—than those that could be discovered by logic or by scientific examination. Both the natural world and the state of childhood were important sources for revelations of "eternal truths." "Romanticism" is also used as a general term to refer to a type of sensibility found in all periods of literary history and usually considered to be in opposition to the principles of classicism. In this sense, Romanticism signifies any work or philosophy in which the exotic or dreamlike figure strongly, or that is devoted to individualistic expression, self-analysis, or a pursuit of a higher realm of knowledge than can be discovered by human reason.

**Romantics:** See *Romanticism*

**Russian Symbolism:** A Russian poetic movement, derived from French symbolism, that flourished between 1894 and 1910. While some Russian Symbolists continued in the French tradition, stressing aestheticism and the importance of suggestion above didactic intent, others saw their craft as a form of mystical worship, and themselves as mediators between the supernatural and the mundane.

# S

**Satire:** A work that uses ridicule, humor, and wit to criticize and provoke change in human nature and institutions. There are two major types of satire: "formal" or "direct" satire speaks directly to the reader or to a character in the work; "indirect" satire relies upon the ridiculous behavior of its characters to make its point. Formal satire is further divided into two manners: the "Horatian," which ridicules gently, and the "Juvenalian," which derides its subjects harshly and bitterly.

**Scansion:** The analysis or "scanning" of a poem to determine its meter and often its rhyme scheme. The most common system of scansion uses accents (slanted lines drawn above syllables) to show stressed syllables, breves (curved lines drawn above syllables) to show unstressed syllables, and vertical lines to separate each foot.

**Second Person:** See *Point of View*

**Semiotics:** The study of how literary forms and conventions affect the meaning of language.

**Sestet:** Any six-line poem or stanza.

**Setting:** The time, place, and culture in which the action of a narrative takes place. The elements of setting may include geographic location, characters' physical and mental environments, prevailing cultural attitudes, or the historical time in which the action takes place.

**Shakespearean Sonnet:** See *Sonnet*

**Signifying Monkey:** A popular trickster figure in black folklore, with hundreds of tales about this character documented since the nineteenth century.

**Simile:** A comparison, usually using "like" or "as," of two essentially dissimilar things, as in "coffee as cold as ice" or "He sounded like a broken record."

**Slang:** A type of informal verbal communication that is generally unacceptable for formal writing. Slang words and phrases are often colorful exaggerations used to emphasize the speaker's point; they may also be shortened versions of an often-used word or phrase.

**Slant Rhyme:** See *Consonance*

**Slave Narrative:** Autobiographical accounts of American slave life as told by escaped slaves. These works first appeared during the abolition movement of the 1830s through the 1850s.

**Social Realism:** See *Socialist Realism*

**Socialist Realism:** The Socialist Realism school of literary theory was proposed by Maxim Gorky and established as a dogma by the first Soviet Congress of Writers. It demanded adherence to a communist worldview in works of literature. Its doctrines required an objective viewpoint comprehensible to the working classes and themes of social struggle featuring strong proletarian heroes.

**Soliloquy:** A monologue in a drama used to give the audience information and to develop the speaker's character. It is typically a projection of the speaker's innermost thoughts. Usually delivered while the speaker is alone on stage, a soliloquy is intended to present an illusion of unspoken reflection.

**Sonnet:** A fourteen-line poem, usually composed in iambic pentameter, employing one of several rhyme schemes. There are three major types of sonnets, upon which all other variations of the form are based: the "Petrarchan" or "Italian" sonnet, the "Shakespearean" or "English" sonnet, and the "Spenserian" sonnet. A Petrarchan sonnet consists of an octave rhymed *abbaabba* and a "sestet" rhymed either *cdecde, cdccdc,* or *cdedce.* The octave poses a question or problem, relates a narrative, or puts forth a proposition; the sestet presents a solution to the problem, comments upon the narrative, or applies the proposition put forth in the octave. The Shakespearean sonnet is divided into three quatrains and a couplet rhymed *abab cdcd efef gg.* The couplet provides an epigrammatic comment on the narrative or problem put forth in the quatrains. The Spenserian sonnet uses three quatrains and a couplet like the Shakespearean, but links their three rhyme schemes in this way: *abab bcbc cdcd ee.* The Spenserian sonnet develops its theme in two parts like the Petrarchan, its final six lines resolving a problem, analyzing a narrative, or applying a proposition put forth in its first eight lines.

**Spenserian Sonnet:** See *Sonnet*

**Spenserian Stanza:** A nine-line stanza having eight verses in iambic pentameter, its ninth verse in iambic hexameter, and the rhyme scheme *ababbcbcc.*

**Spondee:** In poetry meter, a foot consisting of two long or stressed syllables occurring together. This form is quite rare in English verse, and is usually composed of two monosyllabic words.

**Sprung Rhythm:** Versification using a specific number of accented syllables per line but disregarding the number of unaccented syllables that fall in each line, producing an irregular rhythm in the poem.

**Stanza:** A subdivision of a poem consisting of lines grouped together, often in recurring patterns of rhyme, line length, and meter. Stanzas may also serve as units of thought in a poem much like paragraphs in prose.

**Stereotype:** A stereotype was originally the name for a duplication made during the printing process; this led to its modern definition as a person or thing that is (or is assumed to be) the same as all others of its type.

**Stream of Consciousness:** A narrative technique for rendering the inward experience of a character. This technique is designed to give the impression of an ever-changing series of thoughts, emotions, images, and memories in the spontaneous and seemingly illogical order that they occur in life.

**Structuralism:** A twentieth-century movement in literary criticism that examines how literary texts arrive at their meanings, rather than the meanings themselves. There are two major types of structuralist analysis: one examines the way patterns of linguistic structures unify a specific text and emphasize certain elements of that text, and the other interprets the way literary forms and conventions affect the meaning of language itself.

**Structure:** The form taken by a piece of literature. The structure may be made obvious for ease of understanding, as in nonfiction works, or may be obscured for artistic purposes, as in some poetry or seemingly "unstructured" prose.

***Sturm und Drang:*** A German term meaning "storm and stress." It refers to a German literary movement of the 1770s and 1780s that reacted against the order and rationalism of the enlightenment, focusing instead on the intense experience of extraordinary individuals.

**Style:** A writer's distinctive manner of arranging words to suit his or her ideas and purpose in writing. The unique imprint of the author's personality upon his or her writing, style is the product of an author's way of arranging ideas and his or her use of diction, different sentence structures, rhythm, figures of speech, rhetorical principles, and other elements of composition.

**Subject:** The person, event, or theme at the center of a work of literature. A work may have one or more subjects of each type, with shorter works tending to have fewer and longer works tending to have more.

**Subjectivity:** Writing that expresses the author's personal feelings about his subject, and which may or may not include factual information about the subject.

**Surrealism:** A term introduced to criticism by Guillaume Apollinaire and later adopted by Andre Breton. It refers to a French literary and artistic movement founded in the 1920s. The Surrealists sought to express unconscious thoughts and feelings in their works. The best-known technique used for achieving this aim was automatic writing transcriptions of spontaneous outpourings from the unconscious. The Surrealists proposed to unify the contrary levels of conscious and unconscious, dream and reality, objectivity and subjectivity into a new level of "super-realism."

**Suspense:** A literary device in which the author maintains the audience's attention through the buildup of events, the outcome of which will soon be revealed.

**Syllogism:** A method of presenting a logical argument. In its most basic form, the syllogism consists of a major premise, a minor premise, and a conclusion.

**Symbol:** Something that suggests or stands for something else without losing its original identity. In literature, symbols combine their literal meaning with the suggestion of an abstract concept. Literary symbols are of two types: those that carry complex associations of meaning no matter what their contexts, and those that derive their suggestive meaning from their functions in specific literary works.

**Symbolism:** This term has two widely accepted meanings. In historical criticism, it denotes an early modernist literary movement initiated in France during the nineteenth century that reacted against the prevailing standards of realism. Writers in this movement aimed to evoke, indirectly and symbolically, an order of being beyond the material world of the five senses. Poetic expression of personal emotion figured strongly in the movement, typically by means of a private set of symbols uniquely identifiable with the individual poet. The principal aim of the Symbolists was to express in words the highly complex feelings that grew out of everyday contact with the world. In a broader sense, the term "symbolism" refers to the use of one object to represent another.

**Symbolist:** See *Symbolism*

**Symbolist Movement:** See *Symbolism*

**Sympathetic Fallacy:** See *Affective Fallacy*

# T

***Tanka***: A form of Japanese poetry similar to *haiku*. A *tanka* is five lines long, with the lines containing five, seven, five, seven, and seven syllables respectively.

***Terza Rima***: A three-line stanza form in poetry in which the rhymes are made on the last word of each line in the following manner: the first and third lines of the first stanza, then the second line of the first stanza and the first and third lines of the second stanza, and so on with the middle line of any stanza rhyming with the first and third lines of the following stanza.

**Tetrameter:** See *Meter*

**Textual Criticism:** A branch of literary criticism that seeks to establish the authoritative text of a literary work. Textual critics typically compare all known manuscripts or printings of a single work in order to assess the meanings of differences and revisions. This procedure allows them to arrive at a definitive version that (supposedly) corresponds to the author's original intention.

**Theme:** The main point of a work of literature. The term is used interchangeably with thesis.

**Thesis:** A thesis is both an essay and the point argued in the essay. Thesis novels and thesis plays share the quality of containing a thesis which is supported through the action of the story.

**Third Person:** See *Point of View*

**Tone:** The author's attitude toward his or her audience may be deduced from the tone of the work. A formal tone may create distance or convey politeness, while an informal tone may encourage a friendly, intimate, or intrusive feeling in the reader. The author's attitude toward his or her subject matter may also be deduced from the tone of the words he or she uses in discussing it.

**Tragedy:** A drama in prose or poetry about a noble, courageous hero of excellent character who, because of some tragic character flaw or *hamartia*, brings ruin upon him- or herself. Tragedy treats its subjects in a dignified and serious manner, using poetic language to help evoke pity and fear and bring about catharsis, a purging of these emotions. The tragic form was practiced extensively by the ancient Greeks. In the Middle Ages, when classical works were virtually unknown, tragedy came to denote any works about the fall of persons from exalted to low conditions due to any reason: fate, vice, weakness, etc. According to the classical definition of tragedy, such works present the "pathetic"—that which evokes pity—rather than the tragic. The classical form of tragedy was revived in the sixteenth century; it flourished especially on the Elizabethan stage. In modern times, dramatists have attempted to adapt the form to the needs of modern society by drawing their heroes from the ranks of ordinary men and women and defining the nobility of these heroes in terms of spirit rather than exalted social standing.

**Tragic Flaw:** In a tragedy, the quality within the hero or heroine which leads to his or her downfall.

**Transcendentalism:** An American philosophical and religious movement, based in New England from around 1835 until the Civil War. Transcendentalism was a form of American romanticism that had its roots abroad in the works of Thomas Carlyle, Samuel Coleridge, and Johann Wolfgang von Goethe. The Transcendentalists stressed the importance of intuition and subjective experience in communication with God. They rejected religious dogma and texts in favor of mysticism and scientific naturalism. They pursued truths that lie beyond the "colorless" realms perceived by reason and the senses and were active social reformers in public education, women's rights, and the abolition of slavery.

**Trickster:** A character or figure common in Native American and African literature who uses his ingenuity to defeat enemies and escape difficult situations. Tricksters are most often animals, such as the spider, hare, or coyote, although they may take the form of humans as well.

**Trimeter:** See *Meter*

**Triple Rhyme:** See *Rhyme*

**Trochee:** See *Foot*

# U

**Understatement:** See *Irony*

**Unities:** Strict rules of dramatic structure, formulated by Italian and French critics of the Renaissance and based loosely on the principles of drama discussed by Aristotle in his *Poetics*. Foremost among these rules were the three unities of action, time, and place that compelled a dramatist to: (1) construct a single plot with a beginning, middle, and end that details the causal relationships of action and character; (2) restrict the action to the events of a single day; and (3) limit the scene to a single place or city. The unities were observed faithfully by continental European writers until the Romantic Age, but they were never regularly observed in English drama. Modern dramatists are typically more concerned with a unity of impression or emotional effect than with any of the classical unities.

**Urban Realism:** A branch of realist writing that attempts to accurately reflect the often harsh facts of modern urban existence.

**Utopia:** A fictional perfect place, such as "paradise" or "heaven."

**Utopian:** See *Utopia*

**Utopianism:** See *Utopia*

# V

**Verisimilitude:** Literally, the appearance of truth. In literary criticism, the term refers to aspects of a work of literature that seem true to the reader.

*Vers de societe*: See *Occasional Verse*

*Vers libre*: See *Free Verse*

**Verse:** A line of metered language, a line of a poem, or any work written in verse.

**Versification:** The writing of verse. Versification may also refer to the meter, rhyme, and other mechanical components of a poem.

**Victorian:** Refers broadly to the reign of Queen Victoria of England (1837–1901) and to anything with qualities typical of that era. For example, the qualities of smug narrowmindedness, bourgeois materialism, faith in social progress, and priggish morality are often considered Victorian. This stereotype is contradicted by such dramatic intellectual developments as the theories of Charles Darwin, Karl Marx, and Sigmund Freud (which stirred strong debates in England) and the critical attitudes of serious Victorian writers like Charles Dickens and George Eliot. In literature, the Victorian Period was the great age of the English novel, and the latter part of the era saw the rise of movements such as decadence and symbolism.

**Victorian Age:** See *Victorian*

**Victorian Period:** See *Victorian*

# W

*Weltanschauung*: A German term referring to a person's worldview or philosophy.

*Weltschmerz*: A German term meaning "world pain." It describes a sense of anguish about the nature of existence, usually associated with a melancholy, pessimistic attitude.

# Z

*Zarzuela*: A type of Spanish operetta.

*Zeitgeist*: A German term meaning "spirit of the time." It refers to the moral and intellectual trends of a given era.

# Cumulative Author/Title Index

## A

Acosta, Teresa Palomo
  *My Mother Pieced Quilts:* V12
*An African Elegy* (Duncan): V13
*Ah, Are You Digging on My Grave?*
    (Hardy): V4
Ai
  *Reunions with a Ghost:* V16
*Alabama Centennial* (Madgett): V10
*American Poetry* (Simpson): V7
*An Arundel Tomb* (Larkin): V12
*Anasazi* (Snyder): V9
Angelou, Maya
  *Harlem Hopscotch:* V2
  *On the Pulse of Morning:* V3
*Angle of Geese* (Momaday): V2
*Annabel Lee* (Poe): V9
*Anniversary* (Harjo): V15
Anonymous
  *Barbara Allan:* V7
  *Go Down, Moses:* V11
  *Lord Randal:* V6
  *The Seafarer:* V8
  *Sir Patrick Spens:* V4
  *Swing Low Sweet Chariot:* V1
*Anorexic* (Boland): V12
*Any Human to Another* (Cullen): V3
*A Pièd* (McElroy): V3
Arnold, Matthew
  *Dover Beach:* V2
*Ars Poetica* (MacLeish): V5
*The Arsenal at Springfield*
    (Longfellow): V17
*As I Walked Out One Evening*
    (Auden): V4
Ashbery, John
  *Paradoxes and Oxymorons:* V11
*Astonishment* (Szymborska): V15
*At the Bomb Testing Site* (Stafford): V8
Atwood, Margaret
  *Siren Song:* V7
Auden, W. H.
  *As I Walked Out One Evening:* V4
  *Funeral Blues:* V10
  *Musée des Beaux Arts:* V1
  *The Unknown Citizen:* V3
*Auto Wreck* (Shapiro): V3
*Autumn Begins in Martins Ferry,*
    *Ohio* (Wright): V8

## B

*Ballad of Orange and Grape*
    (Rukeyser): V10
Baraka, Amiri
  *In Memory of Radio:* V9
*Barbara Allan* (Anonymous): V7
*Barbie Doll* (Piercy): V9
*Ballad of Birmingham* (Randall): V5
Barrett, Elizabeth
  *Sonnet 43:* V2
*The Base Stealer* (Francis): V12
*The Bean Eaters* (Brooks): V2
*Because I Could Not Stop for Death*
    (Dickinson): V2
*Bedtime Story* (MacBeth): V8
*La Belle Dame sans Merci* (Keats):
    V17
*The Bells* (Poe): V3
*Beowulf* (Wilbur): V11
*Beware: Do Not Read This Poem*
    (Reed): V6
*Beware of Ruins* (Hope): V8
*Bidwell Ghost* (Erdrich): V14
*Birch Canoe* (Revard): V5
*Birches* (Frost): V13
Birney, Earle
  *Vancouver Lights:* V8
*A Birthday* (Rossetti): V10
Bishop, Elizabeth
  *Brazil, January 1, 1502:* V6
  *Filling Station:* V12
*Blackberrying* (Plath): V15
*Black Zodiac* (Wright): V10
Blake, William
  *The Lamb:* V12
  *The Tyger:* V2
*A Blessing* (Wright): V7
*Blood Oranges* (Mueller): V13
*The Blue Rim of Memory* (Levertov):
    V17
Blumenthal, Michael
  *Inventors:* V7
Bly, Robert
  *Come with Me:* V6
  *Driving to Town Late to Mail a*
    *Letter:* V17
Boland, Eavan
  *Anorexic:* V12
Bradstreet, Anne
  *To My Dear and Loving*
    *Husband:* V6
*Brazil, January 1, 1502* (Bishop): V6
*Bright Star! Would I Were Steadfast*
    *as Thou Art* (Keats): V9
Brooke, Rupert
  *The Soldier:* V7
Brooks, Gwendolyn
  *The Bean Eaters:* V2
  *The Sonnet-Ballad:* V1
  *Strong Men, Riding Horses:* V4
  *We Real Cool:* V6

Brouwer, Joel
*Last Request*: V14
Browning, Elizabeth Barrett
*Sonnet 43*: V2
*Sonnet XXIX*: V16
Browning, Robert
*My Last Duchess*: V1
*Porphyria's Lover*: V15
Burns, Robert
*A Red, Red Rose*: V8
*Business* (Cruz): V16
*The Bustle in a House* (Dickinson): V10
*Butcher Shop* (Simic): V7
Byron, Lord
*The Destruction of Sennacherib*: V1
*She Walks in Beauty*: V14

# C

*The Canterbury Tales* (Chaucer): V14
*Cargoes* (Masefield): V5
Carroll, Lewis
*Jabberwocky*: V11
Carver, Raymond
*The Cobweb*: V17
*Casey at the Bat* (Thayer): V5
*Cavalry Crossing a Ford* (Whitman): V13
*The Charge of the Light Brigade* (Tennyson): V1
Chaucer, Geoffrey
*The Canterbury Tales*: V14
*Chicago* (Sandburg): V3
*Chocolates* (Simpson): V11
Clifton, Lucille
*Climbing*: V14
*Miss Rosie*: V1
*Climbing* (Clifton): V14
*The Cobweb* (Carver): V17
Coleridge, Samuel Taylor
*Kubla Khan*: V5
*The Rime of the Ancient Mariner*: V4
*Colibrí* (Espada): V16
*Come with Me* (Bly): V6
*The Constellation Orion* (Kooser): V8
*Concord Hymn* (Emerson): V4
*The Conquerors* (McGinley): V13
*Cool Tombs* (Sandburg): V6
*Courage* (Sexton): V14
*The Courage That My Mother Had* (Millay): V3
Crane, Stephen
*War Is Kind*: V9
*The Creation* (Johnson): V1
*The Cremation of Sam McGee* (Service): V10
Cruz, Victor Hernandez
*Business*: V16
Cullen, Countee
*Any Human to Another*: V3
cummings, e. e.
*l(a*: V1
*i was sitting in mcsorley's*: V13
*maggie and milly and molly and may*: V12
*old age sticks*: V3
*The Czar's Last Christmas Letter. A Barn in the Urals* (Dubie): V12

# D

*Darwin in 1881* (Schnackenberg): V13
Dawe, Bruce
*Drifters*: V10
*Daylights* (Warren): V13
*Dear Reader* (Tate): V10
*The Death of the Ball Turret Gunner* (Jarrell): V2
*The Death of the Hired Man* (Frost): V4
*Deep Woods* (Nemerov): V14
*The Destruction of Sennacherib* (Byron): V1
Dickey, James
*The Heaven of Animals*: V6
*The Hospital Window*: V11
Dickinson, Emily
*Because I Could Not Stop for Death*: V2
*The Bustle in a House*: V10
*"Hope" Is the Thing with Feathers*: V3
*I felt a Funeral, in my Brain*: V13
*I Heard a Fly Buzz—When I Died—*: V5
*Much Madness Is Divinest Sense*: V16
*My Life Closed Twice Before Its Close*: V8
*A Narrow Fellow in the Grass*: V11
*The Soul Selects Her Own Society*: V1
*There's a Certain Slant of Light*: V6
*This Is My Letter to the World*: V4
*Digging* (Heaney): V5
*Do Not Go Gentle into that Good Night* (Thomas): V1
Donne, John
*Holy Sonnet 10*: V2
*A Valediction: Forbidding Mourning*: V11
Dove, Rita
*Geometry*: V15
*This Life*: V1
*Dover Beach* (Arnold): V2
*Dream Variations* (Hughes): V15
*Drifters* (Dawe): V10
*A Drink of Water* (Heaney): V8
*Driving to Town Late to Mail a Letter* (Bly): V17
*Drought Year* (Wright): V8
Dubie, Norman
*The Czar's Last Christmas Letter. A Barn in the Urals*: V12
Du Bois, W. E. B.
*The Song of the Smoke*: V13
Duncan, Robert
*An African Elegy*: V13
Dugan, Alan
*How We Heard the Name*: V10
*Dulce et Decorum Est* (Owen): V10

# E

*The Eagle* (Tennyson): V11
*Early in the Morning* (Lee): V17
*Easter 1916* (Yeats): V5
*Eating Poetry* (Strand): V9
*Elegy for My Father, Who is Not Dead* (Hudgins): V14
*Elegy Written in a Country Churchyard* (Gray): V9
Eliot, T. S.
*Journey of the Magi*: V7
*The Love Song of J. Alfred Prufrock*: V1
Emerson, Ralph Waldo
*Concord Hymn*: V4
*The Rhodora*: V17
Erdrich, Louise
*Bidwell Ghost*: V14
Espada, Martín
*Colibrí*: V16
*We Live by What We See at Night*: V13
*Ethics* (Pastan): V8
*The Exhibit* (Mueller): V9

# F

*Facing It* (Komunyakaa): V5
*Falling Upon Earth* (Bashō): V2
*A Far Cry from Africa* (Walcott): V6
*A Farewell to English* (Hartnett): V10
Fenton, James
*The Milkfish Gatherers*: V11
*Fern Hill* (Thomas): V3
*Fifteen* (Stafford): V2
*Filling Station* (Bishop): V12
*Fire and Ice* (Frost): V7
*The Fish* (Moore): V14
*For a New Citizen of These United States* (Lee): V15
*For An Assyrian Frieze* (Viereck): V9
*For Jean Vincent D'abbadie, Baron St.-Castin* (Nowlan): V12
*For Jennifer, 6, on the Teton* (Hugo): V17
*For the Union Dead* (Lowell): V7
*For the White poets who would be Indian* (Rose): V13
*The Force That Through the Green Fuse Drives the Flower* (Thomas): V8
*Four Mountain Wolves* (Silko): V9

Francis, Robert
    *The Base Stealer:* V12
Frost, Robert
    *Birches:* V13
    *The Death of the Hired Man:* V4
    *Fire and Ice:* V7
    *Mending Wall:* V5
    *Nothing Gold Can Stay:* V3
    *Out, Out—:* V10
    *The Road Not Taken:* V2
    *Stopping by Woods on a Snowy Evening:* V1
    *The Wood-Pile:* V6
*Funeral Blues* (Auden): V10

## G

Gallagher, Tess
    *I Stop Writing the Poem:* V16
*Geometry* (Dove): V15
Ginsberg, Allen
    *A Supermarket in California:* V5
Giovanni, Nikki
    *Knoxville, Tennessee:* V17
Glück, Louise
    *The Gold Lily:* V5
    *The Mystery:* V15
*Go Down, Moses* (Anonymous): V11
*The Gold Lily* (Glück): V5
*A Grafted Tongue* (Montague): V12
Graham, Jorie
    *The Hiding Place:* V10
    *Mind:* V17
Gray, Thomas
    *Elegy Written in a Country Churchyard:* V9
Gunn, Thom
    *The Missing:* V9

## H

H.D.
    *Helen:* V6
Hall, Donald
    *Names of Horses:* V8
Hardy, Thomas
    *Ah, Are You Digging on My Grave?:* V4
    *The Man He Killed:* V3
Harjo, Joy
    *Anniversary:* V15
*Harlem* (Hughes): V1
*Harlem Hopscotch* (Angelou): V2
Hartnett, Michael
    *A Farewell to English:* V10
*Having a Coke with You* (O'Hara): V12
*Having it Out with Melancholy* (Kenyon): V17
*Hawk Roosting* (Hughes): V4
Hayden, Robert
    *Those Winter Sundays:* V1
Heaney, Seamus
    *Digging:* V5
    *A Drink of Water:* V8
    *Midnight:* V2
    *The Singer's House:* V17
Hecht, Anthony
    *"More Light! More Light!":* V6
*The Heaven of Animals* (Dickey): V6
*Helen* (H.D.): V6
Herrick, Robert
    *To the Virgins, to Make Much of Time:* V13
*The Hiding Place* (Graham): V10
*High Windows* (Larkin): V3
*The Highwayman* (Noyes): V4
Hirshfield, Jane
    *Three Times My Life Has Opened:* V16
Holmes, Oliver Wendell
    *Old Ironsides:* V9
*Holy Sonnet 10* (Donne): V2
Hope, A. D.
    *Beware of Ruins:* V8
*Hope Is a Tattered Flag* (Sandburg): V12
*"Hope" Is the Thing with Feathers* (Dickinson): V3
*The Horizons of Rooms* (Merwin): V15
*The Hospital Window* (Dickey): V11
Housman, A. E.
    *To an Athlete Dying Young:* V7
    *When I Was One-and-Twenty:* V4
*How We Heard the Name* (Dugan): V10
Howe, Marie
    *What Belongs to Us:* V15
Hudgins, Andrew
    *Elegy for My Father, Who is Not Dead:* V14
*Hugh Selwyn Mauberley* (Pound): V16
Hughes, Langston
    *Dream Variations:* V15
    *Harlem:* V1
    *Mother to Son:* V3
    *The Negro Speaks of Rivers:* V10
    *Theme for English B:* V6
Hughes, Ted
    *Hawk Roosting:* V4
Hugo, Richard
    *For Jennifer, 6, on the Teton:* V17
*Hunger in New York City* (Ortiz): V4
*Hurt Hawks* (Jeffers): V3

## I

*I felt a Funeral, in my Brain* (Dickinson): V13
*I Go Back to May 1937* (Olds): V17
*I Hear America Singing* (Whitman): V3
*I Heard a Fly Buzz—When I Died—* (Dickinson): V5
*I Stop Writing the Poem* (Gallagher): V16
*The Idea of Order at Key West* (Stevens): V13
*In a Station of the Metro* (Pound): V2
*Incident in a Rose Garden* (Justice): V14
*In Flanders Fields* (McCrae): V5
*In Memory of Radio* (Baraka): V9
*In the Land of Shinar* (Levertov): V7
*In the Suburbs* (Simpson): V14
*Inventors* (Blumenthal): V7
*An Irish Airman Foresees His Death* (Yeats): V1
*Island of the Three Marias* (Ríos): V11
*i was sitting in mcsorley's* (cummings): V13

## J

*Jabberwocky* (Carroll): V11
Jarrell, Randall
    *The Death of the Ball Turret Gunner:* V2
Jeffers, Robinson
    *Hurt Hawks:* V3
    *Shine Perishing Republic:* V4
Johnson, James Weldon
    *The Creation:* V1
*Journey of the Magi* (Eliot): V7
Justice, Donald
    *Incident in a Rose Garden:* V14

## K

Keats, John
    *La Belle Dame sans Merci:* V17
    *Bright Star! Would I Were Steadfast as Thou Art:* V9
    *Ode on a Grecian Urn:* V1
    *Ode to a Nightingale:* V3
    *When I Have Fears that I May Cease to Be:* V2
Kenyon, Jane
    *Having it Out with Melancholy:* V17
    *"Trouble with Math in a One-Room Country School":* V9
*Kilroy* (Viereck): V14
King James Bible
    *Psalm 8:* V9
    *Psalm 23:* V4
Kinnell, Galway
    *Saint Francis and the Sow:* V9
*Knoxville, Tennessee* (Giovanni): V17
Kooser, Ted
    *The Constellation Orion:* V8
Komunyakaa, Yusef
    *Facing It:* V5
*Kubla Khan* (Coleridge): V5
Kunitz, Stanley
    *The War Against the Trees:* V11

## L

l(a (cummings): V1
The Lady of Shalott (Tennyson): V15
The Lake Isle of Innisfree (Yeats): V15
The Lamb (Blake): V12
Lament for the Dorsets (Purdy): V5
Landscape with Tractor (Taylor): V10
Lanier, Sidney
    Song of the Chattahoochee: V14
Larkin, Philip
    An Arundel Tomb: V12
    High Windows: V3
    Toads: V4
Last Request (Brouwer): V14
Lawrence, D. H.
    Piano: V6
Layton, Irving
    A Tall Man Executes a Jig: V12
Leda and the Swan (Yeats): V13
Lee, Li-Young
    Early in the Morning: V17
    For a New Citizen of These United States: V15
    The Weight of Sweetness: V11
Levertov, Denise
    The Blue Rim of Memory: V17
    In the Land of Shinar: V7
Leviathan (Merwin): V5
Levine, Philip
    Starlight: V8
Longfellow, Henry Wadsworth
    The Arsenal at Springfield: V17
    Paul Revere's Ride: V2
    A Psalm of Life: V7
Lord Randal (Anonymous): V6
Lorde, Audre
    What My Child Learns of the Sea: V16
Lost Sister (Song): V5
The Love Song of J. Alfred Prufrock (Eliot): V1
Lowell, Robert
    For the Union Dead: V7
    The Quaker Graveyard in Nantucket: V6

## M

MacBeth, George
    Bedtime Story: V8
MacLeish, Archibald
    Ars Poetica: V5
Madgett, Naomi Long
    Alabama Centennial: V10
maggie and milly and molly and may (cummings): V12
The Man He Killed (Hardy): V3
A Martian Sends a Postcard Home (Raine): V7
Marvell, Andrew
    To His Coy Mistress: V5
Masefield, John
    Cargoes: V5
Matsuo Bashō
    Falling Upon Earth: V2
    The Moon Glows the Same: V7
McCrae, John
    In Flanders Fields: V5
McElroy, Colleen
    A Pièd: V3
McGinley, Phyllis
    The Conquerors: V13
    Reactionary Essay on Applied Science: V9
McKay, Claude
    The Tropics in New York: V4
Meeting the British (Muldoon): V7
Mending Wall (Frost): V5
Merlin Enthralled (Wilbur): V16
Merriam, Eve
    Onomatopoeia: V6
Merwin, W. S.
    The Horizons of Rooms: V15
    Leviathan: V5
Midnight (Heaney): V2
The Milkfish Gatherers (Fenton): V11
Millay, Edna St. Vincent
    The Courage That My Mother Had: V3
    Wild Swans: V17
Milosz, Czeslaw
    Song of a Citizen: V16
Milton, John
    [On His Blindness] Sonnet 16: V3
    On His Having Arrived at the Age of Twenty-Three: V17
Mind (Graham): V17
Mirror (Plath): V1
Miss Rosie (Clifton): V1
The Missing (Gunn): V9
Momaday, N. Scott
    Angle of Geese: V2
    To a Child Running With Outstretched Arms in Canyon de Chelly: V11
Montague, John
    A Grafted Tongue: V12
The Moon Glows the Same (Bashō): V7
Moore, Marianne
    The Fish: V14
    Poetry: V17
"More Light! More Light!" (Hecht): V6
Mother to Son (Hughes): V3
Much Madness Is Divinest Sense (Dickinson): V16
Muldoon, Paul
    Meeting the British: V7
Mueller, Lisel
    Blood Oranges: V13
    The Exhibit: V9
Musée des Beaux Arts (Auden): V1
Music Lessons (Oliver): V8
My Father's Song (Ortiz): V16
My Last Duchess (Browning): V1
My Life Closed Twice Before Its Close (Dickinson): V8
My Mother Pieced Quilts (Acosta): V12
My Papa's Waltz (Roethke): V3
The Mystery (Glück): V15

## N

Names of Horses (Hall): V8
A Narrow Fellow in the Grass (Dickinson): V11
The Negro Speaks of Rivers (Hughes): V10
Nemerov, Howard
    Deep Woods: V14
    The Phoenix: V10
Neruda, Pablo
    Tonight I Can Write: V11
Not Waving but Drowning (Smith): V3
Nothing Gold Can Stay (Frost): V3
Nowlan, Alden
    For Jean Vincent D'abbadie, Baron St.-Castin: V12
Noyes, Alfred
    The Highwayman: V4
The Nymph's Reply to the Shepherd (Raleigh): V14

## O

O Captain! My Captain! (Whitman): V2
Ode on a Grecian Urn (Keats): V1
Ode to a Nightingale (Keats): V3
Ode to the West Wind (Shelley): V2
O'Hara, Frank
    Having a Coke with You: V12
    Why I Am Not a Painter: V8
old age sticks (cummings): V3
Old Ironsides (Holmes): V9
Olds, Sharon
    I Go Back to May 1937: V17
Oliver, Mary
    Music Lessons: V8
    Wild Geese: V15
Ondaatje, Michael
    To a Sad Daughter: V8
On Freedom's Ground (Wilbur): V12
[On His Blindness] Sonnet 16 (Milton): V3
On His Having Arrived at the Age of Twenty-Three (Milton): V17
Onomatopoeia (Merriam): V6
On the Pulse of Morning (Angelou): V3
Ortiz, Simon
    Hunger in New York City: V4
    My Father's Song: V16
Out, Out— (Frost): V10
Overture to a Dance of Locomotives (Williams): V11

Owen, Wilfred
    *Dulce et Decorum Est*: V10
*Oysters* (Sexton): V4

# P

*Paradoxes and Oxymorons*
    (Ashbery): V11
Pastan, Linda
    *Ethics*: V8
*Paul Revere's Ride* (Longfellow): V2
*The Phoenix* (Nemerov): V10
*Piano* (Lawrence): V6
Piercy, Marge
    *Barbie Doll*: V9
Plath, Sylvia
    *Blackberrying*: V15
    *Mirror*: V1
*A Psalm of Life* (Longfellow): V7
Poe, Edgar Allan
    *Annabel Lee*: V9
    *The Bells*: V3
    *The Raven*: V1
*Poetry* (Moore): V17
Pope, Alexander
    *The Rape of the Lock*: V12
*Porphyria's Lover* (Browning): V15
Pound, Ezra
    *Hugh Selwyn Mauberley*: V16
    *In a Station of the Metro*: V2
    *The River-Merchant's Wife: A Letter*: V8
*Psalm 8* (King James Bible): V9
*Psalm 23* (King James Bible): V4
Purdy, Al
    *Lament for the Dorsets*: V5
    *Wilderness Gothic*: V12

# Q

*The Quaker Graveyard in Nantucket* (Lowell): V6
*Queen-Ann's-Lace* (Williams): V6

# R

Raine, Craig
    *A Martian Sends a Postcard Home*: V7
Raleigh, Walter, Sir
    *The Nymph's Reply to the Shepherd*: V14
Randall, Dudley
    *Ballad of Birmingham*: V5
*The Rape of the Lock* (Pope): V12
*The Raven* (Poe): V1
*Reactionary Essay on Applied Science* (McGinley): V9
*A Red, Red Rose* (Burns): V8
*The Red Wheelbarrow* (Williams): V1
Reed, Ishmael
    *Beware: Do Not Read This Poem*: V6
*Remember* (Rossetti): V14
*Reunions with a Ghost* (Ai): V16
Revard, Carter
    *Birch Canoe*: V5
*The Rhodora* (Emerson): V17
Rich, Adrienne
    *Rusted Legacy*: V15
*Richard Cory* (Robinson): V4
*The Rime of the Ancient Mariner* (Coleridge): V4
Ríos, Alberto
    *Island of the Three Marias*: V11
*The River-Merchant's Wife: A Letter* (Pound): V8
*The Road Not Taken* (Frost): V2
Robinson, E. A.
    *Richard Cory*: V4
Roethke, Theodore
    *My Papa's Waltz*: V3
Rose, Wendy
    *For the White poets who would be Indian*: V13
Rossetti, Christina
    *A Birthday*: V10
    *Remember*: V14
Rukeyser, Muriel
    *Ballad of Orange and Grape*: V10
*Rusted Legacy* (Rich): V15

# S

*Sailing to Byzantium* (Yeats): V2
*Saint Francis and the Sow* (Kinnell): V9
Sandburg, Carl
    *Chicago*: V3
    *Cool Tombs*: V6
    *Hope Is a Tattered Flag*: V12
Schnackenberg, Gjertrud
    *Darwin in 1881*: V13
*The Seafarer* (Anonymous): V8
*The Second Coming* (Yeats): V7
Service, Robert W.
    *The Cremation of Sam McGee*: V10
Sexton, Anne
    *Courage*: V14
    *Oysters*: V4
Shakespeare, William
    *Sonnet 18*: V2
    *Sonnet 19*: V9
    *Sonnet 29*: V8
    *Sonnet 30*: V4
    *Sonnet 55*: V5
    *Sonnet 116*: V3
    *Sonnet 130*: V1
Shapiro, Karl
    *Auto Wreck*: V3
*She Walks in Beauty* (Byron): V14
Shelley, Percy Bysshe
    *Ode to the West Wind*: V2
*Shine, Perishing Republic* (Jeffers): V4
Silko, Leslie Marmon
    *Four Mountain Wolves*: V9
    *Story from Bear Country*: V16
Simic, Charles
    *Butcher Shop*: V7
Simpson, Louis
    *American Poetry*: V7
    *Chocolates*: V11
    *In the Suburbs*: V14
*The Singer's House* (Heaney): V17
*Sir Patrick Spens* (Anonymous): V4
*Siren Song* (Atwood): V7
*Small Town with One Road* (Soto): V7
*Smart and Final Iris* (Tate): V15
Smith, Stevie
    *Not Waving but Drowning*: V3
Snyder, Gary
    *Anasazi*: V9
*The Soldier* (Brooke): V7
Song, Cathy
    *Lost Sister*: V5
*Song of a Citizen* (Milosz): V16
*Song of the Chattahoochee* (Lanier): V14
*The Song of the Smoke* (Du Bois): V13
*Sonnet 16 [On His Blindness]* (Milton): V3
*Sonnet 18* (Shakespeare): V2
*Sonnet 19* (Shakespeare): V9
*Sonnet 30* (Shakespeare): V4
*Sonnet 29* (Shakespeare): V8
*Sonnet XXIX* (Browning): V16
*Sonnet 43* (Browning): V2
*Sonnet 55* (Shakespeare): V5
*Sonnet 116* (Shakespeare): V3
*Sonnet 130* (Shakespeare): V1
*The Sonnet-Ballad* (Brooks): V1
Soto, Gary
    *Small Town with One Road*: V7
*The Soul Selects Her Own Society* (Dickinson): V1
*Southbound on the Freeway* (Swenson): V16
Stafford, William
    *At the Bomb Testing Site*: V8
    *Fifteen*: V2
    *Ways to Live*: V16
*Starlight* (Levine): V8
Stevens, Wallace
    *The Idea of Order at Key West*: V13
    *Sunday Morning*: V16
*Stopping by Woods on a Snowy Evening* (Frost): V1
*Story from Bear Country* (Silko): V16
Strand, Mark
    *Eating Poetry*: V9
*Strong Men, Riding Horses* (Brooks): V4
*Sunday Morning* (Stevens): V16
*A Supermarket in California* (Ginsberg): V5

Swenson, May
   *Southbound on the Freeway:* V16
*Swing Low Sweet Chariot* (Anonymous): V1
Szymborska, Wislawa
   *Astonishment:* V15

# T

*A Tall Man Executes a Jig* (Layton): V12
Tate, James
   *Dear Reader:* V10
   *Smart and Final Iris:* V15
Taylor, Henry
   *Landscape with Tractor:* V10
*Tears, Idle Tears* (Tennyson): V4
Teasdale, Sara
   *There Will Come Soft Rains:* V14
Tennyson, Alfred, Lord
   *The Charge of the Light Brigade:* V1
   *The Eagle:* V11
   *The Lady of Shalott:* V15
   *Tears, Idle Tears:* V4
   *Ulysses:* V2
Thayer, Ernest Lawrence
   *Casey at the Bat:* V5
*Theme for English B* (Hughes): V6
*There's a Certain Slant of Light* (Dickinson): V6
*There Will Come Soft Rains* (Teasdale): V14
*This Life* (Dove): V1
Thomas, Dylan
   *Do Not Go Gentle into that Good Night:* V1
   *Fern Hill:* V3
   *The Force That Through the Green Fuse Drives the Flower:* V8
*Those Winter Sundays* (Hayden): V1
*Three Times My Life Has Opened* (Hirshfield): V16
*Tintern Abbey* (Wordsworth): V2
*To an Athlete Dying Young* (Housman): V7
*To a Child Running With Outstretched Arms in Canyon de Chelly* (Momaday): V11
*To a Sad Daughter* (Ondaatje): V8
*To His Coy Mistress* (Marvell): V5
*To His Excellency General Washington* (Wheatley): V13
*To My Dear and Loving Husband* (Bradstreet): V6
*To the Virgins, to Make Much of Time* (Herrick): V13
*Toads* (Larkin): V4
*Tonight I Can Write* (Neruda): V11
*The Tropics in New York* (McKay): V4
*The Tyger* (Blake): V2

# U

*Ulysses* (Tennyson): V2
*The Unknown Citizen* (Auden): V3

# V

*A Valediction: Forbidding Mourning* (Donne): V11
*Vancouver Lights* (Birney): V8
Viereck, Peter
   *For An Assyrian Frieze:* V9
   *Kilroy:* V14

# W

Walcott, Derek
   *A Far Cry from Africa:* V6
*The War Against the Trees* (Kunitz): V11
*War Is Kind* (Crane): V9
Warren, Rosanna
   *Daylights:* V13
*Ways to Live* (Stafford): V16
*We Live by What We See at Night* (Espada): V13
*We Real Cool* (Brooks): V6
*The Weight of Sweetness* (Lee): V11
*What Belongs to Us* (Howe): V15
*What My Child Learns of the Sea* (Lorde): V16
Wheatley, Phillis
   *To His Excellency General Washington:* V13
*When I Have Fears That I May Cease to Be* (Keats): V2
*When I Was One-and-Twenty* (Housman): V4
Whitman, Walt
   *Cavalry Crossing a Ford:* V13
   *I Hear America Singing:* V3
   *O Captain! My Captain!:* V2
*Why I Am Not a Painter* (O'Hara): V8
Wilbur, Richard
   *Beowulf:* V11
   *Merlin Enthralled:* V16
   *On Freedom's Ground:* V12
*Wild Geese* (Oliver): V15
*Wild Swans* (Millay): V17
*Wilderness Gothic* (Purdy): V12
Williams, William Carlos
   *Overture to a Dance of Locomotives:* V11
   *Queen-Ann's-Lace:* V6
   *The Red Wheelbarrow:* V1
*The Wood-Pile* (Frost): V6
Wordsworth, William
   *Lines Composed a Few Miles above Tintern Abbey:* V2
Wright, Charles
   *Black Zodiac:* V10
Wright, James
   *A Blessing:* V7
   *Autumn Begins in Martins Ferry, Ohio:* V8
Wright, Judith
   *Drought Year:* V8

# Y

Yeats, William Butler
   *Easter 1916:* V5
   *An Irish Airman Foresees His Death:* V1
   *The Lake Isle of Innisfree:* V15
   *Leda and the Swan:* V13
   *Sailing to Byzantium:* V2
   *The Second Coming:* V7

# Cumulative Nationality/Ethnicity Index

## Acoma Pueblo
Ortiz, Simon
   *Hunger in New York City*: V4
   *My Father's Song*: V16

## African American
Ai
   *Reunions with a Ghost*: V16
Angelou, Maya
   *Harlem Hopscotch*: V2
   *On the Pulse of Morning*: V3
Baraka, Amiri
   *In Memory of Radio*: V9
Brooks, Gwendolyn
   *The Bean Eaters*: V2
   *The Sonnet-Ballad*: V1
   *Strong Men, Riding Horses*: V4
   *We Real Cool*: V6
Clifton, Lucille
   *Climbing*: V14
   *Miss Rosie*: V1
Cullen, Countee
   *Any Human to Another*: V3
Dove, Rita
   *Geometry*: V15
   *This Life*: V1
Giovanni, Nikki
   *Knoxville, Tennessee*: V17
Hayden, Robert
   *Those Winter Sundays*: V1
Hughes, Langston
   *Dream Variations*: V15
   *Harlem*: V1
   *Mother to Son*: V3
   *The Negro Speaks of Rivers*: V10
   *Theme for English B*: V6
Johnson, James Weldon
   *The Creation*: V1
Komunyakaa, Yusef
   *Facing It*: V5
Lorde, Audre
   *What My Child Learns of the Sea*: V16
Madgett, Naomi Long
   *Alabama Centennial*: V10
McElroy, Colleen
   *A Pièd*: V3
Randall, Dudley
   *Ballad of Birmingham*: V5
Reed, Ishmael
   *Beware: Do Not Read This Poem*: V6

## American
Acosta, Teresa Palomo
   *My Mother Pieced Quilts*: V12
Ai
   *Reunions with a Ghost*: V16
Angelou, Maya
   *Harlem Hopscotch*: V2
   *On the Pulse of Morning*: V3
Ashbery, John
   *Paradoxes and Oxymorons*: V11
Auden, W. H.
   *As I Walked Out One Evening*: V4
   *Musée des Beaux Arts*: V1
   *The Unknown Citizen*: V3
Bishop, Elizabeth
   *Brazil, January 1, 1502*: V6
   *Filling Station*: V12
Blumenthal, Michael
   *Inventors*: V7
Bly, Robert
   *Come with Me*: V6
   *Driving to Town Late to Mail a Letter*: V17
Bradstreet, Anne
   *To My Dear and Loving Husband*: V6
Brooks, Gwendolyn
   *The Bean Eaters*: V2
   *The Sonnet-Ballad*: V1
   *Strong Men, Riding Horses*: V4
   *We Real Cool*: V6
Brouwer, Joel
   *Last Request*: V14
Carver, Raymond
   *The Cobweb*: V17
Clifton, Lucille
   *Climbing*: V14
   *Miss Rosie*: V1
Crane, Stephen
   *War Is Kind*: V9
Cruz, Victor Hernandez
   *Business*: V16
Cullen, Countee
   *Any Human to Another*: V3
cummings, e. e.
   *l(a*: V1
   *i was sitting in mcsorley's*: V13
   *maggie and milly and molly and may*: V12
   *old age sticks*: V3
Dickey, James
   *The Heaven of Animals*: V6
   *The Hospital Window*: V11
Dickinson, Emily
   *Because I Could Not Stop for Death*: V2
   *The Bustle in a House*: V10

"Hope" Is the Thing with
    Feathers: V3
I felt a Funeral, in my Brain: V13
I Heard a Fly Buzz—When I
    Died—: V5
Much Madness Is Divinest Sense:
    V16
My Life Closed Twice Before Its
    Close: V8
A Narrow Fellow in the Grass:
    V11
The Soul Selects Her Own
    Society: V1
There's a Certain Slant of Light:
    V6
This Is My Letter to the World: V4
Dove, Rita
    Geometry: V15
    This Life: V1
Dubie, Norman
    The Czar's Last Christmas Letter.
        A Barn in the Urals: V12
Du Bois, W. E. B.
    The Song of the Smoke: V13
Dugan, Alan
    How We Heard the Name: V10
Duncan, Robert
    An African Elegy: V13
Eliot, T. S.
    Journey of the Magi: V7
    The Love Song of J. Alfred
        Prufrock: V1
Emerson, Ralph Waldo
    Concord Hymn: V4
    The Rhodora: V17
Erdrich, Louise
    Bidwell Ghost: V14
Espada, Martín
    Colibrí: V16
    We Live by What We See at
        Night: V13
Francis, Robert
    The Base Stealer: V12
Frost, Robert
    Birches: V13
    The Death of the Hired Man: V4
    Fire and Ice: V7
    Mending Wall: V5
    Nothing Gold Can Stay: V3
    Out, Out—: V10
    The Road Not Taken: V2
    Stopping by Woods on a Snowy
        Evening: V1
    The Wood-Pile: V6
Gallagher, Tess
    I Stop Writing the Poem: V16
Ginsberg, Allen
    A Supermarket in California: V5
Giovanni, Nikki
    Knoxville, Tennessee: V17
Glück, Louise
    The Gold Lily: V5
    The Mystery: V15

Graham, Jorie
    The Hiding Place: V10
    Mind: V17
Gunn, Thom
    The Missing: V9
H.D.
    Helen: V6
Hall, Donald
    Names of Horses: V8
Harjo, Joy
    Anniversary: V15
Hayden, Robert
    Those Winter Sundays: V1
Hecht, Anthony
    "More Light! More Light!": V6
Hirshfield, Jane
    Three Times My Life Has
        Opened: V16
Holmes, Oliver Wendell
    Old Ironsides: V9
Howe, Marie
    What Belongs to Us: V15
Hudgins, Andrew
    Elegy for My Father, Who is Not
        Dead: V14
Hughes, Langston
    Dream Variations: V15
    Harlem: V1
    Mother to Son: V3
    The Negro Speaks of Rivers: V10
    Theme for English B: V6
Hugo, Richard
    For Jennifer, 6, on the Teton:
        V17
Jarrell, Randall
    The Death of the Ball Turret
        Gunner: V2
Jeffers, Robinson
    Hurt Hawks: V3
    Shine, Perishing Republic: V4
Johnson, James Weldon
    The Creation: V1
Justice, Donald
    Incident in a Rose Garden: V14
Kenyon, Jane
    Having it Out with Melancholy:
        V17
    "Trouble with Math in a One-
        Room Country School": V9
Kinnell, Galway
    Saint Francis and the Sow: V9
Komunyakaa, Yusef
    Facing It: V5
Kooser, Ted
    The Constellation Orion: V8
Kunitz, Stanley
    The War Against the Trees: V11
Lanier, Sidney
    Song of the Chattahoochee: V14
Lee, Li-Young
    Early in the Morning: V17
    For a New Citizen of These
        United States: V15
    The Weight of Sweetness: V11

Levertov, Denise
    The Blue Rim of Memory: V17
    In the Land of Shinar: V7
Levine, Philip
    Starlight: V8
Longfellow, Henry Wadsworth
    The Arsenal at Springfield: V17
    Paul Revere's Ride: V2
    A Psalm of Life: V7
Lorde, Audre
    What My Child Learns of the Sea:
        V16
Lowell, Robert
    For the Union Dead: V7
    The Quaker Graveyard in
        Nantucket: V6
MacLeish, Archibald
    Ars Poetica: V5
Madgett, Naomi Long
    Alabama Centennial: V10
McElroy, Colleen
    A Pièd: V3
McGinley, Phyllis
    The Conquerors: V13
    Reactionary Essay on Applied
        Science: V9
McKay, Claude
    The Tropics in New York: V4
Merriam, Eve
    Onomatopoeia: V6
Merwin, W. S.
    The Horizons of Rooms: V15
    Leviathan: V5
Millay, Edna St. Vincent
    The Courage that My Mother
        Had: V3
    Wild Swans: V17
Momaday, N. Scott
    Angle of Geese: V2
    To a Child Running With
        Outstretched Arms in Canyon
        de Chelly: V11
Montague, John
    A Grafted Tongue: V12
Moore, Marianne
    The Fish: V14
    Poetry: V17
Mueller, Lisel
    The Exhibit: V9
Nemerov, Howard
    Deep Woods: V14
    The Phoenix: V10
O'Hara, Frank
    Having a Coke with You: V12
    Why I Am Not a Painter: V8
Olds, Sharon
    I Go Back to May 1937: V17
Oliver, Mary
    Music Lessons: V8
    Wild Geese: V15
Ortiz, Simon
    Hunger in New York City: V4
    My Father's Song: V16

Pastan, Linda
   *Ethics*: V8
Piercy, Marge
   *Barbie Doll*: V9
Plath, Sylvia
   *Blackberrying*: V15
   *Mirror*: V1
Poe, Edgar Allan
   *Annabel Lee*: V9
   *The Bells*: V3
   *The Raven*: V1
Pound, Ezra
   *Hugh Selwyn Mauberley*: V16
   *In a Station of the Metro*: V2
   *The River-Merchant's Wife: A Letter*: V8
Randall, Dudley
   *Ballad of Birmingham*: V5
Reed, Ishmael
   *Beware: Do Not Read This Poem*: V6
Revard, Carter
   *Birch Canoe*: V5
Rich, Adrienne
   *Rusted Legacy*: V15
Ríos, Alberto
   *Island of the Three Marias*: V11
Robinson, E. A.
   *Richard Cory*: V4
Roethke, Theodore
   *My Papa's Waltz*: V3
Rose, Wendy
   *For the White poets who would be Indian*: V13
Rukeyser, Muriel
   *Ballad of Orange and Grape*: V10
Sandburg, Carl
   *Chicago*: V3
   *Cool Tombs*: V6
   *Hope Is a Tattered Flag*: V12
Schnackenberg, Gjertrud
   *Darwin in 1881*: V13
Sexton, Anne
   *Courage*: V14
   *Oysters*: V4
Shapiro, Karl
   *Auto Wreck*: V3
Silko, Leslie Marmon
   *Four Mountain Wolves*: V9
   *Story from Bear Country*: V16
Simic, Charles
   *Butcher Shop*: V7
Simpson, Louis
   *American Poetry*: V7
   *Chocolates*: V11
   *In the Suburbs*: V14
Snyder, Gary
   *Anasazi*: V9
Song, Cathy
   *Lost Sister*: V5
Soto, Gary
   *Small Town with One Road*: V7
Stafford, William
   *At the Bomb Testing Site*: V8
   *Fifteen*: V2
   *Ways to Live*: V16
Stevens, Wallace
   *The Idea of Order at Key West*: V13
   *Sunday Morning*: V16
Swenson, May
   *Southbound on the Freeway*: V16
Tate, James
   *Dear Reader*: V10
   *Smart and Final Iris*: V15
Taylor, Henry
   *Landscape with Tractor*: V10
Teasdale, Sara
   *There Will Come Soft Rains*: V14
Thayer, Ernest Lawrence
   *Casey at the Bat*: V5
Viereck, Peter
   *For An Assyrian Frieze*: V9
   *Kilroy*: V14
Warren, Rosanna
   *Daylights*: V13
Wheatley, Phillis
   *To His Excellency General Washington*: V13
Whitman, Walt
   *Cavalry Crossing a Ford*: V13
   *I Hear America Singing*: V3
   *O Captain! My Captain!*: V2
Wilbur, Richard
   *Beowulf*: V11
   *Merlin Enthralled*: V16
   *On Freedom's Ground*: V12
Williams, William Carlos
   *Overture to a Dance of Locomotives*: V11
   *Queen-Ann's-Lace*: V6
   *The Red Wheelbarrow*: V1
Wright, Charles
   *Black Zodiac*: V10
Wright, James
   *A Blessing*: V7
   *Autumn Begins in Martins Ferry, Ohio*: V8

## Australian

Dawe, Bruce
   *Drifters*: V10
Hope, A. D.
   *Beware of Ruins*: V8
Wright, Judith
   *Drought Year*: V8

## Canadian

Atwood, Margaret
   *Siren Song*: V7
Birney, Earle
   *Vancouver Lights*: V8
Layton, Irving
   *A Tall Man Executes a Jig*: V12
McCrae, John
   *In Flanders Fields*: V5
Nowlan, Alden
   *For Jean Vincent D'abbadie, Baron St.-Castin*: V12
Purdy, Al
   *Lament for the Dorsets*: V5
   *Wilderness Gothic*: V12
Strand, Mark
   *Eating Poetry*: V9

## Canadian, Sri Lankan

Ondaatje, Michael
   *To a Sad Daughter*: V8

## Cherokee

Momaday, N. Scott
   *Angle of Geese*: V2
   *To a Child Running With Outstretched Arms in Canyon de Chelly*: V11

## Chilean

Neruda, Pablo
   *Tonight I Can Write*: V11

## English

Alleyn, Ellen
   *A Birthday*: V10
Arnold, Matthew
   *Dover Beach*: V2
Auden, W. H.
   *As I Walked Out One Evening*: V4
   *Funeral Blues*: V10
   *Musée des Beaux Arts*: V1
   *The Unknown Citizen*: V3
Blake, William
   *The Lamb*: V12
   *The Tyger*: V2
Bradstreet, Anne
   *To My Dear and Loving Husband*: V6
Brooke, Rupert
   *The Soldier*: V7
Browning, Elizabeth Barrett
   *Sonnet XXIX*: V16
   *Sonnet 43*: V2
Browning, Robert
   *My Last Duchess*: V1
   *Porphyria's Lover*: V15
Byron, Lord
   *The Destruction of Sennacherib*: V1
   *She Walks in Beauty*: V14
Carroll, Lewis
   *Jabberwocky*: V11
Chaucer, Geoffrey
   *The Canterbury Tales*: V14
Coleridge, Samuel Taylor
   *Kubla Khan*: V5
   *The Rime of the Ancient Mariner*: V4

Donne, John
  *Holy Sonnet 10*: V2
  *A Valediction: Forbidding Mourning*: V11
Eliot, T. S.
  *Journey of the Magi*: V7
  *The Love Song of J. Alfred Prufrock*: V1
Fenton, James
  *The Milkfish Gatherers*: V11
Gray, Thomas
  *Elegy Written in a Country Churchyard*: V9
Gunn, Thom
  *The Missing*: V9
Hardy, Thomas
  *Ah, Are You Digging on My Grave?*: V4
  *The Man He Killed*: V3
Herrick, Robert
  *To the Virgins, to Make Much of Time*: V13
Housman, A. E.
  *To an Athlete Dying Young*: V7
  *When I Was One-and-Twenty*: V4
Hughes, Ted
  *Hawk Roosting*: V4
Keats, John
  *La Belle Dame sans Merci*: V17
  *Bright Star! Would I Were Steadfast as Thou Art*: V9
  *Ode on a Grecian Urn*: V1
  *Ode to a Nightingale*: V3
  *When I Have Fears that I May Cease to Be*: V2
Larkin, Philip
  *An Arundel Tomb*: V12
  *High Windows*: V3
  *Toads*: V4
Lawrence, D. H.
  *Piano*: V6
Levertov, Denise
  *The Blue Rim of Memory*: V17
Marvell, Andrew
  *To His Coy Mistress*: V5
Masefield, John
  *Cargoes*: V5
Milton, John
  *[On His Blindness] Sonnet 16*: V3
  *On His Having Arrived at the Age of Twenty-Three*: V17
Noyes, Alfred
  *The Highwayman*: V4
Owen, Wilfred
  *Dulce et Decorum Est*: V10
Pope, Alexander
  *The Rape of the Lock*: V12
Raine, Craig
  *A Martian Sends a Postcard Home*: V7
Raleigh, Walter, Sir
  *The Nymph's Reply to the Shepherd*: V14
Rossetti, Christina
  *A Birthday*: V10
  *Remember*: V14
Service, Robert W.
  *The Cremation of Sam McGee*: V10
Shakespeare, William
  *Sonnet 18*: V2
  *Sonnet 19*: V9
  *Sonnet 30*: V4
  *Sonnet 29*: V8
  *Sonnet 55*: V5
  *Sonnet 116*: V3
  *Sonnet 130*: V1
Shelley, Percy Bysshe
  *Ode to the West Wind*: V2
Smith, Stevie
  *Not Waving but Drowning*: V3
Tennyson, Alfred, Lord
  *The Charge of the Light Brigade*: V1
  *The Eagle*: V11
  *The Lady of Shalott*: V15
  *Tears, Idle Tears*: V4
  *Ulysses*: V2
Williams, William Carlos
  *Queen-Ann's-Lace*: V6
  *The Red Wheelbarrow*: V1
Wordsworth, William
  *Lines Composed a Few Miles above Tintern Abbey*: V2
Yeats, W. B.
  *Easter 1916*: V5
  *An Irish Airman Forsees His Death*: V1
  *The Lake Isle of Innisfree*: V15
  *Leda and the Swan*: V13
  *Sailing to Byzantium*: V2
  *The Second Coming*: V7

## German

Blumenthal, Michael
  *Inventors*: V7
Erdrich, Louise
  *Bidwell Ghost*: V14
Mueller, Lisel
  *Blood Oranges*: V13
  *The Exhibit*: V9
Roethke, Theodore
  *My Papa's Waltz*: V3

## Ghanaian

Du Bois, W. E. B.
  *The Song of the Smoke*: V13

## Hispanic

Cruz, Victor Hernandez
  *Business*: V16
Espada, Martín
  *Colibrí*: V16

## Indonesian

Lee, Li-Young
  *Early in the Morning*: V17
  *For a New Citizen of These United States*: V15
  *The Weight of Sweetness*: V11

## Irish

Boland, Eavan
  *Anorexic*: V12
Hartnett, Michael
  *A Farewell to English*: V10
Heaney, Seamus
  *Digging*: V5
  *A Drink of Water*: V8
  *Midnight*: V2
  *The Singer's House*: V17
Muldoon, Paul
  *Meeting the British*: V7
Yeats, William Butler
  *Easter 1916*: V5
  *An Irish Airman Foresees His Death*: V1
  *The Lake Isle of Innisfree*: V15
  *Leda and the Swan*: V13
  *Sailing to Byzantium*: V2
  *The Second Coming*: V7

## Jamaican

McKay, Claude
  *The Tropics in New York*: V4
Simpson, Louis
  *In the Suburbs*: V14

## Japanese

Ai
  *Reunions with a Ghost*: V16
Bashō, Matsuo
  *Falling Upon Earth*: V2
  *The Moon Glows the Same*: V7

## Jewish

Blumenthal, Michael
  *Inventors*: V7
Espada, Martín
  *Colibrí*: V16
  *We Live by What We See at Night*: V13
Piercy, Marge
  *Barbie Doll*: V9
Shapiro, Karl
  *Auto Wreck*: V3

## Kiowa

Momaday, N. Scott
  *Angle of Geese*: V2
  *To a Child Running With Outstretched Arms in Canyon de Chelly*: V11

## Lithuanian

Milosz, Czeslaw
  *Song of a Citizen*: V16

## Mexican
Soto, Gary
  *Small Town with One Road*: V7

## Native American
Ai
  *Reunions with a Ghost*: V16
Erdrich, Louise
  *Bidwell Ghost*: V14
Harjo, Joy
  *Anniversary*: V15
Momaday, N. Scott
  *Angle of Geese*: V2
  *To a Child Running With Outstretched Arms in Canyon de Chelly*: V11
Ortiz, Simon
  *Hunger in New York City*: V4
  *My Father's Song*: V16
Revard, Carter
  *Birch Canoe*: V5
Rose, Wendy
  *For the White poets who would be Indian*: V13
Silko, Leslie Marmon
  *Four Mountain Wolves*: V9
  *Story from Bear Country*: V16

## Osage
Revard, Carter
  *Birch Canoe*: V5

## Polish
Milosz, Czeslaw
  *Song of a Citizen*: V16
Szymborska, Wislawa
  *Astonishment*: V15

## Russian
Levertov, Denise
  *In the Land of Shinar*: V7
Merriam, Eve
  *Onomatopoeia*: V6
Shapiro, Karl
  *Auto Wreck*: V3

## Scottish
Burns, Robert
  *A Red, Red Rose*: V8
Byron, Lord
  *The Destruction of Sennacherib*: V1
MacBeth, George
  *Bedtime Story*: V8

## Senegalese
Wheatley, Phillis
  *To His Excellency General Washington*: V13

## Spanish
Williams, William Carlos
  *The Red Wheelbarrow*: V1

## Swedish
Sandburg, Carl
  *Chicago*: V3

## Welsh
Levertov, Denise
  *In the Land of Shinar*: V7
Thomas, Dylan
  *Do Not Go Gentle into that Good Night*: V1
  *Fern Hill*: V3
  *The Force That Through the Green Fuse Drives the Flower*: V8

## West Indian
Walcott, Derek
  *A Far Cry from Africa*: V6

# Subject/Theme Index

***Boldface** denotes dicussion in *Themes* section.

## A

**Abandonment**
  *The Singer's House:* 206, 208, 211
**Alcoholism, Drugs, and Drug Addiction**
  *Having it Out with Melancholy:* 100–105, 109
**Alliteration**
  *For Jennifer, 6, on the Teton:* 89
**Ambition**
  *La Belle Dame sans Merci:* 30, 32–33, 35
  *On His Having Arrived at the Age of Twenty-Three:* 168–169
**American Northeast**
  *The Arsenal at Springfield:* 1, 3, 9–10
  *The Rhodora:* 190, 192–196
  *Wild Swans:* 220, 224–225
**American Northwest**
  *For Jennifer, 6, on the Teton:* 86, 89–90
**American South**
  *The Arsenal at Springfield:* 8–9
**American Southwest**
  *The Arsenal at Springfield:* 9
**Anger**
  *I Go Back to May 1937:* 119–121
**Arthurian Legend**
  *La Belle Dame sans Merci:* 31–33
**Artistic Responsibility**
  *The Singer's House:* 208

## B

**Atonement**
  *Having it Out with Melancholy:* 109–110

**Ballad**
  *La Belle Dame sans Merci:* 18, 22, 24, 26–35
**Beauty**
  *For Jennifer, 6, on the Teton:* 93–96
  *I Go Back to May 1937:* 114–116
  *La Belle Dame sans Merci:* 17, 20–22, 24, 30, 32, 35–36
  *The Rhodora:* 192–193, 196, 198–200, 202–203
  *Wild Swans:* 232–233

## C

**Catharsis**
  *I Go Back to May 1937:* 115–116
**Childhood**
  *For Jennifer, 6, on the Teton:* 85–87, 90–91, 94–96
  *I Go Back to May 1937:* 119–121
  *Knoxville, Tennessee:* 137–138, 140
**Christianity**
  *On His Having Arrived at the Age of Twenty-Three:* 167, 169
**City and Country**
  *Driving to Town Late to Mail a Letter:* 65
**Colonialism**
  *The Singer's House:* 206, 210, 212

**Consciousness**
  *Driving to Town Late to Mail a Letter:* 65
**Crime and Criminals**
  *On His Having Arrived at the Age of Twenty-Three:* 161, 164
**Crisis of Faith**
  *On His Having Arrived at the Age of Twenty-Three:* 160
**Cruelty**
  *The Arsenal at Springfield:* 3–7
  *The Singer's House:* 207, 209, 211–212
**Cultural Healing**
  *The Singer's House:* 209

## D

**Death**
  *The Arsenal at Springfield:* 1, 3–7, 10, 13–15
  *The Blue Rim of Memory:* 37, 39, 41, 43
  *The Cobweb:* 49, 51–55
  *Having it Out with Melancholy:* 100, 103–105
  *La Belle Dame sans Merci:* 32–35
  *The Singer's House:* 207–208, 210–212
**Deceit**
  *Poetry:* 186–188
**Depression and Melancholy**
  *Having it Out with Melancholy:* 97, 99–103, 105–110
  *I Go Back to May 1937:* 111–112, 114–117
**Description**
  *The Blue Rim of Memory:* 39, 42

*The Cobweb:* 51–53, 58
*Driving to Town Late to Mail a Letter:* 72
*Early in the Morning:* 77–78
*The Rhodora:* 192–193, 196

**Despair**
*Having it Out with Melancholy:* 99, 102–103, 105
*La Belle Dame sans Merci:* 20, 22

**Dialogue**
*Early in the Morning:* 82
*On His Having Arrived at the Age of Twenty-Three:* 166–167

**Disease**
*On His Having Arrived at the Age of Twenty-Three:* 163–164

**Divinity**
*The Rhodora:* 192

**Divorce**
*I Go Back to May 1937:* 111, 118

**Drama**
*On His Having Arrived at the Age of Twenty-Three:* 162–164

**Dreams and Visions**
*La Belle Dame sans Merci:* 20–21, 24, 26–29, 31–34
*The Singer's House:* 213–214, 216

**Duty and Responsibility**
*The Singer's House:* 208–209, 211, 213

# E

**Ecology**
*For Jennifer, 6, on the Teton:* 89–90

**Education**
*For Jennifer, 6, on the Teton:* 88

**Emotional Exhaustion**
*Wild Swans:* 223

**Emotions**
*The Arsenal at Springfield:* 15
*The Blue Rim of Memory:* 39, 41–42, 44–46
*The Cobweb:* 51, 53, 60–61
*Early in the Morning:* 74–75, 77–78, 81
*For Jennifer, 6, on the Teton:* 91–92, 94
*Having it Out with Melancholy:* 97, 104–105, 109
*I Go Back to May 1937:* 116, 119–121, 123
*Knoxville, Tennessee:* 134
*La Belle Dame sans Merci:* 19–20, 23, 25–26
*On His Having Arrived at the Age of Twenty-Three:* 165
*Poetry:* 178–179, 185
*The Rhodora:* 197–198
*Wild Swans:* 220, 222–223, 225–228, 230–233

**Eternity**
*La Belle Dame sans Merci:* 31–32, 34–35

**Europe**
*The Arsenal at Springfield:* 4, 6, 8–10
*La Belle Dame sans Merci:* 23–24
*On His Having Arrived at the Age of Twenty-Three:* 162–163, 168–169
*Poetry:* 179
*The Singer's House:* 204, 206–218

**Exile**
*The Singer's House:* 204, 206–208

# F

**Farm and Rural Life**
*Driving to Town Late to Mail a Letter:* 62, 64–65, 67
*Knoxville, Tennessee:* 132–134
*Mind:* 147–148
*On His Having Arrived at the Age of Twenty-Three:* 162
*The Rhodora:* 194

**Fate and Chance**
*I Go Back to May 1937:* 124–127
*On His Having Arrived at the Age of Twenty-Three:* 160–161, 164, 170–172

**Film**
*I Go Back to May 1937:* 118

**Folklore**
*La Belle Dame sans Merci:* 21

**Food**
*Knoxville, Tennessee:* 132

**Forgiveness**
*Having it Out with Melancholy:* 109–110
*I Go Back to May 1937:* 119–121

**Free Will vs. Determinism**
*On His Having Arrived at the Age of Twenty-Three:* 161–162

**Freedom**
*Wild Swans:* 223

# G

**Gender**
*Early in the Morning:* 77

**Generosity**
*For Jennifer, 6, on the Teton:* 93, 95–96

**God**
*Having it Out with Melancholy:* 99–100, 102, 106–107, 109–110
*On His Having Arrived at the Age of Twenty-Three:* 158, 160–161, 163–169, 171–172
*The Rhodora:* 190, 192, 194–195, 197–198

**Goodness**
*I Go Back to May 1937:* 119–121
*La Belle Dame sans Merci:* 19–20, 23–24

**Greed**
*For Jennifer, 6, on the Teton:* 87–89

**Grief and Loss**
*I Go Back to May 1937:* 115

**Grief and Sorrow**
*The Arsenal at Springfield:* 13–15
*The Blue Rim of Memory:* 37, 39–41, 43–48
*For Jennifer, 6, on the Teton:* 94–95
*I Go Back to May 1937:* 114–117
*On His Having Arrived at the Age of Twenty-Three:* 164–165

# H

**Happiness and Gaiety**
*Having it Out with Melancholy:* 101–103
*I Go Back to May 1937:* 116

**Heaven**
*Having it Out with Melancholy:* 108–109
*La Belle Dame sans Merci:* 30–35
*On His Having Arrived at the Age of Twenty-Three:* 160–161, 164, 167–169, 171–172

**History**
*Driving to Town Late to Mail a Letter:* 67
*Early in the Morning:* 81–84
*For Jennifer, 6, on the Teton:* 87
*Mind:* 144, 149
*The Singer's House:* 206, 213
*Wild Swans:* 224–225

**Home**
*Knoxville, Tennessee:* 133

**Honor**
*La Belle Dame sans Merci:* 23–24

**Hope**
*Having it Out with Melancholy:* 103–104
*Wild Swans:* 227–229

**Hope and Hopelessness**
*Having it Out with Melancholy:* 102

**Human Condition**
*Driving to Town Late to Mail a Letter:* 65

# I

**Imagery and Symbolism**
*The Arsenal at Springfield:* 3–4, 7–8, 10, 13–15

*The Blue Rim of Memory:* 37, 39–42, 44–45
*The Cobweb:* 49, 51, 53, 55–56
*Driving to Town Late to Mail a Letter:* 68–69, 71, 73
*For Jennifer, 6, on the Teton:* 86, 88, 93–95
*Having it Out with Melancholy:* 100–101, 104–106
*I Go Back to May 1937:* 125–128
*Knoxville, Tennessee:* 142
*La Belle Dame sans Merci:* 29–30, 35
*Mind:* 144, 146–148
*On His Having Arrived at the Age of Twenty-Three:* 160, 171
*Poetry:* 173, 179–181, 186–188
*The Rhodora:* 201–203
*The Singer's House:* 208–210, 213, 216–218
*Wild Swans:* 223, 225, 230–233

**Imagination**
*La Belle Dame sans Merci:* 24–26, 29–30, 32
*Mind:* 144, 147–148, 150–151
*Poetry:* 173, 176–177

**Imagism**
*Poetry:* 178–179

**The Impersonal As Personal**
*The Blue Rim of Memory:* 40

**Introspection**
*The Rhodora:* 199–200

**Irish Culture and Mythology**
*The Singer's House:* 208

**Irony**
*Driving to Town Late to Mail a Letter:* 65, 67–68
*Poetry:* 174, 177–178, 183–184, 186–189

# J

**Journey**
*On His Having Arrived at the Age of Twenty-Three:* 160

# L

**Landscape**
*The Cobweb:* 49, 51, 53
*For Jennifer, 6, on the Teton:* 85–95
*The Rhodora:* 191–193, 195–196, 199–200
*The Singer's House:* 206–207, 210, 212–213

**Language**
*For Jennifer, 6, on the Teton:* 88

**Law and Order**
*Having it Out with Melancholy:* 101, 104–105
*Knoxville, Tennessee:* 134

**Literary Criticism**
*La Belle Dame sans Merci:* 23
*On His Having Arrived at the Age of Twenty-Three:* 164
*Poetry:* 184–185

**Literary Movements**
*The Rhodora:* 196–197

**Loneliness**
*I Go Back to May 1937:* 114–116
*La Belle Dame sans Merci:* 33
*The Rhodora:* 196–197

**Loneliness and Isolation**
*I Go Back to May 1937:* 115

**Love and Passion**
*The Arsenal at Springfield:* 5, 7, 13, 15
*Early in the Morning:* 75, 77, 79
*I Go Back to May 1937:* 114–116, 119–124, 126–127
*Knoxville, Tennessee:* 131, 135
*La Belle Dame sans Merci:* 17, 20–34
*On His Having Arrived at the Age of Twenty-Three:* 164–165
*Wild Swans:* 229–233

**Loyalty**
*La Belle Dame sans Merci:* 17, 23
*The Singer's House:* 211–212

# M

**Marriage**
*I Go Back to May 1937:* 111–112, 114–118, 120

**Memory**
*Early in the Morning:* 77

**Memory and Reminiscence**
*The Blue Rim of Memory:* 37, 39–41
*Early in the Morning:* 74, 76–81

**Modernism**
*Poetry:* 176–180

**Monarchy**
*I Go Back to May 1937:* 118
*La Belle Dame sans Merci:* 26–28, 30, 33
*On His Having Arrived at the Age of Twenty-Three:* 162–164

**Morals and Morality**
*For Jennifer, 6, on the Teton:* 93, 95
*La Belle Dame sans Merci:* 22–23

**Mortality**
*The Cobweb:* 52

**Music**
*The Arsenal at Springfield:* 3–8, 10–11, 13–15
*The Blue Rim of Memory:* 42–43
*Driving to Town Late to Mail a Letter:* 71
*Early in the Morning:* 76–79
*Having it Out with Melancholy:* 102–105
*La Belle Dame sans Merci:* 20–24, 29–34
*Mind:* 146, 150
*The Singer's House:* 204, 207–211, 213–214, 216–218

**Mystery and Intrigue**
*La Belle Dame sans Merci:* 29–31, 33–35

**Myths and Legends**
*La Belle Dame sans Merci:* 17, 20–21, 24, 26–32, 34–35
*The Singer's House:* 207–208, 211–212

# N

**Narration**
*Knoxville, Tennessee:* 136–137
*La Belle Dame sans Merci:* 21–22, 24, 29–32, 34–35

**Nationalism and Patriotism**
*The Singer's House:* 207–208, 211

**Naturalism**
*Wild Swans:* 225

**Nature**
*The Arsenal at Springfield:* 3–5, 7
*The Blue Rim of Memory:* 40, 43–48
*The Cobweb:* 53
*Driving to Town Late to Mail a Letter:* 65, 71–72
*For Jennifer, 6, on the Teton:* 85, 87, 90–91, 93–95
*Having it Out with Melancholy:* 102, 104
*Knoxville, Tennessee:* 141–142
*La Belle Dame sans Merci:* 20–24, 29–34
*Mind:* 144, 147–148, 152–154
*Poetry:* 176
*The Rhodora:* 190, 192, 194–200
*The Singer's House:* 206–207, 217
*Wild Swans:* 226–229, 231–233

**1960s**
*The Blue Rim of Memory:* 42–43

**1970s**
*The Blue Rim of Memory:* 42–43
*Mind:* 148–149

**1980s**
*The Blue Rim of Memory:* 42–43
*The Cobweb:* 49, 53–54
*Early in the Morning:* 78–79
*I Go Back to May 1937:* 117–118

**North America**
*The Arsenal at Springfield:* 4, 8–9
*I Go Back to May 1937:* 113, 117–118

**Nostalgia**
*The Cobweb:* 52

## O

**Ode**
*La Belle Dame sans Merci:* 34–35

## P

**Painting**
*Poetry:* 178–179
**Parent and Child**
*I Go Back to May 1937:* 116
**Passage of Time**
*On His Having Arrived at the Age of Twenty-Three:* 161
**Peace**
*The Arsenal at Springfield:* 6
**Perception**
*Driving to Town Late to Mail a Letter:* 69–70
*La Belle Dame sans Merci:* 31–35
*Mind:* 144, 146–147
**Personal Identity**
*Early in the Morning:* 81–84
*The Singer's House:* 208–210, 212
**Personification**
*For Jennifer, 6, on the Teton:* 88–89
*Having it Out with Melancholy:* 99, 102
**Philosophical Ideas**
*Mind:* 150–151
*On His Having Arrived at the Age of Twenty-Three:* 162
*The Rhodora:* 194–195
**Pleasure**
*Driving to Town Late to Mail a Letter:* 71–72
*La Belle Dame sans Merci:* 30–35
**Poetry**
*The Arsenal at Springfield:* 1, 3, 5–15
*The Blue Rim of Memory:* 37, 39–48
*The Cobweb:* 49, 51–61
*Driving to Town Late to Mail a Letter:* 62–72
*Early in the Morning:* 74–84
*For Jennifer, 6, on the Teton:* 85–96
*Having it Out with Melancholy:* 97, 99–109
*I Go Back to May 1937:* 111–112, 114–127
*Knoxville, Tennessee:* 130–133, 135–143
*La Belle Dame sans Merci:* 17, 19–30, 33–35
*Mind:* 144, 146–152, 154–157
*On His Having Arrived at the Age of Twenty-Three:* 160–172
*Poetry:* 173–189
*The Rhodora:* 190–203

*The Singer's House:* 204, 206–210, 212–214, 216–218
*Wild Swans:* 220, 222–233
**Point of View**
*Early in the Morning:* 74–75, 78
*For Jennifer, 6, on the Teton:* 94–95
*Knoxville, Tennessee:* 137
**Politicians**
*The Arsenal at Springfield:* 8–9
*Having it Out with Melancholy:* 102, 104–105
**Politics**
*The Arsenal at Springfield:* 8 9
*The Blue Rim of Memory:* 42–43
*For Jennifer, 6, on the Teton:* 89–90
*Having it Out with Melancholy:* 104–105
*I Go Back to May 1937:* 117–119
*Knoxville, Tennessee:* 131, 133–135
*On His Having Arrived at the Age of Twenty-Three:* 158, 162–163, 167–169
*The Singer's House:* 207, 211–212, 216–218
*Wild Swans:* 224–225
**Predestination and Free Will**
*On His Having Arrived at the Age of Twenty-Three:* 161
**Pride**
*I Go Back to May 1937:* 114, 116–117
**Protestantism**
*On His Having Arrived at the Age of Twenty-Three:* 162–164
*The Singer's House:* 204, 210–212
**Psychology and the Human Mind**
*The Blue Rim of Memory:* 39
*Early in the Morning:* 77
*Knoxville, Tennessee:* 132, 135
*Mind:* 144, 146–148, 150–156

## R

**Race**
*Early in the Morning:* 78–79, 81–84
*Knoxville, Tennessee:* 132–135
**Reality and Appearances**
*Mind:* 148
**Recreation**
*For Jennifer, 6, on the Teton:* 90
**Religion and Religious Thought**
*The Arsenal at Springfield:* 14–15
*Having it Out with Melancholy:* 102–103, 106–108
*I Go Back to May 1937:* 120–121
*La Belle Dame sans Merci:* 32
*On His Having Arrived at the Age of Twenty-Three:* 161–164, 167, 169

*The Rhodora:* 195, 201–202
*The Singer's House:* 207, 211–212, 216, 218
**Remorse and Regret**
*I Go Back to May 1937:* 121
**Ritual**
*Early in the Morning:* 76
**Roman Catholicism**
*On His Having Arrived at the Age of Twenty-Three:* 162–163
*The Singer's House:* 204, 207, 211, 217–218
**Romanticism**
*The Cobweb:* 52
*La Belle Dame sans Merci:* 22–23
*The Rhodora:* 196

## S

**Salvation**
*On His Having Arrived at the Age of Twenty-Three:* 165–166
**Satire**
*Wild Swans:* 225
**Science and Technology**
*On His Having Arrived at the Age of Twenty-Three:* 162–163
**Security and Insecurity**
*Knoxville, Tennessee:* 133
**Self-Confidence**
*Wild Swans:* 222, 224–226
**Sentimentality**
*I Go Back to May 1937:* 120–121
**Setting**
*The Arsenal at Springfield:* 3, 8
*The Cobweb:* 51–52, 54
*Driving to Town Late to Mail a Letter:* 63–64, 66
*The Singer's House:* 207, 209
**Sickness**
*Having it Out with Melancholy:* 97, 99–101, 102, 104–105, 108–110
**Simple Life**
*Knoxville, Tennessee:* 132
**Simple Pleasures**
*Having it Out with Melancholy:* 104
**Sin**
*For Jennifer, 6, on the Teton:* 89
*Having it Out with Melancholy:* 109
**Slavery**
*The Arsenal at Springfield:* 9
**Solitude**
*Driving to Town Late to Mail a Letter:* 62, 64, 66, 72
*La Belle Dame sans Merci:* 29, 33–34
*Wild Swans:* 230–231
**Sonnet**
*On His Having Arrived at the Age of Twenty-Three:* 158, 160–162, 164–168

**Soothsayer**
*Driving to Town Late to Mail a Letter:* 69
**Sorrow**
*The Blue Rim of Memory:* 41
**Spirituality**
*Having it Out with Melancholy:* 100, 102–103, 105–110
*On His Having Arrived at the Age of Twenty-Three:* 160–162, 166–167, 169
**Sports and the Sporting Life**
*For Jennifer, 6, on the Teton:* 86, 89–90
**Storms and Weather Conditions**
*The Blue Rim of Memory:* 37, 40–41, 44–45
*Driving to Town Late to Mail a Letter:* 62, 64–66, 71–72
*Mind:* 152, 154
**Structure**
*The Arsenal at Springfield:* 10–11, 13
*La Belle Dame sans Merci:* 29–30, 35
*The Rhodora:* 202
*The Singer's House:* 212
**Surprise Inspiration**
*The Rhodora:* 193

# T
**Time and Change**
*La Belle Dame sans Merci:* 29, 31–33, 35
*The Rhodora:* 198–200
**Tone**
*Driving to Town Late to Mail a Letter:* 65–66
*Knoxville, Tennessee:* 137
*Poetry:* 173, 175
*Wild Swans:* 222, 225–226
**Transcendentalism**
*The Rhodora:* 190, 194–198
**Trust**
*Early in the Morning:* 80

# U
**Uncertainty**
*Poetry:* 173, 176–177, 180
*Wild Swans:* 222
**Understanding**
*La Belle Dame sans Merci:* 29, 35
*Mind:* 147–148
*Poetry:* 184
*The Rhodora:* 198, 200
*Wild Swans:* 231

**Unrequited Love**
*La Belle Dame sans Merci:* 21

# W
**War**
*The Arsenal at Springfield:* 5
**War, the Military, and Soldier Life**
*The Arsenal at Springfield:* 1, 4–15
*The Blue Rim of Memory:* 42–43
*Having it Out with Melancholy:* 101, 104–105
*Knoxville, Tennessee:* 133–134
*The Singer's House:* 204, 211–212
*Wild Swans:* 224–225
**Wildlife**
*For Jennifer, 6, on the Teton:* 86–90
*Having it Out with Melancholy:* 102–105
*La Belle Dame sans Merci:* 29, 32–33
*The Rhodora:* 192–193, 196
*The Singer's House:* 207–210, 212–213, 216–218
*Wild Swans:* 220–223, 225, 227–233

# Cumulative Index of First Lines

## A

A brackish reach of shoal off Madaket,— (The Quaker Graveyard in Nantucket) V6:158
"A cold coming we had of it (Journey of the Magi) V7:110
A few minutes ago, I stepped onto the deck (The Cobweb) V17:50
A line in long array where they wind betwixt green islands, (Cavalry Crossing a Ford) V13:50
A narrow Fellow in the grass (A Narrow Fellow in the Grass) V11:127
*A pine box for me. I mean it.* (Last Request) V14: 231
A poem should be palpable and mute (Ars Poetica) V5:2
A stone from the depths that has witnessed the seas drying up (Song of a Citizen) V16:125
A tourist came in from Orbitville, (Southbound on the Freeway) V16:158
A wind is ruffling the tawny pelt (A Far Cry from Africa) V6:60
a woman precedes me up the long rope, (Climbing) V14:113
About me the night moonless wimples the mountains (Vancouver Lights) V8:245
About suffering they were never wrong (Musée des Beaux Arts) V1:148
Across Roblin Lake, two shores away, (Wilderness Gothic) V12:241
After you finish your work (Ballad of Orange and Grape) V10:17
"Ah, are you digging on my grave (Ah, Are You Digging on My Grave?) V4:2
All Greece hates (Helen) V6:92
All night long the hockey pictures (To a Sad Daughter) V8:230
All winter your brute shoulders strained against collars, padding (Names of Horses) V8:141
Also Ulysses once—that other war. (Kilroy) V14:213
Anasazi (Anasazi) V9:2
And God stepped out on space (The Creation) V1:19
Animal bones and some mossy tent rings (Lament for the Dorsets) V5:190
As I perceive (The Gold Lily) V5:127
As I walked out one evening (As I Walked Out One Evening) V4:15
As virtuous men pass mildly away (A Valediction: Forbidding Mourning) V11:201
At noon in the desert a panting lizard (At the Bomb Testing Site) V8:2
Ay, tear her tattered ensign down! (Old Ironsides) V9:172

## B

Back then, before we came (On Freedom's Ground) V12:186
Bananas ripe and green, and ginger-root (The Tropics in New York) V4:255
Because I could not stop for Death— (Because I Could Not Stop for Death) V2:27
Before the indifferent beak could let her drop? (Leda and the Swan) V13:182
Bent double, like old beggars under slacks, (Dulce et Decorum Est) V10:109
Between my finger and my thumb (Digging) V5:70
Beware of ruins: they have a treacherous charm (Beware of Ruins) V8:43
Bright star! would I were steadfast as thou art— (Bright Star! Would I Were Steadfast as Thou Art) V9:44
By the rude bridge that arched the flood (Concord Hymn) V4:30

## C

Celestial choir! enthron'd in realms of light, (To His Excellency General Washington V13:212
Come with me into those things that have felt his despair for so long— (Come with Me) V6:31

Complacencies of the peignoir, and late (Sunday Morning) V16:189

Composed in the Tower, before his execution ("More Light! More Light!") V6:119

# D

Darkened by time, the masters, like our memories, mix (Black Zodiac) V10:46

Death, be not proud, though some have called thee (Holy Sonnet 10) V2:103

Devouring Time, blunt thou the lion's paws (Sonnet 19) V9:210

Do not go gentle into that good night (Do Not Go Gentle into that Good Night) V1:51

Do not weep, maiden, for war is kind (War Is Kind) V9:252

Don Arturo says: (Business) V16:2

(Dumb, (A Grafted Tongue) V12:92

# E

Each day the shadow swings (In the Land of Shinar) V7:83

Each night she waits by the road (Bidwell Ghost) V14:2

# F

Falling upon earth (Falling Upon Earth) V2:64

Five years have past; five summers, with the length (Tintern Abbey) V2:249

Flesh is heretic. (Anorexic) V12:2

For three years, out of key with his time, (Hugh Selwyn Mauberley) V16:26

Forgive me for thinking I saw (For a New Citizen of These United States) V15:55

From my mother's sleep I fell into the State (The Death of the Ball Turret Gunner) V2:41

# G

*Gardener:* Sir, I encountered Death (Incident in a Rose Garden) V14:190

Gather ye Rose-buds while ye may, (To the Virgins, to Make Much of Time ) V13:226

Go down, Moses (Go Down, Moses) V11:42

Gray mist wolf (Four Mountain Wolves) V9:131

# H

"Had he and I but met (The Man He Killed) V3:167

Had we but world enough, and time (To His Coy Mistress) V5:276

Half a league, half a league (The Charge of the Light Brigade) V1:2

Having a Coke with You (Having a Coke with You) V12:105

He clasps the crag with crooked hands (The Eagle) V11:30

He was found by the Bureau of Statistics to be (The Unknown Citizen) V3:302

Hear the sledges with the bells— (The Bells) V3:46

Her body is not so white as (Queen-Ann's-Lace) V6:179

Her eyes were coins of porter and her West (A Farewell to English) V10:126

Here they are. The soft eyes open (The Heaven of Animals) V6:75

Hog Butcher for the World (Chicago) V3:61

Hold fast to dreams (Dream Variations) V15:42

Hope is a tattered flag and a dream out of time. (Hope is a Tattered Flag) V12:120

"Hope" is the thing with feathers— (Hope Is the Thing with Feathers) V3:123

How do I love thee? Let me count the ways (Sonnet 43) V2:236

How shall we adorn (Angle of Geese) V2:2

How soon hath Time, the subtle thief of youth, (On His Having Arrived at the Age of Twenty-Three) V17:159

How would it be if you took yourself off (Landscape with Tractor) V10:182

Hunger crawls into you (Hunger in New York City) V4:79

# I

I am not a painter, I am a poet (Why I Am Not a Painter) V8:258

I am the Smoke King (The Song of the Smoke) V13:196

I am silver and exact. I have no preconceptions (Mirror) V1:116

I am trying to pry open your casket (Dear Reader) V10:85

I became a creature of light (The Mystery) V15:137

I cannot love the Brothers Wright (Reactionary Essay on Applied Science) V9:199

I felt a Funeral, in my Brain, (I felt a Funeral in my Brain) V13:137

I have just come down from my father (The Hospital Window) V11:58

I have met them at close of day (Easter 1916) V5:91

I hear America singing, the varied carols I hear (I Hear America Singing) V3:152

I heard a Fly buzz—when I died— (I Heard a Fly Buzz—When I Died—) V5:140

I know that I shall meet my fate (An Irish Airman Foresees His Death) V1:76

I looked in my heart while the wild swans went over. (Wild Swans) V17:221

I prove a theorem and the house expands: (Geometry) V15:68

I see them standing at the formal gates of their colleges, (I go Back to May 1937) V17:112

I sit in the top of the wood, my eyes closed (Hawk Roosting) V4:55

I'm delighted to see you (The Constellation Orion) V8:53

I've known rivers; (The Negro Speaks of Rivers) V10:197

I was sitting in mcsorley's. outside it was New York and beautifully snowing. (i was sitting in mcsorley's) V13:151

I will arise and go now, and go to Innisfree, (The Lake Isle of Innisfree) V15:121

If all the world and love were young, (The Nymph's Reply to the Shepard) V14:241

If ever two were one, then surely we (To My Dear and Loving Husband) V6:228

If I should die, think only this of me (The Soldier) V7:218

"Imagine being the first to say: *surveillance*," (Inventors) V7:97

In 1936, a child (Blood Oranges) V13:34

In a while they rose and went out aimlessly riding, (Merlin Enthralled) V16:72
In China (Lost Sister) V5:216
In ethics class so many years ago (Ethics) V8:88
In Flanders fields the poppies blow (In Flanders Fields) V5:155
In India in their lives they happen (Ways to Live) V16:228
In May, when sea-winds pierced our solitudes, (The Rhodora) V17:191
In the groves of Africa from their natural wonder (An African Elegy) V13:3
In the Shreve High football stadium (Autumn Begins in Martins Ferry, Ohio) V8:17
In Xanadu did Kubla Khan (Kubla Khan) V5:172
Ink runs from the corners of my mouth (Eating Poetry) V9:60
It is a cold and snowy night. The main street is deserted. (Driving to Town Late to Mail a Letter) V17:63
It is an ancient Mariner (The Rime of the Ancient Mariner) V4:127
It is in the small things we see it. (Courage) V14:125
It little profits that an idle king (Ulysses) V2:278
It looked extremely rocky for the Mudville nine that day (Casey at the Bat) V5:57
It seems vainglorious and proud (The Conquerors) V13:67
It was in and about the Martinmas time (Barbara Allan) V7:10
It was many and many a year ago (Annabel Lee) V9:14
Its quick soft silver bell beating, beating (Auto Wreck) V3:31

## J

Januaries, Nature greets our eyes (Brazil, January 1, 1502) V6:15
Just off the highway to Rochester, Minnesota (A Blessing) V7:24
just once (For the White poets who would be Indian) V13:112

## L

l(a (l(a) V1:85
Let me not to the marriage of true minds (Sonnet 116) V3:288
Listen, my children, and you shall hear (Paul Revere's Ride) V2:178
Little Lamb, who made thee? (The Lamb) V12:134
Long long ago when the world was a wild place (Bedtime Story) V8:32

## M

maggie and milly and molly and may (maggie & milly & molly & may) V12:149
Mary sat musing on the lamp-flame at the table (The Death of the Hired Man) V4:42
Men with picked voices chant the names (Overture to a Dance of Locomotives) V11:143
"Mother dear, may I go downtown (Ballad of Birmingham) V5:17
Much Madness is divinest Sense— (Much Madness is Divinest Sense) V16:86

My black face fades (Facing It) V5:109
My father stands in the warm evening (Starlight) V8:213
My heart aches, and a drowsy numbness pains (Ode to a Nightingale) V3:228
My heart is like a singing bird (A Birthday) V10:33
My life closed twice before its close— (My Life Closed Twice Before Its Close) V8:127
My mistress' eyes are nothing like the sun (Sonnet 130) V1:247
My uncle in East Germany (The Exhibit) V9:107

## N

Nature's first green is gold (Nothing Gold Can Stay) V3:203
No easy thing to bear, the weight of sweetness (The Weight of Sweetness) V11:230
Nobody heard him, the dead man (Not Waving but Drowning) V3:216
Not marble nor the gilded monuments (Sonnet 55) V5:246
Not the memorized phone numbers. (What Belongs to Us) V15:196
Now as I was young and easy under the apple boughs (Fern Hill) V3:92
Now as I watch the progress of the plague (The Missing) V9:158

## O

O Captain! my Captain, our fearful trip is done (O Captain! My Captain!) V2:146
O Lord our Lord, how excellent is thy name in all the earth! who hast set thy glory above the heavens (Psalm 8) V9:182
O my Luve's like a red, red rose (A Red, Red Rose) V8:152
O what can ail thee, knight-at-arms, (La Belle Dame sans Merci) V17:18
"O where ha' you been, Lord Randal, my son? (Lord Randal) V6:105
O wild West Wind, thou breath of Autumn's being (Ode to the West Wind) V2:163
Oh, but it is dirty! (Filling Station) V12:57
old age sticks (old age sticks) V3:246
On either side the river lie (The Lady of Shalott) V15:95
Once upon a midnight dreary, while I pondered, weak and weary (The Raven) V1:200
Once some people were visiting Chekhov (Chocolates) V11:17
One day I'll lift the telephone (Elegy for My Father, Who Is Not Dead) V14:154
One foot down, then hop! It's hot (Harlem Hopscotch) V2:93
one shoe on the roadway presents (A Piéd) V3:16
Out of the hills of Habersham, (Song of the Chattahoochee) V14:283
Out walking in the frozen swamp one gray day (The Wood-Pile) V6:251
Oysters we ate (Oysters) V4:91

## P

Pentagon code (Smart and Final Iris) V15:183
Poised between going on and back, pulled (The Base Stealer) V12:30

## Q

Quinquireme of Nineveh from distant Ophir (Cargoes) V5:44

## R

Red men embraced my body's whiteness (Birch Canoe) V5:31

Remember me when I am gone away (Remember) V14:255

## S

Shall I compare thee to a Summer's day? (Sonnet 18) V2:222

She came every morning to draw water (A Drink of Water) V8:66

She sang beyond the genius of the sea. (The Idea of Order at Key West) V13:164

She walks in beauty, like the night (She Walks in Beauty) V14:268

Side by side, their faces blurred, (An Arundel Tomb) V12:17

Since the professional wars— (Midnight) V2:130

S'io credesse che mia risposta fosse (The Love Song of J. Alfred Prufrock) V1:97

Sleepless as Prospero back in his bedroom (Darwin in 1881) V13:83

so much depends (The Red Wheelbarrow) V1:219

So the man spread his blanket on the field (A Tall Man Executes a Jig) V12:228

So the sky wounded you, jagged at the heart, (Daylights) V13:101

Softly, in the dark, a woman is singing to me (Piano) V6:145

Some say the world will end in fire (Fire and Ice) V7:57

Something there is that doesn't love a wall (Mending Wall) V5:231

Sometimes walking late at night (Butcher Shop) V7:43

Sometimes, a lion with a prophet's beard (For An Assyrian Frieze) V9:120

Sometimes, in the middle of the lesson (Music Lessons) V8:117

South of the bridge on Seventeenth (Fifteen) V2:78

Stop all the clocks, cut off the telephone, (Funeral Blues) V10:139

Strong Men, riding horses. In the West (Strong Men, Riding Horses) V4:209

Such places are too still for history, (Deep Woods) V14:138

Sundays too my father got up early (Those Winter Sundays) V1:300

Swing low sweet chariot (Swing Low Sweet Chariot) V1:283

## T

Take heart, monsieur, four-fifths of this province (For Jean Vincent D'abbadie, Baron St.-Castin) V12:78

Tears, idle tears, I know not what they mean (Tears, Idle Tears) V4:220

Tell me not, in mournful numbers (A Psalm of Life) V7:165

That is no country for old men. The young (Sailing to Byzantium) V2:207

That time of drought the embered air (Drought Year) V8:78

That's my last Duchess painted on the wall (My Last Duchess) V1:165

The apparition of these faces in the crowd (In a Station of the Metro) V2:116

The Assyrian came down like the wolf on the fold (The Destruction of Sennacherib) V1:38

The broken pillar of the wing jags from the clotted shoulder (Hurt Hawks) V3:138

The bud (Saint Francis and the Sow) V9:222

The Bustle in a House (The Bustle in a House) V10:62

The buzz saw snarled and rattled in the yard (Out, Out—) V10:212

The courage that my mother had (The Courage that My Mother Had) V3:79

The Curfew tolls the knell of parting day (Elegy Written in a Country Churchyard) V9:73

The force that through the green fuse drives the flower (The Force That Through the Green Fuse Drives the Flower) V8:101

The green lamp flares on the table (This Life) V1:293

The ills I sorrow at (Any Human to Another) V3:2

The instructor said (Theme for English B) V6:194

The king sits in Dumferling toune (Sir Patrick Spens) V4:177

The land was overmuch like scenery (Beowulf) V11:2

The last time I saw it was 1968. (The Hiding Place) V10:152

The Lord is my shepherd; I shall not want (Psalm 23) V4:103

The man who sold his lawn to standard oil (The War Against the Trees) V11:215

The moon glows the same (The Moon Glows the Same) V7:152

The old South Boston Aquarium stands (For the Union Dead) V7:67

The others bent their heads and started in ("Trouble with Math in a One-Room Country School") V9:238

The pale nuns of St. Joseph are here (Island of Three Marias) V11:79

The Phoenix comes of flame and dust (The Phoenix) V10:226

The rain set early in to-night: (Porphyria's Lover) V15:151

The river brought down (How We Heard the Name) V10:167

The rusty spigot (Onomatopoeia) V6:133

The sea is calm tonight (Dover Beach) V2:52

The sea sounds insincere (The Milkfish Gatherers) V11:111

The slow overture of rain, (Mind) V17:145

The Soul selects her own Society—(The Soul Selects Her Own Society) V1:259

The time you won your town the race (To an Athlete Dying Young) V7:230

The way sorrow enters the bone (The Blue Rim of Memory) V17:38

The whiskey on your breath (My Papa's Waltz) V3:191

The wind was a torrent of darkness among the gusty trees (The Highwayman) V4:66

*There are strange things done in the midnight sun* (The Cremation of Sam McGee) V10:75

There have been rooms for such a short time (The Horizons of Rooms) V15:79

There is the one song everyone (Siren Song) V7:196

There's a Certain Slant of Light (There's a Certain Slant of Light) V6:211
There's no way out. (In the Suburbs) V14:201
There will come soft rains and the smell of the ground, (There Will Come Soft Rains) V14:301
These open years, the river (For Jennifer, 6, on the Teton) V17:86
They eat beans mostly, this old yellow pair (The Bean Eaters) V2:16
they were just meant as covers (My Mother Pieced Quilts) V12:169
They said, "Wait." Well, I waited. (Alabama Centennial) V10:2
This girlchild was: born as usual (Barbie Doll) V9:33
This is my letter to the World (This Is My Letter to the World) V4:233
This is the Arsenal. From floor to ceiling, (The Arsenal at Springfield) V17:2
This is the black sea-brute bulling through wave-wrack (Leviathan) V5:203
This poem is concerned with language on a very plain level (Paradoxes and Oxymorons) V11:162
This tale is true, and mine. It tells (The Seafarer) V8:177
Thou still unravish'd bride of quietness (Ode on a Grecian Urn) V1:179
Three times my life has opened. (Three Times My Life Has Opened) V16:213
to fold the clothes. No matter who lives (I Stop Writimg the Poem) V16:58
Tonight I can write the saddest lines (Tonight I Can Write) V11:187
tonite, *thriller* was (Beware: Do Not Read This Poem) V6:3
Turning and turning in the widening gyre (The Second Coming) V7:179
'Twas brillig, and the slithy toves (Jabberwocky) V11:91
Two roads diverged in a yellow wood (The Road Not Taken) V2:195
Tyger! Tyger! burning bright (The Tyger) V2:263

# W

wade (The Fish) V14:171
Wanting to say things, (My Father's Song) V16:102
We could be here. This is the valley (Small Town with One Road) V7:207
We met the British in the dead of winter (Meeting the British) V7:138
We real cool. We (We Real Cool) V6:242
Well, son, I'll tell you (Mother to Son) V3:178
What dire offense from amorous causes springs, (The Rape of the Lock) V12:202
What happens to a dream deferred? (Harlem) V1:63
What thoughts I have of you tonight, Walt Whitman, for I walked down the sidestreets under the trees with a headache self-conscious looking at the full moon (A Supermarket in California) V5:261
Whatever it is, it must have (American Poetry) V7:2
When Abraham Lincoln was shoveled into the tombs, he forgot the copperheads, and the assassin ... in the dust, in the cool tombs (Cool Tombs) V6:45
When I consider how my light is spent ([On His Blindness] Sonnet 16) V3:262
When I have fears that I may cease to be (When I Have Fears that I May Cease to Be) V2:295
When I see a couple of kids (High Windows) V3:108
When I see birches bend to left and right (Birches) V13:14
When I was born, you waited (Having it Out with Melancholy) V17:98
When I was one-and-twenty (When I Was One-and-Twenty) V4:268
When I watch you (Miss Rosie) V1:133
When, in disgrace with Fortune and men's eyes (Sonnet 29) V8:198
When the mountains of Puerto Rico (We Live by What We See at Night) V13:240
When the world was created wasn't it like this? (Anniversary) V15:2
When they said *Carrickfergus* I could hear (The Singer's House) V17:205
Whenever Richard Cory went down town (Richard Cory) V4:116
While my hair was still cut straight across my forehead (The River-Merchant's Wife: A Letter) V8:164
While the long grain is softening (Early in the Morning) V17:75
While this America settles in the mould of its vulgarity, heavily thickening to empire (Shine, Perishing Republic) V4:161
Who has ever stopped to think of the divinity of Lamont Cranston? (In Memory of Radio) V9:144
Whose woods these are I think I know (Stopping by Woods on a Snowy Evening) V1:272
Why should I let the toad *work* (Toads) V4:244

# Y

You are small and intense (To a Child Running With Outstretched Arms in Canyon de Chelly) V11:173
You do not have to be good. (Wild Geese) V15:207
You were never told, Mother, how old Illya was drunk (The Czar's Last Christmas Letter) V12:44

# Cumulative Index of Last Lines

## A

A heart whose love is innocent! (She Walks in Beauty) V14:268

a man then suddenly stops running (Island of Three Marias) V11:80

a space in the lives of their friends (Beware: Do Not Read This Poem) V6:3

A sudden blow: the great wings beating still (Leda and the Swan) V13:181

A terrible beauty is born (Easter 1916) V5:91

About my big, new, automatically defrosting refrigerator with the built-in electric eye (Reactionary Essay on Applied Science) V9:199

about the tall mounds of termites. (Song of a Citizen) V16:126

Across the expedient and wicked stones (Auto Wreck) V3:31

Ah, dear father, graybeard, lonely old courage-teacher, what America did you have when Charon quit poling his ferry and you got out on a smoking bank and stood watching the boat disappear on the black waters of Lethe? (A Supermarket in California) V5:261

All losses are restored and sorrows end (Sonnet 30) V4:192

Amen. Amen (The Creation) V1:20

Anasazi (Anasazi) V9:3

and all beyond saving by children (Ethics) V8:88

and all the richer for it. (Mind) V17:146

And all we need of hell (My Life Closed Twice Before Its Close) V8:127

and changed, back to the class ("Trouble with Math in a One-Room Country School") V9:238

And Death shall be no more: Death, thou shalt die (Holy Sonnet 10) V2:103

And drunk the milk of Paradise (Kubla Khan) V5:172

And Finished knowing—then— (I Felt a Funeral in My Brain) V13:137

And gallop terribly against each other's bodies (Autumn Begins in Martins Ferry, Ohio) V8:17

and go back. (For the White poets who would be Indian) V13:112

And handled with a Chain—(Much Madness is Divinest Sense) V16:86

And has not begun to grow a manly smile. (Deep Woods) V14:139

And his own Word (The Phoenix) V10:226

And I am Nicholas. (The Czar's Last Christmas Letter) V12:45

*And in the suburbs Can't sat down and cried.* (Kilroy) V14:213

And it's been years. (Anniversary) V15:3

And life for me ain't been no crystal stair (Mother to Son) V3:179

And like a thunderbolt he falls (The Eagle) V11:30

And makes me end where I begun (A Valediction: Forbidding Mourning) V11:202

And 'midst the stars inscribe Belinda's name. (The Rape of the Lock) V12:209

And miles to go before I sleep (Stopping by Woods on a Snowy Evening) V1:272

and my father saying things. (My Father's Song) V16:102

And no birds sing. (La Belle Dame sans Merci) V17:18

And not waving but drowning (Not Waving but Drowning) V3:216

And oh, 'tis true, 'tis true (When I Was One-and-Twenty) V4:268

And reach for your scalping knife. (For Jean Vincent D'abbadie, Baron St.-Castin) V12:78

and retreating, always retreating, behind it (Brazil, January 1, 1502) V6:16

And settled upon his eyes in a black soot ("More Light! More Light!") V6:120

And shuts his eyes. (Darwin in 1881) V13: 84

And so live ever—or else swoon to death (Bright Star! Would I Were Steadfast as Thou Art) V9:44
and strange and loud was the dingoes' cry (Drought Year) V8:78
and stride out. (Courage) V14:126
and sweat and fat and greed. (Anorexic) V12:3
And that has made all the difference (The Road Not Taken) V2:195
And the deep river ran on (As I Walked Out One Evening) V4:16
And the midnight message of Paul Revere (Paul Revere's Ride) V2:180
And the mome raths outgrabe (Jabberwocky) V11:91
And the Salvation Army singing God loves us. . . . (Hope is a Tattered Flag) V12:120
and these the last verses that I write for her (Tonight I Can Write) V11:187
And those roads in South Dakota that feel around in the darkness . . . (Come with Me) V6:31
and to know she will stay in the field till you die? (Landscape with Tractor) V10:183
and two blankets embroidered with smallpox (Meeting the British) V7:138
and waving, shouting, *Welcome back.* (Elegy for My Father, Who Is Not Dead) V14:154
And would suffice (Fire and Ice) V7:57
And yet God has not said a word! (Porphyria's Lover) V15:151
and you spread un the thin halo of night mist. (Ways to Live) V16:229
And Zero at the Bone— (A Narrow Fellow in the Grass) V11:127
As any She belied with false compare (Sonnet 130) V1:248
As ever in my great Task-Master's eye. (On His Having Arrived at the Age of Twenty-Three) V17:160
As far as Cho-fu-Sa (The River-Merchant's Wife: A Letter) V8:165
As the contagion of those molten eyes (For An Assyrian Frieze) V9:120
As they lean over the beans in their rented back room that is full of beads and receipts and dolls and clothes, tobacco crumbs, vases and fringes (The Bean Eaters) V2:16
aspired to become lighter than air (Blood Oranges) V13:34
at home in the fish's fallen heaven (Birch Canoe) V5:31

# B

Back to the play of constant give and change (The Missing) V9:158
Before it was quite unsheathed from reality (Hurt Hawks) V3:138
Black like me. (Dream Variations) V15:42
Bless me (Hunger in New York City) V4:79
But be (Ars Poetica) V5:3
but it works every time (Siren Song) V7:196
But there is no joy in Mudville—mighty Casey has "Struck Out." (Casey at the Bat) V5:58
But, baby, where are you?" (Ballad of Birmingham) V5:17
But we hold our course, and the wind is with us. (On Freedom's Ground) V12:187
by good fortune (The Horizons of Rooms) V15:80

# C

Calls through the valleys of Hall. (Song of the Chattahoochee) V14:284
chickens (The Red Wheelbarrow) V1:219
clear water dashes (Onomatopoeia) V6:133
come to life and burn? (Bidwell Ghost) V14:2
Comin' for to carry me home (Swing Low Sweet Chariot) V1:284

# D

Dare frame thy fearful symmetry? (The Tyger) V2:263
"Dead," was all he answered (The Death of the Hired Man) V4:44
deep in the deepest one, tributaries burn. (For Jennifer, 6, on the Teton) V17:86
Delicate, delicate, delicate, delicate—now! (The Base Stealer) V12:30
Die soon (We Real Cool) V6:242
Do what you are going to do, I will tell about it. (I go Back to May 1937) V17:113
Down in the flood of remembrance, I weep like a child for the past (Piano) V6:145
Downward to darkness, on extended wings. (Sunday Morning) V16:190
Driving around, I will waste more time. (Driving to Town Late to Mail a Letter) V17:63
dry wells that fill so easily now (The Exhibit) V9:107

# E

Eternal, unchanging creator of earth. Amen (The Seafarer) V8:178

# F

fall upon us, the dwellers in shadow (In the Land of Shinar) V7:84
Fallen cold and dead (O Captain! My Captain!) V2:147
Firewood, iron-ware, and cheap tin trays (Cargoes) V5:44
Fled is that music:—Do I wake or sleep? (Ode to a Nightingale) V3:229
For I'm sick at the heart, and I fain wad lie down." (Lord Randal) V6:105
For nothing now can ever come to any good. (Funeral Blues) V10:139
forget me as fast as you can. (Last Request) V14:231

# H

Had anything been wrong, we should certainly have heard (The Unknown Citizen) V3:303
Had somewhere to get to and sailed calmly on (Mus,e des Beaux Arts) V1:148
half eaten by the moon. (Dear Reader) V10:85
hand over hungry hand. (Climbing) V14:113
Happen on a red tongue (Small Town with One Road) V7:207
Has no more need of, and I have (The Courage that My Mother Had) V3:80
Hath melted like snow in the glance of the Lord! (The Destruction of Sennacherib) V1:39

He rose the morrow morn (The Rime of the Ancient Mariner) V4:132
He says again, "Good fences make good neighbors." (Mending Wall) V5:232
Has set me softly down beside you. The Poem is you (Paradoxes and Oxymorons) V11:162
How at my sheet goes the same crooked worm (The Force That Through the Green Fuse Drives the Flower) V8:101
How can I turn from Africa and live? (A Far Cry from Africa) V6:61
How sad then is even the marvelous! (An Africian Elegy) V13:4

# I

I am black. (The Song of the Smoke) V13:197
I am going to keep things like this (Hawk Roosting) V4:55
I am not brave at all (Strong Men, Riding Horses) V4:209
I could not see to see— (I Heard a Fly Buzz—When I Died—) V5:140
I have just come down from my father (The Hospital Window) V11:58
*I cremated Sam McGee* (The Cremation of Sam McGee) V10:76
I hear it in the deep heart's core. (The Lake Isle of Innisfree) V15:121
I never writ, nor no man ever loved (Sonnet 116) V3:288
I romp with joy in the bookish dark (Eating Poetry) V9:61
I see Mike's painting, called SARDINES (Why I Am Not a Painter) V8:259
I shall but love thee better after death (Sonnet 43) V2:236
I should be glad of another death (Journey of the Magi) V7:110
I stand up (Miss Rosie) V1:133
I stood there, fifteen (Fifteen) V2:78
I take it you are he? (Incident in a Rose Garden) V14:191
I turned aside and bowed my head and wept (The Tropics in New York) V4:255
I'll be gone from here. (The Cobweb) V17:51
I'll dig with it (Digging) V5:71
If Winter comes, can Spring be far behind? (Ode to the West Wind) V2:163
In a convulsive misery (The Milkfish Gatherers) V11:112
In balance with this life, this death (An Irish Airman Foresees His Death) V1:76
In Flanders fields (In Flanders Fields) V5:155
In ghostlier demarcations, keener sounds. (The Idea of Order at Key West) V13:164
In hearts at peace, under an English heaven (The Soldier) V7:218
In her tomb by the side of the sea (Annabel Lee) V9:14
in the family of things. (Wild Geese) V15:208
in the grit gray light of day. (Daylights) V13:102
In the rear-view mirrors of the passing cars (The War Against the Trees) V11:216
iness (l(a) V1:85
Into blossom (A Blessing) V7:24
Is Come, my love is come to me. (A Birthday) V10:34
is still warm (Lament for the Dorsets) V5:191
It asked a crumb—of Me (Hope Is the Thing with Feathers) V3:123
it's always ourselves we find in the sea (maggie & milly & molly & may) V12:150
its bright, unequivocal eye. (Having it Out with Melancholy) V17:99
its youth. The sea grows old in it. (The Fish) V14:172
It was your resting place." (Ah, Are You Digging on My Grave?) V4:2

# J

Judge tenderly—of Me (This Is My Letter to the World) V4:233
Just imagine it (Inventors) V7:97

# L

Laughing the stormy, husky, brawling laughter of Youth, half-naked, sweating, proud to be Hog Butcher, Tool Maker, Stacker of Wheat, Player with Railroads and Freight Handler to the Nation (Chicago) V3:61
Learn to labor and to wait (A Psalm of Life) V7:165
Leashed in my throat (Midnight) V2:131
Let my people go (Go Down, Moses) V11:43
life, our life and its forgetting. (For a New Citizen of These United States) V15:55
Like Stone— (The Soul Selects Her Own Society) V1:259
Little Lamb, God bless thee. (The Lamb) V12:135

# M

'Make a wish, Tom, make a wish.' (Drifters) V10: 98
make it seem to change (The Moon Glows the Same) V7:152
midnight-oiled in the metric laws? (A Farewell to English) V10:126
Monkey business (Business) V16:2
More dear, both for themselves and for thy sake! (Tintern Abbey) V2:250
My love shall in my verse ever live young (Sonnet 19) V9:211
My soul has grown deep like the rivers. (The Negro Speaks of Rivers) V10:198

# N

never to waken in that world again (Starlight) V8:213
Black like me (Dream Variations) V15:42
No, she's brushing a boy's hair (Facing It) V5:110
*no*—tell them *no*— (The Hiding Place) V10:153
Noble six hundred! (The Charge of the Light Brigade) V1:3
Not even the blisters. Look. (What Belongs to Us) V15:196
Nothing gold can stay (Nothing Gold Can Stay) V3:203
Nothing, and is nowhere, and is endless (High Windows) V3:108
Now! (Alabama Centennial) V10:2
nursing the tough skin of figs (This Life) V1:293

# O

O Death in Life, the days that are no more! (Tears, Idle Tears) V4:220
O Lord our Lord, how excellent is thy name in all the earth! (Psalm 8) V9:182
O Roger, Mackerel, Riley, Ned, Nellie, Chester, Lady Ghost (Names of Horses) V8:142

of gentleness (To a Sad Daughter) V8:231
of love's austere and lonely offices? (Those Winter Sundays) V1:300
of peaches (The Weight of Sweetness) V11:230
Of the camellia (Falling Upon Earth) V2:64
Of the Creator. And he waits for the world to begin (Leviathan) V5:204
Of what is past, or passing, or to come (Sailing to Byzantium) V2:207
Old Ryan, not yours (The Constellation Orion) V8:53
On the dark distant flurry (Angle of Geese) V2:2
On the look of Death— (There's a Certain Slant of Light) V6:212
On your head like a crown (Any Human to Another) V3:2
One could do worse that be a swinger of birches. (Birches) V13:15
*Or does it explode?* (Harlem) V1:63
Or help to half-a-crown." (The Man He Killed) V3:167
or nothing (Queen-Ann's-Lace) V6:179
or the one red leaf the snow releases in March. (Three Times My Life Has Opened) V16:213
ORANGE forever. (Ballad of Orange and Grape) V10:18
outside. (it was New York and beautifully, snowing . . . (i was sitting in mcsorley's) V13:152
owing old (old age sticks) V3:246

# P

Perhaps he will fall. (Wilderness Gothic) V12:242
Petals on a wet, black bough (In a Station of the Metro) V2:116
*Plaiting a dark red love-knot into her long black hair* (The Highwayman) V4:68
Pro patria mori. (Dulce et Decorum Est) V10:110

# R

Rage, rage against the dying of the light (Do Not Go Gentle into that Good Night) V1:51
Raise it again, man. We still believe what we hear. (The Singer's House) V17:206
*Remember the Giver* fading off the lip (A Drink of Water) V8:66
Rises toward her day after day, like a terrible fish (Mirror) V1:116

# S

Shall be lifted—nevermore! (The Raven) V1:202
Singing of him what they could understand (Beowulf) V11:3
Singing with open mouths their strong melodious songs (I Hear America Singing) V3:152
slides by on grease (For the Union Dead) V7:67
Slouches towards Bethlehem to be born? (The Second Coming) V7:179
So long lives this, and this gives life to thee (Sonnet 18) V2:222
Somebody loves us all. (Filling Station) V12:57
Stand still, yet we will make him run (To His Coy Mistress) V5:277
startled into eternity (Four Mountain Wolves) V9:132
Still clinging to your shirt (My Papa's Waltz) V3:192
Stood up, coiled above his head, transforming all. (A Tall Man Executes a Jig) V12:229
Surely goodness and mercy shall follow me all the days of my life: and I will dwell in the house of the Lord for ever (Psalm 23) V4:103
syllables of an old order. (A Grafted Tongue) V12:93

# T

Take any streetful of people buying clothes and groceries, cheering a hero or throwing confetti and blowing tin horns ... tell me if the lovers are losers ... tell me if any get more than the lovers ... in the dust ... in the cool tombs (Cool Tombs) V6:46
Than that you should remember and be sad. (Remember) V14:255
That then I scorn to change my state with Kings (Sonnet 29) V8:198
That when we live no more, we may live ever (To My Dear and Loving Husband) V6:228
That's the word. (Black Zodiac) V10:47
the bigger it gets. (Smart and Final Iris) V15:183
The bosom of his Father and his God (Elegy Written in a Country Churchyard) V9:74
The dance is sure (Overture to a Dance of Locomotives) V11:143
The eyes turn topaz. (Hugh Selwyn Mauberley) V16:30
The garland briefer than a girl's (To an Athlete Dying Young) V7:230
The guidon flags flutter gayly in the wind. (Cavalry Crossing a Ford) V13:50
The hands gripped hard on the desert (At the Bomb Testing Site) V8:3
The holy melodies of love arise. (The Arsenal at Springfield) V17:3
the knife at the throat, the death in the metronome (Music Lessons) V8:117
The Lady of Shalott." (The Lady of Shalott) V15:97
The lightning and the gale! (Old Ironsides) V9:172
the long, perfect loveliness of sow (Saint Francis and the Sow) V9:222
The Lord survives the rainbow of His will (The Quaker Graveyard in Nantucket) V6:159
The man I was when I was part of it (Beware of Ruins) V8:43
the quilts sing on (My Mother Pieced Quilts) V12:169
The red rose and the brier (Barbara Allan) V7:11
The self-same Power that brought me there brought you. (The Rhodora) V17:191
The shaft we raise to them and thee (Concord Hymn) V4:30
The sky became a still and woven blue. (Merlin Enthralled) V16:73
The spirit of this place (To a Child Running With Outstretched Arms in Canyon de Chelly) V11:173
The town again, trailing your legs and crying! (Wild Swans) V17:221
the unremitting space of your rebellion (Lost Sister) V5:217
The woman won (Oysters) V4:91
their guts or their brains? (Southbound on the Freeway) V16:158
There is the trap that catches noblest spirits, that caught—they say—God, when he walked on earth (Shine, Perishing Republic) V4:162
there was light (Vancouver Lights) V8:246
They also serve who only stand and wait." ([On His Blindness] Sonnet 16) V3:262

They are going to some point true and unproven. (Geometry) V15:68
They rise, they walk again (The Heaven of Animals) V6:76
They think I lost. I think I won (Harlem Hopscotch) V2:93
This is my page for English B (Theme for English B) V6:194
This Love (In Memory of Radio) V9:145
Tho' it were ten thousand mile! (A Red, Red Rose) V8:152
Though I sang in my chains like the sea (Fern Hill) V3:92
or the one red leaf the snow releases in March. (Three Times My Life Has Opened) V16:213
Till human voices wake us, and we drown (The Love Song of J. Alfred Prufrock) V1:99
Till Love and Fame to nothingness do sink (When I Have Fears that I May Cease to Be) V2:295
To every woman a happy ending (Barbie Doll) V9:33
to glow at midnight. (The Blue Rim of Memory) V17:39
to its owner or what horror has befallen the other shoe (A Pied) V3:16
To live with thee and be thy love. (The Nymph's Reply to the Shepherd) V14:241
To strive, to seek, to find, and not to yield (Ulysses) V2:279
To the moaning and the groaning of the bells (The Bells) V3:47
To the temple, singing. (In the Suburbs) V14:201

# U

Until Eternity. (The Bustle in a House) V10:62
unusual conservation (Chocolates) V11:17
Uttering cries that are almost human (American Poetry) V7:2

# W

War is kind (War Is Kind) V9:253
watching to see how it's done. (I Stop Writing the Poem) V16:58
Went home and put a bullet through his head (Richard Cory) V4:117
Were not the one dead, turned to their affairs. (Out, Out—) V10:213
Were toward Eternity— (Because I Could Not Stop for Death) V2:27
What will survive of us is love. (An Arundel Tomb) V12:18
When I died they washed me out of the turret with a hose (The Death of the Ball Turret Gunner) V2:41
when they untie them in the evening. (Early in the Morning) V17:75
When you have both (Toads) V4:244
Where deep in the night I hear a voice (Butcher Shop) V7:43
Where ignorant armies clash by night (Dover Beach) V2:52
Which Claus of Innsbruck cast in bronze for me! (My Last Duchess) V1:166
which is not going to go wasted on me which is why I'm telling you about it (Having a Coke with You) V12:106
white ash amid funereal cypresses (Helen) V6:92
*Who are you and what is your purpose?* (The Mystery) V15:138
Wi' the Scots lords at his feit (Sir Patrick Spens) V4:177
Will hear of as a god." (How we Heard the Name) V10:167
Wind, like the dodo's (Bedtime Story) V8:33
With gold unfading, WASHINGTON! be thine. (To His Excellency General Washington) V13:213
with my eyes closed. (We Live by What We See at Night) V13:240
With the slow smokeless burning of decay (The Wood-Pile) V6:252
With what they had to go on. (The Conquerors) V13:67
Would scarcely know that we were gone. (There Will Come Soft Rains) V14:301

# Y

Ye know on earth, and all ye need to know (Ode on a Grecian Urn) V1:180
You live in this, and dwell in lovers' eyes (Sonnet 55) V5:246
You may for ever tarry. (To the Virgins, to Make Much of Time) V13:226
you who raised me? (The Gold Lily) V5:127